ENCYCLOPEDIA OF
AMERICAN LAW

ENCYCLOPEDIA OF
AMERICAN LAW

DAVID SCHULTZ

■® Facts On File, Inc.

For Mom, who bought me my first encyclopedia

❧

Encyclopedia of American Law

Copyright © 2002 by David Schultz

Facts On File, Inc.
132 West 31st Street
New York NY 10001

Library of Congress Cataloging-in-Publication Data

The encyclopedia of American law/[edited by] David Schultz. p. cm.
Includes bibliographical references and index.
ISBN 0-8160-4329-9
1. Law—United States—Encyclopedias. I. Schultz, David A. (David Andrew), 1958–
KF154 .E528 2002
349.73'03—dc21   2001040206

Text and cover design by Cathy Rincon

Printed in the United States of America

VB Hermitage 10 9 8 7 6 5 4 3 2 1

This book is printed on acid-free paper.

CONTENTS

LIST OF ENTRIES

PREFACE

The law is often an inaccessible doorway through which many people fear to enter. Be it mysterious Latin terms, the seemingly odd rituals in court, or the apparent complexity of the issues that judges and attorneys seem to be addressing, for most the law is depicted as something not for the people but for highly educated and trained specialists.

It should not be that way.

Ultimately, the law is the people's business. Not only should the law reflect the everyday experiences of people, but it should also be understood by all. This is the aim of this volume.

In producing *Encyclopedia of American Law*, the goal was to assemble a collection of issues, terms, concepts, court cases, history, and people that provide a clear overview of the major points of American law that would be of interest to specialists and citizens alike. While this volume is not a definitive or exhaustive review of every aspect of the law, it was written with many audiences in mind.

This is an encyclopedia for teenagers, students, and adults of all ages who want to know more about how the law affects them. It is for people of color—be it African Americans, Native Americans, Hispanics, Latinos, or Asian Americans who want to know about the role they have in our legal system. It is for men, women, and those of different sexual preferences, seeking to understand their constitutional rights. It is also for young and old, those who work, who wish to petition their government, use the Internet, get married, divorced, or live in the United States or become a citizen. And, of course, it is for legal specialists, seeking a richer appreciation of their craft.

Encyclopedia of American Law is the product of many lawyers, judges, academics, and activists, writing on topics that will be of interest to the many audiences this volume is directed toward, and it is written in a style that demonstrates that the law need not be mysterious and confusing, but that instead it should be open to all of us.

David Schultz
Hamline University
Saint Paul, Minnesota
dschultz@hamline.edu

ACKNOWLEDGMENTS

Far more people than I can imagine deserve acknowledgment and thanks for making *Encyclopedia of American Law* possible.

When I was first asked to edit an encyclopedia I was overwhelmed and humbled. Yet Owen Lancer at Facts On File, Inc., challenged me and expressed confidence that I could do it. Only with the help of more than 100 contributors was it possible. From working with these individuals—lawyers, judges, colleagues, and others—not only did I learn more than I ever could have imagined, but I was fortunate to become friends with so many. What I learned from all this was that a passion for the law, learning, and reaching out to the public knew no institutional bounds, with great work and writing being produced by many contributors in all types of schools, law firms, court rooms, companies, and agencies. This diversity is the real strength of *Encyclopedia of American Law.*

Finally, while all effort has been made to acknowledge personally and individually everyone who contributed, no doubt I have missed a few people. To those unintentionally unacknowledged, I apologize for this error and any others in this volume.

CONTRIBUTORS

BRUCE E. ALTSCHULER, State University of New York, Oswego

MARY WELEK ATWELL, Radford University

BRUCE E. AUERBACH, Albright College

GAYLE AVANT, Baylor University

CARLTON BAILEY, University of Arkansas School of Law, Fayetteville

THOMAS E. BAKER, Drake University Law School

WILLIAM D. BAKER, Arkansas School for Mathematics and Science

NANCY WINEMILLER BASINGER, University of Georgia

STEPHEN F. BEFORT, University of Minnesota, School of Law

BERNARD W. BELL, Rutgers University Law School, Newark

SARA C. BENESH, University of Wisconsin, Milwaukee

DANTON ASHER BERUBE, Yale University

BRADLEY J. BEST, Austin Peay State University

MICHAEL W. BOWERS, University of Nevada, Las Vegas

SCOTT R. BOWMAN, California State University, Los Angeles

WILLIAM E. BRIGMAN, University of Houston—Downtown

NATHANAEL CAUSEY, United States Military Academy, West Point

JAMES N. G. CAUTHEN, City University of New York

H. LEE CHEEK, JR., Lee University

DOUGLAS CLOUATRE, Kennesaw State University

CAROLYN E. COCCA, State University of New York, College at Old Westbury

SUSAN COLEMAN, West Texas A&M University

MICHAEL COMINSKEY, Pennsylvania State University

SCOTT COMPARATO, Southern Illinois University, Carbondale

WILLIAM H. COOGAN, University of Southern Maine

JOCELYN CUFFEE, Western New England College of Law

CAROL A. DAY, District Attorney's Office, Eau Claire County, Wisconsin

JAMES W. ELY, JR., Vanderbilt University, School of Law

JEDON EMENHISER, Humboldt State University

FRANCENE M. ENGEL, University of Michigan

MARIE FAILINGER, Hamline University, School of Law

NEIL FERRERA, California State University, Chico

JAMES C. FOSTER, Oregon State University

RICHARD S. FRASE, University of Minnesota, School of Law

RAQUEL J. GABRIEL, City University of New York School of Law

J. DAVID GOLUB, Touro College, New York Institute of Technology, Kean College of New Jersey

SUSAN F. GOODMAN, California State University, Chico

KAREN GOTTLIEB, BioLaw, Nederland, Colorado

STEPHEN E. GOTTLIEB, Albany Law School

JON GOULD, George Mason University

STUART P. GREEN, Louisiana State University

MARTIN GRUBERG, University of Wisconsin, Oshkosh

HANS J. HACKER, University of Maryland

MICHAEL HANNON, Duke University Law School

ROGER HARTLEY, University of Arizona

CRAIG HENNENS, Boise State University

JIM HERRING, United States Military Academy, West Point

CHARLIE HOWARD, Tarleton State University

ROBERT JACOBS, Central Washington University

TIMOTHY R. JOHNSON, University of Minnesota

WARFORD B. JOHNSON III, Daniel, Clampett, Powell and Cunningham, Springfield, Missouri

JAMES H. JOYNER JR., Troy State University

RONALD KAHN, Oberlin College

JUDITH KILPATRICK, University of Arkansas, Fayetteville

ALLISON KNOWLES, California State University, Chico

DAVID THOMAS KONING, Washington University, St. Louis

DANIEL C. KRAMER, College of Staten Island, City University of New York

ANN C. KRUMMEL, Circuit Court, Columbia County, Wisconsin

ASHLYN K. KUERSTEN, Western Michigan University

PAUL KURITZ, Bates College

MARTHA M. LAFFERTY, Tennessee Fair Housing Council

MAURY LANDSMAN, University of Minnesota, School of Law

DANIEL LEVIN, University of Utah

STEPHEN A. LIGHT, University of North Dakota

PAUL D. LINK, Daniel, Clampett, Powell and Cunningham, Springfield, Missouri

MARY F. LOSS, Bowles Rice McDavid Graff and Love PLLC, Fairmont, West Virginia

ROBERT W. MALMSHEIMER, State University of New York College of Environmental Science and Forestry

CHRIS MARKWOOD, University of Central Oklahoma

WENDY L. MARTINEK, State University of New York, Binghamton

JOHN H. MATHESON, University of Minnesota, School of Law

DAVID A. MAY, Eastern Washington University

ANGELA MCCAFFREY, Hamline University School of Law

WM. OSLER MCCARTHY, Texas Supreme Court, University of Texas, Austin

JANE CALABRIA MCPEAK, Hamline University

SUSAN GLUCK MEZEY, Loyola University, Chicago

MARK C. MILLER, Clark University

TYLER MILLSAP, California State University, Chico

VERNON MOGENSEN, Kingsborough Community College, City University of New York

STANLEY M. MORRIS, Attorney, Cortez, Colorado

JEANINE NEHER, California State University, Chico

TIMOTHY J. O'NEILL, Southwestern University

MYRA ORLEN, Western New England College of Law

KAREN ORREN, University of California at Los Angeles

DEMETRA M. PAPPAS, London School of Economics

PATRICK J. PLATTER, Daniel, Clampett, Powell and Cunningham, Springfield, Missouri

VINCENT KELLY POLLARD, University of Hawaii, Manoa

BRIAN L. PORTO, College of St. Joseph, Vermont

STEVEN PURO, Saint Louis University

KATHRYN R. L. RAND, University of North Dakota School of Law

DAVID M. REDDY, Sweet and Reddy, S.C., Elkhorn, Wisconsin

PATRICK K. ROBERTS, Daniel, Clampett, Powell and Cunningham, Springfield, Missouri

NORMAN L. ROSENBERG, Macalester College

GERALD J. RUSSELLO, Covington and Burling, New York

MARGARET R. RYNIKER, State University of New York, Oswego

JORDONNA SABIH, Office of Andrew J. Wistrich, Magistrate Judge, United States District Court, Central District of California

DAVID SCHULTZ, Hamline University

DAVID SELLERS, Administrative Office of the U.S. Courts

CELIA A. SGROI, State University of New York, Oswego

VICTORIA SHABANIAN, office of Andrew J. Wistrich, Magistrate Judge, U.S.

DISTRICT COURT, Central District of California

ELSA M. SHARTSIS, Attorney

STEVEN K. SHAW, Northwest Nazarene University, Nampa, Idaho

CHRISTOPHER SHORTELL, University of California, San Diego

JOSHUA M. SILVERSTEIN, Freeborn and Peters, Chicago

CHARLES ANTHONY SMITH, University of California, San Diego

CHRISTOPHER E. SMITH, Michigan State University

LINDSLEY ARMSTRONG SMITH, Martin and Kieklak Law Firm, Fayetteville, Arkansas

STEPHEN SMITH, University of Arkansas, Fayetteville

ANTHONY SMITH, University of California, San Diego

SHANNON ISHIYAMA SMITHEY, University of Pittsburgh

WILLIAM D. SMOOT, United States Military Academy, West Point

JERRY E. STEPHENS, United States Tenth District Court of Appeals, Oklahoma City, Oklahoma

KRISTEN L. STEWART, J.D.

ROBIN STEWART, Attorney

EDWARD STILL, Lawyers' Committee for Civil Rights Under Law

NORMAN OTTO STOCKMEYER, JR., Thomas M. Cooley Law School

RUTH ANN STRICKLAND, Appalachian State University

PHILIPPA STRUM, City University of New York

RICK A. SWANSON, University of Kentucky

STEVEN R. SWANSON, Hamline University School of Law

BETH S. SWARTZ, Attorney

G. ALAN TARR, Rutgers University, Camden, New Jersey

STEVEN L. TAYLOR, Troy State University

LOUISE ADAMS TYLER, Philadelphia, Pennsylvania (unaffiliated scholar)

GEORGIA WRALSTAD ULMSCHNEIDER, Indiana University-Purdue University, Fort Wayne

JOHN R. VILE, Middle Tennessee State University

MICHAEL H. WALSH, Loyola University, Chicago

ARTEMUS WARD, California State University, Chico

A. J. L. WASKEY, Dalton State College

MARC D. WEINER, Rutgers University, New Brunswick, New Jersey

PAUL WEIZER, Fitchburg State College

STEPHEN WERMIEL, Washington College of Law

KEITH E. WHITTINGTON, Princeton University

KIMBERLY A. WILLIAMS, California State University, Chico

JOY A. WILLIS, Michigan State University

STEVEN WISE, Center for the Expansion of Fundamental Rights

ANDREW J. WISTRICH, Magistrate Judge, U.S. District Court, Central District of California

JAMES WYER, California State University, Chico

LORETTA M. YOUNG, Family Court of State of Delaware

ROSALIE R. YOUNG, State University of New York, Oswego

MARVIN ZALMAN, Wayne State University

abortion rights for women were found to be constitutionally protected in the 1973 Supreme Court ruling of *Roe v. Wade,* 410 U.S. 113 (1973). Nevertheless, the Court's ruling in *Roe* did not end the legal controversy surrounding abortion. The federal government and states continued to enact legislation regulating the procedure in specified circumstances, and much of this legislation was constitutionally challenged in the courts over the ensuing decades.

During the 19th century, many states passed criminal statutes that prohibited all abortions except in cases when necessary in order to save the life of the mother. Because abortion was a dangerous medical procedure, many states enacted laws banning abortions in order to protect the public health, safety, and morals of women. However, as medical technologies improved in the 20th century, abortion also became a safer medical procedure, and consequently, a state's interest in prohibiting most abortions began to appear less legitimate. Many of the constitutional questions surrounding abortion were finally examined by the United States Supreme Court in the landmark case of *Roe v. Wade.*

Roe v. Wade considered the legitimacy of a Texas criminal abortion statute, which prohibited all abortions unless they were performed to save the life of the mother. In *Roe,* the Court found the Texas abortion law to be too rigid. Noting that abortion procedures were now "relatively safe," the Supreme Court ruled that states could not regulate abortions during the first trimester of a woman's pregnancy. However, because abortion became more dangerous after the first trimester, the Court ruled that states could regulate abortions during the second trimester of pregnancy if the regulations were created in an effort to promote maternal health and safety. Finally, the Supreme Court explained that during the third trimester of pregnancy, states could prohibit abortions as long as they provided an exception to save the mother's life. The Court argued that during the third trimester, the fetus was viable outside of the mother's womb, and thus, at that point, the states had an important and legitimate interest to protect the potential life of the unborn.

While *Roe* asserted that states could not regulate abortions during the first trimester of pregnancy, questions still arose as to what types of procedural requirements states could impose on women under the ruling. One of the first issues to come before the Court after *Roe* was the question of parental consent for minors. In the 1976 ruling of *Planned Parenthood v. Danforth,* 428 U.S. 52 (1976), the Court ruled that the parental consent provision in this suit lacked sufficient justification and thus was inappropriate. However, in arriving at this conclusion, Justice Harry Andrew Blackmun emphasized that this ruling did "not suggest that every minor, regardless of age or maturity, may give effective consent for termination of her pregnancy." In fact, soon after the *Danforth* ruling, the Supreme Court upheld laws requiring parental consent for minors in cases such as *Belloti v. Baird,* 443 U.S. 622 (1979) and *H.L. v. Matheson,* 450 U.S. 398 (1981). Similarly, in the 1992 ruling of *Planned Parenthood v. Casey,* 505 U.S. 833 (1992), Justice Sandra Day O'Connor reiterated that states could impose parental consent requirements on minors as long as the juveniles were able to acquire a bypass from a judge in extraordinary circumstances.

The Supreme Court has also upheld state laws that require physicians to inform women of the dangers of abortions, as well as laws that require women to sign informed consent waivers. Likewise, the Court has upheld 24-hour waiting period regulations, which require women who have been informed about the circumstances surrounding abortion to wait at least a 24-hour period after receiving the information before undergoing the procedure. The Court has ruled that these types of restrictions on the abortion process do not cause "an undue burden" on the women seeking the procedure and thus are constitutionally permissible.

The Supreme Court has, however, ruled that spousal notification requirements do place an "undue burden" on women seeking abortions and therefore are invalid. In *Casey,* Justice O'Connor noted that spousal notification requirements would most likely prevent many women from obtaining abortions, especially those women "who fear for their safety" because

of abusive husbands. Moreover, although states have often required spousal notification in an effort to protect the father's rights, the Court rejected this justification. O'Connor states: "It is an inescapable biological fact that state regulation with respect to the child a woman is carrying will have a far greater impact on the mother's liberty than on the father's. . . . Inasmuch as it is the woman who physically bears the child and who is the more directly and immediately affected by the pregnancy . . . the balance weighs in her favor."

While the Supreme Court has generally adopted an "undue burden" analysis for testing the validity of most first trimester abortion procedures, many individuals who support abortion rights for women have been critical of the Supreme Court for not recognizing and appreciating the adverse effects and undue burdens some abortions laws have had on poor women. For instance, in 1976, Congress passed a law called the Hyde Amendment, which prohibited the use of Medicaid funds for abortions. The only exceptions were situations in which the procedure was necessary to save the life of the mother or in cases of rape or incest. In the case of *Harris v. McRae,* 448 U.S. 297 (1980), the Court upheld the constitutionality of the Hyde Amendment, explaining that the *Roe v. Wade* decision did not require the federal government to subsidize abortions for poor women electing the procedure. Thus, while first trimester abortions are constitutionally protected, indigent women often have far greater difficulty acquiring the procedure than middle- and upper-class women.

Members of Congress have often proposed a "Right-to-Life" Amendment to the Constitution to overturn the controversial *Roe v. Wade* decision; however, these proposed amendments to the Constitution have never been successful. There also have been times when it has appeared that the Supreme Court itself may actually be close to overturning (or at least modifying) the *Roe v. Wade* decision. In the decision of *Webster v. Reproductive Health Services,* 492 U.S. 490

(1989), four justices on the Supreme Court expressed an interest in retreating from *Roe*. Since the *Webster* decision, however, *Roe* has remained intact. Moreover, with the appointments of Justices Ruth Bader Ginsburg and Stephen G. Breyer to the Supreme Court, *Roe v. Wade* appears to be on a solid footing. Still, the abortion debate continues to rage on, and only time will tell us where the debate may go from here.

For more information

Craig, Barbara Hinkson, and David M. O'Brien. *Abortion and American Politics*. Chatham, N.J.: Chatham House, 1993.

Devins, Neal. *Shaping Constitutional Values: Elected Government, the Supreme Court, and the Abortion Debate*. Baltimore: Johns Hopkins University Press, 1996.

Tushnet, Mark. *Abortion*. New York: Facts On File, 1996.

Francene M. Engel
University of Michigan

Abrams v. United States 250 U.S. 616 (1919) is most famous for the libertarian dissenting opinion by Justice Oliver Wendell Holmes, Jr., penned in favor of political dissidence by an unpopular minority, an opinion that the Supreme Court has since embraced as part of the law of the First Amendment. The 1919 decision affirmed the convictions of five Russian immigrants who had circulated leaflets objecting to the decision of the United States to send troops to Eastern Europe in response to the Russian Revolution. The leaflets were addressed to "Workers of the World" and called on them to "wake up" to the government's foreign intrigues and were signed "Revolutionists." The defendants' speech had nothing to do with World War I or the draft, yet they were convicted and sentenced to 20 years imprisonment for violating the wartime Espionage Acts, which prohibited the encouragement of draft resistance and con-

spiracies to urge curtailment of war materials production.

Holmes insisted that the defendants had as much right to publish their leaflets as the government had to publish the Constitution. Governmental persecution of speech seemed logical to him in the abstract, if the ruling majority is certain what it wants and has reason to feel threatened that the speech of a minority might get in the way. He observed that history teaches that "time has upset many fighting faiths." But "the theory of our Constitution" is based on the "experiment" that "the best test of truth is the power of the thought to get itself accepted in the competition of the market." Thus, we need to be "eternally vigilant" against attempts to interfere with our nation's "wager" of truth.

For Holmes, only a serious and imminent emergency—a clear and present danger—allowed the government to short-circuit public debate. Otherwise, the First Amendment presumption that "Congress shall make no law" obtains. Therefore, speech, even divisive and controversial and unpopular speech, should have its say to see if it will have its way in the marketplace of ideas.

Despite all this heroic rhetoric, however, Holmes was not actually buying the defendants' "poor and puny anonymities." He believed that most dissident speech amounted to foolish, even silly, opinions of zealous but ignorant people, and the most effective way to marginalize them and their message was to let them have their say so others could recognize them for what they were. In a letter explaining his *Abrams* dissent, he wrote, "To show the ardor of the writer is not a sufficient reason for judging him. I regarded my view as simply upholding the right of a donkey to drool. But the usual notion is that you are free to say what you like if you don't shock me. Of course the value of the constitutional right is only when you do shock people. . . ."

Holmes ends his eloquent dissent with the fulsome lament, "I regret that I cannot put into more impressive words" the importance of the freedom of speech. No other member of the Supreme Court ever has.

For more information

Abrams v. United States, 250 U.S. 616 (1919).

Bezanson, Randall P. *Speech Stories—How Free Can Speech Be?* New York: New York University Press, 1998.

Fish, Stanley. *There's No Such Thing as Free Speech . . . and It's a Good Thing Too.* New York: Oxford University Press, 1994.

Schauer, Frederick. *Free Speech: A Philosophical Enquiry.* Cambridge: Cambridge University Press, 1982.

Smolla, Rodney A. *Free Speech in an Open Society.* New York: Vintage Books, 1993.

Thomas E. Baker
James Madison Chair in Constitutional Law
Drake University Law School

abstention   is the practice of federal court nonintervention in ongoing state legal proceedings. The practice is grounded in both the desire to prevent federal courts from encroaching on state powers and a reluctance to decide issues on a constitutional basis if they can be resolved on narrower legal grounds. As early as 1793, Congress passed an Anti-Injunction Act to prevent federal courts from enjoining state officials from carrying out state laws. However, with the enhanced power of federal courts to protect the right of citizens under the Fourteenth Amendment, federal court involvement in state actions took on a new dimension. In response, the Supreme Court developed the judicial doctrine of abstention to supplement the legislative mandate.

One of the basic principles of constitutional law in a federal system is that federal courts will not determine the meaning of a state law or constitution but instead rely on the interpretation made by the highest state court to rule on the issue. This presents a dilemma with a newly enacted statute which has not been interpreted by a state court. In early years, it was standard practice of federal courts to try to predict how a newly enacted statute would fare in state courts before it could be evaluated on federal constitutional grounds. However, in a series of cases known as the *Pullman Doctrine (Railroad Commission of Texas v. Pullman Co.,* 312 U.S. 496 [1941]), the Supreme Court ruled that federal courts must decline to hear a case and send it to state court if the state statute contains ambiguities or vague language which requires authoritative interpretation.

As a result of the civil rights revolution, the Supreme Court seemed to retreat from the *Pullman* doctrine. In the early 1960s, federal court intervention was allowed when the state legal issues were minor or the state law was so flawed that no reinterpretation could make it constitutional. The most important case was *Dombrowski v. Pfister,* 380 U.S. 479 (1965), which held that abstention was inappropriate when state laws on their face abridged free expression or discouraged constitutionally protected activities.

However, in *Younger v. Harris,* 401 U.S. 37 (1971), the Supreme Court returned to a stricter position. It held that federal courts could not enjoin pending state criminal prosecutions except under extraordinary circumstances where the danger of irreparable loss to federally protected rights is both great and immediate. Subsequently, the *Younger* doctrine has been extended to apply to civil cases except where the state statute involved is clearly unconstitutional or the state case was conducted in bad faith. (*Colorado River Water Conservation District v. United States,* 424 U.S. 800 [1976], sets forth tests to be used by federal courts in civil abstention decision making where both federal and state courts have jurisdiction.)

The most recent major case is *Pennzoil Co. v. Texaco, Inc.,* 481 U.S. 1 (1987), in which a unanimous Supreme Court ruled that a lower federal court could not intervene in an ongoing state civil case, although one of the oil companies contended that the state requirement for posting a

$10 billion bond in order to appeal would bankrupt it. Justice Powell ruled that comity, or federal court respect for the rights of state courts, required federal court abstention. In an era of increased Supreme Court deference to states' rights, the abstention doctrine will remain a bulwark of federal jurisprudence.

For more information

Young, Gordon G. "Federal Court Abstention and State Administrative Law from Burford to Ankenbrandt: Fifty Years of Judicial Federalism under *Burford v. Sun Oil* and Kindred Doctrines," *DePaul L. Rev.* 42 (1993): 859.

Currie, David P. *Federal Jurisdiction in a Nutshell*, 4th ed. St. Paul, Minn.: West Group Publishing, 1999.

William E. Brigman, Ph.D.
University of Houston—Downtown

academic freedom   is a doctrine that protects the right of teachers to be free to research, write, teach, and comment about issues without fear of retribution. The purpose of academic freedom is to preserve the intellectual integrity of persons who research, write, and speak on issues of public interest and who are responsible for educating the young of society. In the United States, a formal, written claim for these rights first appeared in a Declaration of Principles (1915) and a Statement of Principles on Academic Freedom and Tenure (1940) drafted by the American Association of University Professors (AAUP).

The concept has a long history. It was discussed as early as the death of Socrates for teaching ideas not approved by the government. The Declaration and Statement were intended to apply only to teachers in higher education after a national study found that they were in significant danger of having their ideas and speech stifled when they criticized authority (university administrations, local school boards, and local, state, and national governments). This concern

about authoritarian repression in the flow of ideas focused on the individual teacher and not on education as a whole. The claims made in the 1915 and 1940 documents have never been wholly accepted by educational institutions or by the courts, although some aspects of each have been incorporated in teacher employment contracts, in teacher evaluation and performance review structures of universities, and in decisions of the United States Supreme Court and other courts.

It was not until the late 1940s and 1950s that there was substantial court review of the doctrine. Despite its original focus on teachers in higher education, many of the cases have involved grade school and high school teachers. This came about when proponents attempted to link the concept of academic freedom to the individual rights granted in the First and Fourteenth Amendments to the Constitution. Before then, the United States Supreme Court had determined that the First and Fourteenth Amendments protected individuals only against actions by state and federal governments and had no authority when it came to the actions of private individuals and institutions. In addition, the Court had held that the state could place "reasonable conditions" on public employment, which was not a right but a privilege. These interpretations prevailed in teachers' claims of interference with academic freedom until the 1952 decision of *Wieman v. Updegraff,* 344 U.S. 183 (1952), in which the Court declared unconstitutional an Oklahoma law that excluded from state employment any person who would not swear that they did not belong to any subversive organizations.

In 1960 the Court struck down an Arkansas statute that required public employees to provide the state with a list of all their organizational memberships in *Shelton v. Tucker,* 364 U.S. 479 (1960). In *Shelton,* Justice Potter Stewart declared "[t]he vigilant protection of constitutional freedoms is nowhere more vital than in the community of American schools." In *Wieman* the plaintiffs were college teachers while in *Shelton* the case involved teachers at all levels of education. The language of these cases seemed to indicate that it was the atmosphere in which education takes place, not only the rights of the individual teacher, that is entitled to First Amendment protection from authoritarian controls. This notion was borne out in *Dixon v. Alabama State Board of Education,* 294 F. 2d 150 (5th Cir.), cert denied, 368 U.S. 930 (1961), where the Court held that students had a right to due process notice and a hearing before they could be expelled for protesting on school grounds. With this opinion, academic freedom was extended to all persons engaged in education.

Although various portions of the concept of academic freedom now have been given some protection through the courts, the extent of that protection has not been clearly defined. In *Pickering v. Board of Education,* 391 U.S. 563 (1968), the Court held that the First Amendment interest of a teacher must be balanced against the school board's interest in efficient operation of the schools. In that case, the court found no interference in the school's operation as a result of a letter by the teacher criticizing the board and published in a local newspaper. In a later case, the court held that where there were mixed motives for dismissing a teacher, only one of which involved protected conduct, the employer might prevail if it could show that dismissal would have occurred solely on the basis of the unprotected conduct, *Mt. Healthy City School District Board of Education v. Doyle,* 429 U.S. 274 (1977). In *Regents of the University of California v. Bakke,* 438 U.S. 265 (1978), the Court, noting that "[a]cademic freedom, though not a specifically enumerated constitutional right, long has been viewed as a special concern of the First Amendment," defined academic freedom as including "[t]he freedom of the university to make its own judgments as to education." This view was reiterated in *Regents of the University of Michigan v. Ewing,* 474 U.S. 214 (1985), where the Court rejected claims that the school had

acted arbitrarily and refused to interfere with the decision to dismiss a student, stating that it was a "genuinely academic decision."

For more information
Hofstadter, Richard, and William Metzger, *The Development of Academic Freedom in the United States* New York: Columbia University Press, 1955.
Pincoffs, E., ed. *The Concept of Academic Freedom* Austin: University of Texas Press, 1975.

Judith Kilpatrick
University of Arkansas
Fayetteville

accessory   describes one who assists another in the commission of a crime. The word is originally derived from the Latin word *accessio,* meaning something that accompanies or supplements something else. In Roman law, accessory came to mean a mode of acquiring additional property as an outgrowth of or addition to property already owned. This older usage still survives in some contexts. For example, an accessory contract is an agreement entered into between parties to effectuate or bring about the terms of another contract that is more central to the parties' relationship. However, its primary meaning is in the criminal law.

In criminal law, the original distinction between an accessory and a *principal* or main actor was whether the person was present at the scene of the crime. The principals were present at the scene of the crime and either committed the crime themselves or assisted others to do it. The accessory, on the other hand, was not actually present during the commission of the crime but assisted the principal(s) "before the fact" or "after the fact." For example, someone who provided the principal with a weapon or other assistance before the crime could be considered an accessory "before the fact," while someone assisting the principal in escaping from the authorities after the crime was committed would be considered an accessory "after the fact." At common law, the latter crime was called "misprision of felony" but was generally limited to those who failed to disclose or actively concealed the commission of a felony.

An accessory is similar to an *accomplice,* in that both assist the principal in the commission of a crime, and in some states there is little distinction between them. However, an accomplice is usually a greater participant in the crime than an accessory, often being defined as a witness to a criminal action who is determined to have participated in the crime itself. In some states, such as New York, an accessory, even one after the fact, may be found guilty to an equal degree as the actual perpetrator of the crime, so long as the indictment of the accomplice provides enough information as to the crimes charged to prepare a defense.

Contemporary criminal law has generally eliminated the difference between a principal and an "accessory before the fact," and accords them both the same level of culpability. However, most states still accord a lesser degree of culpability to those accessories who did not know of the crime before its commission but offered aid or assistance to the principals "after the fact." Most states require that an accessory after the fact take some intentional action to conceal the crime or aid the principals to escape rather than mere inaction. While at common law an accessory could not be tried or convicted before the principal, the criminal law of most states has now eliminated that requirement and an accessory can be tried and convicted regardless of whether or not the principal of the crime is tried and convicted.

For more information

Kaplan, John, and Robert Weisberg, *Criminal Law: Cases and Materials.* Boston: Little, Brown, 1986, pp. 580–612.

Black's Law Dictionary, 6th ed. St. Paul, Minn.: West Publishing Co., 1990, p. 14.

Gerald J. Russello
Covington and Burling, New York

actus reus   is the action that must be proven in order gain a criminal conviction. When prosecutors wish to prove criminal action, they must prove that the accused did something (actus reus) and that they had criminal intent (mens rea). Actus reus is overt conduct, which can be either a voluntary act or an omission.

Prosecutors must prove that the accused committed an actual deed that was not involuntary. Involuntary acts would include such things as reflex, convulsion, or a bodily movement not under the control of the accused. Under many circumstances, a person acting under duress (i.e., being forced to act at gunpoint or under threat of violence) would not be seen as acting voluntarily. However, some forms of duress (i.e., blackmail) may not be enough to exempt someone from the legal consequences of their actions.

Sometimes actus reus can be an omission or something that is not done. Under American law a person is not required to act to help another except under special circumstances. One such special circumstance would be a relationship such as a parent's obligation to provide food and shelter for a child or an occasion when you have voluntarily assumed care for someone. Another relationship would be a contractual obligation to perform certain acts. Some states also require persons involved in auto accidents to render assistance to others. A person who willfully neglects a child under their care can be criminally prosecuted.

In most criminal cases, the actus reus is not difficult. Only in complicated conspiracy cases, or situations where actions can be interpreted differently, does this rule come into play.

For more information

Hart, H.L.A. *Punishment and the Elimination of Responsibility.* London: University of London, Athlone Press, 1962.

Charlie Howard
Tarleton State University

Adamson v. California   332 U.S. 46 (1947) reopened the great dispute over the "fundamental rights" interpretation of the due process clause of the Fourteenth Amendment and whether the Bill of Rights applies to state governments. A widely noted dissent by Justice Hugo Black argued that the clause should be read to incorporate all of the Bill of Rights guarantees against encroachment by state governments. The majority's position was that only rights which the justices think are "fundamental" should be included.

Admiral Dewey Adamson was convicted of murder in the first degree in California in 1946 and was condemned to death. California's criminal procedure at that time authorized the judge and prosecutor to comment on the defendant's refusal to testify. Adamson had committed earlier offenses which would have been revealed to the jury on cross examination had he testified in his own defense. In his closing argument, the prosecutor pointed out Adamson's refusal to take the stand. After his conviction, Adamson appealed on the ground that the California procedure violated his privilege against self-incrimination under the due process clause of the Fourteenth Amendment.

The Supreme Court decided the case on June 23, 1947. Justice Stanley Reed, writing for a majority of five, held that the privilege against self-incrimination is not part of the right to a fair trial protected by the due process clause of the Fourteenth Amendment. Reed argued that "the purpose of due process is not to protect a defendant against a proper conviction but against an unfair conviction. When evidence is before a jury that threatens conviction, it does not seem unfair to require him to choose between leaving the adverse evidence unexplained and subjecting himself to impeachment through disclosure of former crimes. In short, California's procedure was not "fundamentally unfair."

Justice Felix Frankfurter concurred, arguing that the due process clause of the Fourteenth Amendment was not meant by its framers to include the whole Bill of Rights: "It would be extraordinarily strange for a Constitution to convey such specific commands in such a roundabout and inexplicit way . . ." as the due process clause.

Justice Hugo Black's dissenting opinion argued that inclusion of the entire Bill of Rights in the Fourteenth Amendment had been the intention of its framers. He attached to his opinion a long historical appendix citing many of the speeches of Congressman Jonathan Bingham and other influential members of Congress who had participated in the drafting and ratification of the Fourteenth Amendment. Black argued further that the "fundamental fairness" rule was too open-ended; it gives too much power to judges to include and exclude rights according to their personal wishes rather than on the basis of principled constitutional analysis.

Frankfurter's position prevailed in theory and Black's in practice. By 1970 nearly the entire Bill of Rights had been incorporated in the Fourteenth Amendment. The major exceptions are the Second Amendment's right to keep and bear arms, and the Fifth Amendment's command that criminal defendants are entitled to indictment by grand jury. The Court's specific decision in *Adamson* was changed in 1964 in *Malloy v. Hogan;* state prosecutors may no longer comment to the jury on the defendant's refusal to testify.

The open-ended character of the due process clause of the Fourteenth Amendment permitted later courts to expand personal liberty and privacy rights. *Griswold v. Connecticut* and *Eisenstadt v. Baird* established constitutional rights to receive and use birth control devices and information; *Roe v. Wade* established a constitutional right to an abortion in the first trimester of pregnancy. Had the Supreme Court accepted Justice Black's interpretation of the Fourteenth Amendment, these expansions of individual autonomy would have been much more difficult to achieve.

For more information

Fairman, Charles, and Morrison, Stanley. *The Fourteenth Amendment and the Bill of Rights: The Incor-*

poration Theory. New York: Da Capo Press, 1970. Also see Mark Silverstein's *Constitutional Faiths: Felix Frankfurter, Hugo Black, and the Process of Judicial Decision Making.* Ithaca, N.Y.: Cornell University Press, 1984.

Robert Jacobs
Central Washington University

administrative discretion

administrative discretion describes the freedom of public administrators to make choices, within the limits of their authority, among possible courses of action. Administrative discretion is not necessarily limited to substantive policy decisions. It extends to decisions as to timing of action and the procedures used.

When government officials seek to achieve public goals in legally permissible ways, those officials and the government are exempt from damage claims from those hurt by the government's action. "Administrative discretion" is also sometimes termed the "discretionary function exemption." This exemption gives officials room to make judgment calls and carry them out without fear of being sued, even if their decisions prove to be bad. For example, FBI law enforcement action in 1993 at the Davidian complex outside Waco, Texas, led to the death of 74 members of that religious sect, including many children. A federal district court held that the FBI agents as individuals and the FBI as a federal agency acted within the discretion permitted by law.

"Prosecutorial discretion," a related concept, describes the range of alternatives available to a prosecutor in criminal cases. Alternatives include (1) whether or not to prosecute, (2) the specific charges to be brought, (3) the timing and modes of bargaining with defendant's counsel, and (4) the substance of sentencing recommendations. For example, it is an act of prosecutorial discretion when a district attorney offers to reduce charges against a drug dealer if he will testify against his supplier.

For more information

Davis, Kenneth Culp. *Discretionary Justice.* Baton Rouge: Louisiana State University Press, 1969; Greenwood Press reprint, 1999.

Froomkin, Michael. "In Defense of Administrative Agency Autonomy," *Yale Law Journal* 96 (March 1987): 798.

Gayle Avant
Baylor University

Administrative Procedures Act

Administrative Procedures Act regulates the procedures by which federal government agencies conduct their business. There are many diverse agencies, departments, and commissions of the U.S. government. The duty of each of these administrative units is to oversee and regulate a particular policy area such as communications, transportation, or the environment. Although the substantive area of their expertise differs, most federal agencies follow the same law regulating the procedures by which they operate. That law is called the Administrative Procedures Act (APA). The APA was enacted by Congress in 1946 in order to standardize the procedures by which agencies enact regulation and conduct hearings. The three overall goals of the APA were public information, public participation, and public accountability. The APA standardized and simplified administrative law, making it easier for courts, agencies, and the public to understand the procedures. The APA also was designed to allow more involvement by the public in the way agencies conduct their business, as well as judicial review of agency actions to ensure that the agencies were following the law.

The APA has numerous features. One of the most important requirements of the APA is the rulemaking procedure found in chapter 5 of the *U.S. Code,* section 553. This section requires that agencies wishing to adopt a generally applicable regulation must publicize their intent to do so and then allow a period for public commentary on the agency's proposed regulation. Specifically, although the APA allows for certain exceptions, in most cases the agency must first publish their proposed rule (the actual text or a description of the rule) in the *Federal Register,* along with the time and place of a hearing in which the agency will listen to public comments and debate about the proposed rule. Interested persons may either speak at the hearing or submit written opinions containing data and opinions, as well as legal and policy arguments. After the period of public comment is over, the agency will then announce the final version of the rule along with its basic purpose. Interested persons also have the right to petition for the issuance, amendment, or repeal of a rule.

Another one of the most important elements of the APA is found in section 554. This section requires that when an agency is about to adjudicate a decision that involves the interests of one or more specific individuals or businesses, those parties must be given notice of the intended agency action as well as an opportunity to present their own viewpoints. The requirements are similar to those for rule making described above. The affected party must first be notified of the specific time and place of the hearing along with the specific facts or laws that are being asserted by the agency. Then, at the hearing, the affected party must be given the opportunity to present facts and arguments in favor of or against the specific action the agency wishes to take.

Sections 701 through 706 of chapter 7 of the *U.S. Code* lay out the APA's guidelines for judicial review of agency actions. This review includes both the substance and procedure of an agency's final action. If a party challenges an agency's action in court, the action can be overturned on several grounds. These reasons include instances in which the agency action violated any constitution, statute, administrative regulation, or other law. As another example, a court will reverse an agency's action if the substance of its decision was unsupported by substantial evidence, or was reached in an arbitrary or capricious manner.

The APA is not without its critics. Some believe the APA places too many procedural obstacles in the way of agencies, making it more difficult for them to enact important regulations to protect people's health, safety, or the environment. Others, on the other hand, believe the APA gives too much power to agencies to regulate minute details of behavior, and that compliance with excessive, costly, and confusing regulations ends up choking the private business sector. Either way, the APA's basic elements have probably become a permanent fixture on our legal landscape.

For more information

Aman, Alfred C., and William T. Mayton, *Administrative Law.* St. Paul: West Publishing Co., 1998; The Administrative Procedures Act, 5 U.S.C. §§ 551–59, 701–06, 1305, 3105, 3344, 5372, 7521.

Rick Swanson
University of Kentucky

admiralty law or maritime law is the unique set of substantive and procedural legal rules generally applicable to activities on navigable waterways. The core policy goal is to provide a uniform and predictable legal system that encourages waterborne commerce. Significant substantive coverage areas include ship collisions, personal injury, carriage of goods, maritime liens and ship mortgages, charter agreements, towing, pilotage, limitation of liability, salvage, marine pollution, maritime insurance, and recreational uses.

Admiralty's history extends back to ancient Babylonian, Roman, and Greek law. By the end of the first millennium A.D., maritime trade had expanded to create centralized maritime rules often named for the seaport in which they arose. Of greatest interest to American lawyers was the French island Oléron's sea code, which traveled to England in the 11th century. At this point, continental and English maritime practice took different paths. In most civil law countries, admiralty was incorporated into national codes; while in England, court decisions developed maritime law.

In medieval times, English ports had their own admiralty courts, but as the English government became more centralized, the king gave the lord high admiral the right to create a system of admiralty courts, leading to jurisdictional disputes with local courts. By the 1500s the growth of English shipping had increased the significance of admiralty courts, which commercial interests preferred because substantive admiralty law applied, the process was quicker, the court generally accepted written testimony, and no jury was required. These same benefits threatened the English common law courts, which attempted to take exclusive jurisdiction over many traditional admiralty claims. Ultimately, admiralty and common law courts acted to prohibit each other's jurisdiction. In the 1600s, the common law courts won this battle, severely limiting the admiralty courts' ability to hear commercial cases or any cases that arose on British internal waters or land.

Prior to the Constitution's adoption, the newly independent states of the United States followed English law and created their own admiralty courts. The need for uniform and predictable trade rules and dissatisfaction with the states' decentralized regimes led to the creation of admiralty jurisdiction in the federal courts in Article III, section 2 of the Constitution, which provides, "[t]he judicial Power shall extend . . . to all Cases of admiralty and maritime Jurisdiction. . . ." Congress furthered national uniformity in section 9 of the Judiciary Act of 1789, which provided: ". . . the district courts . . . shall also have exclusive original cognizance of all civil causes of admiralty and maritime jurisdiction . . . saving to suitors, in all cases, the right of the common law remedy, where the common law is competent to give it . . . ." Unlike England, where special admiralty courts were used, the United States allowed regular federal courts to decide maritime disputes, although applying different laws and using different procedures.

The Constitution and the Judiciary Act fail to define "admiralty and maritime jurisdiction," leaving it to judicial determination. Over the years this has led to disputes over exclusive application of federal admiralty law over state law. The strongest statement of federal admiralty supremacy came in the Supreme Court's 1917 decision in *Southern Pacific Co. v. Jensen*, 244 U.S. 205 (1917), which struck down the application of a state workers compensation award to a maritime worker. The Court found that the need for maritime uniformity rendered the state law unconstitutional if it "contravenes the essential purpose expressed by an act of Congress or works material prejudice to the characteristic features of the general maritime law or interferes with the proper harmony and uniformity of that law in its international and interstate relations."

Despite this strong statement, the courts have not provided clear guidance on this important federalism issue. The case-by-case determinations make little attempt to provide a unifying theory, and recent Supreme Court decisions have added to the confusion. For example, in *American Dredging v. Miller*, 510 U.S. 443 (1994), the Court refused to require that the state of Louisiana apply the maritime law's traditional doctrine of *forum non conveniens* because the rule did not originate in admiralty or find its exclusive home in maritime law. Although that case acknowledged the *Jensen* standard, it seemed to create an entirely new approach. In another important case, *Yamaha Motor Corp. v. Calhoun*, 516 U.S. 199 (1996), the Court refused to find that a general maritime remedy preempted a state wrongful death statute for a death that occurred within U.S. territorial waters. Such cases misunderstand the important maritime policies of uniformity and predictability. Similarly, recent congressional enactments have not respected these goals. For example, the Oil Pollution Act of 1990 allows each state to create an unlimited liability regime for oil spills occurring in its territory.

For more information

Benedict on Admiralty (8th ed.), Thomas J. Schoenbaum, *Admiralty and Maritime Law* (2d ed., 1994), or Swanson, Steven R. "Federalism, the Admiralty, and Oil Spills," *Journal of Maritime Law and Commerce* 27 (1996): 379.

Steven R. Swanson
Hamline University School of Law

advisory opinion   is a judicial interpretation of the law that has no binding effect because it does not occur in response to an actual dispute in which the parties have adverse interests. In other words, a court issues an advisory opinion in a "dispute" that is hypothetical, not real. The supreme courts of 12 states have authority to issue advisory opinions, but the courts of most states, and the federal courts, do not.

Federal courts cannot issue advisory opinions because Article III of the Constitution prohibits them from doing so. The United States Supreme Court reached that conclusion in 1793, after President George Washington sought the Court's advice about legal questions that resulted from America's neutrality in the war then in progress between England and France. The Court declined to give President Washington the advice he sought. Chief Justice John Jay replied to the president that Article III restricted courts to deciding "cases" or "controversies," which Jay and his fellow justices interpreted to be actual disputes between adverse parties, in which court decisions could resolve matters. He added that the Constitution allowed the president to seek advice only from the heads of executive departments (i.e., members of the cabinet), not from the Supreme Court.

That reasoning is still good law today. Indeed, ever since 1793, the Supreme Court has held that requests for advisory opinions present "nonjusticiable" issues, in other words, issues that the Constitution does not permit the Court to decide or even to consider. The Court provided a formal statement of its views on advisory opinions in *Muskrat v. United States,* 219 U.S. 346 (1911). Congress had authorized certain Indians to file suit to determine whether a particular law was constitutional and had given the Indians a right of appeal to the Supreme Court. The Court concluded that even though Congress had authorized it, the lawsuit did not present a case or a controversy between adverse parties but instead sought to obtain advisory opinions from the Court about whether certain federal laws were constitutional. The Court stated in *Muskrat* that it was inappropriate for courts "to give opinions in the nature of advice concerning legislative action, a function never conferred upon it by the Constitution and against the exercise of which this Court has steadily set its face from the beginning."

There are two sound reasons why the Constitution limits the power of federal courts to actual disputes between adverse parties. The first reason is a practical one. Judges' training and professional experience qualify them to resolve live controversies between parties with adverse interests but not to decide abstract or hypothetical issues. The second reason is a more formal one that concerns the governmental structure that the Constitution established. When courts decide abstract or hypothetical questions, outside the boundaries of lawsuits, they violate the "separation of powers" principle that underlies our governmental structure and thus invade the domain of Congress and the president. The constitutional prohibition against the issuance of advisory opinions by federal courts honors the separation-of-powers principle by limiting the exercise of judicial power to matters in which it is appropriate, indeed, necessary.

The state courts of 38 states honor the same prohibition on advisory opinions. In the other 12 states, the state supreme court has the authority, under either the state constitution or a law enacted by the state legislature, to issue advisory opinions about proposed actions in response to formal requests by the governor or the legislature. For example, the New Hampshire Constitution permits the governor or either house of the state legislature to seek advisory opinions from the New Hampshire Supreme Court. In 1998 the state senate asked that court for its opinion regarding the likely constitutionality of the governor's plan to reform the way in which New Hampshire finances its public schools. The court advised the senate that the governor's plan would violate the state constitution, which forced the governor and the legislature to search for an alternative solution. Thus, where permitted, advisory opinions can influence public policy in important ways.

For more information

Fisher, Louis. *American Constitutional Law,* 3d ed. Durham, N.C.: Carolina Academic Press, 1999.

Porto, Brain L. *May It Please the Court: Judicial Processes and Politics in America.* New York: Addison Wesley Longman, 2000.

Brain L. Porto
College of St. Joseph (Vermont)

affirmative action policy seeks to overcome past and continuing racial, ethnic, or gender discrimination by increasing educational or employment opportunities through the preferential treatment of targeted groups. Preferential treatment may entail efforts to enlarge the pool of applicants for positions through advertising or other forms of publicity. However, the public and legal dispute over affirmative action centers on programs that provide bonus points for minority or women applicants to improve their chances for selection or that set firm quotas for qualified minority or women applicants.

The conviction that a color-blind policy would overcome the effects of racial discrimination animated the early Civil Rights movement. The theory was that if the stigma of public racism

were removed, then the plight of blacks and other minorities would disappear. The passage of the 1964 Civil Rights Act and the 1965 Voting Rights Act seemed to accomplish this aim. By the late '60s, however, it became clear that racially neutral programs of nondiscrimination failed either to guarantee equal opportunity in employment and higher education or to overcome inequalities in income among racial and ethnic groups. Executive orders issued by the Kennedy and Johnson administrations encouraging efforts to recruit and promote minorities in federally funded programs were unsuccessful. In 1969 President Richard Nixon stiffened existing programs with the implementation of the Philadelphia Plan, a program establishing specific goals and timetables for minority recruitment in the Philadelphia building trades.

By the 1970s affirmative action programs were common in higher education and in employment markets. Legal suits challenging such programs as "reverse discrimination" were also common. The Supreme Court first ruled on the legality of affirmative action in *Regents of the University of California v. Bakke* (1978). A divided Court rejected a University of California, Davis Medical School program because of inflexible quotas but indicated that other forms of affirmative action were permissible. Later cases upheld affirmative action in private (*United Steelworkers v. Weber* [1979], relying on Title VII of the 1964 Civil Rights Act) and public (*Johnson v. Transportation Agency, Santa Clara, California* [1987]) employment and in federal construction contracts (*Fullilove v. Klutznick* [1980], citing Congress's grant of the spending power under Article I of the Constitution). More recent cases such as *City of Richmond v. J. A. Croson* (1989) and *Adarand Constructors, Inc. v. Pena* (1995) suggest that the Supreme Court will approve voluntary affirmative action by governments only when the program passes "strict scrutiny." This test, traditionally applied to government actions affecting "suspect classes" such as race or ethnicity, requires that the state demonstrate that the means it has selected to accomplish its compelling interest are least intrusive on individual rights. Some lower courts have rejected affirmative action outright (*Hopwood v. Texas, 999 F. Supp. 872* [1998]). Voters in California and Washington state banned state and local affirmative action programs during the late 1990s.

Opponents of preferential treatment rely either on the Fourteenth Amendment or Titles VI and VII of the 1964 Civil Rights Act as the legal bases to their challenge. They assert that the Fourteenth Amendment's guarantee of equal protection is unequivocal. The declaration that "No State shall . . . deny to any person within its jurisdiction the equal protection of the laws" rejects racial or ethnic ancestry as a relevant basis for awarding a government benefit. Moreover, they argue, the 1964 Civil Rights Act requires that individual, not group-based, attributes be the only permissible factor when governmental or private goods or opportunities are dispersed. Opponents also invoke policy arguments. Preferences tend to reward the most advantaged members of the targeted groups while hurting the least advantaged members of the non-preferred groups, creating an unjust form of compensation. Preferences also stigmatize minorities as inferior since they may be seen to succeed not through merit but through gift. Finally, opponents fear that preferences encourage racial and ethnic identities as a means to win social goods and services, "balkanizing" rather than uniting the nation.

Supporters of affirmative action appeal to a mixture of policy and legal considerations. The Fourteenth Amendment and the Civil Rights Act permit carefully tailored programs designed to overcome systemic discrimination against minorities and women. They further argue that preferential treatment produces significant social benefits that outweigh the harm inflicted on the supposed victims of reverse discrimination. It preserves social peace by establishing society's sensitivity to the plight of its minority citizens. It stimulates social mobility by provid-

ing role models who will inspire minority youths. It improves access to professional services such as medical and legal care by training minorities to serve traditionally undeserved communities. It enriches the marketplaces of goods and of ideas with a diversity of viewpoints, experiences, and interests. And it responds to the remedial spirit of the Reconstruction amendments, allowing government and private redress for past social wrongs.

The controversy over affirmative action seems to pose a choice between two unpalatable alternatives. Endorsing race- or ethnic-conscious programs may further legitimize these characteristics as means to apportion benefits and burdens in American society. Rejecting such programs on a "color-blind" principle may condemn minorities to a continued status as an underclass.

Whether affirmative action works is further part of the debate. In 1974 the unemployment rate among African Americans was double that of non-Latino whites. In 1999, the rate was still double. In the late 1960s, the proportion of families with incomes below the poverty line was four times greater among blacks than whites. It is still four times greater. There has been some rise in the numbers of minorities in higher education and the professions, but with the exception of women, most groups have not seen appreciable improvement since the mid-1970s, with an actual decline among African-American males entering college.

For more information
Sindler, Allan P. *Bakke, Defunis, and Minority Admissions.* New York: Longman, 1978.

Skrentny, John David. *The Ironies of Affirmative Action: Politics, Culture, and Justice in America.* Chicago: University of Chicago Press, 1996.

Timothy J. O'Neill
Southwestern University

alienage   and immigration are central elements of U.S. national social and economic policies. Aliens are individuals from another nation who seek admission into the United States. Aliens who are U.S. residents generally have the same civil and criminal rights as given to citizens; major exceptions include voting, holding federal elective office, and serving on a jury. Constitutional interpretation permits executive and legislative branches to decide about the presence of foreigners in our nation.

Immigration is an exclusive function of the national government as part of its power over foreign affairs.

In U.S. history there has been frequent societal ambivalence toward immigration. Restrictions on admission of persons from another country began in 1882 with the Chinese Exclusion Act. Since then Congress has passed a variety of acts to limit entry of certain types of individuals, such as criminals, the mentally ill, or persons from particular nations as part of a national origins quota system. The Immigration and Nationality Act of 1952 (McCarran-Walter Act) placed severe restrictions "upon the immigration and naturalization of Communists and other totalitarians." Congress may establish annual limits for immigration and may alter those limits and quotas for persons or their relatives with special skills. In 1965 Congress abolished the national quota system and established a new annual limit of 170,000 persons per year.

The U.S. Congress decides immigration policy as part of its power to regulate foreign commerce. The U.S. Supreme Court has deferred to Congress on immigration matters, and there are few constitutional limits on this legislative power. Congress establishes rules and individual qualifications for naturalization of an alien admitted to citizenship; see Article I, section 8 of the Constitution. Minors become citizens when their parents are naturalized. Naturalization matters, including admission, naturalization, and deportation of aliens, are administered by the Immigration and Naturalization Service (INS) in the U.S. Department of Justice.

There have been frequent constitutional claims against excessive use of force and border searches and seizures by the INS. On administrative issues, there have been claims of arbitrary INS practices concerning individuals seeking entry into the country. Immigration rules for deportation and those seeking admission do not always comply with the full realm of rights under the Constitution. However, the Supreme Court has ruled that due process guarantees apply to INS deportation hearings. An outline of general INS administrative procedures is given in *INS v. Chadha*. Executive departments play an important role in administering immigration laws. Both the Departments of State and Justice have substantial discretion to determine who may enter the United States.

For more information

Aleinkoff, Alexander T. "Federal Regulation of Aliens and the Constitution," *American Journal of International Law* 83 (1989): 862–71.

Gordon, Charles, and Harry N. Rosenfeld, *Immigration Law and Procedure,* rev. ed. New York: Matthew Bender, 1985.

INS v. Chadha, 462 U.S. 919 (1983).

Neuman, Gerald L. *Strangers to the Constitution: Immigrants, Borders, and Fundamental Law.* Princeton, N.J.: Princeton University Press, 1996.

Steven Puro
Saint Louis University

alternative dispute resolution   refers to a broad range of techniques used in settling conflicts between parties outside the arena of a public court. Alternative dispute resolution (ADR) methods may involve relatively few formal procedures, as in negotiation and mediation, or may, in the instance of arbitration, resemble the structure and adversarial format of a civil trial. The ultimate purpose of ADR is to produce an agreement to which the parties will be bound, avoiding litigation. However, ADR proceedings may be either binding or nonbinding and may be court-ordered or entered into voluntarily by the parties. In voluntary ADR, parties may stipulate at the outset whether the results of proceedings, such as an arbitrator's award, will be binding. In court-ordered ADR, parties enjoy the option of entering into a binding agreement at the conclusion of proceedings. Also, parties are allowed to reject the outcome of court-ordered ADR and pursue claims in a judicial forum. Moreover, ADR is favored by many disputants as a procedurally flexible, cost-effective way of resolving conflict while avoiding civil litigation.

Although in use throughout our nation's history, ADR techniques were not widely embraced by American courts until the 1970s. In the 1980s and 1990s, ADR methods became permanent fixtures in the American legal establishment as state and federal legislatures responded to the exigency of burgeoning civil dockets. In 1990 Congress encouraged the use of ADR techniques by passing the Civil Justice Reform Act, providing funds for ADR programs in the federal courts. More recently, Congress passed the Alternative Dispute Resolution Act of 1998. This legislation requires the federal courts to ensure that litigants consider non-adjudicative approaches to resolving civil disputes. As part of a broader plan to streamline government operations, in 1993 the Clinton administration called on federal administrative agencies to enhance efforts at ADR and avoid the costs of litigation. As a result, federal agencies increasingly employ forms of mediation and arbitration in resolving disputes with private citizens.

ADR is used, to varying degrees, in all state court systems. In many instances, state law or court rules require that litigants participate in one or more approaches to ADR before proceeding to trial. State law and court rules often require that parties engage in ADR in cases involving family issues or commercial relationships. Many legal scholars observe that in matters of divorce and child custody, disputants are more inclined to comply with the terms of settlements reached in the non-adversarial settings of

negotiation and mediation. The business community lauds ADR schemes for providing a degree of flexibility and confidentiality in settling legal disputes not ordinarily available through traditional adjudicative processes. Considering that agreements and decisions reached via ADR techniques need not be founded on legal principles, many litigants consider these options better suited to the task of securing a just outcome. ADR strategies are routinely employed in foreign trade disputes where jurisdictional ambiguities often make litigation an unwieldy exercise. Business executives often find that ADR methods are useful in preserving the highly interdependent relationships between firms so typical in today's economy.

The most common forms of ADR include pretrial settlement conferences, the relatively non-adversarial methods of negotiation and mediation, the slightly more adversarial techniques of summary jury trials and mini-trials, and arbitration, the most procedurally complex and formal of non-litigious dispute resolution strategies. Negotiation often takes place between disputing parties prior to the time that attorneys are retained, and this often precludes the need to engage in the expense and delay associated with formal pleadings and discovery. Sometimes, however, parties to a dispute employ legal counsel for the purposes of safeguarding their interests in negotiating a settlement in a civil dispute. Settlement conferences are part of standard pretrial procedures in the federal courts. In a settlement conference, a magistrate, rather than a trial judge, meets with opposing attorneys prior to the scheduled trial date and explores the possibility of a mutually acceptable resolution to the case. When successful, settlement conferences produce a formal, binding agreement between the parties, achieving the goal of avoiding a trial.

Mediation is considered a non-adversarial ADR technique. Mediation sessions are less procedurally rigid than arbitration and are designed to preserve existing legal relationships. Mediation sessions are not intended to gauge the legal strength or evidentiary weight underlying each party's position. Rather, the neutral third party, or mediator, is principally concerned with guiding the disputants toward an agreement to which both parties can accede. Thus, mediators typically seek to highlight points of agreement between parties and narrowly frame issues that produce discord. Doing so often requires that mediators meet with disputing parties in joint sessions as well as in individual meetings, typically referred to as caucuses, in a search for consensus and a sustainable agreement. Mediation sessions may be ordered by a court or arranged voluntarily by the parties. In either case, disputants are free to reject mediation agreements and proceed to litigation.

Summary jury trials are a unique and innovative form of ADR. In a summary jury trial, opposing attorneys present documentary and testimonial evidence, along with brief oral arguments, to a panel of neutral finders of fact. These panels, or "juries," then advise the parties as to the probable outcome of the case were a public trial held. Summary jury trials often occur at a time between the discovery stage of civil litigation and the beginning of an actual trial. Further, summary jury trials are comparatively more adversarial than mediation and are especially useful for litigants as indicators of the viability of their case. Despite the procedural differences between mediation and summary jury trials, both are designed to encourage out-of-court settlements and avoid the delay and expense associated with civil trials. Summary jury trials are occasionally required by court rules.

Mini-trials are similar to summary jury trials in that both settings involve the use of jurors and modifications of conventional trial settings. In addition, mini-trials often involve discovery or information-sharing procedures similar to, yet presumably less costly than, those used in civil trials. Whereas summary jury trials typically use laypersons as finders of fact, mini-trials ordinarily employ a panel of corporate executives representing the disputing parties. Acting as jurors,

these executives enjoy the authority to effectuate a binding settlement in the dispute. Like mediation and summary jury trials, mini-trials serve the goal of fully informing the disputants about one another's position, a strategy designed to increase the probability of an agreement and thus obviate the need for litigation. Although frequently arranged solely by the parties, in some jurisdictions courts require mini-trials as a precondition to litigation.

The most adversarial of ADR methods, arbitration is commonly used in business and international trade disputes. Also, arbitration has proven useful in reconciling labor-management discord in a variety of employment settings. Often, parties to a contract will agree in advance not to litigate disputes over duties and obligations but to have an arbitrator produce a binding decision. If the parties to a dispute elect to participate in arbitration at the time when a disagreement occurs, a neutral third party hears opposing arguments and renders a decision, sometimes referred to as an award. Parties may agree in advance to be bound by an arbitrator's decision. Inasmuch as arbitration awards resemble jury verdicts, the hearings that precede the award often include presentation of documentary and testimonial evidence as well as questioning of witnesses.

In cases of voluntary arbitration, the principle of *res judicata* applies, restricting either party from future litigation in the matter. Moreover, by agreeing to participate in arbitration, disputants may waive their Seventh Amendment right to a jury trial and agree to be bound by an arbitrator's decision. Awards rendered in binding arbitration sessions are enforceable by public courts. Unlike circumstances wherein parties agree to arbitrate a dispute, court-annexed arbitration is nonbinding and either party may reject the neutral's award. In this instance, a trial *de novo* may be held and a court resolves all legal and factual disputes in the matter. Following an arbitrator's decision, however, parties may accept an arbitrator's award and enter into a binding, enforceable agreement.

The popularity of ADR is reflected in the ascendance of several public and private sector organizations that offer standardized procedural frameworks and professional neutrals trained in dispute resolution methods. The American Arbitration Association (AAA), a private sector organization, provides a complete range of mediation and arbitration services. In addition, the AAA monitors the performance and has compiled a lengthy roster of highly qualified mediators and arbitrators with expertise in a variety of fields. The AAA reports that in 1999 the firm administered ADR services in more than 140,000 cases. In addition, the Global Arbitration Mediation Association provides directory services for parties seeking referral to ADR firms and professionals. The Federal Mediation and Conciliation Service is an independent government agency dedicated to mediating labor-management disputes in public and private sector entities. The prevalence of ADR in domestic and international arenas is likely to encourage growth in these and many related organizations.

For more information

Kheel, Theodore W. *The Keys to Conflict Negotiation: Proven Methods of Settling Disputes Voluntarily.* New York: Four Walls and Eight Windows, 1999.

Nolan-Haley, Jacqueline M. *Alternative Dispute Resolution in a Nutshell.* St. Paul, Minn.: West Publishing Co., 1992.

Bradley J. Best
Austin Peay State University

amendments to the U.S. Constitution
are vital both to keeping the document up-to-date and to avoiding violence that can occur when peaceful means of constitutional change are blocked, as the colonists felt they had been at the onset of the American Revolution.

Seeking mechanisms that would respond to widely perceived necessities while resisting temporary currents of opinion, the framers of the U.S. Constitution included amending processes in Article V. This article divides the amending process into proposal and ratification stages and provides two forms of each. An amendment must be proposed by two-thirds majorities of both Houses of Congress or, in a still unused mechanism, by a special convention proposed by two-thirds of the state legislatures. Congress specifies whether amendments will be ratified by three-fourths of the state legislatures or—as in the case of the Twenty-first Amendment repealing national alcohol prohibition—by special state conventions.

Reflecting the importance of the Great Compromise between the small and large states, Article V specifies that no state shall be deprived of its equal vote in the Senate without its consent. Another so-called entrenchment clause provided that Congress would not interfere with the slave trade during the new nation's first 20 years.

Throughout the course of American history, members of Congress have introduced more than 10,000 amending proposals, many of them redundant. Congress has proposed only 33 by the necessary two-thirds majorities and, of these, only 27 have been adopted. Un-ratified proposals have included a provision related to congressional representation, an amendment to strip citizenship from individuals who accepted titles of nobility, an amendment (the Corwin Amendment) that would have guaranteed the continuing existence of slavery in the South, a child labor amendment, an amendment guaranteeing congressional representation for the District of Columbia, and the Equal Rights Amendment.

The initial Congress introduced the first 10 amendments, collectively known today as the Bill of Rights, and the states ratified them in 1791. These amendments emerged from the controversy between Federalist proponents of the Constitution and Anti-Federalist opponents, who had cited the omission of a bill of rights as a key fault in the new document. Although initially resisting, key Federalists, most notably James Madison, agreed to work for a Bill of Rights if the new document were adopted. In the first Congress Madison gathered together scores of state proposals, most guaranteeing individual rights, which were condensed into 12 amendments, 10 of which were ratified in 1791. Key provisions include the protections for freedom of religion, speech, press, peaceable assembly, and petition in the First Amendment; the right to bear arms in the Second Amendment; provisions against the quartering of troops in private residences in the Third Amendment; protections against unreasonable searches and seizures in the Fourth Amendment; protections for individuals accused of, or on trial for, crimes in amendments Five through Seven; and the provision against cruel and unusual punishments in the Eighth Amendment. Reflecting Federalist fears that no set of amendments could adequately provide for all contingencies, the Ninth Amendment refers to unenumerated or unlisted rights, and the Tenth Amendment cites rights retained by the states. When originally adopted, the provisions in the Bill of Rights applied only to the national government, but since the adoption of the Fourteenth Amendment with its protection against state denials of due process, the Supreme Court has applied, or "incorporated" almost all these provisions to the states as well. Unincorporated provisions are the Second Amendment right to bear arms, the Third Amendment provision regarding the quartering of troops, the Fifth Amendment guarantee of grand jury indictment, the Seventh Amendment right to a jury in civil cases, and the Eight Amendment provision against excessive fines and bails.

The Eleventh and Twelfth Amendments were almost contemporaneous with the Bill of Rights. The Eleventh Amendment overturned a Supreme Court decision by limiting lawsuits against the states, and the Twelfth modified the electoral college mechanism for presidential selection so as to prevent unanticipated ties in the voting that the party system had made possible.

The three amendments ratified from 1865 to 1870 responded to the events that precipitated the Civil War. The Thirteenth Amendment permanently abolished slavery. The Fourteenth Amendment overruled the *Dred Scott* decision of 1857 by extending citizenship to all persons born or naturalized in the United States and prohibiting states from denying citizens their rights. The Fifteenth Amendment further specified that race was not to be used to deny individuals the right to vote.

Adopted from 1913 to 1920, the next four amendments are associated with the Progressive Era in U.S. politics, which stressed reform and greater democratic participation. The Sixteenth Amendment overturned a Supreme Court decision and permitted the national income tax. The Seventeenth Amendment provided for direct election of U.S. senators, who had been previously selected by state legislatures. The Eighteenth Amendment mandated national alcohol prohibition, while the Nineteenth extended the right to vote to women, a subject that had been increasingly in the national consciousness since the Seneca Falls Convention of 1848.

The last eight amendments have dealt with a variety of subjects. The Twentieth Amendment changed the dates that new presidents and congresses take office, thus shortening the terms of so-called lame-duck members who had been voted out of office. The Twenty-first Amendment repealed national alcohol prohibition. The Twenty-second Amendment limited presidents to two full terms, or eight years, in office. The Twenty-third Amendment provided representation in the electoral college for the District of Columbia. The Twenty-fourth Amendment limited the effect of poll taxes; the Twenty-fifth Amendment provided for cases of presidential disability; and the Twenty-sixth Amendment reduced the voting age to 18.

The last amendment, the Twenty-seventh, prohibits Congress from giving itself a raise until after an intervening election. Originally proposed in 1789 as part of the Bill of Rights, the states did not ratify the amendment until 1992, after a college student named Gregory Watson became convinced that the amendment was still viable. This amendment points to the fact that Article V specified no ratification deadline. Similarly, Article V does not specify whether states can rescind ratifications of pending amendments or ratify amendments they have previously rejected.

Proposed amendments often become issues even when they are not proposed by Congress by the necessary two-thirds majorities and ratified by the states. Recent decades have witnessed vigorous debates over amendments to reverse Supreme Court decisions regarding prayer and/or Bible reading in public schools, busing, abortion, and flag-burning as well as amendments to balance the federal budget, make English the official national language, and guarantee victims' rights.

Interpretations of the Constitution often change over time through judicial decisions and congressional and presidential practices. Amendments serve, however, as markers for many key changes in the Constitution and evidence of the continuing power that "We the people" can exercise through legal channels.

For more information

Palmer, Kris E. *Constitutional Amendments, 1789 to the Present.* Detroit: Gale Group, Inc., 2000.

Vile, John R. *Encyclopedia of Constitutional Amendments, Proposed Amendments, and Amending Issues, 1789–1995.* Santa Barbara, Calif.: ABC-CLIO, 1996. See also Appendix.

John R. Vile
Middle Tennessee State University

American Bar Association   or the A.B.A. is a private, voluntary association, with headquarters in Chicago, which is the national organization for the legal profession. The A.B.A. is the largest association of professionals in the world, with more than 350,000 members, or approximately half of the lawyers in the United States.

The A.B.A. was established in 1878, in response to the industrialization of the economy, which spurred calls for the creation of stricter standards for entry into the legal profession. The standards for admission to law practice had been lax for more than a hundred years. As late as 1860, only nine of the 39 states had any educational requirements for practicing law. In those states, an aspiring lawyer served a period of apprenticeship in a law office, then sat for a rather casual oral exam, conducted by a judge, which lasted about a half hour. Often, the examinee passed because of a recommendation from a well-known lawyer, not because of professional competence. The A.B.A. urged state legislatures to require candidates for admission to the bar to pass a written "bar exam" that was more rigorous than the earlier oral exams. A.B.A. members viewed written exams as a method of improving the competence of lawyers, which remains one of the association's major goals.

Today the A.B.A. pursues that goal principally by serving as the national accrediting body for U.S. law schools. Most states rely on A.B.A. accreditation to determine whether the law school attended by an applicant for admission to practice meets the educational requirements necessary for admission to the bar. Graduation from a law school that is not A.B.A.-accredited may entitle the graduate to take the bar exam in the state in which the law school is located, but it often disqualifies the graduate from taking the bar exam in other states. Therefore, the customary path to the legal profession nowadays is to earn a baccalaureate degree (B.A. or B.S.) from a four-year college and a juris doctor (J.D.) degree from an A.B.A.-accredited law school. The A.B.A.'s Section of Legal Education and Admissions to the Bar assists aspiring lawyers to find suitable law schools by publishing the *Official American Bar Association Guide to Approved Law Schools* annually.

The A.B.A. also attempts to improve the competence of lawyers by sponsoring continuing legal education programs and by publishing books, articles, pamphlets, and newsletters that address substantive areas of the law, as well as issues such as law office management and the increasing role of technology in the practice of law. Some A.B.A. publications recommend standards of conduct that lawyers should follow when they perform certain legal tasks. For example, *Standards of Conduct: Pleas of Guilty,* Third Edition (1999), establishes guidelines for prosecutors and defense attorneys to use in negotiating "plea bargains" with persons accused of crimes. In a plea bargain, the accused pleads guilty to a less serious offense than the offense that was charged originally, in exchange for receiving a less severe sentence than would have resulted from a conviction on the original charge.

The ethical standards of the legal profession are another focus of the A.B.A., and they have been for many years. In 1908 the A.B.A. adopted a code of professional ethics, and most states either accepted the A.B.A. code or something similar as their official rules for the conduct of lawyers. Today the A.B.A. periodically amends its code of ethics, known as the "Model Rules of Professional Responsibility," which states are free to accept or reject, but which most states adopt, at least in part or in modified form.

One of the most important roles that the A.B.A. plays is as an evaluator of prospective federal judges. The A.B.A.'s "Committee on Federal Judiciary," which is comprised of 15 members who represent each region of the country, screens persons whom the president is considering for nomination to a federal judgeship and assigns each one a rating of "not qualified," "qualified," or "well-qualified," which the committee then makes available to the attorney general and to the Senate Judiciary Committee for their consideration. The major function of the Committee on Federal Judiciary is to try to prevent ill-advised nominations; once the president chooses a nominee, the committee does not actively oppose that choice even if it rated the nominee "not qualified."

Despite its power and prominence, the A.B.A. faces several daunting challenges in the new millennium. Among these are: (1) making legal services more affordable; (2) making the practice of law friendlier to minorities and women, especially mothers of school-age children; and (3) addressing the public perception that our system for compensating injury victims enriches lawyers but diminishes America's economic competitiveness in the global economy. Only time will tell whether the A.B.A. is equal to these awesome challenges.

For more information

Linowitz, Sol, and Martin Mayer, *The Betrayed Profession: Lawyering at the End of the Twentieth Century.* Baltimore, Md.: The Johns Hopkins University Press, 1994.

Porto, Brian L. *May It Please the Court: Judicial Processes and Politics in America.* New York: Addison Wesley Longman, 2000.

Brian L. Porto
College of St. Joseph (Vermont)

American Civil Liberties Union or the ACLU is a nonpartisan citizens' organization dedicated to the preservation and implementation of the Bill of Rights. It was founded in 1920 by political activists reacting to government attempts to stifle dissent during World War I, and it now has 300,000 members, national offices in New York City and Washington, D.C., with a staff of more than 150, affiliate offices in 50 states, and an agenda that covers all the rights protected by the Constitution.

Its underlying premise is that democracy, as embodied in the U.S. system of government and law, has two parts: rule by the majority of the people, through democratically elected representatives, and protection of the rights of the individual and of groups—even when protection means limiting the power of the majority. By this reasoning, it would be undemocratic, for example, to permit the majority to prohibit people from voting, going to certain schools or holding certain jobs because of their race, religion, political views, gender, or other irrelevant character-istics.

While the organization has persuaded state and federal courts to apply this underlying principle, that has not exempted it from the animosity of many. The reasons are twofold.

First, the ACLU has adopted numerous positions that were, and in some cases remain, controversial. Taking the entire Bill of Rights as its mandate, the organization regularly involves itself in issues such as speech (*Reno v. ACLU*, 1997), racial discrimination, separation of church and state (*Santa Fe Independent School District v. Doe,* 2000), lesbian and gay rights (*Romer v. Evans*, 1996), arts censorship, capital punishment, children's rights, education reform, national security, privacy and technology, prisoners' rights, voting rights, women's rights (*Planned Parenthood v. Casey*, 1992), and workplace rights, electronic privacy, rights of the mentally ill, and drug policy and law enforcement issues (*Miranda v. Arizona*, 1966).

Second, the ACLU frequently defends people whose opinions are controversial or extreme (*National Socialist Party of America v. Skokie,* 1977) because it believes that once the government is empowered to violate one person's rights it can use that power against everyone.

The ACLU describes itself as the nation's first public interest law firm. The bulk of its work consists of litigation, with the combined national and affiliate offices handling more than 6,000 cases a year. The majority are the work of volunteer attorneys. They work closely with the legal staff, members of which sometimes argue cases themselves. The organization's boards of directors are similarly made up of volunteers.

In addition to bringing cases itself, the ACLU writes amicus curiae ("friend of the court") briefs in cases it considers particularly important in a specific subject area or in the development of constitutional doctrine. It argues more cases and submits more amicus briefs to the Supreme Court than any other nongovernment organiza-tion. Its high success rate accounts for its impact on both American law and the proliferation of other public interest law organizations.

For more information

Walker, Samuel. *In Defense of American Liberties: A History of the ACLU.* New York: Oxford University Press, 1990.

Cowan, Ruth B. "Women's Rights through Litigation," *Columbia Human Rights Law Review* 8 (1976): 373–412.

Philippa Strum
City University of New York

Americans with Disabilities Act   or the

ADA is a federal statute prohibiting discrimination based on disability in employment, state and local government, public accommodations, commercial facilities, transportation, and telecommunications. President George H. W. Bush signed the Americans with Disabilities Act (ADA) into law in 1990. Any individual who has a disability, or a relationship or association with someone with a disability, is covered by the ADA.

According to the ADA, the term disability refers to a physical or mental impairment that substantially limits major life activities. Anyone who has a history of such impairments, or whom others perceive to have such impairments, is protected by the provisions in the ADA. The ADA does not specify all types of disabilities that the law covers. In fact, after passage of the ADA, AIDS (acquired immunodeficiency syndrome) activists sought, and eventually won, a Court interpretation of the statute that includes AIDS as an ADA qualifying disability.

Congress divided the ADA into titles, and each specifies protections within a particular category. Title I requires employers (employing 15 or more persons) to provide equal opportunities to all employment-related benefits for qualified individuals with disabilities. The Equal Employment Opportunity Commission (EEOC) handles Title I complaints.

Title II applies to state and local governments and requires that all people with disabilities be assured access to public programs and services. The kinds of public programs and services that ADA applies to are, for example: public education, government employment, public transportation, access to the courts, and participation in elections. Title III requires businesses and nonprofit service providers to provide equal treatment to persons with disabilities. Examples of the types of public accommodations covered under Title III include: movie theaters, buses, homeless shelters, hotels, retail stores, and restaurants. Businesses running these sorts of public services are required to provide "reasonable accommodation" for people with disabilities. This is a difficult term to define, and judges have interpreted it in various ways. Generally it means that whenever possible, businesses should make adjustments to accommodate people with disabilities. If an owner can show that he or she has made an honest attempt to provide accommodations, then this will generally put them in compliance with the law. For instance, a business may be required to provide adaptations, like ramps, wider doorways, and braille menus. The U.S. Department of Justice handles complaints under both Titles II and III.

Finally, Title IV of the ADA covers telecommunication services such as television and telephone access for persons who have hearing and/or visual impairments. The purpose of this title is to ensure that people with disabilities have access to interstate and intrastate communications. Therefore, the telephone companies are required to provide devices such as telecommunications devices for the deaf (TDDs). In addition, television broadcasting companies were required to add closed captioning to federally funded public service announcements. Television manufacturers were required to make television sets capable of showing the closed captioning available to the general public. The Federal Communications Commission oversees this title.

Disability advocates heralded the passage of the ADA through Congress, and its signing into law, as a triumph. Many Americans with disabilities have benefited from the provisions of this law at work, in leisure activities, and in exercising their rights as citizens to vote in elections. Many disability interest groups are still working to educate members of the public, and persons protected by the law, on its many provisions.

For more information
(on interest group education) *http://TheArc.org;* and (the law itself) 42 U.S.C. section 12101 et seq.

Nancy Winemiller Basinger
University of Georgia

amicus curiae is Latin for "friend of the court." The plural is amici curiae. As the name suggests, amici curiae are expected to serve the interests of the court. An amicus curiae is anyone, or any group, that has a strong interest in a case but is not one of the direct parties in a case, who seeks to provide information to the court to reinforce the arguments provided in the briefs of the litigants or to provide information that those parties did not include in their briefs. This understanding of amici curiae and their role before the courts may be somewhat misleading. In practice, amici curiae have generally participated to advance their own policy objectives, rather than serving altruistic goals such as serving the needs of the court system to be fully informed.

Amicus curiae briefs can be filed in any court, state or federal, and at any level, trial or appellate. In most instances, the amicus is an attorney filing the brief on behalf of a client, but it need not be. Amicus curiae briefs can only be filed with the consent of the court in which the case is being heard, but this consent is usually granted, particularly when the consent of both litigants is provided. However, if the party submitting the brief is the federal government, state, territory, or commonwealth, consent is not required from the court. In rare circumstances, amici are allowed to participate in oral arguments.

These briefs are filed by interested third parties because decisions of the court, while directly applying only to the parties directly involved in the case, have implications beyond the case being decided. Through the doctrine of *stare decisis,* or precedent, the decision in a case may be of interest to persons, businesses, or interest groups not directly involved in the case. In these instances, those who might be potentially affected may file an amicus curiae brief.

Amicus curiae briefs are more frequently filed at the appellate level than in trial courts. The reasons for this are associated with the cost of filing amicus briefs and the policy impact of becoming involved in the case. The most effective amicus curiae briefs are those with substantial legal research, containing information that the court might not otherwise obtain from the litigants. As a result, the cost to research and prepare the brief can be quite high. In addition, those filing briefs will want to participate as amicus curiae in a court where the decision will have the greatest impact, and will focus on courts of appeal rather than trial courts.

There is no limit on the number of amicus briefs that can be filed in a single case. Those cases that tend to attract the most amicus activity are those that involve issues that are highly salient to the public and involve significant issues of policy that affect large segments of the population. The first amicus brief was filed in the Supreme Court in 1821, and amicus activity was relatively rare for the next century. Even during the first half of the 20th century, amicus briefs were filed in approximately 10 percent of Supreme Court cases. As the Supreme Court heard more cases involving civil liberties, and public interest groups formed to pursue policy, it is now rare for a case to reach the Supreme Court without at least one amicus brief filed. In recent years, more than 80 percent of cases heard by the Supreme Court contain at least one amicus curiae brief.

The record for the most amicus curiae briefs filed in a case heard by the Supreme Court occurred in *Webster v. Reproductive Services,* an abortion rights case decided in 1989. In *Webster,* there were 78 amicus curiae briefs filed by hundreds of pro-choice and antiabortion organizations, breaking the previous record of 57 briefs filed in the affirmative action case *Regents of the University of California v. Bakke* in 1978. The Court may give the arguments in the amicus curiae brief as much or as little weight as it chooses, but with the increasing number of briefs filed, the Court is certainly better informed about the potential legal, social, and political consequences of their decisions than ever before.

For more information

Merrill, Thomas, and Joseph P. Kearney, "The Influence of Amicus Curiae Briefs on the Supreme Court," *University of Pennsylvania Law Review* 148 (January 2000): 743–855.

Ennis, Bruce J. "Effective Amicus Briefs," *Catholic University Law Review* 33 (1984): 603–609.

Krislov, Samuel. "The Amicus Curiae Brief: From Friendship to Advocacy," *Yale Law Journal* 72 (March 1963): 694–721.

Scott Comparato
Southern Illinois University at Carbondale

animal rights   often refers broadly to efforts by advocates of every kind to protect nonhuman animals from exploitation by humans. But to many lawyers it refers specifically to the struggle to obtain legal rights for at least some nonhuman animals.

Twenty-first-century U.S. humans have an assortment of basic legal rights: They cannot be enslaved. Their bodies cannot be used in biomedical research without their consent. They cannot be imprisoned in steel and concrete cages if they have committed no crime. At one time Americans enslaved each other. It was only near the end of the Middle Ages that Europeans began to believe that it was wrong to enslave those who were of their own race or religion. That did not stop white Christians from enslaving Muslims or Africans of any religion, but it was a start. At various times in the history of the United States, Indians, women, children, and blacks all lacked basic legal rights. Human slaves were treated as legal things, scarcely different from a chair, a dish, or a cow. Sometimes they were treated as real estate, such as houses and land. Only legal persons have legal rights and human slaves were not legal persons under the civil law. They were invisible to the civil law and so they lacked all civil rights.

Legal things are often protected by the criminal law, but that does not give them any legal rights. Today a statute might make it a crime to take a baseball bat to the windshield of a car. A wrongdoer might be fined or even sent to prison, but neither the car nor the windshield would be a legal person with civil rights. Before the Civil War, many slave-holding states made it a crime to kill or grievously harm a slave. If a master violated that law, it was a criminal matter between the master and the state, not a civil one between the master and slave. The first major criminal statute that protected nonhuman animals was England's "Martin's Act," passed in 1822 to "prevent the cruel and improper treatment of Cattle." That statute has been expanded, extended, and multiplied throughout the English-speaking world. Every U.S. state has at least one. But, in almost every way, the "legal thinghood" of every nonhuman animal in the United States today is the same as it is for windshields and cars and the same as it once was for black slaves before the Civil War.

Animal rights lawyers are trying to change this. They want at least some nonhuman animals to be declared legal persons with basic legal rights. They want people to be able to protect them against enslavement, biomedical research, and imprisonment. This might be accomplished in several ways. The United States Constitution or state constitutions might be amended, but these are unlikely places to start. More promising

are the legislatures of the 50 states. Perhaps the most promising is the common law.

The common law is what judges make as they decide cases that do not interpret of statutes or constitutions. The rules that one cannot drive negligently or break a contract are just some of a large number of common law rules. How do judges decide what these rules should be? They look to three things—precedent, policy, and principle. Precedents are those cases already decided, whether yesterday or 500 years ago. Policy concerns what judges think will be the impact of their decisions on society. Principle involves what judges believe is right and wrong. By temperament and training, each judge will tend to emphasize one of these three over the others.

Precedent judges, who care most about deciding cases the way they have always been decided and in keeping the law stable will probably not be inclined to change the legal status of nonhuman animals from legal thing to legal person. After all, nonhuman animals have been legal things for many centuries. More common in the United States are policy judges and principle judges. It can be thought that when the basic interests of a being are at stake, they should never be sacrificed to the interests of those who want to exploit them. This is exactly what occurred before the Civil War. Even Northern judges who hated slavery supported the most unfair Fugitive Slave Laws for policy reasons; they wanted to facilitate economic growth and promote national unity by not alienating the slave-holding South. Today we think they did a terrible thing as a matter of principle.

The highest principles of the common law include liberty and equality. Fundamental to liberty is the idea that certain basic interests are of immense importance. One of those interests is "autonomy." Any being able to want things and able intentionally to try to get them, and who has a sense of self complex enough to allow them to realize, however dimly, that they are living a life should have autonomy sufficient to entitle them to the legal rights to bodily integrity and bodily liberty. Their bodies cannot be used in biomedical research. They should not be imprisoned in steel and concrete cages. Species should be entirely irrelevant.

Fundamental to equality is the idea that "likes should be treated alike." We give basic legal rights even to human infants born without a brain who are not conscious or sentient. What about chimpanzees and bonobos? They feel pain and suffer. They are probably self-conscious. They act intentionally. They solve problems insightfully. They use and make tools. They flourish in rough and tumble societies so political that they are routinely dubbed "Machiavellian." They can learn symbols and numbers and understand two or three thousand English words. It is impossible both to comport with equality and give these infants rights, yet deny every legal right to chimpanzees and bonobos. And there are almost certainly others.

For more information

Wise, Steven M. *Rattling the Cage—Toward Legal Rights for Animals.* Boulder, Colo.: Perseus Publishing, 2000.

Steven Wise
Center for the Expansion of Civil Rights

antitrust law   refers to a cluster of federal laws that seek to inhibit private parties from improperly restraining the marketplace through large combinations or trusts of business or capital. Some argue that the goal of antitrust laws can be thought of as promoting allocative economic efficiency. That is, the goal of antitrust is to promote a market system that maximizes societal wealth by deploying resources where they are most highly valued. Others argue that antitrust is primarily designed to protect consumers from monopolists and cartel members. That is, the policy goal is to avoid artificially high prices being charged to the consumer. Whatever the normative policy goal, the laws take the form of

prohibitions on a variety of actions deemed to harm or improperly restrain the market. While many states have enacted legislation that tracks the federal laws, the term generally refers to the Sherman Act, the Clayton Act, and the Federal Trade Commission Act.

The Sherman Act (15 U.S.C. § 1–7) makes contracts or agreements for purposes of the restraint of interstate or foreign trade illegal. The Sherman Act also prohibits monopolies and conspiracies to monopolize. By *monopoly,* the statute contemplates a consolidation of economic power which allows the suspect firm to set a price that is artificially high.

The Clayton Act (15 U.S.C. § 12–27) supplements the Sherman Act by prohibiting price discrimination when the effect is to substantially lessen competition. The Clayton Act also prohibits kickbacks and other commercial bribery or price manipulation as well as any attempt to obtain or grant kickbacks or bribes.

The Federal Trade Commission Act (15 U.S.C.A. § 41–51) creates the commission responsible for preventing the use of unfair methods of competition or deceptive trade practices.

Antitrust laws can be the basis for civil or criminal actions and can be privately or publicly enforced. In the event that a private plaintiff prevails in an antitrust action, that plaintiff is entitled to damages. Damages may take the form of injunctive relief or compensatory relief. Injunctive relief occurs when the defendant(s) is/are ordered to cease and desist engaging in the objectionable behavior that gave rise to the litigation. Compensatory relief seeks to compensate the aggrieved party for the actions of the defendant(s).

The Clayton Act contains a treble damages provision which is designed to discourage bad behavior before it occurs. The Clayton Act awards treble damages, or triple the actual loss, to any successful plaintiff. The treble damages provision has been the principal deterrent to and punishment of anticompetitive conduct. It also serves as an incentive for private enforcement of the antitrust laws and a mechanism for retrieving ill-gotten gains. Still, the treble damages provision is not without its critics. Some economists and legal scholars argue that the statute does not encourage consumers or others to mitigate, or lessen, their damages since it awards three times the actual damages suffered. Further, since the proscribed behavior is somewhat vague, the treble damages may create a disincentive for aggressive competition. The windfall of treble damages may act as an incentive for frivolous litigation. Finally, compensating an injured party beyond their damages while penalizing a defendant in excess of the gains from misbehavior may be unfair.

For more information

Hovenkamp, H. *Federal Antitrust Policy, The Law of Competition and Its Practice,* 2nd ed. St. Paul., Minn.: West Publishing Co., 2000.

Ross, S. R. *Principles of Antitrust Law.* Westbury, N.Y.: The Foundation Press, Inc., 1993.

Sullivan, E. T., and Harrison, J. L. *Understanding Antitrust and Its Economic Implications,* 2nd ed. New York: Matthew Bender and Co., 1994.

Charles Anthony Smith
University of California, San Diego

appeal is a legal procedure by which an unsuccessful litigant in a lawsuit requests a higher court to reverse the decision made by a lower court or agency.

The term *appeal* was originally used in early English law to mean "to accuse." In the 13th century, the term was used to refer to a proceeding by which a superior court tried a case anew, without deference or reference to a lower court's decision. The term now refers to a superior court's examination of possible prejudicial error in a lower court proceeding. Potential errors that appellate courts examine may include, but are not limited to, a lower court's decision about motions, monetary awards or remedies, the admission or suppression of evidence, sentenc-

ing, the application of the law to the facts of the case, or the lower court's overall judgment.

The aggrieved party who is displeased with a lower court decision and initiates an appeal is called the appellant or petitioner. The party who opposes the appeal and is usually satisfied with the lower court's decision is called the appellee or respondent. To commence the appeal, the appellant must file a notice of appeal and other legal documents. An "appeal by application" is an appeal requiring permission by the appellate court before a case may be appealed, whereas an "appeal by right" requires no prior permission.

Rules of appellate procedure applicable to a reviewing court, as well as court practices, local rules, and internal operating procedures, govern an appellate court's review. Federal appellate courts follow the Federal Rules of Appellate Procedure, and state appellate courts follow their own rules of appellate procedure. Such rules and practices determine, for example, the scope of the types of cases that are appealable and to which appellate court they are appealed, the procedure by which the appeal is brought before the court, what procedures the parties must follow when appealing a case, and the standard of review that is used by the appellate court to determine what is required for a reversal of the lower court decision.

Appellate courts review cases to assure that significant and prejudicial errors made by a lower court during pretrial and trial stages are corrected, to develop the law, and to act with the ultimate goal of assuring uniformity of the law. An appellate court does not make the initial decision in a case, accept new evidence, call witnesses, or render judgments that it would have rendered if it had originally tried the case. Instead, an appellate court reviews the record of a lower tribunal proceeding (such as transcripts of testimony, documents, and the lower court's opinion) to determine whether the lower tribunal correctly applied the law to the facts of the case. Appellate review is often restricted to the appellate court's independent determination of the law, which is guided by precedent so that similar cases are similarly decided.

An appellate court rarely alters a trial judge's interpretation of facts and will only alter facts when the trial court's factual findings are clearly erroneous. An appellate court almost never disturbs the trial court's conclusions about the credibility of witnesses or documents. Most appellate courts will not interfere with the discretionary decisions made by a trial court, unless the court abused its discretion. Moreover, an appellate court usually will only review legal issues that were raised in the trial court. Under exceptional circumstances, such as a clear miscarriage of justice, a legal issue that was not preserved for appeal might be reviewed for plain error. Issues that have become moot or cases that have been settled during the time period that the appeal is pending are not reviewable.

Appellate courts usually review issues from a lower court case after a final judgment in that case has been entered. However, under certain circumstances, some issues may be appealable before a trial court has issued a final judgment (known as an interlocutory appeal). The review of nonfinal judgments is limited to legal questions (such as issues of qualified immunity, subject matter jurisdiction, or constitutional questions) that must be answered before the trial court case may properly proceed.

There are different routes an appeal may take through state or federal judicial systems. Cases appealed to state appellate courts usually originate in state trial courts. Most states have more than one level of appellate courts, with the first level called an intermediate appellate court, and the highest court of the state (often called the state "Supreme Court") being on the second level. Cases appealed to federal appellate courts may originate in a U.S. district court, the highest court of a state in which a decision could be received, or a federal agency. The U.S. courts of appeals are intermediate appellate courts in the federal judicial system. Cases appealed to a U.S. court of appeals typically originate in a federal

district court located in the geographic region of the court of appeals. The highest court of the United States is the United States Supreme Court. The United States Supreme Court, outside of narrow exceptions, accepts cases by permission only and selects only a relatively few number of appeals to review during each court term.

An appeal might be reviewed by only an intermediate appellate court; however, some cases can also be reviewed by the highest appellate court in the judicial system after the case was reviewed by an intermediate appellate court; and some cases may bypass the intermediate appellate court and be appealed directly to the highest appellate court of the judicial system. An administrative agency decision is usually reviewed by an administrative law judge before it is appealed to a trial court, and then the case may proceed through the appellate courts, such as an intermediate appellate court and then, perhaps, to the highest court in the judicial system.

Appellate briefs are usually written by both the appellant and appellee and presented to the appellate court to assist the court in understanding the legal questions presented on appeal. The appellate court may grant the appellant and appellee an opportunity to argue their cases orally to a panel of judges, so that the parties may elaborate on the arguments presented in their appellate briefs and answer questions asked by the judges. Oral arguments are subject to time limits that are usually established at the discretion of the appellate court.

If an appellate court affirms a lower court decision, the appellate court agrees with the decision reached by the lower court. If an appellate court modifies a lower court decision, the court agrees with the appellant that prejudicial error exists, and the appellate court changes the result reached by the lower court. If an appellate court reverses a lower court decision, the court agrees with the appellant that a legal error(s) was made, and the appellate court changes the result reached in the lower court proceeding. If an appellate court remands a case back to the lower court, the appellate court generally agrees with the appellant and directs the lower court to determine the relevant issue(s) consistent with the appellate court's decision. An appellate court might also dismiss an appeal, if, for example, the court discovers that it lacks the authority to hear the appeal.

An appellate court need not reach a unanimous decision. The majority of judges on the panel reviewing an appeal determines the result of the appeal. An appellate judge(s) who disagrees with the majority's result may write a dissenting opinion that explains areas of disagreement. A judge(s) who agrees with the result reached by the majority, but disagrees with the reasons for majority's decision, may write a concurring opinion that provides reasons for disagreement.

For more information

Hornstein, Alan D. *Appellate Advocacy in a Nutshell.* St. Paul: West Publishing Co., 1998.

Martineau, Robert J. *Fundamentals of Modern Appellate Advocacy.* Rochester, N.Y.: The Lawyer's Cooperative, 1985.

Neumann, Richard K. Jr. *Legal Reasoning and Legal Writing: Structure, Strategy, and Style.* Boston: Little, Brown, 1994, pp. 327–37.

Lindsley Armstrong Smith
Martin and Kicklak Law Firm

appellate briefs   are written documents that present legal questions about the proceedings and final decision in a lower court case and are intended to persuade an appellate court that an error was or was not made by the lower court.

Appellate briefs assist an appellate court (a superior court of review) in understanding the facts and legal questions presented in an appeal of a lower court case. The briefs must conform to formal stylistic requirements that are established by the appellate court (such as: restrictions on the length of the briefs, size and font of lettering, jurisdictional statement, table of contents, table of authorities, proper legal citations, a concise statement of the relative facts of the case, and an argument section with both headings and subheadings). Appellate briefs are filed with the appellate court and provided to the opposing litigant. Appellate briefs are usually written by attorneys who represent the appellant (the litigant who is dissatisfied with a lower court decision and who brings the case to the appellate court for review) and the appellee (the litigant who is generally satisfied with a lower court decision and opposes the reversal of the decision). A brief written by a litigant, rather than a licensed attorney, is called a *pro se* brief.

An appellant provides the appellate court with a brief that consists of arguments about how the lower court decided a case inconsistently with the law, and it may include arguments that the lower court made erroneous findings of fact. Specifically, the appellant typically provides the legal question presented for review by the appellate court, the relevant facts of the case, arguments supporting reversal of the lower court decision, and legal authority supporting the arguments. The appellee, in turn, writes a brief that refutes the arguments made in the appellant's brief, discusses the deficiencies in the appellant's brief, and urges the appellate court to accept the decision of the lower court. Although the appellee's brief is usually a response to the arguments and legal authority presented in the appellant's brief, the appellee may also present other issues for the appellate court's review in the form of a cross-appeal (appeal by the appellee to modify or reverse a portion of the lower court's decision, which is usually heard at the same time as the appellant's appeal). The appellant, in turn, may then provide the appellate court with a reply brief, which refutes the arguments and/or legal authority discussed in the appellee's brief.

Individuals or associations that are not litigants in a lawsuit may also file an appellate brief, which is referred to as an amicus brief. The people or associations filing such briefs are referred to as "amicus curiae" (a friend of the court). Amici typically write an appellate brief because they wish the appellate court to consider a relevant perspective of the law and society that was not specifically addressed by a litigant, they wish to advance the argument of a litigant or to provide specific expertise on a legal issue that is to be decided by the court. The amici typically wish to influence the court's decision on a legal issue of great importance to the amici.

For more information

Hornstein, Alan D. *Appellate Advocacy in a Nutshell.* St. Paul: West Publishing Co., 1998, pp. 182–226.

Neumann, Richard K. Jr. *Legal Reasoning and Legal Writing: Structure, Strategy, and Style.* Boston: Little, Brown, 1994, pp. 327–37.

Lindsley Armstrong Smith
Martin and Kieklak Law Firm

appellate jurisdiction   is the authority of a higher court to review and revise a case that has already been decided by a lower court.

Appellate jurisdiction is distinguished from "original jurisdiction" (the jurisdiction conferred on or inherent in a court to hear a case initially). For example, if a case is not one designated within the United States Supreme Court's original jurisdiction, the Supreme Court could only hear the case through the exercise of its appellate jurisdiction. Article III, section 2 of the U.S. Constitution vests appellate jurisdiction in the Supreme Court, and 28 U.S.C.A. sections 1291–1295 vest appellate jurisdiction in the federal courts of appeals (intermediate appellate courts in the federal judicial system).

Appellate courts do not have the authority to hear every appeal presented to them. The federal Constitution and statutes, as well as state constitutions and statutes, create courts and designate the types of cases within the appellate jurisdiction of the courts. The structure of judicial systems, federal and in each state, provides a guide as to which court within

a system has the authority to hear an appeal. For example, appellate jurisdiction does not exist in a court where an action is first brought, but it can exist in a higher court. Appellate courts may have concurrent power to hear a certain type of appeal, or a particular appellate court may be vested with the exclusive power to review a particular appeal. In effect, an appellate court must determine whether it has the authority to hear the appeal in the judicial system of which it is a part, as well as determine whether it has the jurisdiction to hear the particular appeal.

The lack of appellate jurisdiction is so important that an appellate court must dismiss an appeal of its own initiative, without the need for a litigant to first argue that appellate jurisdiction is lacking, if the court does not have the authority to hear the appeal (a *sua sponte* dismissal). Appellate courts must also determine the scope of their jurisdiction. Appellate courts have the power to decide only the law and issues presented in the particular case on appeal, rather than pronounce judgment on issues that have no practical effect on the determination of the case being appealed. Appellate courts dismiss a premature appeal—one that was presented for review before the lower court issued a final, appealable order or judgment—however, some nonfinal judgments of a lower court are reviewable under a court's appellate jurisdiction. Moreover, appellate courts lack the power to hear certain appeals, such as those that are moot or present political (rather than judicial) questions.

For more information

"Federal Courts, Original and Appellate Jurisdiction." In *American Jurisprudence,* 2nd ed. Volume 32, Section 549, Rochester, N.Y.: Lawyer's Cooperative, 1995.

Hornstein, Alan D. *Appellate Advocacy in a Nutshell.* St. Paul: West Publishing Co., 1998, pp. 43–47.

Lindsley Armstrong Smith
Martin and Kieklak Law Firm

appointment and removal power (executive) concerns presidential authority under Article II, section 2 of the Constitution— Appointments Clause—to remove subordinates in the executive branch and in administrative agencies.

The Constitution allows the president to nominate, with the advice and consent of the Senate, a wide variety of officers of the United States, including "Ambassadors, other public ministers and Consuls, Judges of the Supreme Court and all other Officers of the United States. . . ." Appointments are divided into two classes: principal and inferior officers. Presidential appointment power to carry out the executive duties of government has received a broad constitutional mandate. The president has clear authority to appoint principal officers—those requiring advice and consent of the Senate— who have major enforcement and administrative duties. Further, the president has discretion in removing administrative officials, both principal and inferior, who are directly responsible to that office. This authority is connected to the presidential requirement to "faithfully execute the laws." Congress may allow the president to appoint inferior officers on his own or through the heads of departments. The president has the authority to remove federal officers, such as local postmasters or members of independent regulatory commissions, who may have a combination of legislative, executive, and judicial powers.

The appointment and removal power can involve issues of separation of powers between the executive and the legislature. A main question is whether congressional statutes interfere with the executive's removal and appointment powers. A major conflict occurred in *Morrison v. Olson*. In this case Congress passed a law establishing the office of special prosecutor. Independent counsels from that office had authority to investigate and prosecute high ranking federal government officials or violation of federal crim-

inal laws. The appointment and removal process was conducted by judiciary and the attorney general, and it was independent of presidential appointment or removal authority. The Court said that special prosecutors are "inferior" officers. However, the Constitution allows for some congressional interbranch appointments, where an officer of one branch is appointed by officers of another branch.

Congressional attempts to increase its own appointment and removal powers at the expense of the executive branch have been ruled unconstitutional. Congress cannot directly remove executive officials without invading the executive's removal powers. Congress can only remove principal executive officials through impeachment and conviction. In several periods of congressional–executive conflict presidential removal power has been the central question of constitutional litigation.

For further information
Bowsher v. Synar, 478 U.S. 714 (1986).
Buckley v. Valeo, 424 U.S. 1 (1976).
Humphrey's Executor v. United States, 295 U.S. 602 (1935).
Morrison v. Olson, 484 U.S. 654 (1988).

Steven Puro
Professor of Political Science
Saint Louis University

arms, right to bear refers to the Second Amendment of the U.S. Constitution which, according to some, guarantees the right of each individual to own firearms. However, the amendment does not guarantee this right.

Historically, the right to bear arms derives from an Anglo-American legal tradition relying on citizens to fulfill many of the functions of government, from serving on juries to policing and protecting communities. Among the unpaid obligations of citizenship was the bearing of arms to suppress civil disorder and repel invasion.

Long before the invention of firearms, Englishmen were required to be ready to assemble as bowmen in defense of the realm, and this requirement was readily transferred to colonial America. From the recruitment of Miles Standish to train and lead a Pilgrim militia to the reliance on state militias in support of the Continental Army in the War for Independence, state and federal governments attempted to maintain a force capable of providing stability and security to communities and the state without recourse to standing armies.

After the Revolution this impulse continued, and it was combined with a pervasive general fear of standing armies. For these reasons the federal Constitution provided for the creation and use of militias "to execute the Laws of the Union, suppress domestic Insurrections and repel invasions," but it also specified that the states appoint militia officers and take control of training the militia "according to the discipline prescribed by Congress" (Article I, section 8). Even so, the Second Amendment attests to a lingering distrust of a consolidated government by guaranteeing the theory that "A well regulated Militia, being necessary to the security of a free State, the right of the people to keep and bear Arms, shall not be infringed." In addition to limits on Congress, many of the new states provided in their own constitutions for protecting the right to bear arms.

Although most states linked this right to a militia duty, Pennsylvania expanded the traditional language and stated, "The people have a right to bear arms for the defence of themselves and the state." As new states joined the union in the following century, many defined the right to bear arms as an individual right to self-defense rather than as a collective one, though not all did so. Mississippi's guarantee of 1817, that "Every citizen has a right to bear arms in defense of himself," became a model for other states before the Civil War, as fear of slave revolts and Indian resistance generated concerns for security.

Even so, individual gun ownership remained rare until after the war, when veterans returned with their mass-produced weapons and manufacturers fueled demand with heavy advertising and low prices.

Over the past century, state legislatures have protected individual gun ownership, but they retain the authority to regulate it. The Supreme Court has upheld state firearms control laws against challenges under the Second Amendment (*United States v. Cruikshank* in 1870 and *Presser v. Illinois* in 1886), as well as a model local ordinance banning handguns (*Quilici v. Village of Morton Grove* in 1983). Current constitutional law continues to define the "right to bear arms" as a collective matter, not an individual right (*United States v. Miller,* 1939).

For more information

Cornell, Saul, ed. *Whose Right to Bear Arms Did the Second Amendment Protect?* New York: St. Martin's Press, 2000.

Cottrol, Robert J., ed. *Gun Control and the Constitution: Sources and Explorations on the Second Amendment.* New York: Garland Publishing, 1994.

David Thomas Konig
Washington University in St. Louis

arraignment is any court appearance that precedes a trial in a criminal proceeding. In a strict sense, it is defined as the hearing before a court having jurisdiction, or judicial power to adjudicate a criminal case, in which the identity of the defendant is established and in which the charges are formally announced. The court informs the defendant of his or her rights and requests the defendant to enter a plea or reply to the charges. There are five possible pleas: Not Guilty (Innocent); Not Guilty by reason of an affirmative defense, such as self-defense, or insanity; Guilty; Nolo Contendere, or 'no contest', which means that the defendant will be convicted; Remain standing silent, which is entered as a plea of "not guilty."

In many states, appearance is required in all events except where a simplified information is presented by the prosecutor in a misdemeanor. The defendant always has the right to the aid of counsel at the arraignment and at every subsequent stage of the action. Appearance by counsel instead of the charged person is permissible in any case in which the defendant is required to appear in court by summons or a traffic appearance ticket.

If the defendant appears without counsel, generally he or she must be informed of the rights listed below. The court must allow the defendant to exercise those rights and must also undertake affirmative action to ensure that those rights have been employed, where the defendant exhibits inaction.

Right to an adjournment for the purpose of obtaining counsel;

Right to communicate, free of charge, by letter or by telephone to obtain counsel or inform next of kin that a criminal charge has been entered against her;

Right to have the court appoint counsel if there is financial impairment.

At the arraignment, in the absence of an intention to dispose of the action in its entirety, the court must issue a securing order either releasing the defendant on his own recognizance or setting bail for a future appearance in the action. In the case of a felony charge, the court must allow the district attorney to object to the bail, or after knowledge or notice of the application and a reasonable opportunity to be heard, a failure to appear constitutes a waiver of the right to do so.

The court must also be furnished with a report from the division of criminal justice services listing the defendant's criminal record, if any, or with a police department report with respect to the defendant's prior arrest record. The report must be presented to the defendant or his legal defense counsel. In New York State, for example, if a local criminal court lacks authority to order

recognizance or bail, or has denied the application for recognizance or bail, or has fixed excessive bail, then defense counsel may make an application or motion to a superior court judge to vacate an existing order and enter a decree for bail or recognizance subject to notice to the district attorney and an open court hearing in the case of a felony charge.

Special statutory criminal procedure provisions exist for the arraignment of corporate defendants. A "corporate summons" is a process issued by a superior court directing a corporate defendant designated in an indictment to appear before it at a designated future time in connection with an indictment. The summons must be served by a public servant, designated by the court, upon the corporation by delivering it to an officer, director, managing or general agent of such corporation authorized by law to receive service of process.

The arraignment process may also be used to ascertain whether a person or individual is a material witness. A court may issue a "material witness" order declaring that a person possesses material information in connection with a pending action and is expected not to be amenable or responsive to a subpoena to appear at a later time. A prospective material witness must be informed in an arraignment about the nature and purpose of the proceeding and is entitled to a prompt hearing upon the issue of whether a decree declaring the person a material witness should be ordered. The court must also instruct the prospective material witness as to the right to legal counsel, including adjournment to obtain counsel or assignment of counsel, in case of financial hardship. If the proceeding is adjourned at the request of the prospective material witness, then the court may set bail to assure future attendance.

In *Garland v. State of Washington,* 232 U.S. 642 (1914), the defendant was retried on two information statements, one charging him for larceny of a $1,000 check, and the second for larceny of 1,000 U.S. dollars. No arraignment or plea was entered on the second information charge. The Court held that the object of an arraignment was to inform the accused of the charged criminal offense and to obtain an answer. Referring to English history, the Supreme Court reviewed the necessity of arraignment to validate the trial. In *U.S. v. Alvarez-Sanchez,* in spite of the absence of a state court arraignment, defendant's confession on other federal criminal acts was upheld.

For more information

Lawrance F. Travis III. *Introduction to Criminal Justice,* 3rd ed. Cincinnati, Ohio: Anderson Publishing, 1998.

J. David Golub
Touro College

arrest   is the depriving of a person's liberty by legal authority because that person has been accused of committed a crime.

Hundreds of arrests are made on television, but what exactly is an arrest, what is required for it to be valid, and what rights does the arrested person have? Although in theory any citizen may make an arrest, due to possible legal and physical dangers law enforcement agents make nearly all arrests. When someone is deprived of freedom by being taken into custody, an arrest has occurred whether that specific word is used or not. If the suspect has no choice about whether to accompany the officer, even when the officer phrases the matter as a polite request, it is considered an arrest. Because arrests are considered seizures of the person, the Fourth Amendment's prohibition of unreasonable searches and seizures applies. Therefore, no person may be lawfully arrested without probable cause, which is defined as adequate evidence to convince a reasonable person that the suspect is likely to have committed a crime. However, most arrests are made without a court-issued warrant. Such arrests are legitimate if made in a public place with proba-

ble cause. When the police go to someone's residence, however, they need an arrest warrant.

Many people incorrectly believe that an arrest is invalid unless accompanied by the Miranda warning. In fact, this warning is required only for custodial interrogation. If it is not given, any responses by the suspect cannot be used as evidence by the prosecutor but, if no questions are asked, the suspect does not have to be told of his/her rights to counsel and silence.

In *Chimel v. California* (1969) the Supreme Court ruled that a lawful arrest allows the police to search the area within the suspect's immediate control even without a search warrant. The justification is to prevent destruction of evidence and to allow the police to safeguard themselves by seizing any weapons the suspect might grab.

The Supreme Court has expanded police power to stop automobiles. Roadblocks to deter and apprehend drunk drivers are permitted if there is no police discretion. This means that either every vehicle or every *n*th vehicle can be stopped to determine sobriety even without probable cause. *Maryland v. Wilson* (1997) held that during routine traffic stops, police could order not only the driver but also passengers out of the car.

Terry v. Ohio (1968) allowed the police to make investigatory stops of suspects on less than probable cause. Any officer with a reasonable suspicion that a crime is about to be committed can stop a suspect, frisk him/her for weapons, and ask a few questions. Only if this results in additional evidence adequate for probable cause can an arrest be made. The recent case of *Illinois v. Wardlow* (2000) held that unprovoked flight from the police in a high crime area justified a *Terry* stop and frisk. On the other hand, *Florida v. Royer* (1983) ruled that a person who ignores the police and goes about his/her business cannot be stopped without additional evidence.

Because evidence obtained as a result of an unlawful arrest is generally excluded from a trial, the legality of an arrest is often critical to its outcome.

For more information

Illinois v. Wardlow, 2000 U.S. Lexis 504.

Podgers, James. "Poisoned Fruit: Quest for Consistent Rule on Traffic Stop Searches," *American Bar Association Journal* 81 (February, 1995): 50–51.

Bruce E. Altschuler
Professor and Chair, Dept. of Political Science
State University of New York, Oswego

arson is a criminal offense defined by the Model Penal Code as the intentional or deliberate starting of a fire or explosion, usually for the purpose of (a) destroying a building or occupied structure of another or (b) destroying any property, whether one's own or the property of another, for insurance proceeds. Although originally a common-law crime, the elements of arson have now been defined by statute, with most states following the Model Penal Code definition. Finding an intent to cause injury to others, or the intent to cause personal harm, is not a requirement, so the definition of arson also includes the act of starting a fire or explosion in a vacant or abandoned building. However, a related offense under the arson provision of the Model Penal Code, "Reckless Burning or Exploding," does include the element of placing another person in danger of bodily harm or death. To accommodate modern realities, "occupied structure" has been expanded—sometimes by implication and sometimes by express statutory language—to include any structure, such as automobiles or watercraft, used for overnight lodging or travel. The Model Penal Code also provides that for multiunit structures, such as apartment buildings, each unit not occupied by the person committing arson is considered as a separate structure.

Because the crime of arson does not require personal injury, some states have developed the offense of "aggravated arson," which includes all the traditional elements of arson but adds the additional element of harm to persons, either intended or actual. One example of this is *State v.*

Williams, 623 A.2d 800 (N.J. 1993). Other states have separated the basic crime of arson into one or more degrees, with the lowest degree being merely reckless starting of a fire, and the greatest involving harm to others. However, the criminal law varies from state to state on whether a person may lawfully burn his own property, if not in order to collect insurance proceeds.

For more information

Black's Law Dictionary, 6th ed. St. Paul, Minn.: West Publishing Co., 1990, p. 111.

Model Penal Code sec. 220.1, St. Paul, Minn.: West Publishing Co., 1974.

Gerald J. Russello
Covington & Burling, New York

Articles of Confederation were adopted in 1781 as the first constitution for the United States after its independence from England.

The Articles of Confederation were drafted in stages from 1776 to 1777 but were not ratified until 1781; the Articles extended and revised the existing understanding of diffused authority and state autonomy. Richard Henry Lee, Samuel Adams, John Dickinson, and Roger Sherman, among others, assisted in the drafting of the document. Although regarded in 1781 as a reliable constitution, the accepted caricature of the Articles portrays the work as a dismal failure in all respects; the Articles could not provide for a system of popular rule or supply the young regime with the security measures that were needed to ensure its survival. Critics of the Articles usually cite the plan's inability to endow a national government with the power to levy taxes or regulate commerce, thereby discouraging all efforts at national cohesion. The Articles, in other words, embodied the political tensions within American politics during the period between the Declaration of Independence and the Philadelphia Convention.

The Articles possessed the means for affirming popular rule, diffusing political authority, and allowing for a system of government. As in the case of the Declaration of Independence, the Articles perpetuated the original design for the territorial division of the country into independent and sovereign states, a "perpetual union." Article Two described the nature of the alliance: "Each state retains its sovereignty, freedom and independence, and every power, jurisdiction, and right, which is not by the Confederation expressly delegated to the United States, in Congress assembled." Articles Three and Four, antecedents of the Tenth Amendment, affirmed the nature of their "league of friendship" and provided for the extradition of fugitives. Article Five presented a system of representation for the states in Congress that allowed for each state to have no less than two and no more than seven delegates. Articles Six and Seven concerned limitations upon the states regarding the conducting of foreign affairs and national security. Article Eight detailed how the costs of war would be defrayed, and Article Nine outlined the powers of Congress, the only branch of government established by the document. The last four Articles discussed various aspects of the "perpetual" union.

The Articles confirmed the centrality of the states, thus maintaining the relationship between the governed and the government at the state level instead of the national level. The Articles also provided that the respective states, not the federal government, would protect citizens' privileges and immunities. As a genuine precursor to the Tenth Amendment, the Articles limited the power of the federal government and strengthened state prerogatives.

For more information

Hoffert, Robert W. *A Politics of Tension: The Articles of Confederation and American Political Ideas.* Boulder: University Press of Colorado, 1991.

Jensen, Merrill. *The Articles of Confederation.* 1940. Reprint. Madison: University of Wisconsin Press, 1970.

Moore, Wayne D. *Constitutional Rights and Powers of the People.* Princeton, N.J.: Princeton University Press, 1996.

H. Lee Cheek, Jr.
Lee University

assault and battery   are two different legal concepts: assault is a threat of violence, and battery is an actual violent attack on another person. In the original common-law conception, assault was a threatened violent physical or verbal attack on another person. No actual physical contact was required. Battery was an unlawful touching or striking of another, either with his own person or by some instrumentality put in motion by the assailant, which touching had not been consented to by the victim and was done without privilege.

There are two kinds of assault and two kinds of battery, each dealing in terms of criminal and civil law. In U.S. law, the most commonly thought of type is criminal battery, often popularly called assault and battery. Many jurisdictions within the United States have combined the two concepts using one label or the other. There has been no consistency among the states as to which name is proper. For example, what Colorado statutes call sexual assault, Florida's call sexual battery, yet both describe the common-law crime of rape as well as other crimes in nearly identical terms.

Since assault as a demonstration of intent can be difficult to define within the common law, most state statutes define assault as the intent to cause bodily injury and include a present ability to do the harm. Aggravating circumstances may include a threat made with a deadly weapon. Some assaults include only a violent outburst, such as threatening to punch someone in the nose. Carrying out the threat then is the element of battery.

Defenses against prosecution for assault and battery are as varied as self-defense and defense of property. A common defense for sexual assault is consent. However, in the case of sexually oriented beatings, consent is usually void because they are against public policy. Similarly, consent is frequently used as a defense in cases of mutual combat. A person consenting to a beating as in a flogging in a religious play or a fight in a bar may not collect civil damages, intent being the controlling concept. If the persons inflicting the blows become overzealous, however, they could be charged with criminal assault and battery.

Civil liability for assault, resulting in the payment of damages to the person assaulted, is an act, other than mere words, that puts the victim in fear of immediate and harmful contact from the actor. Words alone are not sufficient to create an assault. While words do not count as a battery, incitement of another to act may impose liability. On the other hand, mere presence or silent approval will not make a person liable.

Certain other actions such as contact by a physician performing surgery or a police officer arresting a suspect are considered privileged and are exceptions to the rules of assault and battery.

In a criminal case, the court and jury are bound by the statutory definitions, but in a civil case the court has more leeway to determine what facts constitute an assault. The jury then decides what weight to give to the facts and determines the credibility of the witnesses.

Persons other than the actor may be held accountable for an assault, or assault and battery. If the assault is criminal there must be conspiracy on the part of the non-actor. A non-perpetrator can be liable for an assault and battery by an employee or other person acting under his or her authority. Also, a non-perpetrator can be held accountable for an assault because of negligence or because he or she incited the actor to commit the assault or the battery.

An attempt to apologize or to claim that the battery was done out of some laudable motive does not excuse an assault or a battery.

For more information

American Jurisprudence, 2nd ed. Vol. 6, *Assault and Battery.* St. Paul, Minn.: West Group Publishing, 1988–.

Restatement of the Law of Torts, 2d §§13, 21 et.seq. Washington, D.C.: American Law Institute; Consult the statutes in your state.

Stanley M. Morris
Attorney at Law
Cortez, Colorado

assisted reproductive technologies (ART)

have challenged traditional concepts of family law by raising questions involving the legal status of a child that results from ART and the legal rights and duties of the gamete donor(s), surrogate mother, and intended custodial parents.

ART includes both low-tech artificial insemination and higher tech "test-tube baby" procedures where the egg and sperm are brought together outside of the body, such as for in vitro fertilization (IVF), gamete intrafallopian transfer (GIFT), zygote intrafallopian transfer (ZIFT), and intracytoplasmic sperm injection (ICSI).

Laws regulating ART are few and far between except for statutes and court decisions clarifying legal rights and duties in artificial insemination. New legal issues have arisen when a surrogate mother is carrying a child for another couple (who may or may not be the genetic parents) and decides that she does not want to relinquish the child, when the father is deceased and his sperm are used in ART, and when excess embryos are frozen for future implantation and one of the prospective parents no longer wishes to participate.

Surrogate mothers first came to the public's attention with the Baby M case, *In re Baby M*, 537 A.2d 1227 (N.J. 1988), in which the surrogate mother provided both the egg and the uterus. The New Jersey Supreme Court found that the surrogacy contract was invalid because it conflicted with public policy and adoption laws that prohibited the enforcement of preconception agreements. The court gave sole custody of the child to the intended custodial parents but did not terminate the parental rights of the surrogate mother. In *Johnson v. Calvert,* 851 P.2d 776 (Cal. 1993), the surrogate mother provided only the uterus and the intended custodial parents contributed the embryo; the California Supreme Court honored the preconception intention of the parties.

The ability to freeze and store sperm for later insemination after the death of the father has raised legal issues. In Louisiana, Judith Hart was conceived by GIFT three months after the death of her father. Her mother applied for Social Security survivor benefits for her based on the father's Social Security employment and earnings record. Under Louisiana and federal law, the child was not the legal heir of her father because she was not born at the time of his death, nor born within 300 days of his death. The Social Security Administration decided that survivor's benefits would be paid nevertheless, based on public policy reasons, but recognized that there were neither regulations nor law to address this issue.

As an alternative to immediate implantation, pre-embryos can be stored for future implantation by freezing them in liquid nitrogen. Thousands of these frozen pre-embryos are stored in laboratories and IVF clinics across the country. There are no clear laws on who has authority to dispose of them or what becomes of them in case of parental death, divorce, unavailability, dispute, or nonpayment of storage fees. In both *Davis v. Davis,* 842 S.W.2d 588 (Tenn. 1992) and *Kass v. Kass,* 696 N.E.2d 174 (N.Y. 1998), the couple attempted to conceive a child through IVF but divorced before they could do so. In both cases, the husband asked that the court not give the pre-embryos to the wife. In the Tennessee case, there was no prior written agreement regarding pre-embryo disposition, and the Tennessee Supreme Court weighed the procreative interests of the husband and wife and ruled that the party wishing to avoid reproduction should prevail whenever the other party has a reasonable possibility of having offspring through other means. In the New York case, the court ruled that the couple's signed written agreement prior to ART directing the IVF program to use the pre-embryos in approved research should be honored.

Laws are needed for clarifying the status of ART offspring and for assigning rights and duties of parentage in situations when gamete donors and surrogate mothers are used. The spirit and intent of the laws would have to acknowledge that the U.S. Supreme Court has recognized procreation as one of the basic civil rights. An outright ban on ART would be unconstitutional because it would limit the basic right of individuals to reproduce.

For more information

Andrews, Lori B. *The Clone Age: Adventures in the New World of Reproductive Technology.* New York: Henry Holt and Company, 1999.

Evans, Donald, ed. *Creating the Child: The Ethics, Law and Practice of Assisted Procreation.* The Hague, Netherlands: Martinus Nijhoff, 1996.

Gosden, Ralph. *Designing Babies: The Brave New World of Reproductive Technology.* New York: W. H. Freeman, 1999.

Karen Gottlieb, Ph.D., J.D.
BioLaw
Nederland, Colorado

asylum can be sought by a person physically present in the United States who meets the definition of a refugee and fears political persecution if returned to his or her home country. A refugee is defined as "any person who is outside any country of such person's nationality or in the case of a person having no nationality, is outside any country in which such person last habitually resided, and who is unable or unwilling to avail himself or herself of the protection of that country because of persecution or a well-founded fear of persecution on account of race, religion, nationality, membership in a particular social group, or political opinion."

Asylum law was codified in the United States as part of the Refugee Act of 1980. Serious concern for the plight of refugees developed both internationally and in the United States after World War II. The definition of a refugee used by the United States comes from the 1951 United Nations Convention and 1967 Protocol Related to the Status of Refugees, which the United States signed in 1968.

Persons seeking refugee status apply from outside the United States, whereas asylum seekers apply from within the United States. Under current law, applications for asylum must be made within one year of entry unless there are extraordinary circumstances that caused delay or changed circumstances that materially effect the applicant's eligibility for asylum. Persons who meet the definition of refugee may not be granted asylum if they have been firmly resettled in a safe third country before coming to the United States. Additionally, applicants may not qualify for asylum if they themselves were persecutors, if they have been convicted of a serious crime in the United States, if there are reasons to believe they committed a serious crime outside the United States, or if they are a risk to the security of the United States. Similar restrictions apply to spouses or children of asylees who otherwise may be granted asylum if accompanying or following to join the person granted asylum status.

Persons filing for asylum in the United States may request work permission after a several month waiting period. Persons granted asylum status may file for permanent resident status after one year.

For more information

Anker, Deborah E. *The Law of Asylum in the United States,* 3rd ed. Boston: Refugee Law Center, 1999.

Bhabha, Jacqueline, and Coll, Geoffrey, eds. *Asylum Law and Practice in Europe and North America.* Toronto: Federal Publications, Inc., 1992.

The Immigration and Nationality Statute, 8 U.S.C. § 1101(a)(42)(A) and 1158 (2000), and the Code of Federal Regulations, 8 C.F.R. § 208.1–208.31 (2000).

Angela McCaffrey
Hamline University
School of Law

attempt is in general the performance of an act or series of acts with the intention to achieve some end. In criminal law, the attempt to commit a crime usually means that a person acting with the level of culpability or knowledge required to commit the crime (1) purposefully engages in conduct which would constitute the crime if the attendant circumstances were as that person believes them to be (for example, buying drugs from an undercover government agent); (2) when causing a particular result is an element of the crime, does or omits to do something with the purpose of causing that result; or (3) does or omits something where the defendant believes that act or omissions is a "substantial step" in a course of conduct planned to culminate in the commission of a crime. (Model Penal Code § 5.01 [4]). As the New Jersey Supreme Court stated in *New Jersey v. Robinson,* 643 A.2d 591 (1994), "the criminalization of attempt focuses on the intent of the actor to cause a criminal result."

The law of attempts is of relatively recent origin in the common law, commonly dated to the 1784 decision by Lord Mansfield in *Rex v. Scofield.* It is also one of the more complex concepts in criminal law. By definition, an attempt to commit a crime means that the crime itself usually has not occurred. As set forth by the New York Court of Appeals in *New York v. Mahboubian,* 74 N.Y.2d 174 (1989), common rationales advanced for punishing attempts include that it is as appropriate to punish a person who has unsuccessfully committed a crime as one who has committed one, and that law enforcement authorities should be encouraged to stop crimes before they occur. In the case, for example, of one who attempts to commit a crime but fails to do so because of unforeseen circumstances or accident, it seems proper still to punish the perpetrator for the attempt.

In order to protect against punishing thoughts or acts that will not, without more, lead to a crime, attempt statutes as drafted by the legislatures and interpreted by the courts have sought to distinguish between actions taken in order to attempt to commit a criminal offense and actions that, while "preparatory" to a crime, are not themselves sufficient to constitute an attempt. These include the doctrines of "factual" impossibility, in which the attempted crime is unable to be completed due to some factual circumstance unknown to the actor, for example, by picking an empty pocket; and "legal" impossibility, in which the intended result of defendant's actions is not in fact a criminal offense, for example, attempting to receive stolen goods that were not in fact stolen. A person who is found to have attempted a legal impossibility generally is immune from conviction for attempt. However, one who attempted to commit a crime that was factually impossible is still subject to punishment for an attempt to commit the contemplated crime.

While at common law attempt was considered a lesser crime than had the crime been completed, and so was accorded a lesser punishment, the current trend among state attempt statutes is to punish attempt at the same level as the crime attempted.

For more information

Kaplan, John, and Robert Weisberg, *Criminal Law: Cases and Materials.* Boston: Little, Brown, 1986, pp. 509–77.

Gerald J. Russello
Covington and Burling, New York

attorney general, U.S.   is the chief legal officer of the United States or of a state, who gives legal advice to the chief executive and to other officials. In the early years the attorney general of the United States gave legal advice to the Congress when requested. In 1819 William Wirt put a stop to this. The attorney generals serve two masters—the chief executive and the law. From time to time there can be a clash between their responsibilities to their political superior and to the public interest. The attorney general gives both legal and policy/political advice. The attorney general's interpretation of a law stands as authoritative unless overturned by judicial decision. In recent years the attorney general has been legally empowered to appoint an independent prosecutor to investigate cases of high-level wrongdoing in the executive branch.

The U.S. attorney general heads the Department of Justice and, since the time of George Washington, is a member of the president's cabinet. In 1993 Janet Reno became the first woman attorney general in the nation's history. While some state attorneys general have gone on to the governorship (e.g., Bill Clinton in Arkansas), no federal attorney general has become president (though Robert Kennedy ran for the office in 1968, and William Wirt was the candidate of the Anti-Masonic Party in 1832). However, a number of attorneys general (Roger B. Taney, Nathan Clifford, Joseph McKenna, William Moody, James C. McReynolds, Harlan F. Stone, Frank Murphy, Robert H. Jackson, Tom C. Clark) have become justices on the Supreme Court. Henry Stanbery (Andrew Johnson's A.G.) and Ebenezer R. Hoar (Grant's A.G.) were rejected by the Senate when nominated for the Supreme Court.

The attorney general directs the Justice Department with the assistance of the deputy attorney general, the associate attorney general, the solicitor general, and nine assistant attorneys general. On rare occasions the attorney general may represent the government before the Supreme Court, though it is usually the solicitor general who appears. (It was not until December 1996 that Attorney General Reno argued a case before the Supreme Court.) The attorney general directs the work of the U.S. attorneys, the U.S. marshals, and federal penal institutions. The Justice officials also make recommendations to the president concerning appointments to federal judicial positions. The attorney general, acting through the Immigration and Naturalization Service, may grant asylum to applicants who have well-founded fears of persecution in the country to which they would otherwise be returned.

Forty-three states have elected attorneys general; the rest are appointed. Thus it is possible in many states for the attorney general to be a member of a different political party from that of the governor. Sometimes the attorney general may refuse to represent the governor's position before the courts. Governors may need to have their own lawyers represent them where the attorneys general are at arm's length.

For more information

Baker, Nancy V. *Conflicting Loyalties: Law and Politics in the Attorney General's Office, 1789–1990.* Lawrence: University Press of Kansas, 1992.

Clayton, Cornell W. *The Politics of Justice: The Attorney General and the Making of Legal Policy.* New York: M.E. Sharpe, 1992.

Martin Gruberg
University of Wisconsin at Oshkosh

attorneys general Government officials who serve as the chief legal officer of either the national government or a state government. Both the U.S. government and the governments of each of the 50 states have a chief legal officer that represents its legal interests in court. Commonly that official holds the title of the attorney general. Thus, the United States has an attorney general, and most states have an attorney general.

Attorneys general rarely personally appear in court on behalf of their respective governments, although for particularly important cases an attorney general may personally represent the government's interests in court. Rather, attorney generals employ and supervise the lawyers that will actually appear in court in most cases. Thus, much of an attorney general's responsibilities are administrative. While the attorney general of the United States has authority over all federal prosecutors, in many states crimes are prosecuted by the local district attorneys (who are either elected officials or gubernatorial appointees), and thus state attorneys general exercise less control over criminal prosecutions than does the attorney general of the United States. Indeed, on the state level, representing the government in civil lawsuits takes up much more of the attorney general's resources than representing the government in criminal prosecutions.

Attorneys general often have other responsibilities in addition to overseeing the representation of their respective government's interests in court. They often advise the chief executive officer of the government, such as the president or the governor, regarding the legality of the chief executive officer's actions, the constitutionality and wisdom of proposed legislation, or even judicial appointments. However, attorneys general are usually viewed as representing the government rather than the chief executive, and thus there is some tension in the attorney general's various roles. Consequently, chief executives also generally hire lawyers as a part of their personal staffs who are more beholden to them as chief executive. Attorneys general, on the state level at least, often have an obligation to respond to inquiries from the legislature about the constitutionality of potential legislation. In addition, attorneys general may be responsible for governmental entities other than those that are comprised mainly of lawyers. For instance, the U.S. attorney general has responsibility for supervising law enforcement agencies, such as the Federal Bureau of Investigation and the Drug Enforcement Agency. The U.S. attorney general also supervises the Immigration and Naturalization Service, which controls entry into the United States.

The attorney general of the United States is appointed with the approval of a majority of the

U.S. Senate. Many state attorneys general are elected, but some are appointed by the governor with the approval of the state senate. In at least one state where the attorney general is appointed, the attorney general, once appointed, possesses some tenure protection to assure that he maintains some independence from the governor.

Sometimes citizens bring lawsuits to vindicate the rights of themselves and the public in general. In such circumstances the individual is sometimes referred to as a private attorney general.

For more information

Huston, Luther A., et al. *Roles of the Attorney General of the United States.* Washington, D.C.: American Enterprise Institute, 1968.

Ross, Lynne M., ed. *National Association of Attorneys General, State Attorneys General: Powers and Responsibilities.* Washington, DC.: Bureau of National Affairs, 1990.

Bernard W. Bell
Professor of Law
Rutgers Law School (Newark)

B

bail is money deposited to a court or bondsperson to ensure an arrested person's ("arrestee") appearance at trial and to prevent the arrestee from destroying evidence or intimidating witnesses. Traditionally, arrestees charged with noncapital offenses (maximum punishment is less than the death penalty) had an absolute right to be admitted to bail. Today, however, an arrestee's pretrial release may not only be subject to conditions but he may be denied bail altogether. The United States Supreme Court held in *Stack v. Boyle,* 342 U.S. 1 (1951), that it is permissible for a judge to condition pretrial release on an adequate assurance that the arrestee will stand trial and submit to sentence if found guilty. Accordingly, the Court has held that bail set at a figure higher than an amount that is reasonably calculated to fulfill this purpose is excessive. In addition, the Eighth Amendment to the U.S. Constitution prohibits excessive bail.

Beginning with the Bail Reform Act of 1966, Congress passed laws that provided that conditions of release could be imposed if a judge determined that they were necessary to reasonably assure the appearance of the arrestee at trial. Later, the Bail Reform Act of 1984 authorized a judge to consider, for the first time, the extent to which a release would endanger the safety of any other person or the community. More importantly, the 1984 act allowed a judge to detain an arrestee prior to trial.

In order to determine whether any condition or combination of conditions would reasonably assure the appearance of the arrestee or endanger the safety of others, a judge under the 1984 act must consider various factors, including the nature of the offense charged, the weight of the evidence against the defendant, and the history and characteristics of the arrestee. The facts used by a judge to support his/her conclusion must be supported by clear and convincing evidence. However, the arrestee is presumed to be too dangerous to be released if the prosecutor proves that the arrestee has been convicted of one or more of several specific crimes (i.e., crime of violence). In addition, it is presumed that no conditions of release will reasonably assure that the arrestee will not flee if the judge concludes that there is probable cause to believe the arrestee committed an offense involving the use of a gun. A judge must make written findings stating reasons if an arrestee is ordered detained prior to trial. In *United States v. Salerno,* 481 U.S. 739 (1987), the United States Supreme Court upheld the constitutionality of the preventive-detention provision of the Federal Reform Act of 1984.

For more information

Dressler, David. *Understanding Criminal Procedure.* New York: Matthew Bender, 1991.

Carlton Bailey
University of Arkansas School of Law
Fayetteville

Baker v. Carr 369 U.S. 186 (1962) is a "landmark" ruling of the Warren Court that initiated a "reapportionment revolution" in American constitutional law and electoral politics. In his memoirs, Earl Warren, who was chief justice of the United States from 1953 to 1969, wrote that, in his opinion, the most important case during his tenure on the Supreme Court was not the school desegregation case *of Brown v. Board of Education of Topeka, Kansas;* rather, it was *Baker v. Carr.*

Prior to the case of *Baker v. Carr,* which the Supreme Court handed down on March 26, 1962, the Court and virtually all other courts of law in the country had for decades steadfastly refused to hear cases concerning legislative reapportionment. For instance, in the case of *Colegrove v. Green* in 1946, the United States Supreme Court refused to accept, under what is known as the "political question doctrine," a legislative reapportionment case from Illinois concerning that state's congressional districts in the U.S. House of Representatives. In the words of Associate Justice Felix Frankfurter, who wrote the opinion for the Court in *Colegrove,* "Courts ought not to enter this political thicket." What Frankfurter meant is that the issue of legislative reapportionment was one that the political system was equipped to address, but that the judiciary was not able to address the issue in any kind of principled way. By invoking the political question doctrine, as it did in *Colegrove,* the Court

declared that the issue of legislative reapportionment was a "nonjusticiable" issue.

The Court in *Baker v. Carr* changed its mind, overruled *Colegrove,* and clearly stated that, contrary to the ruling in *Colegrove,* legislative reapportionment was NOT peculiarly political and instead was a justiciable issue, one that the judiciary could address through the judicial process using well-established legal principles. Writing for the Court in *Baker v. Carr,* Associate Justice William J. Brennan reasoned that when a legislature, in the light of population increases and shifts over the course of six decades, still did not reapportion legislative seats, the Equal Protection Clause of the Fourteenth Amendment offered a constitutional vehicle by which lawsuits could be brought alleging denial of political equality and voting rights. The Court in *Baker* did not decide the case from Tennessee on the merits; rather, it remanded or sent the case back to the federal trial court, thus empowering federal courts to begin accepting such reapportionment cases.

By holding in *Baker v. Carr* that reapportionment was no longer a nonjusticiable controversy, the Supreme Court soon would find itself bombarded by such cases. Over the next two years, the Court would hear close to 20 such cases, and the principle, under the Fourteenth Amendment's Equal Protection Clause, of "one person, one vote" would soon be enshrined in American constitutional law and electoral politics. Reapportionment cases are still regularly before the Court today and often are no less controversial than they were a generation ago.

Another critical issue confronted by the Court in *Baker v. Carr* was the Court's own role in American law and politics. Dissenting in *Baker,* Justice Frankfurter argued that "there is not under our Constitution a judicial remedy for every political mischief, for every undesirable exercise of legislative power." However, by repudiating Frankfurter's thesis on legislative reapportionment announced in *Colegrove,* the Court in *Baker* not only offered a definitive statement on the meaning of the political question doctrine; the Court also committed itself to defining and ultimately policing a system of fair and responsible government in the United States.

For more information

Baker, Gordon. *The Reapportionment Revolution.* New York: Random House, 1966.

Strum, Philippa. *The Supreme Court and 'Political Questions': A Study in Judicial Evasion.* Tuscaloosa: University of Alabama Press, 1974.

Stephen K. Shaw
Department of History and Political Science
Northwest Nazarene University, Nampa, Idaho

Bakke   See *REGENTS OF THE UNIVERSITY OF CALIFORNIA V. BAKKE.*

bankruptcy   is the legal process by which the assets of insolvent debtors are identified and distributed among their creditors. The purpose of bankruptcy is to provide a fair means to satisfy the claims of creditors and permit debtors to make a fresh start without the burden of debt that brought them to insolvency in the first place. Discharge in bankruptcy is an exclusively federal power that is created and regulated by federal statues; however, because property rights are created and defined by state law, the process of bankruptcy varies from state to state. For example, some states, such as Florida, allow debtors to protect more of their property from creditors than other states. In all cases, however, bankruptcy rearranges and redefines the legal relationships between debtors and creditors.

Both individuals and businesses may declare bankruptcy, and there are several different statutory schemes under which the bankruptcy process may be pursued. The most extreme approach is for the debtor to be declared insolvent and his or her assets (the bankruptcy estate) to be identified, reduced to cash, and distributed among the creditors. Bankruptcy law determines what assets may be distributed, how creditors must make their claims on those assets, and which creditors have priority in being paid from the bankruptcy estate. Once the distribution is completed, the debtor's legal obligations to the creditors are extinguished, even if the debts have not been fully paid. In other cases, bankruptcy is used to prevent individual creditors from seizing the debtor's assets and require the creditors to accept payment according to a plan approved by the bankruptcy court. Under this approach, debtors with an income that is sufficiently stable and regular to make payments can gain protection from their creditors while their debts are being paid off. Both individuals and businesses have access to these types of bankruptcies, and under both approaches creditors are often paid substantially less than the entire amount they are owed.

The bankruptcy laws have been altered several times in recent years in response to pressure, especially from the credit industry, to curb abuses of the bankruptcy remedy. Reformers have argued that the law encourages people to overspend and run up debts by offering them an easy way to discharge their liabilities while still retaining much of their property. Opponents of reform argue that the potential for abuse is already limited by the fact that debtors are entitled to file for bankruptcy only once every seven years. They also claim that the credit industry encourages individuals to spend beyond their means.

The most recent bankruptcy reform effort addresses these concerns by limiting individual debtors' access to the so-called straight bankruptcy (Chapter 7) and forcing them to make use of the less liberal Chapter 13 bankruptcy, which allows debtors to discharge fewer debts and obligates them to enter into payment plans with their creditors. In addition, debtors' ability to shelter their assets is limited by setting a cap on the "homestead exemption," under which individual states determine the value of residential property that the debtor may protect from creditors. The basic goal of such reforms is to limit access to consumer bankruptcy and force debtors to be more accountable. Nevertheless, easy access to consumer credit is likely to continue to encourage debtors to spend beyond their ability to pay.

For further information

Caher, John. "Bankruptcy Reform; Congress Set to Address Perceived Debtor Abuse," *New York Law Journal* (June 1, 2000): 5.

Solomon, Robin. "A Bankruptcy Primer for Paralegals," *The Legal Intelligencer,* September 14, 2000, p. 9.

Celia A. Sgroi
State University of New York, Oswego

Barron v. Mayor of Baltimore   32 U.S. 243 (1833) is the case in which the Supreme Court, under Chief Justice John Marshall, announced that the Fifth Amendment's "Takings Clause," which prohibits the government from taking private property unless it pays the owner "just compensation," applied only to the national government, not state governments.

In *Barron,* 32 U.S. 243, 7 Pet. 243 (1833), the plaintiff was seeking to recover damages for injuries to his "extensive and highly productive wharf" that were the result of changes in the way the city of Baltimore graded and paved streets. The wharf-owner alleged that the city's actions constituted an uncompensated taking of property, and that as a result, those actions violated the "Takings Clause" of the Fifth Amendment, which provides "nor shall private property be taken for public use, without just compensation." The suit was first brought in the Baltimore County Court, where after a trial, the wharf-owner was awarded $4,500 in damages. On appeal, the Maryland Court of Appeals reversed the trial court and dismissed the suit. The case was then appealed to the United States Supreme Court.

The Supreme Court, in an opinion written by Chief Justice John Marshall, held that "We are of [sic] opinion, that the provision in the fifth amendment to the constitution, declaring that private property shall not be taken for public use, without just compensation, is intended solely as a limitation on the exercise of power by the government of the United States, and is not applicable to the legislation of the states." Chief Justice Marshall set forth three arguments in support of this conclusion.

Marshall's first argument is that the Constitution concerns a government created by the people for themselves, not for the states. In the opinion, Marshall writes: "The people of the United States framed such a government for the United States as they supposed best adapted their situation and best calculated to promote their interests. The powers they conferred on this government were to be exercised by itself; and the limitations on power, if expressed in general terms, are naturally, and, we think, necessarily, applicable to the government created by the instrument."

Marshall's second argument is premised on the language of the Takings Clause. Marshall argues that when the Constitution sets forth limitations on the power of the states, as it does in Article I, section 10, it does so expressly ("no state shall pass any bill of attainder or ex post facto law"). More general limitations on power, like those found in Article I, section 9, must only be applicable to the national government, otherwise the language expressly including the states in Article I, section 10 is superfluous. The Takings Clause of the Fifth Amendment is a general limitation and must therefore only be applicable to the national government.

Marshall's last argument is based on the concerns of the public at the time the Constitution was ratified. In the opinion, Marshall writes: "In almost every convention by which the constitution was adopted, amendments to guard against the abuse of power were recommended. These amendments demanded security against the apprehended encroachments of the general government—not against those of the local governments. In compliance with a sentiment thus generally expressed, to quiet fears thus extensively entertained, amendments were proposed by the required majority in congress, and adopted by the states. These amendments contain no expression indicating an intention to apply to the state governments."

The holding in *Barron* has since been reversed (see *Chicago, Burlington and Quincy Railroad Company v. Chicago,* 166 U.S. 226 [1897]). The Supreme Court, based on the Fourteenth Amendment's Due Process Clause, has gradually incorporated most of provisions of the first eight amendments so that they apply to state governments.

For more information

White, G. Edward. *The Marshall Court and Cultural Change 1815–1835* (abridged edition). New York: Oxford University Press, 1991.

Michael H. Walsh
Senior Lecturer, Political Science Dept.
Loyola University, Chicago, Illinois

Batson v. Kentucky 476 U.S. 79 (1986) held that a prosecutor could not use his or her peremptory challenges to strike potential jurors based only on their race, under the Equal Protection Clause.

Batson was an important step in ensuring that criminal defendants have the opportunity to select a jury of their peers, including jurors of all races and backgrounds. The right to a jury not selected on the base of race dates back to *Strauder v. West Virginia,* 100 U.S. 303 (1880), which held that states could not exclude African Americans as jurors by law under the Equal Protection Clause to the Constitution. The *Strauder* court noted that excluding jurors based on race violated not only black jurors' rights to take on equal responsibilities of citizenship but also black defendants' rights to a jury of their peers.

The *Batson* case applies this rule in situations where the law itself does not exclude people from the jury pool because of race, but the prosecutor uses his or her challenges to exclude them from the actual jury selected. *Batson* does not stop the prosecutor from considering the background of potential jurors, including their race, in making jury decisions so long as race is not the only factor for exclusion. It also does not guarantee a defendant that jurors of his race, or any particular race, will be seated on the jury. Since *Batson,* the Supreme Court has gone on to rule that defense counsel may not challenge jurors based solely on race in *Georgia v. McCollum,* 505 U.S. 42 (1992), and that race-based jury exclusion was improper in civil trials as well in *Edmonson v. Leesville Concrete Co., Inc.,* 500 U.S. 614 (1991).

In addition, *Batson* held that when a defense counsel shows that jurors of a particular race were systematically excluded from the jury, the burden shifts to the prosecutor to prove that there was a legitimate nondiscriminatory reason for his or her jury strikes. This ruling was unusual because in most Equal Protection cases, the Supreme Court puts the burden on the plaintiff complaining of racial discrimination to show that exclusion or different treatment of persons based on race was intended by the state before they can win their suit.

Batson also led the way for the Court's ruling that neither the prosecution nor the defense can disqualify potential jurors based only on gender, a ruling that may apply to other groups especially protected by the Equal Protection Clause in *J.E.B v. Alabama ex rel T.B.,* 511 U.S. 127 (1994). In *Hernandez v. New York,* 500 U.S. 352, (1991), the Court upheld a prosecutor's peremptory challenges removing bilingual English-Spanish speakers from a jury because of the concern that they might not listen to the translator's version of the witness testimony, but noted that prosecutors cannot use language as a pretext for excluding people based on race.

For more information

"Batson v. Kentucky," *The Oxford Companion to the Supreme Court of the United States 66.* New York: Oxford University Press, 1992.

Chemerinsky, Erwin. *Constitutional Law Principles and Policies* 572–74. New York: Aspen Publishers, 1997.

Marie Failinger
Hamline University

Beard, Charles A. (1874–1948) was among the most important American political historians of the first half of the 20th century. As a leading member of the "Progressive" school of U.S. historians, Beard was influential and active in both the scholarly and political communities and may be best known for writing *An Economic Interpretation of the Constitution of the United States* (1913).

Beard graduated from DePauw University and studied at the University of Oxford and Cornell University before earning his Ph.D. at Columbia University in 1904. Though raised in a prosperous midwestern family, Beard quickly became involved in the working-class politics of the day, both in Britain and in the United States. Upon completing his Ph.D., Beard joined the Political Science Department at Columbia as a member of the faculty. A prolific author, Beard wrote and edited numerous books and textbooks, as well as a large number of articles and book reviews for both scholarly and popular publications.

The Progressive school of U.S. history emphasized the economic roots of politics and argued that economic conflict between popular and elite classes within society was the central feature of American political history. *An Economic Interpretation of the Constitution of the United States* is the most famous work in that vein. *An Economic Interpretation* argued that the Constitution was part of an elite reaction to the democratizing influence of the American Revolution and was motivated by the economic interests of its supporters. Although controversial even in its own time, it was a pioneering work in examining the motivations of politicians and the political origins of the Constitution and U.S.

Charles A. Beard (Library of Congress)

law. Beard extended this argument in such works as *The Economic Origins of Jeffersonian Democracy* (1915), *The Economic Basis of Politics* (1922), and *The Supreme Court and the Constitution* (1912). With his wife, Mary Ritter Beard, he applied this basic approach to all of American history in the influential narrative *The Rise of American Civilization* (1927). Both Beard's specific analysis of the origins of the Constitution and his general emphasis on economic conflict in U.S. political history were challenged beginning in the 1950s by the "consensus" school, led by such historians as Louis Hartz and Daniel Boorstin, who argued for the importance and persistence of shared values in shaping U.S. politics.

The Progressive political movement, with which Beard was associated, emphasized "good government" reforms to reduce political corruption and democratize politics, while also encouraging a more activist government that would address the social and economic problems associated with industrialism and urbanization. In keeping with those concerns, Beard published such works as *American Government and Politics* (1910), *American City Government* (1912), *American Leviathan* (1930), and *The Myth of Rugged Individualism* (1932). In his early years at Columbia, Beard produced several textbooks and readers on modern European history. In 1917 Beard resigned from Columbia University in protest of the investigation and firing of a number of professors for political activities against World War I. In 1919 he helped to found the New School for Social Research. In his later years, Beard turned much of his attention to criticism of the foreign policy of Franklin Roosevelt and the U.S. entry into World War II.

For more information

Hofstadter, Richard. *The Progressive Historians: Turner, Beard, Parrington.* Chicago: University of Chicago Press, 1968.

Nore, Ellen. *Charles Beard, An Intellectual Biography.* Carbondale: Southern Illinois University Press, 1983.

Keith E. Whittington
Princeton University

Berman v. Parker 348 U.S. 26 (1954) was a decision by the U.S. Supreme Court that broadened federal and state governments' power of eminent domain. This ability to take private property for a public purpose is explicitly established by the Fifth Amendment to the U.S. Constitution:

"No person shall . . . be deprived of . . . property, without due process of law; . . . nor shall private property be taken for public use without just compensation."

Despite the Constitution's old-fashioned language, most of the document is relatively easy to understand. For instance, "just compensation" means that in situations which require a governmental body to seize privately owned land, the owner must be paid a fair price. Unfortunately, the meanings of some portions of the Fifth Amendment, such as the "public use" phrase, have been questioned for 200 years. The Constitution's failure to define this phrase compounds the fact that the wording may be interpreted in many, equally plausible, ways. Because of the confusion surrounding the meaning of "public use," this phrase has become the key issue in many courtroom controversies, including *Berman v. Parker.*

Between the end of World War II and the 1954 Supreme Court decision in *Berman v. Parker,* millions of military veterans returned to the United States, eager to use their very low interest rate, "GI" mortgages, to purchase homes. Because there was a shortage of urban residential space, veterans were forced to use their cheap mortgages on real estate outside the city limits. This non-country, but also non-city, lifestyle quickly became the American ideal, and middle-class Americans flocked to the newly invented suburbs. As a result, the suburbs flourished, while only the lowest income populace remained within city limits. The urban poor had no choice but to live in substandard, unsanitary, poorly maintained housing, owned by absentee landlords. In an effort to remedy this situation, in 1949 Congress established urban renewal as a national priority and, during the next five years, enacted additional laws and allocated federal funds for rehabilitation of blighted, poverty-stricken, urban areas.

During the 1950s, the standard urban renewal project adhered to an inflexible plan which mandated that each project begin with the eviction of all residents and businesses, continue with demolition of all buildings in the project area, and culminate with construction of new, uniformly designed, buildings.

The plaintiff in *Berman v. Parker* was infuriated when he discovered that his profitable, longstanding neighborhood business was in an area scheduled to be razed pursuant to a neighborhood improvement plan. In an effort to halt the demolition of his livelihood, he sued the government agency which administered the plan.

The plaintiff first argued that the ongoing profitability of his business clearly demonstrated that his premises served a "public use." Hence, he stated that his property should be excepted from the plan to demolish the entire neighborhood.

The plaintiff's second argument was based on the urban renewal plan's goals, which were: beautification of the neighborhood by building safe, sanitary, building-code compliant residences; and improvement of the neighborhood's balance of commercial, residential, and municipal land uses. The plaintiff argued that these goals exceeded a reasonable interpretation of the Fifth Amendment's "public use" clause. Hence, the plaintiff stated that the urban renewal plan itself violated the constitutional limitations on eminent domain.

The Supreme Court disagreed with the plaintiff's arguments. The justices decided that even if, within the area to be revitalized, a privately owned parcel of land contains a viable business, the public's interest in completion of the project outweighs the landowner's interest in continuing his business. Furthermore, the justices found that the neighborhood improvement plan in this case would serve the public's interest by encouraging development of a neighborhood with strategically located residential buildings, churches, schools, and commercial enterprises. The Supreme Court concluded that the *Berman v. Parker* project's plan sought to use the plaintiff's land for a public purpose, within the meaning of the Fifth Amendment to the Constitution.

Since *Berman v. Parker,* the Supreme Court has continued to broaden the scope of the Fifth Amendment's "public use" clause. Whereas pre-*Berman* plans limited urban revitalization projects to recreational and residential improvements, these projects may now include, in addition to upgraded residential property, a wide variety of economic improvements, including factories, casinos, shopping malls, parking lots, and high-rise office buildings. Additionally, the trend which began with *Berman v. Parker* has shifted the focus of neighborhood improvement projects from demolition to preservation and rehabilitation of property.

For more information

"City Planning," *Microsoft Encarta Encyclopedia,* 2000 edition.

Klop, Jeremy R. *Eminent Domain.* Chapel Hill: University of North Carolina Press, 1998.

United States Code Annotated, Title 42, Section 1441, 1998 edition.

www.planning.org, website of the American Planning Association.

Beth S. Swartz, J.D.

bill of attainder   is an act of the legislature that inflicts punishment on specifically named persons or groups whose members can easily be determined. The Constitution, in Article I, section 9, prohibits the federal government from passing bills of attainder. The states are prohibited by Article I, section 10. These prohibitions insure that punishments are not imposed without the safeguards present in a judicial proceeding.

Historically, a bill of attainder was an act of the British Parliament that imposed the death penalty on persons or a particular group, usually for treasonous activities. These legislative acts usually were accompanied by a "corruption of blood," prohibiting individuals from inheriting property from attained persons. If the punishment imposed by Parliament was less than death, the act was referred to as a "bill of pains and penalties." Although the Constitution only prohibits bills of attainder, the Supreme Court has recognized that the prohibition extends to these bills of pains and penalties. As a result, a legislative act imposing any type of punishment on individuals or specific groups falls within the prohibition.

A bill of attainder may include punishments like death, imprisonment, or the imposition of a fine, but it also extends to punishments such as the deprivation of rights or the banning of employment. For example, in *United States v. Lovett,* 328 U.S. 303 (1946), the Supreme Court found that a congressional act forbidding payment of funds to three government employees found by Congress to have engaged in subversive activity was an unconstitutional bill of attainder. It oftentimes may be difficult to determine if a legislative act directed to an individual or group is a punishment or a permissible regulation. In determining whether it is a punishment, thereby making it an unconstitutional bill of attainder, the Supreme Court has considered whether the challenged act falls within the historical understanding of punishment, whether the act furthers any nonpunitive legislative purposes, and whether there is evidence of a legislative intent to punish.

For more information

Tribe, Laurence H. *American Constitutional Law,* 2nd ed. Mineola, N.Y.: Foundation Press, 1988, pp. 641–63.

James N.G. Cauthen
The City University of New York

Bill of Rights   is the first 10 amendments to the U.S. Constitution and lists the basic civil liberties possessed by people living in the United States. When the new U.S. Constitution was proposed in 1787, a large group of people argued against the adoption ("ratification") of the proposed federal Constitution. Because of their opposition, they became know as the "Anti-Federalists." One of their main objections was the fact that the proposed Constitution did not put specific limits on government interference with the basic political rights and freedoms of citizens. The Anti-Federalists feared that without a list of specific rights of the people, the national government would have too much power and so might end up oppressing the people by taking away their individual liberties. Supporters of the proposed Constitution, who became known as the "Federalists," publicly proposed a compromise. The Federalists asked the Anti-Federalists, as well as people undecided as to whether to support the new Constitution, to support the ratification. In exchange for their support, as soon as the Constitution was ratified, a list (a "bill") of individual rights would immediately be proposed as amendments to the document. Although only a minority of Anti-Federalists and undecided people were persuaded by this offer to support the Constitution, enough were satisfied with the compromise to tip the scales in a sufficient number of state legislatures in favor of ratification.

In keeping with the understood agreement, immediately after the Constitution was ratified, the new U.S. Congress proposed 12 amendments to the Constitution listing specific limitations on the power of the federal government. Ten of these were ratified by enough states to become amendments to the Constitution. These first 10 amendments to the U.S. Constitution are known as the Bill of Rights. The Bill of Rights lists many of the most basic political rights of persons within the United States. These rights include the freedom of speech, freedom of the press, and freedom of religion, as well as numerous rights of fair procedure given to criminal suspects, such as a right to a jury. These rights were based on the common understanding at the time of which rights were the most important and fundamental rights of individual citizens. These ideas had their origins in earlier legal documents such as the English Bill of Rights of 1689 as well as the variously worded bills of rights that already existed in the constitutions of the individual American states. In fact, the Bill of Rights found in the U.S. Constitution was drafted primarily by James Madison, who used the Virginia Bill of Rights as a rough model.

For more than a hundred years the U.S. Supreme Court, when interpreting the Bill of Rights, generally offered very little protection to the rights listed. However, beginning in the early to mid 20th century, the Supreme Court began to strongly enforce the rights contained in the Bill of Rights. Also, although the Bill of Rights was originally intended to place limits on the power of only the *federal* government, the U.S. Supreme Court has applied most of the limitations on power in the Bill of Rights to *state* governments as well. The court has done this by "incorporating" the Bill of Rights into the Fourteenth Amendment's guarantee that no *state* shall deprive any person of life, liberty, or property without "due process of law." Thus, the amount of liberty protected by the Bill of Rights has seen a slow but steady expansion in the last century.

Most other nations have analogous listings of individual rights in their national constitutions, although in many instances those rights are neither recognized nor enforced to any great degree. Regardless, generally the people of other nations look to the United States as a model of how to write and apply a bill of rights to their government and society.

For more information

Epstein, Lee, and Thomas G. Walker, *Constitutional Law for a Changing America: Rights, Liberties, and Justices,* 3rd ed. Washington, D.C.: CQ Press, 1998.

Levy, Leonard W. *Origins of the Bill of Rights.* New Haven, Conn.: Yale University Press, 1999.

Rick A. Swanson
University of Kentucky

Black, Hugo (1886–1971) served as associate justice for the Supreme Court from 1937 to 1971. He became known as one of greatest "liberals" to serve on the Court during the 20th century. Black supported civil liberties and political equality in numerous opinions over 34 years.

Black was born in Clay County, Alabama, on February 22, 1886. He received a law degree in 1906 and became a police court judge in 1911. He was elected prosecutor for Birmingham, Alabama, and later became an influential trial lawyer in Alabama. During the early 1920s he briefly joined the Ku Klux Klan. In 1925 he was elected to the U.S. Senate where he served until 1937. During his time in the Senate, Black supported the New Deal legislation of President Franklin D. Roosevelt, conducted congressional investigations of the utilities industry and its lobbyists.

In 1937 Roosevelt used his first opportunity to nominate Black to the Supreme Court. Black's participation in the Ku Klux Klan became an issue in his confirmation. He made a national radio broadcast saying his involvement in the Klan was minor and defending his record on racial issues. He stated that he did "number among my friends many members of the colored race. . . ."

Black immediately began to work on reversing the Court's anti–New Deal rulings and voting to support the constitutionality of administration legislation. By the early 1940s he began to develop his reputation as a civil libertarian and free speech advocate. After voting in the majority to uphold suppression of unpopular views in *Chaplinsky v. New Hampshire* (1942) and *Minersville School District v. Gobitis* (1940), Black became the Court's leading advocate of absolute protection for First Amendment freedoms.

Black's change of heart in the middle 1940s led to intellectual and personal feuds with some of his Supreme Court brethren, especially Justices Felix Frankfurter and Robert Jackson. During the period of 1941 to 1953, when conservative pro-government decisions were being handed down, Black was usually in dissent, often accompanied by William O. Douglas, Frank Murphy, or Wiley Rutledge. During the years of Chief Justice Earl Warren, Black often authored majority opinions supporting the rights of minorities, freedom of speech, and the rights of the accused. Black was particularly forceful in

Justice Hugo Black (HARRIS AND EWING, COLLECTION OF THE SUPREME COURT OF THE UNITED STATES)

arguing for an "absolutist" position for First Amendment rights. Dissenting in *Roth v. United States* (1957), he stated, "But I believe this nation's security and tranquility can best be served by giving the First Amendment the same broad construction that all Bill of Rights guarantees deserve. . . ." He was equally forceful in decisions concerning freedom of the press and the right to counsel.

During the final years of his tenure on the Supreme Court, some observers argued that Black moved toward a more conservative position. While Black's absolutist position on the First Amendment never wavered, he occasionally was very limited in what he considered "speech." Black dissented from protecting Paul Cohen's jacket in the case *Cohen v. California* (1971) and in 1965 wrote the dissent *Griswold v. Connecticut* (1965), stating, "[The] Court talks about a constitutional 'right of privacy' as though there is

some constitutional [provision] forbidding any law ever to be passed which might abridge the 'privacy' of individuals. But there is not."

Black entered his final year on the Supreme Court in declining health. He resigned on September 17, 1971, and died eight days later. Black ranks as one of the most important justices of the century, and his support for First Amendment rights has been heralded by scholars as the most devoted and articulate of any Supreme Court justice. It was ironic that Black, a typical southerner in many ways, would be a leader for racial justice and individual liberty.

For more information

Newman, Roger K. *Hugo Black: A Biography.* New York: Pantheon Books, 1994.

Simon, James F. *The Antagonists.* New York: Touchstone, 1989.

Charlie Howard
Tarleton State University

Blackstone, Sir William (1723–1780) was an English judge and law professor whose *Commentaries on the Laws of England* influenced the development of early American law in colonial times and after the Revolution. Blackstone published his *Commentaries* in 1765–70 while he was professor of law at Oxford University. He later served on the Court of Common Pleas in England.

The Blackstone treatise, which organized English law into basic themes, was at the time often the only law book for American lawyers as American courts slowly committed decisions to record. Almost all of the American founders had read Blackstone's *Commentaries,* and his ideas on property law, free speech, contract, and tort law were the main bridge between English common law and the laws that the colonies enforced prior to the revolution. Blackstone's influence after the Revolution was also significant, serving as the basis of early U.S. law in the states, defining provisions of

Sir William Blackstone (LIBRARY OF CONGRESS)

state constitutions, and capturing the mind of many United States Supreme Court justices such as John Marshall and Joseph Story.

For more information
Freedman, Lawrence M. *A History of American Law.* New York: Simon and Schuster, 1973.

Wm. Osler McCarthy
Supreme Court of Texas
University of Texas, Austin

Bolling v. Sharpe   347 U.S. 497 (1954) was a unanimous, 9–0, United States Supreme Court decision declaring racial segregation in the public schools of Washington, D.C., to be unconstitutional.

Bolling basically provided a unique solution and legal rationale to desegregate public schools in the District of Columbia. Interestingly, this case was decided shortly after the landmark Supreme Court decision of *Brown v. Board of Education of Topeka, Kansas,* in which the Court ruled that separate public schools for blacks and whites were inherently unequal and therefore violated the Equal Protection Clause of the Fourteenth Amendment to the Constitution. The *Brown* decision is famous for providing a legal precedent to desegregate public schools around the country and particularly in the South.

On the heels of the *Brown* decision, the *Bolling* case seemed to be simple on its face. If schools were to be desegregated by the *Brown* decision, then why was Washington, D.C., any different? The case is unique and important because the Supreme Court found a problem in the District's special status in America. Washington, D.C., was not a state, so the Equal Protection Clause of the Fourteenth Amendment did not apply, given its language of "nor shall any state deprive . . . the equal protection of the laws." Since Washington, D.C., was not a state, this presented a problem of finding the correct legal authority to rule against segregation (as in *Brown*).

In the unanimous opinion by Chief Justice Earl Warren, the court ruled that the D.C. public schools should be desegregated like other schools throughout America. The problem of finding a controlling legal authority for the District was solved by making use of the Due Process Clause of the Fifth Amendment of the Constitution where it states that "no person shall . . . be deprived of life, liberty, or property without due process of the law." The Fifth Amendment provided a solution that remedied the problems of Washington, D.C., because much of the District is controlled by actions of the U. S. Congress. Since the Fifth Amendment applied to the federal government, it was deemed to be applicable to the District.

Therefore, writing for the Court, Chief Justice Warren argued that while the Fourteenth and the Fifth Amendments are not the same, "both . . . [stem] . . . from our American ideal of fairness,

[and] are not mutually exclusive." Furthermore, "discrimination may be so unjustifiable as to be violative of due process" and it would be unthinkable to "impose a lesser duty" in the District of Columbia than in the rest of the United States. Thus, in a pragmatic fashion the Court used the available law to desegregate the schools throughout America.

For more information

Kluger, Richard. *Simple Justice: The History of Brown v. Board of Education and Black America's Struggle for Equality.* New York: Knopf, 1976.

Roger Hartley
University of Arizona

bond is a widely used and versatile financial instrument, and it appears in an enormous number of varieties. The use of bonds is a common occurrence in commercial transactions, in order to raise money for a corporation or government without diluting equity ownership.

In general, a bond is a written document that certifies or evidences a debt for which the debtor, who is almost always the issuer of the bond, promises to pay interest on the debt at a set rate for a set period. Upon the expiration of the period of the bond, which in general can range anywhere from one to 30 years, the issuer will pay the full, or "face," amount of the debt to the bondholder. However, bonds have been developed into many different types: Some pay no interest at all, some adjust the interest rate during the period, and others pay interest dependent on other factors such as the issuer's financial condition. This flexibility has made issuing bonds a common financial strategy for raising funds.

A bond is therefore a type of security. Unlike stock, however, possession of a bond does not confer on the bondholder equity or ownership in the issuer. Once the bond is paid at the end of the period, the relationship between the issuer and the bondholder is ended. Like stocks, bonds are traded widely in the public markets,

and the markets have developed unique trading procedures for bonds. For example, bonds can be divided into two parts. One part represents the face value paid at the end of the term, and the other represents the stream of interest payments due until the term of the bond expires. These are traded separately and the pieces are "bundled" together with similar pieces from other bonds. There are several companies that rate bonds according to their investment value, with Triple A (AAA) bonds having the highest rating.

When issued by a private company, bonds are generally secured by collateral. The most common form of collateral is mortgages on real property, although any other item of value can serve as collateral, or "security," for a bond. If the issuer defaults on the debt by failing to pay either interest payments or the face amount, the collateral can then be used to repay the bondholders. Bonds are very often issued by the federal government or state governments as well. These types of bonds are generally backed by the "full faith and credit" of that government rather than specific collateral. The most common type of government bonds are called "General Obligation Bonds" and are issued to raise funds for overall governmental operations. Many state and local governments will issue bonds, however, for specific projects, such as highway maintenance, school funding, or building construction.

Aside from this common commercial use, bonds are also used for several purposes in the law. The most common example is the posting of a bond in exchange for the temporary release of a defendant under indictment but not yet tried. The bond is issued, in an amount set by the judge or according to statute, as a security for the defendant to remain available for trial and to prevent flight to escape trial. Bonds are also used in civil disputes. A judge can require a party seeking extraordinary or injunctive relief before a trial to post a bond in order to protect the other party to the dispute should the party seeking the relief fail to prevail on the merits of the case.

For more information

Black's Law Dictionary, 6th ed. St. Paul, Minn.: West Publishing Co., 1990, pp. 178–81, 847.

Reddy, Michael T. *Securities Operations,* 2d ed. Upper Saddle River, N.J.: Prentice Hall, 1995.

Gerald J. Russello
Covington and Burling, New York

Bork, Robert H. (1927–) is best known for being among the most controversial appointments to the Supreme Court in the 20th century. Robert Bork has served as professor of law at Yale University (1962–73, 1977–81), solicitor general of the United States (1973–77), and as a judge for the U.S. Circuit Court of Appeals for the District of Columbia (1982–88). He was nominated for the U.S. Supreme Court by President Ronald Reagan on July 1, 1987, to replace the retiring justice, Lewis Powell. The Senate rejected Bork's nomination on October 23, 1987, by a 58–42 vote. Justice Powell had become known as a relatively moderate justice who held the swing position on the Court on a number of controversial issues. The nomination of Bork to replace Powell seemed to symbolize the Reagan administration's strategy of appointing conservatives to the federal judiciary. Given the importance of Powell's seat to the balance of the Court and the outcome of the 1986 elections, in which the Democrats regained the majority of the Senate, the Senate confirmation process was unusually long, public, and contentious. After being rejected by the Senate for the seat on the Supreme Court, Bork resigned from his seat on the Circuit Court in 1988. Anthony Kennedy was later appointed and confirmed to fill Justice Powell's seat on the Court. Presidents have subsequently been careful to avoid a similar confirmation battle over their judicial nominations by choosing less well-known or less controversial candidates.

Bork is a judicial conservative and a leading advocate of the view that the Constitution should be interpreted in accord with the "original intentions" of the founders who drafted and ratified it. This was also a prominent position of the Reagan administration, but it is generally controversial. This originalist approach to constitutional interpretation urges the Court to enforce the Constitution only as it would have been understood at the time it was adopted and to exercise judicial restraint by refusing to strike down laws that do not clearly violate the Constitution. Critics of originalism argue that such deference to historical understandings is impractical and would have the effect of reducing protections to civil liberties. After leaving the judiciary, Bork further explained and defended his approach to the Constitution in a book, *The Tempting of America.*

Bork received his law degree from the University of Chicago in 1953, and before becoming involved in constitutional issues he worked in antitrust law, concerned with regulating monopolies. At Chicago, Bork was influenced by the early "law and economics" movement, which sought to apply economic theories to the law and often opposed government intervention in the marketplace. His first book, *The Antitrust Paradox,* was a critique of activist antitrust policy and argued that the primary goal of antitrust law should be to benefit consumers. As solicitor general, Bork is best known for carrying out President Richard Nixon's order to fire special prosecutor Archibald Cox, who was investigating the Watergate scandal and had sued to obtain tapes of White House conversations. The public outcry over the dismissal of Cox led to the appointment of a new special prosecutor, the start of an impeachment investigation, and eventual legislation providing for independent counsels to investigate executive misconduct.

For more information

Bork, Robert H. *The Tempting of America: The Political Seduction of the Law.* New York: Free Press, 1990.

Bork, Robert H. *Slouching toward Gomorrah: Modern Liberalism and American Decline.* New York: HarperCollins, 1990.

Keith E. Whittington
Princeton University

Bowers v. Hardwick   478 U.S. 186 (1986) was a case in which the U.S. Supreme Court declared states could criminalize homosexual sodomy and was the first case ever to reach the Supreme Court involving the rights of gays and lesbians. In that case, a police officer had gone to the residence of Michael Hardwick to serve him with a warrant for failure to keep a court date. One of Hardwick's housemates allowed the officer to search the house for him. The officer passed a bedroom door and saw Hardwick engaged in homosexual sodomy (anal sex with another man). The officer arrested Hardwick for violating a Georgia law that prohibited the practice of oral or anal sex. Hardwick challenged the law as violating his constitutional right to privacy.

The Supreme Court, by a 5–4 vote, held there is no constitutional right to engage in "consensual homosexual sodomy." The majority opinion, written by Justice White, declared the right of privacy includes only those rights "deeply rooted in the Nation's history and tradition." Sodomy did not meet that definition because it was a crime under the common law and had been outlawed by all 13 original colonies, all 50 states as recently as 1961, and 24 states as of 1986. Nor did it matter to the court that Hardwick's conduct occurred in the privacy of the home. The Court stated that it could not grant a right to engage in "victimless" crimes between consenting adults in the home because such a right would allow the use of drugs, as well as other sex crimes such as adultery, incest, and prostitution.

The dissenting opinion, written by Justice Brennan, attacked the majority for mischaracterizing the basic issue involved in the case. The real issue according to the dissent was whether adults have a right to control the nature of their intimate relationships with others. The dissent believed "the right of an individual to conduct relationships in the intimacy of his or her own home" is at "the heart of the Constitution's protection of privacy."

Although the *Bowers* case allowed states to continue to criminalize homosexual sodomy, since 1986 many state legislatures have repealed their laws against homosexual sodomy. Several other state supreme courts have ruled that their states' anti-sodomy laws are unconstitutional, based on other constitutional rights such as equal protection under the U.S. Constitution, or based on a right of privacy or equal protection found in their own state constitutions rather than in the U.S. Constitution.

Moreover, a recent Supreme Court case, *Romer v. Evans* (1996), calls into question the continued vitality of the holding in *Bowers*. In *Romer*, the Court declared unconstitutional an amendment to the Colorado Constitution that prohibited local governments within Colorado from offering gays and lesbians protection against discrimination. The Court said this violated the Equal Protection Clause of the U.S. Constitution. The Colorado amendment was so far-reaching in its consequences, it was "inexplicable by anything but animus" toward gays and lesbians, and hostility toward a group, the Court declared, is not a valid reason for denying that group equal protection of the law. However, the majority in *Romer* neither discussed nor even cited *Bowers*. This left unanswered the question of whether the Court would find that anti-sodomy laws, or any other laws that discriminate on the basis of sexual orientation, are based merely on hostility toward gays and thus would be unconstitutional under the Equal Protection clause. Given the increasing pressure across the nation for equal rights under the law for gays and lesbians, it is undoubtedly just a matter of time before the Court will confront this issue again.

For more information

Bowers v. Hardwick, 478 U.S. 186 (1986).
Romer v. Evans, 517 U.S. 620 (1996).

Rick A. Swanson,
University of Kentucky

Bradwell v. Illinois 83 U.S. 130 (1873) is the case in which the United States Supreme Court held that the Illinois Supreme Court's decision to deny Mrs. Bradwell a license to practice law solely because she was a woman did not violate the Privileges and Immunities Clause of the Fourteenth Amendment. However, the case is more often remembered for the concurring opinion written by Justice Bradley wherein he opined "the paramount destiny and mission of woman are to fulfil the noble and benign offices of wife and mother. This is the law of the Creator."

At issue in *Bradwell v. Illinois,* 16 Wall. (83 U.S.) 130 (1873), was whether the Illinois Supreme Court's decision to deny Mrs. Bradwell a license to practice law solely because she was a woman violated the Privileges and Immunities Clause (not the Equal Protection Clause) of the Fourteenth Amendment. The majority opinion, written by Justice Miller, held that "the right to practice law in the courts of a State is one of those powers which are not transferred for its protection to the Federal government, and its exercise is in no manner governed or controlled by citizenship of the United States in the party seeking such license." The holding was based on the extremely narrow construction of the Privileges and Immunities Clause announced by the Supreme Court one day earlier in the *Slaughterhouse Cases* (1873).

Justice Bradley began his opinion with an attempt to undermine the basis of Mrs. Bradwell's claim that women can engage in any and every profession of civil life. He did so by writing "the civil law, and nature herself, has always recognized a wide difference in the respective spheres and destinies of man and woman. *Man is, or should be, woman's protector and defender. The natural and proper timidity and delicacy which belongs to the female sex evidently unfits it for many of the occupations of civil life.*"

He then added that the "constitution of the family organization, which is founded in the divine ordinance, as well as in the nature of things, indicates the domestic sphere as that which properly belongs to the domain and functions of womanhood."

Having laid out these patriarchal notions about the nature of life, Justice Bradley's opinion then focused on the issue of whether denying a woman a license to practice law solely because she is a woman was contrary to the Privileges and Immunities Clause. He reasoned that it did not because the *"paramount destiny and mission of woman are to fulfil* (sic) *the noble and benign offices of wife and mother. This is the law of the Creator. And the rules of civil society must be adapted to the general constitution of things, and cannot be based upon exceptional cases."* Therefore, he concluded the opinion by proclaiming "[i]n the nature of things it is not every citizen of every age, sex and condition that is qualified for every calling and position. It is the prerogative of the legislator to prescribe regulations founded on nature, reason, and experience for the due admission of qualified persons to the professions and callings demanding special skill and confidence. This fairly belongs to the police power of the State; in my opinion, in view of the peculiar characteristics, destiny, and mission of woman, it is within the province of the legislature to ordain what offices, positions, and callings shall be filled and discharged by men, and shall receive the benefit of those energies and responsibilities, and that decision and firmness which are presumed to predominate in the sterner sex."

While the Supreme Court has never altered its restrictive view of the Privileges and Immunities Clause, the decision in *Bradwell* has been overturned as a result of the Supreme Court's holding that the Equal Protection Clause of the Fourteenth Amendment prohibits discrimination against women. It should also be noted that Mrs. Bradwell was later admitted to the bar of the state of Illinois (1890) and, somewhat ironically, to the bar of the Supreme Court of the United States (1892).

For more information
Reed v. Reed, 404 U.S. 71 (1971); *Craig v. Boren,* 429 U.S. 190 (1976); and *Mississippi University for Women v. Hogan,* 458 U.S. 718 (1982).

Michael H. Walsh
Senior Lecturer, Political Science Dept.
Loyola University, Chicago

Brandeis, Louis D. (1856–1941) was a lawyer and Supreme Court justice who helped change the course of law in the United States. Born in Louisville, Kentucky, Brandeis enrolled at Harvard Law School when he was 18. Shortly after he left Harvard in 1878 he opened a law partnership in Boston. There he developed a novel approach to the role of the lawyer.

Brandeis assumed that to assess his small business clients' needs he had to understand not only their immediate problems but the economic context in which they arose. That belief illuminated his legal philosophy, which held that law had to be consistent with societal needs and that societal needs could be assessed only through an accumulation of facts. The fact-filled briefs he presented to courts, a novelty in his day, later became the basis for the modern American approach to law.

He also believed that law had to be moral in order to be valid, and that attorneys had an obligation to work on behalf of the people rather than as employees for wealthy corporations. That led in 1893 to his beginning a simultaneous career in public service, beginning with a 10-year fight against the attempt of the Boston Elevated Railway to acquire a monopoly over Boston's transportation system. His decision not to take fees for public service helped create the American *pro bono* ("for the public good") tradition and led to the media's dubbing him the "People's Attorney." He redesigned Massachusetts' utilities laws, invented Savings Bank Life Insurance so that workers could provide for their families, designed much of President Woodrow Wilson's antitrust policy, advised President Franklin Roosevelt to enact unemployment insurance, and advocated legalization of unions, minimum wage and maximum hours laws, public ownership of Alaska's natural resources, and public works projects during the Depression of the 1930s.

Wilson nominated Brandeis to the Supreme Court in 1916—the first time a Jew had been nominated—and he took his seat later that year. A colleague called Brandeis an "implacable democrat"; another commented that to Brandeis, "democracy is not a political program. It is a religion." His unceasing accumulation of facts had convinced him that freedom was endangered by concentration of power, whether in the hands of government or of corporations. As a justice, therefore, he usually favored action by the states over that by the federal government, balancing corporate power with union power, encouraging competition among businesses, and permitting experimentation with laws designed to aid workers (*New State Ice v. Liebmann,* 1932; *Liggett v. Lee,* 1933). He insisted that the Court exercise self-restraint (*Ashwander v. TVA,* 1936) and not substitute its opinion for reasonable attempts by legislatures to solve societal problems (*Jay Burns v. Bryan,* 1924). At the same time, he joined the Court whenever it struck down what he felt was a level of governmental assumption of power not contemplated by the Constitution or inconsistent with democracy (*Schecter v. U.S.,* 1935).

Brandeis's democratic ideal included an emphasis on the rights of the individual, particularly as they affected human dignity and the ability of people to participate in the democratic process. He and his law partner coined the phrase "the right to be let alone" in an 1890 article about privacy. He drew on it as a justice when the Court upheld what it saw as the government's constitutional power to wiretap at will. A furious Brandeis insisted in dissent that the Founding Fathers had included the "right to be let alone" in the Constitution (*Olmstead v. United States,* 1928). In later years the Supreme Court came to

Justice Louis D. Brandeis (HARRIS AND EWING, COLLECTION OF THE SUPREME COURT OF THE UNITED STATES)

privacy and free speech that gradually became the law of the land, an emphasis on individual dignity, and his certainty that, given the efforts of active democrats, liberty would indeed prevail.

For more information

Mason, Alpheus Thomas. *Brandeis: A Free Man's Life.* New York: Viking, 1946.

Strum, Philippa. *Louis D. Brandeis: Justice for the People.* Boston, Mass: Harvard University Press, 1984.

———, ed. *Brandeis on Democracy.* Lawrence: University Press of Kansas, 1994.

Philippa Strum
City University of New York

agree and has repeatedly cited Brandeis in affirming a constitutional right to privacy.

He considered free speech an absolute necessity if citizens were to have access to ideas and be able to make intelligent choices among them. His dissenting opinions in a number of 1920s cases, arguing that unpopular and even potentially dangerous views had to be permitted to preserve democracy, were adopted by the Supreme Court in the 1960s and are largely responsible for the United States' permissive speech jurisprudence (*Whitney v. California,* 1927; *Brandenburg v. Ohio,* 1969).

When Brandeis resigned from the Court in 1939, he left behind a tradition of lawyers contributing their efforts to public service, a jurisprudence based on interpreting the Constitution in light of societal facts, an insistence on

Brandeis brief   refers to a legal brief that emphasizes sociological and economic information rather than legal principles. It takes its name from Louis D. Brandeis, the lawyer and later Supreme Court justice who created it.

During the late 19th century and the first years of the 20th century American courts developed the doctrine of liberty of contract. They interpreted the word *liberty* in the Constitution's Fourteenth Amendment ("No state shall . . . deprive any person of life, liberty, or property without due process of law") to mean that employers and employees were free to enter into whatever contractual relationship they liked. Liberty of contract therefore precluded state regulation of hours, wages, and other working conditions.

When the courts of Oregon used the doctrine to strike down a state statute establishing a 10-hour workday for women in laundries and factories, the National Consumers' League hired Brandeis to appeal the decision. In 1905 the Supreme Court had endorsed the doctrine (*Lochner v. New York*), saying that a law limiting men's working hours had no relationship to health and safety. Brandeis decided his only hope was to argue that women needed a greater level of protection than did men for the sake of their own health and safety and that of society. He and his colleagues, including his sister-in-law Josephine Goldmark, therefore devised a brief that devoted only two pages to legal precedents and went on to present more than 100 pages containing sociological, economic, and physiological data about the effect of long working hours on the health of women. The tactic worked. Justice David Brewer acknowledged the brief in his opinion for the Court (*Muller v. Oregon*, 1908), and Brandeis won his case.

The Brandeis brief was subsequently utilized by lawyers to sustain other regulations of working conditions. In 1954 attorneys in *Brown v. Board of Education* drew on the social and behavioral sciences to demonstrate the negative effects of segregated schooling on the ability of African-American children to learn, and Chief Justice Earl Warren cited their evidence in his landmark decision overturning the "separate but equal" doctrine.

Brandeis's assumption that the law must reflect societal realities and that one of the lawyer's functions is to present those realities to the court has since gained general acceptance, and the Brandeis brief has become the norm for lawyers arguing constitutional cases.

For more information

Woloch, Nancy. *Muller v. Oregon*. New York: Bedford Books, 1996.

Strum, Philippa. *Louis D. Brandeis: Justice for the People*. Cambridge, Mass.: Harvard University Press, 1984, chap. 8.

Philippa Strum
City University of New York

Brandenburg v. Ohio   395 U.S. 444 (1969)

is an important Supreme Court case that established significant guidelines for free speech under the First Amendment.

In this case the Supreme Court ruled that a statute which purports to punish mere advocacy speech, or which forbids assembly to advocate with others, violates both the First and Fourteenth Amendments. A state may forbid speech or assembly only where advocacy is directed to incite or produce imminent lawless action.

Clarence Brandenburg, the leader of an Ohio Ku Klux Klan group, was convicted, fined $1,000, and sentenced to one to 10 years in prison under Ohio's 1919 criminal syndicalism statute. The Klan leader had invited a Cincinnati television reporter and cameraman to attend and record a rally at which the participants burned a large wooden cross and carried firearms. The Klan leader was taped making derogatory remarks about Negroes and Jews and speaking of the possibility of "revengeance" (sic). In 1919, when the Ohio statute was written, the Constitution did not guarantee a right to speech that advocated illegal acts or violence. Any speech that "tended" to cause a violation of the law could be punished.

With *Brandenburg,* the Court found that the Ohio Criminal Syndicalism Act went beyond the "clear and present danger" standard that Justice Holmes had advocated in *Schenk v. United States,* 249 U.S. 47 (1919). Under that test, speech, even mere advocacy, could be limited if it posed a clear and present danger. The Court found that while Mr. Brandenburg was advocating action, he was not inciting imminent lawless action. With this new test, speech may not be suppressed or punished unless it is intended to produce "imminent lawless action" and it is "likely to produce such action." Otherwise, the First and Fourteenth Amendments protect even speech and assembly which advocate violence.

The *Brandenburg* imminent lawless test that was developed by this case effectively meant an end to most laws that seek to punish the advocacy of ideas, thereby protecting all types of speech and speakers from censorship.

For more information

Greenawalt, Kent. *Fighting Words: Individuals, Communities, and Liberties of Speech*. Princeton, N.J.: Princeton University Press, 1995.

Harrison, Maureen, and Gilbert, Steve, eds. *Freedom of Speech Decisions of the United States Supreme Court.* First Amendment Decisions Series, Carlsbad, Calif.: Excellent Books, 1996.

Wolfson, Nicholas. *Hate Speech, Sex Speech, Free Speech.* Westport, Conn.: Praeger, 1997.

Paul Kuritz
Bates College

Brennan, William J., Jr.

Brennan, William J., Jr. (1906–1997) was one of the most significant justices ever to serve on the U.S. Supreme Court and a dominant force for expanding constitutional rights during his tenure from 1956 to 1990. His decisions advocated a reading of the Bill of Rights that would recognize and expand the "human dignity" of individuals, and his approach to the Constitution called for interpreting it according to society's changing values.

Born in Newark, New Jersey, in 1906, Brennan was the son of a labor organizer who became a successful political leader in Newark. Brennan, who eschewed politics, attended the Wharton School at the University of Pennsylvania and Harvard Law School. He joined a major Newark law firm in the 1930s and developed an expertise in the emerging field of labor law but on the side of management. During World War II, he enlisted in the army and served as a labor and manpower specialist in Washington, D.C. After the war he returned to practice in Newark and became involved in efforts to reform the state judicial system. In 1949 he became a trial judge in the newly revamped state court system, and he advanced quickly to the appeals court and in 1952 to the state supreme court.

In 1956 Brennan, a Democrat, was picked by President Dwight Eisenhower, a Republican, for a seat on the United States Supreme Court to replace the retiring Justice Sherman Minton. Eisenhower wanted to appoint a Catholic and a Democrat to help cement his support among independent and Democratic voters in the north-

Justice William J. Brennan, Jr. (ROBERT OAKES, NATIONAL GEOGRAPHICAL SOCIETY, COLLECTION OF THE SUPREME COURT OF THE UNITED STATES)

east in the 1956 presidential election. Eisenhower's sentiment expressed a few years later, that he was disappointed at how liberal Brennan proved to be, was misplaced since Brennan was chosen for his impact on the election rather than on the Court.

Brennan quickly won the trust of Chief Justice Earl Warren and earned the respect of other justices. He demonstrated a remarkable ability to bring justices together to form important majorities in case after case. His warm, friendly manner and ready accessibility to colleagues made him extraordinarily effective in the Court's internal deliberations and opinion-drafting.

Among his major decisions, Brennan wrote *Baker v. Carr* (1962), which paved the way for the Supreme Court to reapportion state legislatures to achieve "one person, one vote." He authored *New York Times v. Sullivan* (1964), which said that criticism of public officials was protected by the First Amendment guarantee of freedom of speech. He led the court's application of provisions of the Bill of Rights to the states through the due process clause of the Fourteenth Amendment, known as "incorporation." He wrote the decision in *Craig v. Boren* (1976), which subjected gender discrimination to greater scrutiny under the Fourteenth Amendment equal protection clause. He wrote major decisions upholding affirmative action, striking down loyalty oaths for public employees, and requiring due process for individuals receiving welfare, food stamps, and other government assistance. As a dissenter, he argued for the unconstitutionality of the death penalty and for the First Amendment protection of obscene materials.

After Earl Warren retired, and first Warren E. Burger became Chief Justice in 1969 and then William H. Rehnquist in 1986, the court grew more conservative; Brennan found himself more often in dissent, but he continued to muster surprising victories. Brennan retired after he suffered a stroke in 1990, still forging majorities down to his last day on the bench. He died in 1997.

For more information

Cushman, Clare, ed. *The Supreme Court Justices: Illustrated Biographies, 1789–1995,* 2nd ed. Washington, D.C.: Congressional Quarterly Books, 1995.

Rosenkranz, E. Joshua, ed. *Reason and Passion: Justice Brennan's Enduring Influence.* New York: W.W. Norton and Co., 1997.

Stephen Wermiel
American University, Washington College of Law

Breyer, Stephen Gerald (1938–) was nominated to the Supreme Court by President Bill Clinton in April 1994 and was confirmed by Congress in July 1994.

A native of San Francisco, Breyer earned an A.B. from Stanford University in 1959. He continued his education in England, where he earned a B.A. in philosophy and economics at Oxford University in 1961. On his return to the United States, Breyer enrolled in Harvard Law School, from which he graduated magna cum laude in 1964. He has been married since 1967 and has three children. He is an avid bicyclist and also enjoys cooking and recreational reading.

Stephen Breyer started his professional career by accepting a prestigious Supreme Court clerkship, a position coveted by every newly graduated attorney. During his clerkship, Breyer assisted Supreme Court Justice Arthur Goldberg with writing the Court's decision in *Griswold v. Connecticut,* a landmark, right-to-privacy case.

In early 1967 Breyer became an assistant professor at Harvard Law School. He was promoted to a full professorship in 1970. However, in 1967, soon after he started teaching at Harvard, Breyer was offered a Washington, D.C.-based position as assistant U.S. attorney general. Breyer also accepted that employment and continued to commute between Boston and Washington, D.C., until 1980.

Stephen Breyer gained visibility in 1974 by serving as an assistant special prosecutor on the Watergate Special Prosecution Force, a task group formed to investigate the possibility of impeaching President Richard M. Nixon. After the Watergate prosecution team completed its mission, Breyer accepted employment as a senior aide to Senator Edward M. Kennedy, chairman of the Senate Judiciary Committee. Breyer demonstrated that his talent and work ethic enabled him to excel not only with employment in the judicial and executive branches of government but also with work at the legislative branch. Less than one year after starting work with Senator Kennedy, Breyer was promoted to special counsel to the Judiciary Committee. He was promoted to chief counsel to that committee in 1979.

During this time period, Stephen Breyer's unorthodox, creative methods of solving both legal questions and practical problems impressed both Republican and Democratic committee members. Because senators from both sides of the aisle respected Breyer's talent for innovative reasoning and willingness to assert independent, nonpartisan ideas, the senators trusted him to convert legislative stalemates into mutually acceptable solutions. Breyer soon earned a reputation for being Congress's most skillful consensus builder.

During his tenure with the Judiciary Committee, Breyer became well known for his groundbreaking work in deregulating the airline and trucking industries. He also initiated long term projects in the dissimilar fields of prison reform and fair housing law, with the ambitious goal of updating, reorganizing, and rewriting these statutes

In October 1980, during the presidential campaign in which Democratic President Jimmy Carter sought reelection, Stephen Breyer was one of several individuals nominated by the president to fill vacant judicial positions in federal courts. Unfortunately, President Ronald Reagan, a Republican, won the election before Congress had time to finalize these appointments. Following the usual practice of a new president whose political affiliation differs from his predecessor's, in January 1981 President Reagan "cleaned house." With one exception, he nullified the appointments made by Carter but not confirmed by Congress. The exception was the only nominee who had support from both political parties: Stephen Breyer. His new title, "justice of the U.S. Court of Appeals," was confirmed in early 1981.

Throughout his 13-year tenure at the U.S. Court of Appeals, Stephen Breyer's judicial opinions reflected his pragmatism and distrust of broad legal theory. His work also clearly demonstrated that he was a political moderate and an advocate of judicial restraint. Breyer's name became well recognized by the general public as well as by attorneys and politicians because of his unusual talent for expressing complex legal concepts in language that bright high school students could comprehend.

While serving in the Court of Appeals, Breyer participated in the work of the U.S. Sentencing Commission, a group of U.S. Court of Appeals judges who were responsible for the revision of the federal guidelines consulted by judges when imposing criminal sentences. The revised guidelines, which took effect in 1987, reflect Breyer's idea that the sentence recommended for a particular crime should be based on national averages of sentences in similar cases. Unlike his other work, these guidelines have been widely criticized as being too rigid, since they do not permit any input of judicial discretion.

Breyer's performance on the Supreme Court evinces a moderate ideology amid an overall tendency to align with the Court's liberal bloc. He typically assumes a probusiness position in antitrust cases, expressing a suspicion of government regulation of private business activity. His dislike of government regulatory schemes is muted, however, in cases involving environmental protection legislation. Justice Breyer has generally supported affirmative action plans, joining Justice Ginsberg's dissent in the *Adarand Contractors v. Pena* (1995) decision. Several of Breyer's recent decisions angered conservatives who supported his nomination. Justice Breyer wrote the majority opinion in *Stenberg v. Carhart* (2000), the controversial partial-birth abortion case in which the Court reaffirmed the essential features of *Roe v. Wade* (1973). Furthermore, Breyer recorded liberal votes in *Chicago v. Morales* (1999), *Illinois v. Wardlow* (2000), and *Dickerson v. United States* (2000), three highly publicized cases involving the rights of criminal defendants.

For more information

"Justice Steven Breyer," *Encarta* and *Encyclopaedia Britannica:* "Justice Breyer," *National Law Journal*

(June 30, 1997); and *usscplus.com,* the official website of the United States Supreme Court.

Beth S. Swartz, J. D.
Bradley J. Best
Austin Peay State University

brief describes two different types of legal documents. Generally the term refers to written documents submitted to a court to advocate a particular disposition of a motion or a case. Such briefs may be directed to either an appellate court or a trial judge. The term *brief* also refers to a summary of a legal decision setting forth the disposition of the case and its underlying facts; the court's holding, i.e., the rule of law established by the case; and the rationale underlying the court's decision. Briefs are an essential part of the appellate process—the process by which judges' rulings undergo review for errors. Litigants may appeal a judicial decision to an appellate court, which will determine whether the judicial ruling should be upheld, reversed, or resolved in some other manner.

Appellate briefs, briefs submitted to appellate courts, enable the lawyers for the various parties to the lawsuit to give a written explanation of their argument that the appellate court should either uphold or overturn the decision rendered by the lower court. The precise form of appellate briefs varies somewhat depending on the appellate court to which the brief will be submitted. Generally, however, appellate briefs consist of a statement of the legal issues that must be resolved, a description of the relevant factual background, and a legal argument that details the legal bases for ruling in the party's favor. The factual section of an appellate brief includes citations to the portions of the record supporting the factual assertions made in the brief. The record consists of the legal documents filed in the trial court, trial testimony, trial exhibits, and the decisions rendered by the trial court. The argument section of appellate briefs includes citations to cases, statutes, regulations, and other legal authorities that support the statements of law made as a part of the argument. Though lawyers for the parties to a case often have the opportunity to present oral arguments before appellate courts once they have filed their appellate briefs, appellate judges rely much more heavily on briefs than on oral argument.

Briefs submitted at the trial level are ordinarily less formal than appellate briefs, and they are often referred to as memoranda of law. Whenever a party to a lawsuit seeks an order from the court, the party must file a motion and ordinarily must submit a brief justifying the order sought. Such briefs, or memoranda of law, generally consist of a section setting forth the facts relevant to the motion and a legal argument establishing the party's legal entitlement to prevail on its motion, supported by citations to legal authorities. The other parties in the case can then submit responsive briefs or memoranda of law setting forth facts and legal arguments justifying denial of the motion. Sometimes parties also submit trial briefs—briefs to familiarize a judge with the facts parties expect to present and the legal basis for their claims in a trial over which a judge will preside.

Lawyers occasionally use the term *brief* to refer to a formal summary of a legal decision. Such a brief, also known as a case brief, sets forth the issue presented by a case, the disposition of the case, the relevant facts, the legal principle established by the case, and the rationale for the court's decision. Case briefs are not submitted to judges but rather are a form of note taking. Law students often prepare case briefs to prepare for class.

For more information

Shapo, Helene S., Marilyn R. Walter, and Elizabeth Fajans. *Writing and Analysis in the Law,* 4th ed. Westbury, N.Y.: Foundation Press, 1999.

Porter, Karen K., et al. *Introduction to Legal Writing and Oral Advocacy.* New York: Matthew Bender, 1989.

Bernard W. Bell
Professor of Law
Rutgers University Law School (Newark)

Brown v. Board of Education of Topeka, Kansas

Brown v. Board of Education of Topeka, Kansas 347 U.S. 484 (1954) was the case in which the Supreme Court declared that racial segregation in the public schools violated the Constitution of the United States.

The Fourteenth Amendment to the U.S. Constitution states, "No state shall . . . deny to any person within its jurisdiction the equal protection of the laws." The Amendment became part of the Constitution in the immediate aftermath of the Civil War. Soon after its adoption a number of Southern and border states passed laws mandating racial segregation in public facilities. In 1896 the Supreme Court found that so long as the facilities provided for members of different races were equal, segregation itself did not violate the Equal Protection Clause (*Plessy v. Ferguson*). This "separate but equal" doctrine was used as the legal justification for segregation laws for more than half a century.

In 1952, 17 states and the District of Columbia segregated their public schools. Linda Brown was an eight-year-old African-American girl who lived near an all-white elementary school in Topeka. Though her parents wanted her to attend that school, she was not allowed to do so because of her race. Linda sued, through her parents, to have Topeka's school segregation laws declared unconstitutional. The Supreme Court combined Linda's case with four others and issued its decision on May 17, 1954.

On behalf of a unanimous Court, Chief Justice Earl Warren wrote that even if the physical facilities provided to members of different races were equal, modern psychological research demonstrated that legal segregation, itself, conveyed a governmental message to those who were kept out of schools attended by the white majority. "[T]he policy of separating the races is usually interpreted as denoting the inferiority of the negro group. A sense of inferiority affects the motivation of a child to learn. . . . Separate educational facilities are inherently unequal."

Legal segregation did not end with the *Brown* decision. The Court recognized that the states would need time to develop plans for eliminating their dual school systems. In *Brown v. Board of Education II* (1955) the Court told local school boards to move toward that goal "with all deliberate speed."

Some school boards ended segregation quickly. Most did not. Critics of *Brown II* scolded the Court for its failure to foresee the fact that segregationist diehards would treat the decision as an invitation to proceed with "all deliberation and no speed." As late as 1992 the state of Mississippi was before the Court because it was continuing to maintain a dual university system (*United States v. Fordice*).

Though *Brown I and II* did not end legal segregation immediately, they removed its constitutional underpinning and put the full backing of the Constitution behind the Civil Rights movement in the United States.

For more information

Karst, Kenneth L. *Belonging to America: Equal Citizenship and the Constitution.* New Haven, Conn.: Yale University Press, 1989.

Peltason, Jack. *Fifty-Eight Lonely Men.* Urbana: University of Illinois Press, 1971.

Woodward, C. Vann. *The Strange Career of Jim Crow,* 3d ed. New York: Oxford University Press, 1974.

William H. Coogan
University of Southern Maine

Buckley v. Valeo

Buckley v. Valeo 424 U.S. 1 (1976) is the Supreme Court case that established the basic guidelines for the current system of financing campaigns for federal office in the United States.

At issue were the 1974 amendments to the Federal Election Campaign Act (FECA) of 1971. The Court upheld limits on the amounts that individuals and political action committees could contribute to candidates, requirements for reporting receipts and spending by candidates, and the system for publicly financing the presidential election campaigns. The ruling struck down spending limits for candidates and independent persons and groups, as well as restrictions on the use of personal wealth to fund campaign activity.

There are two key results of this ruling pertaining to financing campaigns for federal office. First, it confirmed the right of Congress to legislatively set limits on contributions to candidates. The Court further reinforced the idea that contribution limits were constitutional in *Nixon, Attorney General of Missouri, et al v. Shrink Missouri Government PAC, et al.,* 528 U.S. 1033 (2000) where the Court expressly stated that *Buckley* was the authority on this matter and extended the right of regulating the amount of contributions to state legislatures as well.

The most significant feature of the case is the linkage of money and spending to political speech and the First Amendment. To quote the decision:

> A restriction on the amount of money a person or group can spend on political communication during a campaign necessarily reduces the quantity of expression by restricting the number of issues discussed, the depth of their exploration, and the size of the audience reached. This is because virtually every means of communicating ideas in today's mass society requires the expenditure of money.

This linkage of political speech to money makes any attempt to fully regulate campaign finance extremely difficult, as it would require getting around the First Amendment. As such, Congress has no way of legislating a cap on spending by candidates, nor can it limit the amounts spent by independent groups. A 1996 case, *Colorado Republican Federal Campaign Committee, et al. v. Federal Election Commission,* 518 U.S. 604 (1996), further clarified the issue by ruling that political parties could collect and spend unlimited funds for "party building" exercises. The combined effects of *Buckley* and *Colorado Republican* have created the significant

influx of soft money (i.e., unregulated campaign contributions and spending) into campaigns since the 1996 electoral cycle.

In sum: it is constitutionally allowable to limit how much can be given to a candidate, but the amount that candidate spends cannot be capped. Further, groups and individuals acting independently from a candidate cannot be limited in the amount they spend.

The Court did allow an exception to its strictures against limiting campaign spending. Spending ceilings were upheld in the case of the partial public financing of presidential primaries and the complete public financing of the general election campaign for president on the basis that the system was voluntary in nature. Candidates could choose to receive the funds and therefore be required to conform to limits, or candidates could avoid the limits by not accepting public monies.

Of secondary importance to the basic rules of the game for campaign finance, it is also worth noting that the case struck down the method of selecting the Federal Election Commission (FEC) which gave the president pro tempore and the speaker of the House the authority to appoint two members each to the commission. The Court held that this violated the Appointment Clause of the Constitution (Article II, section 2, cl. 2). As a result, the Court ordered the Congress to reformulate the appointment provisions to the FEC, although the Court did uphold any existing rulings made by that body.

The ruling was *per curiam* (unsigned), in which all members of the Court joined at least in part, excepting Justice Stevens who took no part in the consideration or decision of the case.

For more information
Buckley v. Valeo, 424 U.S. 1 (1976).
Ducat, Craig R. *Constitutional Interpretation,* 7th ed. St. Paul, Minn.: West Group Publishing, 2000.

Steven L. Taylor, Ph.D.
Assistant Professor of Political Science
Troy State University

burden of proof   refers to the duty of one asserting a claim against another to have the responsibility to prove the assertion.

One who asserts a claim against another, alleging that the other has done wrong, is said to have the burden of proof—to have responsibility for proving the assertion. The weight of the burden differs in civil and criminal cases. In both types of cases, the person making the claim must provide sufficient facts, through documents and testimony, to convince a judge or jury that the assertions are correct. So, for example, a civil plaintiff who alleges that the accident in which she was injured occurred because the defendant was negligent in some way must provide enough evidence to convince the jury of the truth of her allegations. A prosecutor must provide enough evidence to prove that the defendant committed the crime with which he is charged.

Even if the defendant does not present any evidence in response, the plaintiff still must provide enough evidence to meet the basic requirements ("elements") of the relevant law, or fail in proving her case. A civil plaintiff's burden of proof in this situation may be relatively perfunctory, but it still is a real one.

When a plaintiff or prosecutor's assertion is contested by the defendant, the plaintiff or prosecutor must meet different burden of proof. A civil plaintiff must carry her burden by a "preponderance of the evidence," which means that the plaintiff must convince the judge or jury that events occurred in the way she has said. It is not merely a matter of balancing the plaintiff's and defendant's stories and evidence against each other. The defendant's burden of refuting the plaintiff's basic evidence need not be by a preponderance of the evidence. Even though a plaintiff's story of how the facts prove her case might be more acceptable, more probable, and more consistent with the facts than the defendant's, it still might be insufficient to convince the jury that events did occur in the way plaintiff says they did.

In a criminal prosecution, the proponent for the state must provide evidence that convinces the judge or jury "beyond a reasonable doubt" that the charges against the defendant are valid. Defining this burden has been difficult. In one case, the United States Supreme Court suggested it was "the kind of doubt that would make a person hesitate to act" on serious and important matters of life.

However, the term *burden of proof* also may be used to indicate a responsibility for "moving the evidence forward." In the example above, if the plaintiff's evidence fulfills the basic elements of the claim, then it commonly is said that the burden of proof "shifts" to the defendant to provide enough evidence to counter the plaintiff's story of what happened. The defendant must assume the burden of moving the evidence forward, or face an adverse judgment. This shifting of responsibility to move forward may occur innumerable times during a trial.

As noted, the burden of moving the evidence forward may be a lesser one than plaintiff's ultimate burden of proof. For example, the defendant may convince the jury that the accident could not have occurred in the way plaintiff has said it did, without having to convince the jury about how the accident did occur. The ultimate burden of proof—proving the allegation that the defendant is responsible for the plaintiff's injuries—remains with the plaintiff. This ultimate burden of proof also is sometimes called the "risk of nonpersuasion."

For more information
Holland v. United States, 348 U.S. 121 (1954).
Rommency v. City of New York, 63 N.Y.S. 186, 49 App.
    Div. 64 (1900).

Judith Kilpatrick
University of Arkansas, Fayetteville

Burger, Warren E.   (1907–1995)   served as the fifteenth chief justice of the United States from June 10, 1969, to July 10, 1986. He was born on Constitution Day, September 17, 1907; he died June 29, 1995.

Burger's life was a Horatio Alger story. The fourth of seven children, he picked tomatoes on the family farm near St. Paul, Minnesota, and he had a number of odd jobs, including a daily newspaper route. He turned down a scholarship to Princeton because he could not have worked to contribute to the family finances. Instead, he attended the University of Minnesota at night and then St. Paul College of Law (now William Mitchell) where he graduated in 1931 magna cum laude. He did so well in law school that the faculty appointed him an adjunct professor, and he taught there for 17 years while practicing law in St. Paul.

His practice was primarily corporate, real estate, and probate. He became active in local civic affairs and Republican Party politics. He was the floor manager for Minnesota governor Harold Stassen's 1948 and 1952 campaigns for the presidential nomination, which brought him to the attention of national party leaders. President Eisenhower's attorney general, Herbert Brownell, named Burger assistant attorney general of the Civil Division at the Department of Justice, where he earned a reputation for industry and loyalty.

In 1955 Burger was appointed to the U.S. Court of Appeals for the District of Columbia. He began speaking and writing about the perennial problems facing the judicial system: crime and corrections, overloaded dockets, and delays. These activities brought him to the attention of President Nixon, who had campaigned against the activism of the Warren Court and for "law and order."

Chief Justice Burger was widely viewed as a conservative jurist who presided over a conservative court. But the Burger Court did not overrule Warren Court decisions on constitutional law, managing only to refrain from extending them. Furthermore, in many new and controversial areas, the Burger Court rushed in where the Warren Court had feared to tread: the issues of

Chief Justice Warren E. Burger (HARRIS AND EWING, COLLECTION OF THE SUPREME COURT OF THE UNITED STATES)

abortion, affirmative action, and the death penalty.

The chief justice seemed to tack back and forth, unwilling or unable to chart a clear course either for his own constitutional jurisprudence or for the Court's. His judicial performance was certainly better than his contemporary critics would allow and not appreciably different from many of his colleagues. Still, he was not a great justice. The Burger Court likely will go down in history as a transitional period between the liberal Warren Court and the conservative Rehnquist Court, both of which enjoyed considerably greater acclaim—and significant controversy—for their visions of the Constitution.

At his Senate confirmation hearing, Burger pledged to take seriously the title of being "chief justice of the United States." He kept this promise by using the prestige and influence of his office to initiate countless reforms of the federal and state courts. Indeed, his indefatigable work to improve the administration of the courts—more than his judicial decisions or opinions—was his most important contribution to justice. History will credit him with leading the modernization of the nation's court system.

Burger's last great public service was as chairman of the Commission on the Bicentennial of the U.S. Constitution. In the foreword to the pocket Constitution the commission published, he wrote, "For 200 years this Constitution's ordered liberty has unleashed the energies and talents of people to create a good life." That describes his own life and career as a jurist, administrator, and public servant to improve the cause of justice.

For more information

Blasi, Vincent, ed. *The Burger Court—The Counter-Revolution That Wasn't*. New Haven, Conn.: Yale University Press, 1983.

Lamb, Charles M., and Halpern, Stephen C. eds. *The Burger Court—Political and Judicial Profiles*. Champaign: University of Illinois Press, 1991.

Schwartz, Bernard, ed. *The Burger Court—Counter-Revolution or Confirmation?* New York: Oxford University Press, 1998.

Woodward, Bob, and Armstrong, Scott. *The Brethren—Inside the Supreme Court*. New York: Simon and Schuster, 1979.

Thomas E. Baker
James Madison Chair in Constitutional Law
Drake University Law School

burglary   is a criminal offense consisting of the breaking and entering in the nighttime of another's dwelling place, with the intent to commit a felony inside. As the old adage states, "a man's home is his castle." It is the enjoyment of this castle, free from the midnight terror of an intruder, that the outlawing of burglary was designed to protect. Thus, the essence of the crime of burglary at common law is the violation of the security of the dwelling house, rather than a crime against property.

To prove common-law burglary, the state must meet all of the elements of the offense, which requires proof that the perpetrator's actions consisted of: (1) breaking, (2) entering, (3) a dwelling house, (4) in the nighttime, and (5) with the intent to commit a felony. To constitute a "breaking," one need not pry a lock or destroy property to gain entry. Pushing open an unlatched or partially opened door or window is sufficient. The breaking may even occur once the perpetrator has entered the house, or it may occur in an outbuilding near the premises. Of course, the entry must be without the consent of the owner of the premises. However, the dwelling need not be occupied at the time of the entry, so long as it is suitable for residential purposes and the occupant has the intent to return. The breaking must occur "at night," which is generally understood to mean that the sky contains insufficient sunlight to discern a person's face.

To be guilty of burglary, the perpetrator need not actually commit the intended felony. He need not carry away any goods. It is enough simply to enter the premises with the requisite intent. The intended felony may be one of a number of offenses, including larceny, rape, assault, or arson. The state generally may prove intent by circumstantial evidence, and if no explanation for the breaking and entering is apparent, a jury may infer the perpetrator's intent was to commit larceny.

Under modern criminal statutes, many of the strict definitional rules of common-law burglary have been relaxed or abandoned. For example, in many states, mere entry into an occupied building or structure is sufficient; the "breaking" requirement has either been abandoned or it is stated as an alternative to entering (e.g., *breaking or entering*). Moreover, the common-law requirement for breaking into a "dwelling house" has been relaxed in many states. Many statutes define burglary to include the entry with intent to commit a crime into any "building," including stores and other business establishments. Indeed, in a number of states, the entry into a motor vehicle, railroad car, or vessel may constitute burglary. Also, the requirement that the offense occur "at night" generally has been eliminated; the unlawful entry may now occur at any time, day or night. Finally, the perpetrator need not intend to commit a felony to be guilty of burglary; it is now sufficient if the perpetrator intents to commit any crime, including petty larceny.

Interestingly, even in those states that have substantially modified the definition of burglary, the impact of the common law is still felt. Many states impose greater penalties on the perpetrator if the burglary occurs at night, or in a dwelling house, or if the perpetrator intended to commit a felony.

For more information

Torcia, Charles E. *Wharton's Criminal Law,* 15th ed. Vol. 3. New York: Clark Boardman Callaghan, 1995.

Nathanael Causey
Assistant Professor of Law
United States Military Academy
West Point, New York

Burton, Harold Hitz (1888–1964) served as an associate justice of the United States Supreme Court in 1945–54, where he represented a moderate judicial approach, neither predictably liberal nor predictably conservative.

Burton was born in 1888 near Boston, where his father served as dean of the faculty at the Massachusetts Institute of Technology. After attending Bowdoin College, where he excelled as a student and as an athlete, Burton graduated from Harvard Law School. He then married Selma Florence Smith and joined her uncle's law firm in Cleveland, Ohio. He served with the Allied forces in Europe during World War II and afterward returned to private practice and civil affairs in Cleveland. He was elected to the Ohio legislature as a Republican in 1929 and became mayor of Cleveland in 1934. There he earned a reputation for integrity and economy. In 1940 Burton won a seat in the U.S. Senate where he served until his appointment to the Court. While in the Senate, Burton was a member of Harry S Truman's special committee to investigate the national defense. In addition to disclosing fraud and abuse in war contracts, the committee fostered a camaraderie between Truman and Burton that doubtless contributed to Truman's decision to make Burton his first appointment to the Supreme Court.

Burton's record in the Senate reflected the same values that would characterize his behavior on the bench. He was a moderate who supported civil rights for African Americans and an internationalist who opposed communism. His character as a tireless worker who paid painstaking attention to detail followed him from the legislature to the judiciary. Truman's nomination of the Republican Burton to the Court was intended as a conciliatory gesture. His name was brought to the Senate in the midst of debate on an unemployment bill. He was confirmed unanimously without hearings, debate, or objection.

Burton served under Chief Justices Harlan Fiske Stone, Fred Vinson, and Earl Warren, and during his tenure he observed the Court becoming more concerned with civil rights and civil liberties. He wrote the Court's opinion in *Henderson v. United States* (1954), holding that segregation in railway dining cars violated the Interstate Commerce Act. He was an early supporter of overturning the "separate but equal" principles of *Plessy v. Ferguson* and outlawing school segregation in *Brown v. Board of Education* (1954). Burton kept a diary during the Court's conferences on segregation, which has been a valuable source for understanding how Warren built consensus for the unanimous ruling. Burton's votes were mixed in cases where the civil liberties of suspected communists were at issue. In *Emspak v. United States* (1955) he voted with the majority to support the Fifth Amendment rights of wit-

Justice Harold Hitz Burton (HARRIS AND EWING, COL-LECTION OF THE SUPREME COURT OF THE UNITED STATES)

nesses before congressional committees. Burton also joined the majority in *Ullman v. United States* (1956), which upheld the Immunity Act limiting the use of Fifth Amendment protections in testimony before grand juries investigating threats to national security. In *Yates v. United States* (1957) Burton voted to limit the application of the Smith Act, which had outlawed the organizing activities of the Communist Party, but Burton's vote was cast on narrow procedural grounds. He did not agree with Justices Black and Douglas that the Smith Act itself violated the First Amendment.

Burton disagreed with one of the Warren Court's early decisions applying the Bill of Rights to the states through the Fourteenth Amendment due process clause. In *Griffin v. Illinois* (1956) Burton dissented when the Court held that denying trial transcripts to indigent defendants violated due process. He would leave criminal procedure to be determined by the states.

Burton's votes on cases related to the economy are also evidence of his independence and nonideological position. He opposed his good friend Truman's seizure of steel mills during a strike in *Youngstown Steel and Tube v. Sawyer* (1952). With the majority of the Court, Burton believed that the president could not seize private property in peacetime. During his first term on the Court, he wrote the opinion in *American Tobacco Company v. United States* (1946), holding that the tobacco industry formed a conspiracy in violation of the Sherman Antitrust Act. In two later dissents he took positions on both sides of the application of the Sherman Act. In *United States v. E. I. DuPont* (1957) Burton held that duPont should not be charged with monopolistic practices for a stock acquisition 40 years earlier. In *Toolson v. New York Yankees* (1953) he was in the minority who argued that major league baseball was a business subject to antitrust laws.

Burton retired from the Court in 1958. He died in Washington, D.C., in 1964.

For more information

Berry, Mary Frances. *Stability, Security, and Continuity: Mr. Justice Burton and Decision Making in the Supreme Court 1945–1958.* Westport, Conn.: Greenwood Press, 1978.

Schwartz, Bernard, with Stephan Lesher. *Inside the Warren Court.* Garden City, N.Y.: Doubleday, 1983.

Mary Welek Atwell
Radford University

C

capital punishment is also known as the death penalty or execution and is the punishment of a criminal offender by killing.

As of 1998, capital punishment in the United States was legal for 38 states and the federal government. Capital punishment is typically reserved for very serious offenses such as premeditated murder, treason, or murder as a byproduct of crimes such as kidnapping. While most of the world once legally practiced capital punishment, today capital punishment is illegal in most countries outside the United States and has been prohibited by law or in practice in all Western European countries. In the United States the practice of capital punishment has existed since the time of its founding. In our history death sentences have been issued in a legal fashion (by courts) and illegally (by lynch mobs). Today the philosophy, process, methods, and results of capital punishment are controversial topics that are often the subject of great debate.

The philosophy of capital punishment is a subject of moral and ethical debate in the United States. When polled, the U.S. public generally favors the practice of capital punishment, but

dissent is often great among opponents. Proponents of capital punishment rely on its history of use in countries throughout the world and refer to the philosophy of retribution or an "eye for an eye." Under this philosophy, the punishment for killing should be the life of the offender. Opponents of the practice of capital punishment often refer to the sanctity of all life and say that the violence of murder should not be met with a violent solution from society. Opponents also refer to state-sponsored execution as a violation of basic individual rights by government tyranny. Finally, Americans argue that the Eighth Amendment of the United States Constitution, with its protection against "cruel and unusual punishment," prohibits the killing of offenders. However, since the 1947 case of *Louisiana ex rel. Frances v. Resweber,* the United States Supreme Court has held that the death penalty is not cruel or unusual. The justices have argued that the death penalty was intended by the framers and that it was used at the time of the writing of the Constitution.

The process of capital punishment is also debated; this refers to the bureaucratic or administrative nature of choosing who is eligible for the death penalty as well as how, when, and where it is implemented. Scholars of criminal justice have often referred to the U.S. variety of capital punishment as the most complicated and bureaucratic of the countries that practice it. As to who is eligible for the death penalty, the states, under the guidance of the United States Supreme Court, have the power to decide what crimes are capital crimes and what type of offender is eligible. For example, debates rage over whether children or the mentally retarded are eligible for the death penalty. In fact, the minimum age that the death penalty can be imposed varies among the states. Eight states have no specific minimum age, 14 states have a minimum age of 18, and 16 states indicate a range of eligibility from 14 to 17. Interestingly, 11 of the 38 death-penalty states outlaw the practice for those who are mentally retarded.

Additionally, the process has led to great debate over the selection of individuals for execution. The death penalty process is considered to be legal because of the United States Constitution's due process clauses of the Fifth and Fourteenth Amendments. These state that no person shall be deprived of life without due process of the law. Under these provisions, if offenders receive a fair trial, then life can be deprived if the offense is serious enough. Many opponents argue that even with due process, some that are innocent are convicted and placed on death row. Some estimate that 350 innocent people were placed on death row between 1900 and 1985. As of 1992, 23 legally innocent people have been executed this century (*See* Johnson, *Death Work,* 1998, page 5.)

Many of the legal challenges to the death penalty, in fact, no longer rest on whether it is "cruel and unusual" but on whether due process rights are violated. In the case of *Furman v. Georgia* (1972), the United States Supreme Court placed a temporary stop to executions until states could show that the process they used was fair and not discriminatory. The opponents who won this case argued that the death penalty *as*

practiced was unfair and that it discriminated against African Americans. After the *Furman* case, states changed their laws of procedure and the Supreme Court reinstated the death penalty in the case of *Gregg v. Georgia* (1976). Interestingly, many still challenge the death penalty today by citing statistics that show minorities and men receive the death penalty in disproportionate numbers. Recent data from the U.S. Bureau of Justice Statistics indicates that from 1977 to 1998, 500 prisoners have been executed. Among these there were 278 white men, 178 black men, 34 Hispanic men, 4 Native American men, 3 Asian men, and 3 white females.

Methods of execution that are still in practice in the United States include electrocution, poisonous gas, hanging, firing squad, and lethal injection. Of the 500 executions held from 1977 to 1998, 344 were by lethal injection, 141 by electrocution, 10 by poisonous gas, 3 by hanging, and 2 by firing squad. Interestingly, the most common method of execution in history was beheading. Today opponents of the death penalty have argued that the method of death employed by some states is more "cruel" than those used by other states. Methods that call for direct physical trauma such as electrocution, hanging, and firing squad are considered less humane than gas or lethal injection.

Finally, the outcome or effects of capital punishment are debated. Proponents have argued that capital punishment provides a real deterrent to future crimes by placing real costs on the committing of serious crimes. Opponents respond that some social science studies show capital punishment is not a deterrent because death sentences seem arbitrary and the practice is not swift or sure. In fact, the average time on death row to execution has steadily increased from an average of 51 months in 1977–83 to 130 months in 1998. As to sureness of sentence, of the 6,089 prisoners sentenced to death from 1977 to 1998 only 500 or 8.2 percent were executed. Those in favor of the death penalty have argued that it would be more of a deterrent if executions were imposed, were more visible, and were carried out swiftly after trial. However, since the reinstatement of the death penalty in 1976, statistics show that there has been an increase in the overall number of persons sentenced to death and executed.

For more information

Johnson, Robert. *Death Work: A Study of the Modern Execution Process,* St. Paul, Minn.: West/Wadsworth Publishing, 1998.

Snell, Tracy. *Capital Punishment 1998.* United States Bureau of Justice Statistics, December 1999.

Van den Haag, Earnest. "The Ultimate Punishment: A Defense," *Harvard Law Review* 99 (May 1986).

Rogen Hartley
University of Arizona

Cardozo, Benjamin (1870–1938) was an associate justice of the United States Supreme Court from 1932 to 1938 who gained an international reputation for his efforts to reconcile constitutional interpretation with the social and economic challenges of the New Deal. Cardozo was born to a prominent Sephardic Jewish family in New York City on May 24, 1870. Educated at Columbia College and Law School, he was admitted to the New York Bar in 1891 at the age of 21 and went into private practice in New York City.

Cardozo was elected to the New York Supreme Court in 1913, where he served briefly before receiving a temporary appointment to the New York Court of Appeals, the state's highest court. He was elected to the Court of Appeals in his own right in 1918 and became chief judge in 1927. Under his leadership, the New York Court of Appeals developed a reputation as one of the leading courts in the nation, and Cardozo was widely regarded as one of the nation's premier common-law judges, especially in the areas of tort and contract law. In *MacPherson v. Buick* (1916), for example, Cardozo established the foundations of modern product liability law,

while *Palzgraf v. Long Island Railroad* (1928) established the principle that negligence must be founded upon the foreseeability of harm to the injured party, and *Ultrameres Corporation v. Touche* (1931) extended protections against fraud to third parties.

On February 15, 1932, President Herbert Hoover appointed Cardozo to replace retiring justice Oliver Wendell Holmes on the United States Supreme Court. Cardozo joined a court that soon found itself sharply divided over how to treat the New Deal legislation emerging from the Franklin Roosevelt administration. As a leading member of the Court's liberal wing, Cardozo often maintained that Congress and the states should be accorded considerable deference in dealing with the nation's economic crises. In attempting to reconcile the traditional principles of U.S. constitutional law to the changed conditions of the 1930s and to uphold key elements of the New Deal, Cardozo often found himself joining justices Louis D. Brandeis and Harlan Fiske Stone in dissent.

Cardozo was instrumental in leading the Court toward a more pragmatic, less abstract interpretation of the nature of federalism, away from the system of mutually exclusive rights and powers that had defined the relationships between the states and the federal governments toward a relationship in which the rights and powers of the two layers of government would be understood as overlapping and concurrent. In *Steward Machine Co. v. Davis* (1937) and *Helvering v. Davis* (1937), Cardozo wrote for the Court in upholding the Social Security Act of 1935 based on Congress's authority under the taxing and spending clauses of the Constitution, while his majority opinion in 1937's *Palko v. Connecticut* laid out the Court's rationale for the incorporation of elements of the Bill of Rights into the Fourteenth Amendment and the application of those constitutional protections to state actions.

In addition to the 150 opinions that he wrote during his six years on the U.S. Supreme Court,

Justice Benjamin Cardozo (HARRIS AND EWING, COL-
LECTION OF THE SUPREME COURT OF THE UNITED STATES)

Cardozo was also the author of *The Nature of the Judicial Process* (1921), *The Growth of the Law* (1924), *Paradoxes of Legal Science* (1928), and *Law and Literature* (1931). He died in Port Chester, New York, on July 9, 1938, following a heart attack and a stroke.

For more information
Kaufman, Andrew L. *Cardozo.* Cambridge, Mass.: Harvard University Press, 1998.
Pollard, Joseph P. *Mr. Justice Cardozo.* 1935. Reprint. Westport, Conn.: Greenwood Press, 1970.

William D. Baker
Arkansas School for Mathematics and Science

cease and desist order   is an official court decree directing a party to refrain from engaging in some conduct or activity that is found to be detrimental to another party, a designated group, or the community as a whole. This order is generally sought by governmental administrative agencies as an enforcement tool to enjoin illegal and harmful conduct committed against people, legal entities, property, and the environment.

Federal agencies that have imposed such orders include but are not limited to the Federal Trade Commission, the National Labor Relations Board, the Securities and Exchange Commission, and the International Trade Commission. For example, the FTC will impose such an order where an entity such as a partnership, corporation, or other person or individual has been found guilty of unfair methods of competition and unfair or deceptive acts or practices, such as "price discrimination," in interstate commerce. Civil penalties for the violations of cease and desist orders may be recovered in subsequent civil proceedings.

After receiving due process in an administrative agency hearing, a defendant ordered by an administrative law judge to refrain from continuing specifically defined illegal practices in violation of a federal statute may contest the findings and the decision by seeking judicial review of any cease and desist order but must continue to comply with the order, which may include the filing of annual or special reports or providing specific disclosure of internal proprietary information. The United States Court of Appeals for the relevant circuit has exclusive jurisdiction to affirm, enforce, modify, or set aside such judicial order. The United States Supreme Court may grant a valid petition to review the validity of such an order.

For more information
The Administrative Procedure Act (APA) 5 U.S.C. § 551 et Seq. Administrative Law and Regulatory Policy: Problems, Text, and Cases, by Breyer, Stewart, and Sunstein.

J. David Golub
Touro College

censorship is legal banning of the publication or distribution of printed or recorded materials by the government.

Once a relatively straightforward constitutional concept, censorship has become an increasingly contested issue. Anglo-American constitutional discourse traditionally saw governmental censorship as a regrettable (though occasionally necessary) departure from the overriding normative goal of providing constitutional protection for the widest possible "free exchange of ideas." Censorship, in this frame, signified external governmental restraint on the internal preferences of individuals to speak or write "their own mind."

More recently, critical theorists who embrace continental literary and political theory have treated censorship as a linguistic practice. By that any one person's expression inevitably depends on shared understandings with others and on culturally constructed conventions of what kinds of utterances count as meaningful discourse. From this perspective, the question is not whether there is censorship but, rather, what kinds of censorship are in force and what is their effect on the existing distribution of power and knowledge.

Debate over censorship emerged in relationship to prior restraints imposed by governmental officials. The English licensing system, in which an official censor decided what publications were allowed to go to press, provided the classic example. Although licensing disappeared during the 17th century, the issue of prior restraints remained a central concern of U.S. constitutional doctrine. Litigation over forms of prior restraint that could seem analogous to licensing appeared in a variety of circumstances: injunctions against libelous publications (*Near v. Minnesota* [1931]); local ordinances that required speakers or persons distributing printed matter to obtain special licenses (*Marsh v. Alabama* [1946]); licensing arrangements aimed at entertainment with sexually explicit content (*Joseph Burstyn, Inc. v. Wilson* [1951]); laws against "hate speech" (*R.A.V v. St. Paul* [1992]); congressional limitations on political expenditures (*Buckley v. Valeo* [1976]); and, in the famous "Pentagon Papers case," an injunction against publication of a secret history of U.S. involvement in Vietnam (*New York Times v. Nixon* [1971]).

Although the U.S. Supreme Court ruled in favor of "freedom of expression" and against "censorship" in all these cases, even celebrants of the anticensorship position acknowledged a countertradition. The Court, for example, allowed public school officials to censor student publications (*Hazelwood School District v. Kuhlmeier* [1980]) and upheld a contractual arrangement that barred current or retired CIA officers from publishing anything that had not been cleared by the agency (*Snepp v. U.S.* [1980]). According to the traditional anticensorship position, decisions such as this simply meant that the Court would, in a few, very narrowly defined, special circumstances, allow governmental censorship.

Critics of this perspective, however, insist that discussions of censorship cannot be limited by the classical concept of governmental action or focused on allegedly neutral constitutional doctrines and on "core principles" such as the requirement that government regulation not "create an external chill" on free discussion. Constitutional debate over censorship has never been simply about expression per se, the critical view argues, but has always involved political decisions about the proper distribution of social power. Expression does not achieve protection because, in some abstract constitutional calculus, it involves the "free" exchange of ideas but because the political agenda to which the expression is connected seems legitimate to those powerful people who possess the potential to censor it. Disputes about expression over the Internet, for instance, have highlighted the ways in which traditional copyright law both restricts and enables expression. Critics also argue that it is no accident that, during the last 30 years, the Supreme Court has struck down governmental measures aimed at reining in large political expenditures and laws designed to combat racist and pornographic speech and has upheld regulations aimed at protecting the national security bureaucracy.

More broadly, critics note that the traditional idea of censorship, with its focus on governmental action, ignores the day-to-day regulation of expression by powerful private groups. Media conglomerates routinely decide what counts as "news" and what kinds of cultural products seem worthy of distribution, while corporations of all kinds possess broad power to regulate—and even effectively silence—the expression of their employees. A marketplace of ideas, even if entirely freed from governmental restraints, would hardly qualify as a "free" one, in this critical view.

The critical perspective on censorship suggests no clear set of constitutional principles or legal doctrines. Indeed, because it emphasizes the complex, social-linguistic networks through which expression is articulated and received, it tends to place in the foreground the inability of universal principles, such as "no prior restraints" or the freest possible "exchange of ideas," to untangle the complex, censorship-related issues such as "hate speech." As a consequence, this critical perspective, though well represented in legal-constitutional scholarship, has yet to find its way into legal-constitutional doctrine, which is still closely tied to the traditional concept of eliminating "governmental censorship" of "the exchange of ideas." This long-established view of censorship, its supporters maintain, still constitutes one of the bulwarks of American constitutionalism.

For more information

Burt, Richard, ed. *The Administration of Aesthetics: Censorship, Political Criticism, and the Public Sphere.* Minneapolis: University of Minnesota Press, 1994.

Jansen, Sue Curry. *Censorship: The Knot That Binds Power and Knowledge.* New York: Oxford University Press, 1991.

Post, Robert C. *Censorship and Silencing: Practices of Cultural Regulation.* Los Angeles: J. Paul Getty Museum Publishers, 1998.

Norman L. Rosenberg
Macalester College

certiorari, writ of   is a discretionary writ—an order with the force of law—that has long been in use in English and American judicial practice. Pronounced *sir-sho-rare-ee*, certiorari is a Latin term literally meaning "to be informed of; to be made certain." As the word suggests, a writ of certiorari requires a lower court to provide a higher court with the record of a specific judicial proceeding so that the higher court can review, "be informed" about that record, and "made certain" that the lower court's judgment is free from legal errors.

In England writs of certiorari originally were issued at the monarch's prerogative to remedy an official's abuse of authority or neglect of duty. English use of such writs evolved gradually to where private individuals could apply to chancery courts beginning in the 14th century and then, in the 16th century, to the Court of Queen's Bench and, after 1857, to the High Court to persuade jurists to issue a writ of certiorari commanding jurists in lower courts to certify—return—their proceedings so that their actions could be reviewed.

In the United States, writs of certiorari (or their equivalent) are an important discretionary avenue of review in state and federal courts. Two states, Oklahoma and Rhode Island, specify writs of certiorari as a possible way to obtain review of provisional (interlocutory) judgments of lower courts. While some states have statutorily abolished the term *certiorari* in lieu of an appellate "petition of review" (Alaska, Idaho), a "writ of supervisory control" (Montana), or commonly a petition for "leave to appeal," these actions are similar in nature and purpose to certiorari. At the federal level, about 90 percent of the cases that come to the U. S. Supreme Court arrive via petitions for a writ of certiorari (or "cert." for short). The procedure governing consideration of writs of certiorari, found in Part III, rule 10 of the Rules of the Supreme Court, specifies: "Review on a writ of certiorari is not a matter of right, but of judicial discretion." The Supreme Court usually decides to "deny cert.," rejecting 90 percent of petitions for writs of certiorari filed. It has not always had complete discretion to choose the cases it would hear. Prior to the Judiciary Act of 1891, which created intermediate federal courts of appeal, the Supreme Court had no control over its docket. The 1925 Judiciary Act ("Judges' Bill") expanded the Court's certiorari jurisdiction while mandatory appeals were severely restricted.

Because the Supreme Court has complete discretion to grant or to deny "cert.," it consequently has broad authority to set its own agenda. The seven formal rules pertaining to its jurisdiction on writs of certiorari (Part III, rules 10–16) provide meager insight into the practical factors shaping how justices determine which cases to decide. Students of judicial decision making have devoted considerable attention to exploring this aspect of the black box that envelops the choices justices make. The prevailing view is that all judicial choices, including decisions on "cert." petitions, result from "strategic" interactions among the justices which entail each jurist pursuing policy goals interdependently with colleagues within the context of internal and external social rules (institutions) which structure judicial practices. Over the past two decades, the Supreme Court has exercised its discretion to deny "cert.," thereby restricting appellate access while, at the same time, the number of cases filed has soared. By the mid-1990s more than 6,500 new cases were filed annually while the Court granted "cert." to fewer than 5 percent.

For more information

Epstein, Lee, and Knight, Jack. *The Choices Justices Make.* Washington, D.C.: Congressional Quarterly Press, 1998.

Provine, Doris Marie. "Certiorari." In Janosik, Robert J., ed., *Encyclopedia of the American Judicial System,* 3 vols. New York: Charles Scribner's Sons, 1987, II: 783–94.

James C. Foster
Department of Political Science
Oregon State University

Chase, Samuel (1741–1811) was an associate justice of the United States Supreme Court and the only member of the Supreme Court ever to be impeached by the House of Representatives.

A native of Maryland, Chase had long been active in state politics and was a leading supporter of the American Revolution in Maryland. He was a member of the state legislative assembly (1764–84), a member of the Continental Congress (1774–78, 1784–85), and a signer of the Declaration of Independence. As a member of the Maryland ratification convention, he opposed the ratification of the U.S. Constitution but later became an ardent Federalist and a supporter of the new Constitution. He was the chief judge of the Maryland General Court (1791–96), during which time he became involved in a brief scandal and was the subject of an impeachment investigation by the Maryland legislature.

In 1796 Chase was appointed to the Supreme Court by President George Washington to fill the seat vacated by John Blair. He was the ninth justice appointed to the Court, and he held the seat until his death in 1811. Chase wrote the lead opinion in the important case of *Ware v. Hylton* (1796), which declared federal treaties to be superior to conflicting state laws. Chase wrote a provocative opinion in the case of *Calder v. Bull* (1798) that foreshadowed the Court's declaration of a power of judicial review in the later case of *Marbury v. Madison* (1803), as well as later debates over "substantive due process." In *Calder,* Chase argued that legislative power was limited by "certain vital principles in our free

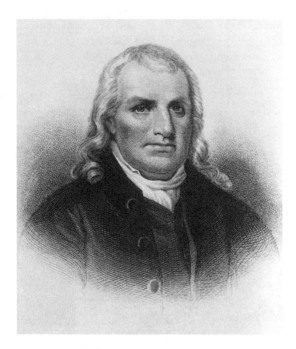

Justice Samuel Chase (PAINTING BY JARVIS, AND ENGRAV-
ING BY H.B. HALL, COLLECTION OF THE SUPREME COURT
OF THE UNITED STATES)

republican government," even if those principles had not been explicitly included in the constitutional text. In the case of *United States v. Worrall* (1798), Chase wrote an early opinion denying the existence of a federal common law of crimes, which would have allowed federal prosecutions based on judge-made law rather than a specific statute.

In 1804 Chase was impeached by the House of Representatives, but he was acquitted by a four-vote margin in a trial by the Senate in 1805. In the two years prior to the elections of 1800, Chase had been particularly aggressive, and some thought biased, in conducting criminal trials of various opponents of the Federalist administration. Chase had also actively participated in the reelection campaign of President John Adams in 1800. In 1803 he delivered an inflammatory political speech to a grand jury in

Maryland. Based on these events, the Jeffersonians, who had won the congressional and presidential elections of 1800, impeached Chase for abusing his judicial office and using it in a partisan manner. His eventual acquittal both eased fears that the impeachment power would be used to undermine judicial independence and discouraged federal judges from further involvement in partisan politics.

For more information

Presser, Stephen. *The Original Misunderstanding: The English, the Americans, and the Dialectic of Federalist Jurisprudence.* Durham, N.C.: Carolina Academic Press, 1991.

Rehnquist, William H. *Grand Inquests: The Historic Impeachments of Justice Samuel Chase and President Andrew Johnson.* New York: William Morrow, 1992.

Keith E. Whittington
Princeton University

chief justice   is the title of the Supreme Court justice nominated by the president to lead the rest of the Court. The chief justice has both formal and informal powers that shape how the Court functions.

The position of chief justice was mentioned in the Constitution under the impeachment clause and was formally created by the Judiciary Act of 1789. Neither, however, mentions the scope of duties or powers of the chief justice. The role of the chief justice has been developed over the course of 200 years by the individuals who have filled the post. The position of chief justice is often referred to as *primus inter pares,* Latin for first among equals. This is not entirely accurate, though. The chief justice does have unique responsibilities and powers that set the position apart from the associate justices. In addition to hearing and deciding cases with the rest of the justices, the chief justice's role can be divided into three parts: formal, informal, and extrajudicial.

The chief justice's formal powers include being able to assign who will write the opinion in a case (if they are in the majority), controlling and managing discussion of the cases in the weekly private conference, and determining whether either side presenting oral arguments in a case can go over their allotted time. Additionally, the chief justice handles a myriad of administrative duties ranging from oversight of the premises of the Supreme Court to reviewing work conditions for Court employees.

These formal powers are just the beginning, though. The chief justice's informal powers are based on his or her ability to lead the rest of the Court. Chief Justices John Marshall, Charles Evans Hughes, and Earl Warren were renowned for their ability to get majorities together for major cases through persuasion, example, and conviction, while Chief Justices Edward White and Fred Vinson are regarded as largely ineffective leaders.

The chief justice is the most highly visible of the justices, and his actions and beliefs carry an added weight not only on the Court but also in the public. It is this visibility that is key to the chief justice's extrajudicial functions. The chief justice is involved in lobbying Congress for funding for the judicial branch, developing standards for judicial ethics at all federal court levels, leading the conference of all the federal court judges, and presiding over impeachment trials in the Senate. These extrajudicial functions are critical to establishing and maintaining the stature of the Supreme Court and play an important role in the operation of the Court.

There have been 16 chief justices since the adoption of the Constitution. In chronological order, they are:

John Jay (1789–1795)
John Rutledge (1795)
Oliver Ellsworth (1796–1800)
John Marshall (1801–1835)
Roger Brooke Taney (1836–1864)
Salmon Portland Chase (1864–1873)
Morrison Remick Waite (1874–1888)
Melville Weston Fuller (1888–1910)
Edward Douglass White (1910–1921)
William Howard Taft (1921–1930)
Charles Evans Hughes (1930–1941)
Harlan Fiske Stone (1941–1946)
Fred M. Vinson (1946–1953)
Earl Warren (1953–1969)
Warren Earl Burger (1969–1986)
William H. Rehnquist (1986–   )

For more information

Fish, Peter Graham, *The Office of Chief Justice.* Charlottesville: White Burkett Miller Center, University of Virginia, 1984.

Steamer, Robert J. *Chief Justice: Leadership and the Supreme Court.* Columbia: University of South Carolina Press, 1986.

Christopher Shortell
University of California, San Diego

child pornography   generally defined as sexually explicit materials made by exploiting children, is not protected by the First Amendment.

Child pornography is a fairly new legal concept. It was not until *New York v. Ferber* (1982) that sexually explicit material involving underage individuals became a separate category outside the confines of mainstream obscenity law. In that case, the Supreme Court found that the involvement of children in the production of child pornography was psychologically and physically harmful to them. Consequently, the constitutional protections required in obscenity prosecutions did not apply in child pornography cases. *Ferber* and subsequent cases held that child pornography had no redeeming social significance and that mere possession or viewing of child pornography could be a crime.

Federal and state laws have tried to keep pace with new concerns and technologies. The original federal law enacted in 1977 criminalized interstate commercial child pornography. However, child pornography was not a major commercial enterprise: Only one person was convicted under the law in nine years. In 1984 Congress broadened the law to include non-commercial sexual exploitation of children. Subsequently the law was modified to outlaw the electronic transmission of child pornography.

Prior to 1996 the actual participation of children in the production of pornography was the *sine qua non* of the regulation scheme. However, in 1996 Congress shifted its focus from defining child pornography in terms of the harm inflicted upon real children to a determination that child pornography was evil in and of itself, whether it involved real children or not. Congress argued that even simulated child pornography increases the activities of child molesters and pedophiles. The law was declared unconstitutional in December 1999 by the Ninth United States Court of Appeals.

Despite the near universal abhorrence of child pornography, its regulation poses several problems. Neither the word *child* nor the word *pornography* has a universal meaning. Different cultures define childhood differently. In some countries a person ceases to be a child at age 13. In other countries marriage at any age makes one an adult. Prior to 1984, U.S. child pornography laws did not apply if the participants were over the age of 16—now it is 18. Even today age requirements are not uniform in the states. The variety of definitions is a major problem if governments attempt to apply their laws to producers or distributors of materials available on the Internet.

Determining what constitutes child pornography is also difficult. For some, any picture of a naked child is child pornography, can have no redeeming social value, and must be outlawed. This perception has led to the prosecution of such works as *Radiant Identities* and *The Last Day of Summer* by photographer Jock Sturges, *The Age of Innocence* by French photographer David Hamilton, and the Academy Award–winning film, *The Tin Drum.*

Most Americans, and the courts, would not go to that extreme. To do so would make all parents with pictures of their naked children criminals. Because drawing the line between the need to prevent the sexual exploitation of children and the right to take nonexploitative pictures of children is critical but difficult, the battle to define child pornography will continue.

For more information

Akdeniz, Yaman. *Regulation of Child Pornography on the Internet: Cases and Materials,* at http://www. cyber-rights.org/reports/child.htm. Last updated December 1999. Copyright Yaman Akdeniz, 1996–1999.

William E. Brigman, Ph.D.
University of Houston—Downtown

citizenship   is defined in the Fourteenth Amendment to the Constitution, which states, "All persons born or naturalized in the United States, and subject to the jurisdiction thereof, are citizens of the United States and of the State wherein they reside." Prior to the ratification of the Fourteenth Amendment in 1868, the Constitution had been silent on the definition of national citizenship, leaving that issue to the states to determine.

The Supreme Court addressed the definition of citizenship in *Dred Scott v. Sandford,* 60 U.S. 393 (1857). In this infamous decision authored by Chief Justice Taney, the Court ruled that persons of African descent could never be citizens of the United States. The Fourteenth Amendment was enacted in part to overturn this decision and thus provide a national definition of citizenship.

After passage of the Fourteenth Amendment, however, some issues regarding the definition of citizenship still remained. In *Elk v. Wilkins,* 112 U. S. 94 (1884), the Supreme Court ruled that native Americans were not automatically citizens, because as members of tribes they were not wholly "subject to the jurisdiction" of the federal government. Congress later reversed this decision. In *United States v. Wong Kim Ark,* 169 U. S.

649 (1898), the Court ruled that persons of Asian ancestry born in the United States were citizens despite the fact that federal laws in force until 1952 prohibited Asians from becoming naturalized citizens.

The Court has also had to face questions regarding the rights of noncitizens. In *Yick Wo v. Hopkins,* 118 U.S. 356 (1886), a unanimous Court ruled that the equal protection clause of the Fourteenth Amendment applies to noncitizens as well as to citizens. In *Graham v. Richardson,* 403 U. S. 365 (1971), the Court held that alienage, like race, was a suspect classification under the Equal Protection Clause, requiring strict scrutiny and analysis. Under strict scrutiny, the state must prove that laws drawing distinctions based on citizenship must serve compelling governmental interests. Thus the Court ruled that it was unconstitutional for states to deny welfare benefits to noncitizens. In *In re Griffiths,* 413 U. S. 717 (1973), the Court also applied the strict scrutiny standard, holding that states may not prohibit noncitizen resident aliens from practicing law.

However, in *Sugarman v. Dougall,* 413 U.S. 634 (1973), the Court stated that noncitizens could be barred from some elective and nonelective positions in state governments, although states could not prohibit noncitizens from holding certain civil service jobs. Justice Blackmun, writing for the Court, stated that noncitizens could be barred from governmental positions that involve the formulation, execution, or review of broad public policy, since these political functions go to the heart of representative government. Later cases upheld state prohibitions on noncitizens becoming state troopers, public school teachers, and deputy probation officers, but rejected such citizenship requirements for notaries public.

For more information

Carens, Joseph H. "Who Belongs? Theoretical and Legal Questions about Birthright Citizenship in the United States," *University of Toronto Law Journal* 37 (1987):413.

Shklar, Judith N. *American Citizenship: The Quest for Inclusion.* Cambridge, Mass.: Harvard University Press, 1995.

Mark C. Miller
Clark University

civil action   is a noncriminal lawsuit filed in a court.

Rule 2 of the Federal Rules of Civil Procedure provides that there shall only be one form of noncriminal action (i.e., lawsuit) known as a "civil action." Most states have a similar provision. To appreciate the significance of having only a single form of action, one must understand how it departs from traditional practice.

Historically, there were two separate judicial systems in Anglo-American law. Courts of law were empowered only to award monetary damages. Courts of equity, on the other hand, could order a party to perform certain actions (like convey a piece of real estate) or not perform certain actions (such as not building a fence which blocks access to someone else's property). Thus, the choice of court and whether one files an "action" at law or a "suit" in equity largely depended upon the type of relief being sought.

In courts of law, there were a wide variety of forms of action with names like *assumpsit* (to recover damages for the breach of a promise) and *trover* (to receive compensation for goods wrongfully used by another person). Each form had technical requirements that could trap the unwary draftsman and cause an action to be dismissed.

Federal courts, as well as the courts in most states, now have jurisdiction over both legal and equitable claims. Moreover, the numerous and complex forms of action have been replaced by a single form—the civil action. To initiate a civil action, one simply files a complaint with the court which contains a "short and plain statement" as to why one is entitled to relief. The technical forms of pleading have been abolished.

For more information
Federal Civil Judicial Procedure and Rules (2000).
Reppy, Alison. *Introduction to Civil Procedure: Actions and Pleading at Common Law.* Buffalo, N.Y.: Dennis, 1954.

Danton Asher Berube
Yale University

civil disobedience   is an unlawful act, committed in public, based on nonviolence and performed in a conscientious manner with a willingness to accept punishment. American author Henry David Thoreau first introduced the idea of civil disobedience in his 1849 essay, "Civil Disobedience." Thoreau's refusal to pay taxes in protest against slavery and the U.S. war against Mexico resulted in his arrest and his acquiescence to punishment typical of a civilly disobedient act.

Civil disobedience involves breaking a law. No one crime category defines a civilly disobedient act. Civil disobedience may involve violation of noise ordinances, trespass laws, tax payment laws, traffic laws, and so on. Any deliberate violations of the law performed in public could represent civil disobedience. Expression of radical viewpoints and vehement oral disagreement with a law are not sufficient. An act of civil disobedience requires the performance of a legally forbidden act. The civil disobedient knowingly breaks the law based on a moral evaluation of the law.

Not every act that violates the law is based on civil disobedience. The act of civil disobedience, unlike the act of armed robbery, is not undertaken for private gain. Instead, those who engage in civil disobedient protests will voluntarily suffer legal punishments, financial losses, and in some instances personal humiliation. Acts of civil disobedience are based on a cause or larger principles for which the civil disobedient is willing to make personal sacrifices. Usually, those who employ civil disobedience have exhausted all legal avenues to change.

A willingness to accept punishment is essential. This distinguishes civil disobedient acts from the acts of common criminals, such as thieves. Civil disobedience, then, is a conscientious act. Conscientious means that the protestor honestly believes that what he or she is doing is correct. Weighing the consequences of violating the law, civil disobedients knowingly break the law based on what they believe is right.

Civil disobedience is an act usually performed in public. To make a statement for the cause or principle for which they stand, those who are civilly disobedient must break the law in public. A protestor who burns his military draft card at home may have broken the law but has not made a public statement of protesting a war. By breaking the law in public, the protestor makes a public statement and expresses a willingness to take responsibility for that act in an attempt to remedy injustice. Some acts of civil disobedience may be clandestine by necessity such as the disobedient protest during the Civil War when Northern citizens systematically violated slave system laws by building the underground railroad. Generally, however, civil disobedience must be public, to educate fellow citizens about the injustices of the law being broken.

Civil disobedience is usually nonviolent. Most protestors who engage in civil disobedience abhor violence. Violent acts often invoke fear and may alienate significant parts of the population to whom civil disobedients wish to make a conscientious appeal. Although violence may attract greater media coverage and public attention, it also scares people and may place those who commit such acts in a negative light. Most adherents to civil disobedience eschew violence and view deliberate use of nonviolent methods, such as passive resistance, as more effective ways to register an honest disagreement with a law. Violence is often associated with revolution and the rejection of authority or repudiation of a regime. Civil disobedience does not seek death, destruction, and the overthrow of government. Its aim is to point out injustices associated with the law or a set of laws, not to create instability.

Civil disobedience has been employed on the left and the right of the ideological spectrum. Antiabortion protestors, large numbers of whom are associated with the Religious Right, employed civil disobedience in the 1980s and into the 1990s by blocking access to abortion clinics. Protestors in the 1960s and 1970s used civil disobedience to register their concerns about the Vietnam War. Environmental protection activists in the 1980s and 1990s have used civil disobedience by laying down their bodies in front of logging trucks. Martin Luther King's Civil Rights movement in the 1960s used the tactics of civil disobedience to overturn Jim Crow segregation laws.

For more information

Cohen, Carl. *Civil Disobedience: Conscience, Tactics and the Law.* New York: Columbia University Press, 1971.

Herngren, Per (trans. Margaret Rainey). *Path of Resistance: The Practice of Civil Disobedience.* Philadelphia, Pa.: New Society Publishers, 1993.

Ruth Ann Strickland
Professor, Political Science and
Criminal Justice Department
Appalachian State University

civil liberties   refer to a person's freedom from arbitrary government interference.

In the United States, civil liberties are based on the Bill of Rights, the first 10 amendments to the U.S. Constitution. "Government," sometimes called "the State," in this sense includes government in all its forms—public schools, police, public health systems, and all government agencies on any level, and may include private persons who act on behalf of the government. The Bill of Rights specifically *denies* government the power to do certain acts and applies to all persons in the United States, not just citizens.

U.S. government is based on two conflicting ideas: (1) that the majority rules, and (2) that the power of the majority must be limited so as to preserve civil liberties. For example, according to (1), the majority of voters can approve a law that bans a certain religion, but under (2) that law would be invalid and unenforceable because of the First Amendment guarantee of freedom of religion. Similarly, even widely accepted civil liberties are not absolute and are limited by the rights of other individuals and by the concept of public safety. It is sometimes very difficult to determine where one person's freedom should end and another person's freedom should begin; courts repeatedly struggle with these limitations and conflicts.

The civil liberties guaranteed by the Bill of Rights and further developed by statute and by court decisions include:

First Amendment rights: freedom of expression, of speech, and of the press; freedom of association and assembly; freedom of religion and freedom *from* religion; freedom to complain to the government and ask for assistance or correction of a problem.

Fourth Amendment: freedom from unreasonable government searches and seizures of one's home, office, personal possessions, documents, and records.

Fifth Amendment: freedom from self-incrimination; freedom from double jeopardy; right to not be deprived of life, liberty, or property without due process of law; right to fair payment for private property that the government takes for public use.

Sixth, Seventh and Eighth Amendments: rights to fair treatment if one is accused of a crime; rights to fair court procedures.

In addition, through laws enacted by legislatures and through court rulings based on the Bill of Rights, civil liberties now include:

Right to equal treatment under law (nondiscrimination): applies in schools, the workplace, the courts, and the voting booth, as well as most public accommodations such as hotels, restaurants, public transportation, and most businesses.

Right to due process: right to be treated fairly when facing criminal charges or other serious accusations that could result in loss of liberty, property, schooling, housing, benefits, or other major interests.

Right to privacy: right to pursue and make decisions about one's personal life without government interference.

For more information

Carey, Eve, Alan H. Levine, Janet R. Price, and Norman Dorsen. *The Rights of Students: ACLU Handbook for Young Americans.* New York: Puffin Books, 1997.

Gara, Joel M., David Goldberger, Gary M. Stern, and Norton H. Halperin. *The Right to Protest: the Basic ACLU Guide to Free Expression.* Carbondale: Southern Illinois University Press, 1991.

Lynn, Barry, Marc D. Stern and Oliver S. Thomas. *The Right to Religious Liberty: the Basic ACLU Guide to Religious Rights,* 2nd ed. Carbondale: Southern Illinois University Press, 1995.

McDonald, Laughlin, and John A. Powell. *The Rights of Racial Minorities: the Basic ACLU Guide to Racial Minority Rights,* 2nd ed. Carbondale: Southern Illinois University Press, 1993.

Ross, Susan Deller, Isabelle Katz Pinzler, Deborah A. Ellis, and Kary L. Moss. *The Rights of Women: the Basic ACLU Guide to Women's Rights,* 3rd ed. Carbondale: Southern Illinois University Press, 1993.

Elsa Shartsis
Attorney

civil procedure   is the body of laws and rules that govern how courts handle noncriminal lawsuits. Each court system has its own set of rules, and there are often significant variations between the federal rules and those of various states. Their fundamental purpose, however, is the same. As stated in Rule 1 of the Federal Rules of Civil Procedure, they seek "to secure the just, speedy, and inexpensive determination of every action."

Civil procedure provides the answers to a number of fundamental questions that arise in almost every civil action, including: Which court has the power to hear the case (jurisdiction)? How are the issues to be litigated or framed (pleadings)? What information must the parties provide to each other (discovery)? What relief may the parties seek from the court short of a trial (motions)? How is the lawsuit itself conducted (trial procedure)?

There is no more fundamental issue in civil procedure than which court has jurisdiction over a given dispute. Jurisdiction is literally "the power to speak," and without it, any action or judgment by a court is wholly invalid. There are two distinct types of jurisdiction—subject matter and personal. Subject matter jurisdiction defines the types of issues and cases a court can hear. Civil courts, for example, generally do not have subject matter jurisdiction over criminal cases. Another common subject matter limitation has to do with the dollar amount at issue—thus in some states a "small claims" court may be prohibited from hearing disputes involving more than $5,000 or $10,000.

Personal jurisdiction, on the other hand, refers to the power of a court to issue an order or render a judgment which is binding upon a particular party. As a general rule, for example, a New York court would lack personal jurisdiction over a person who resided in California. But a state court can acquire personal jurisdiction over nonresidents if they have sufficient contacts with the state, such as doing business there or causing an accident within the state's borders. Moreover, unlike subject matter jurisdiction, a lack of personal jurisdiction may be waived by a party. Without subject matter jurisdiction over the type of dispute and personal jurisdiction over the parties, a court lacks the authority to hear and resolve a case.

Parties to a lawsuit use pleadings to advise each other and the court of the factual and legal questions at issue in the case. The plaintiff—i.e., the person bringing suit—files a complaint, which sets forth the factual allegations that the plaintiff contends give rise to liability on the part of the defendant. The defendant then files an answer, which admits or denies each of the plaintiff's allegations. The answer is also used to raise affirmative defenses to the lawsuit. For example, the defendants might admit that they breached a contract but claim that the plaintiff waited too long to file suit, thereby raising the statute of limitations as an affirmative defense.

Pleadings, however, are merely a rough outline of the facts in dispute between the parties. In order to speed up trials, the rules of civil procedure require that parties exchange detailed information with one another through a process known as discovery. Perhaps the most common of these information-exchanging techniques is the deposition. During a deposition, the witness is asked questions under oath and the answers are transcribed by a court reporter. Other discovery methods include interrogatories—written questions which must be answered by the other party—and requests for production of documents—which identify papers and related items that one party must disclose to the other. Discovery can be the most time-consuming and expensive step in the litigation process. It has the advantages, however, of streamlining the trial itself, avoiding unfair surprises, and even facilitating settlement once the parties understand the proof in each other's favor.

Most civil cases never reach the trial stage. Instead, they are either settled by the parties or disposed of by motion. A motion is simply a request by a party for a court order. If, for example, a defendant needs more time to prepare an answer, he could file a motion with the court asking for an extension. The two most important motions under the rules of civil procedure are the motion to dismiss and the motion for summary judgment. They are called dispositive motions because they allow the court to dispose of a case—i.e., rule on the merits—without having to conduct a trial. In a motion to dismiss, the defendant is asking the court to dismiss the plaintiff's lawsuit because, even assuming the facts are as the plaintiff alleges, she is legally not entitled to any relief. A motion for summary judgment, on the other hand, is generally filed at the conclusion of discovery. It asks the court to render a judgment in favor of the moving party on the ground that the moving party is entitled to win even if all of the disputed facts are construed in the light most favorable to the nonmoving party.

If a case does proceed to trial, the rules of civil procedure describe whether there will be a jury, how the jury is selected, the type of verdict to be rendered, etc. It is important to note, however, that some of the most important issues at trial do not involve civil procedure at all. Instead, questions related to the kinds of information that can be considered by the judge or jury are governed by the law and rules of evidence, which is considered to be a quite distinct field from civil procedure.

Civil procedure, in short, may be thought of as the rules by which the game of litigation is played. Many of the requirements are technical and may even appear arbitrary. For the careless lawyer they can be a trap, while master strategists are able to use them to their clients' advantage. But in the end they are an absolute necessity because without rules, the game could not be played.

For more information
Federal Civil Judicial Procedure and Rules, 2000.
Friedenthal, Jack H. et al. *Civil Procedure,* 3rd ed. St. Paul, Minn.: West Publishing Co., 1999.

Danton Asher Berube
Yale University

Civil Rights movement   was a legal, political, social, and economic struggle for equality for African Americans during the 20th century peaking in the period from the mid-1950s to the mid-1960s. Its effects have permanently changed the legal, political, and social structure of America.

The modern Civil Rights movement began in December 1955, with the Montgomery, Alabama, bus boycott. A year later the Supreme Court declared the policy of racial segregation in public bus seating to be unconstitutional in *Gayle v. Browder,* 352 U.S. 903 (1956). The Reverend Martin Luther King emerged as the leader of the movement and as head of the Southern Christian Leadership Conference (SCLC).

The Civil Rights Act of 1957 (42 U.S.C.A., sect. 1975) established the Civil Rights Commission as an independent agency. Its reports and recommendations have often been the basis of new civil rights legislation.

In the 1950s the movement centered on legal maneuvering. Frustrated with the slow pace of change, some groups took direct action. In 1960 black and white college students in Greensboro, North Carolina, engaged in "sit-in" demonstrations at the "whites only" lunch counter at the local Woolworth store. Quickly the sit-in movement was copied in many other places. Arrests for violating segregation laws were eventually dismissed by the courts on the grounds that these laws were unconstitutional, e.g., *Peterson v. City of Greenville,* 373 U.S. 244 (1963), et al.

The Civil Rights Act of 1960 (42 U.S.C.A., sect. 1971) provided for the appointment of referees to help African Americans register to vote. It also granted the right to sue those obstructing the right.

In 1961 the Congress of Racial Equality (CORE) launched "Freedom Rides" with racially mixed groups on buses traveling through the South in order to demonstrate that segregation at bus stations violated the rights of African Americans engaged in interstate travel. In September 1961 the Interstate Commerce Commission outlawed racial segregation in interstate transportation.

In 1963 Martin Luther King led a march on Washington, D.C., pressing for equal rights. The next summer Congress passed the Civil Rights Act of 1964 (42 U.S.C.A., sect. 2000a et seq.), which outlawed discrimination in public accommodations on the basis of the Commerce Clause of the Constitution (Article I, section 8, clause 3).

In 1965 Congress passed the Voting Rights Act of 1965 (42 U.S.C.A., sect. 1973) prohibiting discrimination in voting and outlawing literacy tests. It also provided federal supervision of voting in the South.

After 1965 the Civil Rights movement began to decline as it changed from a movement to end racial segregation in the South to a movement for social and economic equality throughout the whole country. Demands for affirmative action in employment and other areas of life created a "white backlash" with charges that non-African Americans were now victims of "reverse discrimination." The movement further fragmented with ideological disputes among its leaders.

The movement endured throughout the remainder of the century, steadily achieving its original goal of racial equality.

For more information

Davis, Abraham L., and Barbara L. Graham. *The Supreme Court, Race and Civil Rights.* Thousand Oaks, Calif.: Sage Publications, 1995.

Weisbrot, Robert. *Freedom Bound: A History of America's Civil Rights Movement.* New York; Plume, 1991.

A. J. L. Waskey
Dalton State College

civil rights   mandate equal treatment of citizens by other members of society. In contemporary American political life, a person has a civil right to be treated similarly to all other citizens, without being discriminated against for reasons of (in the language of Title VII of the 1964 Civil Rights Act) race, color, religion, sex, or national origin. This was not always the case. The history of civil rights in the United States is the checkered story of outsiders struggling to be included as equal participants in society.

Civil rights struggles are conventionally traced to the end of the Civil War and ratification of the equal protection clause of the Fourteenth Amendment in 1868. In fact, civil rights are implicit in the language of the 1776 Declaration of Independence: "We hold these truths to be self-evident, that all men are created equal. . . ." In the 1830s William Lloyd Garrison, editor of *The Liberator,* insisted on civil rights for blacks as well as the immediate abolition of slavery. The 1848 Seneca Falls Declaration of Rights and Sentiments was adopted by a group of women gathered to consider the "social, civil, and religious condition and rights of women." It proclaimed "that all men and women are created equal." In the depths of the Civil War, in November 1863, Abraham Lincoln reaffirmed at Gettysburg that the American nation was "dedicated to the proposition that all men are created equal." Thus, the language of the Equal Protection Clause is the heritage of nearly a century of civil rights struggles. That clause holds that "No State shall . . . deny to any person within its jurisdiction the equal protection of the laws."

For more than three-quarters of a century after its ratification—between 1868 and the mid-1940s—the principle of equal citizenship at the core of the equal protection clause was in eclipse. In the late 19th and early 20th centuries, civil rights struggles against Jim Crow laws and for women's suffrage took place in the shadow of the Supreme Court's indifferent neglect and legal defeat of civil rights, and in the teeth of fierce social resistance. Ironically, changing judicial and social attitudes toward civil rights was signaled in a 1944 Supreme Court decision upholding the constitutionality, under the equal protection clause, of the exclusion and confinement of over 70,000 American citizens of Japanese descent. In the course of validating these wartime restrictions in *Korematsu v. the United States,* 323 U.S. 214, the Court observed: "all legal restrictions which curtail the civil rights of a single racial group are immediately suspect" and should be given "the most rigid scrutiny."

Constitutional civil rights, under the equal protection clause, emerged in the second half of the 20th century in conjunction with the Civil Rights movement and the Women's movement. Both these civil rights struggles and the Supreme Court's interpretation of the equal protection clause evolved from initially challenging laws requiring discrimination on the basis of race and sex, to advocating and, in the Court's case scrutinizing, positive government responses to remedy the consequences of past discrimination. As the focus of activism and law shifted in the 1970s, civil rights debates again sharpened. The consensus against segregation and universal suffrage unraveled. Policies such as busing and affirmative action generated controversy and incurred resistance. Further fueling civil rights disputes was the rise of the Gay Rights movement following the 1969 Stonewall riots in New York City. Although disparate treatment of people based on their race or their gender—both characteristics generally and legally assumed to be innate—is widely understood to violate civil rights, many view differential treatment of gays and lesbians as a rejection of their lifestyle choices.

For more information

Evans, Sara M. *Born for Liberty: A History of Women in America.* New York: Free Press, 1997.

Kluger, Richard. *Simple Justice: The History of Brown v. Board of Education and Black America's Struggle for Equality.* New York: Knopf, 1975.

McGlen, Nancy E., and O'Connor, Karen. *Women, Politics, and American Society,* 2nd ed. Upper Saddle River, N.J.: Prentice Hall, 1998.

Wilkinson, J. Harvie III. *From Brown to Bakke: The Supreme Court and School Integration, 1945–1978.* New York: Oxford University Press, 1979.

James C. Foster
Department of Political Science
Oregon State University

class action   is a lawsuit brought by or against a limited number of individuals or entities as representatives of a much larger group of similarly situated individuals or entities too numerous to include each separately.

Class action lawsuits frequently generate significant attention in the media, and because they often involve claims by hundreds, thousands, or even millions of people, the costs to the defendants (usually large corporations) can be tremendous. The objects of recent notable class actions include discriminatory employment practices, leaking silicon breast implants, disease-causing asbestos insulation, and defective automobile tires. A suit has even been filed on behalf of pay-per-view customers who were allegedly shortchanged when Mike Tyson was disqualified for biting Evander Holyfield in their 1997 boxing match.

In federal courts, there are four prerequisites which must be met in order to file a class action lawsuit. (Many states have similar rules.) First, there must be so many members of the proposed class that joining them individually in the lawsuit is impractical. Second, there must be questions of fact or law which are common to all members of the proposed class. Third, the claims or defenses of the selected representatives must be typical of those of the proposed class. Fourth, the selected representatives must be able to fairly and adequately protect the interests of the proposed class.

Even after these four prerequisites are met, a class action will not be permitted unless it also satisfies at least one of following four additional conditions. One, there is a risk that separate lawsuits by individual members of the class would subject the opposing party to inconsistent standards of conduct. Two, there is a chance that separate lawsuits would resolve for all practical purposes the rights or obligations of other class members or would impair their ability to protect their legal interests (when, for example, there is a limited fund which is insufficient to satisfy all of the potential claims). Three, injunctive or declaratory relief is appropriate because the opposing party has treated or refused to treat the members of the class consistently. Four, the suit

is characterized more by common questions of fact or law than by different questions for each member of the class and using a class action is fairer and more efficient than the available alternatives.

In class actions arising under the last condition—i.e., those involving common questions of law or fact—members of the class must be given notice of the lawsuit by the best means practicable. For members who can be specifically identified through reasonable investigation, the notice must be sent to them individually. For others, notice is usually in the form of mass media advertisements. Among other things, the notice must advise the class members that they have the right to withdraw from the class and that, if they fail to do so, they will be bound by the court's judgment.

Judges are given broad discretion to manage class action lawsuits to make them both as fair and efficient as possible. The judge must also agree before a class action can be dismissed or settled, and all members of the class must be given notice of the proposed dismissal or settlement.

Class action lawsuits are often controversial. Defendants sometimes claim that they are filed by greedy lawyers more interested in their own legal fees than they are in protecting the rights of class members. While such abuses undoubtedly occur on occasion, in the modern age where goods and services are delivered to millions of consumers nationally, the class action is often the only feasible mechanism of providing justice for all.

For more information

Dickerson, Hon. Thomas A. *Class Actions: The Law of 50 States.* New York: Law Journal Seminars Press, 2000.

Yeazell, Stephen C. *From Medieval Group Litigation to the Modern Class Action.* New Haven, Conn.: Yale University Press 1987.

Danton Asher Berube
Yale University

Clayton Act refers to a group of federal laws (15 U.S.C. 12–27) which supplement the Sherman Act in proscribing unlawful restraints of trade and monopolies. It is part of the cluster of laws referred to as "antitrust laws." The Clayton Act was enacted on October 15, 1914, and has been amended since only to make technical changes. These changes include allowing plaintiffs to recover interest on damages (1980) and allowing foreign governments to recover treble damages in certain circumstances (1982).

The Clayton Act prohibits price discrimination that may substantially lessen competition or may tend to create a monopoly. By "price discrimination," the statute contemplates different consumers being charged different prices for the same good for reasons not connected to the cost of the good. The rationale behind the policy objective of preventing price discrimination is that it is economically inefficient. The inefficiency leads to higher prices for consumers and a lessening of competition.

Price discrimination can take many different forms and is prohibited regardless of whether the buyer or seller initiates the unlawful pricing. Some examples of price discrimination are tie-ins, bribes, rebates, and discount prices. A tie-in occurs when the purchase of one product is tied to the purchase of another. For example, a seller of printer toner might require customers to also purchase paper as a condition of toner sales. Such a requirement might lessen competition in the paper market. Bribes occur when some customers are given an incentive to purchase not available to all customers in proportionally equal terms. Rebates are similar to bribes but are more directly associated with the product. Sometimes these types of prohibited behavior overlap. For example, a movie distributor might require a chain of theaters to run an unpopular movie in order to run a blockbuster (a tie-in) but give a rebate on advertising associated with the popular movie.

Discount pricing generally arises in the context of either vertical or horizontal integration. Vertical integration occurs when a seller moves up or down in a line of commerce. For example, if a distributor entered the retail sales market it would move down the line of commerce. If that distributor entered the manufacturing market, it would move up the line of commerce. Discount pricing arises when one level in the vertical line offers to another level a discount not available to competitors. Horizontal integration occurs when a seller expands at one level in the line of commerce. For example, if a distributor merged with several other distributors, it would expand at one level in the line of commerce. Discount pricing arises when the newly expanded distributor provides discounts not available to competitors. Only vertical and horizontal integration that substantially lessens competition is prohibited.

The Clayton Act also provides for a private cause of action so that individuals who are injured by the proscribed behavior may sue for damages. The act provides for compensatory damages, injunctive relief, and treble damages. Compensatory damages seek to place the aggrieved party in the position they would have been in had the violations not occurred. Injunctive relief takes the form of a court order prohibiting continued violations of the law. Treble damages serve as a punishment for any violation of the act. The treble damages provision triples the award of actual damages.

For more information

Hovencamp, H. *Federal Antitrust Policy, The Law of Competition and Its Practice,* 2nd ed. St Paul, Minn.: West Publishing Co., 2000.

Ross, S. R. *Principles of Antitrust Law.* Westbury, N.Y.: The Foundation Press, Inc., 1993.

Sullivan, E. T., and Harrison, J. L. *Understanding Antitrust and Its Economic Implications,* 2nd ed. New York: Matthew Bender and Co., 1994.

Anthony Smith,
University of California, San Diego

clear and convincing evidence is a standard of proof that is more rigorous than the one that is generally employed in civil litigation.

In the adversarial process of court proceedings, the litigants on both sides present their versions of incidents or transactions that occurred somewhere else at some time in the past. How is a fact finder (judge or jury) supposed to determine the truth among these conflicting versions of events? What is required is some formula by which fact finders can consider how convinced they are by the proof that has been submitted in the trial or hearing. In court, judges and juries are guided by standards of proof or degrees of belief that govern various types of cases. These range from the least rigorous "preponderance of the evidence" used in most civil cases to the most rigorous "beyond a reasonable doubt" standard used in criminal cases. Somewhere in between is "clear and convincing evidence," a standard of proof that is employed when proof by a preponderance of the evidence is not considered to be demanding enough. Standards of proof are generally established by statutes and case law. According to the U.S. Supreme Court, a standard of proof "serves to allocate the risk of error between the litigants and to indicate the relative importance attached to the ultimate decision" (*Addington v. Texas,* 441 U.S. 418 [1979]). Preponderance of the evidence is the appropriate standard of proof for ordinary civil lawsuits because it allocates the risk of loss equally between the parties. Sometimes, however, rights or interests of such importance are involved in a civil suit that one side deserves greater protection than the other. In such instances, stated the Supreme Court, the clear and convincing evidence standard provides "a middle level of burden of proof that strikes a fair balance between the rights of the individual and the legitimate concerns of the state" (*Addington,* 441 U.S. 418).

Clear and convincing evidence is used in cases in which the rights to be determined or issues to be decided are more serious than whether one party or another is entitled to money, such as a significant deprivation of liberty or the loss of important personal rights. For example, determination of paternity must be by clear and convincing evidence, as must termination of parental rights. Civil commitment of a mentally ill person requires proof by clear and convincing evidence, as does the determination as to whether an incompetent person who is terminally ill may have life-sustaining treatment withheld or withdrawn. The clear and convincing evidence standard is also used in civil cases involving adverse possession of property, libel and slander, and fraud and deceit. In all these instances, it is considered necessary for the fact finder to be more certain of which litigant is right than in ordinary civil cases. But how does a fact finder decide what constitutes proof by clear and convincing evidence? How does a judge instruct a jury about the standard, and how does the judge apply the standard in a bench trial? A survey of judges found that most regarded proof by clear and convincing evidence to be about a 75 percent certainty. According to one recent federal court decision, "'clear and convincing evidence' is that quantum of proof which produces in the mind of the trier of fact a firm belief or conviction as to the truth of the allegations sought to be established, evidence so clear, direct and weighty, and convincing as to enable the fact finder to come to a clear conviction, without hesitancy, of the truth of the precise facts in issue" (*Elliott Associates, L.P. v. Republic of Peru,* 12 F.Supp.2d 328 [1998]). All courts agree that proof by clear and convincing evidence is something less than "beyond a reasonable doubt" and more than "preponderance of the evidence," but the precise meaning of the standard and how it should be applied are issues that must be reevaluated frequently.

For more information

Addington v. Texas, 441 U.S. 418 (1979).

McCauliff, C.M.A. "Burdens of Proof: Degrees of Belief, Quanta of Evidence, or Constitutional

Guarantees?" *Vanderbilt Law Review* 35 (November 1982): 1293–1334.

Santosky v. Kramer, 455 U.S. 745 (1982).

Celia A. Sgroi
State University of New York, Oswego

Clinton v. Jones

Clinton v. Jones 520 U.S. 681 (1997), decided by a unanimous Supreme Court, held that a sitting president has no constitutional right to put off, until he leaves office, a civil lawsuit alleging he engaged in harmful conduct in his private life.

Paula Jones sued President Bill Clinton in 1994 for making "abhorrent," unsuccessful sexual advances toward her in 1991, when Clinton was governor of Arkansas and Jones was a state employee. On two grounds, the president asked the courts to delay all pretrial proceedings and the trial itself until after he left office. First, the president argued that the separation of powers doctrine prevented the courts from imposing on a sitting president by requiring him to defend himself in court. Second, the president claimed that if the case were allowed to proceed, the need to defend himself in court would divert critical time and attention from his presidential duties, a problem that could only grow worse as the Court's decision would encourage others to sue the president.

The Supreme Court rejected these claims, stating that the drain on the president's time and attention would be minimal (at least in this case) and that a decision to allow the lawsuit to proceed would be "unlikely" to encourage many others to sue the president. The Court emphasized that a president may not be sued for his official acts as president in order to protect him from fear that his actions on behalf of the public might result in his being sued—as the Court had ruled in *Nixon v. Fitzgerald,* 457 U.S. 73 (1982). But the justices saw no such public interest in protecting a president from lawsuits based on his private behaviors.

The ruling did not result in further lawsuits against President Clinton in his remaining three and a half years in office. Such lawsuits can, however, severely embarrass a president. The pretrial proceedings in the Jones suit unearthed President Clinton's extramarital affair with Monica Lewinsky while in office. His apparent desire to conceal that relationship and his prevarications while under oath in response to questioning on that subject led to his impeachment by the House of Representatives (but later acquittal by the Senate).

Clinton and Jones eventually settled out of court when Clinton paid Jones $850,000.

For more information

Kasten, Martin. "Summons at 1600: Clinton v. Jones' Impact on the American Presidency," *Arkansas Law Review* 51 (1998): 551–74.

Rozell, Mark J., and Wilcox Clyde, eds. *The Clinton Scandal and the Future of American Government.* Washington, D.C.: Georgetown University Press, 2000.

Weeden, L. Darnell "The President and Mrs. Jones Were in Federal Court: The Litigation Established No Constitutional Immunity for President Clinton," *George Mason Law Review* 7 (winter 1999): 361–87.

Michael Cominskey
Pennsylvania State University

Collin v. Smith

Collin v. Smith 578 F.2d 1197 (1978) is a famous case taking place in Skokie, Illinois, a Chicago suburb, and it was the scene of a two-year struggle in the 1970s over a planned march by an American Nazi group that was strongly opposed by a large group of Holocaust survivors. The bitter dispute put the First Amendment to one of its toughest tests and has come to symbolize the tension between freedom of speech and freedom from unwanted speech.

The village of Skokie had a population of 70,000 in 1977, and by most estimates 30,000 of those residents were Jewish, including 6,000 Holocaust survivors and their families. It was in this community that Frank Collin, leader of the

Chicago-based Nazi group, National Socialist Party of America, planned to march on May 1, 1977. Word of the planned march triggered alarms throughout the Holocaust survivors' community.

A prolonged legal battle ensued; before it was finished, the case went to the Supreme Court three times and up and down in the state and federal courts. The end result was, first, a ruling that an injunction issued to stop the march was unconstitutional, and second, a decision by Collin to call off the march.

Faced with the planned march, Skokie invoked a local ordinance that prohibited distributing materials that promote hate, that barred parade permits to groups portraying or inciting hatred based on religion and other factors, and that disallowed demonstrations by political groups wearing military uniforms.

An Illinois trial judge issued an injunction to stop the march, an appeals court agreed, and the state Supreme Court refused to hear an expedited appeal, meaning the injunction against the march remained in effect. The U.S. Supreme Court, in *National Socialist Party of America v. Village of Skokie,* 432 U.S. 43 (1977), ruled 5–4 that the failure of the Illinois Supreme Court to give expedited review to the injunction had an effect similar to an unconstitutional prior restraint of freedom of speech.

With the march still on hold, the high court sent the case back to the state courts. The Illinois Supreme Court, in *Village of Skokie v. National Socialist Party of America,* 373 N.E.2d 21 (1978), said the First Amendment protected the march, even if there was potential for violence from hostile onlookers, and also protected display of the Nazi swastika. Meanwhile, Collin challenged the constitutionality of the Skokie ordinances and won in a decision of the U.S. Court of Appeals for the Seventh Circuit, *Collin v. Smith,* 578 F.2d 1197 (1978). The Supreme Court refused to hear the case, *Smith v. Collin,* 436 U.S. 953 (1978). Collin's march had been rescheduled, but after winning the principle in various courts that his

demonstration was protected by the First Amendment, he called off the plans to march in Skokie.

Throughout the legal proceedings, courts accepted the view that the First Amendment requires content-neutral regulation and does not permit suppression of speech because of opposition to content. To press this point, Collin enlisted the help of the American Civil Liberties Union, which was criticized by some of its members for representing a Nazi, and which saw a loss of membership and contributions.

For more information
Smolla, Rodney A. *Smolla and Nimmer on Freedom of Speech.* Deer Field, Ill.: Clark Boardman Callaghan, 1996.
Strum, Philippa. *When the Nazis Came to Skokie: Freedom for Speech We Hate.* Lawrence: University Press of Kansas, 1999.

Stephen Wermiel
American University, Washington College of Law

the commerce clause   of the U.S. Constitution gives Congress the power to regulate many activities between the United States and other countries and within the United States. It was the outgrowth of the concern over commercial strife that precipitated the call for the Constitutional Convention. Despite this, the Constitution deals with commerce with deceptive brevity. Article I, section 8, clause 3 states: "Congress shall have the power to regulate commerce with foreign nations, and among the several states, and with the Indian tribes." This positive, but imprecise, grant of power to Congress is limited somewhat by a prohibition against export taxes and a requirement that the ports of no state shall have preferred status.

It should be noted that the terms are not defined. What is "commerce"? What is "commerce among the states"? What is the meaning of "regulate"? Today we have an elaborate framework to answer these and similar questions, but that framework has been developed through experience and adjudication.

Congress began the regulation of foreign commerce immediately but waited almost a century before it began serious regulation of domestic commerce with the Interstate Commerce Act of 1887. As a result, the bulk of constitutional adjudication regarding commerce involved state regulation. That topic is covered elsewhere. In this section, the focus is on federal power over commerce.

In *Gibbons v. Ogden,* 22 U.S. (9 Wheat.)1 (1824), which was the first major commerce case to be decided by the Supreme Court, Chief Justice Marshall broadly defined commerce as "commerce which concerns more States than one." Only those activities that had no effect outside of a single state were beyond congressional jurisdiction. Under this conceptualization, Congress could regulate business that operated within a single state if it had an effect outside the state.

Marshall's "effects" test to determine the limits of congressional power over commerce was subsequently subverted into a dichotomy between "intrastate" and "interstate" commerce. The process began when Chief Justice Taney, a states-righter, in the *License Cases,* 46 U.S. (5 How.) 504 (1847), wrote of "internal or domestic commerce, which belongs to the States, and over which Congress can exercise no control." This apparently innocuous restatement creates a geographic basis for the division of the commerce power between the states and the federal government.

However, since Congress did not actively pursue its powers over "commerce among the States" for almost a century, the interstate/intrastate distinction presented few problems. And when Congress entered the field with the Interstate Commerce Act of 1887, it entered the area of interstate transportation where its domain was largely uncontested. But when Congress attempted to use the commerce power to regulate activities other than transportation, the dichotomy between interstate and intrastate became important.

Under the restrictive concept of interstate commerce, Congress could regulate an activity within a state only if Congress could establish that the local activity had a "direct" effect on interstate commerce. An "indirect" effect would not suffice to authorize congressional action even though that "indirect" effect was nationwide. As a result, mining, manufacturing, and agriculture were beyond congressional control. For example, in 1895 the Supreme Court ruled that a trust which controlled virtually all sugar production in the United States was not subject to federal antitrust laws because manufacture was not commerce (*United States v. E. C. Knight Co.,* 156 U.S. 1 [1895]).

In the early 1900s the Supreme Court ruled that the Chicago stockyards, although located within one city, had a direct impact on interstate commerce and upheld federal regulation. It also upheld prohibitively high federal taxation on oleomargarine colored to look like butter and approved the exclusion of lottery tickets from interstate commerce.

However, few federal laws were upheld, and in 1918 the Court returned to the more restrictive position. *Hammer v. Dagenhart,* 247 U.S. 251 (1918), held that Congress could not exclude child-made products from interstate commerce because it was attempting to regulate manufacture. Congressional attempts to place heavy taxes on companies that used child labor also failed.

Thus, when President Roosevelt and Congress launched the New Deal in 1933, the constitutional status of congressional power over commerce, or the Supreme Court's interpretation thereof, was somewhat ambiguous but generally hostile to federal attempts to use the commerce clause as a way to regulate any aspect of manufacturing, mining, or agriculture. In *Schechter Poultry Corp. v. United States,* 295 U.S.495 (1935), and a series of other cases, the Court used the narrow construction to strike down the major legislation undergirding the New Deal:

Although Congress could regulate railroad transportation, it could not create a pension plan for railroad workers; federal regulation of agricultural production was unconstitutional because production did not have a direct impact on interstate commerce; and production codes regulating working conditions and wages were outside the scope of congressional power because production was not directly related to interstate commerce. In short, the Court refused to acknowledge that local activity had any meaningful or "direct" impact on commerce among the states and ruled Congress had no power to act under the commerce clause.

However, apparently responding to President Roosevelt's threat to pack the Supreme Court, it reversed its position in 1937 and upheld legislation very similar to that which it had voided only a few months before. Abandoning the "direct" and "indirect" distinction, the Court endorsed an "effects" theory that appeared to give Congress virtually unlimited power over all aspects of commercial activity. From 1937 to 1995 the Supreme Court, with one exception that was subsequently overturned, upheld the far-reaching application of the commerce clause to all aspects of life, most notably its use to end racial discrimination at all levels.

In 1995 the Supreme Court suddenly reversed course. In *U.S. v. Lopez,* 514 U.S. 549 (1995), it struck down the Gun Free School Zones Act of 1990, holding that the possession of a gun on school grounds was not an economic activity that would have a substantial effect on interstate commerce. To uphold the law, the Court said, would be to convert congressional commerce clause authority into a general police power of the sort held only by the States. The Court followed up five years later by striking down the federal Violence against Women Act in *U.S. v. Morrison,* 529 U.S. 598 (2000).

The majority opinions in the two cases not only reject the broad power of Congress to regulate commerce, which was uncontested from 1937 to 1995 and appears to resurrect the "direct" and "indirect" effect distinction, but the language is also reminiscent of the rhetoric of dual federalism which dominated prior to the New Deal. *Lopez* and *Morrison* may be the opening rounds in a new constitutional revolution that will dramatically reduce the power of the federal government under the commerce clause. As the 21st century begins, it is impossible to foretell the outcome of the new struggle over the meaning of the commerce clause. An area of constitutional interpretation that had been settled for two-thirds of a century is in flux.

For more information

Gunther, Gerald, and Kathleen M. Sullivan, "The Commerce Power." In *Constitutional Law,* 13th ed. Westbury, N.Y.: Foundation Press, 1997.

William E. Brigman, Ph.D.
University of Houston—Downtown

commercial speech   is defined by the U.S. Supreme Court as speech characterized by: (1) an advertisement (2) that refers to a specific product and (3) the speaker is economically motivated.

In *Valentine v. Chrestensen* (1942), the first commercial speech case to come before it, the U.S. Supreme Court held that "purely commercial advertising" was not entitled to any protection by the First Amendment. However, in two cases in the mid-1970s, the Court rejected the rationale of *Valentine* and began to hold that commercial speech had some First Amendment protection, albeit not to the same degree as "core" political speech.

In *Bigelow v. Virginia* (1975) and *Virginia State Board of Pharmacy v. Virginia Citizens Consumer Council, Inc.* (1976), the Supreme Court concluded that society has a strong interest in the free flow of commercial information, such as the availability of abortions (in *Bigelow*) and the prices of prescription drugs (in *Virginia State Board of Pharmacy*). Therefore, such commercial speech enjoyed the protection of the First

Amendment. At the same time, however, the Court held that certain restrictions on commercial speech would be permissible, such as a prohibition on false or misleading ads or advertisements of illegal products or services.

Since these two landmark decisions, the Supreme Court has held the First Amendment's commercial speech protection to apply to advertising by lawyers (*Bates v. State Bar of Arizona,* 1977), advertisements for contraceptives (*Bolger v. Youngs Drug Products Corporation,* 1983), labels listing alcoholic content (*Rubin v. Coors Brewing Company,* 1995), and the advertisement of liquor prices (*44 Liquormart Inc. v. Rhode Island,* 1996). Conversely, the Court has sometimes accepted restrictions on commercial speech, such as upholding a federal law prohibiting broadcasters from advertising other states' lotteries in states that do not allow lotteries (*United States v. Edge Broadcasting Company,* 1993).

If, under the First Amendment, the government may regulate or even prohibit some forms of commercial speech but not others, it was incumbent upon the Court to develop a test or standard to make that determination; this it did in *Central Hudson Gas & Electric Corporation v. Public Service Commission of New York* (1980). In that case, the justices developed a four-part test to determine when commercial speech could be regulated by the government. The first element of this test is to determine whether the commercial speech is protected by the First Amendment. This is achieved by asking whether the speech concerns lawful activity and is not misleading. If the answer is "yes," then the commercial speech at issue has First Amendment protection. A court would then examine the government's regulation to determine (1) if the government's interest in regulating the speech is substantial, (2) whether the regulation actually works in a way that advances that interest, and (3) whether the regulation is not more extensive than necessary to serve that interest. All three of these elements must be proved by the government in order for it to regulate commercial speech. A single "no" on

any of these three questions will result in the commercial speech regulations being declared an unconstitutional violation of the First Amendment's freedom of speech protections.

Although the Supreme Court backtracked on the four-part *Central Hudson Gas* test in *Posadas de Puerto Rico Associates v. Tourism Company of Puerto Rico* in 1986, 10 years later in *44 Liquormart* it disavowed *Posadas* and returned to the *Central Hudson Gas* test, which remains the standard in commercial speech cases.

For more information

DeVore, P. Cameron. *Advertising and Commercial Speech: A First Amendment Guide.* New York: PLI Press, 1999.

Shiffrin, Steven H., and Jesse H. Choper, *The First Amendment: Cases, Comments, Questions.* St. Paul, Minn.: West Publishing Co., 1991.

Michael W. Bowers
University of Nevada, Las Vegas

comparable worth   is a method an employer can use to determine the proper wage for a worker or group of workers. Using a point rating system, all jobs in a plant or agency are evaluated and given points according to the level of knowledge, skill, and responsibility required to do the job. Workers in jobs with similar point ratings receive the same base or hourly pay. An example taken from a Minnesota state job survey:

COMPARABLE WORTH

Job	Job Rating
Delivery Van Driver (mostly men)	117 points
Clerk Typist (mostly women)	117 points

At the end of the 20th century, women working full-time in the United States earned about 75 cents for every dollar earned by men. Some women's groups, labor unions, and legislators want to use a "comparable worth point system" to remedy this pay inequity in the public sector. Critics charge that implementing comparable worth would drive up the cost of government and pay rates are only one factor motivating a worker to prefer one job over another. They claim women freely choose certain types of lower paying jobs.

Other methods employers use to fix pay levels include:

(a) Equal pay for equal work in which all van drivers are on one pay rate and all secretaries are on another (lower) rate.

(b) Union-Management Contract wage rates which specify the base wage rate for each category of worker.

(c) Market-based "prevailing rate" in which the employer pays van drivers what they can earn elsewhere in the area and uses the same calculation to fix (lower) pay rates for secretaries. Advocates of pay comparability want federal workers to get the same base pay, the prevailing rate, as those doing the same work for nongovernment employers in that area.

(d) Federally mandated wage rates, such as the federal minimum wage, determine the wage rate for many workers.

Since 1963 U.S. courts have embraced equal pay for equal work but have refused to support the concept of "comparable worth." The Department of Justice holds as of 2000 that the comparable worth argument does not establish a cause for action under federal law. The Equal Employment Opportunities Commission (EEOC) consistently has turned aside complaints based on comparable worth arguments. In the *Wards Cove* case (1989), the Supreme Court refused to recognize pay differences by gender as deliberate attempts to discriminate.

For more information

Nigro, Lloyd, and Felix Nigro. *The New Public Personnel Administration,* 5th ed. Itasca, Ill.: Peacock Publishers, 2000.

Gayle Avant
Baylor University

compelling governmental interests are the very important public or governmental objectives that may sometimes allow the state to override constitutional rights even where strict scrutiny is called for. Those values must be so important that they may be termed compelling.

The basic idea is that some public needs are so important that they sometimes justify suspending, limiting, or curtailing constitutional rights. The notion that constitutional rights may have to be limited by public necessity is at least as old as the republic. It was a way of expressing the conviction that the needs of the community override individual needs. In its modern form it entered into constitutional doctrine over a period of years from the era of World War II culminating in a fairly well developed and explicit statement in a Supreme Court opinion in *Shelton v. Tucker* in 1960.

The Court, however, has not elaborated standards for the designation of compelling government interests or overriding public purposes. They are not described in the text of the Constitution. And they are not understood in the Rehnquist Court in the same way they were understood in prior courts. Thus, for example, the Burger Court treated racial integration as a compelling government interest but the Rehnquist Court does not. Thus it is not possible to describe compelling governmental interests with any certainty.

Nevertheless, there are several things that can be said. First, by governmental interests we mean public interests. Compelling governmental interests are only about those things that the government does on behalf of the public.

Second, many, though not all, of the interests that the Court has actually found to be compelling seem to be related to constitutional values like life, liberty, and property. Thus, for example, national security protects all constitutional values, and it has repeatedly been held to be a compelling government interest.

Third, the Court interprets these values as justifying the need to restrict constitutionally

specified rights but not to justify the announcement of fundamental rights. Thus the Court has
overridden protections of the First Amendment
because of what it has treated as the compelling
public interest in indoctrinated schoolchildren,
but it has refused to find that there is any fundamental right to education.

Fourth, compelling interests are part of *strict
scrutiny,* a form of *balancing* designed to protect
constitutional rights from limitation except in
the case of the most important considerations.

There are, however, several justices who have
expressed the view that constitutional issues
should be decided by categories rather than by
balancing. Those justices have been very critical
of the notion of compelling interests. Others
argue that categorical tests merely hide the balancing taking place.

For the present, strict scrutiny and compelling government interests remain a part, if a
somewhat muddy part, of constitutional law.

For more information

Gottlieb, Stephen E. "Compelling Governmental
Interests: An Essential but Unanalyzed Term in
Constitutional Adjudication," *Boston University
Law Review* 68 (1988): 917.

———, ed. *Public Values in Constitutional Law.* Ann
Arbor: University of Michigan Press, 1993.

Stephen E. Gottlieb
Albany Law School

condominium   is a form of ownership of real
property with the following characteristics: (1)
exclusive ownership of a designated unit within
a development, (2) an undivided interest in
common areas, and (3) a common system of governance and assessment for the development.
The word is sometimes used to refer to the entire
development or to a specific unit within the
development.

Condominium developments are often associated with high-rise apartments; however, this
form of ownership has also been used for the
development of detached single family residential neighborhoods and commercial and industrial projects. A development is the entire parcel
subjected to the condominium form of ownership, including all structures on that parcel. The
condominium regime is a creature of statute, and
all 50 states have specific legislation authorizing
condominium ownership.

The two basic documents involved in the
creation of a condominium development are the
declaration and the bylaws. A declaration is a
written document filed with the county records
keeper that includes such items as a legal
description of the development, a general
description of each unit, a description of the
common elements, voting rights of each unit
owner, the creation of an association comprised
of all unit owners, and the method of assessments for common expenses. The bylaws establish the methods by which the condominium
development will be administered, usually
including the method of calling the unit owners
to assemble, the process for the election of a
board of directors of the association, and the
rules for the regulation, maintenance, and repair
of the common areas. Some jurisdictions also
require that a plat survey of the condominium
development be recorded.

Individual unit ownership is central to the
condominium concept. Each unit can be separately owned, mortgaged, and taxed. Utilizing
this concept, an apartment in a high-rise building can be transformed into a separate real estate
parcel. The rest of the condominium development, other than the individual units, is considered the common area or common element. The
common elements are subject to mutual rights
of support, access, use, and enjoyment by all
unit owners. However, limited common elements may be designated which primarily benefit one or more but not all of the unit owners.
Examples of common elements are parking lots
and pools. Examples of limited common elements are specific stalls in the parking lot or
attached balconies.

The extent of a unit owner's undivided interest in the common elements is usually expressed in a percentage. A typical method of determining this percentage is to divide the value of each unit by the value of the property as a whole. Quite often this percentage also establishes the amount of the assessment for which the unit owner is responsible.

The management of a condominium development is usually under the control of an association of unit owners. These unit owners typically have an annual meeting at which time they elect a board of directors. The board of directors are responsible for maintaining, repairing, and insuring the common areas and determining and collecting the assessments to pay for the same.

For more information

American Jurisprudence. 2nd ed. Vol 15A, *Condominiums and Cooperative Apartments.* Rochester, N.Y.: Lawyer's Cooperative, 1976.

Rohan, Patrick J., and Reskin, Melvin A. *Real Estate Transactions: Condominium Law and Practice.* New York: Matthew Bender, 1999.

David M. Reddy
shareholder in the law firm of
Sweet and Reddy, S.C., of Elkhorn, Wis.

consent order is a signed document, approved by a court, which limits or terminates continued prosecution of alleged illegal conduct in exchange for an agreement to refrain from committing future similar acts or violations of some statutory law. It is basically a contract between the plaintiff, usually the prosecutor or attorney representing the government, and the defendant, the alleged wrongdoer, subject to the watchful eye of a judge, in which the parties exchange promises to end civil or criminal proceedings for a pledge not to commit any similar future conduct, alleged to violate federal or state statutory law, such as securities patents, antitrust acts, and employment laws. More often, a consent order is reached at or during the investiga-

tion stage of a proceeding brought by a government agency. The agency agrees to terminate the investigation without a determination as to whether a particular statute has been violated, under authority derived from the Administrative Procedures Act. A settlement agreement is reached, with no further prosecutorial action.

Generally, the defendants refuse to admit wrongdoing, by pleading *nolo contendere,* but acquiesce to sign and adhere to the order to avoid a lengthy court battle. As a matter of public policy, the government has incentives to conserve judicial resources, including court time and taxpayer dollars, in situations that are civil in character, and where the opponents have significant financial resources and legal talent to wage extensive protracted litigation, because the alleged misconduct is open to legal interpretation and differing opinions, or there is a lack of clear and specific judicial precedent found in the case law, or because of the vagueness and ambiguity of the written statutes signed into law by either the United States Congress or the state legislatures. The parties to the consent order may also agree that the defendants, as a condition for the termination of continued prosecution, may be required to undertake some additional corrective measures designed to promote and enhance what is presumed to be in the best interests of the community as a whole.

For example, the New York Times Company and the Equal Employment Opportunity Commission specifically declared in a recent consent order that it was the ". . . aim of the parties to correct the statistical imbalance . . ." of minorities and women employed as junior pressmen at the *Times,* by making a good faith effort to increase employment opportunities for females and members of minority groups and to achieve a goal of 25% minority and female representation. A consent decree may be opposed by intervenors, such as labor unions, which are affected, directly or indirectly, by the actual terms and conditions of the consent order, if they can demonstrate legally tangible, material injury. In most cases courts retain jurisdiction during the stated time period in which the consent decree shall remain in force. The court is also available to enforce the contractual provisions and also permit parties to apply for further relief in the form of orders and directions that may be necessary to effectuate the terms and conditions of the consent decree.

Under the 1988 Omnibus Trade and Competitiveness Act, the International Trade Commission, the agency created and authorized to assist the executive branch of the government in carrying out, executing, and enforcing the federal laws in connection with international commerce, is empowered by its own long-standing practice and specific express statutory authority under 19 U.S.C. §1337 to issue and enforce consent orders. A consent order may be enforced, modified, or revoked by civil penalty proceedings.

A consent agreement between a federal agency and an entity or person, corporate or otherwise, including an individual, constitutes a restraint of federal or state power, and is thus subject to federal or state remedy by penalty or enforcement, in the event of the breach and violation of its contractual terms and provisions.

For more information

Breyer, Stephen. *Breaking the Vicious Circle: Towards Effective Risk Regulation.* Cambridge, Mass.: Harvard University Press, 1995.

J. David Golub
Touro College

conspiracy means an agreement or plan between two or more people to commit an illegal act, or an agreement to do something that is legal but by using illegal methods. A person can be found guilty of both a crime and of conspiracy to commit the crime. A person who does not actually commit the crime himself but only conspires with others who do commit the crime can still be guilty of conspiracy because the crime of conspiracy is committed when the agreement is made. In some states, at least one of the conspirators must take a step toward committing the crime before anyone can be guilty of conspiracy. A very small step is usually enough for all of the parties to be charged with conspiracy. All those involved in the conspiracy are guilty of conspiracy. It is important to note, however, that the crime committed and the conspiracy are two separate crimes. If two people conspire to blow up what they believe is an empty building, and they do blow up that building, they are guilty of conspiracy to blow up the building and of the bombing itself. However, if there are people killed in the building, the bombers may be guilty of murder but not of conspiracy to commit murder, because that was not part of the agreement. Conspiracy is a crime that punishes the agreement itself. Each criminal act is punished separately. If several people conspire to rob a bank, and one steals a car for the getaway without the others participating in the car theft or knowing about it, those others are not guilty of conspiracy to steal a car, and they are also not guilty of stealing the car.

For every crime there must be an act. In a conspiracy, the agreement itself is the act. That agreement does not have to be in writing and does not even need to be spoken. As long as the parties knew they were entering into the agreement to commit an illegal act, they can be found guilty of conspiracy. All of the conspirators don't even need to know each other. Two people may be found to have conspired with each other when they have never even met or spoken, because they each conspired with a third person.

If two people are necessary for a conspiracy, what happens if one is found not guilty? If there were only two conspirators, the other one must also be found not guilty. It takes two to commit a conspiracy, and if one is not guilty, the other cannot be guilty either. Of course if there are more than two conspirators and only one is acquitted, the others can still be guilty of conspiracy.

There are different types of conspiracies. A chain conspiracy involves different events that all lead up to the illegal act. A drug-dealer is usually part of a chain conspiracy. The dealer conspires with another person to get the drugs, which he then sells to a third person. There may be other conspirators in between who package the drugs or deliver them. Each person is a link in a chain. If one link is broken, the conspiracy fails. A hub conspiracy involves one person at the center, or hub, who makes separate illegal transactions with different people. An example of a hub conspiracy is a "fence" for stolen goods. The fence may know all of the people who bring him stolen goods, and is conspiring with all of them, but those people do not know each other. One person could stop bringing in stolen goods, and the hub conspiracy could continue.

Once a person has agreed to commit the illegal act, what happens if he decides not to go through with it? What if he tries to stop the others from committing the act or he informs on them? The court must decide if the person effectively withdrew from the conspiracy before the illegal act was committed. To effectively withdraw from a conspiracy the person must let all of his coconspirators know that he has withdrawn. He must do this in time for his coconspirators to be able to give up trying to commit the crime. He may also effectively withdraw by informing the authorities of the conspiracy and of his participation in it, in time for the authorities to stop the illegal act. If he successfully withdraws, he will not be found guilty of committing the actual crime that was the object of the conspiracy, but he may still be guilty of conspiracy, because the crime of conspiracy is committed at the moment of the agreement. For example, a person may conspire to murder someone but then withdraw and tell the authorities. If the murder takes place, the person who withdrew will not be guilty of murder but may still be guilty of conspiracy. Some courts do acquit the person of conspiracy if he informs the authorities in time to stop the illegal act, or if he himself stops the illegal act from occurring.

Many criminal cases involve conspiracies. One recent case where individuals were found guilty of conspiracy was the Oklahoma City bombing case. Timothy McVeigh was found guilty of murder and conspiracy to commit murder and sentenced to death. Terry Nichols, who was more than 200 miles away when the bomb went off, was not convicted of murder. He was still found guilty of manslaughter and conspiracy. His lawyer argued that Nichols was trying to withdraw from his coconspirator McVeigh during the year before the bombing. If true, that was not enough of a withdrawal to spare him from a life sentence without the possibility of parole.

Many people do not know that the assassination of Abraham Lincoln was a conspiracy. Those charged with conspiracy in the assassination included John Wilkes Booth, an actor, a carpenter at the Ford Theater, and even the doctor who set John Wilkes Booth's broken leg.

For more information

Model Penal Code and Commentaries. Philadelphia American Law Institute, 1985.

The Web of Conspiracy Being News Reports and Coverage of the 1865 Conspiracy Trial Relating to the Assassination of President Abraham Lincoln at http://members.aol.com/ historn/index.htm.

Mary F. Loss, Esq.
Bowles Rice McDavid Graff and Love PLLC
Fairmont, West Virginia

constitution   is a word that Americans redefined at the end of the 18th century to mean the written fundamental law that establishes, organizes, empowers, and limits the government. Every republic ever since—the world over—has borrowed from its principles of government of the people, by the people, and for the people.

By force of arms, the American Revolution repudiated the British constitution. In England the word *constitution* simply referred to the country's history of government and how its institutions developed. The term was merely descriptive of how the Crown and Parliament ruled against a background of great events and great laws, like the Magna Carta and the Bill of Rights of 1689. The English system depended on unwritten understandings and traditions, like the common law, but it was based on the fundamental idea of parliamentary supremacy. This worked to the satisfaction of most Englishmen but certainly not the colonists. Great Britain to this day does not have a written constitutional document. There the word *constitution* still means no more nor no less than how in fact the government is organized and functions.

By force of ideas, American constitutionalism reimagined the relationship between government and the individual and codified the new social compact in a written document that is higher law. "It may be a reflection on human nature that such devices should be necessary to control the abuses of government. But what is government itself but the greatest of all reflections of human nature?" James Madison asked rhetorically in *Federalist Papers number 51.* He continued, "If men were angels, no government would be necessary. If angels were to govern men, neither external nor internal controls on government would be necessary. In framing a government which is to be administered by men over men, the great difficulty lies in this: you must first enable government to control the governed; and in the next place oblige it to control itself." Resolving this difficulty has been the lasting achievement of the Constitution.

Americans had been practiced at writing state constitutions after the Revolution, but their first effort at a national constitution, the Articles of Confederation, left much to be desired. Indeed, the founders became possessed with a sense of crisis about whether their bold experiment in self-government would fail, done in by foreign conquest or undone by domestic corruption.

The novel political theory of the Constitution was to draw legitimacy from popular sovereignty and the consent of the governed. The source of ultimate power was the people rather than the legislature. Consequently, the framers patented the convention as the proper mechanism for constitution-making. They met in the Philadelphia Convention of 1787 to draft the Constitution. They held conventions in each of the states to ratify it. "We the People" ordained and established the Constitution.

"A written constitution" was for its time "the greatest improvement on political institutions," according to Chief Justice John Marshall. The greatest innovation of the American regime was to create a document that was itself normative. The written document constitutes the institutions of government, establishes their powers, and limits their function. The will of the people, expressed in the written Constitution, is superior and paramount to the will of the people's representatives expressed in mere statutes. The institutions of government—the state governments and all three branches of the federal government—must adhere to the rule of law that is the Constitution. This political innovation completed what the Revolution had begun.

Mistrustful of the excesses of both human nature and government power, the framers relied on a wonderful clockwork design of checks and balances to protect individual liberty while at the same time energizing the national government. They put in place a republican democracy, characterized by regular elections and limited terms for representatives. The national government was a government of limited and enumerated powers; what Congress could do and could not do was spelled out in Article I, for example.

Federalism—the idea that two sovereign governments could govern the same territory at the same time—was their invention. The great powers of nationhood—such as waging war and making peace, taxing and spending for the general welfare—were assigned to the national government. Other important powers, however, were left to state governments.

Separation of powers divided the national branches into three branches—legislative, executive, and judicial—with elaborate checks and balances on each other. For example, the president nominates Supreme Court justices with the advice and consent of the Senate. The most powerful branch, Congress, was subdivided into two houses as a further restraint.

It was a government the framers hoped would be strong enough to allow the United States to take its rightful place among the nations of the world and, at the same time, would be restrained enough to preserve individual liberty. In Article V the framers proscribed the process for constitutional change through the amending process, evidencing their expectation that the Constitution would be permanent and paramount. As part of the politics of ratification, the founding generation added a Bill of Rights in 1791 for good measure.

The framers of the Constitution were children of the Enlightenment. They believed in the inevitability of progress through the application of right reason, as exemplified in the Constitution. Their Constitution was the first written constitution in history and today our Constitution remains the oldest written constitution in the world. British prime minister William Gladstone delivered the fitting *dictum* that the Constitution of 1787 was "the most wonderful work ever struck off at a given time by the brain and purpose of man."

For more information

Baker, Thomas E. *"The Most Wonderful Work. . ."—Our Constitution Interpreted.* St. Paul, Minn.: West Publishing Co., 1996.

McDonald, Forrest. *Novus Ordo Seclorum—The Intellectual Origins of the Constitution.* Lawrence: University Press of Kansas, 1985.

Wood, Gordon S. *The Creation of the American Republic, 1776–1787.* New York: W.W. Norton and Co., 1969.

Thomas E. Baker
James Madison Chair in Constitutional Law
Drake University Law School

constitutional interpretation includes both the practical application of the Constitution, the academic study of this process, and the normative study of how the Constitution ought or should be understood. As a matter of practical application, officials in all three branches of government—legislative, executive, and judicial—engage in constitutional interpretation. Congressmen and senators often debate not only whether certain pieces of legislation can survive the courts but also whether that legislation is truly in keeping with the principles of the Constitution. Many issues of recent fierce debate, including abortion rights, school prayer, affirmative action, flag-burning, and hate speech have spurred discussion in Congress and the states about the proper understanding of the Constitution. The executive, the branch of government least identified with constitutional interpretation, also exercises this important function. Issues ranging from war powers to presidential immunity to state power, to constitutional limits on Supreme Court power, all depend largely on the meaning of the Constitution.

Of the three branches of government, under the U.S. Constitution the judiciary, that is, the Supreme Court and lesser federal courts, bears the primary responsibility for interpreting what the Constitution means. In *Marbury v. Madison* (1803) the Supreme Court said it was in the province of the Supreme Court to determine whether an act of Congress violates the Constitution. The next time the Supreme Court declared an act of Congress unconstitutional was in *Dred Scott v. Sandford* (1857), a case that helped to precipitate the Civil War. Although constitutional interpretation is not a power expressly granted to the courts, since *Marbury v. Madison* it has been recognized as a fact of the U.S. political system and has become a major role for the Supreme Court, especially in the 20th century.

State supreme courts also engage in constitutional interpretation when they interpret state constitutions to see if state laws conflict with their state's constitution or with the U.S. Constitution, which they are bound to uphold. However, the Supreme Court does not review cases that are purely questions of state law; rather, it has jurisdiction over cases involving federal law and claims relating to the Constitution. Since so many cases can be seen as having a constitutional dimension, the Supreme Court has a wide berth of cases it may hear and wide discretion to decide whether to hear them.

Two major categories of theory can be identified in constitutional interpretation. The first, originalism, holds that the Constitution has a fixed meaning and that the proper business of the courts is to interpret what that meaning says about a particular constitutional claim. Originalism can be broadly divided into intent originalism and textualism, although there is considerable variety even in these categories. Intent originalism emphasizes historical tradition, particularly the views held at the time of the founding. Intent originalists include Chief Justice William Rehnquist and Judge Robert Bork, who has written extensively on intent originalism. A core criticism of intent originalism is based on the question of which originalists' intent to follow: the framers of the Constitution at the Constitutional Convention or the members of the ratifying conventions in the states. Moreover, can we know what the intent of the framers (and ratifiers) of the Constitution and its amendments mean (such as what they meant by *liberty*) when the words way have meant quite different things to these individuals, and the problems of the nation and the role of government change over time.

Textualism focuses exclusively on the words of the Constitution as a guide to interpretation; it is also called literalism. Both liberals and conservatives have been textualists: Justice Hugo Black on the left, and Justices Antonin Scalia and Clarence Thomas, Supreme Court justices in 2000, on the right. Black's textualism led to the application of the guarantees of the Bill of Rights through the Fourteenth Amendment. Where the meaning of a clause simply could not be determined by its reading, Black opted for the plain meaning by the consensus of the day. Justices Scalia and Thomas, by contrast, use a more historical form of textualism, arguing for the understanding of the phrase in the Constitution at the time of the founding when a simple reading of its words and phrases fails. Black, Scalia, and Thomas all share the view that free speech is an absolute and that the courts have no business defining what life, liberty, and property means in the Fourteenth Amendment due process clause, interpretations that have resulted in the Supreme Court defining a right to privacy and right to abortion choices.

Non-originalism counts an even greater variety of approaches to constitutional interpretation than does originalism. Broadly speaking, these approaches have in common a view of a "living Constitution," enunciated in the words of non-originalist Justice William Brennan, and first described by Chief Justice John Marshall in the following oft-quoted words in *McCulloch v. Maryland* (1819): "We must never forget that it is a constitution we are expounding." The above phrase came after Marshall had argued that the Constitution contained a general outline of the federal government's structure and powers, from which the rest of its powers could be deduced; it was not a complex legal code with detailed rules and powers to meet every exigency.

Pragmatism, postmodernism, critical theory, deconstruction, civic republicanism, liberalism, and economic approaches to law all are schools of non-originalist theories of interpretation. Two of the most important non-originalist theories are representation-reinforcement and the moral reading of the Constitution. Representation-reinforcement, put forth by John Hart Ely in *Democracy and Distrust,* holds that the courts ought to keep the political process open, particularly for minorities. Vigorous enforcement of the equal protection clause and the protection of free speech are hallmarks of representation-reinforcement, which opposes the Court placing into law its definition of what such terms as *life, liberty,* and *property* mean.

Ronald Dworkin, a prominent constitutional theorist and legal philosopher, developed the moral reading of the constitution. In numerous books and articles, Dworkin argues that there are two kinds of constitutional provisions: the specific and the open-ended. The Third Amendment, barring quartering of troops in civilian homes during peacetime, is a specific directive. The Eighth Amendment, in contrast, is open-ended because the phrase "cruel and unusual" has no clear meaning. The meaning, Dworkin argues, can only be determined by strenuous moral argument. Dworkin's theory supports substantive due process.

Non-originalism has many more adherents than does originalism. Justices William O. Douglas and William Brennan are examples of non-originalist justices, as are Earl Warren, Arthur Goldberg, Abe Fortas, Thurgood Marshall, and Harry Blackmun. On the Court in 2000, most of the justices are non-originalists: John Paul Stevens, Sandra Day O'Connor, Anthony Kennedy, David Souter, Ruth Bader Ginsburg, and Stephen Breyer. The originalists are Chief Justice Rehnquist and Justices Scalia and Thomas.

Finally, it is important to note that the U.S. Constitution forbids any action by government officials, at any level, that is not compatible with the Constitution, as interpreted. Therefore every legal question may raise a constitutional question, and any action by public officials may or may not be enforceable, depending on whether or not it has been found to be in violation of the Constitution.

For more information

Bork, Robert. *The Tempting of America: The Political Seduction of Law.* New York: Free Press, 1990.

Dworkin, Ronald. *Law's Empire.* Cambridge, Mass.: Harvard University Press, 1986.

Ely, John Hart. *Democracy and Distrust.* Cambridge, Mass.: Harvard University Press, 1980.

Kahn, Ronald. *The Supreme Court and Constitutional Theory, 1953–1993.* Lawrence: University Press of Kansas, 1994.

Ronald Kahn
Oberlin College

constitutional law is a body of public law that includes the Constitution itself and the amendments to the original document as well as judicial decisions and legislative enactments that apply to and interpret that document and its amendments. All of the different types of constitutional law must be in harmony with the Constitution itself. Any legislative enactment or judicial decision that is in violation of a constitutional provision is deemed to be null and void. Thus, constitutional law is the supreme law of our society. The defining feature of both constitutions and constitutional law is that they provide limitations on the power of government. This branch of law also defines and organizes the powers of government and distributes the authorities and functions of government among various political and legal actors.

In the United States constitutional law is a very large component of the law in existence. While short by some standards, the Constitution of the United States provides for numerous procedural and substantive requirements to which governmental actors must adhere. These requirements are found most clearly explained in the first three articles of the Constitution. Each of these articles lays out the constitutional law respecting one of the three constitutional branches of government.

The amendments to the Constitution are also highly regulative of governmental relationships both in terms of the federal state relationship and with respect to the relationship between the government and individual citizens. These additions to the basic corpus of the Constitution have been added over time, but they represent the same type of fundamental legal authority as the original text of the Constitution.

While the Constitution and the subsequent amendments provide a framework for governmental interaction, they are frequently void and are certainly not self-interpreting rules. As a result of the vagueness of some of the constitutional provisions, courts become involved in determining the meaning of the Constitution. The Supreme Court of the United States has been an important actor in promulgating constitutional law by interpreting and applying that document to specific cases brought to them. Many of the most famous decisions that have been made by the Supreme Court have been interpretations of the Constitution and are therefore part of the body of constitutional law.

Whatever its source, constitutional law is the fundamental law of a nation or state. This area of law defines the general plan for government. Constitutional law defines the spheres of governmental power and places limitations on that power. It defines and regulates the relationship between government and individuals. It is the standard that must be met by all other laws.

For more information

Pritchett, C. Herman. *Constitutional Law of the Federal System.* Upper Saddle River N.J.: Prentice Hall, 1984.

O'Brien, David M. *Constitutional Law and Politics: Struggles for Power and Governmental Responsibility.* New York: W.W. Norton and Co, 1991.

David A. May
Eastern Washington University.

contempt is the offense of disobeying an order issued by a court of law.

U.S. judges have inherent authority to punish contempt, an authority that distinguishes a judicial from an administrative body. Due process requires only that contemners be given fair notice and are afforded a public hearing, which,

however, may take place on the spot and immediately prior to sentencing. Contempt may be charged against anyone present during judicial proceedings, or against persons who, away from the courtroom, act in a manner that interferes with the orderly processes of justice. Both types, respectively "direct" and "indirect," may be punished by any reasonable means, normally fine or imprisonment or both. A contempt order seldom will be overruled by a higher court, and then only if it was committed outside the issuing judge's jurisdiction, not for reasons of error.

Although the division is not precise, judges often categorize contempts as civil and criminal. While all contempt orders vindicate the court's dignity, civil contempts are considered those committed "in the face of the court," punished on a motion by an opposing party and imposed in the latter's interest. Civil punishments are intended to be coercive, and they continue until the court's order is obeyed. Criminal contempts are more frequently committed away from the courtroom and punished in the interests of the public. They are generally fixed in amount and duration. Punishment for criminal contempt may be limited and provided special procedures by statute; Congress first established such limits on federal courts in 1831.

Contempt convictions figure in many of the highlights of American legal history. Famous contemners include Passmore Williamson, abolitionist; Eugene Debs, leader of the Pullman strike; Ross Barnett, anti–civil rights governor of Mississippi; William Jefferson Clinton, president of the United States. (The English tradition is equally notable: Charles I was executed for, among other things, contempt of court.) The first volume of *U.S. Reports* includes a Pennsylvania Supreme Court decision fining and imprisoning a Philadelphia editor for contempt after he publically accused local judges of political bias (*Respublica v. Oswald,* 1 U.S. 319 [1788]). The leading contempt case, *Anderson v. Dunn* (19 U.S. 204 [1821]), upheld the order of Henry Clay, speaker of the U.S. House of Representatives, imprisoning a private citizen during his interrogation by the House for attempted bribery.

One of the longest punishments for contempt in American history, seven and one-half years in Maryland state prison (1988–95), was imposed on Jacqueline Bouknight, a welfare recipient who refused to accede to the court's order that she reveal the whereabouts of her son. Previously accused of child abuse, she claimed her Fifth Amendment right against self-incrimination. However, the U.S. Supreme Court held that the local court's order was for compelling reasons unrelated to criminal law enforcement (*Baltimore City Department of Social Services v. Bouknight,* 493 U.S. 549 [1990]), and denied the appeal.

In 1994 in *International Union, United Mine Workers v. Bagwell,* 512 U.S. 821, the U.S. Supreme Court muted the civil-criminal court distinction in the interests of greater procedural protection. The Court unanimously decided that a punishment of monetary fines, graduated upward over successive incidents of the union's disobedience of an order prohibiting certain disruptive practices associated with a coal strike and payable to the state of Virginia as recompense for policing costs, was criminal, despite having been expressly designated by the issuing court as civil. Because the fines, once incurred, could not be purged in the usual method of compliance with the order, they were punitive, under the Constitution requiring trial by jury.

For more information

Dobbs, Dan B. "Contempt of Court: A Survey," *Cornell Law Review* 56 (1971): 183.

Dudley, Earl C. "Getting Beyond the Civil/Criminal Distinction: A New Approach to the Regulation of Indirect Contempts," *Virginia Law Review* 79 (1993): 1025.

Wells, John. "Authority of the Trial Judge," *Georgetown Law Journal* 88 (2000): 1389.

Karen Orren
UCLA

contingency fee refers to an arrangement between lawyer and client in a civil lawsuit in which the payment of attorney's fees is conditioned upon the successful outcome of the case. In essence, a contingent-fee agreement is a contract whereby the attorney agrees to be paid out of the proceeds of the successful lawsuit or not at all. The lawyer may also agree to advance payment of all fees and expenses connected with the civil action. Contingency fees are considered to be valid except where prohibited by law, considered to be against public policy, or obtained by fraud, mistake, or duress. For example, contingent-free agreements are not permitted in criminal cases, and in most jurisdictions they are not permitted in divorce or alimony proceedings. The fee agreed upon is generally a percentage of the award recovered by the plaintiff in the lawsuit. Contingent fees may range from 25% to 40% of the plaintiff's recovery. The fee must be considered reasonable and not excessive, and courts may and do examine contingent-fee arrangements to determine whether they are reasonable. Contingency fees raise ethical problems for lawyers, who are generally not supposed to have a property interest in litigation they bring on behalf of their clients. Contingent-fee arrangements are an exception to this rule. Moreover, contingency fees are limited by the rule of professional ethics that prohibits the charging of excessive fees. However, the risk the lawyer assumes in a contingent-fee case may be reflected in the amount he can charge. The U.S. Supreme Court has observed: "Fees for legal services in litigation may be either 'certain' or 'contingent' (or some hybrid of the two). A fee is certain if it is payable without regard to the outcome of the suit; it is contingent if the obligation to pay depends on a particular result's being obtained. Under the most common contingent-fee contract for litigation, the attorney receives no payment for his services if his client loses" (*City of Burlington v. Dague,* 505 U.S. 563 [1992]).

Whether a contingency fee will be considered reasonable and not excessive depends on the particular difficulty of the case and the amount of work the lawyer must do, as well as the degree of likelihood that the client will succeed at trial. Civil litigation, especially when it involves large companies, is extremely expensive, and successful attorneys charge high fees for their services. Without contingent-fee agreements, many potential plaintiffs would be unable to sue the persons or companies that injured them. However, contingency fees are controversial and continue to be a hotly debated issue in the legal system. Many people claim that contingent-fee agreements cause excessive litigation and larger demands for damages. According to the many critics of the practice, contingency fees encourage lawyers to pursue weak or frivolous cases and mislead clients about their chances of success. Contingency fee lawyers are seen as "hired guns" who reap enormous fees. Indeed, there have been cases in which contingency-fee lawyers have brought class actions in which the attorney's fees reached $100 million. The question is whether the benefit of opening up litigation to lower-income plaintiffs is outweighed by the potential for abuse. Legislatures and courts regulate contingency fee practices, but the controversy is likely to continue as long as large damages awards and high attorneys' fees are handed out by the courts.

For more information

Kritzer, Herbert M. "Contingency Fee Lawyers as Gatekeepers in the Civil Justice System," *Judicature* 81.1 (July/August 1997): 22–29.

Celia A. Sgroi
State University of New York, Oswego

contract is the term for an agreement between two or more parties to exchange goods or services for money or other goods or services.

For a contract to be formed there must be a promise for a promise. For example, Jones saying "I will sell you my gold fountain pen for $200" has made an offer to hand over the pen in exchange for currency in that denomination in ordinary business terms. If Smith then says, either verbally or in writing, "I will take it at that price," an immediate contract is entered into. But, if Smith says, "I will take it for $195 (or some other sum)," he has made a counter/offer and there is not a contract.

If Smith says "I will take the pen on next Friday if White pays me $200 by then," Smith has made a conditional acceptance, which is nevertheless binding when White pays. If White does not pay the money by the time specified, the condition has not been met and the acceptance is void. Even if Smith receives $200 from some other source, the contract is still void because it specified a payment by White.

In order for a contract to be binding, there must be some consideration, that is, something must be given in exchange for the goods or services received. Thus the $200 is consideration for the pen. Consideration may be something other than money, such as other goods or labor performed for the offer or the object accepted. Labor to be performed may be paid for by money or goods. Among family members or other social relations, the consideration may be "natural love and affection."

Contracts may be mutual or unilateral. Most business contracts that are bargained for, such as commodities or real estate, are said to be "arm's-length" and are mutual. An example of a unilateral contract is an employee manual in which the employer sets the terms.

A contract is usually made between two parties but may be made for the benefit of someone else, called a third party beneficiary. For example, a parent may enter into an agreement with a college to pay an offspring's tuition.

A meretricious contract is one that accomplishes an illegal purpose. Thus, a contract to sell street drugs is illegal and therefore is unenforceable in court. Examples of other meretricious contracts would be for engaging in prostitution or for the sale of fertilized human embryos.

A contract may not be enforceable for a number of reasons. A failure of consideration is the term used when performance on one side is not completed. Jones fails to deliver the gold pen upon tender of $200 in U.S. currency. Smith tenders not cash but a check which is returned for insufficient funds. The pen may have been stolen and Jones cannot deliver, and therefore the contract fails for impossibility of performance. There may be a mutual mistake of fact, such as the pen turning out to be other than gold.

A unilateral mistake of fact may not render a contract unenforceable, particularly if Jones, for instance, did nothing to foster the impression that the pen was gold. On the other hand, a court may declare a contract unenforceable if there was such a disconnection between the perceived bargain and what was exchanged that no reasonable person would make such an agreement.

If the price offered for the pen was $20,000 and the pen turned out to be a salesman's promotional giveaway, the contract would be considered voidable if not actually void because the price offered is substantially in excess of the value of the pen. In this instance the court might consider the contract to be an "adhesion contract," that is, one which so heavily favors one side that a reasonable person might think the contract was coerced or involuntary.

Most contracts are explicit in their terms and are called express contracts, as in Jones being willing sell Smith the pen for an agreed price. Some contract terms, however, are implied. A contract to form a partnership for profit implies a covenant of fair dealing and honesty, such as not disclosing business strategy to a competitor to the disadvantage of the partnership.

Most contracts are in writing, although some are not, particularly those dealing with land or for value in an amount greater than that determined by statute. Agreements for an amount smaller than the statutory amount need not be written. If people do not write the contract but behave as if there is one, the courts may find that a contract existed anyway.

For more information

American Jurisprudence, 2nd ed. Vol. 17A, *Contracts.* St. Paul, Minn.: West Group Publishing, 1988–.

Miller, Roger LeRoy, and Gaylord A. Jentz. *Business Law Today,* 5th ed. St. Paul, Minn.: West Publishing Co., 2000.

Stanley M. Morris
Attorney at Law
Cortez, Colorado

cooperative   is a corporation formed to hold title to real property. The shareholders of the corporation are in turn entitled to long-term proprietary leases for units within the property.

A cooperative is usually set up by a sponsor or promoter. The sponsor must follow the state law regarding incorporation of a cooperative. The cooperative corporation is customarily a nonprofit corporation; it issues stock and is governed by a board of directors.

Generally, there are three documents needed to establish a cooperative: (1) the plan of cooperative organization, (2) the proprietary lease, and (3) the bylaws.

The plan of cooperative organization describes the property and identifies the sponsor. It can specify the method of allocation of the corporation's stock. For example, a certain number of shares of the cooperative can be allocated to each unit of the property. Purchasers of those certain stock certificates are then entitled to long-term proprietary leases for the corresponding unit. The plan also usually contains conditions for the purchase of stock, arrangements that have been made for management of the property, and the corporate details.

Owners of a cooperative do not own real estate. Instead, they own stock which entitles them to use the property according to the terms of their proprietary lease. An essential provision of the proprietary lease is the payment of rent.

The amount of the rent is determined by the board of directors and is used to pay the common expenses of the cooperative. The proprietary lease usually contains a provision that prevents the assignment of the lease to another without approval of the board of directors.

The bylaws establish the operating procedures for the board of directors, including the methods of calling shareholders meetings, the process for the election of the board of directors of the association, and the formula for the determination of the amount of rent. A typical method for determining the amount of rent is for the board of directors to estimate the total amount necessary to pay such expenses as real estate taxes, insurance, wages, and utility costs for the ensuing calendar year. That total divided by the number of shareholders represents the annual rent for the tenant-shareholder.

An important question relating to cooperative corporations is whether the corporation is subject to security regulations. Generally it is unlawful for a promoter to offer stock for sale without first registering such stock with the appropriate securities regulator. Some states specifically exempt cooperatives from such registration. Other states have waived the registration requirement, using the analysis that a security is an investment with an expected return, whereas there is no such expectation with the purchase of stock in a cooperative. This is true because purchasers generally make their decision whether to purchase cooperative stock on the basis of a desire to reside in the cooperative unit, not the prospects of profit.

For more information

American Jurisprudence, 2nd ed. Vol. 15A, *Condominiums and Co-Operative Apartments.* St. Paul, Minn.: West Group Publishing, 1976.

Rabkin, Jacob, and Mark H. Johnson, *Current Legal Forms with Tax Analysis,* New York: Matthew Bender, 1994.

David M. Reddy
Sweet and Reddy, S.C.
Elkhorn, Wis.

The U.S. Courts of Appeals   are the middle-level court of the federal court system.

Established by the Evarts Act in 1891, they were intended as appellate courts only; that is, rather than hold trials they only review the cases from lower courts and establish whether there were any errors at trial. Originally created to alleviate the workload of the higher U.S. Supreme Court and to review the decisions of the lower U.S. district courts, these courts have become increasing important in the federal judicial hierarchy. Because most legal decisions never make it to the Supreme Court (less than 200 cases per year), the U.S. Court of Appeals have been largely charged with *interpreting* doctrines of national policy and ensuring that national policies fit local or regional concerns.

In the century since they were established, they have been constantly restructured to accommodate an ever increasing caseload. This increase in caseload largely reflects the expansion of federal law and litigation, as well as the increasing jurisdiction of federal courts, rate of appeals, quantity of federal litigation, and complexity of federal law. The number of circuits has increased from nine to 13 and the authorized judgeships from 22 to 167 to accommodate the current 54,000 cases filed per year. Law clerks and permanent staff attorneys are another addition; virtually unknown in these courts in the 1930s, there are now more than 800 law clerks and 150 staff attorneys assigned to these courts.

Each of the 13 circuits has its own court. The states and territories are divided into numbered circuits, each of which contains three or more states, with the District of Columbia having a circuit in itself. The number of judges in each circuit ranges from six in the First Circuit (e.g., New England and Puerto Rico) to 28 in the Ninth Circuit (e.g., from Alaska to Arizona), with a total of 167.

For the most part, these courts do not have the option of choosing which cases they will review (unlike the U.S. Supreme Court). Instead, questions of error occurring from the lower courts are mandatorily decided by rotating panels of three judges. However, in cases of great importance or ones that divided the panel of judges (about 100 cases per year), a majority vote can choose to hear (or rehear) a case *en banc,* which is participation by all the judges in that particular circuit. As with all federal judges, these judges are nominated by the president and confirmed by the Senate.

Since the 1960s, the volume of cases coming to these courts has increased dramatically, creating great strains on their ability to handle the caseload; their caseload has increased from approximately 33,000 cases in 1985 to 54,000 in 1998. This increase is largely due to the fact that these courts are the intermediate court of the federal judiciary; they handle the disparity between the less than 200 cases that the higher Supreme Court decides each year and the enormous increase in cases at the lower district court level. Much of the strain between these two levels must be absorbed by the appellate courts if a uniformity of national law is to be maintained. Congress has responded with several measures: increasing the number of appellate judgeships, authorizing *en banc* procedures, splitting circuits, and creating the federal circuit are some examples. Nonetheless, the strains in the workload of these courts continue.

For more information

Kuersten, Ashlyn, and Songer, Donald. *Guide to the U.S. Courts of Appeals.* New York: Garland Press, 2000.

Ashlyn K. Kuersten
Western Michigan University

criminal justice system   consists of those governmental and private agencies and personnel whose main functions are to deter and prevent crime; investigate reported crimes; apprehend, prosecute, and defend criminal suspects; adjudicate criminal charges and sentence convicted offenders; and maintain correctional custody over adjudicated offenders.

The primary components of the criminal justice system are police departments, prosecutors' offices, defense attorneys, courts, correctional departments (including probation and parole divisions and penal institutions), and appellate courts. Criminal justice agencies are distributed among local, state, and federal governments.

There is no one integrated criminal justice system. Each state and the federal government has its separate court systems and its corrections departments. State prosecutors are mostly county elected officials who hire assistant prosecutors as needed, although the attorney general's office in each state may prosecute some crimes. The police are highly fragmented. Most law enforcement agencies are units of local government, although each county has a sheriff's office; each state has a state police organization, and there are approximately 50 federal law enforcement agencies. This complexity causes some friction in criminal justice operations, but a good deal of cooperation and coordination among agencies allows the system to function.

The largest component of the criminal justice system is the police, which in 1996 employed more than 900,000 employees, including more than 700,000 sworn full-time officers, spread among 18,800 federal, state, and local law enforcement agencies. The next largest component is corrections, with about 650,000 employees in 1996. State court prosecutors' offices employed about 71,000 attorneys, investigators, and support staff. The total employment in the judicial branch exceeds 400,000 persons, but the number of judicial officers is smaller. The United States Supreme Court and state courts of last resort are staffed by 360 justices and judges. Below these courts, 39 states have intermediate appellate courts (850 judges) and the 12 circuits of the U.S. Court of Appeals (180 judges). Trial courts are divided between courts of general jurisdiction that try felony cases (9,000 state judges; 650 federal district court judges) and courts of limited jurisdiction (18,000 state judicial officers; 500 federal magistrates).

The governmental expenditure for all criminal justice agencies in 1996 was $120 billion. The largest single component was local law enforcement ($38 billion), followed by state correctional expenditures ($29 billion). Expenditure by function in 1996 was police protection—$53 billion; judicial and legal—$26 billion; and corrections—$41 billion. Local government expends 52.3 percent of the total criminal justice budget, state government 33.2 percent, and the federal government 14.5 percent.

Different models of the criminal justice system help to explain its functioning. A model developed by the President's Commission on Law Enforcement and Administration of Justice in 1967 first popularized the idea of a system by portraying criminal justice as a sort of conveyor belt in a flowchart. It depicted a large number of known crimes that lead to a smaller number of apprehensions that are then processed through the adult and juvenile criminal justice systems. At each point in the process a certain number of individuals drop out because of dismissals or acquittals, and some who are conditionally released on probation or parole are recycled back into the system.

Another model—the wedding cake model—indicates that the popular concept of crime is not accurate; the criminal justice system deals with a much larger number of crimes of minor disorder than serious threats to life and safety. At the top of the wedding cake are those very few notorious and extremely serious crimes that linger in the popular imagination, such as the double murder prosecution and acquittal of O. J. Simpson. The second layer includes the violent felonies of murder, manslaughter, rape, robbery, and aggravated assault. These crimes constituted 4.7 percent of all arrests in 1997. Next in seriousness are burglary and felony property crimes—13.2 percent of arrests. The remaining 82.1 percent of arrests were for misdemeanor assault and property crimes, vice crimes, drug offenses, driving offenses, juvenile runaway and curfew violations, and a large number of miscellaneous offenses.

Clearly, the work of criminal justice system personnel includes hundreds, if not thousands, of different tasks. Nevertheless, criminal justice system operations include several unique or distinctive characteristics. First, the system is based on the government's monopoly of the legitimate use of *force*. Contrary to popular entertainment, most criminal justice processes, including arrest, do not involve the overt use of force—most persons who are arrested go along without physical resistance. Nevertheless the system is pervaded by the show of force, including the police officer's gun, handcuffs, and badge, the judge's somber robes, and prison walls. A suspect, defendant, or convicted person who resists can expect to be subdued with physical force. Next, much of the criminal justice system is *routinized* into administrative subsystems, such as plea bargaining, that make the system more efficient than a full use of the model. Another characteristic is the high degree of *discretion* that is available to criminal justice officers, which goes counter to the popular idea that each important aspect of the criminal justice system is controlled by unambiguous laws. Also, the *effectiveness* of the criminal justice system is determined not only by its ability to suppress crime and identify offenders but by its fairness and *justice*. In this regard it is important that agents of the system follow legal and constitutional mandates, that methods deemed unfair not be used, and that persistent problems, such as racial disparities in arrest and sentencing, be minimized.

For more information

Senna, Joseph, and Larry J. Siegel, *Introduction to Criminal Justice*. Rev. ed. Toronto: International Thompson Publishers, 1999.

Walker, Samuel. *Taming the System: The Control of Discretion in Criminal Justice, 1950–1990*. New York: Oxford University Press, 1993.

Websites: Bureau of Justice Statistics: http://www.ojp. usdoj. gov/bjs/; National Criminal Justice Reference Service (NCJRS): http://www.ncjrs.org/ncjhome.htm.

Marvin Zalman
Wayne State University

cruel and unusual punishment is prohibited by the United States Constitution's Eighth and Fourteenth Amendments and most every state constitution.

The prohibition against the infliction of cruel and unusual punishment was originally drawn from the English Declaration [Bill] of Rights of 1689 in order to curtail inhumane tortures and other barbarous methods of punishment. The Eighth Amendment, however, is not tied just to methods of punishment thought to be cruel and unusual at the time the Constitution was drafted; as concepts of dignity and civility evolve in our culture, and as public opinion in society changes and evolves regarding human justice, so do the notions of what is considered cruel and unusual under the Eighth Amendment.

The prohibition against the infliction of cruel and unusual punishment extends beyond just physically appalling punishments and embodies broad and idealistic ideas of dignity, civilized principles, humanity, and decency, against which a court must evaluate criminal sentencing measures. Punishments considered incompatible with evolving standards of decency or that involve unnecessary and wanton infliction of pain are found to violate the Eighth Amendment.

Also related to Eighth Amendment guarantees is the notion that every punishment should be properly proportionate to the crime. For example, it would be thought inhumane to impose capital punishment for a simple parking violation or evasion of taxes. Thus, an extreme punishment relative to the criminal act may also contravene the Eighth Amendment. A penalty that is more extreme than any previously inflicted will be deemed excessive, cruel, and unusual. Likewise, punishments that never before existed in this country or which modern public sentiments regard as cruel will also be found violative of the Eighth Amendment.

The idea of prohibiting torturous or heinous punishments is largely supported throughout U.S. history. How exactly to define what will constitute such heinous punishment, on the other hand, has been the subject of much debate. For example, in some instances of sex offenses, sterilization of criminals by vasectomy has been found to be cruel and unusual punishment while, in other cases, it has been upheld as a valid punishment. In addition, the death penalty has been said by many to violate the constitutional guarantee against the imposition of cruel and unusual punishment; as such, it is unlawful in several states. Still, the United States Supreme Court has not found that the death penalty necessarily violates the Eighth Amendment, unless it is inflicted in a painful or inhumane manner.

While it has been said that efforts to exactly define the term "cruel and unusual punishment" will prove difficult at best, the courts continue to formulate certain recognizable tests or standards for determining whether a given punishment attains cruel and unusual proportions. For instance, the earliest test, and the one that is still most frequently used for determining whether a punishment offends the Eighth Amendment, is consideration of the "inherent cruelty" of a given punishment. Nevertheless, as society's notion of humanity and decency in penal treatment develops over time, changes will be reflected in limits regarding methods of punishment, resulting in continuous reassessment of cruel and unusual punishment.

For more information

"'Nor Cruel and Unusual Punishments Inflicted'": The Original Meaning," *California Law Review* 57 (1969): 839.

"The Cruel and Unusual Clause and the Substantive Criminal Law," *Harvard Law Review* 79 (1966): 635.

Kristin L. Stewart, J.D.

D

Dartmouth College v. Woodward   17 U.S. 4 (1819) was an important early decision that helped to establish both the supremacy of the Constitution over the state legislatures and the role of the Supreme Court as the Constitution's ultimate interpreter.

Decided in 1819, this famous case paired the legendary advocacy of Daniel Webster and the judicial genius of Chief Justice John Marshall. Their nation-building collaboration set in motion the law of the modern corporation, capitalism, and higher education.

It began as a New Hampshire *cause célèbre*. Dartmouth College had been chartered in 1769, in the name of the Crown, to bring Christianity and education to the Indians; later, it became a Congregationalist Church college for whites. The college had the misfortune, however, to became embroiled in state partisan politics. In 1815 the trustees, who were Federalists, removed the president of the college, John Wheelock, son of the founder and first president. The next year, the governor and legislature—Jeffersonian Republicans and political opponents of the Federalists— determined to oust the Federalist trustees once and for all. They passed new state laws revising the royal charter to transform the private college into a public university with new trustees who would be politically appointed. For a time, the two sets of trustees wrangled for control and the campus became a chaos of altercations and confrontations, including physical occupations and changing of the locks of the buildings. The faculty and students were divided between the old college and the new university. Eventually they took their fight to court.

Before the Supreme Court, Daniel Webster, a loyal graduate of the college, invoked the protection of the contract clause in Article I, section 10 of the Constitution. He contended that the original charter to the college had been a contract, and the 1815 state statute purporting to amend the charter was a "Law impairing the Obligation of Contracts" of the kind prohibited by that clause. In closing, Webster appeared to choke up with emotion to implore the rapt bench, "It is, sir, I have said, a small college, and yet there are those that love it."

Marshall owned the whole of the argument, for himself and for the Court, which ruled that a grant of corporate powers was a contract within the meaning of the Constitution and a state legislature had no power to avoid it. The college was a private corporation with vested property rights. Indeed, for the next 100 years the contract clause was the principal provision the Court would use to invalidate state laws that infringed on private property.

A leading magazine of the day remarked, "Perhaps no judicial proceedings in this country ever involved more important consequences." The decision extended national judicial power at the expense of state legislative power. It afforded constitutional protection to private economic and social actors, business corporations, and nonprofit corporations alike, against regulation by state legislatures. It validated private colleges and consequently encouraged legislatures to charter state institutions of higher education. In its aftermath, the prestige and influence of the Supreme Court and Chief Justice Marshall were enhanced considerably.

For more information

Dartmouth College v. Woodward, 17 U.S. (4 Wheat.) 518 (1818).

Garraty, John A. *Quarrels That Have Shaped the Constitution.* New York: Harper and Row, 1987.

McCloskey, Robert G. *The American Supreme Court.* Rev. 2nd ed. Chicago: University of Chicago, Sanford Levinson, 1994.

Smith, Jean Edward. *John Marshall, Definer of a Nation.* New York: Henry Holt, 1996.

White, G. Edward. *History of the Supreme Court of the United States, vols. 3–4, The Marshall Court and Cultural Change.* New York: Macmillan, 1988.

Thomas E. Baker
James Madison Chair in Constitutional Law
Drake University Law School

The Declaration of Independence was adopted by the Second Continental Congress on July 4, 1776, and it declared and enumerated the reasons for the independence of the American colonies from Great Britain, advocated government by consent of the people, and then defended human rights, the right of self-government, and the right of people to rebel against any tyrannical government.

Drawing from the natural rights doctrine of the English philosopher John Locke, the original draft was written largely by Thomas Jefferson but also included the writings of John Adams, Benjamin Franklin, Roger Sherman, and Robert Livingston. Writing in characteristically eloquent prose, Jefferson sought to capture the authentic revolutionary spirit of the times. Several years after the Revolution, Jefferson stated that the Declaration "was intended to be an expression of the American mind." Jefferson and his coauthors believed that the Declaration embodied political ideals that the great majority of Americans cherished.

The Declaration of Independence is based on a novel theory of the political rights of American colonists within the British Empire. As British subjects, the colonists believed fervently that they possessed the same rights as their "British brethren," but, as subjects, they were also legally obligated to obey King George III and Parliament. This state of affairs posed a problem for those who wished to separate from England. If Americans were British subjects, by what right could they claim to be "one people" who were "separate and equal" from other nations? In an attempt to resolve this dilemma, Benjamin Franklin put forth the theory in 1768 that the American colonies were originally established as separate and sovereign states within the British Empire. Franklin argued that the colonial governments owed allegiance only to the king (as did other states or nations within the British Commonwealth), not to the British Parliament. American colonists, therefore, could justify separation *from the King* by invoking the same rights enjoyed by British citizens. This theory, which is embodied in the Declaration, accounts for the fact that it contains a list of charges against the king, not Parliament, and for the fact that the Declaration justifies separation on the ground that Americans, as a free people, had been denied their rights by the king.

The first four sentences of the Declaration put forth a concise justification of the right of revolution which would appear to be derived from the political philosophy of the 17th-century Englishman John Locke (see Locke's *Second Treatise on Civil Government,* 1690). The first sentence of the Declaration asserts the intention of the American colonies "to dissolve the political bands which have connected them with another, and to assume among the powers of the earth, the separate and equal station to which the Laws of Nature and of Nature's God entitle them." Americans in Jefferson's time would have understood that "the Laws of Nature and of Nature's God" referred to natural laws, that is, universal moral principles based on reason.

The Declaration's second sentence enumerates the specific principles that justify a "separate and equal station": "We hold these truths to be self-evident, that all men are created equal, that they are endowed by their Creator with certain unalienable Rights, that among these are Life, Liberty, and the pursuit of Happiness." Jefferson's phrase, "all men are created equal" (today we would say "all people"), was meant to convey the idea that every person, by virtue of being a human being, possessed the same natural rights. John Locke argued that God created people with equal rights in the "state of nature," which existed before people decided to form governments. Upon leaving the state of nature, people retained certain natural (God-given or unalienable) rights—such as the rights to life, liberty, and property—that cannot be given up or alienated in political society. The concept of natural or unalienable rights therefore assumes that the powers of government must be limited.

In the third sentence, we encounter Locke's theory of legitimate government which resonated strongly with the beliefs and experience of the American colonists: "That to secure these rights, Governments are instituted among Men, deriving their just powers from the consent of the gov-

erned." People left the state of nature, according to Locke, to better secure their natural rights by instituting laws and courts, which would impartially apply the law. In forming a "social contract" among themselves, they agreed to create a government to protect those unalienable rights. American colonists believed, as did Locke, that government should be based upon the consent of the governed and should be held accountable by the people.

The fourth sentence of the Declaration articulates a justification for revolution based on Lockean social contract theory: "That whenever any Form of Government becomes destructive of these ends, it is the Right of the People to alter or abolish it, and to institute new Government, laying its foundation on such principles, and organizing its powers in such form, as to them shall seem most likely to effect their Safety and Happiness." According to Locke's theory, when the terms of the social contract have been violated by the government, the people have the right to "alter or abolish it." Revolution could be justified, according to the Declaration, because the king had violated the terms of the social contract by denying or usurping the natural rights of the colonists. The list of charges against the king in the Declaration enumerate these transgressions, which, among others, included taxation without representation, suspending or dissolving colonial governments, denying the right of trial by jury, and subverting the rule of law by appointing judges that were not impartial.

Jefferson's reference to "men" throughout the Declaration of Independence was understood by his contemporaries to exclude women and males who were not recognized as members of political society, such as slaves and American Indians. This fact cannot be overlooked without seriously distorting the historical context within which the Declaration was written. However, throughout the 19th and 20th centuries, leaders of civil rights movements for women, African Americans, and other disenfranchised groups regularly invoked the universalistic principles of the Declaration in support of their causes. Today, the natural rights language employed by Jefferson is interpreted to include all people regardless of their gender, race, or ethnic heritage. This is perhaps the main reason that the Declaration of Independence continues to be one of the most important statements of basic human rights ever written.

For more information

Becker, Carl L. *The Declaration of Independence: A Study in the History of Political Ideas.* New York: Vintage, 1958.

Maier, Pauline. *American Scripture: Making the Declaration of Independence.* New York: Knopf; Distributed by Random House, Inc., 1997.

Wood, Gordon S. *The Creation of the American Republic, 1776–1787.* New York: W. W. Norton, 1972.

Scott R. Bowman
California State University, Los Angeles

declaratory judgment   refers to a court decision that clarifies the rights and responsibilities of the parties to a lawsuit. It is an articulation of the legal relationships among the litigants.

A declaratory judgment does not, however, require the parties to do anything based on the court's enunciation of those rights and responsibilities. This is in contrast to most court cases in which the litigants are requesting the court to order some sort of active relief for alleged injuries; for example, monetary damages. A litigant may seek a declaratory judgment if she is uncertain about her legal obligations and does not wish to inadvertently run afoul of the law. For example, a party wishing to terminate a complicated sales contract may seek clarification from the courts on the requirements for doing so.

As a general rule, courts are hesitant to issue declaratory judgments. In fact, the United States Supreme Court, in the 1928 case of *Willing v. Chicago Auditorium Association,* 277 U.S. 274, suggested that federal courts were severely limited in issuing declaratory judgments under Article III of the Constitution. The language of Article III can be interpreted to imply that only actual (as opposed to hypothetical) cases with real controversy between the parties are within the purview of the federal courts. The United States Supreme Court has subsequently taken a less restrictive view of the permissibility of declaratory judgments. However, for a federal court to issue a declaratory judgment, there still must be an actual controversy and not merely a hypothetical dispute at issue.

Congress specifically authorized federal courts to issue declaratory judgments with passage of the Federal Declaratory Judgment Act of 1934. Declaratory judgments are permissible for all civil issues except for federal tax cases. In the 1937 case of *Aetna Life Ins. Co. of Hartford, Conn. v. Haworth,* 300 U.S. 227, the Supreme Court explicitly considered the constitutionality of the act. The Court upheld the constitutionality of the act, basing its decision on the fact that it limited the use of declaratory judgments to actual controversies. Deciding what constitutes an actual controversy has proven not to be a straightforward matter to determine, but there is evidence that the Court is less likely to resolve major constitutional questions with their use. For example, the Court declined to issue a declaratory judgment in the 1961 case of *Poe v. Ullman,* 367 U.S. 497, to determine the constitutionality of Connecticut's law against contraceptive devices. However, a scant four year later the Court reversed a doctor's conviction for dispensing contraceptives to a married couple in violation of Connecticut law in the landmark case of *Griswold v. Connecticut,* 381 U.S. 479 (1965).

A declaratory judgment is distinct from an advisory judgment, in which a court addresses a question of law in the absence of an actual controversy, a practice the Court has consistently declined to engage in. While each state regulates the issuance of declaratory judgments by its own courts in accordance with its own laws, state practice generally parallels federal practice.

For more information

Hazard, Geoffrey C. Jr., and Michele Taruffo, *American Civil Procedure: An Introduction.* New Haven, Conn.: Yale University Press, 1993.

Silberman, Linda J., and Allan R. Stein. *Civil Procedure: Theory and Practice.* Gaithersburg, Md.: Aspen Law and Business, 2001.

Wendy L. Martinek
SUNY, Binghamton

defamation   is the law that protects a person's reputation or his or her good name from ridicule.

A statement that defames someone is one that causes others to avoid the defamed person. This area of the law is centuries old. Perhaps its earliest enforcement was in the notorious Court of the Star Chamber in England in the 1400s, when the defamer was ordered to pay money to someone whose reputation he sullied and often would be maimed or imprisoned. Truth was no defense—the fact that that another's reputation was attacked was all that mattered. In the Middle Ages dueling often settled disputes caused by such attacks on reputation. By the mid-1600s two separate types of defamation had emerged in the English law: libel, which was defamation by writing, and slander, which was defamation by spoken word. As they developed, these related torts, or civil wrongs, were largely the same. A person who claimed he was slandered, however, had to prove the slanderous statement led to financial harm—cost him money. That was because spoken insults could be quickly forgotten and were limited by how many people might hear them and, not least, such insults could crowd the courts with people demanding redress. With libel, on the other hand, the written disparagement was more permanent and could be transmitted to large numbers of people.

As with all early American law, the law of defamation was established in the various states by English "common law." Despite free speech guarantees of the U.S. Constitution in the First Amendment, defamation law developed exclusively in state courts. It even encompassed seditious libel, a criminal offense that punished disparaging remarks about government officials. For the most part, however, the free speech heritage of the American Revolution established truth as a defense that took root in U.S. law. A true statement could harm a person's reputation, to be sure, but the defamer would not be liable because it was true. Once the person who claimed to be defamed proved that a false statement was written about him and that by its nature it would call his reputation into question, then the harm was presumed—his defamer had to pay, even if no one believed the statement and even if the defamer made the false statement without knowing it was false.

In most states libel protects the reputation of a person defamed by a television or radio broadcast, even though the defamatory statement is spoken, not written. The reason for this is that the statement reaches a wider audience than the law of slander originally intended and, in theory at least, would cause more damage.

The scope of defamation (at least libel) was radically changed beginning in 1964 with the U.S. Supreme Court's decision in *New York Times Co. v. Sullivan,* 376 U.S. 254, 84 S.Ct. 710, 11 L.Ed.2d 686 (1964). In this decision the Supreme Court for the first time held that state libel laws must meet certain free speech protections under the First Amendment. The *Sullivan* case required what English common law and state law did not, that the person defamed must prove his defamer was at fault. In *Sullivan,* concerned only with libel lawsuits filed by public officials when the defamatory statement related to their public duties, the Court determined that the public official claiming to have been defamed must prove that the person who defamed him knew the statement was false or recklessly disregarded whether it was true or not. Later decisions amplifying the rule in *Sullivan* established that fault must be proven in all libel cases, at least against the mass media.

For more information
Rosini, Neil J. *The Practical Guide to Libel Law.* New York: Praeger, 1991.

Wm. Osler McCarthy
Supreme Court of Texas/
University of Texas Department of Journalism

defense attorney   refers to the legal counsel who represents a defendant in either a civil or criminal case. A defense attorney is also referred to as defense counsel or defense lawyer. In either a civil or criminal case, it is the defense attorney's job to protect the interests of the defendant in the case.

The United States has an adversarial system of justice which places the judge in the position of neutral decision maker and attorneys for plaintiffs against those of the defendant. It is the job of the attorneys to bring forth evidence in support of their position and to argue the law. The plaintiff has the burden of proof in both civil and criminal trials.

In civil trials, the plaintiff must prove by a preponderance of the evidence that the defendant is liable, while in criminal trials the plaintiff (the prosecutor) must prove beyond a reasonable doubt that the defendant is guilty. In either case, it is the job of the defense attorney to counter the claims of the plaintiff and defend the defendant. Defense attorneys do not only work during the trial, rather it is their job to defend their clients from the beginning through the end of the case. They not only appear in court but work with plea bargaining, settlements, answering pleadings, researching evidence, and interviewing witnesses.

In civil trials, defense attorneys appear in any number of types of cases. They may appear as defense counsel for large corporations, for individuals, small businesses, and government agencies. Most lawsuits filed, whether it be against an individual, business, or the government, will require a defense attorney. Defense attorneys are therefore a mixed group of lawyers. Although some civil attorneys specialize in defense work, many may simply be lawyers who represent a client on a regular basis (i.e., doing legal contracts) and find themselves in the position of defending their client as a part of that relationship.

The Sixth Amendment to the United States Constitution protects a defendant's right to counsel in criminal cases. In criminal matters, defense attorneys must counter the prosecution's claim of guilt. Most defense attorneys in criminal matters specialize in criminal law. Many defense attorneys in criminal law are former prosecutors. Some defense attorneys work privately or in law firms, while some work for the state as part of a program to provide legal services for indigent defendants. The most widely used of these programs is called a public defender program.

Defense attorneys in criminal law face a hard decision. In many cases, they know their clients will not benefit from a trial. For some of these defendants, working out a plea bargain may be in their best interests. In this way, a defendant who admits guilt or a defendant who faces a strong prosecutorial case may be able to reduce the time spent in prison through a reduction of charges or sentence. On the other hand, defense attorneys will typically recommend trial for those defendants where either there is a strong chance of acquittal or where there is a very high prison sentence. In either of these cases, a defense attorney may find that his or her client's interests would best be served by a trial by jury (*see* Neubauer, 1997).

Defense attorneys, and especially criminal defense attorneys, often face a particularly harsh public image, which is based on the competing morals in public life. On one hand the public wants to see those who are guilty punished. Defense attorneys often represent clients who they believe to be guilty. For example, a civil lawyer may represent a car manufacturer who caused the death of a child through negligence or a criminal lawyer may represent a murderer found standing over a dead body. In either case, the public may be outraged at the person who defends the actions of the defendant, i.e., the defense attorney, especially when an attorney earns an acquittal for their client.

On the other hand, the public does not want to see innocent people go to jail or pay large fines. In this view, defense attorneys who rigorously defend their clients are only doing their job. After all, most people would want a good defense attorney if they stood accused. In addition, in many cases the lawyer simply does not know whether the client is innocent or guilty but simply must work the case based upon what the client professes to be the truth (*see* Tarr, 1999).

For more information

Neubauer, David W. *Judicial Process: Law Courts, and Politics in the United States.* New York: Harcourt Brace College Publishers, 1997.

Tarr, G. Alan. *Judicial Process and Judicial Policymaking.* Boston: West/Wadsworth, 1999.

Joy A. Willis
Michigan State University
Graduate Researcher

Defense of Marriage Act (DOMA)   defines marriage for federal purposes as "the union between one man and one woman." Passage of this act by Congress in 1996 also added a provision to the *U.S. Code* that permits one state to refuse to recognize a same-sex marriage which is valid under the laws of another state.

Congress passed DOMA primarily in response to *Baehr v. Lewin,* a case in which the Hawaii Supreme Court held that under that state's constitution, a marriage statute which restricts the status and benefits of marriage to male-female couples discriminates on the basis of sex. With the *Baehr* decision in 1993, Congress and advocates on both sides of the same-sex marriage debate assumed that it would only be a matter of time before same-sex marriage was a matter of course in Hawaii. Addressing this potential occurrence became a major issue in the 1996 elections, ultimately leading to the passage of DOMA at the federal level and similar laws in many states.

DOMA is unique in several ways. First, marriage regulations have historically been a matter of state law, not federal. Second, DOMA was passed in response to a perceived problem that does not yet exist. That is, while the law purports to regulate marriage, it was really enacted as a response to the possibility of same-sex marriage, which, as of this writing, has not yet been legalized by any state. Third, on its face this act appears to directly conflict with the Full Faith and Credit Caluse of Article IV of the U.S. Constitution. That clause requires that "Full Faith and Credit shall be given in each state to the public Acts, Records, and judicial Proceedings of every other state" and only gives Congress the power to regulate the "Manner in which such Acts, Records and Proceedings shall be proved and the Effect thereof."

Marriage has been a status that has historically led to some departures from the Full Faith and Credit so that while marriages that are valid in the state where performed are generally valid in any other state, such marriages do not have to be recognized in another state if they violate that state's "strong public policy." However, never before has Congress simply declared that any state may categorically refuse to recognize a marriage that is valid in the state where performed.

On January 31, 2000, the Supreme Court of Vermont ruled in *Baker v. State* that it is discrimination under the Common Benefits Clause of the Vermont Constitution to deny same-sex couples the same benefits as male-female couples. Accordingly the Vermont legislature enacted a law which gives gay and lesbian couples the same benefits that are available to heterosexual couples under state law, such as tax benefits, inheritance rights, and the legal right to make medical decisions on behalf of a partner. Vermont stopped short, however, of conferring the status of "marriage" on same-sex couples and instead allows same-sex couples to register their "civil unions." Unlike marriages, these civil unions are not recognized by other states and confer no benefits under federal law. In light of Vermont's civil union law, it appears only a matter of time before one or more states grant same-sex couples the right to marry. Such an occurrence will undoubtedly lead to legal challenges of DOMA on several grounds, including but not limited to claims that DOMA violates the Full Faith and Credit Clause and regulates an area more appropriately left to regulation by the states.

For more information

Kersch, Ken I. "Full Faith and Credit for Same-Sex Marriage?" *Political Science Quarterly* 112 (spring 1997).

Strasser, Mark P. *Legally Wed: Same-Sex Marriage & the Constitution*. Ithaca, N.Y.: Cornell University Press, April 1996.

Martha M. Lafferty
Staff Attorney
Tennessee Fair Housing Council

deposition   is the term for sworn testimony taken before a court reporter who takes down and eventually transcribes oral testimony.

A deposition is part of the phase of the lawsuit called "discovery," which is the process by which a party to a lawsuit finds out the breadth and scope of the other party's case. A deposition is scheduled shortly after the start of a lawsuit for the purpose of preserving testimony and exploring the strengths and weaknesses of the opponent's witnesses and, by extension, the outline of the case. A party or a witness, the "deponent" is summoned into a private conference room or law library. Lawyers for each party are present, as is a court reporter. The court reporter is a notary public or some other official authorized to administer oaths or affirmations. The reporter is also a skilled stenographic note taker who takes down what is said word-for-word. Except for the swearing in of the deponent, the reporter takes

no other active part in the process beyond recording the proceedings.

Once the witness is sworn, the lead attorney for the opposing side will begin asking questions of the witness. There is no presiding officer present to determine whether a question is proper or not. If a question is thought to be improper, the attorney for the deponent may object, stating his grounds based upon the rules of evidence. The deponent will then answer the question. Later, a judge may decide whether the question was proper. Because a deposition can also be used as an instrument of settlement, by exposing both strengths and weaknesses of a deponent's testimony, judges are often very reluctant to strike questions or answers.

Some jurisdictions impose little or no restriction on the type or number of questions that can be asked or the length of the depositions. If the side being deposed feels that the interrogation is oppressive or is being used only for purposes of pressure, the party can apply to the court for orders restricting the manner, length, or even the nature of the questioning. These are called "protective orders."

During a trial a deposition may be used to "impeach" a witness, which is the process of pointing out differences in the witness's courtroom testimony and his deposition testimony. Depositions may also be used to refresh the memory of a friendly witness. If the person whose deposition has been taken is unavailable because of illness, death, or being otherwise excused, the deposition may be read into the record as if it were the testimony of the person given on that day. As many depositions are now videotaped, this has become popular because the judge or jury not only can hear the witness but observe the witness's demeanor and appearance as well.

Depositions are only one of the tools that attorneys use during the discovery phase. They are used most often because they produce the most immediate response. Other tools are written interrogatories, motions to require production of documents for inspection or copying, production of tangible objects for testing, or inspection of real property. Interrogatories often produce the opponent's "best" answer and therefore lack the spontaneity of an oral deposition.

For more information

American Jurisprudence, 2nd ed. Vol. 23, *Depositions and Discovery.* St. Paul, Minn.: West Group Publishing, 1998.

Consult the statutes and rules of civil procedure in your state.

Stanley M. Morris
Attorney at Law
Cortez, Colorado

deterrence   is a term used to describe the theory that punishment should be used to prevent crime. The interests of society demand that crime be prevented; therefore, supporters of deterrence argue that the experience of punishment should be so negative that the offender will never again try to repeat the offense. Furthermore, the fearful dramatic effect of the suffering caused by punishment upon an offender should be an object lesson so powerful that it will dissuade potential offenders.

Scholars distinguish two categories of deterrence: individual (also called special, specific, or simple) deterrence and general deterrence. Individual deterrence refers to the effect punishment has upon an offender's future behavior. General deterrence points to the preventive effect the threat of punishment has on people at large in society.

Deterrence is grounded in many assumptions. First, individual deterrence assumes that if the punishment is severe enough the offender will not commit crimes in the future. Second, focused on society, general deterrence is based on the assumption that all potential offenders will learn from observing the punishment meted out to others. Crime statistics evoke doubts about these assumptions.

A third assumption is that potential offenders rationally calculate the rewards crime will pay against the price of punishment. Many crimes, however, are unplanned, spontaneous acts of passion, or are otherwise uncalculated. Studies have shown that some prisoners do not view prison as unpleasant. For others prison is simply a cost of being in the crime business.

A fourth assumption is that offenders fear getting caught. However, some studies report that many offenders did not believe that they would be caught, or they calculated otherwise.

A fifth assumption is that if punishment is swiftly delivered in proportion to the crime, then crimes rates will drop. However, in the U.S. criminal justice system, delays and appeals seem to reduce any expected deterrence.

A sixth assumption is that the punishment will be certain. However, in the United States large numbers of crimes go unreported, unprosecuted if reported, plea bargained to a lesser offense if brought to trial, and unconvicted if tried.

A seventh assumption is that potential offenders will be deterred from committing criminal acts by the fear of punishment. However, studies have shown that many criminals do not fear punishment. Studies of drinking and driving, and the death penalty, seem to illustrate this.

There has been no agreement among researchers that fear of punishment is a deterrent to crime. Declines in crime rates following increases in sentence severity may not be due to a deterrent effect but to the incapacitation of potential criminals. The occurrence of new crimes indicates ineffective deterrence; however, effective deterrence is difficult to validate, because it involves what has not happened, namely, no new crimes following strong punishment.

For more information

Jacobs, Nancy R., Mark A. Siegel, and Jacquelyn Quiram, eds. *Prisons and Jails: A Deterrent to Crime?* Wylie, Tex.: Information Plus, 1995.

Schonebaum, Stephen E., ed. *Does Capital Punishment Deter Crime?* San Diego, Calif.: Greenhaven Press, 1998.

A. J. L. Waskey
Dalton State College

discretion   is the professional judgment used by criminal justice authorities to choose a course of action, or not to act at all, based on the particular circumstances of the situation. It is one of the most necessary, yet controversial, concepts in the lexicon of law.

Judges have broad discretion to dismiss a case, grant or deny motions, sign warrants, and sentence criminals. Sentencing guidelines, which set a minimum and maximum sentence for each crime, grant judges the power to use their judgment to decide the appropriate penalty for each case. However, many conservatives believe that judges issue lighter sentences than warranted by the crime committed. Consequently, many states have passed mandatory sentencing laws which require a uniform sentence for all who are convicted of a particular crime.

Prosecutors are granted wide discretionary latitude to decide what charges to file against the accused. They may decide not to prosecute, known as *nolle prosequi,* even where there is sufficient evidence against the accused to proceed. Or, the prosecutor might use his discretionary power to drop the case after the accused has been formally charged. They can also decide whether or not to plea bargain with a suspect, or which members of a crime ring arrested for the same crime will be offered a plea bargain. Prosecutors may not file charges for any number of reasons, including insufficient evidence, reluctant witnesses, and violations of the accused's due process rights. Some have criticized the failure of district attorneys to prosecute more cases, but legislative efforts to reign in prosecutorial discretion have been largely unsuccessful.

Though the law formally grants discretionary power to judges and prosecutors, it expects the police to fully enforce all criminal laws. However, the reality of police work in a free society makes this impractical; officers learn to use their judgment to selectively enforce the laws based on the circumstances of each case. An officer on the beat might find it wiser to disperse a group of unruly teenagers with a warning than to book them on disorderly conduct charges.

Properly utilized, discretion is the power of judges, prosecutors, and the police to make decisions that depart from the letter of the law in situations where the uniform application of the law would not produce a just result. However, discretion can be used in improper ways, including corruption and discrimination. While police routinely develop profiles of certain types of criminals based on the concept of reasonable suspicion, the use of racial profiling is an abuse of this power. Recent revelations that the New Jersey State Police routinely stopped black motorists on the New Jersey Turnpike based on the color of their skin is a prime example of how the abuse of police discretion can demoralize its victims and foment distrust of the police and the law.

For more information

Hawkins, Keith, ed. *The Uses of Discretion.* New York: Oxford University Press, 1992.
Ohlin, Lloyd E., and Frank J. Remington. *Discretion in Criminal Justice: The Tension between Individualization and Uniformity.* Albany: State University of New York Press, 1993.

Vernon Mogensen
Kingsborough Community College, CUNY

district attorney   is the elected or appointed official responsible for conducting criminal proceedings against an accused person. Whether called "district attorney," "state's attorney," "chief prosecutor," "commonwealth attorney," "county attorney," or "solicitor," this person prosecutes criminal cases and defends the state or local bodies in suits brought against them.

The prosecutor has a wide range of choices in the handling of criminal defendants, the scheduling of cases for trials, the acceptance of plea bargains, etc. In states with the grand jury system, the prosecutors are responsible for bringing evidence before that body. (In states where grand juries are not used, the district attorney brings charges in the form of an "information" or "presentment.") Courts have obligated the prosecutors to share evidence with the defense. (The goal is justice, not victory by whatever means. A special power of the prosecutor is to ask the court to dismiss a case if there is insufficient evidence to secure a conviction. Yet a successful record as a prosecutor could lead to high political office or to a judgeship. Thus there is a desire to make a record.)

In all but five states, the district attorneys are elected (generally for four-year terms with the possibility of reelection). Usually, like sheriffs, they are selected in partisan elections (though a case can be made for their being nonpartisan). In three states (Alaska, Delaware, and Rhode Island) there are no local prosecutors; responsibility is centralized at the state level.

Each of the 94 judicial districts of the United States is headed by a U.S. attorney, appointed by the president for a four-year term. It is customary for the U.S. attorneys to resign if the opposition party wins the White House. Ramsey Clark proposed selecting U.S. attorneys from the ranks of career civil servants; this would have insulated them from political pressures and would develop nationally uniform standards of prosecution. (Though nominated by the president, the prerogative of selecting them has largely shifted to the senators in the state where they are to serve, from the same political party as the president.) They prosecute federal crimes in federal courts.

For more information

Eisenstein, James. *Counsel for the United States: U.S. Attorneys in the Political and Legal Systems.* Baltimore: Johns Hopkins University Press, 1978.

Jacoby, Joan E. *The American Prosecutor: A Search for Identity.* Lexington, Mass.: Lexington Books, 1980.

Stewart, James B. *The Prosecutors: Inside the Offices of the Government's Most Powerful Lawyers.* New York: Simon and Schuster, 1987.

Martin Gruberg
University of Wisconsin, Oshkosh

divorce   is the legal dissolving of a marriage by a court of law.

Divorce was unavailable under the jurisdiction of English courts prior to the reign of King Henry VII, and while parliamentary divorces during the latter 17th century did exist, they were very rare. By the early 20th century, however, all U.S. states (except South Carolina, which did not permit permanent divorce until 1948) had enacted laws authorizing courts to dissolve marriages for justifiable legal grounds; these grounds usually included adultery, cruelty, desertion, incurable insanity, or voluntary separation for a period of time.

But it was relatively easy to subvert these state requirements, at least for those with sufficient means. Couples who wished to divorce could establish temporary domicile in a more permissive jurisdiction or stage a courtroom charade to fit one of the justifiable legal grounds for divorce. For those without sufficient resources to stage productions in courts, informal separation was the only alternative. Divorce policy in almost all Western countries was either completely revised or substantially reformed after 1960. In the United States, California adopted the first divorce code in 1969 that dispensed entirely with fault-based divorce; it recognized circumstances for divorce where no fault, responsibility, or offense was attributed by law to either spouse.

There had been examples of no-fault provisions in former divorce codes (e.g., divorce by mutual agreement or reasons of incompatibility, insanity, impotence, and unavoidable absence), yet these grounds for divorce did place responsibility on one of the spouses, even if fault was not actually attributed. No-fault divorce codes are different; fault is not attributed to either spouse, and it does not require one of the spouses to be considered innocent and the other guilty. Simply, it recognizes the permanent breakdown of the marriage. Every state has now instituted no-fault procedures based on a irreparable breakdown of the marriage or on some other no-fault criterion, such as separation for a relatively short interval.

No-fault divorce does not rest on the precise circumstances that produced the breakdown of the marriage but simply on the fact of the breakdown. Most laws specify a period during which a couple must have lived separately and the marriage has ceased to have practical meaning; thus, most of the onus of defining the breakdown is given to the spouses themselves and not the courts. This is a profound change in divorce law because it overcomes the centuries-long principle that divorce must be closely regulated by the church or state. Additionally, other changes have followed; alimony has now been severely limited. Spousal maintenance generally is avoided entirely or limited to only brief rehabilitative periods. In theory, equality between the parties can be more easily accomplished through distribution of existing assets rather than future income. Today, only about a sixth of all divorcing women have received maintenance, and two-thirds of the awards have been for limited duration, averaging about two years.

Today, about half of all contemporary marriages will end in divorce, and 60 percent of all children will spend time in single-parent homes.

For more information

Phillips, Roderick. *Putting Asunder: A History of Divorce in Western Society.* New York: Cambridge University Press, 1988.

Rhode, Deborah L. *Justice and Gender: Sex Discrimination and the Law.* New York: Cambridge University Press, 1989.

Ashlyn K. Kuersten
Western Michigan University

DNA testing   has revolutionized the fields of law enforcement and criminal justice due to its ability to link a suspect's DNA with DNA crime scene evidence by matching "genetic markers." A genetic marker is a segment of DNA that can vary between people. The human DNA (*deoxyribonucleic acid*) molecule is a person's "genetic blueprint" and is composed of more than three billion base pairs. Approximately 99.9 percent of the base pair sequences is identical in all humans. The remaining 0.1 percent of DNA consists of many different repetitive base pair sequences varying in length from individual to individual that can be used as genetic markers. If enough genetic markers are tested, the probability of two people (excluding identical twins) having the same combination is infinitesimally small because of the great amount of variation in the genetic markers.

There are two major DNA testing technologies: restriction fragment length polymorphism (RFLP) and polymerase chain reaction (PCR). Both RFLP and PCR technologies are based on recognition of repetitive base pair sequences, but there are differences between the two technologies. RFLP typing, the older technology, identifies extremely long stretches of DNA segments called variable number tandem repeats (VNTR). The disadvantages of RFLP technology are that relatively large amounts of DNA are needed and the DNA cannot be degraded. PCR technology, which makes many copies of the DNA in a crime scene sample, can handle small (as small as the head of a pin) or degraded biological samples. PCR typing recognizes small stretches of repetitive DNA sequences known as short tandem repeats (STRs) that are too short for RFLP analysis. Geneticists estimate there are more than 30,000 STR regions which makes PCR STR technology a powerful forensic tool. Statistical estimates suggest that typing information from 12 different STR markers allows unique identification of an individual. PCR technology also is used to type mitochondrial (as opposed to the more common nuclear) DNA. DNA testing is usually done on body fluids (for example, blood, semen, or saliva), but mitochondrial DNA (mtDNA) typing also can be performed on bone fragments, tooth, hair, and other biological trace evidence.

In 1986 Dr. Alec Jeffries of England pioneered the use of genetic markers in law enforcement when he first excluded a suspect in a case of rape and murder and later identified the perpetrator through DNA testing. Identification through matching of DNA sequences has been admitted as evidence in U.S. courts since 1989. The United States is currently building a nationwide DNA marker database called CODIS, *CO*mbined *D*NA *I*ndex *S*ystem. CODIS can link serial violent crimes that may have occurred in different jurisdictions and can identify suspects by matching DNA evidence left at crime scenes to convicted offenders whose DNA markers are already in the database. An unforeseen consequence of DNA testing is that closed criminal cases are being reopened because post-conviction DNA testing has exonerated defendants wrongfully convicted and already serving a sentence. This is a dilemma for the U.S. criminal justice system that is based on both the search for the truth and the finality of judgments.

For more information

Inman, Keith, and Norah Rudin. *An Introduction to Forensic DNA Analysis.* Boca Raton, Fla.: CRC Press, 1997.

Coleman, Howard, and Eric Swenson. *DNA in the Courtroom: A Trial Watcher's Guide.* Seattle, Wash.: Genelex Corporation, 1994.

Convicted by Juries, Exonerated by Science: Case Studies in the Use of DNA Evidence to Establish Innocence after Trial. Washington, D.C.: National Institute of Justice, U.S. Department of Justice, 1996.

Karen Gottlieb, Ph.D., J.D.
BioLaw
Nederland, Colorado

domestic partnership law regulates the rights and responsibilities of an unmarried couple who live together in a committed, exclusive relationship and who are financially interdependent. Much, but not all, domestic partnership law applies to same-sex couples only.

Many public and private employers offer fringe benefits to the domestic partners of their employees. Federal law treats the most popular of those benefits—such as medical and dental insurance, moving expense reimbursement, and leave time for bereavement and illness of a partner—differently from spousal benefits. Under the COBRA program, which allows employees to continue medical insurance at their own expense after leaving a company, spousal coverage can be continued; domestic partnership coverage can not. The Family and Medical Leave Act of 1993 allows employees to take up to 12 weeks to unpaid leave to care for ill relatives. Domestic partners are not considered relatives, so they are not covered by the act. The Internal Revenue Service counts the value of the medical, dental, and hospital insurance for an employee's domestic partner as part of the employee's income. It does not do so for an employee's spouse.

Many state statutes and local ordinances establish domestic partnership benefit programs for public employees. Some local governments—the city of San Francisco is one—require contractors doing business with the city to make domestic partner benefits available to their employees. The state of Vermont requires insurance companies doing business in the state to offer the same benefits to domestic partners that they do to spouses.

To be eligible for domestic partner benefits, the couple ordinarily files an affidavit stating that neither is already married, that both are of legal age, are not close blood relatives, share a close personal relationship, are jointly responsible for each other's emotional and financial welfare, live together, and plan to remain in the relationship indefinitely.

The most comprehensive form of domestic partnership is the civil union—a marriage in all but name. Parties to a civil union are subject to the entire body of domestic relations law, including divorce, child custody and support, and property division on the dissolution of the union. The parties can adopt children. If either one has a natural child during the period in which the union is in effect, both parties are considered parents. Each can administer the other's estate. Each has the right to visit the other in a hospital and to make decisions about the other's care. A survivor can collect damages for the wrongful death of a partner. The parties are entitled to file joint state, but not federal, tax returns.

For more information

DeLeon, Richard. "San Francisco and Domestic Partners: New Fields of Battle in the Culture Wars." In Elaine B. Sharp, ed. *Culture Wars and Politics.* Lawrence: University Press of Kansas, 1999.

Rutherford, Elizabeth A. "Domestic Partner Benefits: Are You Doing It Right?" *Employee Relations Law Journal* 23 (summer 1997): 125–32.

Wriggins, Jennifer. "Marriage Law and Family Law: Autonomy, Interdependence, and Couples of the Same Gender." *Boston College Law Review* 61 (March 2000): 265–325.

William H. Coogan
University of Southern Maine

domestic violence   is violence that occurs within a family, quasi family, or intimate relationship. The victim or defendant may be family members by blood or marriage, married couples, former spouses with children, or cohabitants.

In the late 1970s sociologists and psychologists began to recognize and study this societal ailment. Traditionally, victims and perpetrators of domestic violence kept their problems behind closed doors and outsiders did not concern themselves with "the problems of other families." In the 1980s the societal outlook rapidly began to change and domestic violence was recognized as the public and private wrong that it is. This resulted in increased state and federal

activism in the area of domestic violence by enacting new legislation or stringently enforcing existing statutes.

Domestic violence takes several forms. It includes physical abuse such as punching, choking, smacking, pushing, forced sexual acts, and using weapons. The violence can also be verbal or psychological. In such case, the perpetrator threatens to harm the victim or someone close to the victim, repeatedly insults, degrades, and attacks the self-esteem of the victim, tells confidential information, limits the victim's contact with others, controls and monitors the whereabouts of the victim, and/or injures pets and causes damage to other property of the victim. It is not uncommon for victims to simultaneously suffer several forms of abuse at the hands of the perpetrator.

Power and control are the objective of the abuser. When the abuser senses that the power and control are waning, the abuser resorts to the above forms of domestic violence to try to reinforce and reestablish control. Abusive relationships run a continuous and familiar cycle. It begins with a tension-building stage. At this time the batterer is frustrated and becomes increasingly jealous or irritable. The victim tries very hard to pacify the batterer, trying to anticipate the batterer's desires and needs and to avoid any agitation.

Stage two is an abusive incident. Violence is most severe at this point. The victim may make police or other outside contacts at this point. The third stage, often referred to as the "honeymoon stage," involves obsessive attempts by the batterer to reestablish the loving, intimate relationship. It often includes promises to discontinue the abusive behavior, promises to change, great remorse, and sometimes a willingness to attend counseling. The batterer will be extremely apologetic and might admit to having overreacted but usually blames some external stressor. Once the relationship is reestablished, the batterer may continue to exhibit intensely loving and nurturing behavior. At some point in time, the batterer will regress and the couple will return to stage one of the cycle.

Studies on the incidence of violence in homes estimate that at least 30 percent of all women will suffer from some form of violence in an adult relationship. For 10 percent of these women, the violence will be so severe that they worry for their personal safety and life. Police forces across North America report that 95 percent of the victims of domestic violence are women and children.

Victims may file a civil or criminal complaint or both to aid in obtaining relief from a batterer. The primary difference lies in the relief that is available to the victim. Either the victim or the police may file criminal warrants. The police will always prepare either an incident report or a police report. Depending on the nature and circumstances of the incident, the police will obtain a warrant for the arrest of the batterer or will direct the victim to take a copy of the report and make application to the appropriate court for a warrant. The police will take the accused into custody upon execution of the warrant and perform the normal criminal processing (arrest, fingerprinting, presentation for initial bail hearing, arraignment, and finally trial). The end result of a criminal proceeding can be probation, incarceration, or dismissal. The court may also, as part of the bail proceeding or probation, prohibit contact between the victim and the accused. Once a criminal complaint is signed, the state takes control of the prosecution. The victim becomes the state's witness and can no longer solely make decisions regarding the prosecution of the case.

In comparison, when a civil petition/complaint is filed, the batterer is not subject to police involvement. The complaint is always filed by the victim or a representative of the victim (counsel or guardian in some cases). The batterer will not be subject to incarceration or probation, but the court can order that there be no contact with the victim. It should be noted that violation of a civil order will result in criminal charges, which could then subject the accused to penalties and sanctions including incarceration or probation. The victim is afforded a much broader spectrum of remedies under a civil order. For example, victims may request any of the following: no contact with the victim, victim's children, or relatives. In addition to face-to-face contact, the "no contact" may include phone, mail, or third party. Civil relief may also include a prohibition against harassing the victim or those closely connected with the victim; a turn-in of firearms by a specific date and time; staying away from victim's residence, property, or workplace; temporary custody of children; possession of marital property; temporary child support or support for the victim. It may also set forth visitation schedules and circumstances under which visitation will occur, or whether it will occur at all.

For more information

Davidson, Terry, ed. *Conjugal Crime: Understanding and Changing the Wifebeating Pattern.* New York: Hawthorne Books, 1978.

Pfouts, J. H., J. H. Scopler, and H. C. Henley Jr."Forgotten Victims of Family Violence," *Social Work* (July 1982).

Loretta M. Young
Family Court of State of Delaware

double jeopardy   is a fundamental constitutional principle that forbids the prosecution of a person for a criminal offense that has already been prosecuted against that party. Under the Fifth Amendment to the United States Constitution, no person "shall be subject for the same offense to be twice put in jeopardy of life or limb." Most states have enacted criminal procedural statutes and rules to carry out the constitutional principle.

Generally a person may not be twice prosecuted for the same offense, nor separately prosecuted for two offenses, unless:

- The offenses, or crimes, have substantially different elements and the acts or conduct establishing the crimes are materially different and distinguishable;

- A mandatory element or attribute for each offense is required in only one of the two offenses but is not required in both;
- The offenses occurred in two separate states and one of the felony crimes is part of enterprise corruption, or racketeering; Enterprise corruption is defined as a "pattern of criminal activity."
- Each offense involves death, injury, loss or other consequence to a different victim.

Another important aspect for judicial consideration is to establish that a person has been previously prosecuted. For example, mere apprehension by the police, or merely being the subject of a warrantless police search, an automobile search, or a house search, without further charge by an accusatory instrument filed in a state court or jurisdiction in the United States, would not constitute previous prosecution. Even if a warrant were signed by a magistrate or judge, in support of a search and an eventual arrest, and the action does not proceed to trial but charges are dropped or never filed, no prosecution would have been deemed to have taken place.

If a jury trial is impaneled, or a witness is sworn before a judge, in a nonjury court trial, a prosecution would have been deemed to occur. However, if a court were to nullify a proceedings and restore the action to the pre-pleading stage, or direct a new trial on the same accusatory instrument, the defendant would have no grounds to interpose the double jeopardy defense. Therefore, a person "is prosecuted" for a criminal charge or offense when a conviction or acquittal verdict (including one entered into by plea bargain) has been entered on the public records, pursuant to a trial, or prior to or during a trial. Also, a person "is prosecuted" when an indictment or a count of an indictment charging that offense is dismissed, without any additional condition to submit the charge to another grand jury.

Lastly, a person is considered prosecuted when an indictment or a count of indictment charging a criminal offense is dismissed because a court has granted a motion to suppress evidence that was illegally obtained or failed to pass minimum constitutional standards. The prosecutor must be very careful to draft a clear, comprehensive, valid, and formal charging document that includes all specific offenses alleged to have been committed. The grand jury, after careful deliberations, weighs the sufficiency of the evidence, states the facts about the alleged crime including the violations of the penal code, and returns an indictment to the court, listing all joinable offenses, to initiate the trial of a felony case. Irrespective of whether the proceedings were initiated by a prosecutorial information statement or a grand jury indictment, the failure to join all criminal offenses in one accusatory instrument may trigger the double jeopardy clause. If the accusatory instrument is used to initiate a trial, or a plea of guilty is entered, the subsequent prosecution for any omitted uncharged offenses is permanently barred under the double jeopardy principle. However, the omitted charges must have arisen from the same criminal transaction, act, or event. Finally, if an application to consolidate multiple offenses is erroneously denied by a court, subsequent prosecution of the unconsolidated offenses will also be denied.

For more information

Klotter, John C., Jacqueline R. Kanovitz, and Michael I Kanovitz. *Constitutional Law.* Cincinnati, Ohio: Anderson Publishing, 1999.

J. David Golub
Touro College

Douglas, William O.

Douglas, William O.   (1898–1980)   sat on the United States Supreme Court in five different decades from 1939 to 1975 championing individual rights and liberties. Never one to shy away from controversy, his writings both on and off the Court demonstrate a commitment to unpopular causes and underdogs. While admirers point to his fierce independence and many opinions supporting liberal ideals, his critics branded him a judicial activist, more interested in self-promotion than coalition-building.

He was born in Maine, Minnesota, October 16, 1898, and spent most of his youth in Yakima, Washington. His father, a Presbyterian minister, died when he was six, and Douglas experienced a childhood of poverty and illness, eventually overcoming infantile paralysis. After serving in World War I, he worked to put himself through school, earning a B.A. from Whitman College in 1920 and a law degree from Columbia in 1925. After practicing law for two years, Douglas taught at Columbia Law School and then at Yale. An academic at the time of the burgeoning legal realist movement, Douglas was influenced by its main precept that the law is malleable and can be used as an instrument for social change. He began his government service pressing for reform on the Securities Exchange Commission in 1936 and served as its head until President Franklin Roosevelt selected him for the U.S. Supreme Court in 1939.

In his early years as a member of the Court, Douglas joined the other Roosevelt appointees in upholding New Deal policies, largely in the area of labor law and business regulation. During World War II, Douglas struggled with his commitment to individual rights and the war effort. In *West Virginia v. Barnette,* 319 U.S. 624 (1943), he reversed his earlier position on the issue and voted to overturn compulsory flag salute and pledge of allegiance laws for public schools. Though he supported individual rights in *Barnette,* he upheld the constitutionality of Japanese-American internment in *Korematsu v. United States,* 323 U.S. 214 (1944) —a decision he vacillated on and ultimately regretted.

Perhaps Douglas's most important and controversial opinion was written for the Court in *Griswold v. Connecticut,* 381 U.S. 479 (1965). In striking down a state prohibition on aiding, abetting, or counseling the use of contraception, Douglas articulated a broad constitutional

Justice William O. Douglas (HARRIS AND EWING, COLLECTION OF THE SUPREME COURT OF THE UNITED STATES)

right to privacy. He held that the "specific guarantees in the Bill of Rights have penumbras, formed by emanations from those guarantees that help give them life and substance." He argued that the various guarantees spelled out in the Constitution, such as the Fourth Amendment's protection against illegal search and seizure, "create zones of privacy." He asked, "would we allow the police to search the sacred precincts of marital bedrooms for telltale signs of the use of contraceptives? The very idea is repulsive to the notions of privacy surrounding the marriage relationship." Critics argued that Douglas had overstepped his constitutional duty in creating a right that is not found in the document. Despite its controversy, *Griswold* remains good law and has been cited as precedent in other controversial opinions. For example, with Douglas in the majority, the Court declared in *Roe v. Wade,* 410 U.S. 113 (1973), that a woman's right to privacy includes the right to have an abortion.

In his later years on the bench, Douglas became more isolated and seemed to lose interest in the work of the Court. He married four times, traveled the world, championed environmental causes, wrote for popular audiences, and survived an impeachment attempt. At the age of 76 Douglas suffered a debilitating stroke. Though he tried to remain on the bench, he quickly showed that he was not up to the task. Douglas's colleagues formally voted to take away his power, and he retired from the Court eight months after his stroke on November 12, 1975. He died on January 19, 1980, and was buried in Arlington National Cemetery, near the graves of Justices Oliver Wendell Holmes, Jr., Potter Stewart, William J. Brennan, and Thurgood Marshall. His headstone reads, "Private U.S. Army." In his record 36 plus years on the high Court, Douglas proved independent, uncompromising, and controversial.

For more information

Douglas, William O. *The Court Years 1939–1975: The Autobiography of William O. Douglas.* New York: Random House, 1980.

Simon, James F. *Independent Journey: The Life of William O. Douglas.* New York: Harper and Row, 1980.

Urofsky, Melvin I., ed. *The Douglas Letters: Selections from the Private Papers of Justice William O. Douglas.* Bethesda, Md.: Adler and Adler, 1987.

Wasby, Stephen L., ed. *"He Shall Not Pass This Way Again": The Legacy of Justice William O. Douglas.* Pittsburgh, Pa.: University of Pittsburgh Press, 1990.

Artemus Ward
California State University, Chico

Dred Scott v. Sandford　60 U.S. 393 (1857)

is a notorious Supreme Court decision that held that an African-American slave could not sue for his freedom in federal court because he was property and not a citizen. However, in attempting to settle definitively the controversy over slavery in the territories, Chief Justice Roger B. Taney shattered the legislative consensus crafted as a result of the Kansas-Nebraska Act, triggered scathing condemnations and outrage among antislavery forces, and propelled the nation further toward civil war.

In 1846 Dred Scott, a slave, filed suit for his freedom against his owner in a Missouri state court, alleging that, having lived with his former master, an army surgeon, in the free state of Illinois and in Wisconsin Territory, he was legally free under Missouri law. The lower court ruled in Scott's favor, based on several precedents in the state's case law recognizing that slaves in Missouri were entitled to freedom by virtue of prior residence in a free state or territory. However, despite the fact that the established legal principle in Missouri was "once free, always free," the Missouri Supreme Court overturned the lower court decision. Scott, with the backing of white abolitionist supporters, appealed the decision to the United States Supreme Court.

The Court might easily have sidestepped the controversial political issue; an 1851 Supreme Court decision had affirmed that state courts had the power to determine the status of African Americans within their jurisdictions, and the federal merits of the case were questionable. However, Chief Justice Taney, a proslavery jurist from Maryland, was determined that the Court would succeed where the nation's political institutions had failed in resolving unequivocally the national controversy over slavery in the territories.

The Court's decision was handed down on March 6, 1857. Writing for a 7–2 majority, Taney declared that, because Scott was a slave, he was not a citizen of the United States and had no standing to sue in federal court; Scott's suit was therefore dismissed for lack of jurisdiction. Taney asserted that the nation's founders had never envisioned citizenship for African Americans, who he described as "beings of an inferior order" with "no rights which the white man was bound to respect."

Furthermore, the Court's majority affirmed that Scott's status as a slave had not changed as a result of his residency in Illinois and Wisconsin. Because the Fifth Amendment prohibits Congress from depriving citizens of their property without due process of law, Taney wrote, slaves could be taken into any territory, free or otherwise, without affecting their legal status as private property. Therefore, Taney determined that Congress had exceeded its constitutional authority in the Missouri Compromise of 1820 when it had prohibited slavery in part of the territories, and that act was accordingly declared invalid.

Despite the fact that the Missouri Compromise had been repealed by the Kansas-Nebraska Act in 1854, the sectional compromise had enjoyed widespread support in the North for decades, and the Supreme Court's decision was widely denounced and condemned in the media, Congress, and the abolitionist movement as a proslavery conspiracy to extend the "peculiar institution" nationwide. Although popular among proslavery forces in the South, Taney's decision undermined the authority and prestige of the Supreme Court, shattered any possibility of peaceful compromise between pro- and anti-slavery interests, and spurred the growth of the new Republican Party. It would ultimately take the Civil War and the passage of the Thirteenth and Fourteenth Amendments to overturn the effects of the *Dred Scott* decision.

For more information

Ehrlich, Walter. *They Have No Rights: Dred Scott's Struggle for Freedom.* Westport, Conn.: Greenwood Publishing, 1979.

Fehrenbacher, Don Edward. *Slavery, Law, and Politics: The Dred Scott Case in Historical Perspective.* New York: Oxford University Press, 1981.

Potter, David M. *The Impending Crisis, 1848–1861.* New York: HarperCollins, 1976.

William D. Baker
Arkansas School for Mathematics and Science

driving under the influence   or DUI is a criminal offense resulting from operating or having actual physical control of a vehicle while impaired by alcohol or drugs. All states and most countries have enacted laws prohibiting such individuals from operating vehicles on public roadways. Driving is considered a privilege, not a right. Driving privileges can be revoked or suspended for violating the DUI law.

A person is considered to be "under the influence" when their normal faculties are impaired by alcohol or drugs. Most states have established "per se" blood-alcohol limits. These are predetermined amounts of alcohol, which result in a presumption of intoxication. The majority of the states have set the blood-alcohol limit at .10 with the remaining states at .08. Some states impose substantially lower or even "zero-tolerance" limits for drivers under age 21.

A properly executed DUI stop and arrest should follow three steps. Step one is the initial observance. In order to stop a vehicle, police must first have a valid reason. Being involved in an accident, committing a traffic violation, encountering a stationary DUI roadblock, or exhibiting other erratic driving patterns are all valid reasons for the initial stop. Step two requires the police to establish probable cause (a reasonable person could find evidence showing that more likely than not the accused is under the influence). This determination is made after the field sobriety testing. Field tests are structured, formal psychophysical tasks that test the driver's balance, coordination, judgment and decision making, and ability to process information. Testing actually begins at the initial contact with the driver. The driver's manner of speech, demeanor, and ability to respond to questioning will be observed. The officer will look for other clues such as bloodshot or watery eyes, flushed complexion, and odor of alcohol. Commonly used tests are alphabet recital, finger counting, walk and turn, one-leg stand, finger to nose, horizontal gaze nystagmus (following pencil with eyes), and preliminary breath testing by a hand-held device.

If the officer believes that the evidence obtained during steps one and two amounts to probable cause, step three, arrest, will take place. Once in custody, the driver will be transported to the police station to take the intoxilyzer test. If the driver's test results are lower than the statutory threshold, the driver could be released without charges. Refusal to take the test can result in suspension of driving privileges by the Department of Motor Vehicles. By statute, the period of suspension for a refusal is longer than a suspension that would be imposed pursuant to a hearing. At the time of arrest, the officer will take physical possession of the driver's license and issue a temporary license. This license is valid for a short period, usually 10 to 15 days. It is up to the driver to request an administrative hearing with the Department of Motor Vehicles. This process is totally separate from the criminal proceeding but is just as crucial. If the driver fails to request a hearing or is unsuccessful at the hearing, it will result in revocation of driving privileges for the prescribed statutory period.

Regardless of the outcome of the administrative hearing, the driver will still face criminal charges in a court of law. The state will again have to show probable cause to believe the driver was operating or in actual physical control of a vehicle. Failure to do so will result in suppression of the field tests, without which the state cannot prove its case. Even after the probable cause burden is met, the state will have to prove guilt beyond a reasonable doubt before the accused can be convicted.

Penalties for DUI vary according to the laws of the state. In general, a first offense conviction may involve a fine, license suspension or restriction, alcohol counseling or treatment, attendance at a DUI education course, and probation. A short period of incarceration may be imposed by law. Second and subsequent offenses will nearly always result in a period of incarceration and may also require community service and involve greatly enhanced penalties. Many states also have first offender's programs requiring longer, more extensive terms of probation. In exchange, the offender avoids a conviction on the record and is not subject to fines.

For more information

Drunk Driving Defense, 5th ed. New York: Aspen Law and Business, 1995.

DUI Fact Book: Drinking and Driving Can Tear Your Life Apart. Collingdale, Pa.: Diane Publishing Company, 1993.

Loretta M. Young
Family Court of State of Delaware

due process   is the short form of the phrase "due process of law," which has two primary conceptual referents in American constitutional law: "procedural due process" and "substantive due process."

These legal concepts become operative in American constitutional law when the Supreme Court, lesser federal courts, and state courts are required to interpret the due process clause within the Fourteenth Amendment of the Constitution, which applies to states, and the due process clause within the Fifth Amendment, which applies to the national government. At the core of both due process clauses is the principle that "No person . . . shall be deprived of life, liberty, and property, without due process of law."

The primary objectives of procedural due process are to assure fair procedure when government imposes significant burdens on individuals, to limit arbitrary government, to force government to give adequate notice to citizens about criminal charges against them or burdens placed upon them so they can reply to such charges and other burdens, and to ensure that similar principles, rules, and procedures are applied to all individuals faced by similar charges and burdens.

The concept of procedural due process comes from the English Magna Carta (1215), a document through which nobles sought to limit the arbitrary use of the king's authority. It has become an important component of the English common-law tradition as the role of English government in the lives of citizens has expanded.

Procedural due process in U.S. law first took shape as an element of criminal law. As a part of the Fifth Amendment, it is mentioned alongside prohibitions on double jeopardy and forced testimony of a suspect and the requirements that the government provide a grand jury in criminal cases and compensate citizens for taking their property. Although rules of procedural due process in criminal law center on providing fair procedures, their application can affect the outcome of cases.

Procedural due process also has an economic component; government must allow a hearing if it takes a citizen's property. For most of the nation's history, this was strictly defined as applying to the government's taking of traditional forms of property, such as land, under common law. The rise of the welfare state raised questions about whether government benefits, such as welfare, were "new property," which also should not be denied with the protection of rules of procedural due process. In *Goldberg v. Kelly* (1970) the Supreme Court held that welfare benefits were property and recipients were entitled to a hearing concerning the termination of benefits. In *Cleveland Board of Education v. Loudermill* (1985) the Court held that a requirement in a public employee's contract that he could only be fired "for cause" entitled him to a hearing before being fired.

More controversial than procedural due process is the concept of substantive due process. Procedural due process simply requires that the government follow proper procedures when it charges a person with a crime or places important burdens on citizens; substantive due process allows the Supreme Court and lesser courts to define substantively what constitutes a deprivation of life, liberty, and property and to place limitations on government when the Court has identified such deprivations.

The Supreme Court's first important invocation of substantive due process was in *Lochner v. New York* (1908) when it struck down a New York state law that established limits on the working hours of bakery workers. The Court said that New York's limitation on working hours was a denial of the freedom of both employer and employee to make a contract for the labor of employees, and that a denial of the right to contract was a deprivation of liberty that is not permitted by the Fourteenth Amendment due process clause. Thus, the Supreme Court application of the concept of substantive due process permitted the Court to define what liberty meant and use that definition as a limit on the government power to regulate working conditions. In what was to be called the *Lochner* period, 1908 to 1937, the Supreme Court made substantive readings of "life, liberty, and property" in order to strike down a wide range of social and economic regulations and government programs, many of which the government established to first meet the negative social and economic effects of industrialization and later to turn the nation away from the economic depression of the 1930s. However, it must be noted that during the *Lochner* era the Supreme Court allowed many government programs to exist as health and safety measures. It also defined liberty in ways that established the right of parents to send their children to private schools and study in languages of their choice.

The concept of substantive due process was revived in the 1960s, when the Supreme Court established that to deprive citizens of the right of privacy constituted a deprivation of liberty, which is not permitted under the due process clauses. In *Griswold v. Connecticut* (1964) the Court found that to deny married couples the use of contraceptives was to deny them such a right to privacy. In *Eisenstadt v. Baird* the Court extended this protection to include the use of contraceptives between unmarried couples.

In the 1970s the Court moved into considerably more controversial territory as it considered the constitutionality of governmental limitations on abortion choice. In 1973, in *Roe v. Wade,* the Court held that the right of privacy included a right to abortion that the state could not interfere with during the first two trimesters of pregnancy. This case created an incredible backlash, propelling abortion into the political spotlight. Presidents Reagan and Bush appointed several antiabortion choice Supreme Court justices with the hope of overturning *Roe.* They were not successful, and in 1992 the Court upheld the right of abortion choice in *Planned Parenthood of Southeastern Pa. v. Casey.*

The application of the concept of substantive due process continues to raise controversial social questions, including the right to die, and the rights of sexual intimacy and marriage for homosexuals. In *Bowers v. Hardwick* (1986) the Supreme Court rejected a substantive due process claim that bans on homosexual intimacy violated the right of privacy and thus protected liberty interests. In *Bowers,* a five-to-four decision, the Court was divided sharply and very nearly went the other way. In *Romer v. Evans* (1992), though an equal protection case, the Supreme Court struck down a law that discriminated against homosexuals. Justice Scalia, who was in the majority in the *Bowers* decision, argued in dissent that the *Romer* decision calls *Bowers* into question because pure animus by the majority against homosexuals is permitted in Bowers but specifically outlawed in *Romer.*

For more information

Graber, Mark A. *Rethinking Abortion: Equal Choice, the Constitution, and Reproductive Politics.* Princeton, N.J.: Princeton University Press, 1996.

Kens, Paul. *Lochner v. New York.* Lawrence: University Press of Kansas, 1999.

Sunstein, Cass. *One Case at a Time: Judicial Minimalism on the Supreme Court.* Cambridge, Mass.: Harvard University Press, 1999.

Ronald Kahn
Oberlin College

Duncan v. Louisiana   (391 U.S. 145, 1968) was a case decided by the United States Supreme Court in 1968 that imposed on states a requirement to provide jury trials for all defendants charged with serious crimes.

The case involved a young African-American man accused of assaulting a young white man during a dispute. Gary Duncan, a 19-year-old African American, was driving through Plaquemines Parish, Louisiana, in 1966 and saw two of his cousins in a heated discussion with several young white men. Because racial tensions were high in Plaquemines Parish in 1966, Gary decided to pull over and offer his cousins a ride. As he was encouraging his cousins to get into his car, there was some exchange of words between Gary and one of the white men, during which Gary apparently touched or "slapped" the arm of one of the white boys. Three days later, Gary Duncan was arrested on the charge of cruelty to minors.

Before he could be tried on that relatively minor charge, he was rearrested after the parents of the white man swore an affidavit charging him with assault. This second charge was much more serious, carrying a maximum penalty of two years in prison. Because of the severity of the possible sentence, Gary Duncan, through his lawyer, requested that his case be heard by a jury rather than by a single judge. That request was denied, and Duncan was convicted and sentenced to 60 days in prison and a $150 fine.

Believing that the original arrest had been racial harassment and that the denial of a jury trial had violated his rights, Duncan appealed to the Supreme Court of Louisiana. That court denied his appeal and upheld the conviction.

The next step was to appeal to the Supreme Court of the United States. The claim made by Duncan was that the Sixth Amendment required jury trials in any case where the maximum penalty was six months or more in jail. Duncan and his lawyer argued that the right to trial by jury was the only procedural right that was found in both the body of the Constitution and in the subsequent amendments. It must therefore be, they concluded, so fundamental and essential to a fair trial that it should not be denied by any of the states. The underlying issue was whether the Fourteenth Amendment secures the right to trial by jury in the states.

By a 7–2 majority, the Supreme Court upheld the appeal of Gary Duncan. In doing so, they incorporated the Sixth Amendment right to trial by jury against state power as well as federal power. While a victory for Duncan, the true import of this case is the extension of Sixth Amendment rights to citizens of the states. However, this case also left some important questions unanswered. Declaring that a jury trial was a right in "serious criminal cases," the Supreme Court declines to clarify what was included in that term. The Court also left unanswered the question of unanimity in a 12-man jury hearing "serious criminal cases," leaving some areas of state discretion intact for the moment and subject to future litigation.

For more information

Foster, James, and Susan Lesson. *Constitutional Law: Cases in Context.* Upper Saddle River, N.J.: Prentice Hall, 1998.

Stephens, Otis H. Jr., and John M. Scheb II. *American Civil Liberties.* St. Paul, Minn.: West Publishing Co., 1999.

David A. May
Eastern Washington University

E

Eisenstadt v. Baird   405 U.S. 438 (1972) is an important Supreme Court decision that reversed William Baird's conviction for distributing a contraceptive.

Eisenstadt v. Baird bridges the Court's privacy decision in *Griswold v. Connecticut,* 381 U.S. 479 (1965), with its controversial landmark abortion rights decision, *Roe v. Wade,* 410 U.S. 113 (1973). Although concerned with contraception—like *Griswold*—*dictum* (a nonbinding statement made in the course of rendering a decision) in Justice William J. Brennan's plurality opinion in *Eisenstadt v. Baird* broadened the right of privacy in ways that paved the way for *Roe.*

Prominent birth control advocate William Baird was arrested, first for exhibiting contraceptive articles in the course of delivering a lecture on contraception to a group of students at Boston University and, second, for giving a young woman a package of Emko vaginal foam at the close of his talk. He was convicted of violating a Massachusetts statute that provides a maximum five-year term of imprisonment for "whoever . . . gives away . . . any drug, medicine, instrument or article whatever for the prevention of conception. . . ." except "[a] registered physician may administer to or prescribe for any married person drugs or articles intended for the prevention of pregnancy or conception." The Massachusetts Supreme Judicial Court unanimously set aside the conviction for exhibiting contraceptives on the ground that it violated Baird's First Amendment rights, but by a 4–3 vote sustained the conviction for giving away the foam. Baird filed a petition for a federal writ of habeas corpus, which the District Court dismissed. On appeal, however, the Court of Appeals for the First Circuit vacated the dismissal and remanded the action with directions to grant the writ discharging Baird. Eisenstadt, the sheriff of Suffolk County, Massachusetts, appealed to the U.S. Supreme Court.

Eisenstadt v. Baird was decided by a 6–1 vote. Justices Powell and Rehnquist did not participate. Chief Justice Burger dissented. Of the six justices voting to affirm the First Circuit Court of Appeals, two (White and Blackmun) argued that Baird's conviction could not stand because, under *Griswold,* Baird had a constitutionally protected right to distribute contraceptives to married persons and, "nothing has been placed in the [trial] record to indicate [the recipient's]

139

marital Status," thereby depriving "us of knowing whether Baird was in fact convicted for making a constitutionally protected distribution of Emko to a married person."

Three justices (Douglas, Marshall, and Stewart) joined Justice Brennan's opinion. Justice Brennan held that Baird's conviction violated the Fourteenth Amendment equal protection clause because there exists no "ground of difference that rationally explains the different treatment accorded married and unmarried persons under Massachusetts General Laws . . . [and] whatever the rights of the individual to access to contraceptives may be, the rights must be the same for the unmarried and the married alike." Having resolved the constitutional status of the Massachusetts law, Justice Brennan added:

> If under *Griswold* the distribution of contraceptives to married persons cannot be prohibited, a ban on distribution to unmarried persons would be equally impermissible. It is true that in *Griswold* the right of privacy in question inhered in the marital relationship. Yet the marital couple is not an independent entity with a mind and heart of its own, but an association of two individuals each with a separate intellectual and emotional makeup. If the right of privacy means anything, it is the right of the individual, married or single, to be free from unwarranted governmental intrusion into matters so fundamentally affecting a person as the decision whether to bear or beget a child.

Brennan's expansive reading of *Griswold* as bearing on the decision "whether to bear . . . a child" opened the door for the argument in *Roe v. Wade* that women—married or unmarried—had a constitutional right to choose an abortion.

For more information

Goldstein, Leslie Friedman. *Contemporary Cases in Women's Rights*. Madison: University of Wisconsin Press, 1994, chap. 1.

James C. Foster
Department of Political Science
Oregon State University

Ellsworth, Oliver (1745–1807) served as a state judge, representative to the Second Continental Congress, the Constitutional Convention, senator, ambassador, and third Chief Justice of the United States Supreme Court. He was born in Windsor, Connecticut, on April 29, 1745. Graduating from the College of New Jersey (later Princeton University) in 1766, he soon began "reading the law." In 1771 he commenced legal practice in Windsor.

His career developed with a number of legal and political appointments. While serving as state attorney of Hartford County he was chosen in 1777 to represent Connecticut in the Second Continental Congress.

Beginning in May of 1787 Ellsworth served at the Constitutional Convention in Philadelphia. His service is best remembered for coauthoring (with Roger Sherman) the Connecticut Compromise, which resolved conflicts between the small and large states over representation in the two houses of Congress. Ellsworth also contributed the term "United States" to the new Constitution.

In 1789 Ellsworth became one of Connecticut's first two U.S. senators. As chair of the Rules Committee he helped to formulate the new Senate's rules. He also chaired the conference committee, which drafted the Bill of Rights, and he was the principal author of the Judiciary Act of 1789 (1 *Statutes* 73) creating the organizational structure of the federal court system.

On March 4, 1796, President George Washington appointed Ellsworth to the U.S. Supreme Court. His very limited service was solid. With only partial success, he persuaded members of the Court to issue a single *per curiam* decision for a case rather than *seriatim* decisions (i.e., individual members of the court each issuing an opinion). In 1796 Ellsworth issued a decision in the case of *United States v. La Vengeance* (3 Dallas 297) that outlined and increased the boundaries of federal admiralty jurisdiction.

Chief Justice Oliver Ellsworth (ENGRAVED AFTER A POR-TRAIT BY CHAPPELL, COLLECTION OF THE SUPREME COURT OF THE UNITED STATES)

The Ellsworth Court also ruled that its appellate jurisdiction must be prescribed through statutory elaboration by Congress. This view of the Court's appellate jurisdiction arose in a case involving the issue of whether an equity degree should come to the Court by a writ of error or a writ of appeal. Ellsworth reasoned that a writ of appeal is a process of civil law origin and removes a cause entirely, subjecting the facts as well as the law to review and retrial. A writ of error on the other hand is a process of common-law origin, and it removes nothing for reexamination but the law, *Wiscart v. Dauchy,* 3 Dallas 321 (1796).

In 1799 Ellsworth was sent on an ambassadorial mission to stop French privateering of U.S. shipping. While in France his health failed. He resigned his chief justiceship on October 16, 1800, and returned home. He died at Windsor, November 26, 1807.

For more information

Brown, William Garrott. *Life of Oliver Ellsworth.* New York: Da Capo Press, 1970.

Casto, William R. *The Supreme Court in the Early Republic: The Chief Justiceships of John Jay and Oliver Ellsworth.* Columbia: University of South Carolina Press, 1995.

A. J. L. Waskey
Dalton State College

Emancipation Proclamation   declared "forever free" slaves residing in the rebellious Confederate States. In the short term, because the Confederacy was at war with the Union in 1862, the Emancipation Proclamation liberated no one. Its immediate significance was that it served as Abraham Lincoln's adroit tactical response to threatening political pressures being exerted on him from domestic and foreign sources. There actually are two Emancipation Proclamations, Lincoln's more well-known announcement made on September 22, 1862, and his proclamation implementing that preliminary declaration on New Year's Day, 1863.

In 1862 circumstances were dire for both the Union cause and Lincoln's presidency. The Federal Army could find neither military leadership nor battlefield victory. Abroad, European governments were growing impatient with the Union blockade of Southern ports and increasingly inclined to bestow diplomatic recognition on the Confederacy. At home, George B. McClellan, one of Lincoln's own generals, was positioning himself eventually to run against the president in the 1864 election. Constitutionally, Lincoln was hemmed in by the fugitive slave clause (Article IV, section 2), which required federal officials to return runaways, and *Dred Scott v. Sanford,* 19 Howard 393 (1857), where seven Supreme Court Justices had declared, among other inflammatory

Proclamation of Emancipation (Library of Congress)

things, that Congress had no constitutional authority to ban slavery in the territories, which it had done in the 1820 Missouri Compromise. Never one to be deterred from his transcendent goal of preserving the Union—either by the letter of constitutional provisions, or a Supreme Court with which he disagreed—Lincoln chafed to seize the initiative back from his various opponents.

The vehicle he drafted to serve this purpose reflected practical, policy, and philosophical considerations. As a practical matter, Lincoln needed to make a bold move to placate abolitionists complaining that he was soft on the issue of slavery, and to outflank potential electoral opponents like McClellan who were agitating for concessions with the Confederacy. Tenuous foreign relations with England and France required Lincoln to fashion a policy that would provide these wavering nations with a reason for not allying with the Confederacy. Philosophically, Lincoln was torn. On the one hand, he was a long-time opponent of extension of slavery into the territories—a position rooted in his embrace of the "freedom national" doctrine that liberty is the universal human condition, slavery an aberration. On the other hand, Lincoln was deeply skeptical about blacks' capacities and about the ability of freed slaves and whites to live together in a single nation.

His proclamation, drafted in secret in July 1862, began by citing his constitutional authority as "commander-in-chief of the army and navy" and by reaffirming his conviction that the "object" of the Civil War was "practically restoring the constitutional relation between the United States and each of the States." Lincoln then threw down a symbolic gauntlet. By January 1, 1863, "all persons held as slaves within any State . . . the people whereof shall then be in rebellion against the United States, shall be then, thenceforward, and forever free. . . ." Between July and September, Lincoln waited impatiently for an occasion to make his proclamation public. When Union and Confederate forces fought each other to a bloody draw at Antietam Creek, Lincoln declared victory and issued his proclamation. In one grand gesture, Lincoln converted the Civil War from a brutal fratricidal feud into a high moral crusade.

In the short run, the Emancipation Proclamation's effect was largely symbolic because it freed no slaves immediately. It did serve Lincoln's purposes of placating critics at home and undercutting potential enemies abroad. In the longer term, the Emancipation Proclamation galvanized Northerners to persevere until victory was won and, after Appomattox, it laid the groundwork for the 1865 Thirteenth Amendment to the Constitution which declares that "[n]either slavery nor involuntary servitude . . . shall exist within the United States."

For more information

Belz, Herman. *Emancipation and Equal Rights: Politics and Constitutionalism in the Civil War Era.* New York: W.W. Norton, 1978.

Wiecek, William M. *The Sources of Anti-Slavery Constitutionalism in America, 1760–1848.* Ithaca, N.Y.: Cornell University Press, 1977.

James C. Foster
Department of Political Science
Oregon State University

embezzlement is the misappropriation, misapplication, or illegal disposal of legally entrusted property by the person charged with preserving the property with the intent to defraud the owner or the intended beneficiary.

The Supreme Court defines embezzlement in *Moore v. U.S.*, 160 U.S. 268 (1895), as the fraudulent appropriation of property by a person to whom such property has been entrusted, or into whose hands it has lawfully come. Embezzlement is distinguished from other crimes, such as larceny, because the original taking of property was lawful and generally included the consent of the owner, whereas larceny requires a simultaneous felonious intent at the moment of property seizure.

Generally, the person charged with embezzlement has originally obtained the property because he or she holds some official position, as agent, fiduciary, officer, or clerk, in connection with the bailment, or employment with some legal entity, such as a bank, financial institution or government agency, or municipal office, associated with the transaction.

The original state and federal statutes carefully carved out the differences between an indictment charging embezzlement and those depicting other acts of theft or fraudulent misappropriation. In cases cited from historical English courts, the statutes limited the offense to certain officers, clerks, agents, or servants of individuals or corporations, as part of an agency or fiduciary relationship. The property must be specifically identified, and the accused must have received the property as part of a fiduciary capacity and subsequently chose to "convert" or abscond with the identified property for a personal use not expressly or impliedly contemplated in any instrument, agreement, or statement designating or charging the duties, powers, and responsibilities of the accused. The fiduciary relationship creates a position of trust that subsumes the notions of confidentiality, trustworthiness, duties not to commingle with personal assets, and finally, accountability to the principal or true owner of the property.

For more information

Cressey, Donald Ray, *Other People's Money: A Study in the Social Psychology of Embezzlement.* Belmont, Calif.: Wadsworth Pub. Co., 1971.

Williams, Howard E. *Investigating White-Collar Crime: Embezzlement and Financial Fraud.* Springfield, Ill.: Charles C Thomas, 1997.

J. David Golub
Touro College

eminent domain   is the power of the government to take a person's property for public use, even over the objection of the owner.

All variety of governments claim this authority. The power of eminent domain allows for a variety of government projects designed to improve the quality of life for the public generally. For example, the government may need to take someone's property in order to make way for a road to ease traffic congestion, or a farm may have to be flooded in order to build a dam to generate electricity or to create a lake for public recreation. In these situations, the government uses its power of eminent domain to take possession of the property.

Eminent domain gives the government considerable authority to interfere with individuals' property rights. In the United States, this power is constrained by the takings clause, that section of the Fifth Amendment to the U.S. Constitution that declares "nor shall private property be taken for public use, without just compensation." The takings clause requires the government to pay for the property it takes. In *Armstrong v. U.S.* (1960) Justice Black summarized the purpose of the takings clause as assuring that no individual is forced to bear the cost of government projects "which in all fairness and justice, should be borne by the public as a whole." Since the whole community benefits from public projects, it is only fair that the whole community (rather than the individual property owner) pay for them.

The government does not have to come into possession of an owner's property but must merely have deprived him of the ability to use it, in order to have effected a taking. This issue arose in the case *U.S. v. Causby* (1946). The Causby family ran a small chicken farm. When the air corps built a training field next to their house and began flying planes over their property, the Causbys became upset and had difficulty sleeping through the noisy flights. Many of the chickens died from fear, and the productivity of the others decreased, as a result of low flying aircraft. The government argued that it should not have to pay compensation because it had not physically occupied the farm. The Supreme

Court disagreed, arguing that "it is the owner's loss, not the taker's gain, which is the measure of the property taken."

When the government does exercise the power of eminent domain, it is required to pay compensation equivalent to the fair market value of the property. Owners do not always accept that the price offered is sufficient to compensate them for their loss. In such cases, owners may seek arbitration or file suit seeking greater compensation. Owners may then refuse to surrender the property until some compromise has been reached. This can slow the progress of public projects, but it is considered necessary to protect property rights.

Eminent domain is supposed to be exercised for public purposes, not merely for the benefit of a private individual or group. In *Cole v. LaGrange* (1884) the Supreme Court held that property may not be taken "for any but a public object." Owners have objected to government projects that seem designed to benefit private parties. Even so, courts have recently tended to defer to legislative judgments about public purpose. For example, in *Hawaii Housing Authority v. Midkiff* (1984) the Court upheld a state program that transferred property from large landowners to a significant number of private people who had been leasing the land. The Court ruled that breaking up the oligopoly controlling most Hawaiian land was a sufficiently public purpose, even though private individuals would benefit. The power of eminent domain thus gives the government considerable latitude to take property so long as it is willing to pay compensation.

For more information

Epstein, Lee, and Thomas Walker. *Constitutional Law for a Changing America*, 3rd ed. Washington, D.C.: CQ Press, 1998.

Shannon Ishiyama Smithey
Department of Political Science
University of Pittsburgh

Employment Division, Department of Human Resources of Oregon v. Smith

494 U.S. 872 (1990) marked an abrupt shift away from nearly three decades of the Supreme Court's settled position on First Amendment free exercise law, prompting political debate over how government regulates individual religious freedom.

Two Native Americans, Alfred Smith and Galen Black, were members of the Native American Church, whose religious sacraments required ingesting peyote (a hallucinogen produced from cactus plants), a controlled substance in Oregon. Smith and Black were fired from their jobs with a private drug rehabilitation organization and applied for unemployment compensation, but Oregon's Employment Division denied them benefits based on work-related "misconduct." Bringing suit in state court, Smith and Black argued that states could not withhold unemployment benefits because of an individual's religious exercise. Oregon responded that the use of peyote was criminalized by a general statute that incidentally affected religious practices, not by a law enacted specifically to burden religion. Oregon's Supreme Court ruled that the state law violated the First Amendment's free exercise clause, and Oregon appealed to the Supreme Court.

The Court held that Oregon could deny unemployment benefits to Smith and Black for their use of a controlled substance. Writing for the majority, Justice Antonin Scalia ruled that their free exercise claim was invalid because Oregon's criminal law was not specifically intended to infringe upon religious free exercise. The statute was a "valid and neutral law of general applicability" that only incidentally had the effect of burdening free exercise.

Until *Smith,* the Court's settled standard for free exercise claims had been its most rigorous: Laws burdening a person's free exercise of religion must be narrowly tailored to further a "compelling governmental interest." In *Smith* the Court replaced this high threshold that a state had to meet if it burdened an individual's free exercise—the "compelling interest" standard—with a much lower threshold of "neutrality" and "general applicability" that the Court explicitly had abandoned years before.

As a result of this abrupt shift in the Court's interpretation of the free exercise clause, *Smith* catalyzed the mobilization of diverse interest groups concerned with protecting free expression and the free exercise of religious beliefs and practices. These groups lobbied for federal legislation incorporating the "compelling interest" standard for free exercise claims used by the Court prior to *Smith*. Congress listened, enacting the 1993 Religious Freedom Restoration Act (RFRA). The RFRA borrowed the Court's pre-*Smith* language, requiring that laws passed at the state or federal level that burdened an individual's religious exercise meet the "compelling interest" standard. Although the RFRA was intended to return to the pre-*Smith* standard, it gave rise to many more questions than it answered, particularly from states concerned that it unduly burdened the legislative process.

In *City of Boerne, Texas v. Flores,* 521 U.S. 507 (1997), the Supreme Court struck down the RFRA, holding that Congress had overstepped its legitimate lawmaking role by broadening constitutional rights that already had been interpreted by the Court. (A ruling of the Supreme Court can be explicitly overturned only by constitutional amendment.) The Court thus breathed new life into *Smith*'s guidelines for balancing the role of government against individuals' exercise of religious beliefs. However, the Court still has not fully resolved the appropriate standard for free exercise disputes, suggesting the inevitability of future political conflicts over the role of religion.

For more information

Choper, Jesse. *Securing Religious Liberty.* 1995.

Epps, Garrett. *To An Unknown God: The Hidden History of* Employment Division v. Smith. *Arizona State Law Journal* 30 (1998): 953.

Dr. Steven A. Light
University of North Dakota

employment law   is the set of legal rules, other than labor law, that govern the workplace. Employment law differs from labor law in that it regulates the individual employer-employee relationship while labor law regulates the collective rights and obligations resulting from union representation.

Until the 1960s, the employment relationship largely was free from governmental regulation in the nonunion setting. The employment law of today, in contrast, consists of a complex web of federal and state regulation. With no single law governing the employment relationship, a major employment law issue concerns the need to accommodate the sometimes overlapping federal and state laws.

The at-will rule long has served as the principal legal foundation for the employment relationship. In the absence of some contractual understanding to the contrary, the at-will rule gives both employers and employees the right to terminate their relationship without cause or notice. Put another way, an employer may discharge an employee under the at-will rule for any or no reason.

While the at-will rule still survives, it is now subject to a number of exceptions. The principal limitation is provided by antidiscrimination statutes. Three federal statutes ban discrimination in employment based upon certain employee characteristics. Title VII of the 1964 Civil Rights Act prohibits discrimination in hiring or firing on the basis of race, color, religion, sex, or national origin. The Age Discrimination in Employment Act, adopted in 1967, protects employees over the age of 40 years from discrimination in hiring, discharge, and mandatory retirement. Finally, the Americans with Disabilities Act, enacted in 1990, prohibits employers from discriminating against an otherwise qualified disabled person who, with or without a reasonable accommodation, is capable of performing the essential functions of the job.

State courts also recognize certain common-law limitations on an employer's right to terminate an employee. Most states, for example, permit a discharged employee to recover tort damages if he or she is discharged for a reason that offends notions of public policy, such as for refusing to commit an illegal act or for exercising a right conferred by statute. A smaller number of states recognize a covenant of good faith and fair dealing, which prohibits bad faith terminations that frustrate legitimate contractual expectations.

Beyond those laws limiting an employer's discharge right, a number of other federal employment laws regulate the terms and conditions of the employment relationship. These include the following:

Occupational Safety and Health (OSH) Act. The OSH Act authorizes the secretary of labor to adopt workplace health and safety standards. The secretary is empowered to enforce these standards through workplace inspections and by issuing citations for noncompliance.

Employee Retirement Income Security Act (ERISA). ERISA regulates pension and employee welfare benefit plans. It establishes procedural requirements with respect to the reporting, disclosure, and fiduciary responsibilities for such plans and broadly preempts state laws relating to employee benefits.

Worker Adjustment and Retraining Notification (WARN) Act. The WARN Act requires employers with 100 or more employees to provide at least 60 days advance written notice to employees who will suffer an employment loss by virtue of a plant closing or a mass layoff.

Family and Medical Leave Act (FMLA). The FMLA requires employers with 50 or more employees to permit employees to take up to 12 weeks each year of unpaid leave in order to care for a new child or a family member with a serious health condition. The FMLA's leave entitlement also extends to an employee who is incapacitated because of his or her own serious health condition.

Various state statutes provide further regulation of the employment relationship. These include the following:

Unemployment compensation statutes. Every state has a law providing for short-term benefit payments following an involuntary termination of employment that is not the result of misconduct. An employee generally must be actively seeking suitable reemployment in order to qualify for these benefits.

Drug testing statutes. A number of states have statutes that specify the circumstances in which employers may test applicants and employees for the illegal use of drugs.

Whistleblowing statutes. Many states also protect employees from retaliatory acts if they report employer wrongdoing to governmental authorities.

The number of employment law claims has risen substantially over the past 20 years. Employment law disputes now make up approximately 20 percent of the cases on federal court dockets.

For more information

Befort, Stephen F., and Karen G. Schanfield. *Employment Law and Practice* St. Paul, Minn.: West Publishing Co., 1995, 1999–2000 Supp.

Rothstein, Mark A. Charles B. Craver, Elinon P. Schroeder, and Elaine W. Shoben. *Employment Law,* 2nd ed. St. Paul, Minn.: West Publishing Co., 1999.

Professor Stephen F. Befort
University of Minnesota Law School

Engel v. Vitale   370 U.S. 421 (1962) prohibited public school–sponsored prayer. The case concerned a prayer that read, "Almighty God, we acknowledge our dependence upon Thee, and we beg Thy blessings upon us, our parents, our teachers and our Country." Engel sought to overturn a lower court ruling that found the prayer constitutional, arguing that any prayer supported by the state violated the establishment clause of the First Amendment. Engel was represented by William J. Butler and supported by the American Civil Liberties Union and a number of Jewish groups. Vitale sought to uphold the lower court, arguing that the statute was constitutional because it was not coercive and did not spend state funds. Vitale was represented by Wilford E. Neier and Porter R. Chandler and supported by the Board of Regents of the State of New York and 20 state attorneys general. The case was argued in the Supreme Court on April 3, 1962, and decided on June 25. In a 6–1 decision, Justice Black, writing for the Court, ruled in favor of Engel, finding the prayer unconstitutional. Justice Douglas concurred, Justice Stewart dissented, and Justices Frankfurter and White did not take part in the decision.

The constitutionality of the prayer considered in *Engel v. Vitale* depended on the justices' understanding of the establishment clause of the First Amendment, which reads, "Congress shall make no law considering an Establishment of religion." Two separate traditions make very different statements about the establishment clause. One tradition, drawing on the writings of Thomas Jefferson and James Madison, urges strict separation of church and state. The other tradition takes the clause to mean only that the state cannot establish an official religion.

Justice Black's majority opinion finally embraced the tradition of separation. The footnotes in his decision include references to the writings of Jefferson and Madison. Black's opinion is long on history and perhaps a bit short on legal precedent. Black emphasizes the repression of religious minorities by majorities and the role that this fact played in the founding. Black rejects the claim that prohibitions on school prayer constitute a hostility to religion. He argues that the separation of church and state preserves the dignity of religion and the autonomy of religion from state interference.

Justice Stewart took a very different view of the establishment clause. He argued that the clause merely prohibited the state from establishing an official religion. In his dissent, he emphasizes that the prayer is not coercive and is nondenominational. Stewart dismisses Black's detailed historical inquiry as irrelevant and argues that the Constitution mentions no "wall of separation." He also argues that many government institutions, including the Supreme Court and Congress, open their days with prayer, and that the Pledge of Allegiance and National Anthem both mention God.

Engel v. Vitale set a strong precedent against the constitutionality of prayer in schools. Allowing the student to be excused at the request of the student or the student's parents did not constitute proof that the prayer was not coercive. The Court also established that even though prayer may be a part of the country's cultural heritage, it is also essentially spiritual. It is the first decision of many on the controversial issue of school prayer, which continues to be important as a political issue today, as schools seek to have prayers at football games and graduations. The Court reaffirmed the no coercion principle of *Engel* in 1992 in *Lee v. Weisman,* when it refused to permit prayer at graduation, and in 2000, in *Sante Fe Independent School District v. Doe,* in which it refused to allow a school board policy that authorized students to vote, first, whether to allow religious invocations at football games, and then to choose the person to deliver them. Thus, *Engel v. Vitale* has served as a foundation for many other cases, including school prayer, state support to religion, and accommodation of religious practices.

For more information

Fraser, James W. *Between Church and State: Religion and Public Education in a Multicultural America.* New York: St. Martin's Press, 1999.

Ravitch, Frank S. *School Prayer and Discrimination: The Civil Rights of Religious Minorities and Dissenters.* Boston: Northeastern University Press, 1999.

Ronald Kahn
Oberlin College

entrapment   is a defense that may be raised by a person charged with having engaged in criminal activity. By raising the defense of entrapment, the defendant is claiming that he or she was enticed by the police into engaging in unlawful activity, and that absent that enticement, he or she would not have committed the crime.

Specifically, the defendant who raises a defense of entrapment is claiming that the criminal activity was conceived of and planned by a police officer, and that without the officer's enticement, he or she would not have committed the crime. The defense of entrapment was first recognized in state courts but was later defined by the United States Supreme Court in *Sorrells v. United States,* 287 U.S. 435 (1932).

"The defense of entrapment has been asserted in the context of a wide variety of criminal activity, including prostitution, alcohol offenses, counterfeiting, price controlling, and probably most spectacularly, bribery of public officials." (Wayne R. LaFave, Jerold H. Israel, and Nancy J. King, *Criminal Procedure,* vol. 2, section 5.1(c), 401 [2nd ed., West Criminal Practice Series, 1999].) The majority of cases in which a defense of entrapment is raised involve charges relating to drug offenses. (*Ibid.,* at 401–402.)

The use of enticement by law enforcement as a method of detecting criminal activity arose out of the difficulty in ferreting out crimes that are "committed privately between individuals who are willing participants." (*Ibid.,* at section 5.1, 399.) Thus, in addition to other routine methods of detecting criminal activity as methods of exposing consensual criminal activity, "law enforcement officers resort to the use of encouragement. *Encouragement* is a word used to describe the activity of a police officer or agent '(a) who acts as a victim; (b) who intends, by his actions, to encourage the suspect to commit a crime; (c) who actually communicates this encouragement to the suspect; and (d) who thereby has some influence upon the commission of the crime.'" (*Ibid.,* at section 5.1(a), 400

[quoting L. Tiffany, D. McIntyre, and D. Rotenberg, *Detection of Crime* 210 (1967)].)

The United States Supreme Court, in *Sorrells,* defined entrapment as "the conception and planning of an offense by an officer, and its procurement by one who would not have perpetrated it except for the trickery, persuasion, or fraud of the officer." (Wayne R. LaFave, Jerold H. Israel, and Nancy J. King, *Criminal Procedure,* vol. 2, section 5.1(b), 401 [2nd ed., West Criminal Practice Series, 1999] [quoting *Sorrells v. United States,* 287 U.S. 435 (1932)].)

In the evaluation of a defendant's ability to successfully raise the defense of entrapment, two tests have emerged. In the federal courts, a subjective approach has been adopted. Under the subjective approach, the court will assess (1) "whether or not the offense was induced by a government agent" and (2) "whether or not the defendant was predisposed to commit the type of offense charged." (Wayne R. LaFave, Jerold H. Israel, and Nancy J. King, *Criminal Procedure,* vol. 2, section 5.2(a), 407 408 [2nd ed., West Criminal Practice Series, 1999].) Two-thirds of the state courts have adopted the subjective approach (*Ibid.,* at 407).

The second approach, the objective approach, "focuses upon the inducements used by the government agents" (*Ibid.,* at section 5.2(b), 411). The rationale underlying the objective approach is that even if the defendant's guilt is established, certain tactics used by the government to induce the commission of the crime are unacceptable (*Ibid.,* at 413).

Myra Orlen
Western New England College of Law

environmental law   is a complex collection of federal and state statutes and regulations, and common-law principles, which seek to control the impacts of human beings and their activities on the natural environment and natural resources. These laws seek to control the deterioration of the environment by (1) the overuse or depletion of natural resources, such as land, water, and biodiversity, and (2) pollution, such as air and water pollution, and waste production and disposal.

Prior to 1970, the vast majority of environmental litigation was based on common law. Injured parties utilized tort law causes of action, such as nuisance, trespass, strict liability, and negligence to halt environmental degradation and for compensation for environmental injuries. However, tort-based environmental litigation was difficult to initiate because plaintiffs often had difficulty proving who caused their injuries. Even when injured parties could overcome these obstacles, courts were often reluctant to grant injunctions to prevent future environmental harm.

The federal government responded to these common-law problems, and inadequate and inconsistent state and local government environmental laws and ordinances, in the 1970s. While common-law remedies are still available, and state and local government enactments serve an increasingly important role, the most important and effective environmental laws are federal statutes.

Federal environmental statutes usually begin as comprehensive laws designed to remedy an entire environmental problem. These enactments are often followed by a set of amendments that ultimately address manageable aspects of the problem. This pattern defines a key feature of federal environmental laws—complex layers of detailed statutes.

Federal environmental statutes can be grouped into three categories: broad policy statutes, ecological and natural resource conservation statutes, and public health statutes. The National Environmental Policy Act is the most famous broad policy statute. It requires the federal government to consider the environmental consequences of its actions when it plans major projects.

Ecological and natural resource conservation statutes conserve these resources on public and private lands. The Endangered Species Act requires the federal government to safeguard endangered and threatened species on its lands and requires private landowners to protect these species on their lands. The National Forest Management Act specifies how the U.S. Forest Service manages National Forests, and the Wilderness Act dictates the management of wilderness areas.

Congress has enacted scores of statutes to protect the public health, including the Clean Air Act (CAA), the Clean Water Act (CWA), the Resource Conservation and Recovery Act (RCRA), and the Comprehensive Environmental Response, Compensation, and Liability Act (CERCLA). The CAA and CWA use complex regulatory mechanisms to control air and water pollution. RCRA provides for the "cradle-to-grave" regulation of hazardous materials. CERCLA, also known as Superfund, is designed to clean up hazardous waste disposal sites.

While the complexity of environmental law often makes compliance costly, these laws have improved U.S. environmental quality. However, as scientists increasingly demonstrate that many environmental problems are global, rather than national, humanity needs international environmental laws that address these issues.

For more information

Chapman, Stephen. *Environmental Law and Policy.* Upper Saddle River, N.J.: Prentice Hall, 1998.

Kubasek, Nancy, and Gary Silverman. *Environmental Law,* 3rd ed. Upper Saddle River, N.J.: Prentice Hall, 2000.

Robert W. Malmsheimer
SUNY College of
Environmental Science and Forestry
Syracuse, New York

Environmental Protection Agency is a federal independent regulatory agency responsible for the enforcement of numerous federal laws designed to protect the environment. Throughout the 1960s, Americans became increasingly concerned about harm to the quality of the natural environment. Private interest groups formed for the purpose of protecting the environment and began to pressure government to enact laws to do so. In 1970 Congress finally created the Environmental Protection Agency (EPA).

The act combined 15 different agencies and parts of agencies from throughout the federal government to consolidate a variety of research, monitoring, standard setting, and enforcement activities relating to pollution control and abatement. EPA's primary role is to establish and enforce standards for air, soil, and water quality, monitor and analyze the environment, conduct research, and support and coordinate research and antipollution activities carried out by state and local governments, private and public groups, individuals, and among other federal agencies with respect to the impact of their activities on the environment. The EPA is authorized to research possible and known environmental pollutants, adopt regulations limiting the levels of those pollutants, and enforce those regulations through monitoring, legal sanctions, and cleanup supervision.

The EPA at first was given authority only over air and water quality. However, throughout the 1970s and 1980s the EPA was given authority to enforce many more major federal environmental statutes. The EPA now has the primary responsibility for overseeing the implementation of major federal environmental laws such as the Clean Water Act; the Safe Drinking Water Act; the Clean Air Act; the Resource Conservation and Recovery Act; and the Comprehensive Environmental Response, Compensation, and Liability Act (Superfund). The agency now has more than 18,000 employees, and its annual budget is now more than $7 billion and is likely to steadily increase in future years.

The EPA has been responsible for numerous achievements during its relatively short life span. Among the major accomplishments have been a ban on the use of the toxic pesticide DDT, the elimination of lead from gasoline, improved automobile gas mileage efficiency while reducing automobile emissions, a ban on the use of chlorofluorocarbons (CFCs) responsible for ozone destruction, the cleanup of countless toxic waste dumps under the Superfund program, a ban on the dumping of sewage sludge into oceans and coastal waters, substantially improved water and air quality nationwide (especially in areas that were highly polluted beforehand), and the encouragement of widespread recycling programs.

Despite its history of successes, the EPA has been criticized, often severely, by both liberals and conservatives. Liberals argue that the agency is not doing enough to protect the environment, and that the EPA's focus on specific health risks from measurable pollution levels often ignores other equally or more important threats to the environment, such as ecosystem destruction. Liberals also charge the EPA with ignoring issues of environmental justice, such as the problem of hazardous waste sites often being located in poor or minority communities. Conservatives, on the other hand, accuse the EPA of imposing harsh and costly regulations on businesses, when the same goal of pollution reduction could be achieved by giving businesses flexibility in choosing the means by which pollution is decreased. Conservatives also attack the agency's calculations regarding unsafe levels of pollutants as being overly restrictive and not based on sound scientific evidence.

Regardless of whether criticisms from either end of the ideological spectrum are valid, public concern over the environment is likely going to remain high on the political agenda. Issues such as global warming, acid rain, depletion of the ozone layer, the destruction of rain forests and other ecosystems, and the extinction of endangered plant and animal species globally have all shown the need for regional and international solutions to environmental problems. Such problems cannot be solved merely by calculating, for example, the risk of cancer from exposure to a chemical and then restricting the use of that chemical to a safe level. Thus, public pressure will continue for Congress to enact additional environmental laws to address these problems more effectively. Given its tradition of having the primary enforcement responsibility for other major federal environmental laws, the EPA will most likely be involved with the implementation of these future environmental laws as well.

For more information

Landy, Marc K., Marc J. Roberts, and Stephen R. Thomas. *The Environmental Protection Agency: Asking the Wrong Questions.* New York: Oxford University Press, 1990.

Ortney, Paul R., Katherine N. Probst, and Adam M. Finkel. "The EPA at 'Thirtysomething,'" *Northwestern School of Law of Lewis and Clark College Journal of Environmental Law* 21, no. 1461 (1991).

Kristin L. Stewart, J.D.
Rick A. Swanson, University of Kentucky

The Equal Pay Act   is a federal law aimed at eliminating pay discrimination based upon sex. Passed in 1963, it was the first major federal legal measure attempting to remedy the wage differential between men and women. The act requires that employers pay the same wage to men and women workers doing "equal" work. Essentially, equal work requires "equal skill, effort and responsibility, and which are performed under similar working conditions." The courts have interpreted this to mean that jobs should be "substantially identical," though they may have different titles, such as janitor and maid, or nurse's aide and orderly. The act provides employers with four defenses for wages that are not equal—seniority, merit, differences in quantity or quality of production, or any other factor not related to gender.

The act was intended to prevent paying women less than men in the same job classification, and it did confront the most blatant instances of sex discrimination in regard to pay. Still, a sizable wage gap prevails; in 1999 women continued to receive about 20 percent lower pay than men for comparable work. Economists have not been able to account for this gap, even after examining a wide range of productivity-related characteristics that determine wages (e.g., differences in education and training, job tenure, absenteeism, and hours of work). Much of that gap reflects the fact that women tend to work in female-dominated occupations that are lower paying. But even when these occupations involve the same skill, effort, responsibility, and working conditions as the male-dominated jobs, they tend to pay less than the male-dominated jobs.

Part of the problem may be that the act does not include differences in the rate of pay among different jobs, and this may create more subtle forms of wage discrimination in which changes in job description are used to mask sex discrimination and the resulting pay gap. This has given rise to policies of equal pay for work of equal value or "comparable worth." Comparable worth generally requires that male-dominated and female-dominated jobs within the same establishment receive equal pay for work of equal value. The value of a job is determined by gender-neutral, objective procedures like job evaluation.

The Equal Employment Opportunity Commission (EEOC), a federal agency, is charged with enforcing the Act.

For more information

Lindgren, J. Ralph, and Nadine Taub, *The Law of Sex Discrimination,* 2nd ed. New York: West Publishing Co., 1993.

Ashlyn K. Kuersten
Western Michigan University

equal protection of the laws   by state and local governments is guaranteed to all persons within the jurisdiction of the United States by the Fourteenth Amendment. The federal government must also provide equal protection under the Fifth Amendment though that amendment does not explicitly say so, according to the Supreme Court decision in *Bolling v. Sharpe,* 347 U.S. 497 (1954). The equal protection clause guarantees the right of "similarly situated" people to be treated the same by the law. For example, people who commit the same crimes should have similar punishments, and people who have the same qualifications should have an equal chance at government jobs. The equal protection clause also guarantees equal citizenship rights, such as equal treatment in voting, running for office, serving on juries, and bringing cases to court.

The equal protection clause was added to the Constitution as one of the post–Civil War amendments. At first, the Supreme Court interpreted the equal protection clause primarily as a way to protect freed slaves from unfair state laws that did not allow African Americans to vote or serve on juries. The clause was used against state officials who refused legal protection when former slave owners tried to bind former slaves to oppressive employment or land contracts, or when Ku Klux Klansmen and marauding bands threatened African-American lives and homes. In *Plessy v. Ferguson,* 163 U.S. 537 (1896), however, the Supreme Court took a step back from racial equality when it held that separate public accommodations, such as separate seating for black and white travelers, were constitutional so long as they were equal. Eroded by several court cases in the 1940s and early 1950s, this "separate but equal" doctrine was finally overruled in *Brown v. Board of Education,* 349 U.S. 294 (1954), and the Civil Rights Act of 1965 eliminated other "separate but equal" public programs.

By the 1960s, the equal protection clause began to be applied more often to protect citizens against all arbitrary laws, not just those based on race. It has played an important role in outlawing racial and gender discrimination and providing limited protections for lawful aliens, the mentally disabled, gays and lesbians, and other groups. For example, Supreme Court rulings outlawing segregated schools and state practices that discouraged black people from voting, such as literacy requirements and a poll tax, are based on the equal protection clause. Similarly, laws that gave males better Social Security protection for their families, benefits in the armed services, and the right to support from their parents have been struck down as equal protection violations. Some fundamental rights have also been protected under the equal protection clause, such as the right of poor people to a lawyer to help in appealing a court decision, and to travel from state to state without losing welfare benefits.

In reviewing most laws under the equal protection clause, the Supreme Court only asks whether the legislation is rational, or whether it is arbitrary or invidious. Laws passed just because of legislators' desire to harm an unpopular group, such as homosexuals or "hippies," or laws that reflect fears that have no basis in fact violate this "rational basis" test. For laws classifying by race or national origin, and most state laws harming legal aliens, the Court has used the "strict scrutiny" test, which requires that the state show that its reason for the law is "compelling" and that it has "narrowly tailored" the law not to disadvantage any more people than necessary to meet its goals. Gender-based laws are viewed with "intermediate" scrutiny, which has been used to strike down laws that allowed females but not males to purchase 3.2 percent beer, that gave divorcing women but not men alimony, and that made spouses of working women but not men prove dependency in order to get Social Security benefits.

For more information

"Equal Protection." In *The Oxford Companion to the Supreme Court of the United States* 257. New York: Oxford University Press, 1992.

Redlich, Norman, John Attanasio, and Joel K. Goldstein. *Understanding Constitutional Law.* New York: Matthew Bender, 1999, pp. 247–356.

Marie Failinger
Hamline University

Equal Rights Amendment   was first introduced in Congress in 1923 and was reintroduced
at every subsequent session of Congress but never
passed. After passage of the Nineteenth Amendment (in 1920) that gave women the right to vote,
the Equal Rights Amendment (ERA) was an
attempt to give women more equality in the workplace. The ERA read: *Men and women shall have
equal rights throughout the U.S. and in every place
subject to its jurisdiction. Congress shall have power
to enforce this article by appropriate legislation.*

An amendment to the U.S. Constitution may
be proposed by two-thirds vote of both houses of
Congress but must then be ratified by three-
fourths of the state legislatures. Therefore, 38
states (three-fourths of 50) are required for ratification of any amendment. In 1972 the ERA
passed both houses of Congress and was then
sent to the states for ratification. Within a year, 30
states ratified it. Yet by the 10-year deadline set by
Congress (1982) only 35 states had ratified.

Questions continue as to why the amendment
stayed three states short of total ratification. A
majority of those who supported giving women
the right to vote opposed the ERA; they considered it a threat to the interests of poor mothers
and full-time homemakers. Spearheaded by Phyl-
lis Schlafly and her organization, Stop ERA,
which benefited from the conservative backlash
that gained momentum in the mid-1970s, supporters and opponents alike certainly did perpetuate this argument. Supporters tended to be
professional career women with few or no children; opponents tended not to work outside the
home and identified themselves as housewives.
Nonetheless, despite its defeat, public support
for the amendment never fell below 54 percent,
and both political parties included it in their
platforms until 1976.

For more information

Stetson, Dorothy McBride. *Women's Rights in the
U.S.A.: Policy Debates and Gender Roles,* 2nd ed.
New York: Garland Publishing, 1997.

Ashlyn K. Kuersten
Western Michigan University

equitable remedies   are used by courts when
an award of money damages will not sufficiently
aid a plaintiff harmed by the legally wrongful
conduct of a defendant. Also, equitable remedies
are used in cases where the law does not allow
successful plaintiffs to be compensated monetar-
ily. In this sense, equitable remedies are a supplement to common-law remedies, providing
relief to plaintiffs for whom financial compensation will not adequately offset the harm done by
a plaintiff.

Our legal tradition embraces a preference for
common-law remedies, i.e., awards of money
damages, as a way of redressing private or civil
wrongs. Plaintiffs that have suffered losses due
to the tortious actions of another or as a result
of a breach of contract typically seek an award of
money as a way to "make themselves whole
again." Common-law remedies include compensatory, punitive, nominal, and liquidated forms
of money damages.

Compensatory damages are awarded to plaintiffs in order to offset financial losses caused by
the defendant's breach of a duty or failure to perform contractual obligations. When creating a
contract, parties may predetermine the sum of
money to be paid in the event of a breach.
Referred to as liquidated damages, this sum is
paid to the non-breaching party if the other party
fails to perform obligations created by the contractual agreement. Sometimes, when it is found
that a defendant has knowingly or maliciously
harmed the interests of the plaintiff, courts award
punitive damages in addition to compensatory
damages. Punitive damages are not awarded in
cases of negligence but may be awarded in cases
involving intentional torts. Nominal damages
may be awarded to plaintiffs whose rights have
been infringed but who are unable to demonstrate the existence of actual financial losses
resulting from the defendant's behavior.

Before awarding common-law remedies,
courts must identify the existence of a legal duty
owed to the plaintiff, determine that the defendant has breached that duty, and then assign a

dollar value to be paid to the plaintiff by the defendant in recognition of the violation of that duty. In the U.S. courts, juries often participate both in determining whether a legal duty has been violated and in the process of identifying the amount of money damages to be awarded to a successful plaintiff.

By contrast, equitable remedies are fashioned by courts only. Juries consider neither the facts nor the proper remedy to be applied in suits at equity; the law of equity is applied entirely by a judge or magistrate. This method of equity proceeding is rooted deep in the history of Anglo-American law. Although the English common-law system attained maturity in the 13th century, it was not until the 15th century that a structure of equity courts was fully in place. Equitable remedies were initially the prerogative of the chancellor, an official in the English clergy trained not in the legal rules that guided the common-law system but steeped in the law of the Roman Catholic Church. As an increasing number of disputes were referred to the chancellor, the Court of Chancery was developed. The masters in chancery, as they were called, resolved disputes by applying principles of morality and right. Whereas common-law remedies could be awarded only where the courts or Parliament had previously recognized the existence of a right, equitable remedies could be extended to plaintiffs in cases that were factually unique. Moreover, in deciding cases the early equity courts were not bound by precedent or the strict rules that guided the decisions of common-law courts. Thus, the law of equity provided remedies to plaintiffs for whom the rigidities of the common law precluded relief.

English settlement brought the common-law tradition and the doctrines of equity to North America. The tenets of English common law and equity influenced the development of judicial systems and legal practice in the early settlements. Although law and equity remained functionally distinct systems during much of the first 300 years of American history, by the early 20th century most states provided for one court system in which both common law and equity suits were resolved. In 1938 law and equity were fully merged in the federal courts. Today, U.S. courts routinely award combinations of common-law and equitable remedies in resolving a single dispute between litigants. Doing so requires that courts are able to employ the rules of procedure unique to equity at one moment, and, at another moment, observe the rules of common-law actions. Arguably, this procedural flexibility explains the durable nature of the legal system in the United States.

Today, various types of injunctions, the order of specific performance, and the remedies of reformation and rescission comprise the standard forms of equitable relief. Injunctions are court orders requiring a defendant to either stop or start taking some particular action. Specific performance, reformation, and rescission are equitable remedies used in disputes arising out of contractual relationships. When money damages are an unsuitable way of compensating a party harmed by another's breach of a contractual agreement, courts sitting in their equity jurisdiction may issue an order of specific performance—a demand that the breaching party perform the obligations that form the substance of the contract. Plaintiffs often seek the remedy of rescission when wishing to affect the cancellation of a contract because of fraud or deceit on the part of the defendant in making the contract. The remedy of rescission is also applicable in cases where a party entered into a contractual agreement under duress or after relying on another party's innocent, though false, misrepresentation of important facts. If a court grants a request for rescission, each party to the contract must return to the other anything of legal value that was exchanged in the partial or full performance of the agreement. A plaintiff may seek the remedy of reformation in instances where the terms of a contract do not express the exact nature of the agreement between the parties or when key provisions of a contract are written in ambiguous language. When ordering the reformation of a contract, courts redraft the terms of a contract to more accurately reflect the intentions of the parties.

A subtle feature of the relationship between the common law and equity is that the latter is sometimes employed to prevent a use of the common law that would be contrary to a sense of fairness. Litigants may seek an equitable remedy in order to prevent the use of the common law as a vehicle for achieving an unjust result. Herein lies the kernel of equity remedies; equitable remedies do not replace common-law remedies. but exist alongside the common law and, at times, are used to achieve just and fair applications of the common law.

For more information

Plucknett, Theodore F. *A Concise History of the Common Law.* Boston: Little, Brown, 1956.

Potter, Harold. *Historical Introduction to English Law and Its Institutions.* London: Sweet and Maxwell Ltd., 1958.

Bradley J. Best
Austin Peay State University

equity   deals with cases involving individuals and hardships that the law (common or statutory) is unable to remedy. It developed in England, after the Norman Conquest, to mitigate the rigidities of the common-law courts. In that day the king's courts of law had developed highly technical rules, forms, and procedures for bringing cases to court. If an aggrieved person's case did not fit the forms, they would very likely be denied their day in court. Consequently, appeals for justice (equity) made to the king were eventually heard in separate courts of chancery.

The Constitution of the United States (Article III, section 2, clause 1) continued English practice saying, "The judicial power shall extend to all cases, in law and equity, arising under this Constitution. . . ." Alexander Hamilton, *Federalist Papers #80* (et al.), discussed extensively the power of the courts to decide cases of equity. He argued the right to decide cases of equity was needed because people unwittingly enter contracts, with no fraudulent intent, which if enforced upon the original terms would create an injustice.

In the 19th century most states had separate courts of chancery that dealt only with equitable relief. Other states provided some way for equity cases to be handled. Until 1938 federal district courts had two separate sides of "law" and "equity." Today, in U.S. law, it is almost the universal practice to have the same courts that can issue a legal remedy be able to prescribe an equitable one. Efficiency is an important advantage of this merger of the administration of law and equity.

Equity follows the law. It provides a special set of remedies and associated procedures which aim to establish substantive justice or fairness. Equitable relief from some harm is generally only available when a legal remedy is insufficient or inadequate in some way. For instance, an injunction might be issued to prevent an irreparable harm from taking place, such as the demolition of a home by a wrecking crew accidentally at the wrong address.

Other matters for which an individual might seek relief are accountings of money matters and rescission of documents. Remedies, besides an injunction, include specific performance, reformation, contribution, and estoppel. Specific performance is an order to parties to a contract to perform the specifics of a contract. Reformation is an action the court may take when a written agreement does not clearly express the real agreement between the parties. Contribution may be used to distribute loss in a situation. Estoppel is used in contracts to prevent one of the parties from denying certain facts. Trust law conflicts generate many cases of equity. Equity easily may be thought of as the conscience of the law.

For more information

Hill, Myron G., Howard M. Rosen, and Wilton S. Sogg. *Remedies: Equity—Damages—Restitution for Law*

School and Bar Examinations. St. Paul, Minn.: West Publishing Co., 1974.

McClintock, Henry Lacy. *Handbook of the Principles of Equity.* St. Paul, Minn.: West Publishing Co., 1948.

A. J. L. Waskey
Dalton State College

ERISA or the Employee Retirement Income Security Act of 1974 is the primary federal law concerning employee benefits.

Congress passed this legislation in 1974 in order to regulate management of retirement funds. Employers who engage in interstate commerce and provide defined benefit or welfare plans to employees must abide by ERISA requirements. ERISA covers every "employee pension benefit plan" and "employee welfare benefit plan." An employee pension benefit plan is any plan which provides for retirement income for employees. An employee welfare plan is any plan which provides for benefits such as medical, sickness, accident, vacation, and disability for employees and their dependents.

ERISA requires that employers with pension plans provide both the U.S. Labor Department and employees with detailed descriptions of benefits they are to receive once they become eligible. Regulations of the department outline which employees must receive a pension if they are so offered and requires that a percentage of the retirement benefits become vested in the employees after they have worked for a given number of years, reached a given age, or both. ERISA also requires that pension plans pay benefits to survivors of deceased employees. The legislation also requires employers to adequately fund their programs and establishes fiduciary responsibilities that must be followed. The Pension Benefit Guaranty Corporation insures defined benefit plans. Employers must pay premiums so that their plans are covered against insolvency by the PBGC. The Pension and Welfare Benefit Administration enforces fiduciary (decisions on

claims), reporting, and disclosure requirements under ERISA. PWBA requires those who manage plans to meet certain standards of conduct and it is authorized to proceed in civil actions to enforce requirements that retirement funds are protected and that eligible participants receive benefits. Congress has authorized tax breaks to employers who follow the guidelines under the Internal Revenue Code in order to encourage employers to follow pension plan regulations.

Regulations concerning employee welfare benefit plans are also extensive. For example, and importantly, ERISA requires that employees be provided summary plan documents of employee welfare benefit plans. Summary plan documents are intended to summarize the full plan document issued on behalf of the employer and be written in plain language that ordinary persons may understand.

ERISA preempts all state law that relates to employee welfare benefit plans, meaning that ERISA controls the plans, not separate state laws. As a result, ERISA controls the interpretation of funding of benefits such as daycare centers, scholarship funds, apprenticeship or training programs, even prepaid legal services. The purpose behind preemption is that multistate employers may depend upon a consistent interpretation and enforcement of the ERISA, rather than a potentially inconsistent approach among different states. ERISA does not preempt plans such as plans sponsored and funded by government agencies or churches. It also does not preempt workers' compensation or unemployment compensation laws. If an employee welfare benefit plan is an ERISA plan, the administrator may state in the summary plan document that it reserves the right to interpret the meaning of the plan and which beneficiaries are entitled to payment. Federal courts typically defer to the findings of the administrator in such situations. This deference provides considerable advantage to administrators of ERISA plans as opposed to insurers who are subject to actions under state law. While individual participants may file civil actions to seek enforcement of the policy, their chances for success are not high when the administrator is granted deference under the summary plan document. The deference given to administrators to deny or limit medical treatment is one of the many reasons why many consumer groups have advocated in the last several years that Congress pass a "patients' bill of rights."

Other provisions of ERISA include the continuation of employee welfare benefit plans after an employee ceases employment with the employer that provided the plan. Congress required under the consolidated Omnibus Budget and Reconciliation Act of 1986 that employers provide what is commonly known as "COBRA" coverage for a period of 18 months following the end of employment, though at cost to the employee. That legislation also eliminated the ability of employers to limit participation in their retirement plans for new employees who are close to retirement and the ability to freeze benefits for participants over age 65. In 1996 Congress required that such coverage be able to be transferred from one plan to another (essentially one employer to another) under the Health Insurance Portability and Accountability Act. Congress also amended ERISA to generally require that benefit levels for mental disorders be the same as that for physical disorders. It also recently increased the rights of women who seek medical treatment for breast cancer or who are pregnant.

In addition, self-funded ERISA plans (ones in which all operations are funded by employers rather than premiums paid to traditional insurance companies) may under certain circumstances be able to recover amounts paid for benefits when the beneficiary recovers from a third party, such as personal injury actions, workers' compensation claims, or similar actions.

For more information

29 U.S.C. Sections 1001 et seq. Employee Retirement Income Security Act of 1974.

29 CFR Parts 2500 et seq. Pension and Welfare Benefits Administration.

29 CFR Parts 4000 et seq. Pension Benefit Guaranty Corporation.

29 U.S.C. Sections 401 et seq. Tax Considerations.

Patrick J. Platter
Daniel, Clampett, Powell and Cunningham
Springfield, Missouri

Escobedo v. United States　378 U.S. 478 (1964) was a Supreme Court decision that guaranteed accused criminals the right to have an attorney present when the police question them. Specifically, *Escobedo* involves the Sixth Amendment issue of the right to be represented by counsel, and it indirectly involves the Fifth Amendment privilege against self-incrimination.

Escobedo was accused of murdering his brother-in-law and was brought to the police station for questioning. His attorney arrived a short time later and requested that he be allowed to consult with Escobedo. However, the officers in charge, including the chief, did not allow him to do so. During the interrogation, Escobedo admitted to knowledge of the murder and also made statements to the police that implicated himself in the crime. Before, and during, the trial Escobedo tried to have the incriminating statements thrown out of court because he had made them without his attorney present. His requests were denied, and he was ultimately convicted of the murder. After losing in the Illinois Supreme Court, Escobedo appealed to the Supreme Court of the United States, asking that his statements be declared inadmissible at trial.

In a 5–4 decision the Supreme Court ruled that Escobedo's statements, made outside the presence of his attorney, should not be admissible in court. As a result, this case set the precedent that nobody accused of a crime may be interrogated without an attorney, if one has been requested. In making its decision, the Supreme Court made two key arguments about why the accused should have the right to counsel during police interrogations.

First, the Court noted that many confessions are obtained during police interrogations, which suggests that there is a critical need for legal advice at this stage of the process. If attorneys were only guaranteed at trial, and not before, the Court argued that they would be useless because most confessions would already be obtained. This would then make it virtually impossible for the defendant to win once the trial begins.

Second, the justices made a distinction between the investigation of an unsolved crime and the point at which a suspect is accused of committing the crime. That is, when the police focus on one suspect, when they interrogate that suspect, and when the suspect requests to see an attorney, it is a violation of that suspect's Sixth Amendment rights to be denied the right to meet with an attorney. The justices concluded that the Constitution guarantees the accused the right to be advised of his or her right against self-incrimination by an attorney prior to, and during, a police interrogation.

Escobedo is the precursor to another criminal rights case—*Miranda v. Arizona,* where the Court ruled that the police must advise the accused of the right to meet with an attorney during an interrogation. Together, these cases are two of the most important criminal rights cases decided by the Supreme Court. Indeed, *Escobedo* guarantees the right to have counsel present, and *Miranda* set out the framework for enforcing the previous decision.

For more information

Epstein, Lee, and Walker, Thomas. *Constitutional Law for a Changing America: Rights, Liberties, and Justice.* Washington, D.C.: Congressional Quarterly Press, 1998.

Medalie, Richard J. *From Escobedo to Miranda.* Washington, D.C.: Lerner Law Books, 1966.

Timothy R. Johnson
University of Minnesota

establishment clause is in the First Amendment to the Constitution, which was ratified by the states in 1791 as part of the Bill of Rights, the first 10 amendments to the Constitution. The establishment clause reads, "Congress shall make no law respecting an establishment of religion." The establishment clause was developed largely through the efforts of Thomas Jefferson and James Madison, and the philosophy of it is eloquently laid out in the latter's "Memorial and Remonstrance." The establishment clause was their response to the question of whether government should be permitted to establish an official state religion, such as was the case in England with regard to the Anglican Church. Supporters of the establishment clause had three arguments: the establishment of a church by the state corrupted religion, argued by Roger Williams; too much influence on the part of religion can be dangerous to the public interest, argued by Madison; and true religion needs no aid from the state, argued by Jefferson.

For most of the history of the United States, the establishment clause was not a vigorously enforced provision of the Constitution. Prior to the Fourteenth Amendment, the Bill of Rights had been held in *Barron v. Baltimore* (1833) to apply only to the federal government and not to the states. Furthermore, the Protestant religion was simply assumed to be a fact of life and an essential part of American public life. Several factors transformed the establishment clause into the highly contentious issue that it is today. First, the turbulent events in Germany in the 1930s and 1940s affected the whole world, and the United States Supreme Court was no exception. Justice Jackson's service at the Nuremberg trial of Nazi leaders, and Justice Frankfurter's Jewish heritage, among other things, helped bring recognition and increased sensitivity of the importance of pluralism and difference in American society. At the same time, with Justice Black taking the lead, the Court began incorporating the Bill of Rights as part of the definition of liberty in the due process clause of the Fourteenth

Amendment and applying it against intrusion in those liberties by the states.

In 1947 the Supreme Court first applied the establishment clause to the states in *Everson v. Board of Education*. In that case, the Court ruled that parents of both public and Catholic schoolchildren could be reimbursed for the bus fare of students. More importantly, the Court ruled that any issues raised under the establishment clause would have to meet a high standard: The state cannot in any way aid religion, rather it must be neutral between religion and non-religion. In *Everson,* all members of the Court agreed to this high standard. The first statement of the originalist position that the establishment clause meant only that the state may not establish an official church, but could accommodate religion in other ways, came in Justice Potter Stewart's 1962 dissent in *Engel v. Vitale.*

The two most important areas of law under the establishment clause are school prayer and aid to religion. In the area of school prayer the Court has consistently held, from *Engel v. Vitale* to *Lee v. Weisman* (1992), that state-sponsored prayer violates the establishment clause. In the area of educational aid to religion, the Court's rulings are more ambiguous. In the area of released-time programs for religious education, the Court has struck down some, such as in *McCollum v. Board of Education* (1948), which allowed religious instruction in public school classrooms, and upheld others, as in *Zorach v. Clauson* (1952), a program that provided released time in the public school day for students to attend religious classes conducted in non-school buildings. The Court also allowed reimbursement for bus fares for Catholic schoolchildren in *Everson v. Board of Education* in 1947. These indirect forms of aid have survived the courts because they give financial support to parents of schoolchildren directly, not money to schools for religious instruction. For example, in *Mueller v. Allen* (1983), the Supreme Court allowed a Minnesota law which permitted taxpayers to deduct from their gross income taxes the actual expenses for tuition, text-

books, and transportation costs of sending their children to both public and private schools, many of which were sectarian. Most direct aid to primary and secondary religious institutions is not allowed by the Supreme Court. However, in a recent 5–4 decision, *Agostini v. Felton* (1997), the Supreme Court allowed government support for remedial education, guidance, and job counseling by public employees within parochial school buildings to students who reside within the attendance boundaries of a public school located in a low-income area who are failing, or are at risk of failing.

The process of Supreme Court interpretation of the establishment clause, which began in the 1947 *Everson* ruling, culminated in 1971 in *Lemon v. Kurtzman,* when the Supreme Court established the three-pronged *Lemon* test for determining the constitutionality of a law under the establishment clause: For a statute not to be in violation of the establishment clause it must have a secular legislative purpose, its principal or primary effect must be one that neither advances nor inhibits religion, and it must not foster an excessive entanglement of government with religion.

For more information

Kahn, Ronald. *The Supreme Court and Constitutional Theory, 1953–1993.* Lawrence: University Press of Kansas, 1994, chap. 4, "Constituting the Separation of Church and State," pp. 107–138.

Levy, Leonard W. *The Establishment Clause: Religion and the First Amendment.* New York: MacMillan Publishing Co., 1986.

Rosenblum, Nancy L., ed. *Obligations of Citizenship and Demands of Faith.* Princeton, N.J.: Princeton University Press, 2000.

Ronald Kahn
Oberlin College

Ethics in Government Act   is a federal law enacted in 1978 and significantly amended in 1989.

The Ethics in Government Acts of both 1978 and 1989 made major changes in the way in which the federal government regulates the ethical conduct of its elected and appointed officials and employees. The act consists of four main parts: public financial disclosure, conflicts of interest, honoraria and outside income and activities, and post-government employment restrictions.

The public financial disclosure provisions, which apply to certain defined individuals or positions in the executive, legislative, and judicial branches of the federal government, include instruction on what must be reported, how reporting is done, and what the review process is. For example, those covered by the act must report positions they hold as officers, directors, and trustees of certain organizations or institutions.

The conflict of interest laws include definitions of conflicts, such as knowingly and substantially participating in a matter in which the employee has a financial interest; instructions on how to divest oneself of holdings that give rise to a conflict; a process for recusing oneself from participation where a conflict exists; and rules for setting up blind trusts to eliminate the conflict. The restrictions and requirements connected to honoraria and outside income and activity establish specific dollar amounts one may receive, for example, for speaking engagements or as earned income apart from one's federal position.

Finally, there are restrictions on post-government employment of certain elected and appointed officials and employees. These limitations extend from lifetime bans to two-year bans, to a one-year cooling off period. During those periods of time the persons to whom the laws apply may not, for example, represent an organization on a matter in which that person had been substantially involved while working for the U.S. government.

Additionally, the Ethics in Government Act established a process for the appointment of independent counsel charged with investigating alleged criminal conduct by high-level executive branch officials and created the U. S. Office of Government Ethics. Initially located in the Office of Personnel, the Office of Government Ethics later became a federal agency whose responsibilities are to provide guidance, education, regulation, and enforcement.

For more information
Ethics in Government Act and Related Statutes, 5 U.S.C. 101–111; 18 U.S.C. 201–218.
President's Commission on Federal Ethics Law Reform. *To Serve with Honor: Report and Recommendations to the President.* Washington, D.C.: U.S. Government Printing Office, 1989.

Jane Calabria McPeak
Hamline University

Everson v. Board of Education   330 U.S. 1 (1947) first applied the religion clauses of the First Amendment to the states.

The case involved a New Jersey law that allowed local school districts to create their own rules for the transportation of students attending any school, except for students attending private schools operated for profit. Under this law, the Board of Education of the Township of Ewing enacted a resolution that reimbursed parents of public and Catholic schoolchildren for the costs of transportation on the public bus systems. The appellant, Arch Everson, challenged the constitutionality of the resolution, claiming that any use of public funds that affected religion violated the clause of the First Amendment that said that government must not establish religion, known as the establishment clause. Edward R. Burke and E. Hilton Jackson argued Everson's case, supported by the Seventh-Day Adventists, the American Civil Liberties Union, and other groups. The Board of Education argued that the law treated religion and non-religion equally. William H. Speer represented the Ewing School Board, and it was supported by numerous states and some Catholic groups. The case was argued in the Supreme Court on November 20, 1946, and decided on February 10, 1947. In a 5–4 decision,

Justice Black, writing for the Court, ruled in favor of the board, finding that the reimbursement of transportation costs for Catholic as well public school students did not violate the establishment clause. Justice Jackson, joined by Justice Frankfurter, and Justice Rutledge, joined by Justices Frankfurter, Jackson, and Burton, wrote dissenting opinions.

Although Justice Black ruled that the reimbursement did not violate the establishment clause, he set a high standard of judgment in cases involving the establishment clause that would ensure a separation of church and state in most cases. Black outlined the history and theory of the establishment clause from its roots in the thought of James Madison and Thomas Jefferson. He states that not only does the establishment clause prohibit the establishment of a state religion but it also prevents both the federal government and states from aiding religion, coercing worship, discriminating on the basis of creed, and using tax revenues to fund religious institutions. However, Black ruled in favor of the transportation reimbursements in question in *Everson* because, he argued, the state must neither favor nor disfavor religion. The case, he wrote, concerned a law that was neutral between religion and the public sector, treating them equally. Black was a strong advocate of the separation of church and state; *Everson* is one of the few cases in which Black voted to uphold a law favorable to religious institutions.

The dissent in *Everson* agreed with Black that a high standard of state neutrality to religion and non-religion must be established if a law that might conflict with the religion clauses of the First Amendment is to be valid. Like Black, the dissenters invoked the words of Madison and Jefferson. They did not agree with Black, however, that the law in question met that standard. In his dissent, Justice Rutledge argued that any allocation of tax dollars with an effect of promoting religion is unconstitutional. In his dissent, Justice Jackson emphasized that the New Jersey law only provided reimbursement to public and Catholic school students. He argued that by including reimbursement to parents of students attending schools of only one religion and excluding others, the law was impermissibly discriminatory in its effect. Beyond its specific and narrow ruling allowing transportation reimbursement for both public and Catholic schools, *Everson* is important and remains good law, because the case held for the first time that the establishment and free exercise clauses, that is the religion clauses of the First Amendment, are made applicable to the states by the Fourteenth Amendment and set the standard by which the religion clauses are to be interpreted. For most of the history of the country, the guarantees in the Bill of Rights have only been held by the courts to be limits on the federal government. Only in the 1940s did First Amendment guarantees come to be held applicable against actions of the states, and *Everson* is a crucial part of that change.

The *Everson* ruling began the process that would culminate in 1971 in the *Lemon v. Kurtzman* standard: that state financial support for parochial schools violates the establishment clause of the First Amendment unless it can be shown to have a clear secular purpose, the primary effect is not to advance religion, and there is no excessive entanglement between church and state. The *Everson* reimbursement to parents, like later cases involving state reimbursements directly to parents of schoolchildren in all schools, had a secular purpose whose primary effect was not to advance religion but to aid safety, and because the direct payments to parents did not constitute excessive entanglement.

For more information

Fraser, James W. *Between Church and State: Religion and Public Education in a Multicultural America.* New York: St. Martin's Press, 1999.

Rosenblum, Nancy L., ed. *Obligations of Citizenship and Demands of Faith.* Princeton, N.J.: Princeton University Press, 2000.

Ronald Kahn
Oberlin College

evidence is anything that tends to prove or disprove a fact. That is, evidence could take the form of the testimony by a witness, a document, a photograph, a statistic, or any other thing. A thing becomes a piece of evidence once it is offered as proof of a fact. For example, a witness might testify that a traffic light was red to prove that a driver did or did not have the right of way. A will might be entered into evidence to prove the wishes of the deceased. A picture or film might be entered into evidence to prove or disprove that the defendant robbed a bank. An expert witness might testify regarding the market size of a commodity to establish a monopoly position. Generally, in order to be admissible in any legal proceeding, evidence must be relevant, material, and competent.

Evidence is relevant when it logically tends to prove or disprove a fact. That is, there must be a logical nexus between the evidence offered and the fact that the evidence purports to establish. If the evidence is logically probative, it is relevant and admissible unless there is some reason to exclude it. Evidence is material if it tends to prove or disprove a fact which is of some consequence to the outcome of the action. Evidence may prove a fact, but if that fact has no impact on the outcome of the proceeding, the evidence is not material. In short, relevancy goes to the logical nexus between the evidence and the fact, while materiality goes to the logical nexus between the fact and the proceeding.

Evidence is competent if it can be trusted or held up to cross-examination to test its veracity and is not otherwise objectionable. Evidence that can be trusted includes facts that are not in dispute and facts that have been established in an earlier stage of the proceeding.

Evidence that is relevant and material still may be excluded if it is otherwise objectionable. For example, an involuntary confession that was obtained in violation of a suspect's Fifth Amendment constitutional rights against self-incrimination may be relevant and material to the proceeding but excluded because of the constitu-

tional violation. Other ways in which evidence otherwise admissible can be excluded include a violation of some privilege and inherent unreliability. Certain privileges exist such as the attorney-client or accountant-client privileges. In short, a privilege will generally shield evidence from disclosure, except in the case of imminent harm, because of the special nature of the relationship under which the evidence came into existence.

One type of evidence which is inherently unreliable is hearsay evidence. Although there are exceptions, an out-of-court statement, hearsay, is inadmissible to prove the truth of the matter asserted. Because the out-of-court statement would not be made under oath and subject to cross-examination, it is considered inherently unreliable.

Evidence may also be excluded if its probative value is outweighed by a danger of unfair prejudice or confusion to the jury. The danger of unfair prejudice contemplates evidence that is more prejudicial than probative. For example, if a security guard is accused of beating a suspected shoplifter to death, evidence that the security guard had in the past beaten a dog to death might be excluded as more prejudicial than probative. If otherwise admissible evidence will be unduly confusing to a jury, it will be excluded. For example, suppose an action involves a contract written in a foreign language, evidence designed to teach the jury the grammatical structure of the foreign language might be excluded as unduly confusing. Evidence which is overly duplicative or cumulative may also be excluded.

Both federal and state courts have rules of evidence that are similar although not identical.

For more information
Brown, K.S., and W. J. Blakely. *Evidence*. St. Paul, Minn.: Westgroup, 1994.

Waltz, J.R., and R.C. Park. *Cases and Materials on Evidence,* 9th ed. Westbury, N.Y.: Foundation Press, 1999.

Park, R., et al. *Evidence Law: A Student's Guide to the Law of Evidence as Applied to American Trials.*

(Hornbook Series), St. Paul, Minn.: West Publishing Co., 1998.

Charles Anthony Smith
University of California, San Diego

exclusionary rule   refers to a constitutional mandate of the Fourth Amendment that illegally seized evidence cannot be used at a trial to convict someone of a crime.

The Fourth Amendment guarantees the "right of the People to be secure in their persons, houses, papers, and effects, against unreasonable searches and seizures," and that "no Warrants shall issue, but upon probable cause, supported by Oath or affirmation, and particularly describing the place to be searched, and the persons or things to be seized." The purpose of this amendment is to prevent the government or police from randomly stopping and searching people unless there is some reasonable suspicion or belief that they have committed a crime.

Yet despite this Fourth Amendment prohibition, evidence is occasionally seized or obtained and the question is what to do with it. In *Weeks v. United States,* 232 U.S. 383 (1914), the United States Supreme Court developed the exclusionary rule, where it stated that evidence seized in violation of the Fourth Amendment was excluded from use at a trial to convict a defendant. In *Weeks* the Supreme Court explicitly said that the exclusionary rule did not apply to the states. In *Mapp v. Ohio,* 367 U.S. 643 (1961), the Court extended the exclusionary rule to apply to the states, including local governments.

Two arguments are offered in favor of the exclusionary rule. First, the rule protects an individual's right to privacy against unwanted government intrusion or searches. Second, the rule is meant to restrain or prevent the police from engaging in illegal searches. The argument here is that if police know that any evidence they obtain illegally will not be allowed in court, then they will be less likely to violate the Fourth Amendment.

Opponents of the exclusionary rule argue that it is unfair to exclude evidence from court simply because the police made a mistake. It would be wrong to set a criminal free just because of a "legal technicality." In addition, opponents argue that the exclusionary rule does not really restrain the police, that it makes their job more difficult, and as a result many criminals go free.

However, the best evidence suggests that less than 1 percent of all criminal cases have evidence thrown out because of the exclusionary rule. Judges are more likely than not to reject motions to suppress evidence, and, contrary to what critics say and what is depicted in the media, hardly a person accused of a crime is completely set free because of the exclusionary rule, suggesting that the rule may not impede police from doing their job.

Finally, the Supreme Court has made numerous exceptions to the exclusionary rule. For example, no warrant is required if one consents to the search, or to search cars, or to search in public if there is probable cause. No warrant is required if the search is incidental to arrest or if the police need to stop and frisk to search for a weapon. No warrant is required if the evidence is in plain view, or if one is in hot pursuit. No warrant is required for border or routine inventory searches at the police department. Finally, while illegally obtained evidence cannot be used at a trial to convict a defendant, this evidence can be used in grand jury proceedings or at trial to impeach a defendant who testifies.

For more information

Katsh, M. Ethan. *Taking Sides,* 3rd ed. Guilford, Conn.: Dushkin Publishing Group, Inc., 1989.

Walker, Samuel. *Sense and Nonsense about Crime and Drugs: A Policy Guide.* Belmont, Calif.: Wadsworth, 2001.

David Schultz
Hamline University

executive privilege   is the idea that presidents have claimed to shield confidential communications from subordinates against demands by the other branches for its production. Although executive privilege has been often asserted, it has never had the firm constitutional position that its presidential advocates have claimed for it.

Executive privilege is an old doctrine, dating from the first major congressional investigation in 1792, when Congress attempted to investigate the reason for the Indian defeat of an expedition led by General St. Clair. A House committee asked President Washington for all papers and records related to the incident. Although Washington turned over the papers, his cabinet decided, in the words of Secretary of State Thomas Jefferson, that "the Executive ought to communicate such papers as the public good would permit, and ought to refuse those, the disclosure of which would injure the public." Jefferson would invoke executive privilege several years later when he refused to turn over documents that he claimed would show that his former vice president, Aaron Burr, had committed conspiracy against the United States. A decision by Chief Justice John Marshall, sitting as a trial judge in the Burr case, has framed judicial doctrine regarding executive privilege ever since. Marshall found that there is no absolute privilege in criminal cases for communications to which the president is a party and that a court may assess both the need for production of the information and the reasons against its disclosure in a closed examination. Marshall also stated that, if the president refuses to produce material relevant to a criminal case, the court hearing the case may draw inferences in favor of the accused or order that the prosecution be dismissed.

The modern controversy over executive privilege largely dates to early cold war years. President Harry Truman refused to provide documents to the House Un-American Activities Committee investigating allegations of communists in the State Department or to allow testimony by General Omar Bradley regarding their discussions over whether to remove General Douglas MacArthur from his command in Korea. President Dwight D. Eisenhower also invoked executive privilege in response to Senator Joseph McCarthy's investigations into the U.S. Army during the same period.

The most important modern judicial decision regarding executive privilege occurred during the Watergate crisis. In *U.S. v. Nixon* (1974), President Richard Nixon had refused to hand over to the special prosecutor tapes of Oval Office meetings during which Nixon and his advisers had discussed covering up the burglary of Democratic Party headquarters. Nixon's aides, who were facing criminal prosecution, had insisted that the tapes would show that their actions had been authorized by the president. The Supreme Court unanimously decided that the tapes had to be submitted to a judge who would balance the president's interest in confidentiality against his aides' fundamental right to a fair trial through an inspection in chambers.

For more information
Rozell, Mark J. *Executive Privilege: The Dilemma of Secrecy and Democratic Accountability*. Baltimore: Johns Hopkins University Press, 1994.

Daniel Levin
University of Utah

expert testimony   is a crucial component of many criminal and civil trials. This testimony, just like a bloody knife and fingerprints, is considered evidence. Whether or not evidence is admitted at trial can make the difference between winning and losing the case. Both the federal and state courts have rules that determine the admissibility of evidence. Only evidence that assists the jury is allowed to be seen or heard. Judges are responsible for excluding testimony that might confuse, mislead, or prejudice the jury.

One difference between expert and lay witnesses is that experts can testify as to their opinions while laypersons can testify to facts only. Expert witness testimony deals with specialized knowledge beyond the range of an average person's experience. For example, an expert might testify regarding DNA comparisons, economic projections, psychiatric evaluations, or disease causation. There has been an explosion of expert witness testimony in the last two decades due to the increased number of cases that rely on specialized knowledge as evidence. Two good examples are the use of DNA identification in criminal trials and the use of epidemiology and toxicology evidence in toxic tort cases, a type of product liability case. Critics have argued that along with this increase in expert witnesses came a decrease in the standards for expert testimony and some even have accused experts of basing their testimony on so-called junk science.

In the case of *Daubert v. Merrell Dow Pharmaceuticals, Inc.,* 509 U.S. 579 (1993), the United States Supreme Court clarified the standard to be used in deciding admissibility where the expert witness is a scientist. The *Daubert* case was one of more than 1,000 lawsuits alleging that the antinausea drug Bendectin, taken by millions of pregnant women, caused a limb reduction birth defect. Before the *Daubert* ruling, there was inconsistency in the admissibility of expert evidence in the federal and state courts. Approximately two-thirds of American courts applied the older *Frye* test, *Frye v. United States,* 293 F. 1013 (D.C. Cir. 1923), which requires that "novel" scientific opinions offered as evidence must be "generally accepted" by scientists in the relevant field to be admissible. Other courts applied the more liberal Federal Rule of Evidence 702, that "a witness qualified as an expert by knowledge, skill, experience, training, or education" may testify as to their opinion.

Under the *Frye* standard, the judge defers to the opinion of an expert scientific witness as long as the opinion is consistent with conventional scientific wisdom. In *Frye,* the defense wanted to introduce the results of a forerunner of the modern polygraph test that they believed demonstrated the defendant's veracity when he denied killing the victim. The court disallowed the evidence on the basis that the theory and method of the test were not "generally" accepted" by scientists in the relevant fields of psychology and physiology. The introduction of Rule 702 in 1975 left undecided the question of whether *Frye* survived as the standard for specialized testimony. The landmark *Daubert* decision held that federal courts must apply Rule 702, not the *Frye* test, in determining admissibility of scientific evidence. The Supreme Court emphasized the judge's role as "gatekeeper" of scientific evidence testimony, ensuring that "not only relevant, but reliable" testimony be admitted. *Daubert* places the responsibility on the trial judge to determine whether the expert has used sound scientific methodology in arriving at her conclusions and offers guidelines to the judge in his gatekeeping role of excluding unreliable scientific testimony.

The United States Supreme Court decision in *Kumho Tire Co. v. Carmichael,* 119 S. Ct 1167 (1999), extended the *Daubert* holding beyond scientific testimony to include all expert witness testimony. *Daubert, Kumho,* and the *General Electric v. Joiner* opinion, 118 S. Ct. 512 (1997), which held that the trial judge has discretion in deciding whether the studies relied upon by the expert witness are sufficient, form the trilogy of opinions that determine the admissibility of expert testimony in the federal courts. The state courts are free to adopt the federal rules, a modified version, or continue to use the Frye test in determining admissibility of expert witness testimony.

For more information

Faigman, David L. *Legal Alchemy: The Use and Misuse of Science in the Law.* New York: W. H. Freeman, 1999.

Foster, Kenneth R. and Peter W. Huber. *Judging Science: Scientific Knowledge and the Federal Courts.* Cambridge, Mass.: MIT Press, 1999.

Reference Manual on Scientific Evidence. Washington, D.C.: Federal Judicial Center, 2000. Also available at *http://www.fjc.gov.*

Karen Gottlieb, Ph.D., J.D.
BioLaw
Nederland, Colorado

expert witness   refers to an individual who testifies, whether in person or by affidavit, about an ultimate fact at issue or conclusions which can be drawn from other evidence. If scientific, technical, or other specialized knowledge will assist the judge or jury in understanding the evidence or in the determination of a fact, a witness qualified as an expert may testify by giving an opinion. In short, an expert is unlike other witnesses because she can and does give her opinion regarding some aspect of the dispute at hand. Other, nonexpert witnesses are limited to recounting what they have seen, heard, or otherwise experienced.

Experts may testify regarding exceedingly complex phenomena such as DNA evidence or the intellectual property rights to a computer program. Experts also may testify about less complex things such as the cost of used clothing at a yard sale or the price of a commodity on a certain date. Often experts testify regarding hypothetical situations that match or contrast with the issue in dispute. Experts could be engineers, economists, social or natural scientists, doctors, fire marshals, or anyone else with specific detailed knowledge about a discreet topic area. Knowledge, skill, training, or education could be the grounds for asserting that an individual qualifies as an expert.

While the judge must accept the proffered witness as an expert before testimony can be presented to the jury, qualifying as an expert is relatively easy. Often, the parties to litigation will stipulate that the opposing experts meet the "minimal qualifications" necessary to testify. Since experts are subject to cross-examination, few resist any individual being qualified as an expert because the less qualified the opposing expert, the easier the opinion is to impeach. Moreover, cases in which experts are used generally have experts on both sides of the litigation. In such cases, the judge or jury may be persuaded by the more credible expert, or two comparable experts may offset each other with a negligible impact on the proceeding. Importantly, because most experts are paid, usually on an hourly basis, the disclosure of that underlying economic incentive can impact the jury's assessment of the expert's credibility. Many states require disclosure of experts consulted but not retained to avoid litigants simply purchasing the most useful opinion.

In general, the expert may rely on any fact, belief, or premise in order to form an opinion. However, the expert must disclose when asked all that contributed to the formation of the opinion. For example, a doctor on the stand may express an opinion that a certain medical procedure was negligently performed. Whether that expert is a medical doctor or a sports physiologist may impact the credibility of the opinion. Whether the expert has reviewed all medical records in question or only those supplied by the attorney might impact the credibility of the opinion. Indeed, regardless of whether the expert consulted tarot cards, tea leaves, or a psychic hotline friend, any grounds for the opinion must be disclosed. In short, the opinion of the expert is only as good as the foundation upon which that opinion is based.

For more information
Consult Federal Rule of Evidence 702 and the following texts:
Matson, J.V. *Effective Expert Witnessing,* 3rd ed. New York: CRC Press, 1998.
Warren, R.A. *The Effective Expert Witness: Proven Strategies for Successful Court Testimony.* New York: Gaynor Pub., 1996.

Charles Anthony Smith
University of California, San Diego

ex post facto   is Latin for "after the fact"—an ex post facto law is a statute enacted after some previous act or conduct and tries to make it a crime. Ex post facto laws are excluded from the enumerated powers of Congress by Article I, section 9, and likewise explicitly prohibited for the state legislatures by Article I, section 10.

These twin clauses codify the ancient principle of the common law that it is fundamentally unfair to punish a person for having done an act that was not unlawful at the time it was done. They apply only to crimes. But the prohibition on criminal ex post facto laws manifests an underlying mistrust of any retroactive legislation—after-enacted statutes that change the law and then try to make the change apply to past conduct. The contract clause and the bill of attainder clauses in Article I, as well as the due process clauses in the Fifth and Fourteenth Amendments are analogous constitutional provisions on the noncriminal or civil side of the law. The ex post facto clauses apply only to statutes and do not apply to changes in the law affected by judicial decisions.

The ex post facto clauses also prohibit an after-enacted statute that would aggravate an offense and increase the punishment for a crime already committed, beyond the punishment that was on the books at the time of the criminal act. Likewise, an after-enacted statute is unconstitutional if it would remove a defense that would have been available at the time the crime was committed or otherwise would so change the legal rules of evidence and procedure as to subvert the defendant's presumption of innocence.

The ex post facto clauses do not prohibit a legislature from changing the type of penalty within the same category. For example, a state could change the method of execution in a capital crime from electrocution to lethal injection. The clauses do allow a legislature to be more lenient, however, to give a criminal defendant the benefit of a reduction in the punishment after the crime was committed. It also is not a violation of the clauses to impose a punishment on a person who continues a course of unlawful conduct after a legislature enacts a statute to declare it a crime.

"The creation of crimes after the fact, or, in other words the subjecting of men to punishment for things which, when they were done, were breaches of no law," Alexander Hamilton observed in *Federalist Papers number 84*, has had a history of being one of "the favorite and most formidable instruments of tyranny." To our lasting benefit and protection, the framers of the Constitution stood against this brand of tyranny.

For more information
Calder v. Bull, 3 U.S. (3 Dall.) 386 (1798).
Goebel, Julius, Jr. *History of the Supreme Court, Volume I: Antecedents and Beginnings to 1801.* New York: Macmillan Publishing Co., 1971.
LaFave, Wayne R., and Austin W. Scott, Jr. *Criminal Law,* 2nd ed. St. Paul, Minn.: West Publishing Co., 1986.

Thomas E. Baker
James Madison Chair in Constitutional Law
Drake University Law School

extradition   is the surrender of a person charged with a crime by another nation or state to the government seeking the fugitive, pursuant to treaty or the U.S. Constitution. Article IV, section 2, of the Constitution deals with interstate rendition and comity. A National Fugitive Felon Law makes it a crime to travel to another state to escape prosecution. (The Constitution refers to those who "flee from justice." Would someone who was not a fugitive be subject to extradition? States have assumed the constitutional power to enter accommodations for the involuntary return of persons indispensable to the state criminal justice system but not fugitives from justice.) Most states have adopted the Uniform Criminal Extradition Act enacted by Congress in 1926. (The first federal extradition statute was adopted in 1793.)

When an officer of one state makes an arrest of someone sought by another state, the arrestee is held for an extradition process. The prisoner may waive a right to oppose extradition or may contest being transferred to the second state. If contested, the defendant may allege that he is not the fugitive sought, that a mistake had been made regarding his identity. Or else he may claim that he had been denied due process or equal protection under the Fourteenth Amendment, that to send him back would amount to injustice. Where the alleged fugitive has established roots in his new state, acquiring a family and employment, living without breach of the law, his community, the media, and the political leadership may oppose surrendering him and wish to have asylum granted. (For example, in the 1990s a Pennsylvania senior citizen was stopped for a traffic offense. A routine computer search revealed that he was still sought by Florida for a long-ago escape from a prison road gang. The embarrassment of appearing to wish to drag a decent elderly man back to complete his time caused the Florida governor to drop the request for extradition.) To date no federal judge has had to enforce an extradition request.

The United States has extradition treaties with more than 80 countries. (Some treaties provide that a nation granting asylum must itself prosecute the person.) Extradition treaties between nations do not generally apply in the case of political offenses. A country rarely surrenders its own nationals who are fugitives. (Argentina, Great Britain, and the United States sometimes allow their own citizens to be extradited.) International law does not recognize extradition as a duty, except by treaty. (Some countries would not extradite to the United States a person who faced a death sentence.) Because there is no international criminal law, without extradition a criminal could escape punishment by crossing a border. Yielding to international sanctions, Libya eventually turned over for trial in the Netherlands two suspects in the bombing of the Pan Am plane over Lockerbie, Scotland.

For more information

Abbell, Michael. *International Extradition* (vols. 4 and 5 of *International Judicial Assistance*). Washington, D.C.: International Law Institute, 1995.

Gilbert, Geoff. *Aspects of Extradition Law.* Dordrecht, Netherlands: Kluwer Academic Publishers, 1991.

Scott, James A. *Law of Interstate Rendition.* Buffalo, N.Y.: William S. Hein and Co., 1983.

Martin Gruberg
University of Wisconsin, Oshkosh

F

Fair Housing Act prohibits housing discrimination that occurs because the victim is a member of one of seven protected classes. The Fair Housing Act (FHA) was passed by Congress in 1968 in response to the Civil Rights movement, and its coverage was broadened to protect additional classes by amendments passed in both 1974 and 1988.

The seven classes currently protected under the federal act are race, color, national origin, sex, religion, familial status, and disability. Moreover, some states and municipalities have broader fair housing acts that prohibit discrimination based on additional classes such as sexual orientation and source of income. Not only are rental and sales housing transactions covered by the act, but also lending, insurance, and advertising. In addition to prohibiting intentional acts of discrimination, the FHA also prohibits seemingly neutral actions which have a disparate impact on one of the protected classes. So, for example, along with prohibiting an ad that states "whites only," the act also prohibits ad campaigns for housing which use only white models because such ads are likely to create the feeling among minorities that they are not welcome as customers.

Some classic examples of housing discrimination include:

1. Providing false information about the availability of housing due to the applicant's race,
2. Changing rental terms and conditions depending on an applicant's sex,
3. Steering a minority family to properties located in a minority section of town,
4. Refusing to sell homeowner's insurance in certain areas due to high concentrations of minorities,
5. Convincing homeowners to sell their dwellings by creating a fear that members of a protected class will be moving in all around them, and
6. Harassing and intimidating members of the protected classes.

In addition to the above types of housing discrimination, which can affect members of any protected class, there are other types of discriminatory conduct that only affect persons with disabilities. In fact, it is often difficult for a disabled person to even enter a dwelling or to use a dwelling's essential portions, such as a bathroom. In order to combat such accessibility problems, the Fair Housing Act requires that apartment buildings that contain four or more units and an elevator and were built after March 13, 1991, be accessible to persons with disabilities. The act also requires that ground floor units in buildings with four or more units without elevators be accessible.

Along with establishing accessibility requirements for new multifamily housing, the Fair Housing Act also requires that reasonable accommodations in rules and services be granted to disabled individuals. So, if someone is disabled and needs a service dog, a landlord generally must allow the dog even if the complex has a "no pet" rule. Finally, the FHA requires all housing providers to allow tenants with disabilities to make reasonable structural modifications at their own expense, such as installing grab bars in a bathroom.

Because housing discrimination is more subtle today than it was before the passage of the FHA and other civil rights laws, it is often not obvious when discrimination is occurring. Accordingly, many fair housing organizations use volunteer testers in order to investigate housing discrimination. Testers can be used in controlled experiments in which the only significant variable is one of the protected classes. So, for example, if a white tester and a black tester visit the same complex on the same afternoon and the black tester is told nothing is available while the white tester is told there are three vacancies, housing discrimination may be occurring. In *Havens Realty Corp. v. Coleman* (1982) the Supreme Court ruled that testers have a right to truthful information even though the testers have no actual intention of buying or renting a home and may, in fact, expect to receive false information. The Court also held that both testers and fair housing organizations can be harmed by a housing provider's discriminatory conduct.

The federal agency responsible for enforcing the Fair Housing Act is the U.S. Department of Housing and Urban Development (HUD). Individuals who believe their fair housing rights have been violated can file a claim with HUD, an equivalent state or local agency, or in federal or state court.

For more information

Dubofsky, Jean Eberhart. "Fair Housing: A Legislative History and a Perspective," *Washburn Law Journal* 8, no.1. (winter 1969): 149.

Fair Housing Act, United States Code Title 42, sections 3601 et seq.

HUD Website at http://www.hud.gov

National Fair Housing Advocate Online at http://www.fairhousing.com

Martha M. Lafferty
Staff Attorney
Tennessee Fair Housing Council

family   evokes a mental picture of one man married to one woman with their 2.1 biological children. We call this grouping the traditional nuclear family. Although we are brought up to expect this kind of traditional family, it is a stereotype that is no longer the norm in most American households. The term is more than a descriptive noun; it has a legal definition also, which is being challenged.

Although we view the heterosexual married couple with biological children as the definition of family, more and more groups of people are seeking to classify themselves as families. These groups are not necessarily bound by age distribution (two adults and one or more minor children), or biology (all parties being related to one another by blood), or even legal ties (marriage). These are groups of people who have come together due to common lifestyle, kinship bond, or a basic need to belong to a group. A common lifestyle may be based on one's sexual orientation, one's profession (high-stress jobs like the stock market or .com), or one's interests (sports, music).

All of these configurations of peoples or families stay together due to this need to feel a part of a group. This group provides support—emotional and financial—and interdependence. One may borrow money from one's family. One may protect one's family with health and life insurance. Family will provide advice, wanted and unwanted, about life's decisions. Family may help make life and death decisions, including DNR orders or organ donations. Family provides this critical sense of belonging, a part of one's identification.

The law used to be clear in its definition of family. The traditional nuclear family was not only the norm, it was all we recognized. As this group has become less common other groups have demanded acknowledgment.

In 1989 the New York Court of Appeals held in *Braschi v. Stahl Associates Co.* that a homosexual partnership would be included in the definition of family. In that case the surviving partner of a 20-year relationship sued to maintain possession of a rent-controlled apartment in New York City. The court found that the long-term relationship established family inheritance rights between and for the partners. The highest court in the state of New York recognized this relationship as a family.

In Minnesota in the case of *In re Guardianship of Kowalski* an appellate court allowed a homosexual partner to act as legal guardian for her partner following a devastating accident. The injured woman's biological family sought to exclude the lesbian partner. The court appointed the partner as guardian of the accident victim over the challenges mounted by the traditional family. The court viewed the lesbian relationship as family.

Law and society are slowly moving to expand the term *family*. No longer is it constrained by legal and biological lines. Many employers are now offering domestic partnership insurance coverage. This benefit affords one the opportunity to include one's partner, heterosexual or homosexual, under one's health insurance coverage.

Co-parenting is gaining acceptance in American courts. Co-parents are unmarried adults in committed partnerships who are allowed to adopt minor children. Prior to the 1990s only heterosexual married couples and occasional single persons were allowed to adopt children. Several states have allowed heterosexual and homosexual couples to adopt without the prior requirement of a marriage license.

Family still includes married couples with children. It merely encompasses more configurations now. As the traditional family has become less common, society has come to accept and include other groupings.

For more information

Braschi v. Stahl Associates and Co., 544 N.Y.S. 2d 784, 543 N.E. 2d 49 (N.Y. 1989).
In re Guardianship of Kowalski, 478 N.W.2d 790 (Minn. App. 1991).

Margaret R. Ryniker
Assistant Professor, Public Justice Department
SUNY, Oswego

Family and Medical Leave Act extended the principles of the 1978 Pregnancy Discrimination Act (PDA), which specified that discrimination on the basis of pregnancy, childbirth, or related medical conditions constituted illegal sex discrimination under Title VII of the Civil Rights Act of 1964.

The act was signed into law on February 5, 1993, the first piece of legislation of the new Clinton administration. The heart of the PDA, section 701(k), stated that: "women affected by pregnancy . . . shall be treated the same for all employment-related purposes . . . as other persons not so affected but similar in their ability or inability to work."

The Family and Medical Leave Act (FMLA) was first proposed in Congress in 1985. Although a number of Republicans favored the measure, two earlier versions of the bill were vetoed by President George H. W. Bush in 1990 and 1992 at the urging of major business interests such as the U.S. Chamber of Commerce and the National Federation of Independent Business; groups such as these opposed it on the grounds that it mandated benefits that would be too burdensome for employers. Another business group, the National Retail Federation, reversed itself and ultimately supported the bill. With Democratic control of Congress and the White House, the likelihood of the bill's passage increased after the November 1992 election, especially since it was one of President Bill Clinton's chief campaign issues.

In signing the FMLA in a Rose Garden ceremony, President Clinton said, "now millions of our people will no longer have to choose between their jobs and their families." The law provides that workers in companies with 50 or more employees are entitled to take up to 12 weeks of unpaid leave during any 12-month period for the birth or adoption of a child; the illness of a child, spouse, or parent; or the worker's own serious illness. To be eligible, employees must work for the same employer for at least a year and for at least 1,250 hours during the year. The employer must continue to maintain health-care benefits for employees during the leave time; workers must be allowed to return to their former, or equivalent, jobs after their return. However, the bill also allows employers to deny leave to the highest paid 10 percent of their workforce if the worker's absence would cause "serious and grievous injury."

The purpose of the FMLA is to allow workers of both sexes to balance the needs of work and family. However, although it furthers the principle of equal opportunity for women in the workplace, because it provides only unpaid leave, the FMLA does not greatly advance the goal of easing the financial burden of childbirth or family illness on working women. Moreover, in spite of its gender-neutral language, it appears that many more women are taking family leave than are men, suggesting that the primary responsibility for family care remains with women. Thus, although it is an important step in achieving gender equity, for these reasons,

the FMLA represents only the initial stages of the process of making the workplace truly egalitarian.

For more information

Selim, Michael. "The Limited Vision of the Family and Medical Leave Act," *Villanova Law Review* 44 (1999): 395–413.

Susan Gluck Mezey
Department of Political Science
Loyola University, Chicago

Federal Bureau of Investigation   or FBI is the principle investigative arm of the U.S. Justice Department. It has been called "the greatest law enforcement body in the world." It was established in 1908 as the Bureau of Investigation and received its present name in 1935. At first it dealt with antitrust violations, bankruptcy, and fraud. It evolved from a force of examiners at first hired by the attorney general from other departments. In 1910 its jurisdiction was expanded to include organized prostitution (under the Mann Act) and in World War I sabotage and espionage. (Note the Palmer Red Raids of 1920.) After the revelation of the scandals of the Harding administration, the agency was reorganized in 1924. J. Edgar Hoover headed the Bureau from 1924 under eight presidents until his death in 1972. In his 48 years Hoover turned an incompetent and corrupt investigative service into a professional police force. However, the record was tarnished by embarrassments and exposés (spying on political enemies, abusing the First Amendment, harassing organizations with disruptive techniques, blackmailing politicians). In 1976 Congress placed a 10-year, single-term limit on the FBI director. Though no agent has been appointed directly to the post of director, Clarence Kelley and Louis J. Freeh had both been special agents at some point in their careers.

In the late 1920s the Bureau's mission increased to include organized crime, racketeering, and bank robbery. In the 1930s it began to investigate kidnappings and to monitor radical and extremist organizations and in World War II to do foreign counterintelligence. It also investigates attacks on the president or other federal officers. The FBI investigates the backgrounds of presidential nominees and oversees the loyalty-security investigation program for federal employees. In the 1960s civil rights violations were added to its scrutiny (for example, the 1964 murder of three civil rights workers in Mississippi). More recently the Bureau has become concerned with offenses involving high technology. In recent years the Bureau's reputation has been harmed with allegations of flawed performance at Ruby Ridge and Waco and in the work of its laboratory. The FBI investigates more than 200 kinds of federal crimes. Normally the FBI's jurisdiction does not extend to income and tax matters, narcotics, counterfeiting, customs matters, postal laws, and the protection of the president.

The FBI has 59 field offices in the United States and a number of "legal attaché offices" outside the country (maintaining liaison with foreign police and intelligence services). The agency provides cooperative services for other criminal justice agencies (laboratory services, fingerprint identification, police training, etc.) Currently there are about 10,000 special agents of which about 10 percent are women, 5 percent African American, and 5 percent Hispanic. The FBI also employs another 14,000 workers (laboratory technicians, clerks, and secretaries). It has almost a quarter of the employees of the Department of Justice. The FBI has its own merit system distinct from the regular civil service.

For more information

Balcavage, Dynise, and Arthur M. Schlesinger, Jr., eds. *The Federal Bureau of Investigation*. Broomall, Pa.: Chelsea House Publishers, 2000.

Jeffreys, Diarmuid. *The Bureau: Inside the Modern FBI*. Boston–New York: Houghton Mifflin, 1995.

Theoharis, Athan G., ed. *The FBI: A Comprehensive Reference Guide*. Phoenix, Ariz.: Oryx Press, 1999.

Martin Gruberg
University of Wisconsin, Oshkosh

federal court system   occupies a small but unique niche in the U.S. system of government. Most civil and criminal disputes are handled by state and local courts, not federal courts. It is the other two branches—the executive and legislative—that most often are in the news or the subject of teachers' lesson plans. Yet it is the federal courts that have resolved some of the most important disputes in the history of the nation. The origin of the federal courts is traced to the Constitution, which says little about the third branch of the government. The principles it enunciates, however, remain the keystone of the federal courts today.

Article III of the Constitution states that "The judicial power of the United States shall be vested in one supreme court and in such inferior courts as the Congress may from time to time ordain and establish." In other words, while the Constitution established the Supreme Court of the United States, it was Congress that later created courts of appeals and district courts.

Judges who serve on these courts are known as "Article III" judges. The Constitution protects the independence of these judges in two ways. First, judges hold their office during "good behavior." This means that they only can be removed from the bench through impeachment for, in the words of the Constitution, "high crimes and misdemeanors." The Constitution also states that a judge's compensation may not be reduced as long as he or she is a judge. Together these two provisions insulate judges so they can reach fair and impartial decisions free from political and societal pressures. They also protect the citizens because it is independent judges who serve as the guardians of the rights of the people. These two principles set federal judges apart from state and local judges and the judges of other nations.

The Constitution's treatment of the federal judiciary stems from the lessons the new United States learned in breaking away from England, where judges were subservient to the king. In addition to establishing the paramount importance of judicial independence, the drafters of the Constitution set up a delicate system of checks and balances, which continues to serve as the hallmark of our democratic system of government. While the number and types of cases have changed over the last 200 years—the drafters of the Constitution did not foresee the Internet—the function of today's federal courts remains virtually unchanged.

The federal judiciary is relatively small. In addition to the nine Supreme Court justices there are 179 court of appeals judges operating out of 13 regional circuits, and 654 district court judges working in 94 different districts. As stated in the Constitution, it is the job of the president to nominate and the Senate to confirm the judges who occupy these positions. While federal judicial nominees typically are highly respected lawyers, law professors, or state judges, the Constitution sets forth no criteria for judicial service. In fact judges need not be lawyers, although all recent nominees have come from the legal profession.

The district court, which is where trials are conducted, handles about 60,000 criminal cases and 260,000 civil cases a year. About 55,000 of these cases are appealed to one of the regional circuit court of appeals. From here, an appeal may be filed with the Supreme Court. The Supreme Court, however, has what is known as "discretionary jurisdiction." This means that unlike the courts below it, it does not have to accept every appeal that is filed. In fact, it typically agrees to take only about one percent of the cases it is requested to hear —usually only serious Constitutional issues or significant disputes among several lower courts.

Since few federal cases ever reach the Supreme Court, most disputes are resolved either by the district courts or courts of appeals. The subject of "jurisdiction," a court's authority to hear a case, is a complex one. The "docket" or case schedule of state courts involves most local crimes or civil disputes, such as disagreements over contracts, or car accidents. Federal courts, on the other hand, only may decide cases that involve the U.S. government, the Constitution, federal laws, or disputes between the states or the U.S. and foreign governments. For example, it is the responsibility of federal courts to hear most civil rights cases, because the relevant laws are federal laws that were enacted by the U.S Congress. Federal courts also would have authority to hear criminal cases that may have occurred in a national park, on a military base, or on other federal land.

For more information
www.uscourts.gov

David Sellers
Assistant Director for Public Affairs
Administrative Office of the U.S. Courts

federal courts   were established under Article III of the Constitution; however, the founders used vague language in describing the system. The Constitution requires that the president, with the advice and consent of the Senate, appoint judges to the federal judiciary for life. Responsibility for constructing the rest of the system's specifics was left to Congress. The Judiciary Act of 1789 was passed by the first Congress and laid the foundation for the third branch of the federal government.

Today the federal court system is composed of three layers. The first layer is composed of the U.S. District Courts. These 94 courts serve as the trial courts for the criminal and civil cases in the federal system. When a case is brought before this level of the court, one judge hears the case and with the help of a jury makes a judgment on the facts of the case. The district courts do not overlap states. Each state has at least one district court that is unique to that state. Many states have several district courts, serving different geographic regions of the state. For example, the state of Alabama has three districts: the Northern District in Birmingham, the Middle District in Montgomery, and the Southern District in Mobile. Different districts have different numbers of authorized judgeships. Congress approves these judgeships as needed to handle the caseload in the district. In addition to these district courts, there are several specialty federal courts that hear trial-level cases on issues such as bankruptcy, military issues, and international trade. Administrative agencies in the federal government also often have administrative law judges who hear cases regarding decisions made in a specific part of the bureaucracy.

The decisions made in the 94 district courts, the specialty courts, and the administrative agencies may be appealed to the second layer of the federal judiciary, the U.S. Courts of Appeals. This layer is composed of 12 regional circuit courts and one federal circuit court. Cases coming before the U.S. Courts of Appeals are generally heard by a panel of three judges. These collegial courts make a consensus decision on each case based on findings of law. The appellate court does not decide whether the facts of the case are correct, rather they examine the accuracy with which the law was applied to the case. The panel is composed of three judges on the circuit. The number of judges in each circuit varies, as it does at the district court level. For example, the Seventh Circuit hears cases in the federal courthouse in Chicago, Illinois, from three states: Illinois, Indiana, and Wisconsin. While the Seventh Circuit has 11 judges, the much larger Ninth Circuit has 28 authorized judgeships. In some cases, litigants may request that the circuit court hear their case *en banc*, which means all of the judges in the circuit will make up one large panel to hear a case.

Litigants who choose to appeal their cases beyond the U.S. Courts of Appeals must appeal to the third, or top layer of the federal court system, the United States Supreme Court. The nine justices who serve on the Court have a great deal of control, as designated by Congress, over which cases they choose to hear. The cases may come from either state or federal courts, and they usually involve important questions involving either the Constitution or federal laws. The justices hear cases as a panel of nine and are again examining cases only for mistakes made in legal interpretation, not findings of facts.

For more information

An excellent map showing all of the geographic jurisdictions of the federal district and circuit courts is available at the web site of the Administrative Office of the United States Courts at: www.uscourts.gov. For additional information on this topic see also the Federal Judicial Center at: www.fjc.gov.

Nancy Winemiller Basinger
University of Georgia

Federal Rules of Evidence are procedural trial rules by which a court determines what evidence is admissible at trial.

In the United States, the federal courts follow the Federal Rules of Evidence. State courts generally follow their own adopted rules of evidence, which are very closely modeled after the Federal Rules. There are 11 articles or sections under the Federal Rules of Evidence. Article I covers Rules 101 through 106. Rules 101–102 deal with general provisions such as the scope, purpose, and construction of the rules. Rule 103 states the effect of an erroneous ruling by a court as regards the admission of evidence, the rulings on evidence, and the manner in which a court may admit or consider evidence. Rule 104 addresses preliminary questions such as the qualification of a witness or existence of privilege. Limited admissibility is the subject of Rule 105. This rule recognizes that a court may admit evidence for a singular purpose, but that the same evidence may not be considered for other purposes.

Rule 106 is a rule of completeness and addresses misleading impressions that may be created by presenting only portions of statements or records or by taking matters out of context.

Article II contains one rule only, Rule 201, which deals with judicial notice of adjudicative facts. Adjudicative facts are the facts which are particular to a case such as who did what, when, how, and where. Normally, a jury decides these types of matters. The court can take notice of adjudicative facts when the facts are such that there is no reasonable controversy (i.e., dogs are canines; men are humans; wounds sometimes bleed; 911 is an emergency call number).

Article III pertains to presumptions in civil trials. A presumption is an assumed fact. In order to invoke the presumption, the moving party must establish the basic facts giving rise to the presumption. The effect of invoking a presumption is that is causes the opposing party to bear the burden of proving nonexistence of the presumed fact. For example, a statute that makes railroads liable for any damages done, unless the railroad can show that reasonable care was exercised, creates a presumption against the railroad.

Article IV addresses relevancy. Rules 401 through 415 provide guidance as to the definition of legal relevance and discuss the test of whether relevance outweighs the prejudicial effect of the evidence on the jury. This section contains the rules pertaining to character and habit evidence, remedial measures, compromise, payment of expenses, admissibility of plea discussions, existence of liability insurance, and evidentiary limits regarding sexual assault cases.

Article V deals with the privilege of witnesses not to testify. The witness invokes the privilege when called upon to give testimony based on the witness's relationship with another person (i.e., lawyer-client, husband-wife, priest-confessor, trade secrets, psychotherapist-patient, identity of informant).

Article VI treats the matter of witnesses and is the most extensive section. Rules 601 through 706 address who is competent to testify, who may be a witness, administration of the oath, method and order of questioning, proper use of interpreters, matters of impeachment, the effect of religious beliefs or opinions, how to treat witnesses who cannot recall the contents of a document, use of prior statements, when a court may call or exclude witnesses, opinion testimony, expert testimony, and disclosure of facts underlying an expert's opinion.

Article VIII, Rules 801 through 806, addresses hearsay, non-hearsay, and the exceptions to hearsay. Hearsay is explained, in depth, within this publication.

Article IX contains Rules 901 through 903 and deals with authentication and identification as a condition precedent to admissibility. Authentication and identification mean sufficiently showing that the evidence is what the proponent says it is. For example, that the shoe is the shoe the defendant wore on the date in question; the voice is that of the victim; the document is not a forgery and was signed by the grantor.

Article X covers Rules 1001 through 1008 and provides guidance as to how evidentiary writings, recordings, and photographs should be treated. Also addressed are the admissibility of duplicates, public records, summaries of voluminous writings, recordings, or photos. Rule 1008 specifies the parameters of the court and jury.

Article XI contains the miscellaneous Rules 1101 through 1103. This section specifies when the rules apply and when they do not. The Federal Rules of Evidence do not apply at grand jury proceedings, for preliminary questions of fact, extradition, criminal preliminary examinations, sentencings, bail hearings, or applications for warrants. The rules do apply to all U.S. district courts in criminal and civil proceedings.

For more information

Federal Rules of Evidence.

Imwinkelreid, Edward J., ed. *Evidentiary Foundations,* 4th ed. Charlottesville, Va.: Lexis Law Publishing, 1998.

Mauet, Thomas A., and Warren D. Wolfson, eds. *Trial Evidence.* New York: Aspen Law and Business, 1997.

Loretta M. Young
Family Court of State of Delaware

Federal Tort Claims Act

is a federal statute enacted in 1946 that permits citizens to bring tort claims (such as claims for personal injury and property damage) against the U.S. government.

Ordinarily, the United States and its agencies have immunity from suit for money damages, and thus, absent a federal statute waiving such sovereign immunity, citizens cannot bring suits for money damages against the federal government. The Federal Tort Claims Act waives the federal government's sovereign immunity with respect to tort claims, that is, claims such as those involving automobile accidents, products liability, medical malpractice, and negligence. Prior to the enactment of the Federal Tort Claims Act, Congress had to pass private bills awarding government compensation to particular citizens for injuries that resulted from the tortious conduct of the government or its employees.

The Federal Tort Claim Act makes the federal government liable for torts under the same standards that a private person would be liable for when committing a tort, with some exceptions. (The act does not waive the sovereign immunity possessed by states and is irrelevant to tort claims against state and local governmental entities.) Though the Federal Tort Claims Act does not establish a special substantive standard of liabil-

ity for the government, it establishes special procedures for resolution of tort claims against the government. In particular, the act requires that potential claimants file their claims with the federal agency that harmed them before initiating litigation. The agency has six months to decide whether to offer the claimant compensation for his injuries. The act precludes citizens from suing federal employees personally, so long as the federal employee was acting within the scope of his employment at the time he injured the plaintiff. The act also limits that percentage of the plaintiff's award that the plaintiff's lawyer can take as compensation for his services (though this limitation is regularly disregarded). Perhaps most importantly, tort claims must by tried before a federal judge sitting without a jury, unlike tort cases against private defendants, which are generally tried before juries.

The Federal Tort Claims Act precludes citizens from recovering money damages against the government in several situations. The most important exemptions from the act's general waiver of sovereign immunity preclude recovery on claims arising out of military activities that occur during wartime; claims arising in a foreign country; claims involving assault, battery, false imprisonment, false arrest, or malicious prosecution (unless committed by a federal law enforcement officer); claims involving defamation and fraud; and claims involving allegedly tortious conduct that either was required by statute or qualifies as an exercise of discretion.

Many suits are brought under the Federal Torts Claims Act. The suits are varied, involving a wide variety of claims against a wide variety of agencies. Some of the most common claims are for negligent operation of motor vehicles, failure to maintain safe premises, and medical malpractice.

For more information

Culp Davis, Kenneth, and Richard J. Pierce, Jr. *Administrative Law Treatise.* Vol. 3. 3rd ed. Boston: Little, Brown, 1994, pp. 229–252.

Dobbs, Dan B. *The Law of Torts*. St. Paul Minn.: West Publishing Co., 2000, pp. 695–715.

Bernard W. Bell
Professor of Law
Rutgers Law School, Newark

federalism   is one of the basic structural components of our system of government. Along with separation of powers, and checks and balances, federalism defines the relationship between various governmental actors.

Separation of powers and checks and balances describe and regulate the distribution of power within the national government or the state governments. Federalism regulates the relationships of power between the states and the national government. This division of power creates specific areas of government in which the states and the national government each have final decisional authority.

The authors of the Constitution realized, based on the failure of the Articles of Confederation, that there was a need to shift significant power to a new national government. At the same time, they feared creating a central government that was too strong and might tend toward tyranny. The balance that they struck was federalism, a system in which the new more powerful central government would be forced to share power with the states.

Federalism can be viewed as a flexible system that addresses the need for some level of national unity while simultaneously respecting and providing for divergent local needs and concerns. The powers that belong to the federal government are laid out in the Constitution—powers referred to as enumerated powers. Additionally the national government possesses implied powers that are based on the necessary and proper clause. The protection of the power of states can be found in the Tenth Amendment and the declaration of reserved powers.

While the system of federalism created by the framers has worked well, it has not been without its critics. From the beginning, the exact nature of the relationship between the two levels of government has been a source of considerable debate. Immediately after the ratification of the Constitution, Alexander Hamilton began to argue for national supremacy while Thomas Jefferson argued for the rights of states over the national government—rights which he believed included the power to nullify national laws.

The continuation of these debates led eventually to the Civil War. With the defeat of the Confederacy in the Civil War, states lost their power to nullify national laws as well as their power to secede from the Union. Expansion of federal power in the wake of the Civil War brought about changing ideas about the exact nature of federalism. The ongoing debate about federalism has caused the relationship between the two levels of government to evolve over time.

From the original intent of the framers, federalism has evolved through dual federalism, cooperative federalism, and creative federalism and toward the new federalism period of the latter half of the 20th century. Federalism is still an important feature of our government and still a matter of political debate. While the development of federalism in the history of our country has generally been toward increased national power at the expense of the states, recent efforts by conservative political forces have sought to reverse that trend.

Federalism as seen in the Constitution was an attempt to define the relationship of power between the national government and the states. Despite that document, the meaning of federalism and the nature of the relationship has remained politically defined and historically contingent.

For more information
Bowman, Ann, and Kearney, Richard. *State and Local Government*. New York: Houghton-Mifflin, 1999.

Nice, David, and Patricia Fredrickson. *The Politics of Intergovermental Relations*. Chicago: Nelson Hall, 1998.

David A. May
Eastern Washington University

felony is a crime for which the defendant, if convicted, may be punished by death or by imprisonment for more than one year.

Since severe punishments fit graver crimes, felonies typically include the worst sorts of crimes. In order for a crime to be classified as a felony, the severity of the maximum punishment is the deciding factor, not the punishment actually imposed. Thus, if someone is convicted of a crime that carries a maximum punishment of three years in prison, even if he or she is only sentenced to six months in prison, he or she has still been convicted of a felony and is a felon.

In jurisdictions that distinguish between felonies and misdemeanors, felonies are crimes that have graver punishments than misdemeanors. Generally, the distinction between a felony and misdemeanor is determined by the punishment prescribed. Thus, since punishments for crimes differ depending on jurisdiction, what may be a felony in one jurisdiction may be a misdemeanor in other jurisdictions.

Federal and some state laws classify felonies by either classification (A, B, C, etc.) or degree (first, second, third, etc.), depending on the seriousness of the offenses. Sentences vary depending on the classification or degree. Typically, Class A and first-degree felonies receive the most severe punishment authorized in that jurisdiction, while lesser felonies (by degree or classification) receive lesser punishment. As an example, death or life in prison is typically a punishment for Class A felonies and first-degree felonies, while a sentence of not more than three years is a typical punishment for Class E felonies and fifth-degree felonies.

The definition of a felony has changed over the years. In the past, at common law, a felony was a crime punishable by total forfeiture of land and goods, and possibly life and limb. Also under common law, additional punishment could be added depending on the crime. Until recently, many jurisdictions defined a felony as conduct punishable by imprisonment in the state penitentiary. Currently, the federal, English, and the growing states' view is to define a felony as conduct punishable by more than one year's imprisonment.

The impacts of a felony conviction can be severe. In many jurisdictions in the United States, convicted felons may lose the right to vote, be prohibited from holding public office, be restricted in their ability to obtain an occupational or professional license, or sit on a jury, or lose firearms privileges. Many jurisdictions impose reporting requirements, requiring certain felons to report their location and occupation to a state agency.

For more information
18 U.S.C. 3156, 22 C.J.S. Criminal Law section 10.

Captain William D. Smoot
Assistant Professor, Department of Law
U.S. Military Academy, West Point

felony murder occurs when an individual causes the accidental death of another while committing a felony, even though that death would not normally be considered murder if no other felony were being committed.

For example, two individuals sneak up upon a third person with the intent to frighten the third person, resulting in him having a heart attack and dying. These two individuals would not be charged with murder. However, in *People v. Stamp*, 82 Cal. Rptr. 598 (1969), a court ruled that when two individuals are committing a robbery and the third person dies from a heart attack as a result of being frightened, then the two individuals could be charged with felony murder.

The idea behind the felony murder rule is that deaths ought to be treated as murder when they are the result of actions of individuals who commit felonies that are inherently dangerous. Under normal circumstances, a prosecutor needs to show that a death was the product of a specific state of mind, such as a knowing or willful intent to end the life of another, but with felony murder, the requirement to prove this state of mind or intent is not necessary. Instead, the prosecutor need only show that the death was grossly reckless and occurred while a felony was being committed.

The justification for the felony murder rule is to deter individuals from committing felonies; or at least to commit them in a "safer" fashion. Another rationale is that by holding felons strictly liable for deaths that occur while they are committing a crime, the hope is that it will discourage felonies in general, or at least the chance that a felony will involve the loss of life.

Critics of the felony murder rule argue that it makes it too easy for prosecutors to obtain murder convictions and that it pressures defendants and their attorneys to confess or plea bargain to a crime.

Among the crimes that qualify for invoking the felony murder rule when a death occurs are kidnapping, rape, robbery, arson, and supplying heroin or providing methyl alcohol to drink.

For more information
Kaplan, John, and Weisberg, Robert. *Criminal Law: Cases and Materials*. Boston: Little, Brown, 1991.

David Schultz
Hamline University

fingerprinting   is a technique that uses the pattern of the friction ridges found on the fingertip to individually identify people. The "fingerprint" is the image of this ridge pattern transferred to a surface or optically stored in a computer. Each fingerprint has certain characteristics that distinguish its pattern from all other fingerprint patterns. These fingerprint differences lie in the minutiae, or points of identifica-

tion, where ridges end or meet. The use of fingerprints in identification is based on two important fundamentals. No two people, not even identical twins, have the same fingerprint pattern, and a person's fingerprint patterns remain unchanged throughout life.

Fingerprints have been used throughout history as a personal "mark" of an individual, but it was not until Sir Francis Galton, an English scientist, established the uniqueness and permanence of fingerprint patterns in 1892 that systematic fingerprinting of criminals began. Both England and the United States started using fingerprints for criminal identification around 1900. Congress established the Identification Division of the Federal Bureau of Investigation (FBI) as a central fingerprint archive for the United States in 1924 as more law enforcement agencies began using fingerprints. At the present time, the FBI's files contain the fingerprints of more than 173 million persons, the largest collection in the world.

The use of fingerprints in law enforcement is based upon matching an unidentified fingerprint at a crime scene with either a fingerprint record stored in a criminal database or a suspect's fingerprints to establish proof of presence at the scene. A bloody fingertip will leave a visible print, but even clean fingers can leave prints due to finger secretions that leave fingerprints on almost everything we touch. These "latent" prints cannot be seen easily by the naked eye, but they become visible when dusted with a powder or chemically treated. Identification can be made on one finger alone or even a partial print from one finger. U.S. law does not require a specific number of points of identification to match, but the FBI *Manual of Fingerprinting* states that the "standard" is generally eight or more points of identification.

Automated Fingerprint Identification Systems (AFIS) have changed the way fingerprints are compared. Traditionally, a fingerprint expert would compare a crime scene print to an inked impression on a 10-print card. Now, computer-driven technology scans fingerprints and determines the slope and length of ridges and curves to find the minutiae. A typical AFIS classifies the fingerprint into one of eight basic patterns (for example, whorl, loop, arch) and compares the minutiae of an individual fingerprint against every fingerprint in the entire database with 99.9 percent accuracy without any human intervention. A new FBI AFIS site in Clarksburg, West Virginia, has individual computerized fingerprint records for approximately 33 million criminals.

Fingerprints also are used to identify missing persons or victims of mass disasters, prevent welfare fraud, screen job applicants, control the national borders, and identify licensed drivers. Fingerprints are just one type of biometrics—unique biological characteristics that distinguish one person from another and can be used for identification. Other types include DNA variants, hand shape geometry, and iris and retinal patterns.

For more information

The Identification Division of the FBI: A Brief Outline of the History, Services, and Operating Technologies of the World's Largest Repository. Washington, D.C.: Federal Bureau of Investigation, U.S. Department of Justice, 1994.

Durham, Norris M., Kathleen M. Fox, and Chris C. Plato, eds. *The State of Dermatoglyphics: The Science of Finger and Palm Prints.* Lewiston, N.Y.: Edwin Mellen Press, 2000.

Karen Gottlieb, Ph.D., J.D.
BioLaw
Nederland, Colorado

flag burning is a constitutionally protected means of expressing opposition to policies and practices of the federal government that became the subject of a vigorous legal and political debate in the United States during the 1990s. The Supreme Court declared both a Texas law and a federal law that prohibited flag burning unconstitutional because they violated the freedom of speech guaranteed by the First Amendment.

The First Amendment prohibits laws that restrict the freedom of speech. "Speech," as the Supreme Court has interpreted it, includes not only oral and written communication but "symbolic speech," such as wearing a black armband to protest the Vietnam War, or displaying an American flag upside down, with a peace symbol attached to it. Therefore, it is not surprising that the Court has held that burning the American flag in a statement of political protest is symbolic speech that the First Amendment protects. The Court has reached that conclusion twice, in *Texas v. Johnson,* 491 U.S. 397 (1989), which involved a Texas anti-flag-burning law, and in *United States v. Eichman,* 496 U.S. 310 (1990), which featured a federal law that prohibited flag burning.

Texas v. Johnson arose from a protest against the policies of the Reagan administration, which occurred in Dallas in 1984. Gregory Johnson, one of the protesters, unfurled an American flag, soaked it with kerosene, and set it on fire. Johnson was convicted of violating a Texas law that prohibited the desecration of "venerated objects," including the American flag. The law said that to "desecrate" was to "deface, damage, or otherwise physically mistreat in a way that the actor knows will seriously offend one or more persons likely to observe or discover his action." The Texas Court of Criminal Appeals reversed Johnson's conviction, and Texas appealed to the Supreme Court, where it argued that its interest in preserving the American flag as a symbol of national unity justified that conviction. The Supreme Court disagreed. Justice William Brennan, writing for the majority, observed: "If there is a bedrock principle underlying the First Amendment, it is that the Government may not prohibit the expression of an idea simply because society finds the idea itself offensive or disagreeable." He added that government does not honor the flag by punishing those who burn it because to punish speech is to diminish the freedom that the flag represents.

Congress reacted to the Court's decision by passing the Flag Protection Act, which sought to survive First Amendment scrutiny by prohibiting flag burning merely to protect the physical integrity of the flag, not to punish the message associated with burning the flag. The act said: "Whoever knowingly mutilates, defaces, physically defiles, burns, maintains on the floor or ground, or tramples upon any flag of the United States shall be fined . . . or imprisoned for not more than one year, or both." The Supreme Court declared the Flag Protection Act unconstitutional in *United States v. Eichman*. The majority reasoned that although this law did not punish flag burning based on the message that flag burning conveyed, Congress's efforts to protect the physical integrity of the flag rested on a desire to preserve the flag against disrespectful treatment, which amounted to the suppression of symbolic speech, a violation of the First Amendment.

In the years since *Eichman*, Congress has tried several times to pass a constitutional amendment to prohibit flag burning, which would overturn the *Eichman* decision. Thus far, Congress has failed in that effort, and flag burning remains constitutionally protected speech.

For more information

Epstein, Lee, and Thomas G. Walker, *Constitutional Law for a Changing America: Rights, Liberties, and Justice*, 3rd ed. Washington, D.C.: CQ Press, 1998.

Fisher, Louis. *American Constitutional Law*, 3rd ed. Durham, N.C.: Carolina Academic Press, 1999.

Brian L. Porto
College of St. Joseph, Vermont

Fletcher v. Peck 10 U.S. (6 Cranch) 87 (1810) was an important and famous case to determine the scope of the contract clause in the U.S. Constitution. Decided in 1810, it involved judicial determination of the ownership of land fraudulently sold by the 1795 Georgia legislature. The major constitutional question pitted state claims of sovereignty over public land as opposed to constitutional contract clause provisions (Article 1, section 10). A main constitutional question was whether state impairment of obligation of contract applied to public as well as private contracts.

This case involved issues of wholesale bribery and fraud. In 1795 Georgia legislators passed a law under substantial bribery to sell about 35 million acres to four land companies, approximately the states of Mississippi and Alabama, for nearly $500,000. The 1796 Georgia legislature revoked the land grant. In the interim land companies sold some lands to land speculators and prospective settlers. Fletcher, as a good-faith purchaser, sued Peck to recover funds because the land title had been rescinded. The Supreme Court invalidated this portion of the land recision and said that Peck had a valid land title. Further, Chief Justice Marshall ruled for a unanimous court that the vast majority of the land grant was rescinded because this grant, as a state contract, had been obtained through bribery and fraud, which invalidated the legislative act.

Marshall's broad reading of the contract clause argued that the 1795 legislative actions were unconstitutional because state actions violated the contract clause of the U.S. Constitution. The Georgia impairment of contracts meant that public contracts were within the scope of the contract clause. Previously, that clause had been assumed to apply only to private contracts between individuals. The national government could sanction state governments if they reneged upon their public contracts. This decision indicated constitutional and national protection for property rights against actual and potential state interference. In addition this decision showed that federalism principles could restrict state regulatory powers. These two ideas were an important part of early U.S. constitutional doctrine concerning the scope of states' rights and individuals' legal protections.

For more information

Cardozo, Benjamin. *The Nature of the Judicial Process.* New Haven, Conn.: Yale University Press, 1931.

Fletcher v. Peck, 10 U.S. (6 Cranch) 87 (1810).

Magrath, C. Peter. *Yazoo: Law and Politics in the New Republic.* Providence, R.I.: Brown University Press, 1966.

White, G. Edward. *The Marshall Court and Cultural Change, 1815–1835.* New York: Macmillan, 1988.

Steven Puro
Saint Louis University

Food and Drug Administration   or the FDA is an agency of the U.S. government located in the Department of Health and Human Services. With about 9,000 full-time employees and an annual budget of about $1 billion, it is the organization that has the major responsibility for insuring that the foods, cosmetics, drugs, medical devices, and color and food additives purchased by the American public are safe and not mislabeled.

The first major federal law regulating foods and drugs was passed in 1906. It was initially enforced by the Department of Agriculture's Bureau of Chemistry under the direction of Dr. Harvey Wiley, an outstanding civil servant whose crusading had led to its enactment. In 1927 the Food, Drug and Insecticide Administration was created to administer it. In 1930 the organization's name was changed to "Food and Drug Administration"; and in 1940 it was transferred to the predecessor of the Department of Health and Human Services.

The 1906 law prohibited the misbranding and adulteration of foods and drugs only. It was replaced in 1938 by the Food, Drug and Cosmetic Act (FDCA), which extended the FDA's jurisdiction to cosmetics and increased its powers over the marketing of drugs. The agency still has no right to require that a food or cosmetic be proven safe before it can be sold. However, it inspects food and cosmetic manufacturing facilities for cleanliness. Moreover, if it finds that a food or cosmetic on the market is adulterated, is misbranded, or is making people ill, it will ask the manufacturer to recall it; and it will get a court order allowing its seizure if the manufacturer ignores its request. (The Food Safety and Inspection Service of the Department of Agriculture has jurisdiction over contaminated meat and poultry, while it is up to the Federal Trade Commission to take action against misleading advertisements of foods, drugs, cosmetics, and medical devices.)

Under the FDCA as amended, the FDA requires the makers of color and food additives to show that they are safe before they can be used in other products. Also, the agency will not allow certain medical devices and what the FDCA calls "new drugs" (which may be over-the-counter as well as prescription) to reach the market unless the manufacturer can demonstrate that they are both safe AND effective. The FDA insists that the manufacturer of a "new" drug conduct clinical tests that can take up to seven years. Once these are completed, the firm must apply for FDA review, accompanied by data from the tests. Once the application is filed, the agency is supposed within six months to okay or disallow the drug's sale, though in practice a decision takes on average about 15 months. (In a few cases, expedited development and review are possible.) Though most of the FDA's funding comes from Congress, since 1992 it has collected a user fee from drug companies applying for permission to market their products. These fees add $100 million annually to its coffers and enable it to hire more employees and thus to speed up its scrutiny of these applications. If a drug or medical device proves unsafe after it reaches the consumer, the FDA will recall it. Thus in March 2000 it ordered the diabetes drug Rezulin withdrawn from pharmacists' shelves because it had caused liver failure in 90 cases since 1997.

Under the FDCA's Delaney clause, any color or food additive that causes cancer in animals or humans, even a tiny number, must be banned.

Ergo the FDA outlawed a color additive known as "Red #2" because its scientists had found that giving it to female rats at a high dosage caused a statistically significant increase in malignant tumors in these rodents.

Since FDA decisions can cost businesses a lot of money or expose consumers to serious health risks, it is not surprising that it receives a great deal of criticism. Tobacco companies were unhappy when it sought to regulate tobacco as a drug and ban its sale to people under 18. (The U.S. Supreme Court held in *FDA v. Brown and Williamson Tobacco Corp., 98–1152*, March 2000, that the agency lacked authority to take this step.) It has been accused of delaying the approval of drugs for so long that patients suffering from certain diseases cannot get medication they desperately need. Some have charged it with approving dangerous food additives or not carrying out enough inspections of food-processing plants. Despite these attacks, the FDA or a bureau similar to it is likely to be around for many years, since the American public demands protection from dangerous foods, drugs, and cosmetics.

For more information

"FDA Reform: Food and Drug Safety and Availability," *Congressional Digest,* February 1997, pp. 34–64.

Daniel C. Kramer
College of Staten Island, CUNY

Frankfurter, Felix (1882–1965) was a justice of the United States Supreme Court from 1939 to 1962. He was appointed by President Franklin Delano Roosevelt.

He was born in Vienna, Austria, and emigrated to America with his family at the age of 12. He grew up in the Lower East Side ghetto in New York City, was educated at City College, and attended Harvard Law School. His top grades propelled him to the editorship of the *Harvard Law Review.* Upon graduating in 1906 he entered public service as an assistant U.S. attorney in

New York under Henry L. Stimson, a leading Progressive. In 1911 Stimson became secretary of war and Frankfurter went to Washington as his assistant. In 1914 he was appointed to the Harvard Law School faculty, a position he retained until his appointment to the Court.

Not a secluded scholar, Frankfurter's public activities made him a nationally prominent liberal. During World War I, he served on President Wilson's labor mediation commission, where his report on the unfair trial of a labor radical caused a national stir. He attended the Paris Peace Conference after that war, representing Zionist interests. He was a founder of the American Civil Liberties Union. He influenced liberal opinion as a frequent contributor to *The New Republic,* and his coauthored book, *The Labor Injunction,* attacked the federal courts for stifling the labor movement. He spoke out against the due process violations in the trials of convicted anarchists Sacco and Vanzetti and did free legal work for the National Consumers' League. He appeared frequently before the Supreme Court on behalf of unions and other progressive causes.

At Harvard he developed a following among his students that combined a passion for academic excellence and a zeal for public service. He selected law clerks from his former students for Justices Holmes and Brandeis, with whom he had close rapport. During the New Deal, he became an important adviser to President Roosevelt and placed many of his former students in important administrative and policy-shaping positions, thus enhancing his influence.

Given his impeccable liberal credentials, it is a great irony that Frankfurter became a leading judicial conservative. This resulted from his judicial philosophy of *judicial restraint*—the belief that the courts should be passive on great public issues, leaving it to the legislature and administrative agencies to supply the popular will and expertise needed to run a complex modern state and resolve political conflicts. This philosophy

Justice Felix Frankfurter (Pach Brothers Studio, Collection of the Supreme Court of the United States)

was in tune with the beliefs of his fellow New Deal justices regarding economic issues, but as the Court, led by Justices Hugo Black and William O. Douglas, began to impose the Constitution on the states in civil liberties cases, Frankfurter remained true to his original philosophy.

The first great rift occurred in public school flag salute cases during World War II. A majority of the Court eventually held that a law requiring a religious dissenter to salute the flag against his conscience violated the First Amendment. Frankfurter dissented on the basis of the need for national solidarity in time of war. This decision displayed his theory that legal rules are not based on constitutional absolutes but on the balanced reasoning that takes into account many factors.

Other major areas where Frankfurter led a conservative majority included several cases where the Bill of Rights was not applied to state and local criminal justice. In cases in the 1940s the Court denied that indigent state defendants were guaranteed the Sixth Amendment right to counsel, the Fifth Amendment rule against self-incrimination, or the Fourth Amendment (search and seizure) exclusionary rule. Frankfurter also led a split Court to rule that it had no jurisdiction to hear an appeal challenging unequal legislative districts under the equal protection clause of the Fourteenth Amendment because it was a *political question*. In these cases Frankfurter was powerfully opposed by Hugo Black, his main antagonist on the Court.

Black and Frankfurter had opposing judicial philosophies. Black tended to follow the Constitution and the Bill of Rights as literally as possible, while Frankfurter was comfortable in making rulings under the more elastic due process clause of the Fourteenth Amendment. Black, therefore, was guided by an absolutist belief that the text of the Constitution required the Court to extend the Bill of Rights in favor of the individual and against the interests of the state and to hold that disproportionate voting districts violated the equal protection of the laws.

Frankfurter's inherent liberalism would emerge where he felt unconstrained by judicial restraint and believed that Fourteenth Amendment due process could be interpreted to protect the rights of persons. Thus, in cases concerning confessions taken by local officers against the will of suspects, or in cases where local police officers engaged in particularly heavy-handed searches, he was willing to apply a somewhat subjective standard—whether the confession was voluntary or whether the search shocked the conscience—to uphold the rights of the individual.

Frankfurter, the brilliant and irrepressible professor, tried to sway his colleagues on the Court with a steady stream of advice and blandishments. This often backfired, and some of the greatest justices of the era, including Black, Douglas, Chief Justice Warren, and William Brennan, turned against his often patronizing tutelage.

One of the high points of Frankfurter's judicial strategy and approach and cooperation with other justices came in the work surrounding *Brown v. Board of Education* (1954), the most important and the most sensitive case of the 20th century. Frankfurter understood that a case that would reverse school segregation would likely cause a social revolution and a massive negative reaction in the South. Because of this he worked to delay a decision at a time when it appeared that the Court might produce a split decision in the one case where unanimity was essential. When Earl Warren became Chief Justice in 1953 Frankfurter was able to provide meaningful support, although the major credit to achieving unanimity goes to Warren for his personal leadership and his ability to draw Justices Robert Jackson and Stanley Reed into the majority.

When appointed, Frankfurter was seen potentially as being rated a great justice. In retrospect, most of his conservative decisions in the 1940s and 1950s were discarded by the Court in the 1960s. In that decade the Court ruled that disproportionate legislative districts violated the equal protection clause, that the Fourth Amendment exclusionary rule applied to unconstitutional search and seizure by local officers, that the Sixth Amendment guaranteed the right to counsel in state courts, and that the privilege against self-incrimination applied to the states. Some of his liberal positions, especially on economic nationalism, are not congenial to the Court's present conservative majority, and his overlong, somewhat pedantic opinions have not stood the test as great examples of legal literature.

For more information

Burt, Robert. *Two Jewish Justices: Outcasts in the Promised Land.* Berkeley: University of California Press, 1988.

Hirsch, H. N. *The Enigma of Felix Frankfurter.* New York: Basic Books, 1981.

Parrish, Michael. *Felix Frankfurter and His Times.* New York: Free Press, 1982.

Marvin Zolman
Wayne State University

fraud   is the deliberate misrepresentation of a material fact, made with the intention of inducing reliance in another person, that causes a loss of money or property. It can have both civil and criminal consequences.

Fraud forms the basis of the tort of misrepresentation, a civil action sometimes called deceit. The victim is entitled to recover compensatory damages based on one or another of three measures. The most common is the "out of pocket" measure, which is the difference between the price paid and the actual value of the item received. A second, more generous measure is the "benefit of the bargain," being the difference between the value of the item as it was represented to be and its actual value. If the item can be made to correspond to the representation, a third measure used is the cost to do so, or "make good" damages.

Because it is a tort, fraud may also be the basis for punitive damages, which are awarded to punish and deter intentional wrongdoing. If the representation was merely reckless, rather than intentional, punitive damages would not be recoverable.

Fraud is also a basis for several forms of judicial relief in contract law. It may provide grounds for rescinding a contract, for recovering restitution of what was exchanged under a contract, or for reforming the terms of a contract to conform to representations made.

To rescind a contract is to "undo" it. If one party to a contract has been misled by the other party's fraud, a court can refuse to enforce the contract and order it rescinded. If a victim of the fraud has paid money or transferred property under the contract, a court can order its restoration to the victim, a remedy called restitution.

In the alternative, under certain circumstances a victim of fraud in the execution of a contract may ask for reformation. Reformation is an equitable remedy in which the court literally rewrites the contract language to make it conform to what was represented. Fraud may also be used in the writing of a will or trust.

Fraud can be the basis for criminal prosecutions under both state and federal law. Several closely related crimes exist in most states to deter fraudulent conduct. The crime of false pretenses occurs where a wrongdoer obtains title to property (which includes money) by intentionally defrauding a victim. Another crime predicated on fraud is larceny by trick, where a wrongdoer causes the victim to transfer possession of property, intending to steal it. Embezzlement is the fraudulent taking of property by one trusted with its possession. Such crimes generally are divided into degrees and punished more or less severely depending upon the value of the property taken.

A number of federal statutes punish fraudulent conduct, such as the False Claims Act, the Mail Fraud Act, and statutes aimed at preventing securities fraud. In addition, the Federal Trade Commission (FTC) has been given jurisdiction to investigate and formulate rules against fraudulent practices that are aimed at consumers. Many states have passed "little FTC acts" that provide penalties such as treble damages for fraudulent business practices.

For more information

Dunn, Robert L. *Recovery of Damages for Fraud.* Westport, Conn.: Lawpress Corp., 1995.

Freedman, Warren. *The Business Tort of Fraud and Misrepresentation.* Stoneham, Mass.: Butterworth Publishers, 1989.

Norman Otto Stockmeyer, Jr.
Thomas M. Cooley Law School

freedom of assembly and association is an essential part of the U.S. Constitution's First Amendment guarantees that restrict federal government regulation of a person's ability to present ideas or create organizations.

Freedom of assembly is directly mentioned while the right of association derives from a variety of First Amendment guarantees of speech and assembly. The assembly and association portions of the First Amendment protect democracy by enhancing discourse; moreover, they permit political advocacy and formation of interest groups as part of our fundamental freedoms. Interest groups are significant in national, state, and local political processes. Both freedom of assembly and association are subject to reasonable government regulations. These provisions do not allow assembly or association for unlawful purposes. Rights of association and assembly are often balanced against other societal interests, such as breach of peace or incitement to riot.

Individuals' ability to assemble and associate ranges from groups such as the Communist Party of the United States to Massachusetts Citizens for Life to labor unions. For example, in the 1930s and 1940s First Amendment rights to assemble and organize were essential for constitutional support of organized labor movements. The United States Supreme Court has often decided against government rules that would make political association ineffective; e.g., *NAACP v. Alabama ex rel. Patterson,* which prohibited Alabama from forcing the NAACP to disclose its membership lists. These lists were connected to individuals' rights of association. This part of the First Amendment also involves a freedom not to associate; see *Abood v. Detroit Board of Education,* which allows teachers not to associate with a union. In the 1980s the Supreme Court established connections between associational rules and discriminatory practices. Due to their public and business purposes both the Jaycees and Rotary International could not use freedom of association as the basis for discriminating against female members; see *Roberts v. United States Jaycees* and *Board of Directors of Rotary International v. Rotary Club.*

Political, social, and economic interests' ability to associate and assemble to petition government are seen as essential to a regime based upon representation. James Madison in *Federalist Papers* number 10 asks whether the structure of government should thwart these political movements. Instead, he argues that freedom of assembly and association principles provide responsiveness to interests of different societal parts, which permit fragmentation of power concerning political and economic interests. These constitutional provisions permit advocacy of ideas, often controversial ideas, without government interference.

U.S. Supreme Court cases have considered rights of association of national and state political parties. Major political parties have maintained their rights to partisan primary elections. Some election laws have been ruled unconstitutional when imposing restrictions on the associational rights of minor political parties or supporters of an independent candidate.

For more information

Abood v. Detroit Board of Education, 431 U.S. 209 (1977).

Board of Directors of Rotary International v. Rotary Club of Duarte, 481 U.S. 537 (1987).

Horn, Robert A. *Groups and the Constitution.* Stanford, Calif.: Stanford University Press, 1956.

NAACP v. Alabama ex rel. Patterson, 357 U.S. 449 (1958).

Roberts v. United States Jaycees, 468 U.S. 609 (1984).

Schwartz, Bernard. *Super Chief: Earl Warren and His Supreme Court—A Judicial Biography.* New York: New York University Press, 1983.

Texas v. Johnson, 491 U.S. 397 (1989).

Steven Puro
Professor of Political Science
Saint Louis University

freedom of conscience   See *WEST VIRGINIA V. BARNETTE.*

Freedom of Information Act   or FOIA is a federal law that provides for public access to records of the U.S. government. The act, which was passed by Congress in 1966, has increased government accountability and information availability. It established the presumption that documents of the federal government should be available to interested citizens and the press, rather than placing a burden on the requester to prove to the government that the information should be released. Indeed, prior to the passage of the FOIA, there were no statutory guidelines dealing with information release and no judicial remedies for those denied access. With the FOIA, the "need to know" standard has been replaced by a "right to know" doctrine. The government now has to justify the need to keep the information secret. The foundation of the act is the belief that the government is accountable for its actions and that the public possesses a right to obtain information about those actions. The act was further strengthened in 1974 following the Watergate scandal.

The FOIA exempts such records that are deemed crucial to foreign policy, national defense, confidential trade and financial information, and private personnel or medical files. If documents are requested that are partially exempt from FOIA disclosure, the agency is under no obligation to release the confidential parts merely because it must release the nonexempt material. Instead, it may edit or redact (usually, by literally blacking out) those portions that are exempt but must still produce those portions that are not exempt. Material obtained from such agencies as the Central Intelligence Agency or the Federal Bureau of Investigation is often redacted to avoid disclosure of sensitive information or to avoid revealing the nature or identity of confidential sources.

The FOIA provides that each government agency publish descriptions of its operations and procedures. Each agency must also make available opinions, orders, and statements of policy that affect the public. Any person or organization can also obtain data from a government agency through a FOIA request. Agencies have 10 working days to comply with a request but may extend this deadline if the search requires them to collect records from field facilities, examine voluminous files, or consult with other agencies having a substantial interest in the matter under investigation.

Under FOIA, agencies may withhold nine categories of records, ranging from national defense information and matters under litigation to medical files. Agencies also may leave out identifying details to avoid unwarranted invasions of personal privacy. Federal courts, however, have jurisdiction to block efforts to withhold records. The Office of Personnel Management also has the power to take disciplinary action against officials who withhold information contrary to the law.

Federal agencies annually spend more than $100 million to process these requests. FOIA's critics charge that the act diverts government personnel from their principal work and that those requesting files all too often use the information they receive at taxpayer expense for commercial purposes. Others charge that the process is too cumbersome, time consuming, and expensive to provide much practical benefit to average citizens. Indeed, although the original purpose of FOIA was to provide ordinary citizens with better access to information about the activities of their government, private companies seeking government records now account for as much as 75 percent of FOIA searches.

For more information

A Citizen's Guide on Using the Freedom of Information Act and the Privacy Act of 1974 to Request Government Records, 3rd report. Washington, D.C.: U.S. Government Printing Office, 1989.

Freedom of Information Act (5 U.S.C., section 552), July 4, 1967, as amended.

Montana, John. "The Freedom of Information Act," *Records Management Quarterly* (April 1998): v32 n2 p46(4).

Theoharis, Athan G. *A Culture of Secrecy: The Government Versus the People's Right to Know.* Lawrence: University Press of Kansas, 1998.

James H. Joyner, Jr., Ph.D.
Assistant Professor of Political Science
Troy State University

freedom of speech is that uniquely American right guaranteed by the U.S. Constitution that the government may not, without extremely good reason, interfere with the political and social speech of its citizens. The Constitution states that Congress "shall make no law . . . abridging the freedom of speech, ..." The courts have interpreted speech to include almost all spoken, written, or printed words as well as many other kinds of expression. Included in speech are pictures such as paintings, drawings, or photographs; dramatic productions such as plays, movies, song lyrics; advertisements; demonstrative acts which express ideas or opinions such as parades, flag burning, refusal to salute a flag; and any expression that has literary, artistic, political, or scientific intent.

All these kinds of expression are protected by the First Amendment under the free speech clause, and the courts have ruled that government may not restrict any of these kinds of speech unless it can demonstrate a "compelling interest" in making the restrictions. The major kinds of restrictions on speech that the courts have allowed are those that come under the clear and present danger principle formulated by Justice Oliver Wendell Holmes. For example, no one can falsely shout fire in a crowded theater nor can someone utter fighting words such as threatening to punch someone.

Other forms of restricted speech include obscenity, which is defined as "Works which when taken as a whole, appeal to the prurient interest in sex, which portray sexual content in a patently offensive way, and which, taken as a whole do not have serious literary, artistic, political or scientific value. . . ." Generally, governmental attempts at restricting obscenity and pornography are aimed at protecting children; but when Congress attempted to ban "indecent material" from the Internet, the Supreme Court struck down the statute as vague and unenforceable because the government was unable to demonstrate that the stated purpose of protecting children did not interfere with the rights of adults to receive information and engage in discourse.

Commercial speech may also be restricted because it promotes the interest of a purveyor of goods or services, but any regulations must advance the governmental interest and only in the least restrictive manner. For example, a state cannot ban the publishing of prices of alcoholic beverages unless it can show some rational relationship between the ban and government's desire to discourage excessive drinking. Most attempts by the government to restrict freedom of speech have been struck down by the courts even when the expression is offensive to the general public. Justice John Marshall Harlan best summarized the precedent when he said that one man's vulgarity is another's lyric.

No other country has so resolutely adhered to a Bill of Rights as has the U.S. citizenry. The Constitution expressly prohibits the government from restricting a citizen's right to express his or her opinion, even when that opinion is offensive to the majority of the people. Only in certain limited circumstances may the government restrict its citizens' right to free expression. Private individuals and institutions, however, are not under these constitutional restraints.

For more information

American Jurisprudence, 2nd ed. Vol. 16A, Constitutional Law. St. Paul, Minn.: West Group Publishing, 1998.

Cox, Archibald. Freedom of Expression. Cambridge, Mass.: Harvard University Press, 1980, 1999.

Hentoff, Nat. Free Speech for Me—But Not for Thee. New York: HarperPerennial, 1993.

Irons, Peter, ed. May It Please the Court: The First Amendment. New York: The New Press, 1997.

Stanley M. Morris
Attorney at Law
Cortez, Colorado

freedom of the press is a subdivision of freedom of speech and generally refers to the protection given to the dissemination of speech expressing news, information, or opinion. The "press" includes such media as newspapers, television, radio, the Internet, and books. As with other clauses of the First Amendment, the purpose is to declare to the federal government what it may not do. Although the words of the Constitution are sparse, the courts, by way of their declared duty to interpret or discover the intent of the framers in placing such conditions on the Congress, determine what the Congress may or may not legislate. The courts have also ruled that the First Amendment applies to the states because of the adoption of the Fourteenth Amendment. Therefore, no state legislature or other governing body may enact a law contrary to the First Amendment

One of the most meaningful restrictions on the government is that it may not stop publication of a newspaper or book in advance of publication. This prohibition is called "prior restraint." There are exceptions such as national security or public health and safety. An example of attempted prior restraint that failed was the "Pentagon Papers," in which the government attempted to enjoin the publication of documents detailing the various policies of the Vietnam War and its prosecution by the U.S. government. The Supreme Court unanimously refused to impose any restraint on what the justices determined to be political speech. This was not the case when a magazine called the *Progres-*

sive sought to publish details of a working hydrogen bomb. In that instance, security and safety overrode the requirements of the First Amendment.

Broadcast media have special requirements because of the regulation of the broadcast spectrum. The restrictions are usually on the basis of time of broadcast. The arrangement that the government and broadcasters have entered into is a modification of the freedom available to print media. In exchange for use of the electronic spectrum, the broadcasters submit to licensing, agreements to air "public service announcements," and some content restrictions. An example of content restrictions is the case involving George Carlin, a comedian popular in the 1960s and 1970s who made a recording called "The Seven Dirty Words You Can't Say on Television." This routine was played over various radio stations and eventually the Supreme Court ruled that the routine could not be broadcast. Just to make sure that everyone knew what words could not be used, the Court thoughtfully appended a transcript of the routine to the written opinion.

Print media, and more recently the Internet, would not be subjected to content restrictions, and any attempt to impose such restrictions would be met with stiff resistance. The main restraint on the press is that neither print nor broadcast media may disseminate libel. Libel consists of publication of false or injurious information about an individual or enterprise such that it damages that individual. If the individual is not a public figure, then the publication need only be negligent to cause the publisher liability and subject him or her to a claim for damages. If the individual is a public figure, then to show liability and damages, the person libeled must show that the publisher had actual malice in disseminating the falsehood.

In general, subject only to the constraints of libel, a publisher of news, information, or opinion may not be restrained from printing, broadcasting, or posting to the Internet what he or she wants.

For more information
Leonard W. Levy. *Emergence of a Free Press*. New York: Oxford University Press, 1985.

Stanley M. Morris
Attorney, Conter, Colorado

Frontiero v. Richardson   411 U.S. 677 (1973) was a Supreme Court decision that addressed the proper standard of review in cases of gender discrimination. A plurality of the Court held that classifications based on gender were inherently suspect and, therefore, should be subjected to a "strict scrutiny" analysis. However, this approach was not adopted by a majority of the Court in subsequent decisions.

The case came to the Court after Sharron Frontiero, a lieutenant in the Air Force, was denied additional housing and medical benefits available under federal law when, as required under the law, she was unable to demonstrate that her husband was dependent on her for over one-half of his support. The law awarded the additional spousal benefits to servicemen without evidence of dependent support. Frontiero filed suit, claiming that the difference in treatment was an unconstitutional gender discrimination violating the equal protection component of the due process clause of the Fifth Amendment. A three-judge district court upheld the constitutionality of the law, applying the less stringent "rational basis" analysis and finding that the saving of administrative costs that would be incurred if servicemen were required to prove dependency of their spouses justified the distinction, given that only a small percentage of their spouses would be ineligible.

In an 8–1 vote, the Court struck down the law as unconstitutional. While Justice Rehnquist was the lone dissenter, believing that the district court's decision should stand, a majority of the justices could not agree on the standard to apply in gender discrimination cases. Writing for the plurality of four justices, Justice Brennan argued that sex discrimination cases should be analyzed under a strict scrutiny analysis, requiring the government to show a compelling interest to justify the distinction. Justice Brennan believed the Court's most recent decision on gender discrimination, *Reed v. Reed,* 404 U.S. 71 (1971), supported the adoption of this more stringent analysis because that decision appeared to signal a departure from the then applicable and less stringent rational basis analysis. In addition, he asserted that a strict scrutiny analysis was justified to remedy the long his-tory of sex discrimination and because gender discrimination imposed a legal burden unre-lated to individual responsibility. Finally, he argued that the recent increased sensitivity of Congress to gender discrimination, in part evidenced by the proposal of the Equal Rights Amendment in 1972, justified the greater level of protection.

Justice Powell, joined by Chief Justice Burger and Justice Blackmun, agreed that the statute was unconstitutional but rejected Justice Brennan's view that gender-based classifications should be inherently suspect and subjected to a strict scrutiny analysis. Justice Powell disagreed with Justice Brennan's reading of *Reed* and also believed it would damage both the Court and democratic institutions if the Court found that gender classifications were inherently suspect while the Equal Rights Amendment was being considered for ratification.

The level of review of classifications based on gender was later addressed in *Craig v. Boren,* 429 U.S.190 (1976), where the Court adopted a standard between the rational basis and strict scrutiny tests. Under this intermediate scrutiny approach, the gender classification "must serve important governmental objectives and must be substantially related to those objectives." The Court has followed this approach in more recent decisions, including *United States v. Virginia,* 518 U.S. 515 (1996).

For more information

Baer, Judith A. *Women in American Law: The Struggle Toward Equality from the New Deal to the Present.* New York: Holmes and Meier, 1991.

Frontiero v. Richardson, 411 U.S. 677 (1973).

Goldstein, Leslie Friedman. *The Constitutional Rights of Women,* 2nd ed. Madison: University of Wisconsin Press, 1988.

James N. G. Cauthen
The City University of New York

Fuller, Melville W. (1833–1910) Chief justice of the United States between 1888 and 1910, was born in Augusta, Maine, in 1833 and educated at Bowdoin College. He received most of his legal education through law firm apprenticeship but also attended lectures at Harvard Law School. Fuller moved to Chicago and established a successful law practice focused on appellate advocacy. He often represented banks, railroads, and members of the Chicago business elite.

Reared in the Jacksonian political tradition emphasizing limited government, Fuller early became active in Democratic Party affairs. He developed a close relationship with President Grover Cleveland. In March of 1888 Cleveland nominated Fuller to replace the deceased Morrison R. Waite as chief justice. Fuller was not well known nationally, but after some delay he was confirmed by the Republican-controlled Senate.

Fuller was an outstanding judicial administrator. A genial man with an urbane sense of humor, he fostered a harmonious working relationship among the justices. Fuller wrote 840 majority opinions, speaking for the Court more often than any other justice during his period of service. He was also instrumental in reducing the huge backlog of appeals and in bringing about the creation of the circuit courts of appeals to ease the work burden of the Supreme Court.

As Chief Justice Fuller guided the Supreme Court to greater judicial solicitude for the rights of property owners against governmental incursions. The Fuller Court established judicial review of railroad rate regulation, gave a new vitality to the takings clause, strengthened the doctrine of substantive due process, and vigorously expanded the reach of judicial authority. In *Pollock. v. Farmers' Loan and Trust Company* (1895), for example, Fuller struck down the 1894 income tax as an unconstitutional direct tax. In *United States v. E.C. Knight Company* (1895) Fuller distinguished between commerce and manufacturing and thus restricted application of the Sherman Antitrust Act. The Supreme Court also ruled that just compensation for private property taken for public use was an essential element of due process as guaranteed by the Fourteenth Amendment. Fuller viewed property rights and individual liberty as closely related, and he sought to protect liberty by restraining government. Dedicated to economic liberty as a crucial constitutional value, Fuller and his colleagues were generally in accord with the prevailing public sentiment of the age. It should also be noted that the Fuller Court upheld many regulations to protect the public safety and health.

Under Fuller the Supreme Court generally deferred to state control of race relations and criminal justice. Thus, in *Plessy v. Ferguson* (1896) the Court approved the emerging practice of racial segregation in the South. It likewise refused to apply the Bill of Rights to state criminal proceedings. With respect to federal criminal prosecutions, however, Fuller and his associates tended to give an expanded meaning to the procedural safeguards in the Bill of Rights.

Melville Fuller died in July of 1910. He had served as chief justice for 22 years during a pivotal era of American history.

For more information

Ely, James W., Jr. *The Chief Justiceship of Melville W. Fuller, 1888–1910.* Columbia: University of South Carolina Press, 1995.

Fiss, Owen M. *Troubled Beginnings of the Modern State.* New York: Macmillan Library Reference 1888–1910, 1993.

James W. Ely, Jr.
Vanderbilt University Law School

Furman v. Georgia 408 U.S. 238 (1972) was the case in which the Supreme Court found that the death penalty violated the Eighth Amendment's prohibition of cruel and unusual punishment. A Georgia jury had convicted Furman of murder and imposed the death penalty under a law that did not provide the jury with any specific guidance regarding when the death penalty might be properly imposed or when alternative sentences, such as life imprisonment, were appropriate. Furman, and the two other petitioners, who had been sentenced to death for rape, were all African American.

The five justices in the majority were divided in their reasoning. Justices Douglas, Stewart, and White found the existing application of the death penalty to be applied in arbitrary or inconsistent manner and thus unconstitutional. Douglas was particularly concerned that capital punishment was disproportionately imposed on African Americans and the poor, and he found its application to violate the equal protection clause of the Fourteenth Amendment as well as the Eighth Amendment. Stewart's concurrence emphasized the randomness of the death penalty, comparing a death sentence to being struck by lightning, and concluded that its arbitrary imposition violated the Eighth Amendment's prohibition of "unusual" forms of punishment. White's concurrence took up where Stewart's left off, concluding that the punishment's rarity had undermined its value as a deterrent to criminal activity and thus one of its major justifications.

Justices Brennan and Marshall found the death penalty to be inherently unconstitutional because of its cruelty and indifference to human dignity. Rejecting the historical acceptance of the death penalty in the United States, they found that it was unique among modern punishments in its capacity to degrade those on which it was imposed and that it violated contemporary standards of decency. Both Brennan and Marshall would oppose the death penalty in every case they considered for the rest of their careers on the Court.

The four justices who dissented were more united in their arguments, with all four writing separately and all four joining each other's opinions. Chief Justice Burger wrote that the original intent of the Eighth Amendment was to prohibit torture, and that the determination that capital punishment was cruel should be left to legislatures and juries, while Justice Powell noted a wide variety of historical and contemporary opinions supporting the death penalty. Justice Rehnquist's dissent focused on the Court's responsibility to restrain its use of judicial review. In a particularly personal concurrence, Justice Blackmun argued that, while he would prefer to see capital punishment abolished, he did not believe that it was the Court's role to end the death penalty while there was both historical and contemporary support for its imposition. In his last year on the Supreme Court, Blackmun would change his mind and argue that the death penalty could not be imposed in a fair manner and that it should be found unconstitutional in all cases.

The Court's ban on the imposition of the death penalty stood until its decision in *Gregg v. Georgia* (1976), which allowed the use of the death penalty so long as juries decided each case based on guidelines that include the consideration of specific aggravating and mitigating circumstances of the criminal act being punished.

For more information

Amnesty International. *Killing with Prejudice: Race and the Death Penalty*. New York: Amnesty International USA, 1999.

Sarat, Austin. *When the State Kills: Capital Punishment and the American Condition*. Princeton N.J.: Princeton University Press, 2001.

Daniel Levin
University of Utah

G

In re Gault 387 U.S. 1 (1967) was a milestone U.S. Supreme Court case in juvenile justice.

The case began when 15-year-old Gerald Gault of Globe, Arizona, was charged with making lewd telephone calls to his neighbor. After he was found guilty in a hearing before a juvenile court judge, Gault was committed to the Arizona Industrial School until he reached majority, that is, for six years. An adult convicted of the same offense would have been sentenced to a maximum of two months in jail or a fine of $5 to $50.

Gault's appeal claimed that he was denied constitutional rights stemming from the due process clause of the Fourteenth Amendment, including the right to an attorney and the privilege against self-incrimination. His appeal was denied by the Arizona state courts, including the state supreme court.

In an 8–1 opinion, the Supreme Court reversed the state supreme court and imposed new procedural requirements on juvenile courts throughout the nation. Speaking for the majority, Justice Abe Fortas began with the reminder that juvenile offenders are entitled to constitutional protections; he said, "neither the Fourteenth Amendment nor the Bill of Rights is for adults alone" (p. 13).

The Court recapitulated the history of juvenile courts, noting that the impetus behind their creation was to insulate juveniles from the harshness of the adult justice system. The relationship between the child and the state was intended to be non-adversarial, the Court pointed out, with the state conceiving its role as the child's parent, under the doctrine known as *parens patria*. Also, because the juvenile court's primary purpose was to rehabilitate the child, not ascertain guilt or innocence, it did not have to apply adult criminal procedures.

Although the theory is admirable, said Fortas, the practice is less so. Because juvenile court hearings are adversarial, children such as Gerald Gault are deprived of their liberty without the due process protections given to adult offenders. Acknowledging the advantages inherent in a separate juvenile court system with its special procedures, the Court held that the Constitution requires the state to provide procedural safeguards, largely stemming from the Fifth and Sixth Amendments, to juvenile offenders. Under the rules announced in *Gault,* states must provide juveniles with specific notice of the charges against them and allow adequate time to prepare a defense; states must notify juveniles of the right to an attorney and provide one if the parents are unable to afford it; juveniles have a right against self-incrimination, and states cannot rely on confessions without showing that they are voluntary; and at trial, juveniles have the right to confront and cross-examine witnesses against them.

Applying these rules to Gerald Gault's case, the Court found that there was insufficient notice of the charges against him; he was not offered counsel; he was not told he did not have to make a statement, so his confession was not truly voluntary; and since the complainant was not called as a witness against him, he was deprived of his Sixth Amendment right to confront his accuser.

For more information
Manfredi, Christopher P. *The Supreme Court and Juvenile Justice.* Lawrence: University of Kansas Press, 1998.

Susan Gluck Mezey
Department of Political Science
Loyola University, Chicago

gay rights   refers to the political and social struggle of homosexuals, bisexuals, and trans-gender individuals to achieve the same legal rights as other Americans regardless of sexual orientation. Although recently debated in the context of gay marriage, gay rights extends to such issues as raising and adopting children, as well as the right to be free from bias in the workplace.

The birth of the modern gay rights movement is often traced to the raid and subsequent riot at the Stonewall Inn in Greenwich Village, a neighborhood in New York City. There in the summer of 1969 patrons of a local gay bar protested what they saw as police harassment. Although few knew about it at the time, the now famous "Stonewall Riot" has become symbolic of the political and social movement for equal rights by gays and lesbians over the last three decades.

The very expression "gay rights" is controversial—and not simply because Americans remain split in their acceptance of gay, lesbian, and trans-gender lifestyles. Rather, the term has come to mean two different concepts in popular culture, often dependent on individual views of homosexuality. To most gays, lesbians, and their supporters, gay rights means constitutional protection against discrimination on the basis of sexual orientation; to opponents, however, the term means "special rights" for homosexuals. This debate was highlighted in the United States Supreme Court case of *Romer v. Evans,* a 1996 challenge to a Colorado initiative prohibiting legal protection for gays and lesbians. Supporters of the law said that it merely put gays and lesbians on the same level as all other persons: just as red-haired people were not entitled to legal protection against discrimination, neither should gays and lesbians claim special rights. The Supreme Court ruled, however, that Colorado could not prohibit a class of people from ever seeking legal protection from discrimination. Noteworthy in the Court's decision was its conclusion that the law was "inexplicable by anything but animus toward the class that it affects."

The *Evans* decision was a departure for the Supreme Court, which 10 years earlier had upheld a Georgia anti-sodomy law that punished two adult men for engaging in consensual sex in a private home. In that case, *Bowers v. Hardwick,* gay rights supporters had urged the Court to grant homosexuals the same constitutional protection it had given other minority groups with a history of exclusion and discrimination. But, rather than using the case to extend civil rights protections to gays and lesbians, the Court narrowly interpreted the Georgia statute as being simply about sodomy. Since *Bowers* a few states have instituted antidiscrimination statutes that apply to gays and lesbians, and at least one state supreme court—Hawaii's—has created legal pro-

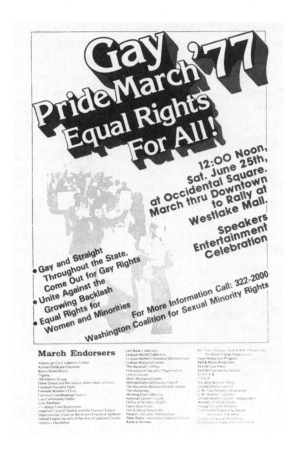

Gay Pride March '77 (LIBRARY OF CONGRESS)

opposed equal rights for gays and lesbians, including, especially, same-sex marriage. In the face of such opposition a few cities and the state of Vermont have enacted civil unions statutes, which allow committed gay and lesbian couples to receive the legal benefits and protections usually reserved for spouses. In addition, gay and lesbian groups are pressuring Congress to enact the Employment Non-Discrimination Act (ENDA), a statute to extend the civil rights laws to gays and lesbians in the workplace. At this writing, the fate of the ENDA is at best uncertain; nonetheless, public support for gay rights is rising in the United States. Perhaps in another decade or two Americans will look back on the struggle for gay rights the way we now consider the Women's Rights and Civil Rights movements: as a campaign to provide equal protection of the laws to a group previously hounded simply for being who they are.

For more information

Newton, David E. *Gay and Lesbian Rights: A Reference Handbook*. Santa Barbara, Calif.: ABC-Clio, 1994.

Marks, Robert B. *The Gay and Lesbian Movement: References and Resources*. New York: G. K. Hall, 1996.

Jon Gould
George Mason University

tection for homosexuals under state constitutional law. The vast majority of states, however, have not.

The election of Bill Clinton as president in 1992 was hailed by many gay rights supporters as an opportunity to enact legislation to protect gays and lesbians. While Clinton campaigned to advance gay rights, the result of his administration is the often-criticized "don't ask, don't tell" policy. Under this policy homosexual men and women may serve in the armed forces so long as they do not engage in any homosexual activities.

Clinton has been criticized by gay rights supporters for failing to actively advance their concerns, but it is also true that Congress has

Gibbons v. Ogden   22 U.S. 1 (1824) is the case in which the Supreme Court held that the national government's power to legislate in the area of commerce is very broad.

Gibbons was the first case in which the Supreme Court attempted to interpret the commerce clause of the U.S. Constitution. The Court, in an opinion written by Justice Marshall, held that the monopoly granted by the New York legislature to Robert Fulton and Robert Livingston regarding steamboat navigation in the waters of New York violated Article I, section 8 of the Constitution, which gives Congress the

"Power . . . To regulate Commerce . . . among the several States."

The case arose when Ogden, a successor to the monopoly rights held by Livingston and Fulton, filed suit in the New York courts seeking an injunction against Gibbons's operation of a steamboat that ran from New York City to Elizabethtown, New Jersey. The highest court in New York to hear the case upheld the request for an injunction, holding that the license granted to Gibbons by the U.S. government to navigate the waters of any particular state did not preempt the New York state legislature's grant of the monopoly. In his appeal to the United States Supreme Court, Gibbons argued that the state had no right to grant the monopoly because navigation is commerce among the states and therefore only Congress can legislate on that subject.

The case raised several important issues. First, what is interstate commerce; second, what is the extent of Congress's power to regulate interstate commerce; and third, what is the effect on the states as a result of the Constitution's express grant of power in this area to Congress? Marshall's opinion clearly resolves the first two questions, but it only hints at the answer to the third.

In answer to the first question, Marshall wrote that commerce is not just buying and selling, but that it comprehends "every species of commercial intercourse." Marshall went on to note that such an expansive definition of commerce encompasses navigation.

As to the second question, Marshall opined that Congress's power was "complete in itself, may be exercised to its utmost extent, and acknowledges no limitations other than are prescribed in the Constitution." In other words, Congress possessed the power "to prescribe the rule by which commerce is to be governed."

Marshall's answer to the third question is as hazy as the answers to the first questions are clear. Marshall wrote that the argument that the commerce power was exclusive, meaning that the states had no authority to regulate in the area

of commerce, had "great force." However, he avoided answering the question definitively by finding that the New York legislature's grant of a monopoly was in conflict with the federal statute under which Gibbons operated his steamboats, and therefore the New York legislation violated the supremacy clause and was thus not enforceable.

By not providing a definitive answer to the third question, Marshall left open the possibility that some state legislation in the area of commerce would be tolerated, thus avoiding huge controversy for the Supreme Court. Marshall's opinion in *Gibbons* is widely viewed as a classic display of his foresight and keen political sense.

For more information

McCloskey, Robert G. (as revised by Sanford Levinson). *The American Supreme Court.* Chicago: University of Chicago Press, 1994.

White, G. Edward. *The Marshall Court and Cultural Change 1815–1835* (abridged edition). New York: Oxford University Press, 1991.

Michael H. Walsh
Senior Lecturer, Political Science Dept.
Loyola University, Chicago

Ginsburg, Ruth Bader (1933–   ) is a leading legal advocate for women's rights and the second woman to be appointed to the Supreme Court.

Although Ginsburg graduated at the top of her 1959 class at Columbia Law School, Supreme Court Justice Felix Frankfurter turned her down for a clerkship, considering a woman clerk unthinkable. No law firm in New York City would hire her either, but a federal district court judge chose her as his clerk.

She subsequently taught at Rutgers Law School, where some of her students asked her to offer a course on women and the law. Surprised at how little had been written about the subject, she and two colleagues put together one of the nation's first casebooks on gender-based discrimination (1974).

At the same time, Ginsburg was helping to create and direct the ACLU Women's Rights Project. She argued six major Supreme Court gender equality cases for it between 1973 and 1979, winning five of them and remaking U.S. law in the process (*Frontiero v. Richardson,* 1973; *Kahn v. Shevin,* 1974; *Edwards v. Healy,* 1975; *Weinberger v. Wiesenfeld,* 1975; *Califano v. Goldfarb,* 1977; *Duren v. Missouri,* 1979).

One of her goals was to persuade the Court to view gender-based legal distinctions as suspect on their face. It was a difficult task. "The response I got when I talked about sex-based discrimination," she recalls, "was 'What are you talking about? Women are treated ever so much better than men.'"

The pervasiveness of that assumption led Ginsburg to utilize a cautious and incremental approach with the Court. She selected a number of cases with male plaintiffs to show the justices that when working women were discriminated against, it was their families, husbands included, who suffered. While the Court did not go as far as she would have liked, it did create a somewhat tighter standard for evaluating whether gender-based laws were constitutional.

President Jimmy Carter named Ginsburg to the D.C. Circuit Court of Appeals in 1981. She made a solid record there as a hardworking and nonideological "judge's judge," and when President Bill Clinton nominated her to the Supreme Court in 1993, she was confirmed by a Senate vote of 97–3.

Throughout her career she has concentrated on the real people involved in a case. As an advocate, she frequently began an argument before the Supreme Court by telling the story of the plaintiff and the discrimination he or she had suffered; her opinions from the bench emphasize the facts and human dimensions of a case as well as legal principles. As a judge she has tended to respect precedent and to support the government's power to regulate. She favors leaving pol-

Justice Ruth Bader Ginsburg (HULTON ARCHIVE)

icy matters to the president and legislature, although she has written that "when political avenues for redressing political problems become dead-end streets, some judicial intervention in the politics of the people may be essential in order to have any effective politics."

One of the crowning moments of Ginsburg's career came in 1996, when she wrote the Supreme Court's opinion ordering the Virginia Military Institute to admit women (*U.S. v. Virginia*). In it, she drew on the precedents she had gotten the Court to set in her days as an advocate and took them further to establish a new and more stringent standard for the adjudication of gender discrimination cases.

It seemed a fitting vindication for the woman whose gender had once kept her from working for the Court.

For more information

Merritt, Deborah Jones. "Hearing the Voices of Individual Women and Men: Justice Ruth Bader Ginsburg," *Hawaii Law Review* 20 (1998): 635.

Rosen, Jeffrey. "The New Look of Liberalism on the Court," *New York Times Magazine,* October 5, 1997.

Philippa Strum
City University of New York

Gitlow v. New York 268 U.S. 652 (1925) was the first Supreme Court decision to hold that the Bill of Rights limited the states' power to regulate free speech and press.

Benjamin Gitlow was indicted for the felony of advocating criminal anarchy, defined by New York as "the doctrine that organized government should be overthrown by force or violence . . . . or by any unlawful means." Gitlow, a Socialist Party activist, arranged for the printing and distribution of the party's "Manifesto," which advocated "proletarian revolutionary struggle" and a "mass political strike" directed at "the overthrow of the political organization upon which capitalistic exploitation depends."

Gitlow's lawyers argued that the statute was unconstitutional. The Fourteenth Amendment to the Constitution prohibits states from denying anyone "life, liberty, or property without due process of law." One of the elements of the liberty protected, Gitlow contended, was liberty of speech and press, as it was referred to in the First Amendment ("Congress shall make no law . . . abridging the freedom of speech, or of the press"). Speech was a right that could be restrained only when its exercise was likely to cause a substantive evil. As the statute did not require a showing of such a connection between speech and an illegal result, it was unconstitutional.

The argument was rejected by the courts of New York. The case reached a Supreme Court that had adopted Justice Oliver Wendell Holmes's formulation in *Schenck v. United States* (1919) that Congress could punish speech if it constituted a "clear and present danger." Justice Edward T. Sanford, writing for the Court, relied on that in rejecting Gitlow's appeal. It was up to the legislature to decide if the articulation of particular ideas constituted a clear and present danger, he declared, and by passing the statute, New York had declared speech like Gitlow's to be such a danger.

Justices Holmes and Brandeis dissented, saying there was no clear and present danger here.

Rejecting Sanford's holding that the manifesto was an incitement rather than mere advocacy, Holmes wrote, "Every idea is an incitement," because it is offered in the hope that the listener will accept and act upon it. Holmes denied that the state could punish speech because of its content, for "the only meaning of free speech" as guaranteed by the Constitution was that Gitlow's speech had to be allowed in the absence of a "present danger of an attempt to overthrow the government by force."

While Gitlow went to prison, his case was important because the entire Supreme Court agreed in it that the Fourteenth Amendment's due process clause protects the rights of speech and press from state action. Until then, the law had been that the First Amendment limited the powers only of Congress, not the states. In subsequent years the new doctrine would be utilized to minimize state restrictions on speech. *Gitlow* would be heralded as the case that began the process of incorporating most of the Bill of Rights into the Fourteenth Amendment's due process clause, thereby extending protection against civil liberties violations by the states as well as the federal government.

For more information

Murphy, Paul L. *The Shaping of the First Amendment: 1791 to the Present.* New York: Oxford University Press, 1992.

Wermiel, Stephen J. "Rights in the Modern Era: Applying the Bill of Rights to the States," *William & Mary Bill of Rights Journal* 1 (1992): 121.

Philippa Strum
City University of New York

grand jury is a group of citizens, usually selected from lists of registered voters and drivers, whose task it is to decide whether a prosecutor has presented enough evidence against a person accused of a crime to justify a trial on the charges presented. If the grand jury decides that there is sufficient evidence for a trial, it issues an "indictment" (a.k.a. a "true bill"), and the prosecution is permitted to go forward.

An indictment expresses no opinion on the guilt or innocence of the accused; it merely states the grand jury's conclusion that the prosecutor has presented sufficient evidence of criminal behavior to justify a trial. If a trial is held, a separate group of people, known as a "petit" jury, will hear the evidence and render a verdict.

The term "grand jury" refers merely to the size of the accusatory body, which has historically been larger than the petit jury. Today, state grand juries can have as few as five and as many as 23 members, while federal grand juries have between 16 and 23 members. A grand jury's term can last from one month to one year, but a typical term lasts three months, during which time the grand jurors meet periodically to consider cases that the prosecutor presents to them, and to conduct other investigations. A court can extend a grand jury's term if the grand jury is conducting a major investigation, such as one of organized crime or official corruption.

The grand jury's major task is to evaluate the evidence that the prosecutor presents to it in order to decide whether or not to issue an indictment. Toward that end, it can issue a reluctant witness a subpoena, which requires the recipient to appear before the grand jury, and it can offer the witness immunity from prosecution in exchange for testimony. A witness who refuses to testify before the grand jury despite a grant of immunity is subject to a citation for "contempt of court," which can result in the witness being jailed until either the witness testifies or the grand jury's term ends. A grand jury proceeding is unlike a trial. There is no judge present; only the prosecutors, the witness, and the grand jurors are present. The prosecutor directs the process, and the grand jurors hear only the prosecutor's version of the evidence, as no defendant(s), defense witnesses, or defense attorneys are present. This arrangement gives the prosecutor an enormous advantage in the search for an indictment, and, more than 95 percent of the time, it results in a decision by the grand jury to return an indictment. After the grand jurors consider the evidence presented, if a majority (e.g., twelve of twenty-three federal grand jurors) votes to indict, it issues a "true bill," which forms the basis for prosecution; if a majority votes not to indict, it issues a "no bill," which ends the case.

In the federal court system, a grand jury is constitutionally required to indict an accused before a prosecution can proceed. That is not true in most states, though; indeed, most states do not use grand jury indictments to determine that there is sufficient evidence for a trial. In 30 states, most or all prosecutions begin by means of an "information," which is a document in which the prosecutor argues that there is enough evidence against the accused to warrant prosecution. A judge scrutinizes the information at a "preliminary hearing," where the judge must decide whether there is "probable cause" to believe that a crime occurred and that the accused committed it. If the prosecutor's case satisfies the judge, the judge will approve the information, and the prosecution will go forward.

The current predominance of the information procedure reflects the controversial nature of grand juries, which do not live up to their promise. There are two traditional arguments in support of grand juries. One argument is that they check prosecutors who would otherwise harass innocent persons for political or personal reasons. Another argument is that they force prosecutors to gather enough evidence to justify holding a criminal trial. There is some truth to these arguments, but not as much as their supporters think there is. Moreover, there is substantial evidence that prosecutors so dominate the grand jury process that a grand jury's check on prosecutorial bad faith, laziness, or incompetence is likely to be minimal. Still, grand juries are an established institution in U.S. law and are likely to remain so indefinitely.

For more information

Neubauer, David W. *Judicial Process: Law, Courts, and Politics in the United States,* 2nd ed. Fort Worth, Tex.: Harcourt Brace College Publishers, 1997.

Schmalleger, Frank. *Criminal Justice Today: An Introductory Text for the Twenty-First Century,* 4th ed. Englewood Cliffs, N.J.: Prentice Hall, 1996.

Brian L. Porto
College of St. Joseph, Vermont

Green v. New Kent County School Board

391 U.S. 430 (1968) was the most important Supreme Court case dealing with school desegregation after *Brown v. Board of Education* in 1954.

In 1954 the Supreme Court declared racially segregated public schools unconstitutional under the Fourteen Amendment's equal protection clause. A year later the Court sought to give courts and school boards guidance by requiring the dismantling of racially segregated schools "with all deliberate speed" (*Brown v. Board of Education* [II], 349 U.S. 294, at 301 [1955]). In *Green* the Court repudiated *Brown's* 13-year-old strategy and moved from demanding an end to segregation to demanding the immediate integration of public schools.

New Kent was a lightly populated rural county in Virginia whose county school board participated in the South's resistance to court-ordered desegregation of its public schools. Threatened by the withdrawal of federal moneys for segregated public schools, the school board introduced a "freedom-of-choice plan" in 1965 allowing students to choose to attend either the formerly all-white New Kent School or the formerly all-black Watkins School. After three years no white student attended Watkins School and only 15 percent of the county's black students attended New Kent.

Justice Brennan, writing for a unanimous Court, held that "it is against this background" of resistance to *Brown* that school boards had an "affirmative duty to take whatever steps might be necessary to convert to a unitary system in which racial discrimination would be eliminated root and branch" (437–38). Brennan dismissed the "freedom-of-choice" plan as a mere token effort, impermissibly transferring the burden of dismantling the outlawed dual school system from the school board to the students (441–42). The school board must "fashion steps which promise realistically to convert promptly to a system without a 'white' school and a 'Negro' school, but just schools" (442).

The finding in *Green* was later expanded to include state action hindering desegregation even though there was no discriminatory motive or purpose (*Wright v. Council of the City of Emporia,* 407 U.S. 501 [1972]). *Green's* emphasis on achieving racial balance eventually led the Court in *Swann v. Charlotte-Mecklenburg Board of Education* (402 U.S. 1 [1971]) to approve school busing.

Justice Rehnquist, dissenting in *Keyes v. Denver School District No. 1,* 413 U.S. 189, 254 (1973), challenged what he considered to be *Green's* mandate for racial balance in public schools. While never winning a majority for his position, in 1991 the now Chief Justice Rehnquist made the issue irrelevant when he wrote for a majority of the Court that once a school district eliminated "the vestiges of prior discrimination," it no longer had to maintain racial balance (*Oklahoma City Board of Education v. Dowell,* 498 U.S. 237, at 250 [1991]).

For more information

Kluger, Richard A. *Simple Justice: The History of* Brown v. Board of Education *and Black America's Struggle for Equality.* New York: Knopf, 1975.

Timothy J. O'Neill
Southwestern University

Gregg v. Georgia

428 U.S. 153 (1976) is a 1976 Supreme Court case that upheld the constitutionality of the death penalty and ruled that a two-part proceeding—one for deciding guilt and

another for determining the sentence—meets the objections raised in *Furman v. Georgia.*

In *Furman v. Georgia* (1972), the U.S. Supreme Court rendered a 5–4 decision holding that the death penalty as administered in the United States was cruel and unusual punishment and therefore unconstitutional. The majority opinion in *Furman* stated that the death penalty was applied capriciously and that judges and juries had too much discretion when imposing the death penalty. This decision prevented the execution of 631 death row inmates in 32 states. Yet a clear consensus was not reached in the *Furman* case. Only a slim majority of justices agreed that the death penalty as administered in the states in 1972 was unconstitutional. They did not say that the death penalty was unconstitutional under all circumstances. This allowed states to revise their death penalty procedures for the purpose of passing constitutional muster in later years.

Four years later in 1976, the Supreme Court reviewed five capital punishment cases from five different states. Each of these states had enacted new death penalty laws. Three states—Georgia, Florida, and Texas—adopted guided discretion statutes. Guided discretion statutes require juries and judges to consider various aggravating and mitigating circumstances when deciding whether a defendant should receive the death penalty. The two other states—North Carolina and Louisiana—passed mandatory death penalty laws which held that anyone convicted of a capital offense would automatically receive the death penalty. The Court decisions that followed addressed the constitutionality of these new laws and the death penalty itself. Collectively, this series of five companion cases became known as the death penalty cases.

Gregg v. Georgia was one of these five landmark capital punishment cases. Like its predecessor *Furman v. Georgia* (1972), it addressed two basic constitutional rights—the equal protection of the laws requirement in the Fourteenth Amendment and the prohibition of cruel and unusual punishment provision in the Eighth Amendment. In *Gregg* a seven-justice majority agreed that capital punishment was not cruel and unusual in all circumstances. The Court upheld the new guided discretion statutes of Georgia, Florida, and Texas. Justice Potter Stewart, writing for the majority, stated that 35 states and the federal government had established new death penalty laws since the *Furman* ruling. He further argued that this augured against the petitioners' claims that the American public would no longer tolerate the death penalty due to evolving standards of decency.

Georgia's new guided discretion statute would be held up as a model for other state legislatures to emulate. Three features of Georgia's statute were regarded by Justice Stewart as sufficient safeguards against capricious or arbitrary application of the death penalty—a two-phased trial system or bifurcated trial, a statutory list of aggravating and mitigating circumstances from which the jury would make its sentencing decision in each case, and automatic review of every death penalty sentence by the state supreme court. The bifurcated or two-phased trial system requires the jury to decide a defendant's guilt first, and then in a separate phase the jury determines the sentence. In the second phase of a death penalty trial, jurors must consider aggravating and mitigating circumstances. This was seen as an important procedural protection. The circumstances of the crime—the way the crime was committed—may have life or death consequences for someone accused of a capital offense. Aggravating circumstances weigh toward a harsher penalty—imposition of the death penalty—whereas mitigating circumstances weigh against application of the death penalty in a particular case. The fact that the state supreme court was required to review every capital punishment case further prevented the arbitrary imposition of the death penalty by a jury.

In contrast to Georgia's guided discretion statute, the mandatory death penalty laws were struck down because they did not focus on the individual circumstances of imposing the death penalty in each case. The *Gregg* ruling precipitated reform in other state legislative death penalty enactments and cleared the way for states to overcome the objections noted in *Furman v. Georgia.*

For more information

Bedau, Hugo Adams. *The Death Penalty in America: Current Controversies.* New York and Oxford: Oxford University Press, 1997.

Vila, Bryan, and Cynthia Morris, eds. *Capital Punishment in the United States: A Documentary History.* Westport, Conn.: Greenwood Press, 1997.

Ruth Ann Strickland
Professor, Appalachian State University
Department of Political Science and Criminal Justice

Griggs v. Duke Power Company 401 U.S. 424 (1971) is a major early ruling holding that certain employment discrimination practices based on race violate Title VII of the Civil Rights Act of 1964.

Decided in 1971, in a unanimous decision written by Chief Justice Burger, the Supreme Court ruled for the black plaintiffs. It argued that consequences of employer practices is the key test of whether those practices fall within Equal Employment Opportunity Commission (EEOC) guidelines.

In this case, the employer used job tests that were not performance-related and had the effect of screening blacks from supervisory jobs. If employers use systematic employment discrimination practices, Title VII "required the removal of all barriers perpetuating the benefits that white employees obtain at the expense of blacks." In *Griggs* the Court held that invalid practices, however neutral in intent, caused a disparate impact upon a group protected by the act. The Griggs disparate impact concept was based on the court's analysis of section 702 (a) (2) of Title VII and required that tests used for hiring and promotion must be job related and validated under EEOC guidelines. In *Griggs* the Supreme Court held that the statutory standard should also be the constitutional standard. Under Title VII the EEOC exercises jurisdiction on matters of employment discrimination and can initiate charges and enforce regulations. Often the EEOC reaches a settlement between the parties, thereby avoiding a lawsuit in federal court.

Following this case, lawyers became aware of Title VII as a potential remedy for claims based upon employment discrimination. The central constitutional question was whether an employer's employment practices or activities, such as preemployment tests, constituted a disparate impact or other impermissible forms of employment discrimination. These activities include those that have consequences of discrimination even if selection criteria did not intend to have discriminatory purposes.

Supreme Court decisions and congressional statutes have altered which party has the burden of proof in employment discrimination cases. *Griggs* placed that burden upon the employer and as of *Ward's Cove Packing Co.* (1989) the Court shifted that burden to the employee. Employees faced a difficult task to show evidence of racial discrimination. Congress has the authority to revise Supreme Court decisions that are based upon congressional statutory provisions. In the Civil Rights Act of 1991 Congress reversed the Court decision and required employers to sustain the burden of proof that their practices do not racially discriminate.

For more information

Griggs v. Duke Power Company, 401 U.S. 424 (1971).

Ward's Cove Packing Co. v. Antonio, 490 U.S. 642 (1989).

Steven Puro
Professor of Political Science
Saint Louis University

Griswold v. Connecticut 381 U.S. 479

(1965) was a Supreme Court decision in which the Court recognized that the right of privacy was a fundamental constitutional right, even though it was not expressly set out in the Constitution. The Court did not address the scope of the right of privacy it its decision but did decide that the right protected married couples from governmental interference in their consensual sexual relations.

The case came to the Supreme Court after Estelle Griswold, executive director of the Planned Parenthood League of Connecticut, and Dr. C. Lee Buxton, the medical director at the League's center in New Haven, gave birth control advice and devices to married couples. Griswold and Buxton were convicted as accessories in the violation of a Connecticut law that made it a crime to use any drug or medical device or instrument for the purposes of preventing conception. After the Connecticut appellate court upheld their convictions, they brought their case to the Supreme Court, asserting that the Connecticut law violated the Fourteenth Amendment.

In a 7–2 vote, the Supreme Court reversed the convictions and struck down the law as an unconstitutional intrusion into the right of privacy. While a majority of the Court recognized that such a right existed even though not expressly set out in the Bill of Rights, there was disagreement among the justices about the location of the right in the Constitution. In his majority opinion, Justice Douglas concluded that the right flowed from the "penumbras" of express rights provided in the First, Third, Fourth, Fifth, and Ninth Amendments and applied to the states through the Fourteenth Amendment. These penumbras, Justice Douglas wrote, were "formed by emanations from those guarantees that help give them life and substance." They provided for a constitutionally protected zone of privacy, and the Connecticut law outlawing the use of contraceptive devices infringed on the marriage relationship that fell within the zone.

In his concurring opinion, Justice Goldberg, joined by Chief Justice Warren and Justice Brennan, believed that the source of the right of privacy was the Ninth Amendment, because its language evidenced that fundamental rights existed although not expressly set out in the first eight amendments. By contrast, Justices Harlan and White, in their concurring opinions, believed that the Connecticut statute infringed on a right of privacy found in the due process clause of the Fourteenth Amendment, which protected basic values "implicit in the concept of ordered liberty."

Like the majority, the dissenters, Justice Black and Justice Stewart, were critical of the Connecticut law; however, they did not believe it infringed upon any fundamental right. They rejected the view that a right of privacy existed in the Constitution, whether under the penumbras of express rights, the Ninth Amendment, or under the Fourteenth Amendment's due process clause. To them, the recognition of a right not expressly set out in the Constitution was beyond the power of the courts.

The right of privacy recognized in *Griswold* was extended in subsequent Supreme Court decisions to other social relations, including a woman's right to choose to have an abortion (*Roe v. Wade*, 410 U.S. 113 [1973]). However, the status and scope of the right continue to be debated by legal scholars and among members of the Court.

For more information

Dionisopolous, P. Allan, and Craig Ducat. *The Right to Privacy: Essays and Cases.* St. Paul, Minn.: West Publishing Co., 1976.

Emerson, Thomas I. "Nine Justices in Search of a Doctrine," *Michigan Law Review* 64 (1965): 219–34.

Griswold v. Connecticut, 381 U.S. 479 (1965).

James N. G. Cauthen
The City University of New York

group standing (also known as associational standing or third-party standing). Group standing is a term describing the set of rules judges use to decide whether a group can participate in a court case as a litigant. Sometimes a group of individuals with a similar claim against one individual or legal entity file a case and ask that it be made into a class action suit. This means that the characteristics the claimants have in common become the basis for a legal class. Anyone fitting those criteria specified in the definition of the class is entitled to join the suit. In other cases, groups that already exist seek to gain standing in the courts. These are usually interest groups like the NAACP (National Association for the Advancement of Colored People) or the Sierra Club. The members of these groups usually have something in common. That commonality may be their race, as is the case with the NAACP, or a love of the environment, like members of the Sierra Club. The groups are usually involved as litigants because they want the court to provide an interpretation of a law, or even to overturn a law. Generally we assume that the group wants this change in public policy because it would be beneficial to most of their members. Unlike the groups in class action suits, these groups exist with a membership base outside of the lawsuit. Their court involvement is only one area of the group's activities.

The term *standing* refers to a set of legal rules used to decide whether a particular litigant may present a specified case in court. These ground rules apply to every case filed in any court in the United States. The judicial system prefers to hear cases from people who have real disputes and not from groups who solely wish to change laws. The origin of modern standing precedent in federal courts comes from *Association of Data Processing Service Organizations v. Camp* (1970). Here the Supreme Court established a two-prong test for claimants who rely on the Constitution for standing. The plaintiff must (1) claim that they fall within the zone of interests protected or reg-

ulated by the relevant statute and (2) allege an injury-in-fact.

When the litigant is a group, the requirements for standing are even more stringent. The rules for third-party standing are complex. First, a group cannot gain standing by claiming that they are enforcing the rights of others. Therefore they cannot claim that they are enforcing the rights of a member of the group, rather, they must claim that the group itself has a constitutional or statutory right to be heard. In addition, group litigants have no right to prevent diffuse harms. Second, the group cannot claim that it is filing the case to prevent diffuse harms. For example, a group cannot file a case against the government alleging that they are filing to remedy infringements on the rights of all taxpayers. Finally, a group does not have a right to an undistorted market. In other words, the group cannot enter the courts simply because a change in public policy would benefit them. The access to the courts is limited to groups who are alleging that an actual injury, not simply an inequity, has resulted from the law.

The NAACP is one example of a group that has often been granted standing in the courts. The Legal Defense Fund of the NAACP gained standing as a group and fought the restrictive covenants neighborhoods put in place to block African Americans from buying houses in their area. In more recent times, a number of AIDS (acquired immunodeficiency syndrome) groups were granted standing as litigants in their efforts to expand the provisions of the Americans with Disabilities Act to include persons living with AIDS.

Groups are frequently involved in the courts. It is important to remember that before groups can participate as litigants, they must meet the stringent standing regulations discussed above.

For more information
Adler, Jonathan H. "Stand or Deliver: Citizen Suits, Standing, and Environmental Protection," *Duke*

Environmental Law and Policy Forum 12 (fall 2001): 39.

Stearns, Maxwell L. "From *Lujan* to *Laidlaw:* A Preliminary Model of Environmental Standing," *Duke Environmental Law and Policy Forum,* II (spring 2001): 321.

Nancy Winemiller Basinger
University of Georgia

guardian ad litem   is a special guardian for a minor child who is appointed by the court in connection with a particular litigation. The guardian ad litem is very different from a regular guardian. A guardian, or custodian, has physical custody of the child. The guardian makes decisions regarding where the child will live and go to school and provides all monetary support for the child. The guardian ad litem has a relationship with the child that is limited in scope and duration. He or she simply advises the court on what is in a child's best interests. The words *ad litem* mean "for the lawsuit."

The guardian ad litem is charged with performing assigned duties competently and should be prompt and diligent and give attention to detail in making recommendations to the court regarding the child's best interests and has great leeway in doing so. Guardians are entitled to receive copies of all pleadings, notices, discovery, and correspondence relating to the child (the same as any party to the litigation). They can independently conduct investigations on behalf of the child by interviewing specialists such as physicians, psychologists, counselors, or other treatment providers who were involved with the child. The guardian can review records, talk to the police or agency officials concerning the child, and should interview and have regular contact with the child. They may take information obtained during the investigation to experts or specialists in order to obtain further recommendations on what is best for the child. The guardian can also monitor agencies that were court ordered to provide services to the child to assure that orders of the court are being followed. They can act as a buffer, shielding the child from insensitive questioning and preventing the child from feeling that he or she is at the heart of the controversy. A guardian assures that the child's wishes are heard. In short, the guardian ad litem is the ears and eyes of the court in determining what is in the best interests of the child.

At the conclusion of the investigation and prior to trial, the guardian makes a written report to the court. The judge is not bound to follow the recommendations of the guardian, but usually the court gives the report great consideration. The guardian makes his or her own decision about what is best for the child. They do not work in conjunction with any agencies or for the court.

The recommendation of the guardian to the court might not be exactly what the child wants. In some circumstances, the guardian may require independent representation. This is normally reserved for cases where the guardian and the child, who is of sufficient age and mental maturity, have a material conflict in position or interest. A guardian ad litem does not have to be a lawyer and does not perform this role for the child. If the guardian is not a lawyer, the court may also appoint counsel to represent the child's legal interests. Any person who possesses good judgment and common sense can be a guardian ad litem. In most states guardians must complete a training program and be certified before being permitted to act on behalf of a child. The court may waive the training qualification upon finding the guardian is qualified due to prior service or is otherwise qualified.

The guardian ad litem will be expected to continue their assigned duties until the litigation is concluded or until relieved by the court. Guardians may be removed from a case, upon proper motion to the court, if they are not acting in the child's best interest. The decision to remove would be made by a judge or other hearing officer assigned to the case.

Guardians may be volunteers, appointed by the court, or hired through private means. If the guardian is court-appointed, he or she will be awarded a reasonable fee for their services in an amount to determined by the court and paid from public funds.

For more information

Alschuler, Jain N., et al. *The Guardian Ad Litem Handbook*. Madison, Wis.: ATS-CLE, State Bar of Wisconsin, 1987 (loose-leaf supplementation).

Heartz, Rebecca H. "Guardians Ad Litem in Child Abuse and Neglect Proceedings: Clarifying the Roles to Improve Effectiveness," *Family Law Quarterly* 27 (fall 1993): 327–47.

Loretta M. Young
Family Court of State of Delaware

H

habeas corpus is Latin for "you have the body." A habeas corpus petition is filed with a court by a person who objects to his own or another's detention or imprisonment. A writ of habeas corpus is a judicial command directed at an individual, usually a prison official, ordering that an inmate be brought to the court so it can be determined whether or not that person is unlawfully imprisoned, and whether or not he should be released from custody. The petition must show that the court ordering the detention or imprisonment made a legal or factual error.

The idea of the writ of habeas corpus was brought to the United States by colonists from England, where they enjoyed the common-law right against unlawful imprisonment. This protection is outlined in Article I, section 9 of the Constitution, which provides: "The privilege of the Writ of Habeas Corpus shall not be suspended, unless when in Cases of Rebellion or Invasion the public Safety may require it." If allowed to suspend the writ of habeas corpus during these times, the government could imprison anyone thought to pose a threat, without any role being played by the courts to caution against unwarranted or reckless use of the power of the government.

The Constitution is not the only repository of the habeas corpus protection. The Judiciary Act of 1789 gave federal courts the jurisdiction to authorize writs of habeas corpus when individuals were being detained or imprisoned by the federal government. This right was expanded in 1867 to include prisoners of state governments as well. The intent was to protect the newly freed slaves, but it was used by a Southern sympathizer in the case of *Ex parte McCardle* to challenge his imprisonment by the military. The Supreme Court had invalidated President Lincoln's use of military tribunals two years earlier, and fearing a similar result here, Congress withdrew the Court's ability to hear cases arising under the Habeas Corpus Act. Though not required by the Constitution, all states now provide for habeas corpus protections, either through their constitutions or by statute.

Originally, writs of habeas corpus only allowed a prisoner to challenge a conviction in state court on constitutional grounds that involve the jurisdiction of the state court. However, the Supreme Court has expanded the use of writs of habeas corpus, which now include all constitutional challenges. Habeas corpus serves as an important check on the manner in which state courts pay respect to federal constitutional rights. Because the process of filing and hearing habeas corpus petitions is time consuming and costly, in recent years the Supreme Court has attempted to limit use of the writ to protect the rights of individuals while at the same time preventing its abuse.

Anyone who believes that they are being detained illegally can apply for a writ of habeas corpus. However, it should be understood that writs of habeas corpus are remedies to be used in extraordinary situations, when relief cannot be obtained any other way. Habeas corpus is largely unavailable when there have been procedural errors made in the prosecution of the individual. Following the doctrine of exhaustion of remedies, the writ of habeas corpus will not be issued when there is an alternative adequate remedy available to the individual being detained.

For more information

Fairman, Charles. *History of the Supreme Court of the United States.* Vol. 7, *Reconstruction and Reunion.* New York: Macmillan, 1971.

Hanson, Roger A., and Henry W. K. Daley. *Federal Habeas Corpus Review: Challenging State Court Criminal Convictions* Washington, D.C.: U.S. Department of Justice, Bureau of Justice Statistics, NCJ-155504, 1995.

Neely Jr., Mark E. *The Fate of Liberty: Abraham Lincoln and Civil Liberties.* Oxford: Oxford University Press, 1992.

Scott Comparato
Southern Illinois University at Carbondale

Hammer v. Dagenhart   247 U.S. 251 (1918)

was a U.S. Supreme Court decision invalidating a congressional law regulating the interstate shipment of goods produced by child labor.

Since 1937 the Supreme Court has liberally interpreted congressional exercises of power under the clause in Article I, section 8 of the U.S. Constitution, granting Congress power "to regulate Commerce . . . among the several States." From about 1890 to 1937, however, the Court often invalidated such laws for unduly interfering with state police powers. *Hammer v. Dagenhart* is such a decision.

Although children have long worked on houses and farms with their parents, the rise of mass production meant that children could work in factories without parental supervision and protection. Such labor could prove physically injurious and keep children out of school. State child labor laws varied from one state to another, giving industries incentives to locate in states with lax laws.

Congress accordingly adopted the Keating-Owen Bill in 1916. This law enacted a 30-day prohibition on the transportation of goods produced by companies employing children under the age of 14 or violating standards set for children from 14 to 16. Dagenhart, a father with two sons employed in a North Carolina cotton mill, sued a U.S. district attorney named Hammer to prevent enforcement of the law.

Justice William Rufus Day authored a 5–4 decision in which the Supreme Court struck down the congressional law for impermissibly interfering with state police powers. Justice Day distinguished this case from others where the Court had upheld congressional laws regulating the interstate transportation of lottery tickets, impure food and drugs, prostitutes, intoxicating liquors, and other such goods. Justice Day ruled that, whereas these goods were in and of themselves harmful, the products of child labor were not. Justice Day further distinguished between the manufacturing of goods and subsequent control over the commerce of such items. Manufacturing, Day argued, was a local matter subject to state prerogatives, guaranteed by the Tenth Amendment of the Constitution.

Dissenting, Justice Oliver Wendell Holmes, Jr., argued that the congressional law was within the language of the commerce clause and should be upheld. Challenging the distinction between goods that were inherently harmful and those that were not, Holmes argued that civilized countries agreed on the evil of child labor.

Rebuffed in *Hammer,* Congress adopted an amendment to the Revenue Act of 1919 taxing goods produced by child labor. The Supreme Court voided this law in an 8–1 decision in *Bailey v. Drexel Furniture Company* (1922). Congress proposed a child labor amendment in 1924, but a sufficient number of states never ratified.

During the New Deal, Congress again incorporated child labor provisions into laws, including the Fair Labor Standards Act of 1938. The Supreme Court upheld this law and repudiated *Hammer* in *United States v. Darby* (1944). Although the Supreme Court has struck down provisions of the Gun-Free School Zones Act of 1990 and the Violence against Women Act in recent cases on the grounds that they exceed national authority under the commerce clause, current child labor laws appear more closely related to control over interstate commerce and do not appear to be in similar jeopardy.

For more information

Bittker, Boris I. *Bittker on the Regulation of Interstate and Foreign Commerce.* Gaithersburg, Md.: Aspen Law and Business, 1999.

John R. Vile
Middle Tennessee State University

Hand, Learned (1872–1961) was a federal judge who is widely regarded as one of the most important figures in the history of American law. He served on the federal bench for more than 50 years, beginning his tenure in 1909 when President William Howard Taft appointed him to the federal district court in New York. In 1924 Hand was tapped by President Calvin Coolidge to serve on the federal appeals court for the Second Circuit. He became chief judge of that court in 1939 and served until his formal retirement in 1951. He continued, however, as a federal judge in sen-

ior status and continued to decide cases until his death in 1961 at the age of 89.

Despite his stature as a distinguished jurist, politics, timing, and bad luck kept Hand from being selected for a seat on the U.S. Supreme Court. In the 1920s William Howard Taft kept Hand from getting a nomination largely due to Hand's support of Theodore Roosevelt in the election of 1912. When Franklin Roosevelt had numerous opportunities to make High Court appointments, he passed over Hand partly because he was inundated with pleas to nominate Hand and partly because he wanted younger men. Even though he never advanced to the nation's highest tribunal, Hand was still able to leave a lasting legacy in the law.

Hand's judicial philosophy was not unlike that of Supreme Court Justice Felix Frankfurter. Both studied under the same law professors at Harvard Law School and on the bench espoused a limited role for courts and judges. Like Frankfurter, Hand argued that judges ought to leave important decision up to the people through their elected branches of government. Though this philosophy of judicial restraint did not hold sway over more activist justices like Hugo Black and William O. Douglas, Hand has proved influential with a new generation of jurists like William H. Rehnquist and Antonin Scalia.

Hand's greatest contribution as a judge came in the area of statutory interpretation where he saw his role as developing legal rules to interpret legislative aims. For example, he developed an influential formula used in tort cases for analyzing negligence. As a lower court judge, Hand felt that he did not enjoy the freedom that his colleagues on the Supreme Court had to interpret the Constitution in new areas of the law. Despite his own judicial views, he saw his role as applying the precedents handed down by the High Court. However, in one area of constitutional interpretation, free speech, Hand played an important role in that doctrine's development.

Hand viewed the First Amendment as a strong protection of free speech rights and in the

Learned Hand (LIBRARY OF CONGRESS)

case of *Masses Publishing Co. v. Patten,* 244 F. 535 (1917), he argued in a controversial opinion that all speech short of direct incitement to illegal action was permissible. Two years later, in *Schenck v. United States,* 249 U.S. 47(1919), the Court used a less protectionist "clear and present danger" test articulated by Justice Oliver Wendell Holmes. Though Hand was critical of the Holmes standard as too restrictive of speech, he set aside his personal views and applied the "clear and present" danger test in *United States v. Dennis,* 183 F.2d 201 (2d Cir. 1950) in upholding the conviction of Communist Party leaders for conspiring to overthrow the government. Eventually, in 1969, a more liberal Supreme Court moved away from its earlier cases and adopted the "incitement to imminent lawless action" standard in *Brandenburg v. Ohio,* 395 U.S. 444, which is generally viewed as virtually identical to the

rule Hand had established over 50 years earlier in *Masses.*

For more information
Griffith, Kathryn. *Judge Learned Hand and the Role of the Federal Judiciary.* London: Jonathan Cape, 1973.
Gunther, Gerald. *Learned Hand: The Man and the Judge.* New York: Knopf, 1994.

Artemus Ward
California State University, Chico

Harlan, John Marshall (1833–1911) was perhaps the most significant U.S. Supreme Court justice of the late 19th and early 20th centuries. Harlan's significance was in his advocacy of strong national power in regulating interstate commerce and in promoting expanded rights against individual state power, especially for African Americans after the Civil War. Because both positions went against the grain of U.S. legal thought and Supreme Court decisions of most of his 34-year tenure on the Court, Harlan's influence on development of constitutional law was waged in hundreds of dissenting opinions.

Harlan, a unionist opposed to Kentucky's secession from the United States to the Confederacy, served as the state's attorney general during the war and unsuccessfully ran for governor twice after the war ended. President Rutherford B. Hayes appointed him to the Court in 1877.

On the Court Harlan advocated substantive due process rights under the Fourteenth Amendment, one of the so-called Civil War amendments that guaranteed due process of law to citizens of the states. Harlan believed this amendment "incorporated" the protections that citizens had against the national government under the Bill of Rights. He also was a strong proponent of antitrust law passed by Congress, believing that concentrated power in trusts was destructive to a free market economy.

Harlan's most famous opinion was his dissent in *Plessy v. Ferguson,* 163 U.S. 537, 16 S.Ct. 1138,

41 L.Ed.256 (1896). The Supreme Court in *Plessy* upheld a Louisiana law that required separate passenger coaches on trains for whites and African Americans and made it a crime for someone of one race to enter a coach reserved for the other race. "[I]n view of the Constitution, in the eye of the law, there is in this country no superior, dominant, ruling class of citizens," he wrote. "There is no caste here. Our Constitution is color-blind, and neither knows nor tolerates classes among citizens."

A half-century later, the U.S. Supreme Court would strike down the rule in *Plessy* that state laws maintaining segregation of the races were constitutional if they assured "separate but equal" opportunity for the races. Before that, in 1925, the Court began the first in a series of cases that held that protections under the Bill of Rights like the right to a jury trial for a criminal offense applied to the states—under the Fourteenth Amendment. Harlan, one of the Court's greatest dissenters, had persuaded a majority in the end.

For more information
Beth, Loren. *John Marshall Harlan: The Last Whig Justice.* Lexington: University Press of Kentucky, 1992.

Wm. Osler McCarthy
Supreme Court of Texas
University of Texas Department of Journalism

hate crimes   are offenses that are committed because of the actual or perceived race, color, religion, national origin, or sexual orientation of another individual or group of individuals.

The rate of crimes involving hate-related attacks on minorities, especially African Americans and Jews, in the 1980s prompted many states to pass hate crime legislation. Critics of hate crime statutes argue that adding extra penalties to a crime based upon the offender's motive or prejudicial statements is an unconstitutional abridgment of free expression.

On June 22, 1992, the U.S. Supreme Court decided its first case dealing with hate crime laws in *R.A.V. v. City of St. Paul,* 501 U.S. 1204 (1991). In that case, the prosecution charged someone with violating St. Paul's "Bias-Motivated Crime Ordinance" after he burned a cross in the yard of an African-American family. The Minnesota Supreme Court had upheld the ordinance on the grounds that it reached only "fighting words," a category of speech that is not considered free speech, like yelling "fire!" in a crowded theater. The Supreme Court ruled that the government cannot regulate certain types of fighting words and leave other types of fighting words free from criminal liability.

Based on the Court's decision, many states reviewed the constitutionality of their own hate crime laws. Some statutes were found, indeed, to have punished the offender's motivation for a criminal act. By punishing someone's motivation, the state is actually prohibiting bigoted thought—not the criminal act itself. Various state courts found that, since the U.S. Constitution's First Amendment protects speech and thought, even when that speech or thought is offensive, any law criminalizing thought should be rendered unconstitutional.

Proponents of hate crime laws have attempted to compare the need for hate crime laws with the need for laws against discrimination. On the other hand, some have noted that civil rights laws target discriminatory behavior, not the prejudice behind the behavior.

For more information
"Sticks and Stones Can Put You in Jail, but Can Words Increase Your Sentence?" *UCLA L. Rev.* 39 (1991): 333, 339.

Kristin L. Stewart, J.D.

hearsay   is a statement, other than one made by the declarant while testifying at the trial or hearing, offered in evidence to prove the truth of the matter asserted.

Hearsay cannot be admitted into evidence under state or federal rules of evidence. Trials are a search for the truth based on reliable information. The prohibition against hearsay is a safeguard; it permits the trier of fact to consider evidence only from the original source, under oath. It provides an opportunity to view the witness's demeanor, test the credibility and memory, and clarify any ambiguity about the statement. Objections to hearsay are a common issue at trial. The analysis of a statement to determine whether it is hearsay can be very involved and lengthy.

Begin the analysis by checking to see if all components of Federal Rules of Evidence (FRE) 801 are present. If not, the statement cannot be hearsay. Second, check FRE 801 (d) (1) to see if the statement is one that has been specifically identified in the rule as "non-hearsay," then make sure it is not any of the five types of admissions that are also not considered hearsay, and lastly, turn to the exceptions to hearsay.

FRE 801 requires that "a person" make the statement. The barking, whining, and sniffing of a bomb dog cannot be objected to on the basis of hearsay. However, the handler's statement that the dog's behavior indicated the presence of a bomb could be objected to if offered in the handler's absence. Statements, as defined under FRE 801, can be spoken, written, or nonverbal such as pointing, gesturing, or nodding. No matter what form the statement takes, the rule further requires that it must have been made with the intent or purpose of communicating with someone. For example, when A tells B that she was catching a plane and meeting her brother, it is an intended oral assertion. When A writes a letter to B explaining why she had to meet her brother, it is an intended written assertion. When the police ask A if she purchased a plane ticket to Hawaii and A nods her head "yes" and points to the ticket stub in her wallet, this is intended nonverbal conduct intended to be an assertion.

Most conduct, as opposed to a statement, is not intended as an assertion. For example, evidence that five employees chose to take the steps rather than the elevator is nonassertive conduct and cannot be admitted to show that the employees had knowledge of the faulty elevator system. The conduct of the employees was not intended to be a communication. Therefore, it is not a statement and it cannot be hearsay. The third step of the analysis is whether the statement is "one made by someone other than the declarant while testifying at the trial." The hearsay rule comes into issue only when a statement was made out of court and repeated by a witness. For example, it is permissible for a witness to testify that "the pink car did not signal before turning" because he is simply saying what he saw. On the other hand, if that witness were to testify that "Danny told me that the pink car didn't use a signal," this is hearsay. It is an out of court statement made by someone other than the witness. The witness is just repeating what Danny said at some other time.

The final analysis under FRE 801 is whether the statement is offered to prove the truth of the matter asserted. If the reason for offering the out of court statement is to prove that the statement is true, it is hearsay. If the party offers the statement for any other relevant purpose, it is not hearsay. For example, in a will contest, the witness testifies that the decedent stated that her niece was a wonderful business manger and a competent horsewoman. This statement would be admissible to prove donative intent on the part of the decedent, but not the actual truth of the statement.

Certain kinds of out of court statements are non-hearsay. FRE 801 (d) (1) lists three types: (1) those that are inconsistent with the declarant's testimony but only if the prior statement was made under oath, (2) those that are consistent with the declarant's testimony offered to rebut an accusation of recent fabrication or improper motive or influence, and (3) identifications of persons. Another group of statements are labeled non-hearsay under FRE 801 (d) (2). Admissions made by a party to the action are not hearsay when offered against that party. The five specific types of admissions are: (1) the party's own statement or one made by a representative of the party, (2) a statement on which the party has acted upon showing the party's belief in its truth, (3) a statement by a person authorized by the party to make a statement concerning the subject, (4) a statement by the party's agent or employee concerning a matter within the scope of agency or employment, or (5) a statement by a coconspirator of a party in the course of the conspiracy.

Federal Rules 803 and 804 contain 22 specific hearsay exemptions and one catchall provision. The underlying premise is that the evidence is either firmly rooted in law or meets a certain degree of trustworthiness. The specific rules should be consulted for greater detail, but the general categories addressed under Rule 804 are spontaneous statements, prior statements, records, reputation and character evidence, treatises, and the catchall provision.

For more information

Federal Rules of Evidence, Rules 801–806.

Imwinkelried, Edward J., ed. *Evidentiary Foundations,* 4th ed. New York: Michie Contemporary Legal Series, 1998, pp. 305–384.

Mauet, Thomas A., and Warren D. Wolfson, ed. *Trial Evidence.* New York: Aspen Law and Business, 1997.

Loretta M. Young, Esq.
Family Court of State of Delaware

Holmes, Oliver Wendell (1841–1935)

served as an associate justice of the Supreme Court from 1902 to 1932 and influenced the transition in jurisprudence from formalism to realism.

Holmes was born in 1841, the son of a prominent Boston physician and essayist. After completing studies at Harvard College, Holmes served in the Union Army. When the Civil War ended, he studied law at Harvard, was admitted to the Massachusetts bar, entered private practice, and lectured part-time at his alma mater. Holmes wrote for legal periodicals and edited Kent's *Commentaries on American Law.* In 1880 he delivered a series of lectures that were published the following year as *The Common Law.* The work has been considered one of the most important pieces of U.S. legal scholarship. In it, Holmes argued that human experience, public institutions, moral and cultural beliefs, and judicial attitudes had a greater impact on the meaning of the law than pure logic. He advised the courts to do what he would later do as a jurist, to make legal determinations based on the public interest. For Holmes, the definition of the public interest would grow from an understanding of history, science, and the evolutionary process.

After the publication of *The Common Law,* Holmes was appointed to the Supreme Judicial Court of Massachusetts, where he served for 20 years, the last three as chief justice. In 1902 President Theodore Roosevelt nominated Holmes to the U.S. Supreme Court. He remained on the Court for 30 years, during which he wrote 873 opinions and served under four chief justices. Although a number of his opinions seem anachronistic, Holmes is remembered most for his dissents, which often seemed to anticipate the majority rulings of future Courts.

Holmes believed in the principle of competition and in several cases he objected that the Sherman Antitrust Act was an "imbecile statute." He also supported the application of human eugenics in *Buck v. Bell* (1927) where he wrote the 8–1 opinion upholding a Virginia law providing sterilization of the "feebleminded." Justice Holmes's reputation as a progressive comes more from his dissents in *Lochner v. New York* (1905) and *Adkins v. Children's Hospital* (1923). In both cases, Holmes argued for judicial deference to the will of elected legislatures. The Court majority in *Lochner,* he stated, would substitute their own beliefs in laissez-faire economics for the reasonable determination of the New York legislature that working hours were a public health concern and within the police powers of the state. Likewise, in *Adkins,* the justice upheld their definition of "freedom of contract" against Congress's reasonable effort to provide a minimum wage for women workers in the District of Columbia. Holmes again maintained that it was not the Court's job to strike down the reasonable acts of elected representatives.

On the question of freedom of speech, Holmes was less willing to defer to the political process. Two cases arising out of World War I restrictions on free expression gave rise to several of Holmes's most quoted principles of free expression. In *Schenck v. United States* (1919), he upheld Congress's power to prohibit speech that presents a "clear and present danger." The same year in *Abrams v. United States* he dissented, claiming that in the absence of imminent danger, opinions must be allowed free expression to compete in the marketplace of ideas.

Holmes retired from the Supreme Court in 1932 and died in Washington, D.C., in 1935.

For more information

Frankfurter, Felix. *Mr. Justice Holmes and the Constitution,* 2nd ed. New York: Cambridge, University Press, 1961.

Novick, Sheldon M. *Honorable Justice: The Life of Oliver Wendell Holmes.* Boston: Little, Brown, 1989.

Mary Welek Atwell
Radford University

Hoover, John Edgar (1895–1972) was the director of the Federal Bureau of Investigation (FBI) from 1924 to 1972, turning a relatively obscure government agency into one of the top law enforcement organizations in the world. In his youth, Hoover applied himself to his schoolwork, being named valedictorian of his high school class. He graduated from the law school at George Washington University and took a job in the U.S. Department of Justice in 1917. There he distinguished himself for his attention to detail and his ambitious career goals. During World War I, Hoover made his mark investigating opposition to the Wilson administration and its role in the war. In 1924 he was selected to head the Justice Department's Bureau of Investigation.

Though the agency was small, Hoover quickly set about establishing it as a well-respected national policing unit. He set up an academy to train future personnel, modernized criminal investigation techniques such as fingerprinting and forensics, and gained national attention in the arrests of notorious gangsters. In 1935 the organization formally became known as the FBI. The Bureau's jurisdiction was increased during Franklin Roosevelt's administration and Hoover set out to uncover evidence of espionage. After World War II, Hoover became an outspoken anticommunist and his agency set about exposing American communist operatives and sympathizers. Hoover's most notorious method of keeping track of alleged misconduct and impropriety was by establishing a "file." The FBI kept track of the activities of many prominent individuals by the information obtained and placed into their files.

One such individual that Hoover was particularly preoccupied with was Martin Luther King. Hoover engaged in such activities as bugging King's phones, following his movements, and even urging colleges not to award him honorary degrees, suggesting that he was affiliated with communists.

Under Hoover, the FBI's power began to wane following the 1960 election of John F. Kennedy as president. Kennedy appointed his brother Robert to head the Justice Department and it soon became clear that the Kennedys intended to scale back the power that Hoover had amassed over the years under far more receptive administrations. The press was also involved in efforts to demystify Hoover and the Bureau's activities.

Following Hoover's death in 1972 at the age of 77, the FBI continued to lose much of its

J. Edgar Hoover (LBJ LIBRARY)

power. Under the Freedom of Information Act, many of the controversial files that Hoover had amassed were made public. They reveal the great lengths, which some would say were unethical and even illegal, that the FBI went to in their zeal for uncovering sabotage and subversion. The files also reveal a government agency that was transformed from a small inept group of government bureaucrats into a respected, and even feared, professional organization.

For more information

Deloach, Cartha D. *Hoover's FBI: The Inside Story by Hoover's Trusted Lieutenant.* Washington, D.C.: Regnery Publishing, 1995.

Powers, Richard Gid. *Secrecy and Power: The Life of J. Edgar Hoover.* New York: Free Press, 1987.

Artemus Ward
California State University, Chico

House Un-American Activities Committee

was an investigatory committee in the U.S. House of Representatives charged with discovering the extent of communist infiltration in the government, the labor movement, and various other areas of American life. The members of this committee used its investigations primarily to expose to the public persons suspected of

belonging to or being affiliated with the Communist Party. The committee was created as a special or select committee in 1938, but it became a permanent committee of the House in 1945 and remained so until it was disbanded in 1975 (it was renamed the Internal Security Committee in 1969). From 1945 to 1957, the committee held at least 230 public hearings, at which more than 3,000 persons testified. During this period, 135 of these witnesses were cited for contempt of Congress, usually for refusing to answer all the committee's questions.

Thus the committee's investigations produced several U.S. Supreme Court decisions that helped to define the limits of Congress's investigatory powers. The first case was *Watkins v. United States,* 354 U.S. 178 (1957), which provided a sharp rebuke to Congress. Watkins was a regional officer of the Farm Equipment Workers Union. Appearing before the committee in 1954, Watkins answered fully the questions pertaining to his affiliation with the Communist Party. He also answered questions about people he knew to be current members of the party, but he refused to answer questions about individuals who had disassociated themselves from the party. In a 6–1 decision, the Supreme Court threw out Watkins's conviction for contempt of Congress. The ruling articulated broad constitutional limits on congressional investigatory powers by balancing the congressional need for particular information with the individual's interests in privacy. The Court also reaffirmed a previous holding that the questions asked by a congressional committee must be pertinent to the stated matter under inquiry, and the purpose of the hearing could not solely be to expose individuals who held unpopular political beliefs or associations.

The second case regarding this committee was *Barenblatt v. United States,* 360 U.S. 109 (1959). Barenblatt, a former professor at the University of Michigan, refused to answer questions regarding communist infiltration into higher education. He appealed his conviction for con-

J. Parnell Thomas, chairman of the House Un-American Activities Committee (right) and Robert E. Stripling, committee investigator, examine films to be shown to the committee investigating the degree of communist infiltration in the motion picture industry.

tempt of Congress based on the *Watkins* precedent and based on his First Amendment rights. In a 5–4 decision, the Court's majority upheld his conviction, retreating from the broad limits on congressional investigations detailed in its earlier decision. The *Watkins* decision had produced concerted efforts in Congress to curb the Court's authority over congressional investigations. Although these efforts were not successful, the Court cited a need for self-preservation when it pulled back from its former defense of the rights of witnesses. Although this decision was never overturned, in later cases the Court did reverse the convictions of various uncooperative congressional witnesses.

For more information

Beck, Carl. *Contempt of Congress: A Study of the Prosecutions Initiated by the Committee on Un-American Activities, 1945–1957.* New Orleans: The Hauser Press, 1959.

Bigel, Alan I. "The First Amendment and National Security: The Court Responds to Governmental Harassment of Alleged Communist Sympathizers," *Ohio Northern University Law Review* 19 (1993): 885.

Mark C. Miller
Clark University

Hurtado v. People of California   110 U.S. 516 (1884) was one of the earliest cases heard by the Supreme Court of the United States that interpreted the meaning of the Fourteenth Amendment to the U.S. Constitution. In this 7–1 decision authored by Justice Matthews, the Supreme Court held that the words *due process of law* in the Fourteenth Amendment do not require an indictment by a grand jury in a state prosecution for murder. Thus the Court's majority refused to apply to the states the federal grand jury requirements found in the Fifth Amendment.

This criminal case arose when the defendant was tried for murder in the California state courts and sentenced to death. A provision in the California constitution authorized prosecutions for felonies by "information," which means that the prosecutor presents the charges directly to a magistrate without ever presenting the charges to a grand jury. The Fifth Amendment, however, requires in federal capital cases that the charges be presented to a grand jury. The defendant argued that, after the passage of the Fourteenth Amendment, the Fifth Amendment provisions should also apply to the states. The defendant also argued that even if the Fifth Amendment did not apply to the states, the term *due process of law* in the Fourteenth Amendment would require the prosecutor to present the charges to a grand jury in a capital case. The Supreme Court majority disagreed with both of these arguments.

The defendant's Fifth Amendment arguments were based on what is known as the incorporation doctrine. Before the adoption of the Fourteenth Amendment, the Supreme Court had ruled in *Barron v. Baltimore,* 7 Pet. 243 (1833) that the guarantees of the Bill of Rights only restricted the actions of the federal government and did not apply to the states. After the passage of the Fourteenth Amendment, Justice Bradley, in his dissent in the *Slaughterhouse Cases,* 16 Wall. 36 (1873), advanced the theory that the Fourteenth Amendment's due process clause fully incorporates all of the guarantees in the Bill of Rights, thus applying them to the states. The Supreme Court majority rejected this theory in both the *Slaughterhouse Cases* and in *Hurtado v. California*. In *Hurtado* the Court also stated that the meaning of "due process" in the pre-colonial common law did not require the use of grand juries in capital cases.

Although the Court has never accepted the total incorporation theory, in a variety of decisions mostly from the 1960s the Court has selectively incorporated many of the guarantees of the Bill of Rights, thus applying them to the states. The Court, however, has never overturned *Hurtado v. California*. Thus today state prosecutors are still not required to use grand juries in capital cases, even though federal prosecutors must do so.

For more information

Fisher, Louis. *American Constitutional Law,* 3rd ed. Durham, N.C.: Carolina Academic Press, 1999.

Israel, Jerold H. "Selective Incorporation: Revisited," *Georgetown Law Journal* 71 (1982): 253.

Mark C. Miller
Clark University

I

illegal alien refers to a foreign-born person not a citizen or national of the United States who is physically present within the United States unlawfully. An alien may lack legal immigration status because he or she entered the United States illegally, or because he or she remains here illegally after having entered legally.

Immigration status is governed by federal law. Currently, lawful forms of admission include, but are not limited to, (1) admission for permanent residence; (2) admission for a temporary stay for authorized purposes, such as diplomacy, business, pleasure, education, cultural and artistic activities, athletics, and certain employment; (3) admission as a refugee or asylum seeker; and (4) temporary parole into the United States for urgent humanitarian reasons or for reasons in the public interest. Once an illegal alien is present within the United States, that individual may be eligible for an adjustment of status to that of a legal resident.

Admission into the United States may be denied or restricted on a variety of grounds, including, but not limited to, (1) numerical limitations based on worldwide levels of immigration, country of origin, familial status, employment status, immigration status, and other factors; (2) health-related grounds, such as a physical or mental disorder that may pose a threat to the safety, welfare, or property of the alien or the public; (3) criminal grounds, such as conviction for crimes of moral turpitude, crimes relating to controlled substances, prostitution, or commercialized vice; (4) security grounds, related to espionage, sabotage, terrorism, violent overthrow of the government, membership in the Communist Party, participation in genocide, or other proscribed activity; (5) the likelihood that the alien will become a "public charge," based on factors such as age, health, family status, financial resources, education, and skills; (5) the alien seeks to enter the United States to perform skilled or unskilled labor, where the performance of such labor may adversely affect workers in the United States, or the alien lacks prescribed professional credentials and qualifications, or certain conditions imposed upon the prospective employer of the alien have not been met; (6) the alien lacks proper documentation, such as a valid immigrant or nonimmigrant visa issued by the United States, or a valid passport or similar document; (7) the alien has violated certain provisions of the immigration laws relating to admission into the United States; (8) the alien has committed some other specified offense(s), such as draft evasion, polygamy, or child abduction.

Illegal aliens who are physically present in the United States, and thus within its territorial jurisdiction, are bound to obey the law, and they also are entitled to the protection of the law. Although the civil rights enjoyed by illegal aliens are not necessarily coextensive with those afforded citizens and legal residents, illegal aliens are entitled to protection under the U.S. Constitution. For example, illegal aliens enjoy freedom of speech and of the press under the First Amendment, and freedom from unreasonable searches and seizures (with notable limitations relating to entry and deportation) under the Fourth Amendment. Illegal aliens may not be deprived of life, liberty, or property without due process of law under the Fifth and the Fourteenth Amendments. The Sixth Amendment's provisions securing certain rights to the accused in criminal proceedings apply to illegal aliens, as do the Eighth Amendment's prohibitions against excessive bail and cruel and unusual punishment. Illegal aliens are entitled to equal protection of the law under the Fourteenth Amendment. Illegal aliens may sue to enforce their civil rights under federal civil rights statutes.

Despite enjoying these and other legal rights under federal and state law, illegal aliens also face significant legal disabilities and penalties. Illegal entry into the United States is a crime punishable by fines, imprisonment, and civil penalties. Illegal aliens who are apprehended are subject to detention and may be ordered removed from the country unless eligible for a waiver or for an adjustment of immigration status. Illegal aliens (like all noncitizens) do not have the right to vote. Unless granted employment authorization, an illegal alien may not lawfully be employed. Illegal aliens may be disqualified from receiving some public welfare benefits.

For more information
8 U.S.C., sections 1101 *et seq.* 3A–3C.
Aliens and Citizens. St. Paul, Minn.: West Group Publishing, 1998.

Victoria S. Shabanian
Law clerk to the Hon. Andrew J. Wistrich,
Magistrate Judge
U.S. District Court, Central District of California

Immigration and Naturalization Service

or INS deals with the admission, naturalization, and deportation of aliens. It also patrols the Canadian and Mexican borders to prevent illegal entry of aliens. In addition it monitors immigrants living in the United States as resident aliens. The INS issues permits ("green cards") that allow nonresidents legally to obtain employment in the United States.

The first immigration office in the federal government was created in 1864. There was a commissioner of immigration within the State Department. (At the time each state had officials responsible for immigration.) The commissioner's office was abolished four years later. In 1891 Congress established complete and definite national control over immigration and the INS was created. At first it was housed in the Treasury Department. In 1903 it was transferred to the Department of Commerce and Labor. Its jurisdiction was expanded in 1933 to include naturalization functions. In 1940 it was moved to the Department of Justice. The INS includes immigration examiners, patrol agents, and deportation officers. The U.S. Border Patrol is a part of the INS. The INS is headed by a commissioner appointed by the president.

INS operations are divided between two major program categories: enforcement and examinations. The former prevents aliens from entering the country illegally. It finds and removes them. The latter deals with evaluating applications of foreign nationals who wish to come to the United States temporarily or permanently and with resident aliens who want to become U.S. citizens. The INS also works with the Department of State, the UN, and the Department of Health and Human Services in the admission and resettlement of refugees. It enforces provisions of the Immigration Reform and Control Act of 1986 relative to sanctions against employers who knowingly hire aliens not authorized to work in the United States.

The 1996 Illegal Immigration Reform and Immigrant Responsibility Act called for a doubling of border patrol agents over three years and allowed for cooperation between local police and the INS. Congress made it harder for asylum seekers to enter the United States and stripped the courts of their power to review arbitrary decisions by immigration officers and mandated the deportation of legal immigrants for even minor criminal offenses committed decades ago. (Immigrants whose countries refused to take them back are now locked up indefinitely in federal detention.) The INS has long been accused of being notorious for arbitrary action. While there is public concern about protecting our porous borders, the agency has been accused of overzealousness through ethnic profiling. The INS has a mediocre record of defending its actions in federal courts, a success rate of 56 percent (cf. the FTC's record of 91 percent, the NLRB's of 75 percent, and the IRS's of 73 percent).

Each year 800,000 legal immigrants arrive. The booming economy and concomitant labor shortages resulted in 2000 in proposed legislation to provide some form of amnesty for up to one million undocumented aliens. The pendulum was swinging away from the anti-immigrant fervor of a few years before. Even labor unions, historically wary of immigrants as a cheap-labor threat, supported the proposed Latino and Immigrant Farmers Act. They saw immigrants as a new source of stable union membership and energy and noted that when immigrant workers whose legal status was in doubt tried to unionize, employers sometimes called in the Immigration

and Naturalization Service to haul away the troublemakers.

For more information

Gimpel, James G., and Edwards, James R. Jr. *The Congressional Politics of Immigration Reform*. Boston: Allyn and Bacon, 1999.

Juffras, Jason. *Impact of the Immigration Reform and Control Act on the Immigration and Naturalization Service*. Santa Monica, Calif.: The RAND Corporation and the Urban Institute, 1991.

Martin Gruberg
University of Wisconsin, Oshkosh

immigration law controls which persons are allowed to enter the United States. It has evolved from an open-door policy during the country's first century to a highly regulated system today. States do not regulate immigration; it is a power retained by the federal government. Congress makes the law and the federal courts exercise limited review. The executive branch enforces immigration law with the assistance of five major departments, the Departments of State, Justice, Labor, Health and Human Services, and the U.S. Information Agency. Immigration law is extremely complicated and the subject of constant political debate and changing legislation.

The early immigration laws were designed to exclude certain persons, including, for example, convicts, prostitutes, and persons likely to become public charges. Another early exclusionary law, the Chinese Exclusionary Act of 1882, discriminated against persons from China. This law was not repealed until 1943.

The goals of the current immigration law are promotion of family unity, strengthening of the U.S. workforce, and protection of the national interest and borders. Immigration laws regulate travel to the United States by nonimmigrants and immigrants. Nonimmigrants come to the United States for a limited period of time and purpose, immigrants intend to reside in the country permanently.

Nonimmigrants generally apply for visas at U.S. embassies in their home countries for permission to come to the United States. There are 18 nonimmigrant categories, including ambassadors, members of foreign press, students, fiancées, religious workers, scholars, persons of extraordinary ability and national acclaim, and certain workers coming to the United States to perform temporary labor in jobs for which workers cannot otherwise be found. Nonimmigrants must prove their financial ability to support themselves in the United States and demonstrate the ties to their homeland that make it certain that they will return home after their temporary visa.

Immigrants come to rejoin family members, engage in skilled jobs for which there are inadequate U.S. workers, or as a result of winning a lottery designed to promote diversity and immigration from countries that have been adversely effected by U.S. immigration policies. Congress sets worldwide limits on the number of persons who may come to the United States each year in each of these categories. In addition, there are per country limits.

Spouses and children under 21 of U.S. citizens and parents of U.S. citizens who are over 21 are considered immediate relatives and may immigrate to the United States without being subject to a waiting period. Four other categories of relatives may immigrate to the United States including:

1. unmarried sons and daughters of citizens,
2. spouses, children, and unmarried sons and daughters of permanent resident aliens,
3. married sons and daughters of citizens, and
4. siblings of citizens.

Due to demand for visas and INS limits there are substantial waiting periods in some of these categories. For example, the waiting period for sibling visas is more than 10 years.

Petitions for family members are filed at INS offices in the United States. Before the relative may immigrate to the United States the sponsor must sign an affidavit of support. A recent immigration law change made these affidavits legally enforceable contracts.

For humanitarian reasons refugees can be admitted to the United States each year. The president in consultation with Congress sets the numerical limit. Refugees are persons outside their country of nationality who are unwilling or unable to return due to well-founded fear of persecution on account of race, religion, nationality, membership in a particular social group, or political opinion. Similarly, persons who meet the same definition and are present in the United States may file for asylum.

Immigration law has significant intersections with other areas of law such as family, employment, public benefits, and criminal law. For example, employers who fail to properly document a worker's permission to work in the United States face potential civil and criminal liability. Criminal defense lawyers need to be familiar with immigration law so that they can properly advise clients who are not citizens of the immigration consequences of plea bargains or convictions. Recent immigration law changes make a large number of crimes deportable offenses.

For more information

Ira Kurzban, *Immigration Law Sourcebook*. Washington, D.C.: American Immigration Law Foundation, 1998.

Weissbrodt, David. *Immigration Law and Procedure in a Nut Shell*. St. Paul, Minn.: West Group Publishing, 1998.

8 U.S.C. sections 1101–1537 (2000).

Angela McCaffrey
Hamline University School of Law

immunity   protects a person from criminal prosecution by preventing a prosecutor from using his prior statements or testimony against him. A witness in a criminal case, who is involved in criminal activity, often will receive some level of immunity in exchange for his cooperation or testimony. A prosecutor may promise immunity to a witness because the prosecutor believes the witness's information or testimony is more valuable to the government than the unimpeded prosecution of the witness for his own crimes.

There are three levels of immunity. "Transactional" immunity offers the most protection: The witness is immune from criminal prosecution for all crimes related to his testimony or statements. "Use plus derivative use" immunity prevents the prosecutor from using the substance of the witness's testimony or statements, and any leads or evidence derived from them, to prosecute the witness. In other words, the prosecutor may use only evidence obtained independently of the witness's statements to prosecute the witness. Under a promise of "use" immunity, which offers the least protection, the prosecutor is prohibited from using the substance of the witness's testimony or statements to prosecute the witness, but the prosecutor may use the witness's statements to develop investigative leads and may use evidence obtained through those leads to prosecute the witness.

A witness may be granted immunity from criminal prosecution based on his incriminating statements either formally (by a court order) or informally (by a prosecutor's promise). If a witness refuses to testify in a court proceeding on the basis of his Fifth Amendment right not to incriminate himself, the prosecutor may ask the court to grant the witness formal immunity. If the court grants immunity, then the witness must testify. If the witness refuses to testify after a formal grant of immunity, he may be held in contempt of court.

A witness may be granted informal immunity by a prosecutor's promise, usually contained in a "proffer letter," which sets forth the terms of the witness's cooperation with the government. Often, if a witness is cooperating in a criminal investigation, the prosecutor will promise immunity in exchange for the witness's statement to investigators and testimony in court proceedings. The prosecutor's promise is treated like a contract between the government and the witness, and it is enforceable to the same extent as a formal grant of immunity. However, with informal immunity, the prosecutor is free to tailor the terms of the proffer letter to a particular case or a particular witness. Generally, prosecutors will promise either "use" or "use plus derivative use" immunity, but because the prosecutor has broad discretion in prosecutorial decisions, the prosecutor may promise other levels of immunity, including transactional immunity or even a promise not to prosecute the witness at all.

For more information

18 U.S.C. sections 6001–6005. *Kastigar v. United States,* 406 U.S. 441 (1972).

"The Granting of Witness Immunity" (Symposium), *Journal of Criminal Law and Criminology* 67 (1976): 129.

Prof. Kathryn R. L. Rand
University of North Dakota School of Law

impeachment is the constitutional procedure by which the president, vice president, and all civil officers may be removed from office: Article II, section 4. "Civil officers" includes federal judges, who hold their office for tenure during "good behaviour," Article III, section 1, but does not include members of the Congress, who must answer to their respective houses for their contretemps: Article I, section 5, clause 2.

The most dramatic impeachment proceeding, of course, involves the president, which has been described as the gravest task assigned to Congress next to declaring war. The procedure itself is essentially political; it applies to political officials; it charges political crimes; it imposes political penalties. Alexander Hamilton explained in *Federalist Papers* number 65: "The subjects of its jurisdiction are those offenses which proceed from the misconduct of public men, or, in other words, from the abuse or violation of some public trust. They are of a nature which may with peculiar propriety be denominated political, as they relate chiefly to injuries done immediately to the society itself."

Article I, section 2, clause 5 assigns "the sole Power of Impeachment" to the House of Representatives. Impeachment by the House essentially is a decision to charge the president, roughly comparable to a grand jury's authority to indict a person for a criminal offense. According to the rules of the House, initially the Judiciary Committee decides whether to adopt a resolution seeking the authorization of the full House before conducting an inquiry. If the full House approves an inquiry, the committee conducts its investigation, holds hearings, and decides whether to prepare formal articles of impeachment. The entire House of Representatives then considers and debates the articles of impeachment and votes whether to approve each individual article or charge by a simple majority vote. If any single article of impeachment is approved by the full House of Representatives, the president is "impeached" and he is subject to trial in the Senate.

Article I, section 3, clause 6 assigns the "sole Power to try all Impeachments" to the Senate. The Senate sits as a court and the proceedings resemble a trial; senators take a special oath. The chief justice presides over presidential impeachments but does not vote or participate in the deliberations. Members of the House of Representatives act as "prosecutors" and the president is represented by counsel and may introduce evidence. At the end of the trial, the Senate votes whether to remove the president. A super-majority vote of two-thirds is required—thus, 67 of the current 100 senators must vote to remove a president. In a proceeding against a federal judge, Senate rules call for testimony and arguments to be heard by a committee, which then reports to the full Senate for further deliberation and voting.

The House of Representatives may impeach and the Senate may convict and remove a president for "Treason, Bribery, or other High Crimes and Misdemeanors," Article II, section 4, a standard of majestic generality and political opportunity. In 1970, then-representative Gerald Ford made the famous claim—in an unsuccessful effort to persuade the House to impeach Supreme Court Justice William O. Douglas—that an impeachable offense "is whatever a majority of the House [considers it] to be at a given moment in history; conviction results from whatever offense or offenses two-thirds of the other body [Senate] considers to be sufficiently serious to require removal of the accused from office." History and tradition, however, demonstrate that impeachment ought to be understood as an awesome constitutional duty more than merely base partisan politics.

Punishment is limited by Article I, section 3, clause 7 to removal from office and disqualification from holding any other constitutional office. But it is possible for a president to be impeached and removed from office and then charged and convicted in a criminal proceeding in the regular courts; there is no double jeopardy. If the president is convicted and removed then the vice president assumes the presidency under the Twenty-fifth Amendment.

Three presidents have felt the lash of House impeachment, but each managed to avoid Senate conviction and removal from office. Andrew Johnson was impeached in 1868, but he was narrowly acquitted by only one vote in the Senate. In 1974 the House Judiciary Committee did vote out articles of impeachment against Richard M. Nixon, but he resigned before the full House of Representatives could vote on them. Most recently, more a memory than history, the House of Representatives voted to impeach William J. Clinton in December 1998 and he was put to trial before the Senate, which acquitted him in February 1999.

For more information

Gerhardt, Michael J. *The Federal Impeachment Process—A Constitutional and Historical Analysis.* Princeton, N.J.: Princeton University Press, 1996.

Posner, Richard A. *An Affair of State—The Investigation, Impeachment, and Trial of President Clinton.* Cambridge, Mass.: Harvard University Press, 1999.

Rehnquist, William H. *Grand Inquests—The Historic Impeachments of Justice Samuel Chase and President Andrew Johnson.* Boulder, Colo.: William Morrow, 1992.

Thomas E. Baker
James Madison Chair in Constitutional Law
Drake University Law School

in forma pauperis **petitions** are filed at the United States Supreme Court by persons unable to afford an attorney yet seeking review of a lower federal court or state supreme court decision. *In forma pauperis* petitions comprise a large percentage of the applications for review received each year by the Supreme Court. Of the nearly 8,000 cases that arrive at the Court during each term, more than one-half are placed on the "miscellaneous" docket of *in forma pauperis* ("in the form of a pauper") filings.

Seeking to avoid the expense of hiring an attorney, litigants proceeding *in forma pauperis* also request a waiver of filing fees required by Supreme Court rules. Most *in forma pauperis* petitions are filed by prisoners held in state or federal correctional institutions. Typically, these applications for review deviate from Supreme Court rules concerning the format of incoming petitions. In fact, many *in forma pauperis* petitions arrive at the Court in handwritten form. Although Supreme Court rules are relaxed when handling these petitions, persons who wish to proceed *in forma pauperis* must comply with several guidelines.

Supreme Court Rule 39 requires that persons may proceed *in forma pauperis* only when granted permission to do so by the Supreme Court. Permission may not be obtained until the party files 10 copies of a motion requesting the privilege of proceeding *in forma pauperis* along with a document supporting the party's claim of indigent status. Also, parties wishing to proceed in this manner must file with the Supreme Court clerk an original draft plus 10 copies of their petition for issuance of the writ of certiorari.

Less stringent guidelines are applied to *in forma pauperis* petitions filed by state and federal prisoners. Prisoners are allowed to provide to the Court only one draft of a petition for certiorari. Should the Supreme Court decide to grant the writ of certiorari, indigent petitioners are provided at public expense an attorney to both assist in the preparation of an appellate brief and represent the petitioner should the Court schedule the case for oral argument.

Most requests for Supreme Court review are denied. During the early years of the 20th century, the writ of certiorari was granted in fewer than 20 percent of cases placed on the "paid" docket—the group of petitions filed under standard Supreme Court rules and procedures. Since the late 1970s, the justices have granted review to fewer than 10 percent of "paid" cases filings. In recent years the justices have agreed to hear an even smaller percentage of requests for review. For example, in the 1997 term, the justices granted review to only 75 (3.1%) of the 2,432 cases placed on the "paid" docket.

Petitions filed *in forma pauperis* are even less likely to be granted review. All but a few petitions placed on the "miscellaneous" docket are denied or dismissed without comment by the justices. During the 1990s, less than one percent of all petitions filed *in forma pauperis* were placed on the Court's docket of cases decided with written opinions.

Although only a small percentage of indigent cases are accepted for review, some of the most significant decisions in Supreme Court history involved appellants proceeding *in forma pauperis*. The most prominent of these decisions is that which resulted from the case brought by Clarence Earl Gideon. Accused of a felony, denied counsel at his trial, and unable to secure a hearing from the Florida Supreme Court, Gideon filed a petition with the U.S. Supreme Court and asked to proceed *in forma pauperis*. Granting his petition, a unanimous Court handed down a landmark decision, ruling for the first time that persons tried for felonies in state courts are guaranteed a right to counsel under the Sixth and Fourteenth Amendments of the Constitution. Moreover, the decision in *Gideon v. Wainwright* (1963) expanded the scope of constitutional protections enjoyed by indigent defendants in all criminal courts and fueled a growth in *in forma pauperis* filings that continues today.

For more information

Geoffrey C. Hazard, Jr., and Michele Taruffo, *American Civil Procedure: An Introduction.* New Haven Conn.: Yale University Press, 1993.

Silberman, Linda J., and Allan R. Stein. *Civil Procedure: Theory and Practice,* Gaithersburg, Md.: Aspen Law and Business, 2001.

Bradley J. Best
Austin Peay State University

in loco parentis   is a legal doctrine describing a relationship whereby an adult, who is not the natural parent of a minor, elects to temporarily undertake the care and control of that child, acting in the place of the minor's natural parents.

This doctrine of substitution of parental guidance and supervision surfaces in many different situations. When a school or university set curfews for residents, establishes guidelines for "appropriate behavior," or bans alcohol from the campus, this is acting in the stead of a parent. The university is substituting for the guidance that a prudent parent might exercise. This doctrine imposes a duty upon schools to maintain a safe environment for students and is the legal rationale behind permitting warrantless searches of school lockers or book bags.

Caregivers in a day care setting have the delegated authority to act as a careful and prudent parent would. They are expected to exercise adequate supervision, keep the child safe from obvious dangers, give appropriate advice and guidance, and recognize when medical attention is needed. The responsibilities of a careful parent are not legally defined, but it can be expected that there is a duty to exercise adequate supervision given the age, ability, needs, and experience of the child.

The doctrine of in loco parentis can also be an element in certain custody, visitation, and adoption cases. In cases where there is no allegation that the biological or current custodial parent is unfit, the individual who is seeking a custody or visitation order must initially show that they have more than a bond by mere blood or affection. The plaintiff must show that they have been a "psychological parent." That is, they acted as a parent over some period of time, and the child, in return, recognizes and depends on that control and guidance.

Existing case law in the area of custody, visitation, and adoption indicate that in determining whether the individual stepped into the parents' shoes, the following factors be considered: (1) the age of the child; (2) percentage of financial support contributed to the child's maintenance requirements; (3) whether the relationship between the person and child was one of a continuous nature and whether the parties' expectation was one of permanence; (4) whether the scope and nature of the decision making has been broad and has concerned major issues in the child's life.

While a finding that a person or group has acted in loco parentis may bestow many rights, entitlements, and privileges, it should be noted that this may also impose expansive and continuing duties and might be a basis for liability should the party fail to act appropriately.

Litigation has ensued over a school's duty to protect and provide a safe environment for students based on the doctrine of in loco parentis. In both cases, the school failed to implement reasonable security measures and was sued when other students or outsiders on the school grounds injured students.

In another case, a claim for negligent failure to control a minor child was based on the doctrine of in loco parentis. Under the facts, the defendant was sued when his girlfriend's minor son inflicted serious injury on a neighbor child who came to play for the afternoon. The complaint alleged that the defendant stood in loco parentis by assuming custody and control, that he knew of the child's violent nature, and that he failed to use ordinary care to control the child so as to prevent him from intentionally harming others.

In nearly all instances, a person who acts as stepparent to his spouse's minor children does not incur an ongoing obligation to the children if the marriage terminates. However, some courts have opined that where that person has actually stood in loco parentis, they cannot unilaterally terminate that status.

For more information

In re Custody of D.M.M., 404 N.W.2d 530 (1987). Court considered whether the word *parent* also meant a person in loco parentis.

In Interest of L.I. v. Circuit Ct. of Washington County, 280 N.W.2d 343 (Ct. App. 1979). Court described state's authority to supervise children during school hours in loco parentis.

In re Montell v. Dept. of Soc. And Health Servs., 775 P2d 976, 978 (Wash. App. 1989).

Lipscomb v. Lipscomb, 660 So.2d 986, 986 (Ala. Civ. App. 1993).

Loretta M. Young
Family Court of State of Delaware

incorporation doctrine   refers to the belief that the due process clause of the Fourteenth Amendment makes the provisions of the Bill of Rights applicable to the states. Adherents to the incorporation doctrine hold that the first eight amendments to the U.S. Constitution (which contain the substantive guarantees of the Bill of Rights) apply to the states exactly as they do to the federal government. This is to say that whatever is forbidden to the federal government by the Bill of Rights is likewise forbidden to the states by the due process clause of the Fourteenth Amendment, which incorporates the Bill of Rights and makes it applicable to the states.

Adherents to the doctrine of incorporation differ among themselves as to whether the due process clause of the Fourteenth Amendment incorporates all the provisions of the first eight amendments to the Constitution, or only some of those provisions. Some justices, most notably Hugo Black, held that the first eight amendments are incorporated in their entirety. Others, such as former Chief Justice Warren, held that only those provisions of the Bill of Rights which the Supreme Court has found to be fundamental principles of liberty and justice are incorporated into the due process clause and made applicable to the states. Other provisions, deemed by the Court not to be fundamental, are not made applicable to the states.

Advocates of the first view are known as full or total incorporationists. Advocates of the second view are known as selective incorporationists. At no time in the Court's history was there a majority of justices who believed in the total incorporation of the Bill of Rights. Indeed, until the 1950s, a majority of justices held to a different doctrine, known as ordered liberty. According to this doctrine, the meaning of the due process clause is independent of the Bill of Rights. It is thus the responsibility of the Court to determine on a case-by-case basis whether a state procedure is consistent with "due process of law." Justice Felix Frankfurter was one of the foremost advocates of this view that "due process of law is a summarized constitutional guarantee of respect for those personal immunities which, . . . are 'so rooted in the traditions and conscience of our people as to be ranked as fundamental,' . . . or are 'implicit in the concept of ordered liberty,'" *Rochin v. California* (342 U.S. 165).

From the 1950s through the 1970s a coalition of both full and selective incorporationists nationalized the Bill of Rights by incorporating most of its provisions one at a time. By the 1960s the doctrine of selective incorporation had become the dominant view on the Court. Since the mid-1970s, selective incorporation has been the unchallenged doctrine of the Supreme Court.

Although the process of incorporating provisions of the Bill of Rights has not necessarily ended, no additional provisions of the Bill of Rights have been incorporated since the 1970s. More importantly, no provision of the Bill of Rights has been unincorporated. At this point, most of the Bill of Rights has been incorporated, including all of the First, Fourth, and Sixth Amendments, most of the Fifth (except for the requirement that indictments be by grand jury), and that portion of the Eighth Amendment which prohibits "cruel and unusual punishment." The Second, Third, and Seventh Amendments have not been incorporated. Other rights, such as the right to privacy, have also been protected by the due process clause of the Fourteenth Amendment. However, despite Justice Douglas's efforts in *Griswold v. Connecticut,* 381 U.S. 479 (1965) to read a right to privacy into the penumbras of the emanations of the Bill of Rights, the better view is that protection for the right to privacy lies outside the doctrine of incorporation.

For more information

Abraham, Henry, and Barbara A. Perry. *Freedom and the Court: Civil Rights and Liberties in the United States,* 7th ed. London: Oxford University Press, 1998.

Auerbach, Bruce E. "Incorporation and the Bill of Rights." In David Schultz, ed. *Law and Politics: Unanswered Questions.* New York: Peter Lang Publishing, 1994.

Bruce E. Auerbach, Ph.D.
Albright College

Indian rights   are rooted not in race but in sovereignty: They derive from the inherent sov-

ereign powers of the tribes as preexisting political entities. Rights belonging to Native Americans and tribes largely are determined according to a few general principles of federal Indian law: First, Native American tribes are sovereign nations with inherent powers of self-government; second, tribal sovereignty is subject to Congress's power to regulate the tribes; third, Congress, rather than the states, has the power to regulate the tribes; and fourth, the federal government serves as a guardian to the tribes.

Both federal regulation and tribal sovereignty stem from the historical context of America's colonization. As the "New World" was colonized, settlers sought lands belonging to the tribes. Recognizing that the vast frontier prevented effective defense against "hostile" tribes, the newly formed federal government negotiated massive land cessions (transfers of lands) with the tribes through treaties and agreements, with certain rights promised in return. Necessary to the treaty-making process was the treatment of tribes as sovereign nations—political entities with valid rights to the lands they occupied. These treaties remain in force, providing the basis for current protection of Indian lands and reserved rights relating to hunting, fishing, gathering, and water usage.

By the time the Constitution was ratified, a long tradition of dealing with the tribes as sovereign nations was in place. In the "Indian Commerce Clause," found in Article I, section 8, the Constitution expressly confers to Congress power "to regulate Commerce . . . with the Indian Tribes."

The Supreme Court further defined the relationship of the federal government and Native American tribes through a series of decisions. First, in *Johnson v. M'Intosh,* 21 U.S. (8 Wheat) 543 (1823), the Court held that although tribes retained the right to occupy their lands, ownership belonged to the United States under the doctrine of discovery, which gave "discoverers" rights over aboriginal peoples. In *Cherokee Nation v. Georgia,* 30 U.S. (5 Pet.) 1

American Indian Movement (AIM) activist Leonard Peltier, who was convicted in 1976 of the murder of two FBI agents, c. 1985 (HULTON ARCHIVE)

(1831), the Court recognized that tribes were self-governing and distinct political entities but held that tribes were not foreign nations. Instead, tribes were "domestic dependent nations" existing as wards to the federal government's guardianship. In *Worcester v. Georgia,* 31 U.S. (6 Pet.) 515 (1832), the Court explained that tribal sovereignty necessarily was limited by the federal government's status as the "protector" of tribes, so that they were subject to federal law. Taken together, these cases hold that Native American tribes are not entitled to sovereignty in the traditional sense of the word (as a foreign country would be) but are afforded only limited sovereignty as domestic dependent nations subject to limitations set by the federal government.

The federal government's relationship with the tribes has varied with federal interests and political climate. In the mid-1800s, the federal government forcibly removed Native Americans from their land, culminating in the Trail of Tears and the death of more than 4,000 Native Americans. At the turn of the century, the federal government transferred title of Indian lands from tribes to individual Native Americans in an effort to weaken tribal governments and to require assimilation.

In the 1930s the federal government attempted to encourage, rather than force, assimilation of Native Americans, but in 1953 Congress adopted a resolution calling for the termination of the tribes' special status as wards of the federal government. Under this policy, Native Americans were treated simply as citizens of the United States, without any recognition of tribal sovereignty. Although not all tribes were terminated under the policy, forced assimilation was widespread.

The Civil Rights movement influenced federal Indian policy, leading to the protection of individual rights through the 1968 Indian Civil Rights Act. President Nixon called for the end of the termination era and urged Congress to return control of federal Indian programs to the tribes. In 1978 Congress passed the Indian Child Welfare Act, intended to protect tribal interests in custody decisions affecting Native American children. Most recently, the federal government has encouraged tribes to undertake economic development as a means of strengthening tribal sovereignty.

Native American tribes are either federally recognized or nonfederally recognized. Federal law sets out mandatory criteria that a tribe must meet before it is recognized by the federal government and thus entitled to federal benefits and rights. There are 557 federally recognized Native American tribes in the United States. Many tribes have their own governments, laws, and court systems that are separate from their state or federal counterparts. Whether tribal, state, or federal law will apply usually depends on whether the people involved in a dispute or crime are Native American, and whether the events at issue took place within "Indian country"—within a reservation or on other Indian land.

For more information

Cohen, Felix S. *Handbook of Federal Indian Law,* updated ed. Washington, D.C.: U.S. Government Printing Office, 1982.

Wilkinson, Charles F., ed. *American Indians, Time and the Law.* Buffalo, N.Y.: William S. Hein, 1988.

Prof. Kathryn R. L. Rand
University of North Dakota School of Law

injunction   is an order a court issues prohibiting someone or some entity from doing a specified act or commanding that some action be reversed.

A court issues an injunction only when necessary to protect against substantial interference with a right and not over trivial matters where the injury is small or technical. The applicant for the injunction must show two essential elements to justify a court issuing one. The applicant must first show that real or personal property or some other legal right is subject to irreparable harm, and next that there is no adequate remedy at law. Generally, "irreparable harm" means an injured party cannot be readily, adequately, and completely compensated with money. The term "adequate remedy at law" means that a later suit for damages will not adequately compensate the applicant for the threatened injury or that the applicant would be faced with multiple lawsuits.

Typically, there are three possible stages in an injunction proceeding: (1) temporary restraining order granted against defendant with or without notice or hearing; (2) preliminary injunction granted after notice and brief hearing; and (3) permanent injunction granted after a full hearing of the evidence.

A judge typically issues a temporary restraining order, without notice to or hearing the defendant, primarily as a means for stopping a defendant's act. Usually, a temporary restraining order is effective for only 10 days unless the judge for good cause extends the time or the defendant agrees to a longer period.

An injunction may be preliminary or permanent. A judge may issue a preliminary injunction only after notice to the defendant. The judge may hear brief argument and conduct limited hearing of evidence, or join the hearing on the preliminary injunction with the hearing on the permanent injunction.

A permanent injunction is the final order the judge issues after a complete hearing of the evidence on the issues determined by the pleadings. Since an injunction often stops a defendant from conducting his business, the court will, in most cases, not grant an injunction without proof that the applicant is likely to suffer irreparable injury if the defendant is not stopped.

For more information

Federal Rule of Civil Procedure 65.

"Injunction." In *Black's Law Dictionary,* 7th ed., 1999, p. 788.

Paul D. Link
Daniel, Clampett, Powell and Cunningham
Springfield, Missouri

insanity   is a criminal defense asserting that at the time of the commission of the acts which constitute the offense, the defendant was unable to appreciate the nature and quality or the wrongfulness of his acts. Willful intent is an essential part of most offenses in criminal law. A person who is not capable of forming such intent is not, therefore, liable for commission of the crime.

The defense of insanity is available to all defendants in all criminal trials. Further, insanity is a complete defense, not just a mitigating factor. That is, insanity is either a complete defense to a criminal charge or no defense at all—courts will not recognize various degrees of insanity or of responsibility for a crime committed by an insane person.

However, the law does not require full mental soundness as a condition of criminal responsibility. Mental deficiency or derangement will not necessarily provide a legal defense in criminal law. The term *insanity,* when it refers to absence of legal responsibility for acts that would otherwise be criminal, is recognized not as a medical term but as a distinct legal concept. Thus, from a medical standpoint, one may be insane by reason of a mental disease or mania and be diagnosed with a mental illness such as psychosis; from a legal standpoint, however, that person's mental condition must be such that he is unable to distinguish right from wrong and is unable to know the nature and consequences of his actions.

The fact that a defendant has demonstrated bizarre or unusual behavior or made delusional statements dos not necessarily mean he will be found legally insane. Likewise, confusion, disorientation, paranoia, and psychosis do not require that a defendant be found insane and thus exempt from criminal responsibility for his acts.

Some courts have termed insane delusions "partial insanity" and have attempted to formulate rules dealing with these circumstances different from those applicable to general insanity. For example, a defendant's belief that the act charged as a crime was one commanded by God has been held as a defense on the ground that, under these circumstances, the defendant could not have known that the act was wrong, although he may have known that it was illegal. On the other hand, some courts have held that knowledge that an act was in violation of the law was sufficient to quash an insanity defense. As for the cause of legal insanity, whether the defendant is found to have been insane at the time of a criminal act generally constitutes a viable defense, regardless of how the condition may have come about. However, temporary insanity arising from, for example, voluntary intoxication or drug use is no defense to a criminal charge.

When the insanity defense is raised in a criminal trial, the question on the issue must be directed to the defendant's capacity at the time the act was committed. If the accused was sane at the moment of the criminal act, it matters not that he may have been legally insane at any other time, whether before or after the act occurred.

For more information

Insanity Defense, 41 Am. Jur. Proof of Facts 2d 615 (1985).

Kristin L. Stewart, J.D.

insider trading   refers generally to all trading in a stock or other security by people who possess material, nonpublic information. This definition applies to corporate insiders (e.g., directors and officers) who buy or sell securities on the basis of nonpublic corporate information. The definition also applies to trading by noninsiders, such as accountants or lawyers, who are not employees of the corporation but who have obtained access to such information. The regulation of insider trading comes under the Securities Exchange Act of 1934. More specifically, the 1934 act addresses insider trading directly in Section 16(b) and indirectly in Section 10(b).

Section 16(b) regulates insider trading by imposing trading restrictions on directors, officers, and 10 percent owners of any class of equity securities (e.g., stock) of publicly traded companies. These insiders must regularly report their registered equity holdings and any changes in such holdings. In addition, Section 16(b) prohibits these insiders from engaging in "short swing trading" by regulating offsetting transactions. If one of these persons either (1) buys and sells or alternatively (2) sells and then buys stock of their company within a six-month period and makes a profit, they are subject to suit. There is no requirement that the officer, director, or 10 percent shareholder actually have inside information at the time of the trades; it is presumed. Section 16(b) allows the issuer of the traded stock to sue to recover any profits the insider earns from trading in violation of this section.

Section 10(b) of the Securities and Exchange Act of 1934 is the general "catchall" prohibition of fraudulent activity under which most insider trading cases are brought. Section 10(b) is implemented by the SEC under Rule 10b-5. This rule requires an insider to either disclose material inside information to the public before trading in a company's securities or refrain from trading on the basis of this information. This has become known as the "disclose or abstain" concept. This rule applies to anybody under a fiduciary duty to the company, such as corporate officers, directors, and employees, as well as other agents in whom a company or shareholders places trust and confidence.

Insider trading violations may also occur under the "misappropriation theory." Under this theory, a non-insider commits fraud under the 1934 act "when he misappropriates confidential information for securities trading purposes, in breach of a duty owed to the source of the information." This theory extends the reach of Section 10(b) to those who are not fiduciaries of the issuing company but who are outsiders trading securities while breaching a duty to the source of the material, nonpublic information.

Tipper/tippee liability is another manner in which trading activity may be insider trading. A person who is furnished with or "tipped" material nonpublic information by an insider and then subsequently uses this information to conduct trades in the securities may be liable for insider trading under Rule 10b-5. Further, the person who furnished the tip—the tipper—may be liable for insider trading violations as well. However, a tippee may only be held liable for insider trading under Rule 10b-5 if his tipper breached his fiduciary duty by disclosing the information in the first place. Two elements must be met to show the tipper breached his fiduciary duty. First, the tipper must have disclosed the information for the purpose of receiving a personal benefit, such as money or goodwill attributed to giving information to business associates, relatives, or friends. Second, the tippee must know or should have known that the tipper breached his duty of confidentiality. In most circumstances these elements are easily shown, so that when an individual receives a "tip" from someone connected with a corporation and then acts on the tip by buying or selling the corporation's stock, both tipper and tippee are subject potentially to both civil and criminal liability.

For more information
Speech by SEC Staff: *Insider Trading—A U.S. Perspective* (T. Newkirk, M. Robertson, September 19, 1998), http://www. sec.gov/news/speeches/spch221.htm.

John H. Matheson
Melvin C. Steen and Corporate Donors
Professor of Law
University of Minnesota Law School

intent   refers to a purpose, aim, or determination to act; a mental attitude to use particular means to effect a certain result.

The term implies a willing consent to engage in a course of action—a free will to do the act. Of course, it is often difficult or impossible to prove a person's subjective intent. For this reason, courts generally hold that intent may be proved by logical deductions made from the person's acts, declarations, and the surrounding circumstances. As one court has explained, a person intends "whatever he voluntarily does."

The civil law of torts recognizes both intentional and unintentional wrongs. Intentional torts include such actions as assault, battery, and false imprisonment. To be liable for an intentional tort, the defendant need not intend to actually injure the plaintiff, so long as the defendant intends to do the act that causes the injury. For example, if I shove another person in jest but without his consent, I have committed a battery. If the other person falls and sustains an injury as a result of my shove, I will be liable for his injury even though I did not intend to inflict any harm. The law presumes that a person intends the natural and probable consequences of his acts. In contrast, if I shove another person because I accidentally trip while walking down the sidewalk, I have not committed a battery. I am not liable for the injuries sustained by the other person (assuming I was not negligent) because I had no intent to do the act. An accident is an act done without any purpose or state of mind to effect the result.

Criminal law is also concerned with the mental state of the defendant. Generally, a person commits a crime only if the person engages in prohibited conduct *and* possesses a culpable mental state, or "mens rea." In criminal law, the term *intent* is an elastic one that describes a variety of these culpable mental states, such as purpose, knowledge, recklessness, or negligence.

The mere commission of an act, even though harmful, is generally insufficient to warrant criminal punishment in the absence of an intent to do the act. For this reason, a person incapable of forming the requisite intent due to mental incapacitation generally may not be found guilty of the offense. However, a person need not intend to commit a "crime," or even be aware that his conduct is illegal, to be guilty of committing an offense. It is normally sufficient if the state proves that the defendant engaged in a prohibited act with the intent to do so.

Some crimes require more than just a general intent to commit the offense. For example, the crime of burglary is defined under many statutes as the breaking or entering into a building *with the intent to commit a felony inside.* For this offense, the state must prove not only that the defendant intended to enter the building, but also that the defendant specifically intended to commit a felony once inside the building. As with tort law, this intent may be proved by circumstantial evidence.

Intent should be distinguished from attempt. Intent is the mental state of planning to achieve a goal, while attempt is an actual effort to achieve the goal. Thus, an attempt to commit a crime requires some action on the part of the defendant. Intent should also be distinguished from

motive. Motive refers to the underlying reasons that explain a person's act, rather than the will to do the act itself. Proof of motive is generally unnecessary in a criminal case.

For more information

Kadish, Sanford H., et al. *Words and Phrases,* "Intent," vol. 22, Perm. ed., St. Paul, Minn.: West Publishing Co., 1994.

Kadish, Sanford H., and Stephen J. Scholhofer. *Criminal Law and Its Processes,* 4th ed. New York: Aspen Publishing, 1983.

Nathanael Causey
Assistant Professor of Law
United States Military Academy, West Point

international law   is the compilation of rules and principles that nation-states regard as binding upon them and that they are expected to observe in their relations with one another. International law is that whole body of law impacting the international community.

Modern international law stems from three main sources: treaties and international conventions, customs and customary usage, and the generally accepted principles of law and equity. Additionally, judicial decisions made by international and domestic courts are important to the overall lawmaking process of the international community. Furthermore, United Nations resolutions also impact the growing body of what is known as customary international law.

International law today is based on the concept of sovereign states. Thus, it is within each country's discretion whether they wish to participate in the negotiation of, or to sign or ratify, any international treaty. Similarly, each member state of an international agency, such as the United Nations, is free to ratify any convention adopted by that agency.

Treaties and conventions were, at first, restricted in application only to those countries that ratified them. Nevertheless, regulations and procedures contained in treaties and conventions have frequently developed from "particular" international law into general customary usage; that is, they have come to be considered binding on even those countries that did not sign or ratify them. Customs otherwise may become part of international law because of continued acceptance by the great majority of nations, even if they are not part of a written treaty instrument.

International conferences have played an important role in the development of international law since the 19th century. For example, the Congress of Vienna reorganized Europe after the defeat of Napoleon and contributed greatly to the body of international law by establishing rules for diplomatic procedure and the treatment of diplomatic representatives.

The League of Nations was established at the end of World War I by the covenant signed in 1919 as part of the Treaty of Versailles. As a result of this covenant, the Permanent Court of International Justice was established in 1921. The League of Nations was created as a permanent organization of independent nations for the purpose of maintaining peace and preventing war. However, membership in the League of Nations was not universal, and unstable relations led to World War II. Nonetheless, in 1945, after the end of the war, the United Nations Charter created a new organization with a highly structured system for solving disputes among countries and for further development of international law.

Since World War II, international law has become increasingly concerned with issues ranging from trade, finance, and business to the protection of human rights, the global environment and ecosystems, and indigenous peoples issues. Continually emerging global issues call for new international responses. Examples include the conventions against acts of terrorism and the distribution of drugs. With the development of modern multilateral treaties, customary international law maintains a central role in the legal system of the international community.

For more information

International Law and Its Relation to United States Law, Restatement of Foreign Relations Law of the United States, 3rd. ed., section 101. Washington, D.C.: American Law Institute, 1986.

Kristin L. Stewart, J.D.

Internet and World Wide Web　are a decentralized transnational telecommunications medium and their development and use raise important legal issues, including taxation, free speech, and copyright law.

Originating in a Department of Defense network but largely under civilian control today, the Internet enables wired and wireless e-mail, file transfers, the graphical World Wide Web, chat, telephony, fax, video, and cybercash. The Internet is transforming law and governance.

Spurred by an expanding Internet, the Telecommunications Act of 1996 overhauled federal telecommunications law for the first time since the 1930s. The act's expansive goal is to let anyone enter any communications business and to compete in any market against any firm. This statute has left open or created several legal issues.

For example, if e-commerce remains a tax-free haven, will state and municipal governments feel forced to hike non-sales taxes since states can't force out-of-state businesses to serve as their tax collectors? To answer these questions, an Advisory Commission on Electronic Commerce was set up in 1998 to examine the issue of e-commerce taxation and to make recommendations to Congress on tough questions like price-setting cases where government assistance to platform products and encouragement of monopolies is hurtful to peripherals.

If "trespass theory" prevails in the short run, restricted information access and speech may inhibit general portals, search engines, and other aggregators of information. The Patent and Trademark Office issued 399 Internet-related business method patents in 1999, more than doubling the previous year's total. However, uploading and downloading of compact discs can become larceny, as charged in *Napster v. Recording Industry Association of America* (2000). Under *U.S. Code* Title 47, Sec. 227(b) (1) (C), broadcasting unsolicited commercial e-mail ("spamming") can be illegal.

Under the "fair use" portions of the 1976 Copyright Act, unauthorized use of "crucial" excerpts of a work invites remedial litigation. By exposing an author's work to all of cyberspace, the Internet raises the stakes, giving copyright holders greater incentive to sue college teachers for infringement.

Computer and Internet crime of all types doubled between 1998 and 2000. During the same period, the Securities and Exchange Commission and Federal Bureau of Investigation utilized the Internet to crack an insider trading ring.

In June 1997 the U.S. Supreme Court invalidated portions of the 1996 Communications Decency Act, rejecting government arguments that the Net should be as highly regulated as broadcast media. On June 22, 2000, a federal appellate court in Philadelphia declared unconstitutional the 1998 Child Online Protection Act's attempted criminalization of speech. Meanwhile, the Children's Online Privacy Protection Act of 2000 requires Internet site operators of Internet sites targeted to preteens to get parental permission.

Will citizen resistance to state intrusiveness survive antiterrorism campaigns? Will Fourth Amendment privacy rights erode in the face of supervisors reading employees' e-mail, "Carnivore" FBI surveillance, anti-encryption statutes, and on-line entrapment? Long-term effects of Internet socialization on civic life also remain uncertain.

For more information

Lemley, Mark A., Peter S. Mennel, Robert P. Merges and Pamela Samuelson. *Software and Internet Law.* New York: Aspen Publishers, 2000.

The Filter <http://cyber.law.harvard.edu/>, The Berkman Center for Internet and Society, Harvard Law School.

Vincent Kelly Pollard
University of Hawaii at Manoa

Interstate Commerce Commission   or ICC was established in 1887 as the first independent regulatory agency in response to demands to create order in the railroad industry. From then until its demise in 1995, the ICC had authority over all commercial traffic that crossed state boundaries, whether by rail, truck, bus, or boat. The ICC's duties began to diminish in the late 1970s and 1980s during a period of intense deregulation under the Carter and Reagan administrations. It was finally abolished by Congress in 1995, and its few remaining functions were transferred to other agencies.

The ICC was historic as the first independent regulatory agency. Like its successors, such as the Federal Communication Commission (FCC), Federal Trade Commission (FTC), the Securities and Exchange Commission (SEC), and the Occupational Safety and Health Administration (OSHA), the ICC was not subordinate to a cabinet agency and was largely autonomous even of the president. These agencies were created with the idea of being apolitical, professional regulators of key sectors of the national economy. Independent regulatory agencies are in a sense minigovernments, having some measure of legislative (rule-making), executive (enforcement and administration), and judicial (hearings and appeals) authority over the narrow sectors under their purview.

The ICC was created in response to a chaotic environment in interstate commerce brought on by rapid westward expansion and the proliferation of railroads. While regulation of interstate commerce had always been a federal function, enshrined in Article I, section 8, clause 5 of the Constitution, it was a relatively minor power in an era dominated by subsistence agriculture and before the creation of a national transportation infrastructure. The issue came to a head in 1886, when the Supreme Court ruled in *Wabash, St. Louis and Pacific Railroad v. Illinois* that the states had virtually no authority to regulate interstate commerce, declaring it an exclusive power of the central government. The ICC was created the very next year after demand by both industry and consumer groups, who all argued that a national economy required some standardization and central management. This included some rather fundamental regulations, such as setting a uniform gauge for railroad tracks and allowing for uniform pricing for commercial shipping by limiting price gouging.

The power of the ICC expanded rapidly in the first decades of the 20th century. The agency aggressively managed the railroad industry, forcing the consolidation of several smaller networks into a few large ones and even gaining the authority to regulate prices. By the middle of the century, its power had grown to include all types of surface transportation and most shipping. Eventually, however, the emergence of cheap air travel and the completion of the interstate highway system proved too much for the now-antiquated rail system to compete with. Efforts to reduce rates and introduce greater efficiencies came too late. The portion of the economy under the regulation of the ICC fell precipitously during the 1950s and 1960s and diminished even further with the deregulatory fever that emerged in the 1970s. By the time Congress passed the ICC Sunset Act in 1995, the commission had shrunk to a fraction of its former size. Its few remaining functions were transferred to other agencies, including the new Surface Transportation Board in the Department of Transportation created by that legislation.

For more information

Hoogenboom, Ari, and Olive Hoogenboom. *A History of the ICC: From Panacea to Palliative.* New York: W. W. Norton, 1976.

Interstate Commerce Act (24 Stat. 379), February 4, 1887.

James H. Joyner, Jr., Ph.D.
Assistant Professor of Political Science
Troy State University

Iran-Contra affair   refers to a 1987 political and constitutional scandal involving the illegal sale of military arms to Iran by members of President Reagan's administration in order to finance military aid to the Nicaraguan Contras.

The Iran-Contra affair, falling between the Watergate "crisis" of 1974–75 and the Clinton impeachment of 1998, provides a fascinating example of postmodern constitutional politics. Despite a lengthy congressional inquiry and Herculean efforts by a special prosecutor, Iran-Contra seems destined to fade, as a distinct event with consequences of its own, from both popular memory and constitutional history. Any attempt to narrate definitively Iran-Contra or to assess its constitutional significance initially founders on the shadowy nature of the events and the contested meanings that can be attributed to them.

Most accounts begin in 1985 with a secret arrangement by certain members of President Ronald Reagan's National Security Council (NSC)—particularly Robert McFarlane, John Poindexter, and Lieutenant Colonel Oliver North—to sell U.S. military arms to Iran. The hope, it appears, was that these sales might help, albeit indirectly, to secure the release of American hostages being held by various groups throughout the Middle East. Here, the NSC apparently worked with a vaguely defined collection of international arms merchants and with officials from several Middle East nations, including Israel. Later, Colonel North diverted money from the Iranian sales to the right-wing forces, the "Contras," who were working with the Reagan administration to overthrow the left-leaning Sandinista government in Nicaragua.

This global effort, which clearly clashed with the professed aims of the Reagan administration and seemingly violated U.S. law, apparently was known to the president, Vice President George Bush, and other high-ranking American officials. Opponents of the administration and much of the media dubbed the affair "Iran-Contragate," likening it to the Watergate episode of the Nixon years. This analogy, however, never effectively signified this Reagan-era controversy that increasingly seemed more of a made-for-TV spectacle than a constitutional crisis.

Iran-Contra became public knowledge in a curious, circuitous, and ultimately incomplete manner. During the fall of 1986, an obscure periodical in Lebanon exposed the Iranian part of the plan. The Reagan administration, after a brief delay, confirmed the Lebanese paper's story and also announced the hitherto secret relationship of the Iranian deal to the effort to aid the Contras. Congress immediately launched an inquiry, and a special prosecutor, Lawrence Walsh, eventually began a criminal investigation. Congressional hearings, which began during the spring of 1987, featured the televised testimony of Colonel North. Capitalizing on his military bearing, his quick wit, and his timely destruction of relevant documents, "Ollie" North decisively won his showdown with the committee and emerged as an antibureaucratic hero in the mold of John Wayne and Clint Eastwood's "Dirty Harry." Unable to untangle labyrinthine machinations of North and his cohorts, the congressional inquiry failed to produce an authoritative chronicle of events and, consequently, to establish convincingly that Iran-Contra involved constitutional misdeeds on the scale of Watergate. In contrast to the Watergate hearings, for example, there was no John Dean to answer questions such as "what did the president know, and when did he know it?"

Lawrence Walsh's lengthy investigation, as he himself bitterly conceded, could not break through the conflicting, vague, and perhaps even perjured testimony offered by participants such as North. President Reagan acknowledged that "mistakes had been made," but both he and Bush successfully maintained that they could not recall having known about the Iran-Contra arrangement. Walsh did secure convictions against Poindexter and North, but appellate courts overturned these, in part because of immunity provisions that had covered their congressional testimony. Although several others, including McFarlane and Eliot Abrams, were convicted of lying to Congress, President George H. W. Bush pardoned them, and several others who were awaiting trial, before leaving office in 1993.

A decade later, the Iran-Contra episode seemed to blend into a series of trials and hearings—such as the Supreme Court confirmation hearings of Robert Bork and Clarence Thomas, the O. J. Simpson trial, the Rodney King case, the Clinton impeachment, and the Elian Gonzalez dispute—that lay somewhere on the border between constitutional law, partisan politics, popular drama, and postmodern spectacle.

For more information

Lynch, Michael, and Bogen, David. *The Spectacle of History: Speech, Text, and Memory at the Iran-Contra Hearings.* Durham, N.C.: Duke University Press, 1996.

Walsh, Lawrence E. *Firewall: The Iran-Contra Conspiracy and Cover-Up.* New York: W. W. Norton, 1998.

Norman L. Rosenberg
Macalester College

J

Jay, John (1745–1829) was the first chief justice of the United States, serving from 1789 to 1795. Beyond his term on the Court, Jay had a varied and distinguished career in public life. Indeed, other than those who served as president, few founding fathers provided the breadth of service to the new country as Jay.

Jay was born in New York City on December 12, 1745. He entered King's College (later renamed Columbia University) at age 14 and graduated with honors in 1764. After serving as a clerk in the legal office of Benjamin Kissam, a prominent New York attorney, Jay was admitted to the bar in 1768 and began a very successful private law practice in New York.

Jay served in the First Continental Congress, but he was not an early supporter of independence, favoring more of a conciliatory approach toward Great Britain. Jay shifted his views after the adoption of the Declaration of Independence and became a strong backer of the Revolution. In 1777 he was appointed chief justice of the New York Supreme Court; however, his period on the court was brief, as he was elected to the Second Continental Congress in late 1778 and served as its president. The next year Jay was sent to Spain to obtain support for independence and economic aid for the war, and he later traveled to Paris to help negotiate the treaty with Britain to end the war. Upon returning from Europe, Jay became secretary of foreign affairs. Although not a delegate to the Constitutional Convention because of his federalist leanings, Jay became a strong proponent of ratification, contributing five essays to what later became known as the *Federalist Papers.*

Jay began his tenure as chief justice in 1789. The Court, sitting in New York, had very little work during its initial terms, but the justices also held court sessions in the circuits. Once the caseload increased, the Court rendered a number of important decisions in such areas as the scope of federal judicial power and the sovereignty of the United States. For example, in *Chisholm v. Georgia,* 2 Dall. 419 (1793), the Court held that citizens of one state could sue another state in federal court, rejecting the view that a state was immune from suit because of its sovereignty. Believing that the decision would severely damage the states, Congress responded by proposing the Eleventh Amendment, removing from the jurisdiction of the federal courts suits by a citizen

Chief Justice John Jay (H.B. HALL, COLLECTION OF THE SUPREME COURT OF THE UNITED STATES)

of one state against another state or a foreign country. Also, in *Glass v. The Sloop Betsy,* 3 Dall. 5 (1794), the Court recognized that representatives of foreign governments in the United States had no authority to resolve admiralty claims. Jay's opinions while riding circuit also influenced later decisions of the Court. For example, his dissenting opinion arguing for the enforceability of provisions of the Treaty of Paris was later adopted by the Court in *Ware v. Hylton,* 3 Dall. 199 (1796).

Jay continued his involvement in foreign affairs even while on the Court. He was sent to England in 1794 to resolve lingering problems and concluded what is known as the Jay Treaty, which, although ratified by the Senate, was criticized by many for favoring the British. Upon his return from England, Jay found that he had been elected governor of New York, and he resigned from the Court to assume office. He served as governor for two terms.

Jay was asked by President Adams in 1800 to resume his position as chief justice, but he declined, in part because he believed the Court lacked authority and respect, and he was not fond of riding circuit. He spent his later years on his farm in New York and continued to work on a number of different causes until his death in 1829.

For more information
Monaghan, Frank. *John Jay.* New York: Bobbs-Merrill, 1935.
Morris, Richard B. *John Jay, the Nation and the Court.* Boston: Boston University Press, 1967.

James N. G. Cauthen
The City University of New York

Jim Crow laws   refer to the system of de jure racial segregation enacted in the late 19th century, particularly in the U.S. South. Although racial separation had been prevalent in the North before the Civil War, under slavery there had been no need for Southern states to require segregation. In fact, during the antebellum years, interaction between blacks and whites occurred at whatever level served the interest of the slaveholding class.

After emancipation removed the structure of race relations defined by slavery, however, southern whites feared the loss of power and status that would accompany an integrated society. An immediate response came in 1865 in the form of the Black Codes passed by the provisional legislatures of the former Confederate states. Among other things, these laws provided for separate railroad accommodations and separate schools. The Fourteenth Amendment, ratified in 1868, was intended to supersede the Black Codes by providing that states could not deny citizens due process or equal protection of the laws. Had the Fourteenth Amendment been consistently applied to protect the rights of the former slaves in the late 19th century, Jim Crow laws might not have evolved to isolate the races in the interest of white supremacy. But after 1877, when Reconstruction was ended and federal troops were withdrawn, the Southern states were left to sort out their own racial arrangements. By the 1890s all had adopted some form of legal segregation. While the motivation for such legislation ranged from paternalism to outright racial hatred, Jim Crow laws united aristocrats and poor whites in the goal of maintaining racial privilege. To assure that African Americans would not use the political process to rectify the situation, Southern states passed restrictions such as literacy tests, poll taxes, grandfather clauses, and white primary rules preventing former slaves and their descendants from exercising their right to vote.

Thus by the end of the 19th century, the segregated society was firmly anchored in the south. It included separate schools, trains, waiting rooms, homes for orphans and the aged, restaurants, hotels, places of recreation, hospitals, housing, and public telephones. More significantly, segregation reinforced discriminatory employment practices and a criminal justice system in which all the major players, with the exception of the defendant, were likely to be white.

A series of decisions by the U.S. Supreme Court allowed the Jim Crow laws to withstand Fourteenth Amendment challenges. In the *Civil Rights Cases* (1883), the Court struck down a federal civil rights law that prohibited racial discrimination in public accommodations. *Plessy v. Ferguson* (1896) involved the Court's ruling that segregation did not violate the Fourteenth Amendment's equal protection guarantee. The majority of justices held that separation of the races was necessary for public order. They denied that segregation involved notions of racial superiority and inferiority; instead, the Court blamed African Americans for choosing to perceiving the laws that way. Laws requiring racial separation remained constitutionally sanctioned until *Brown v. Board of Education* (1954) when the Supreme Court ruled that "segregation is inherently unequal."

For more information

Nieman, Donald G. *Promises to Keep: African Americans and the Constitutional Order, 1776 to the Present.* New York: Oxford University Press, 1991.

Woodward, C. Vann. *The Strange Career of Jim Crow.* New York: Oxford University Press, 1974.

Mary Welek Atwell
Radford University

Johnson, Lyndon Baines (1908–1973)

Johnson, Lyndon Baines (1908–1973) was a career politician who began in the Texas state government and rose to become president of the United States. His varied political career led him to become an expert on the workings of government. While Johnson used this expertise to great advantage in domestic affairs, his undoing was foreign policy and the Vietnam War. Johnson's achievements were largely the realization of a Democratic Party that came of age and ultimately fully realized Franklin Roosevelt's New Deal.

Johnson began his career in 1931 as a private secretary to a member of the U.S. Congress. He then became director of the National Youth Administration in Texas. This position put him in the public eye and vaulted him to a seat in the U.S. House of Representatives in 1937. He held this seat until 1948, except for a brief time spent in the naval reserve in 1940. In 1948 he won election to the U.S. Senate and grew in power on the Washington scene. He was the Senate minority leader for two years and then majority leader from 1956 through 1960. In 1961, after an unsuccessful bid for the Democratic presidential nomination, he was elected to the vice presidency under John F. Kennedy. Johnson served as vice president until November 22, 1963, the day of JFK's assassination. On that day Johnson became president and held the office until January 20, 1969. He completed the term he was elected to with JFK and was reelected in 1964 but chose not to run for reelection in 1968.

Johnson was able to accomplish many things during his six years as president. The Twenty-

Lyndon B. Johnson (LBJ LIBRARY)

fourth Amendment to the Constitution, which banned poll taxes in federal elections and made voting more accessible to African Americans in the South, was ratified shortly after Johnson took office. Passing the civil rights bill that Kennedy had started was another early priority for Johnson. The controversial Civil Rights Act of 1964 became law only after Johnson twisted and cajoled members of Congress to support it. This act forbade discrimination in public accommodations on account of race, secured voting rights for African Americans, and forbade discrimination by employers and unions on the basis of color or gender. Johnson also helped establish the Equal Employment Opportunity Commission, which he had headed as vice president, to help enforce the Civil Rights Act. Under this

commission the attorney general was given the power to challenge local discriminatory practices in court.

Shortly after the passage of the Civil Rights Act, Johnson pushed his Economic Opportunity Act through Congress; it became law on August 20, 1964. The "domestic Peace Corps" known as Volunteers in Service of America (VISTA), the Job Corps, and Head Start came from the Office of Economic Opportunity and were funded by the act, a major step in Johnson's "War on Poverty."

After being reelected in 1964, Johnson had strong support from Congress and was able to pass a number of important bills. On October 3, 1964, Johnson signed a bill revising immigration laws, which liberalized the national origin quota system. Soon afterward, he established the National Foundation of the Arts and Humanities. The end of 1964 also saw the passage of the Highway Safety Act and the National Traffic and Motor Vehicle Safety Act. All of these acts, bills, and foundations were created as part of Johnson's vision of a "Great Society."

Johnson continued this trend in the following year. On July 30, 1965, he signed the Medicare Bill, which gave federally supported medical health services for the elderly, improved health services for children, the mentally retarded, and the disabled, and also gave federal money for medical research. Next, Johnson signed into law the Education Act of 1965, which aided public schools, financed scholarships for needy students, and helped small colleges. On August 6 Johnson approved the Voting Rights Act, which helped to remove impediments to the registration of African-American voters in the South. The Appalachian Regional Development Act of 1965 was passed to help improve socially and economically deprived areas. Two new cabinet posts were established under Johnson, the Department of Transportation and the Department of Housing and Urban Development. Johnson appointed Robert C. Weaver to chair the Department of Housing and Urban Development, the first African American to hold a cabinet post.

Johnson also appointed Thurgood Marshall as solicitor general, the first African American to hold that position, and in 1967 elevated him to the U.S. Supreme Court. Marshall, the great-grandson of a slave, was the first African American to sit on the High Court. Johnson also nominated Abe Fortas, a Tennessee Democrat, to the Supreme Court in 1965. Fortas served until 1969. Johnson appointed a total of 224 federal judges, nearly all Democrats. Six of his appointees were African American, two were Hispanic, one was Asian, and one was female. Johnson's appointments to the federal bench as well as the landmark legislation he signed continue to have a lasting impact on the United States.

For more information

Goodwin, Doris Kearns. *Lyndon Johnson and the American Dream.* New York: St. Martin's Press, 1991.

Unger, Irwin, and Unger, Debbie. *LBJ: A Life.* New York: John Wiley and Sons, 1999.

Tyler Millsap and Artemus Ward
California State University, Chico

judge refers to a public official appointed or elected to decide questions of law and to manage trials and other proceedings in a lawsuit that is pending in a court.

Judges play an important role in American political life. Alexis de Tocqueville's 19th-century observation that "Scarcely any political question arises in the United States that is not resolved, sooner or later, into a judicial question" remains accurate today.

The judicial branch of government generally has at least three levels: (1) trial courts in which cases are filed in the first instance and either settled or decided; (2) intermediate appellate courts in which a trial court decision must be reviewed if requested by any aggrieved party; and (3) a final appellate court with discretionary jurisdiction charged with the function of providing guidance regarding the law to lower courts and correcting a few egregious or enormously important errors that have persisted despite the scrutiny of an intermediate appellate court. Intermediate appellate courts are usually called courts of appeal and final appellate courts are usually called supreme courts, but the terminology varies from one jurisdiction to another.

Each level of the justice system is occupied by judges with distinct responsibilities. Trial court judges generally act alone, intermediate appellate court judges usually act in groups of three, and final appellate court judges usually act in groups of seven or nine. The tasks performed by appellate judges are limited to reading written briefs, hearing oral argument, studying the record compiled in the trial court, and issuing a written opinion explaining the reasons for the court's decision. The tasks performed by trial court judges, by contrast, are more diverse. In civil cases, trial court judges supervise the collection of information during discovery, manage pretrial proceedings, rule on written or oral motions, mediate compromises or settlements, determine what evidence may be admitted at trial, and preside over jury trials and nonjury trials. In criminal cases, trial court judges perform many of those same functions and also accept guilty pleas and sentence convicted offenders.

The paradigmatic model of the judicial function at the trial court level is presiding over a trial, but as the justice system has evolved, that still important function has taken up less and less judicial time. Because only a small fraction of civil and criminal cases are tried, today most trial court judges spend the majority of their time on other tasks.

There are limits on the scope of judicial power. For example, the jurisdiction of trial court judges typically is limited to a specified geographical territory. The jurisdiction of an intermediate appellate court usually is limited to a broader geographical territory, which encompasses several trial courts. In addition, most trial court judges have general jurisdiction to handle all types of criminal and civil cases, but some have only specialized jurisdiction, which may be limited to criminal cases, probate cases, matrimonial cases, bankruptcy cases, tax cases, and so on. Appellate courts usually have no subject matter limits on their jurisdiction.

The formal titles of judges at the various levels of the judicial branch vary. Although it is technically proper to refer to them all as judges, some are accorded other titles, such as justice, particularly at the intermediate appellate court or final appellate court levels. Although trial court judges are usually simply called judge, terms such as magistrate, commissioner, or justice of the peace are used in some jurisdictions.

A judge pro tempore is a person who is appointed to act as a judge on a temporary basis. Lawyers typically perform this service to assist a court in handling a heavy caseload, or while a judge is disabled or a judicial vacancy is being filled.

The term *private judge* refers to a person who is selected by the litigants to provide adjudication services of the type normally provided by a judge, but to do so privately out of court pursuant to an agreement between the litigants rather than pursuant to a grant of governmental authority. Private judges provide the same types of services as do arbitrators. During the past few decades more and more litigants have opted out of the expense and formality of the court system, and the importance of arbitration and other types of private judging has increased.

Judges are representatives or surrogates of the community entrusted with acting on the community's behalf in managing and resolving disputes between members of the community, or between the community and one or more of its members. The manner in which a judge represents the community, however, is circumscribed and, in particular, is more narrow than the way in which a legislator represents his or her constituency.

Judges make different types of decisions than do legislators. Judges merely react to disputes that are presented to them by litigants, based solely on the information presented by the litigants. They see through a microscope rather than through a telescope or a wide-angle lens. Legislators, by contrast, may be proactive, addressing broad policy issues and existing or incipient problems based upon information gathered from a diverse array of sources. In addition, when presented with a dispute, judges almost always are required to make a decision, while legislators usually can decline to act or defer action if they choose.

Judges and legislators also base their decisions on different kind of reasons. Legislators may properly base their votes on the policy preferences of their constituents, their personal policy preferences, or both. The judicial role, by contrast, is more limited. Judges assume a professional obligation to base their decisions on the guiding principles contained in authoritative, preexisting expressions of the policy preferences of the community, such as the Constitution, a statute, or case law precedent. They must not base their decisions on reasons that those sources of law declare illegitimate. Only if the guidance provided by these sources is insufficient may a judge legitimately rely on his or her own judgment about what would make the most sense in rendering a decision. This is sometimes unavoidable because even well-designed rules cannot unambiguously dictate the outcome of every case, especially in a changing world.

Judging, then, is choice largely governed by externally imposed standards applied by the judge in particular cases, without regard to the judge's personal views as to the appropriateness of the standards or the result of their application. Legal realists, such as Appellate Judge Jerome Frank, thought that this view of the judicial function was naive and believed that judicial decisions inevitably are based at least in part on "the political, economic and moral prejudices of the judge." There is force to this criticism, but although judges are human beings and lack the ability to achieve the ideal in every case, it is their obligation to try. As Supreme Court Justice Benjamin Cardozo once observed, "The judge . . . is not a knight-errant roaming at will in pursuit of his own ideal of beauty or goodness. He is to draw his inspiration from consecrated principles."

Judges are obligated to apply the authoritative principles in a manner that is impartial, that is, free from any bias or prejudice either for or against any party. Judges are disqualified from hearing cases in which they have a financial interest or such strong personal feelings about the litigants or the issues that they cannot be fair to both sides.

One of the goals of the justice system is to strike an appropriate balance between independence from a popular will and responsiveness to the popular will. Judges customarily are elected or appointed to relatively lengthy terms of service, in the state courts usually between 8 and 14 years, and in the federal courts for life, in order to insulate them from undue popular influence or coercion. Similarly, judges enjoy absolute immunity from civil liability for most mistakes, or incorrect decisions, or even wrongful acts performed in their judicial capacity. On the other hand, in some states judges may be recalled before their tenure in office has been completed, or not elected or appointed for an additional term if the public or the executive branch believes that their decisions are too divergent from either the dictates of the law or the popular will. In addition, in most jurisdictions, there is a procedure for removing a judge from office for misconduct by impeachment of the legislative branch of the government or by discipline imposed by an administrative commission. Also, judges may be subject to criminal prosecution for accepting bribes or other serious misconduct.

Not surprisingly, the role of politics in the selection and retention of judges is substantial. In some states, judges are simply elected by the public. In other states, judges are appointed by the executive branch of the government, typically by the governor of the state. Federal judges are appointed by the president of the United States with the advice and consent of the Senate. Typically, judges are appointed only after having gone through a screening process during which the candidate's qualifications, and often the candidate's political views, are considered. In most jurisdictions, a person is not eligible to serve as a judge unless he or she is an attorney licensed to practice law in that jurisdiction.

One very important function judges perform is judicial review of statutes enacted by the legislature or referenda or initiatives adopted by the electorate. Judicial review involves comparing what the legislature or the electorate did to the limits on such action set forth in the Constitution. If a court determines that a decision of the legislature or the electorate transgresses the limits contained in the Constitution, then the decision of the legislature or the electorate is invalid. Judicial review is antidemocratic, or at least counter-majoritarian because it may thwart the popular will, but it helps to check and balance the power of the executive and legislative branches, and to ensure that the basic structure of government set forth in the Constitution is respected and preserved. Understandably, judicial review is controversial.

Some, such as Supreme Court Justice John Marshall, believed that courts should play an active role in adapting the Constitution to the needs of a changing world by abandoning or reformulating outdated legal rules when necessary to match new conditions and attitudes. Others believe that the limited role of the judiciary and its institutional constraints demand that courts exercise great restraint, and they generally defer to interpretations of the Constitution by the legislative branch or the executive branch. As Supreme Court Justice Harlen Fiske Stone once said, "courts are not the only agency of government that must be assumed to have the capacity to govern."

For more information

Abraham, Henry J. *The Judicial Process,* 7th ed. New York: Oxford University Press, 1998.

Cardozo, Benjamin N. *The Nature of the Judicial Process.* New Haven, Conn.: Yale University Press, 1921.

Horowitz, Donald L. *The Courts and Social Policy.* Washington, D.C.: The Brookings Institution, 1977.

Keeton, Robert E. *Judging in the American Legal System.* Charlottesville, Va.: Lexis Law Publishing, 1999.

Resnick, Judith. "Managerial Judges," *Harvard Law Review* 96 (1982): 376.

Sattler, Robert. *Doing Justice: A Trial Judge at Work.* New York: Simon and Schuster, 1990.

Andrew J. Wistrich, Magistrate Judge
United States District Court
Los Angeles, California

judicial review   is a power that state and federal courts, especially the United States Supreme Court and state supreme courts, exercise in cases in which the outcome depends on the meaning of constitutional language.

Judicial review is controversial because it can nullify the will of a majority of the people's elected representatives. For example, in *United States v. Eichman,* 496 U.S. 310 (1990), the Supreme Court held that a federal law that prohibited burning an American flag deprived one who did so of the freedom of expression guaranteed by the First Amendment. The Court's majority opinion reasoned that the flag law violated the First Amendment because it "suppresse[d] expression out of concern for its communicative impact," namely, damage to the flag's value as a national symbol. That conclusion restricted the power of a congressional majority to govern a country, one of the founding principles of which is representative democracy based on majority rule. Nevertheless, the Court's conclusion in *Eichman* honored another founding principle of American democracy, namely, respect for the freedom of speech, especially speech that expresses a minority viewpoint.

Judicial review is important because it strikes the balance of power between the three branches of the federal government, between the federal government and the states, and between government and individuals. Courts determine the limits of power that each branch of the federal government possesses because the "separation of powers" is a fundamental principle of the Constitution. The separation-of-powers principle assigns to each branch of government an important duty and then places each branch beyond the direct control of the other two. Consequently, no branch is able to force its will on the others and act effectively without their compliance. For example, the Constitution gives legislative power to the Congress but also gives the president power to veto legislation.

Such interdependence between the branches leads to conflicts about whether a particular branch has acted outside the bounds of its powers. The Supreme Court often resolves such conflicts by means of judicial review, as in *United States v. Nixon,* 418 U.S. 683 (1974), wherein it held that President Richard Nixon's constitutionally protected privilege of confidentiality did not permit him to withhold evidence in a criminal trial.

Court decisions also determine whether the federal government or a state exceeded its constitutional authority relative to the other because "federalism" is another fundamental principle of the Constitution. Federalism resulted from a compromise at the Constitutional Convention in 1787, whereby the delegates agreed to increase the power of the federal government substantially, but to retain the states as sovereign, although inferior, political entities.

That compromise spawned a continuing debate about where federal power ends and state power begins, which produces lawsuits that the Supreme Court resolves, sometimes by exercising judicial review. For example, in *South Dakota v. Dole,* 483 U.S. 203 (1987), the Court upheld

Congress's denial of highway construction funds to states that failed to adopt 21 as their minimum drinking age. In *United States v. Lopez,* 514 U.S. 549 (1995), though, the Court invalidated a federal law that made it a crime to possess a firearm in or near school because the law exceeded Congress's power to regulate interstate commerce.

Last but not least, court decisions attempt to balance government's interests in public safety, order, and health with the individual's interest in personal and political freedom, which the "Bill of Rights" (first 10 amendments to the Constitution) protects. "Civil liberties" cases present conflicts between public order and personal freedom. *United States v. Eichman,* cited above, is a civil liberties case. So is *Brigham v. State,* 166 Vt. 246, 692 A.2d 384 (1997), wherein the Vermont Supreme Court invalidated the state's property tax-based system for funding public schools because it violated the Vermont constitution's guarantee of an equal educational opportunity for all children.

Thus, the power of judicial review places courts at the center of controversial public policy disputes because it makes courts the final determinants of what constitutional language means. Indeed, judicial review ensures that courts are as important to public policy making in the United States as legislatures are.

For more information

Peltason, J. W. *Understanding the Constitution,* 13th ed. Fort Worth, Tex.: Harcourt Brace College Publishers, 1994.

Porto, Brian L. *The Craft of Legal Reasoning.* Fort Worth, Tex.: Harcourt Brace College Publishers, 1998.

Brian L. Porto
College of St. Joseph, Vermont

jurisdiction   refers to the authority or power of an entity to exert control over activities or controversies within its boundary. The term is most often used in connection with a court's authority to hear a dispute and to make a decision about it, but it also may be used for other agencies of government that have such authority. Jurisdictional authority, whether of a court or some other entity, is granted only by the constitution or legislation of the government that created the entity and, on the whole, is limited to a particular geographic area over which that government is sovereign. The remainder of this discussion will be focused on the jurisdiction of courts.

In the United States, both the federal government and the individual state governments have power to create courts and to designate their individual jurisdictions, either through constitutional provisions or by legislation. Each system of courts operates independently and cannot interfere directly with the operation of the other, although there is some overlap between the two in certain types of cases; e.g., the United States Supreme Court has jurisdiction to review certain cases decided in a state's court system, and some federal laws give both federal and state courts jurisdiction to hear disputes based on that law. When there is overlapping jurisdiction, a disputing party may select which court it wishes to use.

A court's jurisdiction generally is comprised of three elements: personal jurisdiction, subject matter jurisdiction, and jurisdiction to grant the judgment requested by the parties. However, a court may have authority in all three areas as to a particular case, yet be deprived of jurisdiction because a party has failed to follow rules that properly present the case to the court. Personal jurisdiction exists when a person has appeared before the court voluntarily and accepted its authority, or has been brought before the court by another person by means of a legal summons to appear (service of legal process). There is an entire body of law and case decision that sets out the limits and extent of personal jurisdiction. Subject matter jurisdiction exists when the court's authority to hear and decide matters includes the particular type of dispute involved in a claim. Jurisdiction to grant the judgment requested by the parties exists when all of the procedural rules have been properly used to present the dispute to the court and the prevailing party has asked for sanctions that are within the court's power to give.

Jurisdiction is a fundamental requirement. The court has a duty to determine whether it has authority at the outset of any request for a hearing. In some instances, where emergency orders are requested by a party, a court may issue the orders and later decide whether it has jurisdiction over the dispute. In such a situation, if the court decides it has no jurisdiction, it will vacate any orders previously issued and refuse to perform any further acts in connection with the case (dismiss it). If the court has jurisdiction over a dispute, the court may not decline to act in the matter. (A distinction must be made between the "court" and a "judge." An individual judge may decline to hear a matter under certain circumstances, but the court in which he or she sits retains jurisdiction over it and another judge will be appointed to hear and decide the matter.) If the court is incorrect about its jurisdiction over any particular dispute, any judgment it renders is void and without legal effect.

There are different aspects to a court's jurisdiction. "Original" jurisdiction is the power to hear and decide a dispute when it first is presented to a court. "Appellate" jurisdiction exists when a court may consider a dispute only after it has been heard by a court with original jurisdiction. Some courts, usually the highest court within a geographic area, may have both original and appellate jurisdiction. "Derivative" jurisdiction exists when a court obtains the power to hear a dispute through another court; e.g., an appellate court derives its jurisdiction from the court of original jurisdiction (the trial court).

Jurisdiction may also be general or limited. "General" jurisdiction is the authority to decide every type of dispute that occurs (although even the widest general jurisdiction has its limits in law). "Limited" jurisdiction is authority limited to certain types of disputes, e.g., tax cases. Jurisdiction also may be exclusive or concurrent. "Exclusive" jurisdiction is sole authority to decide a particular type of disputes. "Concurrent" jurisdiction exists when another court or courts also may decide the same type of cases. Although a court's authority to decide certain types of disputes may be limited, every court has "ancillary" jurisdiction that it may use in the course of exercising its primary jurisdiction. Such ancillary jurisdiction includes the authority to order or control things that are related to its primary jurisdiction, e.g., ordering a party to deposit money with the court, controlling the way in which the trial is conducted, and enforcing its decision once made.

The term *jurisdiction* also may be used in connection with the "effect" that a court's decision will have. Jurisdiction "in personum" means that the person against whom the decision is directed must obey the decision or be subject to legal consequences. Jurisdiction "in rem" affects, or exerts authority over, property or "res" that is located within the geographic area in which the court operates. A third term that relates to the effect of jurisdiction is "quasi in rem." This last is used for cases where property or status is indirectly affected by a decision involving a person; e.g., a person's marital status is indirectly affected when a divorce is granted to the person.

A court's jurisdiction over a dispute, once found to exist, continues until the court has done everything it can to resolve, or decide, the dispute. If the parties to the dispute appeal the court's decision to a higher court, the trial court loses its jurisdiction and the appellate court gains it.

For more information

20 *American Jurisprudence* 2d 372–421, sections 54–129 (1995).

Ford, Richard T. "Law's Territory (A History of Jurisdiction)," *Michigan Law Review* 97 (1999): 843.

Judith Kilpatrick
University of Arkansas, Fayetteville

jury refers to a group of citizens chosen from the community to decide a question of fact or to render a verdict in a criminal or civil case.

The jury's role is to hear and see the evidence presented by both sides during a trial in a courtroom open to the public, and then to make a decision by applying the law described by the judge to the facts of the case. A jury usually consists of 12 citizens, who must reach a unanimous verdict. Smaller juries and nonunanimous verdicts, however, are now allowed in some jurisdictions. The right to a trial by a jury of one's peers in both civil and criminal cases is guaranteed by the Seventh Amendment to the U.S. Constitution, except in a few civil cases based on equity or admiralty rather than on common law, and in criminal cases involving minor or petty offenses.

The jury system is a hallmark of American democracy. It represents a way in which ordinary citizens can participate directly in exercising part of the power of government decision making, bypassing by design the elected or appointed government officials in the judicial branch. In this sense, it might be analogized to the referendum or initiative process, in which ordinary citizens can displace the role of government officials in the legislative branch by directly enacting proposals into law. The involvement of ordinary citizens as jurors allows the community to intercede in disputes between the state and its citizens, or between citizens.

Although versions of the jury may be traced back to ancient Greece, the jury has never been widely used throughout the world. During the last one thousand years, it has principally been a feature of Anglo-American jurisprudence, although it exists in a few other countries as well. Even England has begun to turn away from the jury, largely restricting it to only the most serious criminal cases. Many countries that preserve some form of citizen participation in judicial decision making typically have citizens sit with a smaller number of judges as part of the group that renders the decision.

Even in the United States, the role of the civil jury has been shrinking. There has been a steady shift in the allocation of decision-making responsibility away from juries and toward judges during the latter half of the 20th century. In addition, given the small number of cases that actually go to trial, the percentage of cases decided by a jury in the United States may be as low as two percent of the civil cases that are filed. Therefore, the role of the civil jury, while still important in a few cases and as a framework for settlement bargaining, may have become more symbolic than real, even in the United States. In criminal cases, by contrast, the jury has retained its vitality. Although most criminal cases are resolved by a guilty plea, the majority of the serious criminal cases that are tried are tried in the United States by a jury.

The jury has changed a great deal over time. During the Middle Ages, persons selected as jurors were generally knowledgeable about the dispute, or at least about the parties to the dispute. They were expected to rely at least in part upon their preexisting knowledge of the events and people in reaching their decision. As the centuries passed, the jury evolved away from this model toward a model in which the jurors have no preexisting knowledge of the events or people involved in the dispute and are required to make their decision based solely on the evidence presented in the courtroom during the trial. Some believe this enhances impartiality and fairness; others, however, believe that it yields juries comprised of the least talented and least informed members of the community.

The value of the jury has long been debated. Some question the ability of jurors to understand the judge's instructions regarding the law, their willingness to apply the law, their ability to understand scientific testimony or other complex facts, and their lack of decision-making expertise. Supreme Court Justice Byron White, for example, once described a jury trial as "little better than a roll of the dice." Others believe that juries usually return sound verdicts and enable the community to leaven or temper the interpretation and application of law with popular, commonsense justice. Supreme Court Justice Joseph Storey called the jury "essential to political and civil liberty."

There have been many important studies of jury decision making. Perhaps the most famous, which was conducted by professors at the University of Chicago, concluded that judges and juries agree on the outcome about 80 percent of the time, a rate of agreement that compares favorably with the rate of agreement between doctors diagnosing diseases. Other studies have concluded that jurors are prone to making errors of various types, but the question of whether judges also are prone to making similar errors has not been fully explored.

Another source of controversy about juries is the notion of "jury nullification." That term refers to instances in which a jury may have disregarded the judge's instructions regarding the law and made a decision based upon different criteria. Juries usually are instructed that they must apply the law described by the judge whether they agree with it or not. But, unlike judges, juries do not have to explain the reasons for their decisions, so they may not always follow that instruction. For example, a jury might acquit a defendant rather than returning a verdict of guilty if the jurors believe that the law defining a criminal offense was too strict or that the resulting sentence would be too harsh. If a judge did this openly, the judge's decision would be viewed as illegitimate.

The power of a jury to nullify the law raises the age-old issue of whether the dispensation of justice should depend on rules of law or the discretion of the decision maker. Generally, we believe that decisions in the justice system should be based, insofar as reasonably possible, on legal principles set out in advance and applied consistently to all parties and across all disputes, recognizing that this is an ideal that cannot always be perfectly achieved. Appellate

Judge Jerome Frank argued that "the jury is the worst possible enemy of that ideal of the 'supremacy of law.'" On the other hand, jury nullification may keep the law applied in particular cases from straying too far from the current popular will. This may be desirable, especially in a democracy, if sparingly used. As Professor Susan Estrich has observed, "The ability of a jury to acquit a guilty man and thus nullify the law is a safeguard of liberty when rarely used, and an invitation to anarchy when used too often."

There is also another sort of jury. Unlike a trial jury or petit jury, a grand jury discharges its function only in criminal cases, and only before an indictment or other formal charging document is filed to commence a criminal prosecution. It typically consists of 23 citizens who are selected to serve for six months or more. A grand jury deliberates after receiving in secret only such information as the prosecutor chooses to reveal to them. The responsibility of a grand jury is to determine whether there is sufficient evidence to warrant the filing of a criminal charge against the accused. Since there is no grand jury in civil cases, the two-layer system of petit jury and grand jury exists only in criminal cases. The right to the charged by a grand jury in federal criminal cases is protected by the Fifth Amendment to the U.S. Constitution.

The enduring importance of the grand jury is debatable. There are a few famous examples of grand juries who refused to authorize the filing of an indictment, thus preventing prosecution of an individual. On the other hand, in present practice, the grand jury almost always returns an indictment when requested by the prosecution. According to one study, 99.9 percent of indictments requested by the prosecutor are returned by the grand jury. Therefore, the once valuable role of the grand jury in preventing government oppression of dissidents seems to have been greatly diminished. Perhaps for this reason, many states have restricted or eliminated the use of grand juries.

For more information

Abramson, Jeffrey. *We, the Jury.* New York: Basic Books, 1994.

Few, J. Kendall. *In Defense of Trial by Jury.* Greenville, S.C.: American Jury Trial Foundation, 1993.

Hans, Valarie P., and Neil Vidmar. *Judging the Jury.* New York: Plenum Press, 1986.

Kalven, Harry Jr., and Hans Zeisel. *The American Jury.* Chicago, Illinois: University of Chicago Press, 1971.

Andrew J. Wistrich, Magistrate Judge
United States District Court
Los Angeles, California

justice   in the context of the legal or justice system refers to the fair and proper administration of the law to the situations presented in particular lawsuits. To do justice is to give each litigant his or her due. It has been described by Alexander Hamilton as the "end of government" (*see* Alexander Hamilton, *The Federalist Papers* number 51, 2:121 [1788]), and as an unattainable ideal.

Different cultures, and different people within the same culture, view justice differently, if, in evaluating the justice system, they tend to assume that one standard of justice applies to all people and entities at all times. Similarly, as one philosopher observed, "if justice goes, there is no longer any value in men's living on earth." (Immanuel Kant, The Metaphysics of Morals, 141 [Mary Greger, translator, 91].)

To facilitate analysis, justice has been divided into several categories, each of which is discussed briefly below.

Distributive justice concerns the allocation of all things, whether good or bad, across the persons and entities comprising the community. It concerns questions of the initial allocation of things, and also the question of whether a different allocation would be more just or fair.

Corrective justice concerns the manner in which a community responds to events that alter the distributive status quo. For example, if one

person is injured by another, the role of corrective justice is to re-create the presumably just distribution that occurred prior to the wrongful act by shifting the cost represented by the injury from the victim to the wrongdoer.

Retributive justice addresses the same disturbance in the distribution of things within the status quo but from a different perspective than does corrective justice. While corrective justice focuses on compensation of the victim by the wrongdoer, retributive justice focuses on punishing or inflicting suffering upon the wrongdoer. Both corrective justice and retributive justice may have the effect of discouraging wrongdoing in the future both by depriving wrongdoers of the games that may result from their wrongful acts and by making them worse off—not just no better off—than they would have been had they not performed the wrongful act.

This may achieve both specific deterrents (that is, discouraging the wrongdoer from committing wrongful acts in the future) and general deterrence (discouraging persons other than the wrongdoer from following the wrongdoer's example in committing wrongful acts in the future). Both corrective and retributive justice have an element of readjusting the balance of things after the wrongful acts so that the balance more closely approximates the balance that existed prior to the wrongful act. Unlike distributive justice, however, corrective justice and retributive justice do not address the question of whether the status quo prior to the wrongful act was itself inherently just or unjust. They simply aim, in whole or in part, to return to the status quo that existed prior to the wrongful act.

Commutative justice is similar to corrective justice. It concerns the inequality that may be caused when there is an apparently voluntary exchange that unfairly disturbs the status quo that existed prior to the exchange. Again, like corrective justice and to some degree retributive justice, the aim of commutative justice is to reestablish the balance that existed prior to an event that is regarded by the community as wrongful.

Another form of justice is procedural justice. It concerns the procedures by which a disturbance and the allocation of things is addressed or remedied. Unlike the other forms of justice, procedural justice largely abandons efforts to define the correct or fair outcome, focusing instead on the method by which that outcome is produced. An outcome reached by what is considered to be a fair process is conclusively presumed to be fair or just, regardless of how it addresses the disturbance in the status quo.

In the Anglo-American tradition, fair procedures are largely synonymous with due process of law. The irreducible elements of due process of law are generally considered to be the following: (1) an unbiased tribunal; (2) notice of the proposed action and the grounds asserted for it; (3) opportunity to present reasons why the proposed action should not be taken; (4) the right to present evidence, including the right to call witnesses; (5) the right to know the opposing evidence; (6) the right to cross-examine adverse witnesses; (7) decision based exclusively on the evidence presented; (8) right to counsel; (9) requirement that the tribunal prepare a record of the evidence presented; and (10) requirement that the tribunal prepare written findings of the facts and reasons for its decision. Other terms are commonly used to describe types of justice. Natural justice refers to moral, usually historically or religiously based, rather than strictly legal notions of justice. Popular justice is what satisfies currently prevailing public opinion as fair. Positive justice is justice as defined by the legal system. Substantial justice refers to the proclivity toward deciding cases based upon their merits under the substantive law, rather than by resolving them on the basis of failure to comply with the rules regulating the litigation process, procedural default, or other matters that are popularly viewed as "technicalities."

For more information

Aristotle. *The Nicomachean Ethics,* trans. D. Ross. New York: Oxford University Press, 1925, pp. 1129–1134.

Fletcher, George P. *Basic Concepts of Legal Thought.* New York: Oxford University Press, 1996, pp. 79–94.

Friendly, Henry J. "Some Kind of Hearing," *University of Pennsylvania Law Review* 123 (1975): 1267.

Rawls, John. *A Theory of Justice.* Cambridge, Mass.: Belknap Press of Harvard University Press, 1971.

Solomon, Robert C., and Murphy, Mark C., eds. *What Is Justice?* New York: Oxford University Press, 1990.

Andrew J. Wistrich, Magistrate Judge
United States District Court
Los Angeles, California

Justice, United States Department of (DOJ)

was established in 1870 (though the office of attorney general began in 1789). Until 1870 the responsibility for enforcement of national laws was scattered among the various agencies of the federal government.

The U.S. DOJ includes the Federal Bureau of Investigation, the Drug Enforcement Administration, the Immigration and Naturalization Service, the Federal Bureau of Prisons, the Antitrust Division, and the Civil Rights Division. In addition to protecting the economy from monopolistic practices that reduce competition, the Antitrust Division advises governmental bodies such as the Nuclear Regulatory Commission, agencies that regulate bank mergers, and agencies that lease mining rights on federal lands. The DOJ's Consumer Affairs Section works with the Food and Drug Administration, the Federal Trade Commission, and the Consumer Products Safety Commission. The Civil Division does litigation in which the United States is the defendant being sued for injury and damages allegedly inflicted by a government official. The Justice Department also includes the Bureau of Justice Statistics and the National Institute of Justice, agencies researching and analyzing various aspects of crime.

The DOJ conducts all suits in the Supreme Court in which the United States is concerned. The solicitor general represents the United States in these cases. When the solicitor general petitions the Supreme Court to review an opinion of a lower court, his request is usually granted. The request may come in the form of an amicus curiae brief. Several times during the year the solicitor general comes to the Supreme Court to withdraw a case with the admission that the government had made an error. The department also renders legal advice and opinions, upon request, to the president and to the heads of the executive departments through its Office of Legal Counsel. An assistant attorney general heading up the Office of Legal Counsel is the principal legal guardian in the executive branch of the constitutional prerogatives and powers of the presidency. In addition, the department monitors misconduct by local police and electoral officials.

Throughout the history of the Justice Department, there have been up-and-down relations between its political leadership and the career lawyers who staff the department. Allegations recur of political meddling in criminal, antitrust, and other cases. However, the political leaders often infuse the department with new energy and new ideas.

For more information

Burnham, David. *Above the Law: Secret Deals, Political Fixes, and Other Misadventures of the US Department of Justice.* New York: Scribner, 1996.

McGee, Jim, and Brian Duffy. *Main Justice: The Men and Women Who Enforce the Nation's Criminal Laws and Guard Its Liberties.* New York: Simon and Schuster, 1996.

Martin Gruberg
University of Wisconsin, Oshkosh

K

The Kansas-Nebraska Act, introduced by Illinois senator Stephen F. Douglas and passed by the U.S. Congress in 1854, shattered the national consensus over the spread of slavery in the territories that had prevailed since the Missouri Compromise of 1820, galvanized antislavery sentiment in the North, unleashed a wave of violence in the Kansas Territory, split the Democratic Party and destroyed the Whigs, and set the nation on a course that would lead to civil war seven years later.

During the early 1850s, the prospect of constructing a transcontinental railroad linking California with the eastern states gained momentum and provoked sectional rivalries that had been simmering since the nation's inception. The United States had acquired from Mexico 30,000 acres south of the Gila River as a result of the Gadsden Purchase of 1853, and Southern interests, led by Secretary of State Jefferson Davis, proposed a railroad route through this region that would link New Orleans with the west coast. Northern interests, on the other hand, favored a route through unorganized Indian territory that would link Chicago and San Francisco.

As Congress debated the merits of the various proposals, Senator Douglas, chairman of the Senate Committee on Territories, with an eye on the presidency, sought to facilitate the selection of the northern route by introducing legislation in January 1854 to organize the territories west of Missouri and Iowa as the Nebraska Territory. In order to win support for the measure among southern lawmakers, Douglas proposed settling the issue of slavery in the new territories through popular sovereignty, a democratic concept that had been included in the Compromise of 1850 and enjoyed broad support among westerners.

Unfortunately for Douglas and his supporters, the Missouri Compromise of 1820 had prohibited slavery in the territories of the Louisiana Purchase from latitude 36° 30′ to the Canadian border, a vast region that included the Nebraska Territory. To allow the question of slavery to be decided through popular sovereignty would require the de facto repeal of the Missouri Compromise, the sectional accord on slavery that had maintained a tenuous peace within the nation for 34 years. Although many in the North had come to regard the "sacred pact" as almost a part of the Constitution itself, Southern congressmen were anxious to be rid of the compromise and to establish the right of slaveholders to take their slaves into any territory.

Although he was personally opposed to slavery and believed that the climate and geography of the Great Plains would prove inimical to plantation agriculture, Douglas was forced to offer a number of concessions on the issue of slavery to garner support for his legislation among southern lawmakers: the repeal of those portions of the Missouri Compromise prohibiting slavery north of 36° 30′, a popular sovereignty provision whereby the question as to whether to allow slavery in the new territories would be decided by representative territorial assemblies, and the organization of two territories, Kansas and Nebraska. It was presumed that Kansas, which lay west of slaveholding Missouri, would opt for slavery, while Nebraska, lying west of free-soil Iowa, would become a free state.

However, Douglas had underestimated the degree to which his compromises with the southerners would inflame antislavery and abolitionist sentiments nationwide. Throughout the North, outrage over Douglas's willingness to discard the Missouri Compromise and to allow the spread of slavery into the new territories filled editorial pages and issued from pulpits, and the senator was burned in effigy in a number of communities. Nevertheless, despite the emergence of organized opposition to the Kansas-Nebraska Act from among his fellow Democrats in Congress, Douglas had the support of President Franklin Pierce and ultimately succeeded in pushing the legislation through Congress. The Kansas-Nebraska Act passed by a vote of 37–14 in the Senate and 113–100 in the House and was signed into law by President Pierce in May 1854.

For more information

Freehling, William W. *The Road to Disunion: Secessionists at Bay, 1776–1854.* New York: Oxford University Press, 1991.

Holt, Michael F. *The Political Crisis of the 1850s.* New York: W. W. Norton, 1983.

Potter, David M. *The Impending Crisis.* New York: HarperCollins, 1977.

William D. Baker
Arkansas School for Mathematics and Science

Katz v. United States

Katz v. United States 389 U.S. 1 (1967) is among the most important decisions of the Supreme Court regarding the implied right of privacy found in the Fourth Amendment.

In 1967 Charles Katz was tried and convicted for placing sports bets over the telephone. This seemingly insignificant event led to one of the most far-reaching Supreme Court opinions in history regarding the scope of what constitutes a legal search and seizure.

Agents of the FBI, suspecting that Katz was engaged in illegal activity, observed him leave his home and go to the same public phone booth every day at approximately the same time. The agents then placed recording devices on the top of the phone booth and microphones on the outside of the booth, thus recording Katz's side of his conversations. These recordings did reveal that he was making bets and they were the key piece of evidence used to convict him at trial.

This type of evidence gathering, known as wiretapping, had long been allowed as a means of law enforcement by the Supreme Court, going back as far as *Olmstead v. United States* in 1928, and had been repeatedly reaffirmed. Nonetheless, Katz appealed his conviction, claiming that his Fourth Amendment rights had been violated.

The Fourth Amendment says that "The right of the people to be secure in their persons, houses, papers, and effects, against unreasonable searches and seizures, shall not be violated, and no warrants shall issue, but upon probable cause, supported by oath or affirmation, and particularly describing the place to be searched, and the persons or things to be seized."

Katz's contention was that although there had been no physical intrusion by the agents, listening to his conversations should still be considered a search. He felt that the government had invaded his private realm and seized his words to be used against him. The fact that the conversations took place in a phone booth rather than his home should not matter, nor should the fact that the listening devices were outside the phone booth minimize the intrusion. Katz felt that since he intended his conversations to be private, and took steps such as closing the door to the booth to keep them private, the government had crossed the line.

By a vote of 7–1, the Supreme Court agreed that the wiretapping in this case was a search under the terms of the Fourth Amendment and, therefore, could only be conducted pursuant to a judicially authorized warrant. Speaking for the majority, Justice Stewart explained that the Fourth Amendment protects "people rather than places" and therefore it does not require a physical trespass by the police into any given place.

Justice Harlan's concurring opinion, which has subsequently been relied upon for precedent in determining the scope of the Fourth Amendment, applied a two-part test for determining under what circumstances the amendment's protections apply. First, "a person must exhibit an actual (subjective) expectation of privacy and second, that the expectation be one that society is prepared to accept as reasonable."

This test of reasonableness is still relied upon today in many Fourth Amendment cases to determine when a warrant is needed and serves as an important check on governmental intrusions into the lives of its citizens.

For more information

Hall, Kermit. *The Oxford Guide to United States Supreme Court Decisions.* New York: Oxford University Press, 1999.

James, Foster, and Leeson, Susan. *Constitutional Law: Cases in Context.* Upper Saddle River, N.J.: Prentice Hall, 1992.

Paul Weizer
Fitchburg State College

Kennedy, Anthony M. (1936–) is currently an associate justice of the U.S. Supreme Court and is widely regarded as a key swing vote in contentious constitutional cases. He was born in Sacramento, California, on July 23, 1936, to a middle-class, professional family of practicing Irish Catholics. His father, Bud, was a lobbyist and his mother, Gladys, was active in civic causes. Kennedy received his B.A. at Stanford in 1958 and J.D. at Harvard Law School in 1961. He worked in private practice in San Francisco and Sacramento where he also taught at the McGeorge School of Law from 1965 to 1988. In 1975 he was appointed by President Gerald Ford to the Ninth Circuit Court of Appeals, where he remained until his appointment to the High Court in 1988 by President Ronald Reagan. Kennedy took his place on the bench as Reagan's compromise third choice after the Democratic Senate rejected controversial nominees Robert Bork and Douglas Ginsburg.

Often the deciding vote in high-profile cases, Kennedy's record as a justice has been mixed. Though he has generally been supportive of the Rehnquist Court's conservative majorities, he has occasionally sided with the Court's more liberal members on such issues as religious freedom, speech and expression, and discrimination.

Kennedy was one of the joint authors of the Court's 1992 decision in *Planned Parenthood v. Casey,* 505 U.S. 833 (1992), which upheld a woman's constitutional right to an abortion. The opinion, however, also allowed states to place certain restrictions on that right as long as those restrictions did not create an "undue burden." "Some of us as individuals find abortion offensive to our most basic principles of morality," the opinion explained, "but that cannot control our decision. Our obligation is to define the liberty of all, not to mandate our own moral code." Eight years later Kennedy sided with the dissenters in *Sternberg v. Carhart,* No. 99–830 (2000), where the Court narrowly struck down state laws banning so-called partial birth abortions. In a separate opinion, Kennedy argued that citizens should be able to "address these grave and serious issues" through their state governments.

In the area of free exercise, Kennedy's record has been varied. In *Church of the Lukumi v. Hialeah*, 508 U.S. 520 (1993), Kennedy wrote the majority opinion invalidating a local ordinance that sought to prevent animal sacrifice for religious purposes, affirming the "Nation's essential commitment to religious freedom." But four years later in *City of Boerne v. Flores*, No. 95-2074 (1997), he wrote the majority opinion that struck down the Religious Freedom Restoration Act, which sought to protect the free exercise of religion. Kennedy held that Congress had exceeded its power in passing the bipartisan legislation.

In cases involving religious establishment, Kennedy has been both accommodationist and separationist depending on the specific issue at hand. In *Lee v. Weisman*, 505 U.S. 577 (1992), Kennedy wrote for a narrow Court majority in striking down nondenominational prayers at public school graduation ceremonies as fostering "subtle coercive pressure." He reaffirmed that position in *Santa Fe Independent School District v. Doe*, No. 99-62 (2000), where he sided with the majority in striking down school-sponsored prayers before public high school football games. But writing for a Court majority in *Rosenberger v. University of Virginia*, 515 U.S. 819 (1995), Kennedy held that public schools can provide monetary and other support to campus religious groups as long as the support is allocated on a neutral basis.

Throughout his tenure, Kennedy has generally been protective of free speech principles. In *Texas v. Johnson*, 491 U.S. 397 (1989), Kennedy provided the fifth vote to strike down flag desecration statutes in 48 states as well as at the federal level. Stating that the free speech clause of the First Amendment protects political expression, he explained that the Constitution compelled a ruling that he found personally distasteful. He added, "It is poignant but fundamental that the flag protects those who hold it in contempt." In *Madsen v. Women's Health Center,*

Inc., 512 U.S. 753 (1994), and *Hill v. Colorado*, No. 98-1856 (2000), Kennedy was in dissent, holding the view that states should not be able to prohibit the "unpopular speech" of protesters outside abortion clinics.

As in other areas, Kennedy has stayed away from extreme positions in cases involving affirmative action. In *City of Richmond v. J.A. Croson Co.*, 488 U.S. 469 (1989), and *Adarand Constructors, Inc. v. Pena*, 515 U.S. 200 (1995), he sided with the majority in disallowing governmental use of racial quotas but at the same time allowing race to be taken into account as one factor in contracting, hiring, and school admissions. In *Croson* he wrote "The State has the power to eradicate racial discrimination and its effects in both the public and private sectors, and the absolute duty to do so where those wrongs were caused intentionally by the State itself." Still, he added, "any racial preference (by the government) must face the most rigorous scrutiny by the courts."

Kennedy has continued to employ a cautious conservative jurisprudence in the area of gay rights. He authored the Court's opinion in *Romer v. Evans*, No. 94-1039 (1996), which struck down a Colorado measure that barred ordinances extending gays legal protection from discrimination, such as in housing or employment. Citing the amendment's de facto prohibition on homosexuals from participating in the political process, Kennedy stated, "The amendment imposes a special disability. Homosexuals are forbidden the safeguards that others enjoy or may seek without constraint." But four years later in *Boy Scouts of America v. Dale*, No. 99-699 (2000), he provided the fifth vote to allow the Boy Scouts to bar homosexuals from serving as troop leaders. The Court cited the organization's rights of free expression and free association under the Constitution's First Amendment.

In all, Kennedy's record on the Court has been one of moderate conservatism. His pragmatic approach and cautious nature are reflected in his voting record. While generally sympathetic to the more conservative positions of his colleagues like Chief Justice William H. Rehnquist and Antonin Scalia, Kennedy has found his own voice toward the Court's center. He once commented, "It's easier to be a Rehnquist or a Scalia than a Kennedy."

For more information

Savage, David G. *Turning Right: The Making of the Rehnquist Supreme Court.* New York: John Wiley, 1992.

Simon, James F. *The Center Holds: The Power Struggle Inside the Rehnquist Court.* New York: Simon and Schuster, 1995.

Yarbrough, Tinsley. *The Rehnquist Court and the Constitution.* New York: Oxford University Press, 2000.

Artemus Ward
California State University, Chico

Kennedy, John Fitzgerald (1917–1963)

was elected 35th president of the United States in 1960 by one of the narrowest margins in history. His tenure in the White House symbolized a generational shift in American law and politics and paved the way for important advances in civil rights. Kennedy had several years of experience as an elected official, having served in the U.S. House of Representatives and Senate before defeating Richard Nixon for the presidency.

Kennedy entered the White House with a plan that was termed the "New Frontier." This plan proposed significant changes for the nation's social laws. The Kennedy plan intended to raise the minimum wage, liberalize social security benefits, improve housing, and provide temporary compensation for unemployment. Kennedy encountered difficulties in his efforts to pass this legislation. He initially had visions of accomplishing these tasks immediately after his election, but opposition in Congress forced the postponement of most of the bills.

At the time of Kennedy's election, hostilities in the South were growing due to the Civil Rights movement. Kennedy initially avoided the issue but was aware that action would soon have to be taken. In response to the Civil Rights movement the Kennedy administration proposed a plan that would make it illegal for employers to discriminate on the basis of race. Discrimination would be illegal in all forms of public facilities and public accommodations like hotels and restaurants. The plan also imposed a withholding of federal funds where discrimination occurred. The other major element was the eradication of arbitrary voter discrimination laws. This was by far the most sweeping piece of civil rights legislation in the 20th century. The opposition to the proposal was fierce, but the bill eventually passed as the Civil Rights Act of 1964. Kennedy was assassinated before it was signed into law.

Working with his brother, Attorney General Robert Kennedy, the administration brought significant changes to the Justice Department. The Kennedys stepped up enforcement of voting rights laws and encouraged a voter education project. The Department of Justice was implementing these plans as an effort to bring about changes in the South in a voluntary and peaceful manner. JFK also increased the number of African Americans employed in the Justice Department by 500 percent. His efforts to integrate did not stop there. He appointed 10 African Americans to federal judgeships. Thurgood Marshall, who later became the first African American appointed to the U.S. Supreme Court, was one of the judges that Kennedy appointed to a federal seat. For all his pro–civil rights appointees, Kennedy also appointed some judges to federal seats who were staunch segregationists, such as W. Harold Cox, E. Gordon West, and Robert Elliot.

During Kennedy's abbreviated presidential term he made two appointments to the High Court. In 1962 Arthur J. Goldberg was selected. Goldberg's liberal voting tendencies meshed well with the Kennedy administration's vision for the country. For example, Goldberg supported privacy rights in *Griswold v. Connecticut*, 381 U.S.

John Fitzgerald Kennedy (JFK LIBRARY)

479 (1965), and the rights of the accused in *Escobedo v. Illinois*, 378 U.S. 478 (1964).

President Kennedy also appointed Byron R. White to the Supreme Court. White served on the Court for more than 30 years but did not always side with the liberals. One area where White did vote as Kennedy had hoped was in discrimination cases. For example, White voted to uphold the Civil Rights and Voting Rights Acts. Still, toward the end of his tenure he voted to strike down affirmative action and set aside programs. On individual liberty issues, White was generally conservative, for example, voting against a woman's right to an abortion in *Roe v. Wade*, 410 U.S. 113 (1973) and upholding a state criminal sodomy statute in *Bowers v. Hardwick*, 478 U.S. 186 (1986).

On November 22, 1963, at the age of 46, Kennedy was assassinated in Dallas, Texas. Though his tenure in office was brief, it symbolized an important break with the past. Taking office after eight years of Republican control under Dwight Eisenhower, the Kennedy administration embodied a generational shift in American politics and laid the groundwork for important changes in American law.

For more information
Navasky, Victor S. *Kennedy Justice.* New York: Atheneum, 1971.
Schlesinger, Arthur M., Jr. *A Thousand Days: John F. Kennedy in the White House.* New York: Fawcett Books, 1991.

Artemus Ward, California
State University, Chico

King, Dr. Martin Luther, Jr. (1929–1968) who has been hailed for his embrace of nonviolent strategies to end legally sanctioned racial segregation of African Americans, is widely regarded as the pivotal figure in the Civil Rights movement. He stands as one of the towering political leaders of the 20th century.

King was born on January 15, 1929, in Atlanta, Georgia. After entering historically black Morehouse College at the age of 15, King joined the Christian ministry. Ordained in 1948 at the age of 19, King began his doctoral studies in theology at Boston University in 1951. In 1953 King married Coretta Scott, and the following year he became pastor of the Dexter Avenue Baptist Church in Montgomery, Alabama. King's move to Alabama catapulted him into the forefront of the struggle for African-American civil rights, political equality, and the end of legalized racial segregation in America.

After Rosa Parks refused to give up her seat to a white man and move to the back of a city bus, King was thrust into the spotlight as president and coordinator of the yearlong Montgomery Improvement Association Bus Boycott.

Culminating in a 1956 Supreme Court decision outlawing Alabama's bus segregation laws, the boycott's citizen involvement and nonviolent tactics received national attention, as did King for his stirring speeches and courageous leadership.

King's vision for the Civil Rights movement built upon what had transpired in Montgomery, incorporating grass-roots organizing, African-American churches, nonviolent political protest, and coalitions with progressive whites. In 1957 King founded the Southern Christian Leadership Conference (SCLC) to coordinate protests throughout the South. The SCLC advocated nonviolent "direct-action" campaigns for social change, even as boycotts, marches, lunch counter sit-ins, and peaceful negotiations increasingly met with massive resistance from southern whites in the form of harassment, mass arrests, police brutality, firebombings, and murders.

King maintained that nonviolent protest was both morally correct and politically wise, in that it would create the conditions for local change as well as generate federal intervention to bring about the end of legalized racial segregation. A philosophy that law is meant to promote social justice provided the underlying rationale for King's practical defiance of laws codifying white supremacy, as when he was arrested in 1963 for protesting segregation in Birmingham, Alabama. While imprisoned, King wrote his famous "Letter from the Birmingham Jail," further documenting his belief in nonviolent confrontation as a strategy to catalyze social change.

At the 1963 March on Washington, King delivered his most famous speech, "I Have a Dream." "I have a dream," he thundered, "that my . . . children will one day live in a nation where they will not be judged by the color of their skin but by the content of their character." King hearkened to his commitment to a model of equality under law rooted in social justice. If laws themselves were discriminatory, the principle of equality under law was meaningless. Until race no longer was a barrier to social, legal, polit-

ical, and economic equality for African Africans—King's "dream"—King advocated the use of color-conscious laws and policies to level the playing field for blacks and whites.

King's notoriety continued to grow. He was named *Time* magazine's 1963 "Man of the Year" and was awarded the 1964 Nobel Peace Prize. Yet the Civil Rights movement was splintering into factions advocating different political goals and tactics—some of which dramatically deviated from King's nonviolent vision for change. In the aftermath of congressional passage of the 1964 Civil Rights Act, King's final successful civil rights campaign invoked the democratic ideal of full political participation in the electoral process. A series of demonstrations on behalf of voting rights in Alabama met with significant white resistance, culminating in a public confrontation that prompted President Lyndon B. Johnson to introduce federal legislation that became the Voting Rights Act of 1965.

Victories in the form of federal civil rights legislation prompted King to shift his focus away from the South to issues of poverty and racial discrimination against northern African Americans. King's influence continued to wane, however, while newly militant civil rights organizations gained adherents, and violent forms of political protest escalated as the 1960s drew toward a close.

As part of the Poor People's Campaign he announced in 1967, King went to Memphis, Tennessee, to lend support to a strike by city sanitation workers. On April 4, 1968, while standing on the balcony of the Lorraine Motel, King was assassinated. James Earl Ray, a white segregationist, was convicted of the shooting, a tragedy that shook the faith of people of all backgrounds in America's promise of freedom and equality.

King's vision of social justice shaped the overarching goals and nonviolent tactics of the Civil Rights movement. But racial justice, King warned in his "I Have a Dream" address, would come about only when the "whirlwinds of revolt" shook "the foundations of our nation." As

Dr. Martin Luther King, Jr. (NATIONAL ARCHIVES)

a social reformer, a political leader, and an African-American activist, King embraced both a radical vision of mass political protest as the impetus for social change and a heartfelt belief in democracy's capacity to live up to the promise that "all men are created equal." To the very end of his life, cut short before he could see his dream fully realized, King's faith in the human spirit coincided with the Constitution's guarantees of equality and justice under law. Through the national holiday established in 1986, Americans annually celebrate King's birth, and Atlanta's Martin Luther King, Jr., Center for Nonviolent Social Change carries on King's mission of peace and freedom.

For more information

Branch, Taylor. *Parting the Waters.* New York: Touchstone Books, 1988.

———. *Pillar of Fire.* New York: Simon and Schuster, 1998.

"The Martin Luther King, Jr., Papers Project at Stanford University," http://www.stanford.edu/group/King.

Dr. Steven A. Light
University of North Dakota
Neil Ferrera and Artemus Ward
California State University, Chico.

King, Rodney (1976–) was an African American who was beaten by Los Angeles police officers, thereby triggering a significant controversy regarding the role of race in the criminal justice system.

Rodney King was speeding while driving through the city of Los Angeles on March 3, 1991. A cruising team of Los Angeles Police Department (LAPD) officers followed King and repeatedly signaled him to stop, but he failed to do so. Then, in an obvious attempt to evade the officers, King increased his speed. The resulting eight-mile, high-speed chase through city streets was finally curtailed with the help of two additional officers driving a second LAPD vehicle.

When the LAPD officers asked King to leave his vehicle, he refused to move. Hence, the officer, acting in accordance with regular LAPD procedures, dragged King from the car while he repeatedly threatened to harm the officers. King then refused to comply with the officers' request to lie, face down, on the street.

All of the preceding actions led to the officers' decision to treat this as a clear-cut "resisting arrest" situation. Hence, per LAPD rules, the officers used physical force to gain control of the situation. The officers from the second LAPD vehicle watched while the officers who initiated the chase subdued King by striking him with a baton 56 times and forcefully kicking him six times. This beating caused 11 skull fractures, several broken bones and teeth, kidney injuries, and permanent brain damage.

A neighbor who was using a video camera in his apartment heard the scuffle and ran to his terrace, camera in hand. Although sickened by the scene, he taped 81 seconds of the LAPD officers' actions.

Worldwide distribution of the videotape created international outrage at the LAPD's actions, as well as enormous sympathy for Rodney King. Throughout the three trials that were eventually generated by the alleged police brutality in the King situation, the public consistently sympathized with King and opposed the LAPD actions.

In April 1992 the four LAPD officers present during Rodney King's arrest were tried in California state court for the criminal offense of assault with a deadly weapon. The jury, consisting of 10 Caucasians, one Filipino American, and one Hispanic American, rendered a verdict of "not guilty" for each of the four officers.

Less than two hours after these verdicts were announced, the predominantly black, south central section of Los Angeles erupted in violence. When the rioting finally ended, 70 hours later, 60 people were dead and more than 2,100 were injured. The rioters also caused approximately $1 billion worth of property damage.

The rioting exacerbated public criticism of LAPD's chief, Daryl F. Gates. He was accused of failing to prepare the LAPD for civil unrest, and of making poor decisions during the first four hours of the rioting. Gates eventually resigned in June 1992, after an independent commission, chaired by Warren Christopher, recommended replacement of Gates because of his officers' brutality.

The 1992 riots also ended the political career of Thomas Bradley, who served as the mayor of Los Angeles for five consecutive terms from 1974 through 1994. Although Los Angeles consistently grew and thrived throughout Bradley's first four terms, during his fifth term the 1992 racial strife, loss of lives, and debt of $1 billion for riot-related property damage completely overshadowed Bradley's earlier accomplishments. Bradley retired from politics in 1995.

In August 1992 the four LAPD officers were tried in federal court. The federal court first determined that although this trial and the April 1992 state court trial were based on the same facts, conducting the second trial would not violate the constitutional prohibition against double jeopardy. The state court had tried the LAPD officers for criminal assault according to state law. The federal trial was concerned with a completely separate issue: the federal offense of violation of Rodney King's civil rights.

The federal court jury handed down two verdicts. First, the two LAPD officers who helped to end the vehicular chase observed but did not participate in King's beating and were found not guilty. Second, the pair of LAPD officers who initiated the chase and then used excess physical force to arrest King were guilty of violating his civil rights. This guilty verdict carried a sentence of two and a half years in prison.

In January 1994 Rodney King returned to state court to sue the city of Los Angeles for personal injury. Again, the prohibition on double jeopardy was not violated. The first two trials were for criminal matters, in which the district attorney sought prison sentences for the accused. The January 1994 trial was sought civil damages to help heal the injuries caused by the defendant. King requested both compensatory damages, which ask the defendant to pay a certain sum to the plaintiff to remedy for plaintiff's physical injuries; and punitive damages, which seek to punish the defendant for causing injuries to the plaintiff. The jury denied punitive damages, but awarded King $3.8 million in compensatory damages.

The Rodney King trials have had a nationwide impact on police departments because of the extensive press coverage of the LAPD officers' use of unnecessary physical force. Previously, most police departments handled a "rough treatment" complaint against an officer by sending him to the internal affairs division, which would then issue a meaningless sanction. Since the 1992 Los Angeles riots, internal affairs divisions have added skilled, experienced investigators, whose duty is to seriously examine complaints about "rough treatment." Progressive police departments have also created civilian review boards, staffed by community volunteers. These boards are responsible for tracking complaints about law enforcement officers' use of excessive force. A civilian review board can recommend a departmental reprimand for an officer who has used excessive force.

The King cases and the 1992 riots motivated the U.S. Department of Justice to address the nationwide problem of hate crimes. These cases are now given priority on federal court schedules. To mitigate the conditions that foster hate crimes, the Justice Department coordinates the efforts of other federal, state, and local agencies with the work of neighborhood associations and other public interest groups. Additionally, in 1993, Congress enacted an updated Juvenile Justice and Delinquency Prevention Act. This statute requires that each state's delinquency prevention plan include a component designed to combat hate crimes. The Justice Department also created its own Office of Juvenile Justice and Delinquency Prevention to conduct a national assessment of young persons who commit hate crimes.

The Los Angeles riots of 1992 also motivated the Justice Department to create the Community Relations Service, a federal agency that assists communities in addressing intergroup disputes and preventing hate crimes. This new agency has helped to train hundreds of law enforcement officers who are responsible for teaching school officials how to use peer mediation to address racial tension and conflict.

For more information

Adams, Kenneth, et. al. *Police Use of Force: Overview of National and Local Data,* Research Report, NCJ 176330. Washington, D.C.: Department of Justice, 1999.

Lawrence A. Greenfield, Patrick A. Lanyan, Steven K. Smith Washington, D.C.: U. S. Department of Justice.

A Policymaker's Guide to Hate Crimes, Washington, D.C.: U.S. Department of Justice, 1998. National Institute of Justice.

Beth S. Swartz, J.D.

Korematsu v. United States 323 U.S. 214 (1944), which upheld the wartime internment of Japanese Americans, stands as a rare case in which the Supreme Court has upheld a statute disadvantaging a specific racial minority, and it is one of the Court's most widely disparaged decisions of the 20th century.

In February 1942, soon after declaring war against Japan in World War II, President Franklin Roosevelt authorized military commanders to designate "military areas [from] which any or all persons may be excluded, and . . . the right of any person to enter, remain in, or leave shall be subject to whatever restrictions" imposed by the commanders. A month later Congress passed a law criminalizing any violation of a commander's order under this authority. In May 1942 General John DeWitt ordered persons of Japanese descent to leave their homes and report to assembly and relocation centers, or internment camps, where they could not leave without permission.

Fred Korematsu, an American-born citizen, had been fired by his employer at the beginning of World War II as a result of his Japanese ancestry. After being convicted for remaining in his home instead of reporting to a relocation center, Korematsu appealed to the Supreme Court.

The Court upheld Korematsu's conviction. Writing for the majority, Justice Hugo Black asserted that although "all legal restrictions which curtail the civil rights of a single racial group are immediately suspect" and should receive "the most rigid scrutiny," such restrictions were not necessarily unconstitutional. After drawing the distinction that "[p]ressing public necessity may sometimes justify the existence of such restrictions; racial antagonism never can," Justice Black nonetheless rea-

Japanese-American family awaiting relocation to a camp, Hayward, California, 1942 (HULTON ARCHIVE)

soned that the necessities of wartime and the possible disloyalty of some Japanese Americans constituted a "military urgency" that justified the government's comprehensive internment program.

The program's impacts were unprecedented and devastating. Approximately 120,000 people, including 70,000 American citizens, were deported to 10 relocation centers throughout the West. With little warning, many were forced to leave their homes, businesses, and communities. Entire families lived in single rooms, surrounded by barbed wire fences and guarded by armed soldiers. The internment program ended in 1946, but for those imprisoned, the aftereffects lasted a lifetime.

In 1982 Fred Korematsu successfully filed a petition to overturn his conviction. A congressional commission found that the government's claim that "military necessity" justified the internment of all persons of Japanese ancestry was false; instead, the internment program was motivated by racial prejudice and wartime hysteria fanned by governmental and military leadership. In 1988 Congress enacted a law apologizing for the internment program and providing repa-

ration funds to those who had been unjustly incarcerated.

Korematsu frequently is cited as a historical example of a wrongly decided case. In his dissent at the time, Justice Robert Jackson warned that judicial sanction of racial discrimination in the form of internment "for all time . . . lies about like a loaded weapon ready for the hand of any authority that can bring forward a plausible claim of an urgent need." In the decades since *Korematsu,* the Court has declined to explicitly overrule it. However unlikely might be the detention of American citizens based on their race or ethnicity, *Korematsu* remains on the books, a striking example that no political outcome, however disturbing, is impossible during times of national turmoil.

For more information

Irons, Peter. *Justice at War.* New York: Oxford University Press, 1983.
Tateishi, John, ed. *And Justice for All: An Oral History of the Japanese American Detention Comps.* Seattle: University of Washington Press, 1999.

Dr. Steven A. Light
University of North Dakota

Ku Klux Klan is America's oldest hate group, and it has fostered racial and ethnic discrimination, religious intolerance, and violence from the end of the Civil War to the present.

The Klan (whose name may have been derived from the Greek word *kyklos,* or "circle") was founded in December 1865 in Pulaski, Tennessee. The small social club quickly evolved into an organization dedicated to undermining the federal government's program of Radical Reconstruction and to restoring white supremacy in the South. Klansmen, frequently whites of high social standing, shielded their identities with robes and sheets while developing a mystical organizational hierarchy headed by "grand wizards."

Parade of the Ku Klux Klan through counties of Virginia bordering on the District of Columbia (LIBRARY OF CON-
GRESS)

Klan groups terrorized and murdered African-American freedmen and -women, as well as white supporters of the expanded agenda of rights and liberties stemming from Reconstruction. The 1870 Force Act and the 1871 Ku Klux Klan Act granted President Ulysses S. Grant sweeping powers to combat the Klan, but local chapters remained strong through the end of Reconstruction and the restoration of southern white supremacy.

D. W. Griffith's influential film *The Birth of a Nation* (1915) stirred a revival of Klan pride, while the Bolshevik Revolution in Russia and a massive wave of Eastern European immigration to America raised the specter of dimin-

ished American strength abroad and "watered-down" national identity at home. In addition to African Americans, the Klan spewed its venom at Jews, Roman Catholics, foreigners, trade unions, homosexuals, and communists. Klan chapters sprang up throughout the Midwest as well as the South. Membership reached a peak of approximately 3 million, and the Klan achieved mainstream political power in the mid-1920s through the sponsorship of candidacies or voter drives in several states. However, the Great Depression and World War II provided little space for the Klan on either local or national agendas, and its strength waned.

Southern African Americans mounted organized challenges to Jim Crow in the 1950s and 1960s through voter registration drives, protest marches, lunch counter sit-ins, and boycotts, threatening white supremacy and catalyzing the Klan's resurrection. During the Civil Rights movement, southern Klan groups resumed their infamous "night rides," intended to terrorize black families and white supporters alike, and Klan members were responsible for countless beatings, shootings, and racially motivated bombings throughout the South. In response, state and local governments passed laws against cross burnings and masks, while the overwhelming tide of the Civil Rights movement and federal intervention through various civil rights statutes irrevocably changed southern political culture, relegating the Klan to the extremist fringe through the 1970s and much of the 1980s.

The specter of hooded Klan members rallying around a burning cross is more symbolic of the Klan's past than of its 21st-century guises. Today's hate groups are splintered by multiple agendas. The fall of communism and the continuing globalization of culture and commerce have fueled nativist paranoia among extremists. Antigovernment is on the rise. Racial and ethnic bigotry stems from the ongoing immigration of Latino and Asian populations, as well as the increased civic participation of African Americans and other groups traditionally regarded as outside the mainstream, such as gays and lesbians.

As documented by such reputable watchdog organizations as the Anti-Defamation League and the Southern Poverty Law Center's Klanwatch Project, the number and type of hate groups are increasing. In 1999 Klanwatch identified 163 existing Klan organizations, several of which have been involved in plotting and engaging in terrorist acts against banks, refineries, and African-American churches. The Klan eagerly has turned to the Internet as a means of propaganda and member recruitment, particularly among college-bound teens. As in the past, the Ku Klux Klan threatens to continue to fan the flames of intolerance, discrimination, and violence in the United States.

For more information

"A Hundred Years of Terror," Southern Poverty Law Center, http://www.splcenter.org.

Sims, Patsy. *The Klan.* Lexington: University Press of Kentucky, 1996.

Wade, Wyn Craig. *The Fiery Cross.* New York: Oxford University Press, 1998.

Dr. Steven A. Light
University of North Dakota

L

labor law   is the set of legal rules governing labor-management relations in the workplace. Labor law differs from employment law in that it regulates the collective rights and obligations resulting from union representation, while the latter regulates the individual employer-employee relationship.

The National Labor Relations Act (NLRA), adopted by Congress in 1935, is the principal statute regulating labor-management relations in the private sector. The NLRA, however, is not the exclusive source of U.S. labor law. The Railway Labor Act, also a federal statute, regulates union-management relations in the railway and airline transportation industries. In addition, most states have enacted statutes concerning public sector labor-management issues. While these statutes differ from the NLRA in certain respects, the NLRA serves as the predominant U.S. model of labor law regulation.

Broadly speaking, the NLRA protects three types of employee conduct. First, it protects the right of employees to engage in organizational activities. The NLRA specifically prohibits an employer from interfering with an employee's right to join a union or to engage in activities that urge fellow employees to join a union. Accordingly, an employer commits an unlawful labor practice by such acts as discharging an employee organizer or making threats of reprisal for union support. A union generally attains representational status only after first establishing its majority status among the employees at issue in a representation election.

A second right conferred by the NLRA is the right of employees to bargain collectively through their selected union representative. Mandatory subjects of bargaining include wages, hours, and other terms and conditions of employment, but not matters that go to the core of an employer's entrepreneurial control such as plant closings and product advertising. The NLRA obligates both parties to negotiate in good faith with a present intention to find a basis for agreement, although that obligation does not compel either party to agree to a proposal or offer a concession.

Finally, the NLRA protects the right of employees to engage in "concerted activity for mutual aid or protection." This includes a ban on an employer's ability to discharge or otherwise retaliate against an employee who participates in a lawful strike. Most collective bargaining agreements waive the union's right to strike during the contract term in favor of a grievance arbitration mechanism for dispute resolution.

Collective rights arising under the NLRA are enforced through administrative procedures. The NLRA prohibits various "unfair labor practices" committed by either employers or labor unions. Administratively, the NLRA established a National Labor Relations Board (NLRB) with two distinct functions. One branch of the NLRB, under the direction of the NLRB's general counsel, investigates and prosecutes unfair labor practice proceedings on behalf of complaining unions, employees, or employers. Independently, the NLRB, as a five-member, quasi-judicial body, reviews the unfair labor practice decisions of administrative law judges.

Enforceable rights also may be created by collective bargaining agreements negotiated pursuant to the NLRA. The vast majority of such agreements provide for a "just cause" limitation on employee discipline and discharge. Most contracts also establish a grievance procedure culminating in binding arbitration to resolve contract interpretation disputes.

In 1954, 35 percent of the U.S. nonagricultural workforce belonged to unions. Owing to various factors, union membership declined to less than 15 percent by 2000. Nonetheless, the AFL-CIO, an umbrella organization to which most American labor unions belong, continues to have considerable influence with respect to legislative and political issues.

For more information

Sharpe, Ray, and Robert N. Strassfield. *Understanding Labor Law*. New York: Matthew Bender, 1999.

Professor Stephen F. Befort
University of Minnesota Law School

land use law   emerges out of the power of state and local governments to regulate the ways that land can be used. Although landowners have general control over their property, the government may limit the uses to which it can be put. For example, zoning ordinances often restrict the sort of property that may be erected in specific areas. If an area is restricted to residential uses, a landowner may not open a commercial operation there.

State and local governments have considerable authority to regulate the ways land can be used. Regulation of land use is one of a broad range of state "police powers," which give state and local governments the power to protect the health, safety, morals, and welfare of their citizens. States may determine that some uses to which owners want to put their land conflict with the public good and therefore exercise their police powers by forbidding the land to be used as the owner would otherwise want. For example, state and local governments often forbid the sale of alcoholic beverages within several miles of a school, in order to decrease the risk that children will be killed by drunk drivers. No landowner is authorized to operate a bar or a liquor store on land within the forbidden zone. State regulatory claims are particularly strong when owners seek to devote land to dangerous or "noxious" uses, such as building a power plant on top of an earthquake fault.

Landowners sometimes object to restrictions on land usage because regulations may decrease property values. Owners are particularly likely to object when regulations are adopted after the land is purchased. What appeared to be a good investment, likely to bring in significant profit, may lose considerable value if land may not be developed as the purchaser had planned.

To challenge regulations that decrease the value of land, owners have brought suit, relying on the takings clause of the Fifth Amendment. This provision declares "nor shall private property be taken for public use, without just compensation." Although the clause applies most directly to government actions that confiscate or destroy property, owners have argued that they should be compensated for reductions in the value of their land. The Supreme Court dealt with this sort of argument in the case of *Euclid v. Ambler Realty Company* (1926). Ambler Realty bought a parcel of land in the village of Euclid, intending to develop it for industrial use. After a number of years in which Ambler Realty waited to develop its land, the village adopted zoning regulations that forbade industrial development on most of the property. Because this significantly lowered the value of the land, Ambler Realty sued for compensation under the takings clause. The Court ruled in favor of the village, holding that the creation of residential zones was sufficiently related to the health and safety of the community to justify the ordinance. Since this decision, courts have generally upheld zoning ordinances in the face of takings clause challenges.

Recently, the Supreme Court has expanded the rights of owners to challenge land use regulations. In *Nollan v. California Coastal Commission* (1987) and *Dolan v. Tigard* (1994), the Court ruled that requiring owners to leave a section of their land open to the public, even for environmental reasons, constituted a taking that had to be compensated. The Court agreed that land use regulations are not takings if they "substantially advance legitimate state interests" and if they do not "deny an owner economically viable use of his land." However, the Court decided that since the owners would not be allowed to deny access to the relevant sections of their property, the regulations affected "permanent physical occupations" and should be compensated.

For more information

Foster, James, and Susan Leeson. *Constitutional Law: Cases in Context,* Vol. 1. Upper Saddle River, N.J.: Prentice Hall, 1998.

Shannon Ishiyama Smithey
Department of Political Science
University of Pittsburgh

law   is the authoritative regulation of human behavior and interaction within a given society. There are a wide variety of legal systems and sources of law, but their common element is that they provide rules for resolving conflicts within society. The government is the source of most law, but it is not the only possible source of law. Many societies have recognized natural law and church law, for example, which regulate human activities based on religious requirements and are not necessarily enforced by the government. Somewhat differently, international law regulates the relationships between nations and often develops through the agreements of multiple governments.

The U.S. legal system is derived from the common-law system inherited from England. In the common-law system, the law is built up over time through the resolution of individual cases. Legal reasoning works by example as later cases are resolved based on the decisions in earlier, similar cases, known as precedents. In the United States, statutory law, or legislation, has generally replaced the common law. Rather than waiting for particular conflicts to arise and declaring a rule to resolve that conflict, legislatures create written rules in advance that address society as a whole. Judge-made law, or case law, is generally restricted to clarifying or filling in the details of the written law, rather than creating entirely new law with no prior foundation in the actions of the legislature. Even so, some areas of the private law in many states still rely on common law, and the statutory law frequently adopts the same rules that had been previously developed by judges.

A basic distinction can be made between the public law, which regulates the various parts of government and the relations between individuals and the government, and the private law, which regulates the relations among individuals. The most fundamental branch of the public law is constitutional law—the rules derived from the Constitution. Constitutional law stands above all the other types of law and determines the organization and limits of government power. Through the power of judicial review, the courts refuse to enforce government actions that violate the constitutional law. The law that regulates the bureaucracy is known as administrative law. It defines the powers, limits, and decision-making procedures of administrative agencies and authorizes the courts to monitor the bureaucracy for compliance with those rules. Another branch of the public law is the criminal law. Criminal law defines some individual actions as violations against the public order and authorizes the government to punish those crimes in order to secure peace for the society as a whole.

Private law is composed of the civil law. Civil law facilitates cooperation and resolves conflicts between individuals and deals with the rights and duties individuals possess relative to one another. Civil law addresses such particular issues as contracts. property, family relationships, and accidents. Individuals may use the courts to enforce their rights against other individuals, for example, by requiring someone to fulfill a contract, pay compensation for causing a personal harm, or assume responsibility for a child.

For more information

Abraham, Henry J. *The Judicial Process: An Introductory Analysis of the Courts of the United States, England, and France.* New York: Oxford University Press, 1998.

Levi, Edward H. *An Introduction to Legal Reasoning.* Chicago: University of Chicago Press, 1949.

Keith E. Whittington
Princeton University

law clerk   is a graduate of a law school hired by a state or federal judge to assist in the various administrative and legal research responsibilities of the individual judge. These law clerks ordinarily have no statutorily defined duties but do the work assigned to them by the supervising judge.

The work of most law clerks is, however, concentrated in the areas of legal research and writing. For example, the federal judiciary's policies and procedures manuals describe the range of duties assigned to law clerks as typically including legal research, preparing bench memoranda, drafting and proofreading orders and opinions, verifying citations, maintaining the chambers library, assembling documents, and handling exhibits during trial.

These seemingly innocuous legal assistants have frequently been the subject of both interest and concern. Edward Lazarus, in his book *Closed Chambers,* describes the behind-the-scenes work and actions of the U.S. Supreme Court's law clerks. Lazarus had direct experience as a clerk for the late Supreme Court Justice Harry Blackmun from 1988 to 1989. But *Closed Chambers* has been criticized by many commentators as a violation of the need for confidentiality that exists between a law clerk and the supervisory judge. The publication of *Closed Chambers* later led to a revision of the Supreme Court's code of conduct for law clerks to emphasize that this need for confidentiality remains even after the law clerk leaves the Court. A more scholarly description of the work of law clerks can be found in Richard Posner's book, *The Federal Courts: Challenge and Reform.* Posner observes that concern about federal law clerks ranges from the effectiveness of delegation and supervision of their work by the judge to the degree of influence law clerks may exert on the judge's own decision making.

For more information

"Law Clerks: The Transformation of the Judiciary," *The Long Term View: A Journal of Informed Opinion* vol. 3, no.1 (spring 1995), an issue of a legal journal published by the Massachusetts School of Law devoted to the role and influence of law clerks to the judiciary.

Posner, Richard. *The Federal Courts: Challenges and Reform.* Cambridge, Mass.: Harvard University Press, 1996.

Rubin, Alvin B. *Law Clerk Handbook: A Handbook for Law Clerks to Federal Judges.* Washington, D.C.: Federal Judicial Center, 1989.

Jerry E. Stephens
U.S. Court of Appeals (10th Circuit)
Oklahoma City

law school   is a three-year, full-time graduate program that leads to the "juris doctor" (J.D.) degree, which qualifies one to take the "bar exam" which is required for admission to practice law in state and federal courts. Today nearly all future lawyers attend law school before seeking admission to the bar; still, Alaska, California, Maine, New York, Vermont, Virginia, and Washington states permit candidates for admission to substitute several years of law office study for law school. Law schools developed late in the 19th century and replaced apprenticeships in law offices as the principal method of training future lawyers. U.S. lawyers had learned their craft by means of apprenticeships for a hundred years before law schools began to open. The first law schools were undergraduate departments in universities; they did not become graduate programs until approximately 1920.

The leader among law schools during their early days was Harvard, where Dean Christopher Columbus Langdell revolutionized legal education, beginning in 1870. His most important innovation was the "Socratic method" of teaching law, which remains the standard method today. The Socratic method replaced lectures with classroom discussions of court decisions that illustrated legal principles that the professor wished to convey. The professor asked the students questions about the decisions, and each answer prompted another question, until the class had examined a decision thoroughly and had uncovered the principle(s) of law for which it stood. The Socratic method was unpopular with Langdell's students initially because it required them to read assigned cases carefully, and to answer detailed, probing questions in class, with their classmates watching and listening attentively. Modern law students have the same complaints about the Socratic method. Nevertheless, it became the dominant method of teaching law early in the 20th century, and it remains so today.

Despite the continued preeminence of the Socratic method, much about law school has changed since Dean Langdell's day, and many of those changes have occurred since the 1960s. The most significant change has been the growth of "clinical studies," elective courses in which students earn academic credit by representing, under the guidance of a faculty member, low-income clients in civil matters, such as landlord-tenant disputes, or persons who are accused of crimes and who cannot afford to hire lawyers. Another important change in legal education has been the creation of courses that relate law to issues or to academic fields that law school curricula used to avoid, such as "Law and Psychology," "Law and Economics," or "Law and Sports." Professors teach "law and" courses in the same way that they teach the required first-year courses, so the "law and" courses are a less significant innovation than clinical studies, but they are important nevertheless because they enliven the curriculum, and they may help students to discover areas of interest in which to work after graduation.

Curricular changes have not diminished the significance of traditional courses such as corporations and income taxation, though; their presence on bar exams ensures that law schools will continue to offer them and that law students will continue to enroll in them. Law school graduates who intend to practice law must pass a bar exam in the state(s) where they plan to practice. The bar exam is a two-day affair in most states. On the first day, 47 states and the District of Columbia administer a "Multistate Bar Examination," which consists of 200 multiple-choice questions on contracts, torts (personal injury law), property, civil procedure, criminal law, and constitutional law. Every examinee who attended law school took a required course in each of those subjects during the first year. On the second day, the examinees answer essay questions that test their knowledge of the law in the respective states where they seek admission to the bar. Only examinees who pass the bar exam will gain admission; those who are unsuccessful will have to take the exam again.

The requirement that one pass a bar exam in order to obtain a law license helps to make law school part "trade school" and part graduate school in liberal arts. Law school attempts to offer both preprofessional training and a forum for the exchange of ideas. This hybrid status can frustrate both practice-oriented and academically oriented students; the former complain that law school does not prepare them for practice, while the latter complain that it overemphasizes preparation for practice. Law school is likely to remain a hybrid because students enroll for a variety of reasons, and institutions want to attract a diverse student body. Thus, the tension between the study and the practice of law will continue.

For more information

Goodrich, Chris. *Anarchy and Elegance: Confessions of a Journalist at Yale Law School.* Boston: Little, Brown, 1991.

VanAlstyne, W. Scott, Jr., Joseph R., Julin, and Larry D. Burnett. *The Goals and Missions of Law Schools.* New York: Peter Lang, 1990.

Brian L. Porto
College of St. Joseph, Vermont

legal ethics   refers to the set of rules and regulations that govern the professional conduct of lawyers. Legal ethics is also referred to as professional responsibility. The legal ethics rules in each state differ in some respects from those of other states. Most federal courts rely on state legal ethics rules to govern the conduct of lawyers who appear in the federal system. In different states bar associations, special state supreme court committees, local ethics committees, courts, and administrative agencies enforce legal ethics rules. The vigorousness of enforcement, the mechanism of enforcement, and the penalties for violation also may differ from state to state. Violation of the rules of legal ethics is not the same as legal malpractice.

The rules that govern lawyers' professional conduct come from a number of sources: Each state has adopted rules that are based upon models written by the American Bar Association (ABA). Most states have adopted a form of the ABA Model Rules of Professional Conduct. A much smaller number of states have adopted rules based on the ABA Model Code of Professional Responsibility. Other sources of legal ethics rules are rules of particular courts, both state and federal, and rules of administrative agencies.

Legal ethics rules embody a number of core principles that are supposed to govern lawyers' professional conduct. Subject to certain exceptions, lawyers should put their own clients' interests ahead of their own interests and the interests of non-clients. This means that lawyers should keep the confidences and secrets of their clients, should not represent clients with conflicting interests, and should not let their own interests outweigh those of their clients. Thus a lawyer or a law firm may not represent both sides of a dispute in court and may not represent one client when that client's interest is opposed to a former client in a related matter.

Lawyers should represent their clients diligently, communicate with them, and keep them informed of the status of their case. They should not take on more work than they can reasonably do. They should return phone calls, comply with requests for information, and explain matters to clients in ways that they can understand.

There are, however, limits to what lawyers can do for their clients. For instance, a lawyer cannot counsel or help her client to break the law. A lawyer may not talk to another person in a lawsuit that the lawyer knows is represented by someone else without the other lawyer's permission. A lawyer may not knowingly lie to a court or misrepresent her position in a matter to a third person in the course of representing a client.

Lawyers also have positive obligations to provide legal services to people who cannot afford them. Legal ethics rules make the profession "self-policing" so that a lawyer who knows that another lawyer has committed a serious violation of the rules of legal ethics should report this to the appropriate authorities.

Sometimes a lawyer's professional ethical obligations put her in conflict with other ethical or moral obligations that most people believe non-lawyers have. For example, if a client tells a lawyer that he has killed someone and buried their body in a field, the lawyer may not tell the relatives of the victim, even though it causes the relatives emotional distress. Most people would think that nonlawyers have an ethical obligation to relieve another person's suffering if it is possible. A lawyer in this situation may counsel his client to tell the family or to let him tell the family, but the lawyer must follow the client's decision.

For more information

Freedman, Monroe. *Understanding Lawyer's Ethics.* New York: Matthew Bender, 1990.

Hazard, Geoffrey, and Hodes, William. *The Law of Lawyering: A Handbook of the Model Rules of Professional Conduct.* Englewood Cliffs, N.J.: Prentice Hall, 1990.

Maury Landsman
University of Minnesota Law School

legal malpractice   refers to the legal claim made by a person against his or her lawyer when the negligence or fault of the lawyer results in injury to the person.

Legal malpractice is often also called legal negligence. It may be one of a number of legal wrongs known as torts or may be a breach of a contract to perform services. In order to prove a legal malpractice case, a person (called "the plaintiff") must prove the following: (1) that an attorney-client relationship existed; (2) the lawyer owed a duty to or had a contract with the

plaintiff; (2) the lawyer was negligent, i.e., did not perform to the appropriate standards, or broke the terms of the contract; (3) the lawyer's negligence or breach of contract was the cause of damage to the plaintiff; and in certain cases (4) the plaintiff would have been successful if the lawyer had performed correctly.

A plaintiff must show that an attorney-client relationship existed. Thus, if a non-client is damaged or injured by the failure of a lawyer to perform her job, the injured person may not bring a legal malpractice suit. An exception to this rule may sometimes be found where the lawyer and client enter a contract with the intention of benefiting a third person. Thus, in some cases, if a lawyer fails to properly draft a will, a person who is left out of the will because of the lawyer's negligence may be able to bring a legal malpractice suit.

In order to establish a contract, the plaintiff must show that there was a binding oral or written contract between her and the lawyer. This contract may be shown by the existence of a written document or by testimony of witnesses including the plaintiff and/or the lawyer. Alternatively, the plaintiff may show that the lawyer owed her a duty or obligation growing out of the relationship between lawyer and client. When a lawyer undertakes to represent a client, the lawyer and client enter an agreement or contract specifying what the lawyer is to do for the client and what the lawyer will be paid for her services.

When the relationship is formed, the lawyer takes on certain obligations such as loyalty and competence. Typically, when a lawyer is sued for malpractice, the plaintiff is claiming that the lawyer did not perform adequately.

If a plaintiff proves the existence of a lawyer-client relationship and shows that there was an express contract to obtain a particular result, then she will have to show that the lawyer did not attain the result. This is not, however, the usual case. Usually, the plaintiff will have to show that the lawyer did not fulfill her obligation to the client. In order to show this the plaintiff usually needs to present testimony of an expert witness, someone with specialized knowledge of law practice. The expert is almost always another lawyer or law professor, who will testify that the lawyer's actions were negligent or, in other words, that the lawyer's actions fell below the generally accepted standards for lawyers engaged in the particular kind of work.

Finally, to prevail in a legal malpractice claim, a plaintiff must show that if the lawyer had performed in a reasonably competent manner, the plaintiff would have won the case or obtained the agreed-upon result. When a legal malpractice case involves accusations of negligent handling of a lawsuit, the plaintiff must prove the "case within a case," that is, the jury must determine both the lawyer's negligence and the outcome of the original lawsuit.

For more information
Mallen, Ronald E., and Jeffrey Smith, *Legal Malpractice*. St. Paul, Minn.: West Publishing Co., 1996.

Maury Landsman
University of Minnesota Law School

legal realism was an intellectual movement that declared that the law was what a judge said it was.

Legal realism reached prominence among legal scholars and political scientists during the 1930s but enjoyed its greatest influence decades later, when it became "gospel" among judges and practicing lawyers. Legal realism revolutionized thinking about the law because it argued that when judges decided cases, they "made law" by choosing between conflicting values, according to their public policy preferences. That may not sound revolutionary today, but it did in the 1930s.

Legal realism appeared revolutionary in the 1930s because the "classical view" of the judicial process was dominant among lawyers then. The classical view held that a court decision was the predictable, indeed, almost mechanical, result of a judge's application of a clear rule of law, which

was stated in legislation, constitutional language, or a prior court decision, to the facts of the case at hand. Classical theorists argued that a judge had little or no discretion to interpret such rules. A famous statement of the classical view was the majority opinion that Justice Owen Roberts wrote for the Supreme Court in *United States v. Butler,* 297 U.S. 1 (1936), in which the Court declared the Agricultural Adjustment Act of 1933 (AAA) unconstitutional because Congress lacked the power, under the Constitution, to regulate agricultural production.

Justice Roberts observed that judges had little power in constitutional cases, and the power they had was divorced from politics. He wrote that when the Supreme Court considered a case that presented a constitutional challenge to an act of Congress, "all [it] does, or can do, is to announce its considered judgment upon the question." He added that the Court "neither approves nor condemns any legislative policy." Instead, he wrote,

> When an act of Congress is appropriately challenged in the courts as not conforming to the constitutional mandate the judicial branch of the Government has only one duty-to lay the article of the Constitution which is involved beside the statute which is challenged and to decide whether the latter squares with the former.

According to this view, the AAA was unconstitutional because the Constitution permitted Congress to regulate "commerce," but the AAA sought to regulate "production," which was not commerce; therefore, Congress could not regulate production. Legal realists criticized Justice Roberts's view by noting that the Constitution mentioned commerce but not production, so it was not clear that commerce excluded production. If commerce included production, then Congress could regulate production pursuant to its power to regulate commerce. Therefore, the distinction that Justice Roberts drew between commerce and production was not nearly as clear as he had suggested it was. That distinction was not the result of a constitutional command but, instead, of the distaste that Roberts and a majority of his fellow justices had for governmental regulation of business.

Thanks to legal realism, modern lawyers and judges recognize that to judge is not merely to apply a fixed legal rule to the facts of a case but, instead, to choose which rule to apply and how to apply it. The legacy of legal realism, then, is that lawyers and legal scholars recognize that judges' policy preferences can and do influence the outcomes of cases. To be sure, there is disagreement about the degree to which judges' policy preferences influence case outcomes. Some political scientists, known as "judicial behaviorists," argue that the greatest influence on a judge's decisions is the judge's political philosophy; some law school faculty, who belong to the "critical legal studies movement," even argue that judges' decisions are merely their political philosophies expressed in legal language. Other scholars offer a "neo-institutionalist" perspective, which admits that judges' political philosophies influence their decisions but also argues that case facts, legal principles, court rules, and judges' views about the role that courts should play in the American political system influence their decisions too. Still, there is nearly unanimous agreement today that the legal realists were right, and the classical theorists were wrong. Indeed, it is almost impossible to find a modern lawyer or political scientist who does not believe that judges' political philosophies can and do influence the outcomes of the cases they decide.

For more information

Porto, Brian L. *May It Please the Court: Judicial Processes and Politics in America.* New York: Addison Wesley Longman, 2000.

Rumble, Wilfrid E. *American Legal Realism: Skepticism, Reform, and the Judicial Process.* Ithaca, N.Y.: Cornell University Press, 1968.

Brian L. Porto
College of St. Joseph, Vermont

Legal Services Corporation (LSC) is a private, nonprofit corporation established in 1974 by Congress to provide civil legal assistance to the poor.

Early in U.S. history, legal aid to the poor was decentralized among private and municipal legal aid organizations. In the 19th century some states established legal assistance to the poor as part of poor relief regulation. After the Civil War in 1865 and until 1868, the federal government provided some legal aid to indigent blacks in criminal and civil proceedings. A few local legal aid organizations existed for the poor after the Civil War, but counsel for the poor generally was unavailable. By 1917 only 41 legal aid societies supplied a mixture of civil and criminal representation for poor people. The legal aid movement in the early 20th century provided legal advice to indigent in areas such as wage and contract disputes, landlord-tenant disputes, and domestic relations cases. By the 1960s, legal aid still was found primarily in the largest cities with an estimated 400 full-time legal aid lawyers available to assist almost 50 million indigent.

In 1964 President Lyndon B. Johnson, as part of the War on Poverty, persuaded Congress to create the Office of Economic Opportunity (OEO). In 1965 the OEO funded grants to local legal aid organizations and mobilized lawyers to provide legal services to the indigent. By 1971 OEO greatly strengthened legal assistance to the poor with the support of more attorneys and funding of legal aid organizations in a wider array of communities. Still, critics of the OEO claimed their efforts were characterized by too much local control. This precipitated a movement to create a national Legal Services Corporation.

In 1971 members of Congress introduced legislation to establish the Legal Services Corporation. The Legal Services Corporation Act was passed in 1974 on the eve of President Richard Nixon's resignation. As established, the private, nonprofit Legal Services Corporation (LSC) could not provide direct legal representation to the poor. Instead, the LSC would give financial assistance to qualified local programs. At this time, several restrictions were imposed on LSC-sponsored legal assistance programs, including no participation in abortion, school desegregation, and selective service cases. Limits were also placed on involvement in class action suits and various types of juvenile representation. LSC-funded programs do not handle criminal cases and will not accept fee-generating cases that private attorneys take on a contingency basis.

Subject to annual appropriations from Congress, funding for the LSC initially grew in the 1970s, and a concomitant expansion of LSC-funded local programs occurred, which funded access to legal services for indigent in every state in the United States. The election of Ronald Reagan to the presidency in 1980, however, created a new series of challenges for the LSC. President Reagan attempted to terminate the Legal Services Corporation, advocating increased reliance on pro bono legal assistance, and he obtained budget cuts and restraints on "cause-oriented" work of LSC offices supported by federal funds. In the debates over LSC funding, critics assert that LSC attorneys should be limited to client-based representation. Opponents of the LSC in Congress claimed that LSC attorneys have used LSC funds to promote politically liberal agendas and to force social change. In the Legal Services Reform Act of 1996, opponents of using LSC funds for cause-oriented legal work were successful in placing additional restrictions, including funding of alien representation, legislative redistricting, prisoners' rights, and public-housing evictions of alleged drug criminals.

The Legal Services Corporation has provided substantial support for the poor in civil litigation. It continued to exist with a slight increase in funding under Bill Clinton's presidency. Taking inflation into account, the funding of the Legal Services Corporation never returned to the funding levels seen in the 1970s. In addition to budget cuts at the federal level, state and local funding levels have also decreased. Supporters of the LSC note its continued importance in assisting the poor in child support, spousal abuse, veteran assistance, consumer fraud, employment, victim assistance during natural disasters, debt collection, contract, and many other types of cases.

For more information

Mentor, Kenneth W., and Richard D. Schwartz. "A Tale of Two Offices: Adaptation Strategies of LSC Agencies," *The Justice System Journal* 21 (2000): 143–69.

Quigley, William P. "Symposium–Legal Services: The Demise of Law Reform and the Triumph of Legal Aid: Congress and the Legal Services Corporation from the 1960s to the 1990s," *Saint Louis University Public Law Review* (1998): 241–62.

Ruth Ann Strickland
Professor, Appalachian State University
Department of Political Science and
Criminal Justice

Lemon v. Kurtzman   403 U.S. 602 (1971), the landmark United States Supreme Court case in the area of church-state relations, sets forth the constitutional test of contacts between government (state, local, or national) and religious institutions or practices. Such contacts are governed by the "religion clauses" of the First Amendment to the U.S. Constitution: "Congress shall make no law respecting an establishment of religion, or prohibiting the free exercise thereof."

In *Lemon v. Kurtzman* the Court considered whether two state laws violated the "establishment" part of the religion clause. One law provided for a salary supplement for teachers in nonpublic schools that were underfunded as compared to the funding of public schools. The other law provided that public schools could purchase secular educational services from nonpublic schools and directly reimburse the nonpublic schools for teacher's salaries, textbooks, and instructional materials. The Court found that virtually all of the nonpublic schools that benefited from both laws were religious schools, and it ruled that both laws violated the religion clauses of the First Amendment.

The *Lemon* Court acknowledged that the religion clauses are vague and general, and that religious issues are an extraordinarily sensitive area of constitutional law. The *Lemon* Court stressed that it could not require total separation between church and state; total separation is not possible in an absolute sense. For example, religious institutions are subject to some taxes and most municipal ordinances and to fire inspections and building, safety, and zoning regulations; and they are entitled to police and fire protection. Religious schools are subject to attendance and accreditation standards. Resolving these apparent contradictions, the Court established three analytical criteria, all three of which must be met if a church-state contact (a state statute, a local ordinance, a practice, a measure, or contact in any other form) is permissible:

- the statute must have a secular legislative purpose;
- its principal or primary effect must be one that neither advances nor inhibits religion; and
- the statute must not foster an excessive government entanglement with religion.

Failure to meet any one of these criteria means that the contact is unconstitutional.

The *Lemon v. Kurtzman* criteria remain the constitutional test in religion clauses cases, and they have been applied, with mixed results, to a variety of contacts between the state and religious institutions or activity. Many, but not all, of these religious institutions are schools. Contacts include state loan of textbooks to religious schools; issuance of municipal bonds for the benefit of religious schools; tax exemption for places of religious worship; prayer in public schools; state-funded bus transportation for reli-

gious-school students; state-funded lunches in religious schools; state-funded health services for religious school students; state-funded special education programs for religious school students; and religious displays on state property.

For more information

Lynn, Barry, Marc D., Stern, and Oliver S. Thomas. *The Right to Religious Liberty: The Basic ACLU Guide to Religious Rights,* 2nd ed. Carbondale: Southern Illinois University Press, 1995.

Elsa M. Shartsis, B.A., M.S., J.D.

libel   is a false statement written about someone that damages the person's reputation. That means that the false statement must so ridicule or so disparage the person about whom the statement was made that a person who reads it would want to avoid the person who was the subject of the false statement.

Until recently, a libel lawsuit could be won by a person who showed that a reputation-damaging statement was made about him, without needing to show whether the statement was false or the person who made it had good reason to believe it was true or that it really caused his reputation to suffer. For the most part, the U.S. Supreme Court changed libel law by deciding that the person who libeled another had limited protection under the First Amendment to the U.S. Constitution, the guarantee of free speech.

The Court held, first in *New York Times Co. v. Sullivan,* 376 U.S. 254, 279–80, 84 S.Ct. 710, 11 L.Ed.2d 686 (1964), then in cases that followed it, that a person who sues for libel must prove (1) that the statement about him was false and (2) that his reputation was actually damaged—that is, that someone who read the statement caused him to be injured in a tangible way, by losing business, for example. The Supreme Court also changed libel law by requiring that, under the First Amendment, the person who claimed he was libeled had to prove that the defamer did not have a reasonable basis for believing the statement to be true. Before the *Sullivan* decision, state law was the only authority on libel and, in most states, a person could be legally responsible for making a false statement about someone else that hurt his reputation even if the person who made the statement acted without fault. The Supreme Court's decisions were in lawsuits against newspapers or broadcast news organizations, but the First Amendment principles upon which the Court relied seem to apply to libel claimed by a private person against a person or company not publishing news.

For more information

Rosini, Neil J. *The Practical Guide to Libel Law.* New York: Praeger Publishers, 1991.

Wm. Osler McCarthy
Texas Supreme Court
University of Texas Department of Journalism

liberty of contract   also known as "freedom of contract," is the right to create and enter into legally binding agreements with others, based on mutual agreement and free will.

Liberty of contract is a fundamental principle of American contract law. In this manner, people are able to create their own promissory obligations and liabilities, which the state will enforce under most circumstances. This freedom of contract principle rests on the idea that it is in the public interest to allow individuals to structure their affairs through binding agreements free from government interference. According to freedom of contract, a contract's legitimacy comes from the intent of the parties and their expectations rather than the government's policies. Under modern freedom of contract in the United States, federal, state, and local government's ability to interfere with these private dealings is limited.

People's right to bind themselves through exercise of their right to freedom of contract is protected by the courts. One of the primary functions of the court system in the United States is to maintain and enforce these binding legal agreements. Although courts are generally required to enforce contracts, there are several exceptions to freedom of contract that permit courts to refuse to enforce all or part of an agreement. For example, courts will not enforce an illegal contract.

Contracts for slavery, murder, or other crimes are obviously not protected by freedom of contract. Contracts in violation of a strong public policy are likewise not protected by freedom of contract, but only if the public policy being violated is stronger than the public policy of freedom of contract itself—one of the most powerful policies of all. An example of a public policy strong enough to overcome freedom of contract is the policy against restraint of trade. Certain noncompetition or price-fixing agreements are an example of contracts "in restraint of trade," and these are not protected by freedom of contract. Another major exception to freedom of contract concerns those who cannot make contracts because of their status. Courts will not enforce contracts made by minors, the mentally ill, or persons otherwise without power to contract.

In addition to being a contract principle, liberty of contract is also a constitutional-law doctrine. Liberty of contract is protected in part by the U.S. Constitution, as well as most state constitutions. Although not explicitly mentioned in the Fifth or Fourteenth Amendments, liberty of contract is part of both due process clauses. This means that federal and state legislatures are not allowed to make laws that unreasonably limit the liberty of contract. This liberty of contract doctrine was used to hamper social and economic reform in the late 19th and early 20th centuries, by making legislation like minimum-hour and minimum-wage requirements illegal because they interfered with the freedom of contract between employers and employees. This strict application of the doctrine was overruled, and after the 1930s, the liberty of contract doctrine was no longer widely used to strike down social or economic legislation.

For more information

Farnsworth, E. Allan. *Contracts,* 3rd ed. New York: Aspen Publishers, 1999.

Scheiber, Harry N., ed. *The State and Freedom of Contract,* Stanford, Calif.: Stanford University Press, 1998.

John H. Matheson
Melvin C. Steen and Corporate Donors
Professor of Law
University of Minnesota Law School

library book banning   is a First Amendment constitutional violation of the right of students when public school libraries are ordered to remove certain books from their collections because school boards find them offensive or objectionable.

In *Board of Education v. Pico,* 457 U.S. 853 (1982), at issue was whether a public school board could direct a high school and junior high school libraries to remove certain books that it found to be "anti-American, anti-Christian, anti-Sem[i]tic, and just plain filthy," It sought to remove these books in response to pressure from a parents' committee that found several of the books in the library to be objectionable for the above reasons. These books included *Slaughterhouse Five,* by Kurt Vonnegut, Jr.; *The Naked Ape,* by Desmond Morris; *Down These Mean Streets,* by Piri Thomas; *Best Short Stories of Negro Writers,* edited by Langston Hughes; *Go Ask Alice,* of anonymous authorship; *Laughing Boy,* by Oliver LaFarge; *Black Boy,* by Richard Wright; *A Hero Ain't Nothin' but a Sandwich,* by Alice Childress; *Soul on Ice,* by Eldridge Cleaver; *A Reader for Writers,* edited by Jerome Archer; and *The Fixer,* by Bernard Malamud.

The school board directed that several of these books either be removed from the school libraries or that they be placed on restricted access to students.

In a very closely divided opinion, the Supreme Court ruled 5–4 that while school boards have broad discretion to manage school affairs, the power does not extend to their ability to violate the First Amendment rights of students to freedom of expression and inquiry. According to the Court:

> But we think that the First Amendment rights of students may be directly and sharply implicated by the removal of books from the shelves of a school library. Our precedents have focused "not only on the role of the First Amendment in fostering individual self-expression but also on its role in affording the public access to discussion, debate, and the dissemination of information and ideas." (457 U.S. 867)

Drawing upon its decision in *Stanley v. Georgia,* 394 U.S. 557 (1969), the Court stated that "the Constitution protects the right to receive information and ideas" and that this right placed limits on the ability of a school board to remove objectionable books from its libraries. The Court was careful to distinguish the power of the board to select books and materials for curriculum in the classroom versus removing non-required books from the library. In the latter case, the First Amendment rights of students were very important.

The importance of *Pico* was in affirming the right of libraries, including public libraries, to fight efforts to ban books that they already own. To what extent this ruling also extends to stopping school boards from preventing their libraries from buying books they find offensive was not explicitly answered in this case.

For more information

Yudof, Mark. "Library Book Selection and Public Schools: The Quest for the Archimedean Point," *Indiana Law Journal* 59 (1984): 527.

David Schultz
Hamline University

Lincoln, Abraham   (1809–1865) was a lawyer, legislator, and president of the United States during the Civil War. Lincoln's four-year tenure in the White House ushered in a new era in U.S. law and politics. The age of Jacksonian, state's rights policies lost out to a new regime of national citizenship and rights anchored in the Emancipation Proclamation and the Thirteenth, Fourteenth, and Fifteenth Amendments to the U.S. Constitution.

In 1857, under Chief Justice Roger B. Taney, the Supreme Court held that slaves could never be citizens under the Constitution. When Lincoln took office four years later, he was confronted with a divided nation and hostility on the Supreme Court. When war broke out, Lincoln and Taney clashed over the president's wartime policies. Taney's circuit opinion in *Ex parte Merryman,* F. Cas. 9487 (1861), criticized the president's conduct of the war, including his orders to arrest disloyal civilians. Lincoln countered that the Constitution allowed the elected branches wide latitude in conducting war. Despite Taney's opposition, the Court as a whole narrowly upheld most of Lincoln's orders as commander in chief. For example, in *The Prize Cases,* 67 U.S. 635 (1863), the Court rejected a challenge to Lincoln's order for a naval blockade of southern ports.

The Emancipation Proclamation spelled out Lincoln's desire to win the war and end slavery. In late 1863 Lincoln gave an address at Gettysburg, Pennsylvania, that exemplified his administration's commitment to such national rights as literacy, property, and legal remedies. He invoked the Declaration of Independence and the Constitution in the speech, reaffirming his commitment to broad principles of equality.

Lincoln was able to appoint five justices to the High Court who shared his legal and political philosophy. All were pro-Union and generally sympathetic to the president's long-term goals. For example, when Taney died in 1864, Lincoln named his treasury secretary, and longtime abolitionist, Salmon P. Chase as chief justice. Despite his appointments Lincoln worried that the Court might not sustain his postwar agenda, including the conditions he set for the

Abraham Lincoln (LIBRARY OF CONGRESS)

readmission of southern states to the union. Lincoln felt that the Thirteenth Amendment, outlawing slavery, would be the catalyst toward achieving increased civil and political rights for former slaves. But when Andrew Johnson became president following Lincoln's death, it soon became clear that the forces opposing Lincoln's postwar plans were formidable. For example, Johnson appointed numerous federal judges, particularly in the southern states, who were pardoned ex-Confederates. The Court retreated from its wartime deference and formally limited the push for broad national rights. For example, In the *Slaughterhouse Cases,* 83 U.S. 36 (1873), a narrow majority strictly interpreted the Thirteenth and Fourteenth Amendments as only outlawing slavery in a formal sense. Despite the setbacks following his death,

Lincoln's pragmatic repudiation of the old regime and prophetic vision of national civil and political rights won out.

For more information

Donald, David Herbert. *Lincoln*. London: Jonathan Cape, 1995.

Hyman, Harold M. and William M., Wiecek. *Equal Justice under Law: Constitutional Development, 1835–1875*. New York: Harper and Row, 1982.

Artemus Ward
California State University, Chico

Lochner v. New York

Lochner v. New York   198 U.S. 45 (1905) is the infamous case in which the Supreme Court found that laws regulating bakers' working hours infringed the "liberty of contract" that the Court found in the Fourteenth Amendment. The case was decided by a margin of 5–4, and Justice Holmes's dissent in *Lochner* has become far more famous and widely read than the majority opinion of Justice Peckham.

New York's Bakeshop Act was adopted in 1895 through the combined efforts of the Journeymen Bakers' and Confectioners' International Union and a larger coalition of reformers concerned over the conditions in bakeries. It required that employees of bakeries work not more than 10 hours per day or 60 hours in a single week.

Justice Rufus Peckham's majority opinion held that the Bakeshop Act violated the "right to contract" found in the Fourteenth Amendment's statement that states might not deprive any person of liberty without due process of law. This theory became part of "substantive due process," the idea that some restrictions violated due process rights because they had no legitimate purpose. Comparing baking to other types of work, Peckham reasoned that bakers were as capable as other workers to decide how many hours they should work and did not deserve any more protection than doctors, lawyers, or other workers. The Bakeshop Act therefore violated bakers' "liberty of contract" because they should be able to make their own decisions regarding the number of hours they wished to work. Because Peckham could not find a particular hazard in baking, he was able to distinguish this case from the 1898 case of *Holden v. Hardy*, where the Court had allowed maximum hours regulation of mining because of the danger involved.

Justice Oliver Wendell Holmes's dissent argued that the Constitution does not embody any particular economic theory, including the free market understanding that underlay the majority's opinion. Holmes noted that many other state laws also interfered with the right to contract, such as liquor laws, Sunday closing laws, and prohibitions on lotteries. Holmes also objected to the Court's activist stance, preferring that legislatures decide which values should inform public policy.

Justice John Marshall Harlan also dissented, but he was willing to allow for liberty of contract. However, Harlan argued, when the legislature had decided a policy question such as workers' hours, the courts should defer to its decision unless the law plainly violated a provision of the Constitution. Harlan also found the evidence that harm resulted from bakers working too many hours to be more compelling than the majority had.

The right to contract was used to strike down many other laws protecting labor and workers during the first part of the 20th century until the Supreme Court abandoned the doctrine in the 1937 case of *West Coast Hotel v. Parrish*. However, the Court allowed regulation of workers' hours in special cases, such as women working factory jobs in *Muller v. Oregon* (1908), and allowed a law setting a maximum 10-hour day for all workers in *Bunting v. Oregon* (1917).

For more information

Kens, Paul. *Lochner v. New York: Economic Regulation on Trial*. Lawrence: University Press of Kansas, 1998.

Daniel Levin
University of Utah

M

malice   is simply a state of mind.

The term is thought to connote hatred, hostility, or ill will by one person toward another. More specifically, the legal term *malice,* or malicious, is defined as an intentional commission of a wrongful act by one person toward another without legal justification or excuse; or, put another way, malice is a state of mind that prompts a conscious violation of law to the prejudice and injury of another. The Supreme Court defined malice in *Allen v. United States,* 164 U.S. 492, as a condition of the mind showing a heart devoid of social consciousness and bent upon mischief.

The determination of the existence of malice can become important in both criminal cases and civil causes of action. In criminal law, when malice is an essential factor in a case, the courts permit a wide range of evidence designed to show the state of mind a criminal defendant had during the commission of some criminal act. For example, evidence of threats or hostility is admissible to show that a criminal act was done willfully and maliciously.

When malice or ill will becomes an issue in a civil action, the court will also consider a party's acts, statements, and conduct, which have a bearing on his state of mind, to determine the presence of malice. In a civil action, however, malice does not necessarily mean that a person acted with spite but that he can be shown with conduct that injured another, through proceeding with an ill-regulated mind, not sufficiently cautious before causing injury to another.

Furthermore, the term *actual malice,* or malice in fact, has been defined as a positive desire and intention to annoy or injure another person. Unlike legal malice that, as we have seen, connotes spite or ill will, the term *actual malice* often refers to publication of defamatory material with knowledge that it was false or with reckless disregard of whether or not it was false. The knowledge of falsity is enough to satisfy the requirement for "actual malice" in that case, and no spite or ill will need be proven.

For more information

Action for Malicious Prosecution Based on Institutions of Bankruptcy, Insolvency, or Receivership Proceedings. 40 A.L.R. 3d 296 (1971).

Libel and Slander: What Constitutes Actual Malice, Within Federal Constitutional Rule Requiring Public

Officials And Public Figures To Show Actual Malice. 20 A.L.R. 3d 988 (1975).

Kristin L. Stewart, J.D.

Mapp v. Ohio   367 U.S. 643 (1961) is the landmark case in which the United States Supreme Court applied the exclusionary rule to state police actions through incorporation of the Fourth Amendment via the due process clause of the Fourteenth Amendment.

The Fourth Amendment provides individuals protection against "unreasonable searches and seizures." But originally that protection covered only the actions of federal authorities, not state authorities. In the earlier case of *Weeks v. United States,* 232 U.S. 383 (1914), the Supreme Court developed the exclusionary rule, in which evidence seized in violation of the Fourth Amendment was excluded from use against a criminal defendant.

In *Weeks,* the Supreme Court explicitly said that the exclusionary rule did not apply to the states. The Supreme Court again addressed the applicability of Fourth Amendment protections to state action in the 1949 case of *Wolf v. Colorado,* 338 U.S. 25. While the Supreme Court declined to require states to abide by the exclusionary rule, the majority opinion in *Wolf* did enhance protections for individuals by declaring that the "core of the Fourth Amendment" did apply to state police actions through the due process clause of the Fourteenth Amendment. In a later case, *Elkins v. United States,* 364 U.S. 206 (1960), the Supreme Court characterized the protections afforded individuals under the due process clause of the Fourteenth Amendment as equivalent to those afforded individuals under the Fourth Amendment. *Etkins* did not, however, give the Court the opportunity to apply the exclusionary rule to the states because it did not involve state action. The Court subsequently applied the exclusionary rule to the states in *Mapp v. Ohio.*

Dollree Mapp, whose first name has been variously noted as Dolree and Dolly, resided in the upstairs of a duplex in Cleveland, Ohio. On the afternoon of May 23, 1957, three police officers came to the house and asked to speak to her. On the advice of an attorney she had engaged to deal with a separate civil matter then in progress, Ms. Mapp declined to allow the officers to enter her home unless they produced a valid search warrant. The police originally went to Ms. Mapp's home on a tip they received that a fugitive was hiding there. Interestingly, the fugitive was a suspect in the bombing of a man who would later become well known as a boxing promoter, Don King.

For the next few hours the police remained outside her home, with several additional officers joining them. Ms. Mapp's attorney appeared, at which point the police said they did have a valid search warrant but they refused to produce it. The police then broke into the home. The police waved a paper they claimed to be a search warrant in front of Ms. Mapp, but when she grabbed the paper the police took it from her, handcuffed her, and forced her to accompany them upstairs to her apartment. The police conducted a full search of her apartment as well as the basement of the house. In the process of conducting this search, they found allegedly pornographic material, which Ms. Mapp said belonged to a man who had recently boarded with her.

After the Ohio Supreme Court upheld Ms. Mapp's conviction in the state trial court for possession of pornographic materials, she appealed to the United States Supreme Court, which agreed to hear her case. Although the attorney representing Ms. Mapp focused on the obscenity issue, the disposition of the case hinged on the legality of the search and the application of the exclusionary rule to the states. The police were never able to produce the alleged search warrant. In a 6–3 decision, with Justice Clarke writing for the majority, the Supreme Court held not only that the protections embedded in the Fourth Amendment covered state action, but that the exclusionary rule applied to the states as it did to their federal counterparts.

While not overruling its decision in *Mapp,* the Supreme Court has imposed limits on the protections extended in that decision. For example, the Court has declined to require application of the exclusionary rule in grand jury proceedings. It has also refused to require federal judges to employ the writ of habeas corpus to enforce the exclusionary rule on the states. Further, the Court has recognized a good faith exception to the exclusionary rule under several situations, including the seizure of evidence with a warrant subsequently found to be technically flawed in some way and searches that would not have been made but for the innocent mistakes of judicial personnel.

For more information

Kamisar, Yale. "The Swing of the Pendulum: Warren Burger's Supreme Court and Criminal Law," *The Nation,* vol. 239, no. 4, Sept 29, 1984.

Katsh, M. Ethan. *Taking Sides,* 3rd ed. Guilford, Conn.: Dushkin Publishing Group, 1989.

Wendy L. Martinek
State University of New York, Binghamton

Marbury v. Madison   5 U.S. 137 (1803) was the first case in which the United States Supreme Court asserted its right to review and overturn acts of coequal branches of government for violating the federal Constitution. This power of the Supreme Court is known as "judicial review." To understand the *Marbury v. Madison* case fully, it is important to recognize the political situation surrounding it.

In 1800 there were two major political parties: the Democratic-Republicans and the Federalists. While the Federalist Party had had political control since the founding of the nation, the election of 1800 brought about a political change when Thomas Jefferson was elected president and the Democratic-Republicans won a majority of seats in the House of Representatives. Fearful of the power its party would lose, the Federalists attempted to sustain power in the federal government through the judicial branch. Two days before his term in office was about to expire, President Adams nominated 42 Federalists to positions as justices of the peace. However, because these nominations were confirmed at the 11th hour, 17 of the 42 commissions for judgeships were not delivered to their recipients before the Adams administration ended.

When President Jefferson took office, he instructed James Madison, who as attorney general was responsible for delivering the commissions, to stop delivery of the remaining commissions. One of the 17 men who did not receive his commission before Jefferson took office was William Marbury. Wanting to force Madison to deliver his commission, Marbury sought a *writ of mandamus* from the Supreme Court under section 13 of the Judiciary Act of 1789. If the Supreme Court agreed to issue a writ of mandamus in Marbury's case, the Jefferson administration would be required by law to give Marbury his commission for a judgeship.

Marbury's request for a mandamus put the Supreme Court in a political dilemma. At this early stage in the U.S. republic, it was important that the federal judiciary did not appear weak in order to reinforce the concept of three coequal branches of government. If the Supreme Court refused to issue Marbury a mandamus, which would force Jefferson to give him his commission, the Court indeed would appear weak because Marbury had a legal right to his commission. On the other hand, the Court's reputation and power most likely would be undermined as well if the Court did agree to grant Marbury the mandamus, since President Jefferson probably would not comply with the Court's decision. Chief Justice John Marshall, nevertheless, was able to maneuver his way out of this political bind, while asserting an even greater power for the Court—the right to exercise judicial review.

Marshall explained that Marbury had a legal right to his commission, which he demanded. Moreover, the chief justice stated that under the law, Marbury had a right to a remedy. However, Marshall argued that the proper remedy for Marbury was not a mandamus issued by the Supreme Court, since the Court lacked the power, or jurisdiction, to grant the mandamus under the Constitution. Although section 13 of the Judiciary Act gave the Supreme Court the power to issue writs of mandamus under its original jurisdiction, Marshall pointed out that the congressional law was at odds with Article III of the Constitution. Article III stated that the Supreme Court only had original jurisdiction "in all cases affecting ambassadors, other public ministers and consuls, and those in which a state be a party." Furthermore, Article III declared that "[i]n all other cases, the Supreme Court shall have appellate jurisdiction." Because section 13 gave the Supreme Court original jurisdiction in a situation which was inconsistent with Article III, Marshall declared section 13 to be unconstitutional, or null and void.

With this ruling, Marshall secured the power of the federal judiciary. The Court appeared strong by ruling that Marbury had a legal right to his commission. Marshall also did not have to worry about President Jefferson undermining the authority of the federal judiciary by refusing to enforce his ruling, since Marshall ruled that he did not have the power to issue a mandamus on Marbury's behalf. Even more importantly, though, Marshall ensured the federal judiciary's power in political practice, by asserting the Court's right to exercise judicial review against coordinate branches of government.

Prior to the *Marbury v. Madison* decision, the right to judicial review had been asserted by Alexander Hamilton in the *Federalist Papers* number 78. Hamilton's position, however, was not explicitly written into the Constitution and certainly was not accepted by everyone during the founding era. Thus, when Marshall stated in the *Marbury* decision that "[i]t is emphatically the province and duty of the judicial department to say what the law is," he asserted a rather grand power for the Court, which was not universally accepted or settled in U.S. political practice. In asserting the power of judicial review, Marshall proclaimed that the judicial branch, like the political branches, had a right to interpret the Constitution. Moreover, Marshall asserted that the federal judiciary had the right to invalidate congressional legislation if the Court believed the legislation to be inconsistent with the United States Constitution. Marshall noted that "a law repugnant to the Constitution is void; and that *courts* as well as other departments, are bound by that instrument." In an attempt to emphasize the supremacy of the Constitution in the American political system, Marshall explained that the Constitution was the "paramount law of the nation," and consequently, any act of legislation that was inconsistent with the document had to be considered null and void.

The *Marbury v. Madison* decision is a significant case in our constitutional history. Even though the Supreme Court did not once again exercise its power of coordinate judicial review after *Marbury* for another 54 years, over the course of history the Supreme Court's exercises of judicial review have increased steadily. Today judicial review is commonplace in judicial decision making. While there are many people who believe that the Supreme Court's contemporary exercises of judicial review should be more restrained, the general practice of judicial review has nevertheless become an accepted feature of political practice.

For more information

Alfange, Dean. "*Marbury v. Madison* and Original Understanding on Judicial Review," *Supreme Court Review* (1993): 329–446.

Hobson, Charles M. *The Great Chief Justice: John Marshall and the Rule of Law.* Lawrence: University Press of Kansas, 1996.

Van Alstyne, William. "A Critical Guide to *Marbury v. Madison*," *Duke Law Journal* (1969): 1–47.

Francene M. Engel
University of Michigan

Marshall, John (1755–1835) was the fourth chief justice of the United States. He served for 34 years and is widely regarded as the most important jurist in U.S. history.

Marshall was born on September 24, 1755, near Germantown (now Midland), Virginia. His father, Thomas Marshall, was a surveyor, justice of the peace, sheriff, vestryman, militia leader, and burgess of the county, and his mother, Mary Randolph Keith, was the daughter of a clergyman. Young John was enrolled for a year at a school in Westlandmore County, then was home schooled for a year by the local parish priest who temporarily resided with the family. As important as Marshall's formal education was his exposure to the colonial Virginia gentry, a school for training future statesmen.

When the war broke out, John took up service first in the county militia, then as an officer in the Virginia line of the Continental army. He participated in numerous battles and survived the harsh winter's encampment at Valley Forge in 1777–78. During the spring and summer of 1780, on a break from the war, Marshall attended a course on law and natural philosophy at William and Mary College, lectured by Thomas Jefferson's law mentor George Wythe. The education Marshall had received sufficed to qualify him for a law license. In 1783 he married Mary Willis Ambler (1766–1831), daughter of Rebecca Bruwell and Jacquelin Ambler, the state treasurer. John and his "dearest Polly" had 10 children, six of whom survived to adulthood. By the end of the 1780s Marshall's reputation, after joining a small group of lawyers who practiced in the superior court of the state and serving in the House of Delegates, placed him at the top of the bar. His beliefs in fairness, a strong central government, and acute intellect prompted John Adams to call on Marshall to serve his country. In 1797 Marshall served as an envoy in the "XYZ" Affair in an attempt to compromise differences with the revolutionary Republic of France. Though the mission was a failure, it proved to be a personal triumph for Marshall, returning home a national hero.

In 1799 Adams offered Marshall a seat on the Supreme Court, but he refused, opting for service in the House of Representatives. Establishing himself as a formidable spokesman for the Adams administration, he was rewarded with a place in Adams's cabinet as secretary of state from May of 1800 through the remainder of Adams's term. Marshall was then appointed to chief justice and confirmed by the Senate on January 27, 1801.

Scholars generally hold that Marshall was the founder of American constitutional law, calling

Chief Justice John Marshall (Alonzo Chappell, Collection of the Supreme Court of the United States)

him "the great chief justice." Upon joining the Court, he immediately set about unifying its members. The practice of each justice delivering individual opinions in each case was abandoned in favor of a single opinion, usually written by Marshall himself. Almost immediately, Marshall strengthened the judicial branch of government with his landmark ruling in *Marbury v. Madison,* 5 U.S. 137 (1803). In his unanimous opinion, Marshall established the Supreme Court's power to review, and if necessary invalidate, acts of Congress. The opinion greatly enhanced the prestige and importance of the Court, placing it on a coequal level with the executive and legislative branches.

The most important, and controversial, theme in Marshall's opinions is the issue of federalism. In nearly every important case he decided, he ruled against the states, thereby increasing the power of the national government. For example, in *McCulloch v. Maryland,* 17 U.S. 316 (1819), he ruled that states could not tax instruments of the national government, such as U.S. banks. He read the "necessary and proper" clause of the U.S. Constitution to establish implied powers that could be used by the national government in carrying out its specified constitutional functions. In *Gibbons v. Ogden,* 22 U.S. 1 (1824), he broadly construed the Constitution's commerce clause to prohibit states from passing legislation that burdened the free flow of goods across state lines. Near the end of his tenure, and faced with a Court and nation becoming increasingly sympathetic to state's rights, he retreated from his strong nationalist position in a case involving the Fifth Amendment to the Constitution. In his last constitutional opinion, in *Barron v. Baltimore,* 32 U.S. 243 (1833), he wrote that the protections of the Bill of Rights were only applicable to the national government and not the states. It was not until after the Civil War and the passage of the Fourteenth Amendment that the Court changed course and began applying the Bill of Rights to the states.

As a complement to his strong nationalist views, Marshall was also a supporter of property rights. He interpreted the contract clause of the Constitution as a protection for individuals against state action. In *Fletcher v. Peck,* 10 U.S. 87 (1810), he tied the contract clause to theories of natural law and vested rights that state governments could not infringe. Similarly, in *Dartmouth College v. Woodward,* 17 U.S. 518 (1819) he ruled that once a state entered into a charter or grant, it could not unilaterally alter the original terms of the agreement.

Marshall's expansive reading of the Constitution and leadership of the Court has made him one of the most important figures in American history. His ideas on constitutional interpretation are regarded as authoritative as the *Federalist Papers,* on which he relied frequently. In his opinions he cited natural law, common law, the intent of the framers, and drew on America's revolutionary and political history. He defined the role of chief justice and greatly enhanced the power and prestige of the Court. His opinions are still read and cited today as definitive statements on the meaning of the U.S. Constitution.

For more information

Beveridge, Albert J. *The Life of John Marshall,* 4 vols. Boston: Houghton Mifflin, 1916–19.

Hobson, Charles F. *The Great Chief Justice: John Marshall and the Rule of Law.* Lawrence: University Press of Kansas, 1996.

Allison Knowles and Artemus Ward
California State University, Chico

Marshall, Thurgood   (1908–1993)   was the first African-American justice of the United States Supreme Court, on which he served from 1967 to 1991. Even without holding that position, Marshall would still be remembered as one of the most important attorneys of the 20th century, for his courtroom battles to end legal segregation in the United States had already earned him the nickname of "Mr. Civil Rights."

Born into a middle-class family at Baltimore, Maryland, on July 2, 1908, Marshall attended the local segregated schools, then graduated from Lincoln University and Howard Law School in Washington, D.C. Marshall entered private practice in Baltimore in 1933, then joined the field staff of the National Association for the Advancement of Colored People (NAACP) in 1936 as assistant counsel, becoming counsel in 1938 and, at age 30, the most prominent black attorney in the United States. He served as director-counsel of the NAACP Legal Defense Fund (1941–61), planning and winning the legal assault on segregated America, overcoming barriers to voting, serving on juries, attending public educational institutions, equalizing teacher salaries, and racial covenants against purchasing property. Marshall was victorious in 29 of the 32 Supreme Court cases he argued, the most important of which was the landmark case of *Brown v. Board of Education* (1954), wherein the Supreme Court unanimously declared that separate educational facilities were inherently unequal.

In 1961 Marshall was appointed by President Kennedy to the U.S. Court of Appeals for the Second Circuit. During his four years as an appellate judge, none of his opinions were overruled by the Supreme Court. In 1965 he was appointed by President Johnson as solicitor general of the United States, serving for two years as the government's advocate before the Supreme Court and winning 14 of the 19 cases he argued there.

In 1967 President Johnson nominated Marshall as the first black associate justice of the Supreme Court, a position he held for 24 years until he retired in 1991. He believed that the Constitution was a living document to be read and interpreted through the lens of contemporary social realities and real-life experiences. As a member of the Warren Court, Marshall wrote important First Amendment opinions in *Amalgamated Food Employees Union v. Logan Valley Plaza* (1968) and *Stanley v. Georgia* (1969), and he joined the majority in *Furman v. Georgia* (1972) and *Roe v. Wade* (1973),

Justice Thurgood Marshall (HARRIS AND EWING, COLLECTION OF THE SUPREME COURT OF THE UNITED STATES)

establishing himself as a consistent supporter of economic justice and civil and constitutional rights for individuals. During the more conservative Burger and Rehnquist years, however, Marshall often dissented on cases limiting affirmative action, restricting freedom of speech, and denying appeals in cases involving the death penalty, which he believed to be unconstitutional.

Thurgood Marshall died at the National Naval Medical Center in Bethesda, Maryland, on January 24, 1993, and he is buried in Arlington National Cemetery.

For more information
Smith, Stephen A. "Thurgood Marshall." In *African American Orators: A Biocritical Sourcebook.* Westport, Conn.: Greenwood, 1996.

Tushnet, Mark V. *Making Civil Rights Law: Thurgood Marshall and the Supreme Court, 1936–1961.* New York: Oxford University Press, 1994.

———. *Making Constitutional Law: Thurgood Marshall and the Supreme Court, 1961–1991.* New York: Oxford University Press, 1997.

Williams, Juan. *Thurgood Marshall: American Revolutionary.* New York: Times Books, 1998.

Stephen Smith
University of Arkansas

martial law   exists when military authorities exercise governmental authority in place of civil government due to the civil government's inability to properly function as a result of war or domestic disturbance.

A declaration of martial law renders the military independent of, and superior to, the civil government. Martial law should terminate when civil authorities can once again preserve order, punish offenders, and compel obedience to the laws and other ordinary functions.

When martial law is in effect, the military commander has the power, within his jurisdiction, to suspend all civil rights and remedies, subject citizens as well as soldiers, and substitute military force for, and to the exclusion of, the laws; only his superiors may restrain him. Martial law should supercede local law only to the extent necessary, and only for the preservation of order.

Martial law may be declared over any geographic area where the civil government cannot function. Thus, martial law may be exercised over an entire country, state, or territory, or over a smaller portion or region thereof.

In the United States the authority to declare martial law is shared by the legislative and executive branches of government, but it may be delegated. The basis for the president's declaration of martial law is found in the Constitution. Article II, section 2, makes the president commander in chief of the armed forces. Article IV, section 4 provides that the United States shall protect the states against invasion "and on application of the Legislature, or of the Executive (when the Legislature cannot be convened) against domestic violence."

Federal and military regulations outline situations in which military commanders may be delegated the authority to impose martial law. Commanders may act without higher authority only when immediate action is demanded and available communications do not permit contact with higher authority. For U.S. forces, modern communications are likely to make these circumstances rare.

In the United States, martial law has been declared infrequently, and only during time of war. One notable example was President Lincoln's declaration of martial law during the Civil War, an act that led to a famous constitutional law case—*Ex parte Milligan.* In September 1862, President Lincoln declared that in order to suppress the insurrection, "all rebels and insurgents, and their aiders and abettors . . . shall be subject to *martial law.* . . ."

Lamdin Milligan was a citizen of Indiana who was convicted by a military tribunal on charges ranging from conspiracy to insurrection. The Supreme Court found the declaration of martial law unconstitutional as the civilian government was in power and the civilian courts were open. The Court said that when the courts are actually closed, in the theater of active military operations "where war really prevails, there is a necessity to furnish a substitute for the civil authority . . . to preserve the safety of the army and society." Consequently, there is no power left but the military and it is allowed to govern by martial law until civil government can operate.

For more information

Ex parte Milligan, 18 L.Ed. 281 (1866); 93 C.J.S. War and National Defense, section 40.

Ochikubo v. Bonesteel, 60 F. Supp 916 (S.D. Cal. 1945).

U.S. v. Minoru Yasui, 48 F. Supp 40 (D. Or. 1942).

Captain William D. Smoot
Assistant Professor, Department of Law
U.S. Military Academy, West Point

McCleskey v. Kemp 481 U.S. 279 (1987) was a U.S. Supreme Court case that represented the last major constitutional challenge to the death-sentencing process in the United States.

In *McCleskey* the Court rejected the defendant's claim that his death sentence was unconstitutional because it was based on racial discrimination.

The defendant, Warren McCleskey, was an African American convicted of murdering a white police officer during a robbery attempt of a furniture store in 1978. He admitted to participating in the robbery but denied that he was responsible for the killing. Amid conflicting evidence, the jury convicted him and proceeded to the penalty phase of the trial where it deliberated on his appropriate punishment—life imprisonment or death. The jury decided that because the killing occurred during the course of a felony— the armed robbery—and the victim was a law enforcement officer (two factors known as aggravating circumstances), he deserved the death penalty for the murder charge; he was sentenced to consecutive life sentences on the robbery charges. The trial judge concurred with the jury's recommendation.

After several appeals were rejected, McCleskey's case reached the U.S. Supreme Court. He argued that his death sentence was racially discriminatory and violated the equal protection clause of the Fourteenth Amendment. His claim of racial discrimination was supported by a statistical study of more than 2,000 murder cases that had occurred in Georgia during the 1970s. The study, which analyzed 230 variables, showed that race was an important factor in capital punishment. First, it is imposed more frequently on African-American defendants than white defendants. The study also demonstrated that the race of the victim is key in determining whether a defendant is sentenced to death; in Georgia, African-American defendants convicted of killing white victims stand the greatest chance of being sentenced to death. One of the authors of the study, Professor David Baldus of the University of Iowa, testified at the lower court hearing that the effect of race is primarily felt in the mid-range cases where the jury and judge typically exercise the most discretion in sentencing.

McCleskey argued that the racial disparity in sentencing, as demonstrated by the study, created an inference that the sentencing procedure was discriminatory. The problem he faced, however, was that in order to make a successful claim of an equal protection violation, he was required to prove that the sentencing in his case was a product of intentional racial discrimination.

In a 5–4 ruling, the Supreme Court rejected his claim. Speaking for the majority, Justice Lewis Powell held that the study, known as the Baldus study, was not sufficient to prove the existence of unconstitutional racial discrimination against McCleskey. Although the district court judge had criticized the methodology of the Baldus study, the Supreme Court did not dispute the statistical validity of the findings. Rather, the Court found that the study did not show that McCleskey's sentence was a product of purposeful racial discrimination. Because McCleskey was unable to prove that he was discriminated against, the Court upheld the Georgia capital punishment procedure.

For more information

Lee, Cynthia K. Y. "Symposium on Race and Criminal Law: Race and the Victim: An Examination of Capital Sentencing and Guilt Attribution Studies," *Chicago-Kent College of Law* 73 (1998): 533–58.

Susan Gluck Mezey
Department of Political Science
Loyola University, Chicago

mediation is one of several possible alternative dispute resolution mechanisms that may be employed in the course of, or instead of, litigation. The proposition is to have the parties resolve the issues with each other, with the direction of a mediator. This paradigm purports to have the parties develop for themselves a win-win situation, as opposed to the win-lose outcome of litigation and adjudication.

A standard exemplar of mediation is the "orange." Two siblings each want the sole orange in the family refrigerator and are found arguing over it. A parent, rather than simply decide to give it to one or the other based on any particular rationale (such as finding it first, being older, etc.), asks the siblings *why* they each want the orange. To this query, one replies that the peel of an orange is required to bake a cake, whereas the other replies that the orange will abate hunger and slake thirst. Thus, by having facilitated discussion with each other, the siblings learn that they can both have the orange they want, with both winning and neither losing.

The concept of mediation—and indeed of alternative dispute resolution processes in general—as an alternative to traditional litigation became mainstream in the latter half of the 20th century. Indeed, mediation is frequently used in disputes ranging from landlord-tenant to complex civil litigation and insurance. Among the more frequent types of programs are labor disputes, small claims, parent-child status offense disputes (such as truancy), property matters, and domestic relations. In some countries, particularly in Africa and China, mediation was considered a natural extension of customary law.

In mediation, the goal is to empower the parties, who by virtue of "private ordering," or shared solving of a dispute, also remove cases from court dockets. The mediator in a sense teaches communication skills to the parties, as well as acting as a strategist for them. Confidentiality is key to the process, although the final agreement is written up as a contract between the parties. Along the way to this final agreement, the mediator can employ a number of techniques that are largely absent from a traditional courtroom; one of these is caucusing with the parties separately, which would be barred in court as *ex parte* communication. Unlike a traditional litigation technique, where lawyers often try to widen the dispute and add to issues, a mediator will seek to progressively narrow the dispute and to subtract from it areas of common ground.

However, in some cases adjudication should actually be viewed as the preferred mode of dispute resolution. For instance, if mediation is mandatory, there is an inherent power imbalance and coercion is, ultimately, inextricably intertwined with the process. Likewise, where a mediator is overly directive (rather than acting as a facilitator for communication, negotiation, and agreement), one or more parties can be disempowered, rather than empowered. It is inappropriate for a mediator to act as a final arbiter or to inject his or her own views over those of the parties. Moreover there is a danger that the parties will perceive themselves as having been relegated to a lesser forum, without even the benefit of a jurist.

Risk is particularly problematic in family and domestic cases. There is a growing literature to the effect that power imbalances may be inherent in such cases, especially where there is domestic violence, sexual abuse, or emotional abuse of a spouse or child. Indeed, these are the very cases where adjudication is most required, not least required. This example shows that while mediation is a powerful tool when properly employed, improper deployment can lead to physical and emotional harm to those who need protection the most.

For more information

Murray, John S. Alan Scott, Rau, Edward F. Sherman. *Processes of Dispute Resolution: The Role of Lawyers,* 2nd ed. (*University Casebook Series*). Westbury, N.Y.: The Foundation Press, 1996.

Pappas, Demetra M. "Direction or Conciliation: The Theory and Reality of Preliminary Directions Hearings Conducted in Croydon, England under the Children Act 1989," *Family and Conciliation Courts Review 31* (1993): 327–33.

Demetra M. Pappas, J.D., M.Sc.
London School of Economics and Political Science

medical examiner refers to an individual appointed within a jurisdiction to be responsible for the overall investigation into any suspicious deaths within that jurisdiction. While the term has been used interchangeably with the term *coroner,* the two may have different sources of authority from which to conduct their respective investigations and may have slightly different roles.

In most cases, a coroner is a public official, who is either elected to office or appointed by a government body. A coroner may not necessarily have any medical training, nor, depending on the jurisdiction, be required to have such a background. A coroner's main responsibility is to determine whether or not a death involved possible criminal, suspicious, or undetermined circumstances that warrant further investigation. A coroner may order a forensic autopsy, which is authorized by law, in order to determine a cause of death for an individual and will often oversee the investigation into the circumstances surrounding any death not attributable to natural causes. In such cases, a coroner may supervise a team of physicians and other forensic scientists to find the cause of death. Finally, a coroner may be responsible for issuing and completing the cause of death on the death certificate.

In contrast, a medical examiner is often a physician, appointed within a particular jurisdiction, and charged with many of the same duties that a coroner assumes, including the determination of cause of death. However, a medical examiner, by virtue of his/her training, is expected to bring medical expertise to the evaluation. A medical examiner may investigate further into a victim's medical background as well as to the manner in which an individual died. It is assumed that a physician will more readily be able to ascertain whether or not a suspicious death has taken place, given his/her medical background. A medical examiner may not necessarily be an expert in the field of forensic pathology, which is the branch of medicine dealing with the examination of death due to violent or unexpected circumstances. Most jurisdictions that employ medical examiners will encourage further training of physicians appointed to the position.

As noted previously, the decision as to whether there is a medical examiner or coroner who ultimately decides to open an investigation into a suspicious death is dependent upon jurisdiction. In many smaller jurisdictions, law enforcement officials often act as coroners, in an effort to conserve resources and streamline investigations.

For more information
National Association of Medical Examiners website, at http://www.thename.org.

Raquel J. Gabriel
Associate Professor
Reference/Government Documents Librarian
City University of New York School of Law

mens rea refers to state of mind or criminal intent.

In most crimes prosecutors must prove that the accused not only committed a criminal act (actus reus) but that they did so with a specific criminal intent (mens rea).

In some criminal cases prosecutors do not have to prove state of mind. In regulatory crimes, often involving food, a defendant is strictly liable for the act committed and no criminal intent need be shown to obtain a conviction.

In most cases criminal charges can be changed and punishments can be affected by whether the accused had a criminal intent, and what type the state of the mind of the accused was at the time of the crime. For example in tax fraud cases prosecutors will need to determine whether the accused acted with willful intent to cheat or was just careless. In military justice the difference between being Away Without Leave (AWOL) and desertion revolves around the person's intent.

Many criminal statutes, including the Model Penal Code, distinguish among four different levels of mens rea or culpability in addition to strict liability. One acts "purposely" when one consciously desires to bring about a certain result, such as the death of another. One acts "knowingly" when one is aware that his conduct will bring about a result. "Reckless" behavior involves the conscious disregard of an unjustifiable risk that brings about some conduct. Finally, to act "negligently" is when one could have been unaware of a substantial and unjustifiable risk. Depending on the state of one's mind, a person might be charged with a different crime, or a different level of crime. For example, depending on the circumstances surrounding a death, one could be charged with first or second degree murder, manslaughter, or another crime.

Mens rea is proven by the circumstances surrounding the events in question. Prosecutors must show a chain of acts that point to the person's intent and motivation. Some examples of actions that would be used to prove mens rea would include: how hard did a person try to cover up their activities, did they lie to police or investigators, did they do things in a specific sequence to facilitate the ultimate criminal act.

For more information

Hart, H.L.A. *Punishment and the Elimination of Responsibility.* London: Athcone Press, 1962.

Charlie Howard
Tarleton State University

Mexican American Legal Defense and Educational Fund   or MALDEF is a national organization dedicated to advancing the civil rights of Latinos in the United States. Headquartered in Los Angeles, California, it has regional offices in Chicago, Illinois; San Antonio, Texas; San Francisco, California; and Washington, D.C.

Founded in San Antonio, Texas, in 1968, MALDEF utilizes litigation as a primary tool to secure civil rights for Latinos. It sponsors, coordinates, and directs civil rights lawsuits brought on behalf of the Latino community. MALDEF's founders, like African-American leaders before them, believed that such an organization was needed because traditional political activity alone was insufficient to secure civil rights for Latinos. Moreover, MALDEF's founders noted that litigation on behalf of Latinos had been sporadic and underfunded. Accordingly, they sought out and received help from the successful NAACP Legal Defense and Educational Fund (LDF) in creating their organization. With the aid of the LDF, MALDEF received a $2.2 million, five-year start-up grant from the Ford Foundation.

Modeled after the LDF, MALDEF appointed Texas attorney Peter Tijernia, a driving force behind MALDEF, as its first executive director, and Texas assistant attorney general Mario Obledo as its first general counsel. Like the LDF, MALDEF hoped to draw its staff and its network of cooperating attorneys—independent attorneys who work on MALDEF lawsuits—from the community it serves. However, it quickly became apparent to MALDEF that this plan was not to be. There were simply not enough Latino attorneys with sufficient civil rights experience or independent incomes to staff its positions or act as cooperating attorneys. Hence, early on MALDEF relied heavily on non-Latino attorneys and began its scholarship program for Latino law students.

In its early years MALDEF also faced other challenges besides attorney recruitment. MALDEF was overwhelmed with routine legal cases that did not involve larger constitutional civil rights issues it wished to pursue in litigation. Moreover, a perception emerged that some of MALDEF's San Antonio staff were "too militant."

These challenges signaled a change for MALDEF. Acting upon the Ford Foundation recommendation, it moved its headquarters, first to San Francisco and then to Los Angeles.

With this move MALDEF began to work with the LDF on employment discrimination cases and to bring more cases before the U. S. Supreme Court.

By 1973 MALDEF had succeeded in its Supreme Court effort. In 1973 it participated in eight cases before the Court. The results of its efforts were mixed. In *San Antonio Independent School District v. Rodriguez,* MALDEF failed in its attempt to establish that education was a fundamental right protected by the Fourteenth Amendment. However, in *White v. Regester,* MALDEF achieved victory. This case, involving the constitutionality of single-member election districts, assisted in bringing Texas into compliance with the 1965 Voting Rights Act.

Spurred on by this victory and despite its losses, MALDEF has continued its litigation efforts in the areas of education and political access and has achieved other successes. In 1982 in *Plyler v. Doe,* MALDEF convinced the United States Supreme Court that children of undocumented aliens may not be charged a fee for attending public school. MALDEF also instituted lawsuits in the 1970s and early 1980s which resulted in increased voter registration among Latinos. In 1989 it achieved success in *Edgewood ISD v. State of Texas,* in which the Texas Supreme Court found Texas's public school financing system unconstitutional. More recently MALDEF was instrumental in stalling California's implementation of Proposition 187, a measure which effectively cut off, among other social services, education to the children of undocumented immigrants.

Finally, while continuing to press its litigation efforts in the areas of employment, education, immigration, and political access, MALDEF also seeks to advance its civil rights agenda through lobbying and community outreach. It has continued its scholarship program for Latino law students, developed leadership training programs, and has initiated a Census 2000 Education Outreach Program aimed at encouraging Latino participation.

For more information

"Mexican American Legal Defense and Educational Fund." The Handbook of Texas Online <http://www.tsha.utexas.edu-/handbook/online/articles/ view/MM/ joml.html> [Accessed Wed Sep 13 9:22:05 US/Central 2000].

O'Connor, Karen, and Epstein, Lee. "A Legal Voice for the Chicano Community: The Activities of the Mexican American Legal Defense and Educational Fund, 1968–82," *Social Science Quarterly* 65 (June 1984): 245–56.

Georgia Wralstad Ulmschneider
Indiana University-Purdue University, Fort Wayne

Minor v. Happersett 88 U.S. 162 (1875) raised the question of whether the adoption of the Fourteenth Amendment required states to grant women the right to vote as one of the privileges and immunities of citizenship.

Virginia Minor, who was the president of the Missouri Woman Suffrage Association, brought the suit before the Supreme Court in an attempt to acquire a woman's right to vote in political elections, contending that laws in the state of Missouri, which limited voting rights to men, violated the U.S. Constitution. Specifically, Minor argued that since both native-born and naturalized women are citizens of the United States as well as citizens of the states in which they reside, then under the "privileges and immunities" clause of the Fourteenth Amendment, these women have the right to vote. Moreover, Minor argued that since this right to suffrage was constitutionally guaranteed by the Fourteenth Amendment, no state could make laws that would abridge this guaranteed right of citizenship.

The Supreme Court, however, rejected Minor's arguments. The justices argued that "citizenship" is defined as "conveying the idea of membership of a nation, and nothing more." In an opinion written by Chief Justice Waite, the Court explained that while "there is no doubt that women may be citizens," it is not the Fourteenth Amendment that gave women their citizenship status. The Court stated:

[S]ex has never been made one of the elements of citizenship in the United States. In this respect men have never had an advantage over women. . . . . The fourteenth amendment did not affect the citizenship of women any more than it did of men. In this particular, therefore, the rights of Mrs. Minor do not depend upon the amendment. She has always been a citizen from her birth, and entitled to all the privileges and immunities of citizenship.

Consequently, the Court noted that the question that had to be answered in this case was "whether all citizens are necessarily voters," and the Court concluded that this was not the case. The Court asserted that the framers of the Constitution did not intend "to make all citizens of the United States voters." Moreover, the Court explained that if voting rights and citizenship went hand-in-hand, then all citizens, including women, should be able to vote in each of the individual states. However, the justices pointed out that "women were excluded from suffrage in nearly all of the States by the express provision of their Constitution and laws." Therefore, it was clear to the Supreme Court that all United States citizens were not meant to possess voting rights. Finally, the Court explained that the ratification of the Fourteenth Amendment did not create any new voters. If this indeed had been the intent of the amendment, the justices explained that such a major change would have been "expressly declared" and not left to implication. Furthermore, it was noted that if the privileges and immunities clause of the Fourteenth Amendment had intended to extend the rights of suffrage to all citizens, then the Fifteenth Amendment, which guaranteed that suffrage could not be denied by the United States or any state based on "race, color, or previous condition of servitude," would not have been necessary. In short, the Supreme Court concluded that the privileges and immunities clause did not grant women the right to suffrage.

The *Minor v. Happersett* ruling indicated that women would not be successful in acquiring new rights under the Constitution via the privileges and immunities clause of the Fourteenth Amendment. As a result, the women's suffrage movement recognized that they needed to secure an amendment to the Constitution in order to achieve nationwide suffrage for women. Women finally did obtain the right to vote in 1920 with the passage of the Nineteenth Amendment of the Constitution.

For more information

Isenberg, Nancy. *Sex and Citizenship in Antebellum America.* Chapel Hill: University of North Carolina Press, 1998.

Kerber, Linda K. *No Constitutional Right to Be Ladies: Women and the Obligations of Citizenship.* New York: Hill and Wang, 1998.

Lister, Ruth. *Citizenship: Feminist Perspectives.* New York: New York University Press, 1997.

Francene M. Engel
University of Michigan

Miranda v. Arizona 348 U.S. 436 (1966) is an important Supreme Court case that protects the rights of people arrested and accused of committing a crime by requiring that the police read these individuals their constitutional rights at the time they are arrested. In this case the Court held that the Fifth Amendment requires this reading of rights.

The case began in a Phoenix police station. The complaining witness identified Ernesto Miranda as the person who had sexually assaulted her. Miranda was then taken to an interrogation room where he was questioned by two police officers. After two hours, the detectives emerged from the room with a written confession signed by Miranda. The confession statement was headed by a typed paragraph stating that the confession was made voluntarily, without threats or promises of immunity, and with full knowledge of Miranda's legal rights.

This confession was admitted into evidence at the trial, which led to Miranda's conviction on rape and kidnapping. The Supreme Court of Arizona ruled that Miranda's rights were not violated; nevertheless, the U.S. Supreme Court reversed the decision because he was not advised of his right to consult with an attorney, to have one present during the interrogation, and of his right not to be compelled to incriminate himself.

Miranda v. Arizona accepted the argument that custodial interrogations are inherently coercive. It rejected after-the-fact assessment of the voluntariness of confessions as insufficient protection for the Fifth Amendment privilege. The Supreme Court announced that the Fifth Amendment requires police to give suspects basic warning of their rights prior to custodial questioning. The Court then described specific warnings that would protect the suspect's Fifth Amendment rights. These basic warnings came to be known as the Miranda warnings.

When suspects are taken into police custody or otherwise deprived of their freedom, they must be warned prior to any questioning (1) that they have the right to remain silent; (2) that anything they say may be used against them in a court of law; (3) that they have the right to the presence of an attorney; and (4) that if they cannot afford an attorney one will be appointed for them prior to any questioning if they so desire. After the warnings have been given an individual may waive these rights and agree to answer questions or make a statement. However, to waive one's rights, one must do it in a voluntary, knowingly, and intelligent fashion.

Confessions or statements given in violation of *Miranda* are inadmissible in a court of law. However, these statements may be used in grand jury proceedings and at trial to impeach the credibility of a defendant who chooses to testify.

The *Miranda* decision has been controversial. Some have argued that the *Miranda* warnings have made it harder for the police to solve crimes and secure confessions. Others have argued that these warnings have improved policing and ensure that confessions are real and innocent people do not confess to crimes out of fear or force. While there have been several efforts to overturn *Miranda, Dickerson v. United States,* 120 S.Ct. 2326 (2000), upheld and reaffirmed this decision.

For more information

Baker, Liva. *Miranda: Crime, Law and Politics.* New York: Atheneum, 1983.

Leo, Richard A., and George C. Thomas III, eds. *The Miranda Debate: Law, Justice, and Policing.* Boston: Northeastern University Press, 2000.

Paul Kuritz
Bates College

Miranda warnings See *MIRANDA V. ARIZONA.*

misdemeanor refers to any crime that carries a lesser punishment than a felony, or for which no penalty is imposed.

In many jurisdictions a misdemeanor is defined as any crime that is not a felony. Thus, as a felony is typically defined as a crime that has an authorized punishment of death or imprisonment of more than one year, a misdemeanor is a crime whose authorized punishment does not exceed one year in prison. Punishments for misdemeanors range from no punishment to fines, penalties, and imprisonment of one year or less. Since misdemeanors are usually less severe crimes than felonies, they thus deserve less punishment.

Some jurisdictions classify misdemeanors based on the severity of the possible punishment. Typically, Class A misdemeanors receive greater punishment than do Class B misdemeanors. As an example, in those jurisdictions that classify misdemeanors, a Class A misdemeanor may receive a prison term of not more than one year, a Class B misdemeanor may receive a prison term of not more than six months, etc.

Just as misdemeanors are distinguished from felonies based on the degree of authorized punishment, so too, many jurisdictions distinguish misdemeanors from petty offenses and infractions. The distinction is again based on the authorized punishment. In those jurisdictions that recognize petty offenses and infractions, the punishment for these violations is less severe than the punishment for misdemeanors. Petty offenses and infractions often authorize minimal jail time and a light fine as punishment.

For more information
22 C.J.S. Criminal Law section 11; 18 U.S.C. 1 (repealed).

Captain William D. Smoot
Assistant Professor, Department of Law
U.S. Military Academy, West Point

Model Penal Code   is an enormously important and influential document in modern criminal law.

Compiled during a 10-year period ending with a proposed official draft in 1962, the code is the product of a collaboration by a large group of criminal law scholars assembled by the American Law Institute and working under the direction of Professor Herbert Wechsler, the code's chief reporter. The code has had a remarkable impact since its completion, having been used as the basis for codifications or revisions in some 30 or more states and discussed in countless judicial opinions. It consists of four parts: general provisions, definitions of specific offenses, treatment and correction, and organization of correction. Each part contains model provisions that are intended for adoption by state legislatures. A commentary on the special part was published in 1980 and on the general part in 1985.

Perhaps the code's most important innovation can be found in its provisions concerning the mental element necessary to commit an offense. The pre-code common law used a complex and confusing collection of terms to designate mens rea. In their place, the code offers a concise and ostensibly simple hierarchy of mental states that define modes of acting with respect to the material elements of an offense: purposely, knowingly, recklessly, and negligently. Another significant general part provision is that concerning the controversial issue of strict criminal liability. The code takes a compromise approach by allowing for the possibility of such offenses but classifying them as "violations" punishable only by fines.

The code also contains a number of important innovations in the definition of special offenses. Among its most significant achievements is the consolidation of a notoriously complex collection of common-law crimes such as larceny, false pretenses, and embezzlement into a small number of theft provisions. The code also seeks to reform the law of homicide by, among other things, developing a coherent system for grading homicide offenses, and transforming the much-criticized common-law felony murder rule (which allowed a defendant to be held strictly liable for a death that occurs during the perpetration of a felony) into a mere presumption that the offender has acted with recklessness and indifference.

Despite criticism of various specific provisions in the Model Penal Code, its influence on U.S. criminal law has undoubtedly been a salutary one. If nothing else, it has given lawyers, judges, scholars, law students, and state legislators a common conceptual framework for thinking about the criminal law. But the code is also beginning to show signs of age. In the wake of several decades of changes in patterns of criminality, social mores, and sentencing and constitutional law, a comprehensive revision of the code may well be in order.

For more information
American Law Institute. *Model Penal Code: Official Draft and Explanatory Notes,* 7 vols. (1980 & 1985).

"Symposium on the Model Penal Code," *Columbia Law Review* 63 (1963): 589–686.

"Symposium on the Model Penal Code," *Rutgers Law Journal* 19 (1988): 519–954.

"Symposium on the Model Penal Code," *Buffalo Criminal Law Review* 4 (forthcoming, 2000).

Stuart P. Green
Louisiana State University

motive　in criminal law is the reason why a person (usually the defendant) acted in a certain way or, conversely, did not act in a certain way. It is the willful desire that leads a person to commit a criminal act.

The prosecution in a criminal case often tries to show that the defendant had a certain motive because this helps to support the belief that the defendant committed the crime. As an example, take the case of a defendant accused of committing arson by burning down his own warehouse. Suppose that during the investigation it is discovered that the defendant's business was doing very poorly and that the defendant had taken out a large insurance policy on the warehouse. The prosecution may try to use these facts to argue that the defendant had the motive to commit arson. In another case, a defendant may argue that the lack of a motive supports his argument that he did not commit the crime.

Although motive is often important in criminal trials, the prosecution is not required to prove motive because motive is not an essential element of a crime. In a criminal trial the fundamental consideration is whether the defendant committed the crime and not why the criminal committed the crime. Thus a distinction must be drawn between motive and intent. Usually the prosecution must prove criminal intent by proving that the defendant intended to commit the crime. Criminal intent is the intent to commit a criminal act without any defense such as justification or excuse.

An important exception to the principle that the prosecution does not have to prove motive is when a defendant is charged with a hate crime. In a hate crime trial, the prosecution must prove that the defendant was motivated by hate toward the victim because of the victim's race or nationality or some other protected status.

The motive of the defendant may be important during the police investigation of a crime. Law enforcement investigators often try to discover possible motives for a crime because this can help them focus on the most likely perpetrators. The motive for a crime may also be considered by the judge during sentencing to enhance a sentence because the convicted person acted with a bad motive.

For more information

West's Encyclopedia of American Law, vol. 7. St. Paul, Minn.: West Publishing Group, 1998.

Michael Hannon
Duke University Law Library

Muller v. Oregon　208 U.S. 412 (1908) is an important case for understanding the relationship that often exists between the law and gender.

The *Muller v. Oregon* case demonstrates that when society believes "physical differences" exist between the sexes, laws often are constructed to treat women differently from men in order to "protect" women. At issue in this 1908 case was an Oregon law that mandated that women could not work more than 10 hours a day "in any mechanical establishment . . . factory, or laundry." When the constitutionality of this statute was questioned in Court, attorneys for the plaintiff in error argued that the Oregon law was inconsistent with the Supreme Court's decision three years earlier in *Lochner v. New York*, which ruled that a New York law setting maximum work hours for bakers violated workers' Fourteenth Amendment rights to freedom of contract.

Supporters of the Oregon work hours law, however, argued that *Lochner* should not be a guiding precedent in this case, since the Oregon law was specifically geared toward women, and they believed important differences existed between the sexes. Progressive lawyer Louis Brandeis wrote a famous brief in defense of the Oregon law, which traditionally is referred to as the "Brandeis brief." In defending the maximum work hours law for women, Brandeis used social science data to support the position that long work hours posed a serious and unique health risk to women. Quoting a physician who had studied women in the workforce, the "Brandeis brief" explained that "[w]oman is badly constructed for the purposes of standing eight or ten hours upon her feet . . . [due] to the particular construction of the knee, . . . the shallowness of the pelvis, and the delicate nature of the foot as part of a sustaining column." Other physicians noted that prolonged work hours could have an adverse effect on women's "female functions" in life. For example, one doctor contended that long work hours could make women "sterile." Another physician argued that the children of women who worked long hours often suffered because the infant had to be "bottle-fed" or because the woman's "milk [was] unfit for the child's nourishment" due to her exhaustion from overworking.

The Supreme Court accepted the social science data put forth in the "Brandeis brief" and ruled that the "inherent differences between the two sexes, and in the different functions in life they perform" justified treating men and women differently under the law. Consequently, the Court decided that the *Lochner v. New York* decision, which rejected maximum work hours for men working as bakers, did not apply when judging the Oregon law.

In an opinion written by Justice Brewer, the Court explained that because "healthy mothers are essential to vigorous offspring, the physical well-being of woman becomes an object of public interest . . . in order to preserve the strength and vigor of the race." Justice Brewer went on to conclude that a woman "is properly placed in a class by herself, and legislation designed for her

protection may be sustained, even when like legislation is not necessary for men and could not be sustained."

The *Muller v. Oregon* decision shows the importance social science can play in Supreme Court decision making. Likewise, feminists have argued the *Muller v. Oregon* demonstrates how the law often has viewed women as inferior by "nature" and in need of "protection." Feminists have pointed out that society's belief that the law must protect women because of their physical differences has been instrumental in maintaining women's subordination in society.

For more information

Ericson, Nancy. "Historical Background of 'Protective' Labor Legislation: *Muller v. Oregon.*" In Kelly Weisberg, ed. *Women and the Law: The Social Historical Perspective,* vol. 2. Cambridge, Mass.: Schenkman Publishing, 1982, pp. 155–86.

Otten, Laura A. "The Writing on the Wall: No Constitutional Protection for Women." In *Women's Rights and the Law.* Westport, Conn.: Praeger, 1993, pp. 55–79.

Francene M. Engel
University of Michigan

murder   is the unjustified killing of another human.

Murder is the most serious of all homicide offenses. At common law, murder was a homicide committed "with malice aforethought," a technical term that referred to the mental state of the offender. Curiously, it required neither malice nor forethought. Rather, the term came to denote killings that were committed with intent to kill, intent to cause serious bodily injury, extreme recklessness, or during the perpetration or attempted perpetration of certain serious felonies. Murder statutes today typically do not use the term *malice aforethought.* Instead, they define murder more straightforwardly as the intentional or purposeful killing of a human being by another human being, without justification, excuse, or other mitigating circumstances.

In many jurisdictions, murder also includes homicides committed with intent to cause serious injury, with extreme recklessness, or during the commission or attempted commission of certain enumerated felonies. Murder typically carries the most serious sanctions that the criminal law allows, whether it be the death sentence, life imprisonment, or imprisonment for a substantial number of years.

At early common law, the penalty for murder was invariably death. In an effort to alleviate the harshness of this regime, the Pennsylvania legislature in 1794 enacted the first statute dividing murder into two degrees: first degree murder (for which the death sentence was still applied) and second degree murder (for which a lesser sentence was imposed). First degree murder required a killing that was either "willful, deliberate, or premeditated," committed by means of poison or lying in wait, or that occurred during the perpetration or attempted perpetration of certain enumerated felonies.

All other forms of murder were regarded as second degree, including intentional homicides that were not premeditated, homicides committed with intent to inflict serious bodily injury rather than death, and homicides that occurred during the commission of unenumerated felonies. The Pennsylvania scheme proved enormously influential, with some version of it being adopted in a large majority of the states during the next century and a half. Under one form of the Pennsylvania-inspired scheme, murder is considered first degree if it involves factors such as the use of torture, use of an explosive, murder for hire, or the killing of a public official or police officer.

Today the law of murder continues to evolve, reflecting changes in society's views about violence, the death penalty, and sentencing, as well as various developments in constitutional law. One particular trend worth noting, attributable to the influence of the Model Penal Code, is a moving away from the statutory classification of different degrees of murder. Under the code's approach, there is only one degree of murder, although certain "aggravating" and "mitigating" circumstances are taken into account in determining what the sentence should be. Aggravating circumstances include factors such as elderly or juvenile victims, and multiple victims. Mitigating circumstances include factors such as the youth of the defendant or a lack of criminal history.

For more information

Pillsbury, Samuel. *Judging Evil: Rethinking the Law of Murder and Manslaughter.* New York: New York University Press, 1998.

Wechsler, Herbert, and Jerome Michael, "A Rationale of the Law of Homicide," *Columbia Law Review* 37 (1937): 701–61, 1261–1325.

Stuart P. Green
Louisiana State University

N

National Association for the Advancement of Colored People (NAACP) is one of the most prominent organizations in the United States lobbying and litigating on behalf of African Americans and other minority groups.

The mission of the NAACP is twofold: to achieve the legal, social, cultural, and economic equality of minority groups, and to eradicate racial prejudice. Begun in 1905 by a group of social activists, the organization initially called for the elimination of all distinctions in law and policy based on race or color. The first official meeting of the NAACP was held in 1909. By 1945 the NAACP could boast more than 300,000 members and 1,600 branches. More importantly, the organization had begun to achieve credibility among lawmakers and to exert its influence in the courts.

Although the NAACP is most closely associated with the Civil Rights movement of the 1960s, its first effort to achieve racial equality began as a coordinated legal strategy during the 1920s and 1930s to overturn the legality of "restrictive housing covenants." These covenants were part of property deeds enforced by courts. They required present and future owners to restrict sale of property only to people of the Caucasian race. During this period, the association retained the services of highly visible attorneys, including Clarence Darrow, Moorfield Storey, and Louis Marshall. These prominent volunteers failed in their efforts to outlaw housing discrimination (*Corrigan v. Buckley*, 271 U.S. 323 [1926]). However, they did see impressive gains in the acknowledgment of rights for minorities. During the 1940s, NAACP attorneys led by Charles Houston and Thurgood Marshall developed and oversaw national litigation strategy. In the case *Shelley v. Kraemer*, 334 U.S. 1 (1948), they succeeded in convincing the Supreme Court that restrictive housing covenants were legally unenforceable.

Beginning with the incorporation of the NAACP Legal Defense Fund in 1939, the association launched its first full-scale legal attack on racial segregation in education and transportation. The Legal Defense Fund (LDF) provided full-time legal staff to work on civil rights litigation and achieved extraordinary results within a few years. LDF general counsel Thurgood Marshall successfully implemented a long-

NAACP – One Society (LIBRARY OF CONGRESS)

term legal strategy, appealing a large number of important cases to the U.S. Supreme Court. These cases include *Morgan v. Virginia,* 328 U.S. 373 (1946), the case outlawing segregation in interstate travel accommodations, and *Sweatt v. Painter,* 340 U.S. 846 (1950), in which the Court effectively banned segregation in graduate education.

Arguably, the NAACP's greatest legal triumph came in *Brown v. Board of Education I,* 347 U.S. 483 (1954). In this case the Court ruled that segregating public school children by race was unconstitutional. In addition, the Court overturned the segregationist doctrine of separate but equal. Thus, within 15 years of instituting a fully funded litigation campaign against discrimination in education and public accommodations, the NAACP and its Legal Defense Fund achieved their core objectives. NAACP lawyers successfully argued to overturn legally

sanctioned segregation in public schooling and some accommodations.

In the 1960s the NAACP began to shift its emphases to lobbying for passage of the federal Civil Rights Act (1964) and Voting Rights Act (1965). The association was instrumental in the passage and implementation of these acts, which guarantee freedom from discrimination in employment, accommodations, and voting. Despite encountering savage resistance (including the assassination of NAACP field director Medgar Evers), federal marshals and NAACP civil rights volunteers successfully registered more than 300,000 black voters in southern states. More recently, the NAACP has continued to organize support for antidiscrimination policies and to encourage minority voters registration and participation.

For more information

Kluger, Richard. *Simple Justice.* New York: Random House, 1976.

NAACP website: www.naacp.org.

Vose, Clement. *Caucasians Only.* Berkeley: University of California Press, 1959.

Hans J. Hacker
Adjunct Professor of Public Law
University of Maryland

National Institute of Justice   or NIJ is an important center for criminal justice research. It conducts local, national, and international studies aimed at revising criminal justice policies, practices, and standards. It also investigates ways to improve the training, assessment, and professionalism of law enforcement personnel. It funds studies to reduce or alter criminal conduct with more effective ways of controlling crime.

The National Institute of Justice was created in 1968 by the Omnibus Crime Control and Safe Streets Act (*U.S. Code,* 42 U.S.C. sections 3721–3722). This law was enacted in response to recommendations made to President Lyndon B. Johnson by the Presidential Commission on Law

Enforcement and Administration of Justice (1967).

The Omnibus Crime Act created the Law Enforcement Assistance Administration (LEAA). The LEAA then created, as a unit of itself, the National Institute of Law Enforcement and Criminal Justice as a research agency.

After the LEAA was abolished (April 15, 1982), the Justice Department transferred the LEAA's responsibilities to the Office of Justice Assistance, Research, and Statistics (OJARS, 1982–84). OJARS was in turn abolished by the Justice Assistance Act of 1984 (98 Stat. 2077), which created the Office of Justice Programs as a coordinating agency for the National Institute of Justice (NIJ), Bureau of Justice Statistics, Office of Juvenile Justice and Delinquency Prevention, and the newly created Bureau of Justice Assistance.

At the end of the Clinton administration the NIJ was a unit of the Office of Justice Programs of the Department of Justice. The NIJ, headed by the institute director, a position appointed by the president and confirmed by the Senate, was divided into three offices—Office of Development and Communications, Office of Research and Evaluation, and Office of Science and Technology.

The NIJ's original mandate was to challenge the conventional wisdom of the day by testing assumptions about crime prevention and control. NIJ sponsored research and investigated many questions and issues dealing with crime, including victims, juries, architecture and crime prevention, street lighting, proposals to reorganize the handling of minor traffic cases that were clogging court systems, police training to deal with family crisis management, crime mapping, studies of correctional theory, and many other subjects.

NIJ's responsibilities expanded with passage of the Violent Crime Control and Law Enforcement Act of 1994 (Crime Act)—Public Law 102–322. Section 3721 authorizes the NIJ to provide for and encourage research efforts that can improve federal, state, and local criminal justice systems and related aspects of the civil justice system. NIJ is also charged with researching ways to prevent and reduce crimes, to aid in developing citizens' dispute-resolution forums, and to pioneer advances in science and technology that help deter, identify, and apprehend offenders. NIJ studies are valuable tools for criminal justice policymakers.

For more information

Russell, Michael J. *Data Resources of the National Institute of Justice.* Collingdale, Pa.: Diane Publishing Co., 1999.

Siegel, Larry J., and Laura Beaudoin, eds. *American Justice: Research of the National Institute of Justice.* St. Paul, Minn.: West Group Publishing, 1990.

A. J. L. Waskey
Dalton State College

New Jersey v. T.L.O. 469 U.S. 325 (1985)

was a U.S. Supreme Court decision expanded the authority of school officials to search students' possessions and established different standards for protecting the privacy rights of children and adults.

The case began when two students were discovered smoking in the school bathroom—in violation of school rules—in a Piscataway, New Jersey, high school. When they were brought to the assistant vice principal's office, one of the students admitted that she had been smoking. The other student, 14-year-old T.L.O., denied that she had been smoking and insisted that she did not smoke at all. The school official asked to see her purse and, upon opening it, found cigarettes. As he removed them, he noticed cigarette rolling papers, which, in his experience, were associated with marijuana. Suspecting that he would uncover additional evidence of drug use, he conducted a more thorough search of the purse and found various drug paraphernalia, including a pipe, marijuana, empty plastic bags, and a bundle of one dollar bills, as well as documents suggesting that she was involved in selling marijuana.

T.L.O. subsequently confessed that she sold marijuana.

A New Jersey juvenile court held that the search was reasonable and admitted the evidence against T.L.O. On the basis of this evidence, she was found delinquent and sentenced to one year's probation. Her conviction was later reversed by the state supreme court, which held that there were no reasonable grounds for the search and it was therefore unconstitutional.

In a 6–3 opinion, the U.S. Supreme Court reversed the state supreme court. Speaking for the majority, Justice Byron White steered a middle ground between those who argued that school searches were not within the Fourth Amendment and those who wanted to apply the rules for adult searches to students. As applied to adults, the Fourth Amendment requires the authorities to have probable cause before undertaking a search of the person or property. Absent probable cause, evidence obtained from a search is excluded in court.

The Court first determined that school officials are subject to the Fourth Amendment's prohibition against unreasonable search and seizure. However, unlike the police, they need not obtain a warrant before conducting a search. In determining the standard for conducting a proper Fourth Amendment search, the Court weighed the student's privacy interests against the school's need to maintain discipline and order. It ruled that a search is justified if the school authorities have "reasonable grounds" to suspect that it will produce evidence of a violation of school rules. Therefore, unlike a police search of an adult, a school official is not required to have probable cause that the student has committed an illegal act before conducting the search. Finally, the Court concluded that the search of T.L.O.'s purse was reasonable and the material found in it could be used as evidence against her.

The case of *New Jersey v. T.L.O.* became the basis for later Supreme Court rulings on student searches, including the 1995 case of *Vernonia School District 47J v. Acton*. In *Acton* the Court balanced the student's right to privacy against the school's need to combat drug use and held that the Fourth Amendment allowed school officials to conduct drug tests among its student athletes even though they had no individualized suspicion of drug use.

For more information

Book, Michael. "Group Suspicion: The Key to Evaluating Student Drug Testing," *Kansas Law Review* 48 (April 2000): 637–61.

Susan Gluck Mezey
Department of Political Science
Loyola University, Chicago

New York Times Co. v. Sullivan　376 U.S. 254 (1964) is the most important U.S. Supreme Court decision in the history of American libel law, if not in the history of free press and free speech rights.

In *Sullivan* the Court laid the groundwork for constitutional protections, under the First Amendment, in what had been exclusively a state law concern. The Supreme Court decided that the First Amendment required a public official who sued a critic for libel must prove that the critic knew his statement about the official was false or that he recklessly disregarded whether it was true or not.

Sullivan was the beginning of a wholesale revision of libel law. The Court in essence abolished strict liability in libel by holding that a government official must prove a person who defamed him acted with fault. Before the *Sullivan* decision a person who proved that a false statement damaged his reputation could collect money damages from the person who defamed him, regardless of whether the defamer even knew that the statement was false or had been reasonably careful in believing it was accurate. By itself, this was more than just imposing a requirement to prove that the defamer was at fault. It was a high hurdle for public officials that the Court said the U.S. Constitution demanded to assure free speech about public affairs. Within three years the Court applied the same "actual malice" standard of fault—that is, knowing falsity or reckless disregard for the truth—to public figures (well-known people such as movie stars and famous athletes) in *Curtis Publishing Co. v. Butts,* 388 U.S. 130, 87 S.Ct. 1975, 18 L.Ed.2d 1094 (1967). Then in 1974 the Court in *Gertz v. Robert Welch Inc.,* 418 U.S. 323, 94 S.Ct. 2997, 41 L.Ed.2d 789 (1974), required that a private person defamed must prove at least that the person who defamed him acted negligently in making the false statement. Negligence, or the lack of making reasonable efforts to assure that the statement was truthful, was not as high a standard as actual malice, but it was proof of fault that had never been required in a libel lawsuit before.

The *Sullivan* decision ended a lawsuit by the elected police commissioner in Montgomery, Alabama. The commissioner, L. B. Sullivan, claimed that an advertisement signed by national civil rights leaders in the *New York Times* in 1960 falsely portrayed Montgomery police tactics against African-American college students. The false statements reflected minor deviations from what happened, but Sullivan said they nonetheless harmed his reputation. The Alabama Supreme Court upheld the decision in a trial that the *Times* libeled Sullivan, despite proof by the newspaper that it had determined that the reputation of the leading signers assured its veracity. The U.S. Supreme Court decided that the First Amendment guarantee of a free and robust press in pressing public debate needed room for error, so long as the error was not published when the person publishing it knew it was wrong or was so careless as to be reckless about whether it was true or not.

For more information

Lewis, Anthony. *Make No Law: The Sullivan Case and the First Amendment.* New York: Random House, 1991.

Wm. Osler McCarthy
Supreme Court of Texas
University of Texas Department of Journalism

Ninth Amendment is one of the most interesting, least understood, and infrequently applied provisions in the U.S. Constitution. This amendment, which has been almost interpreted out of existence, reads, "The enumeration in the Constitution, of certain rights, shall not be construed to deny or disparage others retained by the people."

For almost 175 years, the Ninth Amendment essentially was a dead letter in American constitutional law. It never figured decisively in any decision by the United States Supreme Court, and lower federal and state courts followed the lead set by the Supreme Court when it came to taking the Ninth seriously.

However, in 1965, in the case of *Griswold v. Connecticut,* 381 U.S. 479 (1965), the Supreme Court resurrected the Ninth Amendment. In *Griswold* the Court discovered the fundamental right of marital privacy in striking down a Connecticut law that banned the use of and the giving of advice on how to use contraceptives. Associate Justice Arthur Goldberg, in a concurring opinion joined by Associate Justice William J. Brennan and Chief Justice Earl Warren, wrote, "The language and history of the Ninth Amendment reveal that the Framers of the Constitution believed that there are additional fundamental rights, protected from governmental infringement, which exist alongside those fundamental rights specifically mentioned in the first eight constitutional amendments." Justice Goldberg's use of the Ninth Amendment to protect marital privacy constituted the first major judicial treatment of the Ninth.

Eight years later, in the 1973 case of *Roe v. Wade,* in which the Supreme Court decided that a woman had the fundamental right to decide whether to terminate her pregnancy, Associate Justice Harry Blackmun, in his opinion for the Court, concluded that the right of privacy, "whether it be founded in the Fourteenth Amendment's concept of personal liberty . . . or, . . ., in the Ninth Amendment's reservation of rights to the people, is broad enough to encompass a woman's decision whether or not to terminate her pregnancy."

In spite of the handful of cases in which the Ninth Amendment played any kind of prominent role in the Court's decision making, by no means do all scholars or jurists accept the invitation sent by the U.S. Constitution to take the once-forgotten provision seriously. One scholar refers to the Ninth as "that constitutional jester," and former federal judge Robert H. Bork, in his ultimately unsuccessful attempt to join the Supreme Court in 1987, told the Senate Judiciary Committee that the Ninth Amendment was "an ink blot" on the Constitution. Late Supreme Court Associate Justice Robert H. Jackson wrote in the 1950s that he could not even recall what the Ninth was about.

Clearly, the Ninth Amendment has experienced periodic if not chronic neglect. Yet, it is and should be seen as a significant part of the Constitution, our fundamental law. When he introduced in the first session of Congress in 1789 what became known as the Bill of Rights, James Madison inserted the language of the Ninth Amendment at least as a "rule of construction"; he was addressing the fear of granting away rights because an exhaustive list of all civil liberties could not be produced.

The Ninth Amendment is a constitutional command issued to those who interpret the Constitution: Search for unlisted or "unenumerated" rights. The language of the Ninth is imperative— the listing of individual rights "shall not" be taken to mean that those are the only rights that exist and are worthy of legal protection. Also, the Ninth is directed toward the future. In the words of law professor Charles Black, Jr., the Ninth Amendment "was put where it is by people who believed they were enacting for an indefinite future." With the continuing concern about privacy, especially in the information age, the Ninth Amendment is a critical reminder of some of the concerns that motivated the framers of the Constitution, especially James Madison, the father of the Constitution and the Bill of Rights.

For more information

Barnett, Randy, ed. *The Rights Retained by the People: The History and Meaning of the Ninth Amendment.* Fairfax, Va.: George Mason University Press, 1989.

Shaw, Stephen K. *The Ninth Amendment: Preservation of the Constitutional Mind.* New York: Gancano Publishers, 1990.

Stephen K. Shaw
Department of History and Political Science
Northwest Nazarene University, Nampa, Idaho

nuisance is a cause of action governing the use of one's land and the effect of that use on others' property that was established in English jurisprudence by the 13th century.

There are two types of nuisance—private and public. Private nuisance deals with the use of a person's land in such a manner that it interferes with another's use and enjoyment of his or her property. In other words, a private nuisance is a civil wrong that stems from a disturbance of rights in land; it allows the injured landowner to collect money for the damage or to obtain an injunction to compel discontinuation of the objectionable practice. For example, a company that produces a noxious odor could be required to pay damages to the adjacent landowners because the smell impairs the enjoyment of the property or could be mandated to modify its procedures to prevent the emissions.

A nuisance may be caused intentionally or negligently. An oil drilling company that routinely dumps brine (a by-product of the drilling process) onto a neighbor's field acts intentionally or knowingly, although not always maliciously. The company is aware that the field's productivity will be substantially diminished but continues the practice with full knowledge of the resulting harm. Inadvertent acts or omissions that result in failure to meet the ordinary standard of care for landowners may also result in liability. To illustrate, a landowner that does not maintain a fence may be liable if her wandering dog destroys a neighbor's prizewinning flowers or vegetable garden.

A landowner that engages in an activity that is likely to create a substantial risk of harm may incur liability solely because of that activity even though the landowner acted with reasonable care. A defense plant that stores radioactive substances can be held legally responsible for contaminated water wells despite the fact that all possible efforts to protect the local water supply from seepage were taken.

Early common law recognized only private nuisances, that is, causes of action that were tied directly to the land and applied only to persons directly affected by the act. However, by the middle of the 16th century, the tort of public nuisance had been established. A public nuisance is an activity that is dangerous to or annoys the community as a whole. It includes interference with public health (establishing conditions where insects breed), with public safety (storing explosives), with public morals (keeping illegal gambling houses), with public peace (shooting firecrackers), with public convenience (obstructing a road), or with public comfort (creating noise from planes landing at a nearby airport). Many of the public nuisances are viewed as violating the peace of the general public and are criminalized. Recently, environmental pollution has been treated as a public nuisance, subject to penalties imposed by the government on behalf of the general public, rather than as private nuisances.

The law of nuisance does not seek to remedy all petty annoyances and inconveniences. The interference must be "unreasonable" as determined by reasonable persons and must have a fairly substantial impact on the enjoyment of the neighbors' property.

For more information

Keeton, W. Page, Dan B. Dobbs, Robert E. Keeton, and David Owen. *Prosser and Keeton on The Law of Torts.* Hornbook Series. St. Paul, Minn.: West Publishing Co., 1984.

Calvi, James, and Susan Coleman. *American Law and Legal Systems,* 4th ed. Upper Saddle River, N.J.: Prentice Hall, 2000.

Susan Coleman
West Texas A&M University

O'Brien v. United States 391 U.S. 367 (1968) is the U.S. Supreme Court's most influential ruling dealing with symbolic speech, that is, the use of conduct (as opposed to words) to convey a message.

During the antiwar protests of the 1960s, opponents of the Vietnam War burned their draft cards (issued to all men potentially eligible for the draft) to demonstrate their opposition to the war. Among these protesters was David O'Brien, who in 1966 burned his draft card on the steps of the South Boston Courthouse in front of a large crowd. FBI agents in the crowd immediately arrested O'Brien, who was charged with violating a congressional statute, enacted in 1965 after the protests had begun, under which any person "who forges, alters, knowingly destroys, knowingly mutilates, or in any manner changes any such certificate" was subject to fine and imprisonment.

O'Brien readily admitted that he had destroyed his draft card but claimed that the statute had been adopted to stifle antiwar protest and that his expressive conduct was protected by the First Amendment's guarantee of freedom of speech. Although O'Brien's argument did not prevail at trial, a federal appeals court declared the statute unconstitutional and overturned his conviction. The case was then appealed to the U.S. Supreme Court.

By a 7–1 vote, the Supreme Court vote reversed the appeals court and affirmed O'Brien's conviction. Chief Justice Earl Warren, speaking for the Court, insisted that "we cannot accept the view that an apparently limitless variety of conduct can be labeled 'speech' whenever the person engaging in the conduct intends to express and idea." He proposed a four-step test for determining whether a governmental regulation of conduct ran afoul of the First Amendment. Under this test, to survive constitutional scrutiny, enactments had to: (1) be within the constitutional power of the legislature, (2) further an important or substantial governmental interest, (3) further an interest unrelated to the suppression of speech, and (4) impose incidental restrictions on alleged First Amendment freedoms no greater than were essential to achieving that purpose.

Applying this test, Chief Justice Warren concluded that because Congress had the constitutional authority to raise armies and because its requirement that potential draftees carry draft cards promoted a more efficient draft system, the statute did not violate the First Amendment. To O'Brien's contention that Congress enacted the restriction to stifle opposition to the war, Warren responded that the Court would not inquire into the motivations underlying otherwise-valid legislation.

In upholding the law, the Supreme Court also upheld O'Brien's conviction and his prison sentence. The decision discouraged opponents of the Vietnam War from burning their draft cards, although this form of protest had declined even prior to the Court's ruling. O'Brien's most lasting effect, however, was on First Amendment law. The Court's ruling confirmed that First Amendment protection was not limited to the spoken word. It also supplied standards for determining whether laws impinging on symbolic speech are consistent with the First Amendment. In the decades since *O'Brien,* the Supreme Court has applied the *"O'Brien* test" in cases involving bans on "sleep-ins" in national parks and laws forbidding flag burning and flag desecration.

For more information

Alfange, Dean. "Free Speech and Symbolic Conduct: The Draft Card Burning Case," *Supreme Court Review* (1968): 1.

Nimmer, Melville. "The Meaning of Symbolic Speech under the First Amendment," *U.C.L.A. Law Review* 21 (1973): 29.

G. Alan Tarr
Rutgers University, Camden, New Jersey

obscenity is a type of speech that has never been considered to be protected by the First Amendment.

Traditionally, obscenity deals with materials that are sexually explicit and whose purpose is to arouse sexual excitement. Over a 100-year period legislatures and courts have struggled to agree on a definition of obscenity that balances community values with First Amendment freedoms.

The Supreme Court, in the 1942 case *Chaplinsky vs. New Hampshire,* said that speech that was "worthless" as a step toward truth did not deserve First Amendment protection. One of the categories of worthless speech was speech that was lewd, obscene, or profane.

In 1867 British courts declared that the test of obscenity was "whether the tendency of the matter charged as obscene is to deprave and corrupt those whose minds are open to such immoral influences and into [whose] hands a publication of this sort may fall." This rule, known as the Hicklin rule or the bad tendency test, was the standard in English and American common law for many years. During the 20th century, several judges began to question the effectiveness of the Hicklin rule, but no revised test was forthcoming until the 1950s.

In 1957, in a case styled *Roth v. United States,* the Supreme Court issued a new test for obscenity that stated that in order to be considered obscene, material must be (1) utterly without redeeming social value, and (2) the average person applying contemporary community standards finds that the dominant theme of the material taken as a whole appeals to prurient interest. Despite several attempts to define the somewhat vague language in the Roth test, no Supreme Court majority could agree until the early 1970s.

The next stage in the saga to define obscenity came in 1973 with the case *Miller v. California.* In this case, Chief Justice Burger, on behalf of a five-person majority, issued a new test for obscenity. The steps in this test are: (1) whether the average person, applying contemporary standards of the state or local community would find the work, taken as a whole, appeals to prurient interest; (2) whether the work depicts in a patently offensive way sexual conduct specifically defined by applicable state law; and (3) whether the work lacks serious literary, artistic, political, or scientific value. This test remains the standard for defining obscenity, but problems have arisen in the application of the test to new media.

In 1978 the Supreme Court stated that the Federal Communications Commission could hold radio and television broadcasters to "decency standards" that were more restrictive than the obscenity standard (*FCC v. Pacifica*). By 1989 the Court had ruled that the decency standards were unsuitable for telephone conversations (*Sable Communications v. FCC*) and that private telephone messages had to meet the obscenity standard. In 1997 in response to Congress's passage of the Communications Decency Act the Supreme Court ruled that the Internet must meet the obscenity standard (*ACLU v. Reno*).

For many years, authorities have tried to suppress material that was deemed immoral, lewd, pornographic, or obscene. In recent years, authorities have used zoning laws and liquor licensing to suppress certain outlets for sexually explicit material. However, with the pervasiveness of computer technology, the goal of ridding society of sexually lewd material has had little success.

For more information

Tedford, Thomas. *Freedom of Speech in the United States*. State College, Pa.: Strata Publishing, 1997.

O'Connor, Sandra Day (1930–) made history on August 19, 1981, when President Ronald Reagan nominated the Arizona appellate court judge to fill the vacancy on the United States Supreme Court created by the retirement of Associate Justice Potter Stewart. Approximately one month later O'Connor's nomination was approved by the Senate Judiciary Committee by a vote of 17–0–1, and on September 21, 1981, she was confirmed as an associate justice of the Supreme Court by the U.S. Senate by a vote of 99–0. She took her seat on the nation's highest court on September 26, 1981, and became the 102nd associate justice and first female member of the Court.

Sandra Day O'Connor, native of Texas and longtime resident of Arizona, completed her undergraduate degree in economics and her law degree from Stanford University in five years, graduating third in her class of 102 students from Stanford Law School in 1952, magna cum laude and a member of the Stanford Law Review. However, she was unable to find work as an attorney upon graduation; the only job offer she received was as a legal secretary at the firm where an attorney by the name of William French Smith worked. Smith would later, as President Reagan's attorney general, screen O'Connor's nomination to the Supreme Court.

Justice O'Connor is the only member of the current Court with previous political experience in all three branches of the government. In Arizona she served in the executive branch as state

Supreme Court Judge Sandra Day O'Connor, the first woman to achieve the office, c. 1970 (Hulton Archive)

attorney general; in the legislative branch as a member of the Arizona State Senate, including a stint as majority leader of the Senate; and in the judiciary as a member of the Arizona Court of Appeals. She also is the only member of the current Court to have served in elective public office, given her time in the Arizona State Senate.

In her time on the U.S. Supreme Court, O'Connor has distinguished herself as a justice who avoids ideological extremism. She is known for practicing a restrained jurisprudence; she sees her work to be that of a judge rather than as a crusader, philosopher, or knight-errant bent on fixing all of society's ills. O'Connor's written opinions normally emphasize continuity of legal doctrine and respect for judicial precedent. She is widely viewed as one of the hardest-working and best-respected members of the Court. A few years ago she survived breast cancer surgery and returned to the bench in 10 days following the surgery.

Justice O'Connor practices a relatively conservative approach to constitutional law, especially with respect to civil liberties, with the major exception of gender discrimination. In recent years she has become the critical "swing vote" on the Court in cases involving the religion clauses of the First Amendment, affirmative action, abortion, and the death penalty. Her "undue burden" test concerning the constitutionality of laws regulating abortion has become a major approach on the Court, and her "endorsement" test with respect to the establishment clause of the First Amendment is one of the key tools used by the Court.

Justice O'Connor has been and continues to be a vital voice for American federalism during her time on the Court. She is an outspoken advocate of federalism, seeking to safeguard the reserved powers of the states under the Tenth Amendment. She is not reluctant to strike down activities of the federal government, especially legislation enacted by Congress, that in her opinion intrude upon state sovereignty.

Justice O'Connor is third in seniority on the Supreme Court, behind Chief Justice William H. Rehnquist and Associate Justice John Paul Stevens. Her name is often prominently mentioned as one who might retire from the Court soon. In 1983, speaking of her nomination and confirmation to the Court, she remarked, "Stated simply, you must be lucky."

For more information

Savage, David G. *Turning Right: The Making of the Rehnquist Supreme Court*. New York: John Wiley and Sons, 1992.

Abraham, Henry J. *Justices, Presidents, and Senators*. Lanham, Md.: Rowman and Littlefield, 1999.

Stephen K. Shaw
Department of History and Political Science
Northwest Nazarene University, Nampa, Idaho

Oklahoma City v. Dowell   111 S.Ct. 630 (1991) is the name of a series of cases seeking the elimination of a public school system divided along racial lines in Oklahoma City, Oklahoma. The *Dowell* cases followed in the path of the landmark decision in *Brown v. Board of Education* (1954) in which the U.S. Supreme Court addressed the problem of legal segregation in America's public schools.

A number of racial segregation laws had existed in Oklahoma since territorial days. These constitutional and legislative measures had created a system of social and political apartheid. Oklahoma's legalized segregation extended to the public schools. As a result, minority children were generally forbidden from attending public schools with majority white children. It was in this historical context that the Dowell family unsuccessfully petitioned the Oklahoma City School District to allow their son to attend the high school in which majority students in their residential attendance area were ordinarily assigned. A lawsuit naming the Oklahoma City School District as defendant was filed by the

Dowell family in the federal district court in Oklahoma City in 1963.

Following a trial to the court, U.S. District Judge Luther L. Bohanon concluded that the Oklahoma City School District was operating a dual school system in violation of the equal protection clause of the Fourteenth Amendment. Judge Bohanon issued orders directing the desegregation of the school district with individual schools to reflect the minority population of the district. The district court's desegregation orders were, however, immediately and actively resisted by the school district and its majority race school patrons. Judge Bohanon later ordered the school district to develop a plan for cross-district busing of students following the expert advice of Dr. John Finger, a professor at Brown University in Rhode Island.

The adopted school attendance plans and changing residential patterns were the subject of further litigation and appeals from 1977 until 1991. Judge Bohanon determined in 1977 that the Oklahoma City School District had achieved "unitary" status and that the school district was free of any trace of state-imposed school segregation. Appeals from the district court's decisions challenged the unitary schools determination and the standards used by the district court in finding such unitary status. Finally, in 1991, the U.S. Supreme Court directed the district court to conclusively determine whether or not the Oklahoma City School District was

a unitary district and one in which the original segregated conditions were no longer the prevailing conditions. The Supreme Court also accepted the less rigorous standard that had been applied by the district court in making its unitary determination. Following the directions of the Supreme Court, Judge Bohanon held that the Oklahoma City School District was unitary in operation. He then released the school district from further direct federal court supervision.

At the conclusion of the lengthy litigation, the Oklahoma City School District became one of the first in the nation to return to neighborhood schools after years of court-ordered cross-district busing of students.

For more information

Jellison, Jennifer. *Resegregation and Equity in Oklahoma City.* Cambridge, Mass.: Harvard University Press, 1996.

Orfield, Gary, and John T. Yun, *Resegregation in American Schools.* Cambridge, Mass.: Harvard University Press, 1999. For biographical information and a description of the reaction of the white community to Judge Bohanon's desegregation orders and student attendance plans, see Weaver, Jace. *Then to the Rock Let Me Fly.* Norman: University of Oklahoma Press, 1993.

Jerry E. Stephens
U.S. Court of Appeals (10th Circuit)
Oklahoma City

P

Palko v. Connecticut 302 U.S. 319 (1937) is a criminal case that raised the question of whether individuals enjoyed the same set of rights against the state governments as they enjoyed against the federal government under the U.S. Constitution.

Traditionally, the requirements of the Bill of Rights, the first 10 amendments to the U.S. Constitution, were understood to apply only against the federal government, not the states. The Fourteenth Amendment to the U.S. Constitution, however, requires that states not deprive individuals of life, liberty, or property without "due process of law." The Fifth Amendment of the U.S. Constitution prohibits "double jeopardy," putting an individual on trial for the same crime twice. The state of Connecticut allowed individuals to be tried again under certain circumstances, such as if the judge in the first trial made mistakes that damaged the prosecution.

In Frank Palko's particular case, the Connecticut courts had determined that the trial judge had improperly excluded Palko's confession and given bad instructions to the jury, and so Palko could be prosecuted again for first-degree murder despite his previous conviction

for second-degree murder. The question raised in *Palko* was whether the Fourteenth Amendment's "due process" requirement included a prohibition against double jeopardy, implicitly imposing the same constitutional obligations on the state of Connecticut that the Fifth Amendment explicitly imposed on the federal government.

Writing for a majority of the Supreme Court, Justice Benjamin Cardozo argued that the Fourteenth Amendment's due process clause did not "incorporate" all the requirements of the Bill of Rights. "Due process" only included those provisions of the Bill of Rights that were "of the very essence of a scheme of ordered liberty." Not every aspect of the Bill of Rights is essential to the preservation of liberty. The states could employ different procedures to protect individual liberty from those the federal government could under the Constitution. As a result, an individual's constitutional rights relative to the state government might be slightly different from his rights relative to the federal government. In Palko's particular case, the Court held that the Fifth Amendment's absolute prohibition of "double jeopardy" did not apply to the states. Connecticut could try individuals more than once while still satisfying the Fourteenth Amendment's due process of law requirement.

Palko was an important case in clarifying the requirements of the Fourteenth Amendment's due process clause and the rights of individuals against the states. Cardozo's argument that the Fourteenth Amendment selectively "absorbed" only those elements of the Bill of Rights that embodied "fundamental principles of liberty and justice" has been highly influential and helped frame how the Court thought about, and expanded, individual rights under the due process clause for decades. In 1969, however, the Court changed its mind about the specific holding in *Palko* and decided that the prohibition against double jeopardy is so essential to liberty as to be required by the due process clause after all. The double jeopardy rule now applies to both the states and the federal government.

For more information

Cortner, Richard C. *The Supreme Court and the Second Bill of Rights: The Fourteenth Amendment and the Nationalization of Civil Liberties.* Madison: University of Wisconsin Press, 1981.

Keith E. Whittington
Princeton University

pandering   is inducing a person by menacing or criminal intimidation to commit prostitution or knowingly arranging or offering to arrange a situation in which a person may practice prostitution.

The crime is often commonly referred to as pimping, although pimping is actually defined as living off the proceeds of, and being supported by, one or more prostitutes. Pimping often generates a greater penalty than pandering. Some jurisdictions refer to both pandering and pimping as being the same crime. The difference, set out above, is the historical distinction. The crimes had, in the past, applied only to men who exploited women through prostitution. Now they generally apply to persons who are in a position of control over the person being prostituted. Penalties are usually increased if the panderer coerces the person prostituted.

A mere panderer is one who may serve as a "broker" to arrange sexual activities for a fee, whether in money or something else of value. For example, a corporate manager who offers the sexual favors of a subordinate to a customer as an incentive to do business with the company is as guilty of pandering as is a common street thug who uses violence or withholding addictive drugs to coerce a homeless street kid to become a prostitute.

Age of the person prostituted is always a consideration where the prostitute's age is younger than the statutory age of consent and the panderer is the older. Typically, 16 years is considered the age of consent and the age of the panderer is four years or more than that of his victim. Bringing a 16-year-old of either gender into a house of prostitution to live is often prima facie evidence of pandering. There may not be a requirement that the person being procured perform a sex act for money or other value.

Keeping a house of prostitution is considered in some states to be pandering, although a defense to the criminal charge is that of demonstrating that the house was owned and managed by someone else. Even providing a motel room for the purpose of the sex act has been held to be keeping a house of prostitution.

A conviction for pandering may stand if the panderer turns custody of the person prostituted over to a third person who then exercises control for the purpose of procuring sex. In each and every case, to make an accurate determination, state and federal statutes must be consulted to make an appropriate judgment as to what constitutes a crime of pandering. As can be seen in many of the statues concerning sexual mores, definitions are expanding and contracting with reevaluation of those statutes in light of contemporary thought.

For more information
American Jurisprudence. 2nd ed. Vol. 63A, *Prostitution,*
St. Paul, Minn.: West Group Publishing.
Consult the statutes in your state.

Stanley M. Morris
Attorney at Law
Cortez, Colorado

paralegal is a person qualified through education, training, or experience to perform legal work under the direction and supervision of a licensed attorney.

Paralegals carry out many tasks attorneys would otherwise do. They work only for attorneys and not directly for the public. The paralegal profession is fairly new, and no state currently requires paralegal licensing. The titles "paralegal" and "legal assistant" mean the same thing. Some employers use their own job titles. Paralegals work for solo practitioners, small and large law firms, federal, state, and local government agencies, and corporations, and as "free-lance" paralegals on an as-needed basis.

Paralegals perform a wide variety of legal work with attorneys' supervision. State regulation of law practice prevents paralegals from representing clients in court, counseling clients, and giving legal advice. Paralegals, as an attorney directs, may investigate facts, interview clients and witnesses, research issues, draft documents, gather and organize information, draft interrogatory questions and answers, assist at depositions, assist in trial preparation, and assist at trial.

Many paralegals receive their education from a college that offers specialized courses for paralegals. Some receive their education without completing an undergraduate degree, while some receive it as part of a college undergraduate or graduate degree program. Others attend paralegal training programs after earning an undergraduate degree. Some receive on-the-job training. Although educational requirements may vary, most paralegals learn investigation, legal research and writing, and litigation. They may take classes in specific areas of law, such as torts, contracts, family law, property, and business. Paralegals also maintain and improve their skills by attending seminars and workshops.

The American Association for Paralegal Education (AAfPE) and the American Bar Association (ABA) maintain standards for paralegal education. An ABA-approved program requires at least 60 hours of classroom study. AAfPE has endorsed the ABA's standards and has developed a set of core competencies for paralegal education. These include instruction in:

(a) professional ethics,
(b) legal research,
(c) analysis of legal materials,
(d) drafting legal documents,
(e) judicial and administrative procedures,
(f) substantive areas of law,
(g) office systems and technology,
(h) oral and written communication skills.

For more information
Standing Committee on Legal Assistants
American Bar Association
750 North Lake Shore Drive
Chicago, Ill. 60611
Website: www.abanet.org

American Association for Paralegal Education
"How to Choose a Paralegal Education Program"
P.O. Box 40244 Overland Park, Kans. 66204
Website: www.aafpe.org

National Association of Legal Assistants, Inc.
1516 South Boston Street, Suite 222
Tulsa, Okla. 74119
Website: www.nala.org

Patrick K. Roberts
Daniel, Clampett, Powell and Cunningham
Springfield, Missouri

pardon is the power of a government official such as the president or a governor to forgive a person for crimes they have committed. First recognized in American jurisprudence by Chief Justice Marshall as an "act of grace," a pardon not only removes the punishment imposed for an offense but also an offender's guilt.

The power to pardon convicted criminals is one of the most ancient powers exercised by government. Usually reserved for a monarch, the power to pardon was utilized so as to provide a sense of mercy and justice to the law. Roman emperors, upon claiming the throne, issued general amnesties or specific pardons to their predecessor's enemies. During medieval times pardons were issued to rebels as an incentive to lay down their arms. In Britain the monarch utilized pardons to dilute the rigidity of the common law.

In the United States the pardoning power was granted to the president in Article II, section II of the Constitution, in which he is given the power to grant reprieves or pardons for crimes against the United States. The sole restriction on the pardoning power is the prohibition against pardoning for impeachment. The framers of the Constitution rejected proposals to allow the Senate or the judiciary to oversee the power, specifically refusing to place controls on the pardoning power.

Included among the definition of the power to pardon is granting general amnesties. These were used by presidents including Washington and Lincoln, who pardoned those involved in rebellion so as to effect reconciliation. One of the most controversial of the amnesties was granted to Vietnam War draft dodgers by President Carter. The amnesty was challenged in Court and upheld as a proper use of the pardoning power.

The range of scope of pardons has been tested frequently in the judiciary. These legal decisions, along with presidential use, have established recognizable boundaries for the power. Pardons can be used for violations of federal law. In the case of *Ex parte Grossman* (1925) the Supreme Court found pardons extended to include individuals cited for contempt of court by federal judges. Lower federal courts also upheld President Gerald Ford's pardon of Richard Nixon, with judges recognizing that the power extended to cases of future prosecution for violation of federal law.

Pardons are considered public acts that are an acceptance of guilt by the individual pardoned. But pardons do not have to be accepted by the individual in order to be in force. Pardons cannot be overridden by Congress or the court, and once given the convictions are considered wiped from the individual's record. In *Ex parte Garland* (1867), the Supreme Court ruled that President Andrew Johnson's pardon of former Confederates prohibited Congress from requiring loyalty oaths from those who sought to practice law before federal courts.

The pardoning power extends to the country's governors. Their power, though, is limited to violations of state laws. Pardons are also restricted in some states to recommendations of parole boards. In recent times, pardons have been most widely used to commute death sentences.

For more information

Moore, Kathleen Dean. *Pardons: Justice, Mercy and the Public Interest.* New York: Oxford University Press, 1989.

Steiner, Ashley. "Remission of Guilt or Removal of Punishment? The Effects of a Presidential Pardon," *Emory Law Journal* 44 (1997): 959.

Ann C. Krummel, JD
Judicial Commissioner
Circuit Court for Columbia County
Wisconsin Douglas Clouatre
Kennesaw State University

parole is the early conditional release of a prisoner after the convicted inmate has served part of a sentence. Upon the recommendation of a parole board or as a result of legislation that mandates release after a defined period of incarceration, inmates are released with specific conditions under the supervision of a parole officer.

Failure to adhere to these conditions may result in a return to prison.

Alexander Maconochie, director of the English penal colony on Norfolk Island off the coast of Australia from 1840 to 1843, is generally described as the father of parole. Early release for "good behavior" served as a deterrent for misbehavior in recognition of the developing belief that offenders were rational people who would respond to positive incentives. By 1944 every jurisdiction in the United States had some form of parole to help keep order in prisons and reduce the inmate population. The percentage of a sentence which must be served and the amount of credit that can be granted for good behavior vary from state to state.

Eligibility for parole does not guarantee an early release. Corrections and/or parole officials determine whether the inmate is ready to be released. Parole boards, sensitive to negative publicity, evaluate the probability that the inmate will reoffend. Other inmate factors that appear to influence the parole board are age, race, health, media attention, length of time served, and behavior within the correctional facility. Approximately 75 percent of inmates are granted conditional release under the supervision of a parole officer.

Since the U.S. Supreme Court has determined that parole is a privilege rather than a right, the full range of due process rights may not be available at a parole hearing. (See *Greenholtz v. Nebraska Penal Inmates*, 99 S. Ct. 2100 [1979].) Once parole is granted, however, the Supreme Court has expanded the due process rights available to parolees in jeopardy of parole revocation. (See *Morrissey v. Brewer*, 408 U.S. 471 [1972] and *Gagnon v. Scarpelli*, 411 U.S. 778 [1973].) If parole is not granted, the inmate is given a date for the next review. A board may recommend that an inmate alter his or her behavior in specific ways before the next review.

Commonly, while on parole, parolees must remain within the geographic jurisdiction to which they are paroled, report to their parole officer as specified, permit the parole officer to visit as desired, work or engage in education, avoid contact with known felons and illegal substances, and refrain from new criminal activity. Parolees may be returned to prison to complete their original sentence if they violate the conditions of parole. Two hearings must be granted before revocation, one to establish that probable cause exists to believe that the conditions of parole were violated and the second to determine whether or not parole should be revoked.

Advocates suggest that supervised parole, in addition to relieving prison crowding and providing an incentive for positive inmate behavior, helps inmates reintegrate back into the community. Some jurisdictions require the monthly payment of a supervisory fee by the parolee to transfer the cost of supervision from the community to the offender.

Opponents of parole have complained that early release has not served to reduce recidivism, deter further crime, or protect the public. Citizens and the media protest vociferously when an inmate who is released early perpetrates a violent crime. Despite the cost, many states have implemented "get tough on crime" programs, which have limited judicial sentencing discretion, indeterminate sentencing, and early release. Parole is no longer available to newly sentenced federal prisoners.

For more information

Abadinsky, Howard. *Probation and Parole: Theory and Practice,* 7th ed. Englewood Cliffs, N.J.: Prentice Hall, 2000.

Latessa, Edward J, and Harry E. Allen. *Corrections in the Community,* 2nd ed. Cincinnati, Ohio: Anderson Publishing, 1999.

Rosalie R. Young
Public Justice Department
State University of New York, Oswego

petit jury   is a trial jury for criminal or civil cases.

While most states use 12-person juries, jury size ranges from six members to 12. Federal juries have a dozen persons. The Supreme Court has upheld juries with as few as six persons in state trials, except for cases involving the death penalty. The highest court ruled that a five-person jury was too small. Many states permit a verdict to be less than unanimous. Unanimity is necessary for six-person juries. The choice of using a jury is often left to the defendant in a criminal case or the parties in a civil case.

Trial by jury is a right mentioned in the Magna Carta. Initially jurors were persons familiar with the events and persons brought to trial. Two celebrated trials that exemplified the independence of jury members were that of William Penn (in 17th-century England) and John Peter Zenger (in 18th-century New York). Both sets of jurors resisted executive branch pressures to ratify trumped up charges. At least 80 percent of criminal trials by jury take place in the United States.

An estimated 80,000 criminal jury trials take place in the United States each year. More than 1.5 million Americans per year serve as jurors. Jurors are selected from voter registration lists, lists of taxpayers, driver registrations, phone listings, welfare lists, etc. Jurors may be dismissed for cause (if the judge believes the prospective juror might have a bias in the case) and be challenged peremptorily (based on a hunch an attorney has that the juror would not be favorable to his client). The courts have made it impermissible to "strike" jurors solely because of their race. However, that still occurs.

Attorneys for both plaintiffs and defendants try to screen the panel of jurors to select those likely to learn to their side of the case and to weed out those likely to be less supportive. Sometimes they use trial consultants to advise on jury selection.

The ideal is "a jury of one's peers." Critics have faulted the jury system for reflecting community biases and for persons lacking the ability to understand complex evidence or the judge's instructions. Cases involving accidents, negligence, property, and contracts are often too complicated for laypersons. The adversary proceedings, presenting conflicting testimony, may be confusing to the average juror. Jurors often do not understand the judge's instructions. Some juries act like philanthropists (giving disproportionate monetary awards against those with deep pockets) or engage in jury nullification (deciding despite the law or the evidence).

Since the jurors are laypersons, it is up to the judge to instruct them on the law. It is alleged that laypeople may become confused over legal technicalities and cannot follow instructions or the testimony of expert witnesses. Some favor instead trial by judge or by blue-ribbon juries (made up of those with more education or sophistication) or by professional jurors (trained to function effectively, hearing one case after another). The British system has the judge select the jury. The objection to these alternatives is that it would deny to the defendants a jury of their peers. Another argument for jury independence is that it can overrule incompetent or biased judges.

The longest jury trial in U.S. history was the *McMartin Preschool* case. It began with 109 charges of sexual molestation in 1984 and concluded with not guilty verdicts in 1990. There were 124 witnesses. Six of the original 12 jurors and six alternates were excused for health or job reasons during the long, tedious trial.

Another lengthy notorious case was that of O. J. Simpson. There was a criminal trial and a civil trial. The criminal court jury had to be unanimous in finding guilt "beyond a reasonable doubt," whereas the civil court jury had to reach a verdict of guilt by a "preponderance of the evidence." In the latter only seven of the 12 jurors had to vote for the verdict.

Some states, such as Arizona, are making changes in jury rules. Judges allow jurors to take notes, question witnesses, and even discuss evidence among themselves while the trial is under way.

For more information

Abramson, Jeffrey. *We the Jury: The Jury System and the Ideal of Democracy.* New York: Basic Books, 1994.

Guinther, John. *The Jury in America.* New York: Facts On File, 1988.

Lehman, Godfrey D. *We the Jury. . . .: The Impact of Jurors on Our Basic Freedoms.* Amherst, N.Y.: Prometheus Books, 1997.

Martin Gruberg
University of Wisconsin, Oshkosh

physician-assisted suicide   is the ending of the life of a patient with the assistance of a medical doctor.

Physician-assisted suicide differs from euthanasia in that it is the patient, rather than the doctor, who commits an act which is life shortening—although the physician provides the means (such as a doctor prescribing lethal doses of painkillers or barbiturates, which the patient then takes, either orally or by injection. Thus, the doctor, while chargeable for acting in concert or accomplice liability in a criminal case (in jurisdictions where physician-assisted suicide is a crime), is a secondary actor, while the patient is the primary actor. Nevertheless, a doctor in such cases may find him/herself facing criminal charges relating to homicide and/or drug delivery. Note that in these cases the patient cannot be criminally charged, in view of the fact that suicide (and its attempt) have been decriminalized in Anglo-American law.

For purposes of this discussion, patients are assumed to have attained the age of majority and to be competent. They are also presumed to have a medical diagnosis of a terminal illness (such as cancer, which serves as the classic paradigm) with a projected life span of six months or less (the currently applied standard in American discussions, although in the United Kingdom the life span prediction utilized is frequently a period of one year). An alternative diagnosis of a chronic degenerative disease (such as AIDS, Huntington's Disease, or Alzheimer's Disease), which will inevitably result in a total loss of mental and/or physical capacities, sometimes serves as the basis of a patient request for physician-assisted suicide (this is currently not a legal standard in the United States).

In prosecutions for assisted suicide, the two central issues regard the cause of the patient's death and/or the intent of the physician. Causation, for example, must be proved to be from the physician's acts relating to the assisted suicide, and the possibility of the underlying illness causing the death must be ruled out, beyond a reasonable doubt. While this sounds relatively easy, consider the case where a patient is imminently terminally ill and is given an overdose of morphine, sleeping pills, or even, in the case of some of Dr. Jack Kevorkian's clients, noxious gases or potassium chloride (which stops the heart). A plausible argument can (and has) been made that either the illness or the drug could have caused the death, and that the cause of death cannot be proved beyond a reasonable doubt to flow from the physician's acts. Such favorable facts might even be elicited from prosecutorial witnesses, such as a medical examiner or from documented medical records.

The question of intent is most frequently the central issue in cases where a physician is being prosecuted for assisted suicide. A doctor's intent is deemed noncriminal in cases where the primary intent is to provide relief from pain or to give the patient palliative or comfort care, even if there is a secondary effect (presumably unintended) of shortening the patient's life. This principle of double effect is one which is frequently employed in defense against prosecution, most often where the death results from (shockingly) massive doses of painkillers, such as morphine. The lethality of the drugs is generally not in dispute in these cases. Furthermore, there is no reason why defenses such as lack of causation and lack of intention (which are not necessarily inconsistent with each other) cannot be raised simultaneously.

For more information

Humphrey, Derek, and Mary Clement. *Freedom to Die: People, Politics and the Right-to-Die Movement.* New York: St. Martin's Press, 1998.

Otlowski, Margaret F. A. *Voluntary Euthanasia and the Common Law.* Oxford: Clarendon Press, 1997.

Demetra M. Pappas, J.D., M.Sc.
London School of Economics and Political Science

Planned Parenthood v. Casey 505 U.S. 833 (1992) was the Supreme Court decision reaffirming but limiting the constitutional right to abortion.

During the years after *Roe v. Wade* (1973), the Court came under great pressure to overturn its ruling. It initially struck down most state-imposed limitations other than the requirement that abortions be performed in state-approved facilities and that minors obtain parental or judicial consent, but it was more divided in its abortion rights decisions by the late 1980s.

In *Casey* abortion providers challenged a 1982 Pennsylvania statute requiring a woman to wait at least 24 hours after having given her consent for an abortion, in order to obtain either parental or judicial consent if she was a minor, or to inform her husband if she was married. The Supreme Court found itself too divided to fashion a majority opinion. Justices O'Connor, Kennedy, and Souter wrote a plurality "opinion of the Court," and Justices Blackmun and Stevens agreed with enough of it to make a 5–4 majority.

The opinion affirmed *Roe's* holding that under the Fourteenth Amendment women have the right "to have an abortion before [fetal] viability and to obtain it without undue interference from the State." It recognized both that there was societal disagreement "about the profound moral and spiritual implications of terminating a pregnancy" and that the right to abortion had become part of the national fabric. "For two decades of economic and social developments," the Court said, the citizenry had come to count on the availability of abortion, and "the ability of women to participate equally in the economic and social life of the Nation has been facilitated by their ability to control their reproductive lives."

Speaking of the Court's legitimacy as "grounded truly in principle, not. . . . . compromises with social and political pressures," the plurality stated that "to overrule under fire in the absence of the most compelling reason to reexamine a watershed decision" would subvert that credibility. While it therefore affirmed what it described as the core of *Roe,* it also criticized that decision for giving too little consideration to the state's "substantial interest in potential life." It rejected *Roe's* trimester standard and instead established the rule that regulations of abortion rights were to be overturned only if they constituted an "undue burden" on the right to abort a nonviable fetus.

Applying that criterion to the Pennsylvania statute, the Court upheld the 24-hour and parental consent provisions but struck down the spousal notification requirement. It did so in a lengthy section describing the extent of domestic violence in the nation and the undue burden caused by placing some women in the position of choosing between an unwanted pregnancy or additional physical abuse.

Casey thus confirmed the constitutional right to abortion but gave the states greater leeway than had *Roe* to regulate it. As indicated in the discussion of domestic violence, the new standard was fact-based and would require a showing that a regulation was unduly burdensome if it was to be invalidated.

For more information

Craig, Barbara Hinkson, and O'Brien, David M. *Abortion and American Politics.* Chatham, N.J.: Chatham House, 1993, chap. 10.

Philippa Strum
City University of New York

plea bargaining   is an agreement in a criminal case between the attorney for the government and the attorney for the defendant.

It is estimated that more than 90 percent of all criminal cases are eventually resolved through a negotiated plea. A guilty plea results in sentencing discounts.

The court is usually not permitted to participate in such discussions and may not go along with the agreement, though some states allow judicial participation in the plea bargaining process. The prosecutor may not renege on the promise of leniency.

Plea bargaining first began to appear in American courts in the early or mid-19th century and became a major element of criminal case proceedings in the late 19th century. Prosecutors (and defense lawyers) lacked the resources to go to trial on more than a fraction of the cases. Also plea bargains eliminate the risk of jury trials ending in acquittal. For the prosecutor, plea bargaining juices up the conviction rate. He is more likely to negotiate if he has a weak case. (A guilty plea would void all prior constitutional investigatory errors.) Plea bargaining can also be used in order to obtain information about other people or factors involved in the case where the evidence is insufficient to get a conviction if tried. Judges and prosecutors want high disposition rates in order to prevent backlogs and to present a public impression that the process is running smoothly. The judge's main motive is that justice not be delayed.

There are different types of deals. One form is "charge bargaining." Here the prosecutor either downgrades (from a felony to a misdemeanor) or eliminates some of the charges in exchange for a guilty plea to the reduced charges. "Count bargaining" is a situation in which the defendant pleads guilty to one or more criminal charges and in return the prosecutor dismisses all remaining charges. "Sentence bargaining" involves a plea of guilty exchanged for a fixed lenient sentence term. The prosecutor may be conceding little if the defendant has been "overcharged"

in the first place. Defendants plea guilty to avoid a perceived risk of a more severe punishment after a trial. In states with three-strike laws, defendants are more likely to go to trial unless the new offense is bargained down to a misdemeanor.

Critics attack plea bargaining both as a form of self-incrimination made under considerable pressure and as resulting in sentences that are disturbingly lenient. Innocent persons may agree to pleading guilty to a criminal charge because of what seems an uphill effort to be exonerated at a trial. Defendants who can afford to hire a private attorney are in a more favorable position to plea bargain. Career criminals are often more effective in the process than amateurs. Critics also assert that rehabilitation is adversely affected if after the bargain the defendant has a negative perception of the judicial system.

Victims do not play a key role in plea bargaining decisions (which led California voters in 1982 to vote for a Victims Bill of Rights proposition). Police also feel left out of the process.

In Maricopa County, Arizona, plea bargaining was phased out for a wide range of felony crimes including homicide, robbery, kidnaping, sale of narcotics, burglary, rape, and child molestation. The number of trials did not substantially increase and most defendants, even without plea negotiation, pleaded guilty.

In 1975 Alaska's attorney general abolished plea bargaining. Yet defendants pleaded guilty about as often as they had before. Though the number of trials increased about 500 percent, the total remained quite small. The conviction and sentencing of persons charged with serious crimes of violence appeared completely unaffected by the change in policy. (However, over time charge bargaining returned. Without deals the system would be overwhelmed.)

For more information

Herrmann, Milton. *Plea Bargaining: The Experience of Prosecutors, Judges, and Defense Attorneys.* Chicago: University of Chicago Press, 1978.

Rosett, Arthur, and Cressey, Donald R. *Justice by Consent: Plea Bargains in the American Courthouse.* Philadelphia: Lippincott, 1976.

Martin Gruberg
University of Wisconsin, Oshkosh

Plessy v. Ferguson

Plessy v. Ferguson 63 U.S. 537 (1896), decided by the United States Supreme Court in 1896, upheld the constitutionality of mandating separate facility for blacks and whites.

The decision in *Plessy,* by a 7–1 majority, is often referred to as the "separate but equal case." The decision in *Plessy,* under the rhetoric of separate but equal facilities for the black and white races, legitimized racial segregation/domination in the United States. The decision remained law for 62 years until it was overturned in *Brown v. Board of Education.*

The case was orchestrated by a Louisiana group, which called itself the Citizens' Committee. It was agreed and arranged that Homer Plessy, a man of mixed parentage, would board a "whites only" compartment of a New Orleans train and then be taken to jail for violating the segregation laws. The case would then be tried mainly under the equal protection clause of the Fourteenth Amendment. The Citizens' Committee set out to prove that the segregation laws violated the United States Constitution.

Plessy's lawyer, Albion Tourgee, brought the case before the Supreme Court in 1896. Tourgee's brief argued that the Louisiana law of segregation violated the Thirteenth and Fourteenth Amendments in limiting "the natural rights of man."

The Supreme Court ruled 7–1 (one justice did not participate) that Homer Plessy's constitutional rights had not been violated. Justice Henry Billings Brown, writing for the majority, stressed: "We consider the underlying fallacy of the plaintiff's argument to consist in the assumption that the enforced separation of the two races stamps the colored race with a badge of inferiority. If this be so, it is not by reason of anything found in the act, but solely because the colored race chooses to put that construction upon it. . . . . The argument also assumes that social prejudices may be overcome by legislation, and that equal rights cannot be secured to the Negro except by enforced commingling of the two races. We cannot accept this proposition. If the two races are to meet upon terms of social equality it must be the result of natural affinities, a mutual appreciation of each other's merits, and a voluntary consent of individuals." The Court thus sanctioned the legitimization of racism under state law.

The sole dissenter, Justice John Marshall Harlan, recognized the consequences the decision would meet. In his dissent he stated, "Everyone knows that the statute in question had its origin in the purpose, not so much to exclude white persons from railroad cars occupied by blacks, as to exclude colored people from coaches occupied by or assigned to white persons. . . . . If a white man and a black man choose to occupy the same public conveyance on a public highway, it is their right to do so; and no government proceeding alone on grounds of race, can prevent it without infringing the personal liberty of each." Justice Harlan continued, "Our constitution is color-blind, and neither knows nor tolerates classes among citizens. In respect of civil rights, all citizens are equal before the law. The humblest is the peer of the most powerful. The law regards man as man, and takes no account of his surroundings or of his color when his civil rights as guaranteed by the supreme law of the land are involved. It is therefore to be regretted that this high tribunal, the final expositor of the fundamental law of the land, has reached the conclusion that it is competent for a state to regulate the enjoyment by citizens of their civil rights solely upon the basis of race. In my opinion, the judgment this day rendered will, in time, prove to be quite as pernicious as the decision made by this tribunal in the Dred Scott Case."

For more information

Higginbotham, Leon, Jr. *Shades of Freedom: Racial Politics and Presumptions of the American Legal*

Process. New York: Oxford University Press, 1998.

Louise Adams Tyler
Unaffiliated Scholar

Plyler v. Doe 457 U.S. 202 (1982) is a U.S. Supreme Court case that overturned a 1975 Texas statute banning students of undocumented immigrants from attending public school. Under this law, local school districts could admit these children on a tuition-paying basis but they would not be counted in the formula used to obtain state funding for the local school districts.

Plyler v. Doe and its companion case, *In re Alien Children Litigation,* are precedent cases of special significance to public school officials and children of illegal immigrants. Only a few Supreme Court cases actually raise constitutional questions about the provision of public education. *Plyler v. Doe* questioned the constitutionality of the Texas statute and its implementation in the Tyler school district, which prohibited children of illegal immigrants from attending school unless their parents paid the full cost of tuition—$1,000 per year.

Plyler v. Doe, filed in U.S. District Court in September 1977, was a class action suit on behalf of school-age Mexican children living in Smith County, Texas, who could not document that they were legally admitted into the United States. The case involved a 1975 Texas law that withheld state funds from local school districts for the education of illegal alien children. Texas law allowed local education agencies to deny enrollment to these children. The state started charging tuition to students who could not document their citizenship of the United States. In *Plyler v. Doe* U.S. Supreme Court justices examined whether illegal immigrant children have the right to a tuition-free public education. Supporters of the Texas law argued that it deterred illegal aliens from entering Texas, saved the state money, and helped the state provide better education to children of legal residents.

In its 5–4 ruling the Supreme Court reaffirmed that a free public education is not a right granted by the Constitution. At the same time, Justice William Brennan, writing for the majority, claimed that undocumented immigrants are still protected by the equal protection clause of the Fourteenth Amendment. He also argued that even illegal aliens are "persons" who are guaranteed due process of law under the Fifth and Fourteenth Amendments.

Next, Justice Brennan addressed the constitutionality of the 1975 Texas statute. He expressed particular concern for the children involved in the class action suit, claiming that they were being punished for a legal circumstance beyond their control. The Court rejected the state's argument that illegal immigrants imposed a significant burden on the Texas economy or the ability of the state to provide quality education services to its citizens. He also noted the importance of public education to the maintenance of American political and cultural heritage and to social and economic mobility. Because the denial of a free public education would deny children of illegal aliens, perpetuating a subclass of illiterates who in turn would be a burden to society, the majority of the Supreme Court struck down the Texas law as a violation of the equal protection clause of the Fourteenth Amendment. The Court held that states could not use state residency requirements to deny undocumented children access to tuition-free public education.

After the *Plyler* ruling, numerous illegal alien children started to attend public schools in the United States. Teachers, administrators, and staff of public schools have found ways to accommodate undocumented students. Controversy related to the *Plyler* ruling still exists. California's Proposition 187, passed in 1994, was in part a reaction to undocumented immigrants' access to welfare services The 1975 Texas law and Proposition 187 share commonalities, and many believed that if Proposition 187 were reviewed by the Supreme Court, it too would be declared unconstitutional.

For more information

Calhoun, Frederick S. *Supreme Court Decision on Right to an Education.* Arlington, Va.: Educational Research Service, 1982.

Cooper, Phillip J. "Plyler at the Core: Understanding the Proposition 187 Challenge," *Chicano-Latino Law Review* 17 (fall 1995): 64–87.

Salinas, Norberto P. "Proposition 1987 and *Plyler v. Doe.*" In *Legalis,* (spring 1977.) http:www.wabash.edu/bop/legalis/issues/1997/Spring/187.html (September 11, 2000).

Ruth Ann Strickland
Professor, Department of Political Science
and Criminal Justice
Appalachian State University

police power   is the power of states and their subdivisions to protect the public's health, safety, welfare, and morals. These responsibilities are inherent attributes of sovereignty. The states may exercise the police power in any way they see fit, so long as they do not violate a provision of their own state constitution or the U.S. Constitution.

The police power is used to protect public health when a state requires that its school children be vaccinated against disease, when it establishes a system of public hospitals, when it regulates the practice of medicine, or when it prohibits cigarette sales to minors.

The state promotes public safety by enacting and enforcing its criminal code, by maintaining fire departments, and by licensing automobile drivers. Some states require drivers to wear seat belts and motorcycle operators to wear helmets. States also have adopted comprehensive building codes. Firearms regulation, including laws that prohibit the possession of guns near schools, are examples of the exercise of the police power. So are the protective actions of child welfare offices.

When the state legislates in the area of marriage and divorce, it is promoting the public welfare. It promotes public welfare when it bans billboards from its highways. When the state enacts zoning laws, it is doing so in order to promote the good of the entire community—even though in doing so it may limit the latitude of some property owners. When a state wishes to build a highway, it may advance the general welfare by requiring landowners to sell their property to the state.

Public morality is the subject of a great deal of state attention. State and local governments regulate, and sometimes prohibit, the sale or consumption of liquor. States also establish penalties for the use of drugs. Some states allow gambling; others do not. Some states ban sales of obscene materials; others do not. Nearly every state outlaws prostitution.

The federal government is a government of delegated powers. Since the Constitution does not grant police power to the United States, it may not legislate in the areas of health, safety, welfare, and morals unless if it does so pursuant to a power specifically enumerated in the Constitution or implied by it. Because of its power to regulate interstate commerce, for example, the federal government has been able to establish a minimum wage, thus enhancing employee welfare. On the other hand, when Congress gave women the right to sue their assailants in federal court, it had to justify that effort to protect women's health and safety by pointing to the aggregate effects of such violence on interstate commerce. The Supreme Court found the connection too fanciful and declared the law unconstitutional (*United States v. Morrison* [2000].)

For more information

Beer, Samuel H. *To Make a Nation: The Rediscovery of American Federalism.* Cambridge, Mass.: Harvard University Press, 1993.

Berger, Raoul. *Federalism: The Founders' Design.* Norman: University of Oklahoma Press, 1987.

Hamilton, Alexander, et al. *The Federalist Papers.* New York: Penguin, 1987.

William H. Coogan
University of Southern Maine

political corruption refers to the abuse of power by government leaders who exploit their positions of public trust for financial gain, personal ambition, or immoral purposes.

In the United States, political corruption has been an issue of public concern since the revolutionary period when colonists rebelled against what they perceived to be a corrupt British government intent on depriving Americans of their rights. To guard against corruption, the Constitution of the United States contains numerous checks and balances and provides for impeachment of federal officers.

More often than not, political corruption in the United States has resulted from "influence peddling," which refers to the "buying" of influence over elected officials (usually through campaign contributions) in order to affect the content of legislation or government policies. During the late 19th and early 20th centuries (what historians refer to as the Progressive Era), widespread political corruption inspired a broad-based reform movement that produced enduring changes in U.S. political life. The major reforms of that era sought to eliminate the tremendous political influence enjoyed by wealthy individuals, especially owners and managers of large corporations. For example, many states instituted methods of direct democracy such as the initiative, referendum, and recall in an effort to make political leaders accountable to voters. Civil service procedures were implemented in the federal government to reduce the control of political parties over government agencies. In addition, state and federal legislation was passed to limit corporate influence in electoral politics. However, this problem proved difficult to remedy.

Although Congress passed the Tillman Act in 1907 to prohibit corporations from making direct contributions to candidates running for federal office, not a single conviction for illegal corporate contributions had been obtained by 1971, when the Federal Election Campaign Act (FECA) was passed. The Federal Corrupt Practices Act of 1925 had imposed additional constraints on labor and business campaign contributions but was filled with loopholes and exceptions, thus proving to be equally ineffective. Until the 1970s, federal election laws were so vague and enforcement so lax that there was usually little difficulty in hiding campaign contributions. The FECA, as amended in 1974 and 1976, changed this state of affairs by requiring strict financial disclosure requirements for candidates in federal elections and by imposing limits on the amount that individuals, political parties, and political action committees (PACs) could contribute to a candidate. Although FECA prohibited corporations and unions from giving directly to candidates in federal elections, it did not prevent corporate and union PACs from making such contributions.

In 1978 the Federal Election Commission issued a ruling that left a loophole for "soft money," which refers to (unlimited) contributions that individuals or organizations can make to state and local political parties (technically, for various nonfederal party expenditures), that can be spent by the parties to help finance elections of candidates in federal elections, a result that is clearly inconsistent with the intent of FECA's contribution limitations. Many political analysts and activists believe that "soft money" corrupts the political process by allowing special interests to spend huge sums to influence elections and "buy" politicians. As of 2000, Congress had not remedied this problem despite the fact that many of its members had been elected on the promise of reforming campaign finance laws.

For more information

Lewis, Charles. *The Buying of Congress: How Special Interests Have Stolen Your Right to Life, Liberty, and the Pursuit of Happiness.* Washington, D.C.: Center for Public Integrity, 1998.

Sorauf, Frank J. *Inside Campaign Finance: Myths and Realities.* New Haven, Conn.: Yale University Press, 1994.

Scott R. Bowman
California State University, Los Angeles

polygraph test is a scientific method developed to determine the truthfulness of a person.

Polygraphs are most typically associated with use by the legal community, such as law enforcement, to narrow a list of suspects in a crime. It can also be used in business as a way for employers to verify information or determine drug use, or by private citizens engaged in civil disputes. The accuracy and reliability of polygraph examinations has been established for many years. It is important, however, that such examinations be performed by experienced, trained, and licensed professionals using proper equipment.

The polygraph instrument measures physiological body functions that control blood pressure, pulse rate, respiration, perspiration, and muscle movement and will register changes when a person is being untruthful. Lying triggers an emotional reaction, which in turn causes a physical reaction, such as an increase or decrease in blood volume and heart rate, and changes in respiration and perspiration. All of these changes can be measured when a person is being deceptive. These reactions will be different from a person's *normal* body patterns. Measurements are collected on a series of charts, which are then analyzed by an examiner who renders an opinion on truthfulness.

An average polygraph examination will take two to three hours. A great deal of time is spent on pretest preparation by the examiner with the person to be tested. This preparation is crucial to the accuracy of test results. Before the actual examination takes place, the examiner will fully explain the process including: the equipment and how it works, the test person's legal rights, and the issue for the examination. The examiner reviews with the person all questions that will be asked during the examination. It is critical to the integrity of the test that any areas of concern or issues making the person feel uncomfortable be discussed with the examiner in the pretest phase of the examination. It is not unusual for the person being tested to be nervous. The pre-examination interview and preparation should reduce the level of nervousness, and being nervous will not affect the overall test results. The examiner assesses the emotional state and medical condition of the person and makes adjustments that might otherwise affect the test results. Once the pre-examination assessment is completed, and if the examination proceeds, the examiner attaches measuring devices to the person. These consist of two elastic tubes across the upper chest and abdomen, one or two metal plates on the end of the fingers, and a blood pressure cuff around the upper arm. All of these attachments are completely painless to the subject. During the testing phase, the same questions will be asked of the person three or four times to produce multiple charts for analysis.

While the polygraph technique is highly accurate, errors can occur for a variety of reasons, including: examiner error in preparation of the subject, lack of training and experience of the examiner, equipment malfunction, and countermeasures from the subject being tested. For the most part, studies show polygraph tests are highly accurate. A subject cannot "fool" properly functioning equipment and an experienced examiner. If a subject *knows* they are lying, their body patterns will react and the lie will be detected. If there is ever a question that an error has occurred, a second examination or a different examiner may be used for a second opinion.

Polygraph results can only be released to authorized persons. The use of polygraph testing is frequently challenged in court. Some states and federal jurisdictions allow polygraph testing and the results to be admitted in court, others limit their use, and still others prohibit polygraph tests entirely.

For more information
Abrams, Stanley. *The Complete Polygraph Handbook,* Lexington, Mass.: Lexington Books, 1989.

Carol A. Day
Victim/Witness Services Coordinator
of the District Attorney's Office
Eau Claire County, Wisconsin

pornography   is a word given to material of a sexually explicit nature. Often people use the words *pornographic* and *obscene* synonymously but there is a difference. Obscene materials are unprotected by the First Amendment and must conform to the test laid out by the Supreme Court in *Miller v. California* (1973). Pornography is a generic term used to describe a host of sexually explicit material that may or may not be legally obscene. Pornographic materials are protected by the First Amendment.

Explicit images of sexuality are as old as prehistoric humans. Images of sexual behavior have been found in all early civilizations, including the golden age of Athens and the Roman Empire. Since before the Middle Ages most societies have made a distinction between works of art that contained nudity and works that were designed to arouse lustful thoughts.

In the United States the first federal law aimed at regulating the sale of pornographic material was the Comstock Law, passed in 1873. The law, named after antipornography crusader Anthony Comstock, made it a crime to send through the mail not only "obscene" material but any information regarding birth control or abortion. Both the post office and the United States Customs office were enlisted in the effort to prevent books, pictures, or any other sexually explicit material from being sold. Works by such celebrated authors as Daniel Defoe, Voltaire, Walt Whitman, James Joyce, and D. H. Lawrence were prosecuted as pornographic.

As society changed, attitudes about sexually oriented material changed as well. An underground economy in sexually arousing images started at least by the 1860s and continued until the 1950s. In 1953 the underground became more mainstream with the publication of *Playboy* magazine and its many imitators. In 1970 the President's Commission on Pornography concluded that pornography caused little harm and recommended a decriminalization approach. However, in the 1980s several factors led to more conservative attitudes about the regulation of pornography.

By the 1980s some feminist groups began to charge that sexually explicit material, even if not legally obscene, was contributing to the denigration and inequality of women. They attempted to pass laws to redefine pornography as a civil rights violation and allow women to sue distributors for damages. In *American Booksellers Association v. Hudnut* the Seventh Circuit Court of Appeals struck down an Indianapolis ordinance along these lines.

In 1984 the Court ruled that sexually explicit materials involving minors did not have to meet the standards of obscenity. The case *Farber v. New York* allowed governments to criminally prosecute makers and distributors of any sexually explicit materials that involved minors.

In 1986 a new presidential commission on pornography was convened. After much controversy the so-called Meese Commission (named for Attorney General Edwin Meese), issued a report arguing for greater enforcement of obscenity laws and new laws protecting children. The Meese Commission was so divided and riddled with controversy that its report had little impact.

In recent years, advances in technology have created new concerns for those attempting to regulate sexually explicit material. The Internet is replacing adult theaters and bookstores and efforts to regulate pornography on the Internet have proved difficult. However, efforts to suppress images of sexuality will continue no matter what forms those images take.

For more information
Hixson, Richard. *Pornography and the Justices: The Supreme Court and the Intractable Obscenity Problem.* Carbondale: Southern Illinois University Press, 1996.

Charlie Howard
Tarleton State University

Powell v. Alabama   287 U.S. 45 (1932), or the Scottsboro Boys Case, established the principle that a state must provide effective assistance of counsel to indigent persons accused of capital crimes.

In March of 1931 a freight car carrying two groups of youths—one black and one white—ambled slowly across Alabama. A fight broke out, and the white boys were thrown off the train. The black boys remained on board, along with two white girls. When the train stopped, the blacks, ranging in age from 12 to 20, were arrested, brought to the county seat in Scottsboro, and accused of raping the white girls. The charge carried the death penalty.

The judge set the trial date for April 6, 12 days after the alleged offense. Because Alabama law required the appointment of counsel for indigent defendants in capital cases, the judge appointed "all members of the bar" to help the defendants through their arraignments. It remained unclear what role the local bar would play in the trials themselves. On the morning of April 6 a lawyer from Tennessee appeared to help defend the accused. He had not had an opportunity to prepare their defenses. One member of the local bar stepped forward to help. The defendants faced hostile, all-white juries. All were convicted on the strength of the two girls' testimony. The trials lasted just one day.

The cases were eventually appealed to the U.S. Supreme Court, which asserted that the role of the criminal defense lawyer was fundamental to a fair trial. The Court commented on the youth and illiteracy of the defendants; the fact that they had been held incommunicado while awaiting trial; the racial hostility of the community; the frantic pace of the arraignments, trials, and convictions; the trial judge's failure to assign specific responsibility for representing the defendants to any particular lawyer; and the capital nature of the charges. These factors taken together, the Court said, meant that the defendants had not had effective assistance of counsel and were thus deprived of the due process of law guaranteed by the Fourteenth Amendment. The convictions were overturned, and new trials were scheduled.

The defendants were retried three times. Four were eventually convicted and imprisoned. The last of the Scottsboro Boys was released from prison in 1950.

Years later one of the girls retracted her testimony. The other had given such conflicting and unlikely testimony that it is probable that she perjured herself.

Powell v. Alabama stood for the principle that the state must provide effective assistance of counsel in capital cases in order to fulfill its responsibilities under the Fourteenth Amendment's due process clause. *Powell* was the first in a line of cases that extended the right to counsel to defendants in every stage of a criminal case, from police interrogation to the appeal of a conviction.

For more information

Carter, Dan T. *Scottsboro: A Tragedy of the American South,* rev. ed. Baton Rouge: Louisiana State University Press, 1979.

Russell, Katherine K. "The Racial Hoax as Crime: The Law as Affirmation," *Indiana Law Journal* 71: (1996): 593–621.

William H. Coogan
University of Southern Maine

prayer in public schools   is not constitutionally permitted when it is led, initiated, or sponsored by the school, its officials, or students because it is a violation of the First Amendment establishment clause. However, the First Amendment does not prevent students or other individuals at school from praying on their own.

The First Amendment states that "Congress shall make no law respecting an establishment of religion." While there is a lot of controversy as to what it means to establish a religion, in a series of decisions commencing in the 1960s the United States Supreme Court has ruled that school-sponsored or initiated prayer in public schools violate the First Amendment prohibition on the government sponsoring or endorsing a religion.

In *Engel v. Vitale*, 370 U.S. 421 (1962), the Supreme Court declared unconstitutional a New York State Board of Regents rule that required a public school day to begin with a reading of a "nonsectarian" prayer read in class. Two years later in *Abington v. Schempp*, 374 U.S. 203 (1963), the Court struck down a Pennsylvania rule requiring 10 verses of the Bible to be read at the start of every school day, even though any child who objected to the reading could be exempt from the reading upon written parental request. In both cases the Court reached the same conclusion—that these activities were clearly violations of the establishment clause. In *Engel v. Vitale*, the Court clarified its reason for its decisions:

> [T]he State's use of the Regent's prayer in its public school system breaches the constitutional wall of separation between Church and State. We agree with the contention since we think that the constitutional prohibition against laws respecting an establishment of religion must at least mean that in this country it is no part of the business of government to compose official prayers for any group of the American people to recite as a part of a religious program carried on by the government (370 U.S. 421, 425).

Both of these decisions were very controversial. Supporters of them argued that the government, including schools, does not have the right to sponsor religion or force others to believe something they do not accept. In the first case it would be a violation of the establishment clause; in the second instance, it would be a violation of freedom of conscience. Critics claimed that the Supreme Court was trying to kick "God out of the schools," and they sought ways to get around these opinions. However, the Court has continuously reaffirmed this ban on school-sponsored prayer in schools.

In *Wallace v. Jaffree*, 472 U.S. 38 (1985), at issue was an Alabama law that mandated that each school day would start with a moment of silence. This moment could be used for prayer, silent meditation, or whatever the students preferred. The Court struck this law down as unconstitutional, noting that the records of the Alabama legislature indicated that the sponsor of this law authorizing the moment of silence saw this bill as a first step toward returning prayer to public schools.

In *Lee v. Weisman*, 505 U.S. 577, (1992), the Court ruled unconstitutional the delivery of a state-written nondenominational prayer at public junior and high school graduation ceremonies. This case tested the applicability of school prayer cases to school activities that take place outside of the normal school day. Finally, in *Santa Fe Independent School District v. Doe*, 530 U.S. 290 (2000), student-led, student-initiated invocations prior to football games, as authorized by policy of public school district, were held to violate the establishment clause ban on prayer in public schools. In this case, the invocations were given over a school's public address system by a speaker who was elected by majority of student body. The invocations took place on government property at government-sponsored, school-related events. The Court stated that the expressed purposes of school prayer policy encouraged selection of a religious message that the audience would perceive as being delivered with the school district's approval.

Overall, the Supreme Court has consistently struck down efforts to permit school-sponsored prayer in public school, both during school and in school-sponsored events. However, contrary to critics, these decisions did not ban all prayer in public schools. Students, for example, still may pray anytime they want on their own.

For more information

Levy, Leonard W. *The Establishment Clause: Religion and the First Amendment*. New York: Macmillan, 1986.

Schultz, David. "Church-State Relations and the First Amendment." In David Schultz, ed. *Law and Pol-*

itics: Unanswered Questions. New York: Peter Lang Publishing, 1994, pp. 235–56.

David Schultz
Hamline University

precedent is a court ruling that is relied upon in future cases.

Phrases in statutes and constitutions are often open to interpretation. A person accused of a crime is entitled to "due process of law." If the meaning of that phrase were to be determined anew each time a judge presided over a criminal trial, there would be no rule of law as we know it. Law must be predictable in order for society to function.

When a matter requiring interpretation of a provision in a statute or constitution comes before a court—or in those instances in which there is no relevant statute or constitutional provision—judges will examine previously decided cases. If the facts in an earlier case are similar to those in the present one, the judge will apply the earlier ruling. The doctrine requiring judges to do so is called *stare decisis,* or "let the decision stand."

Stare decisis operates in two ways. First, lower courts must always follow the decisions made by higher courts in the same jurisdiction. Thus, state supreme courts and the U.S. Supreme Court are the final arbiters of the meaning of state and federal law, respectively.

Second, judges rely on precedents decided by other judges at their own levels, but they do so with a freer hand. Nineteenth-century courts deciding who owned the branches of a tree whose trunk was on one side of a property line, but whose mulberries contaminated the pond on the other, determined that the boundaries of a person's real estate extended from its outline on the surface of the earth upward to the outermost reaches of the universe. Then came airplanes. Soon judges redrew the upper boundaries closer to the treetops.

Judges do follow precedents most of the time, even after they have become shopworn. There are several reasons for doing so. First, many of society's institutions—the family, business, government, contractual relations, and land ownership—could not function without stability in the meaning of the laws. Second, individuals order their affairs—wills, trusts, gifts—on the basis of their expectation that the laws governing inheritance and the interpretation of the language in wills is going to persist after their deaths. Third, the use of precedents reduces the burden on judges by making it unnecessary for them to ponder the meaning of every provision of the law open to competing interpretations each time they hear a new case. Fourth, the U.S. Constitution requires courts to apply the law equally to everyone. Therefore the law must mean the same thing in every case. Fifth, by following precedent judges reassure litigants that the law is impartial. As U.S. Supreme Court Justice Harlan Fiske Stone said, "It is often more important that a rule of law be settled than that it be settled right."

For more information

Currier, Thomas S. "Time and Change in Judge-Made Law: Prospective Overruling," *Virginia Law Review* 51 (1965): 235–38.

Hart, Henry M., and Sacks, Albert M. *The Legal Process: Basic Problems in the Making and Application of Law,* tentative ed. Cambridge, Mass.: Harvard University Press, 1958.

Levi, Edward. *An Introduction to Legal Reasoning.* Chicago: University of Chicago Press, 1947.

William H. Coogan
University of Southern Maine

pregnancy disability act also commonly referred to as the Pregnancy Discrimination Act, or PDA, mandates that pregnancy-related disabilities be treated the same as any other medical disability.

Under PDA, discrimination based upon the fact that a woman is pregnant constitutes illegal sex discrimination. The PDA was passed by the U.S. Congress and signed into law by President Jimmy Carter in 1978 as a direct response to two U.S. Supreme Court decisions in the mid-1970s that had held it legally permissible for company-paid health insurance plans to exclude pregnancy, miscarriage, and childbirth from their coverage.

The first of these two cases, *Geduldig v. Aiello* (1974), involved a constitutional challenge to a California disability insurance plan that covered many health problems common to men and women and some applicable only to men, such as prostatitis and circumcision. It specifically excluded, however, any coverage of normal pregnancy and delivery. Carolyn Aiello argued that, since only women can become pregnant, the pregnancy exception embodied in the California insurance plan discriminated against women in violation of the equal protection clause of the Fourteenth Amendment to the U.S. Constitution ("No state . . . shall deny to any person within its jurisdiction the equal protection of the laws"). The Supreme Court, however, held that the program did not exclude anyone from benefits eligibility because of gender. Indeed, the justices concluded, the distinction made was not between men and women, but between pregnant women and nonpregnant persons. The Court, consequently, applied its lowest level of constitutional scrutiny and found that the plan did have a "reasonable basis" for excluding pregnancy: high costs.

The second of the two cases, *General Electric Company v. Gilbert* (1976), was similar to *Geduldig* with one exception: Rather than challenging the program on equal protection grounds, Martha Gilbert challenged it based on Title VII of the Civil Rights Act of 1964, which makes it illegal to engage in employment practices that discriminate on the basis of "race, color, religion, sex, or national origin." Again, however, the Supreme Court held that General Electric's disability benefits plan, which like that in *Geduldig* excluded pregnancy but included

disabilities common to both men and women and some particular to men, such as a vasectomy, was not a sex classification per se, but one between pregnant women and nonpregnant persons. Whereas the former would have violated Title VII, the latter did not.

Almost immediately after the *Gilbert* decision, a coalition of more than 300 feminist, union, and church organizations calling itself the Campaign to End Discrimination against Pregnant Workers began lobbying Congress to amend Title VII. That is, if the Supreme Court held that Title VII did not include protection for pregnancy-related disabilities, these groups would convince Congress to amend the act so that such disabilities would be included. As noted above, they were successful in 1978 when Title VII was amended by the PDA to say that "The terms 'because of sex' or 'on the basis of sex' [in Title VII] include, but are not limited to, because of or on the basis of pregnancy, childbirth, or related medical conditions." In 1983 the Supreme Court conceded that their previous distinction between pregnant women and nonpregnant persons had been overridden by Congress when the Court held in *Newport News Shipbuilding & Dry Dock Co. v. Equal Employment Opportunity Commission* that "discrimination based on a woman's pregnancy is, on its face, discrimination because of her sex." The PDA applies not only to health benefits plans but to all employment decisions, including compensation and the terms and conditions of employment generally.

In 1987 the Supreme Court answered one of the questions unanswered by Congress in its passage of the PDA. Clearly the PDA prohibits discrimination against pregnant employees; however, could the individual states provide preferential treatment to pregnant employees? In *California Federal Savings & Loan Association v. Guerra* a California statute allowed pregnant employees, but not other disabled employees, up to four months of unpaid leave for disability due to the pregnancy. The Court held that this preferential treatment did not violate the PDA. The purpose of the PDA, the Court concluded, was to prohibit discrimination based on pregnancy; states could, however, provide preferential treatment in such cases if they chose to do so.

Further protecting pregnant women and their spouses, Congress in 1993 passed and President Bill Clinton signed into law the Family and Medical Leave Act, allowing pregnant women and their husbands to take up to 12 weeks of unpaid leave from their jobs for the birth of their child.

For more information

Goldstein, Leslie Friedman. *The Constitutional Rights of Women: Cases in Law and Social Change.* Madison: University of Wisconsin Press, 1988.

Mezey, Susan Gluck. *In Pursuit of Equality: Women, Public Policy, and the Federal Courts.* New York: St. Martin's Press, 1992.

Michael W. Bowers
University of Nevada, Las Vegas

preponderance of evidence   is the standard of proof used to decide most civil lawsuits.

Decision making by judges and juries is guided by standards of proof or degrees of belief that govern various types of cases. In a civil lawsuit, the plaintiff is generally required to prove all the elements of his or her claim by preponderance of the evidence. Although standards of proof are generally a matter of state or federal statutory and case law, the constitutional issue of due process of law must also be considered. As noted by the U.S. Supreme Court, standards of proof allocate the risk of error between the litigants. In ordinary civil suits involving money damages, the preponderance of evidence standard allocates the risk of error equally between the contending parties.

In cases in which one party's loss in the case of error would be more serious than mere loss of money, the standard of proof may need to be set higher. "Because the 'preponderance-of-the-evidence' standard results in roughly equal alloca-

tion of the risk of error between litigants, we presume that this standard is applicable in civil actions between private litigants unless 'particularly important individual interests or rights are at stake'" (*Grogan v. Garner,* 498 U.S. 279 [1991]). Thus, a litigant facing deportation or loss of parental rights, for example, is entitled to the higher "clear and convincing evidence" standard.

In the great majority of civil cases, however, proof of the elements of the respective claims must satisfy the preponderance of the evidence standard. In trials or hearings, the judge must instruct the jury how to apply the standard or apply it him/herself in a bench trial. Although standards of proof are difficult to summarize in words, there is more agreement among courts about the meaning of preponderance of evidence than about the meaning of the more rigorous standards of clear and convincing evidence and beyond a reasonable doubt.

In 1997 the Supreme Court explained that: "the burden of showing something by a preponderance of the evidence simply requires the trier of fact to believe that the existence of a fact is more probable than its nonexistence before he may find in favor of the party who has the burden to persuade the judge of the fact's existence" (*Metropolitan Stevedore Co. v. Rambo,* 521 U.S. 121). According to many courts, preponderance of the evidence means that the plaintiff has shown that his or her version of events is "more likely true than not." One federal court elaborated by observing that: "The plaintiff carries the burden of preponderance of evidence if she proves facts that make the scales tip, however slightly, in favor of the proposition she seeks to establish" (*Camus v. Supermarkets General Corp.,* 903 F.Supp. 668, S.D.N.Y. 1995). In civil litigation, due process of law provides protection for litigants based on the seriousness of the loss that they face.

Many people may be surprised to find that the loss of $10 million is considered to be less serious than the loss of parental rights. However, the requirement of proof by preponderance of evidence in civil cases in which "mere money" is at stake, no matter how great the amount may be, demonstrates that private litigants in such cases are accorded the minimum protection against risk of error.

For more information

Orloff, Neil, and Stedinger, Jery. "A Framework for Evaluating the Preponderance-of-the-Evidence Standard," *University of Pennsylvania Law Review* 131 (April 1983): 1159–74.

Celia A. Sgroi
State University of New York, Oswego

preventive detention   is the holding in custody of someone charged with a crime while the judicial process is still not concluded.

If a defendant poses a danger to the community (for example, by committing serious crimes) or a danger that the accused would flee in order to evade trial, judges may deny bail before trial and after conviction. All states and the District of Columbia use preventive detention in juvenile courts. Juveniles are detained if they represent a "clear and immediate danger to themselves and/or to others." (The criteria varies from "a danger," to "a substantial danger," to "a significant peril," to "an unreasonable danger." Is the danger to "the community" or to "any other person"? Is it from "physical harm" or "serious crime"?)

Under the traditional system of bail, poor defendants often were detained while awaiting trial. Some judges deliberately set unaffordable bail in order to detain some defendants, especially if there was likelihood of flight.

Some students of criminal justice argue that incapacitation of chronic offenders for a long time would lead to a meaningful reduction of the crime rate. They use the analogy of quarantining those with contagious diseases or confining psychotics. In the late 1980s Juan Segarra Palmer, a Puerto Rican New Yorker, charged with conspir-acy and planning a robbery, was incarcerated for more than 28 months.

Critics attack preventive pretrial detention as contrary to the legal principle that the accused person should be presumed innocent until proved otherwise. Attorneys worry that it is hard to get a fair trial after being officially declared "dangerous." Some of those detained would have lost employment and reputation in the community and had their families undermined. Conditions of confinement would be as bad as or worse than those under which convicted felons would be imprisoned. Those who are detained are less able to assist their counsel in preparing for trial. Pretrial detention may itself increase recidivist tendencies in detainees. Their experience may make them hardened, embittered, and more savvy as criminals. Even if they are acquitted, they have been stigmatized.

In 1970 there was a preventive pretrial detention statute for the District of Columbia. In 1984 Congress passed the Bail Reform Act, authorizing federal judges to deny bail to criminal suspects who might pose a threat to the community. More than 34 states followed suit. The Supreme Court upheld the federal law with Chief Justice Rehnquist denying that detaining a person amounted to the government imposing punishment under the Fifth or Eighth Amendment. Justice Stevens dissented, arguing that by the standard of dangerousness, why should defendants be released even if they are acquitted?

For more information

American Bar Foundation. *Preventive Detention: An Empirical Analysis.* Chicago: American Bar Foundation, 1972.

Martin Gruberg
University of Wisconsin, Oshkosh

prior restraint   is a doctrine allowing censorship of materials prior to publication.

The concept of prior restraint elaborates on Blackstone's analysis that "the liberty of the press is indeed essential to the nature of a free state; but this consists in laying no previous restraints upon publications, and not in freedom from censure for criminal matter when published."

In *Near v. State of Minnesota,* 263 U.S. 697 (1931), the Supreme Court heard the case of a Hennepin County attorney seeking to enjoin the publication of articles making serious accusations against public officers. The defendant, Near, claimed that the articles were not malicious, scandalous, or defamatory and invoked the protection of the due process clause of the Fourteenth Amendment. The Court held that while, "protection even as to prior restraint is not absolutely unlimited," it is "better to leave a few of its [the press's] noxious branches to their luxuriant growth, than, by pruning them away, to injure the vigor of those yielding the proper fruits."

The issue of prior restraint came under review again with *New York Times v. United States,* 403 U.S. 683 (1971). Justice Black declared that the government cannot "halt the publication of current news of vital importance to the people of this country," as it sought to due when the *New York Times* sought to publish the Pentagon Papers of the Vietnam War. The Court did, however, leave open the possibility of prior restraint in the case of a threat to national security. Various justices thought prior restraint of publication possible to prevent "inevitable harm" (Brennan), to protect the national interest (Stewart), or to defend national defense and foreign policy (Harlan, Burger, Blackmun). The Court rejected on the one hand the claim that classified information automatically deserves prior restraint and on the other that the First Amendment barred all prior restraint.

The only instance where a court has permitted the prior restraint of a newspaper was in *United States v. Progressive, Inc.,* 467 F. Supp. 990 (W.D. Wis. 1979), where a federal court enjoined a magazine from publishing the directions on how to make a hydrogen bomb. The government feared that publishing the recipe for the bomb would threaten national security because a terrorist might then be able to make a nuclear weapon and threaten the United States. Eventually a federal court of appeals decision lifted the injunction on publication of the directions and the *Progressive Magazine* published the hydrogen bomb recipe in an article.

Overall, for prior restraint of any publication, the government has a "heavy burden" to prove.

For more information
Rudenstine, David. *The Day the Presses Stopped. A History of the Pentagon Papers Case.* Berkeley: University of California Press, 1996.

Paul Kuritz
Bates College

prisoners' rights necessarily are limited by legal imprisonment, but prisoners retain some constitutional rights. After a person has been convicted of a crime and imprisoned, he is deprived of his freedom, as well as other constitutional rights incompatible with the needs of prison security and the penal objectives of deterrence and rehabilitation. For example, although inmates retain the fundamental right to marry, the right of access to the courts, the right to due process, the right to free exercise of religion, and the right to equal protection of the laws, these rights are subject to limitations imposed by the prison's legitimate interests.

Prisoners may sue prison officials for civil rights violations (under, for example, 42 U.S.C. section 1983, one of the federal civil rights statutes). Civil rights suits filed by prisoners are governed by the Prison Litigation Reform Act of 1995, which limits when prisoners may proceed *in forma pauperis* (that is, without paying court fees) and bars inmates from bringing section 1983 suits for damages based on only mental or emotional injuries. The act also created a "three strikes" provision for frivolous,

Old cell block, Sing Sing Prison (LIBRARY OF CONGRESS)

malicious, or legally insufficient claims filed by prisoners.

Actions of prison officials that limit an inmate's constitutional rights are generally valid if they have a rational relationship to legitimate penological interests. In determining the reasonableness of a prison regulation, a court will consider whether (1) there is a valid, rational connection between the regulation and penological interests; (2) there are alternative ways for inmates to exercise their constitutional rights; (3) accommodating the inmates' rights will negatively affect guards, other inmates, or prison

resources; and (4) there is an obvious alternative to the regulation.

The Eighth Amendment protects prisoners from "cruel and unusual punishments" and is violated where inmates are subjected to the unnecessary and wanton infliction of pain. In claims involving excessive force, a prisoner must allege that the force was applied maliciously and sadistically. In claims challenging a prisoner's conditions of confinement, the prisoner must allege that officials were deliberately indifferent to his health or safety, meaning that officials were aware of and disregarded a substantial risk of serious harm. In both kinds of cases, the prisoner also must allege a sufficiently serious injury.

Inmate civil rights actions have brought about institutional reform of prisons. Beginning in the 1960s, federal courts used the Eighth Amendment to address appalling conditions in then-existing state prison systems through institutional reform. Although courts traditionally had left prison administration to prison officials, the deplorable conditions in many prisons led to court-ordered change. By the end of the 1970s, prisons in nearly half the states were operating under court orders mandating certain minimum levels of acceptable conditions.

For more information

Calhoun, Emily. "The Supreme Court and the Constitutional Rights of Prisoners: A Reappraisal." *Hastings Constitutional Law Quarterly* 4 (1977): 219.

A Jailhouse Lawyer's Manual, 5th ed. *Columbia Human Rights Law Review,* 2000.

Prof. Kathryn R. L. Rand
University of North Dakota School of Law

privileges and immunities clauses are located in Article IV and in the Fourteenth Amendment of the Constitution. Article IV states that: "Citizens of each State shall be entitled to all Privileges and Immunities of Citizens in the several States." Essentially, the privileges and immunities clause protects individuals from the possibility of state encroachment upon rights associated with "national unity." However, these protections apply only to those rights that are considered fundamental and essential to the concept of national citizenship. These fundamental rights center around protecting freedom of commerce. For example, Article IV protects the right of citizens to be employed, to practice a chosen profession, and to engage in business relationships generally.

Even if the state were to infringe on an individual's protected right under the privileges and immunities clause, it may still be found a valid exercise of state power if the state could meet a two-pronged test. First, the state must show that the restriction placed on the individual is an attempt to remedy a "peculiar source of evil" that the person from out-of-state represents. Second, the state must show that the solution employed is "substantially related" to the evil against which they are trying to protect their citizens. In addition, the offending statute, or practice, in question must be shown to be the least restrictive method for carrying out the state's objective.

The protections afforded by the privileges and immunities clause should not be confused with those protections guaranteed to citizens of the United States by the equal protection clause. Several differences between the protections afforded by each are key. First, the equal protection clause can be applied to businesses as well as individuals. Second, the standard under the privileges and immunities clause is much more strict than that of the equal protection clause. Unlike the privileges and immunities clause, which requires that the state restriction be closely tied to the stated purpose of combating a "peculiar source of evil," the equal protection clause only requires that the statute in question be held to a standard of "mere rationality." The equal protection clause is more expansive in terms of those that can claim protection under it, but it applies a standard that is easier for states to meet than that required by the privileges and immunities clause.

The Fourteenth Amendment protects rights of national citizenship, such as the right to travel from state to state without restriction. The Fourteenth Amendment states, in part: "All persons born or naturalized in the United States, and subject to the jurisdiction thereof, are citizens of the United States and of the state wherein they reside. No state shall make or enforce any law which shall abridge the privileges or immunities of citizens of the United States. . . ." Soon after its adoption in 1868, the

Supreme Court was faced with a challenge to the Fourteenth Amendment.

Faced with increased pollution of the Mississippi River by New Orleans slaughterhouses, the Louisiana legislature created a state-run slaughterhouse and forced all butchers in the New Orleans area to use those facilities. The butchers sued, arguing that the legislature was preventing them from pursuing their right to conduct business, a right guaranteed by the privileges and immunities clause. The Supreme Court did not agree. In what came to be known as the *Slaughter-House Cases,* the Court ruled that the only privileges that the Fourteenth Amendment protected against were those "which owe their existence to the Federal Government, its National character, its Constitution, or its laws." Article IV already granted those rights, and the Court's decision suggests that the privileges and immunities clause of the Fourteenth Amendment was redundant and offered no more protection than that already enjoyed by citizens.

However, this interpretation of the privileges and immunities clause does not appear to be shared by current members of the Supreme Court. In 1992 the state of California amended its Aid to Families with Dependent Children (AFDC) program by limiting new residents to only those benefits that they would have received in their previous state during their first year of residence in California. The Supreme Court ruled that the changes to the AFDC program initiated by California restricted the right to travel of citizens, thus violating the equal protection clause of the Fourteenth Amendment. In addition, the California program denied newly arrived residents the same privileges and immunities that other residents of the state enjoyed. The Court relied on the reasoning provided in the *Slaughter-House Cases,* holding that their status as citizens of the United States and of a particular state entitled them to the same treatment as long-time citizens of California.

For more information
Gunther, Gerald, and Sullivan, Kathleen M. *Constitutional Law,* 13th ed. Mineola, N.Y.: Foundation Press, 1997.
Schwartz, Bernard, ed. *The Fourteenth Amendment: Centennial Volume.* New York: New York University Press, 1970.

Scott Comparato
Southern Illinois University, Carbondale

probable cause   refers to the quantity of evidence that must exist in order for an arrest or search for evidence conducted by law enforcement to be considered reasonable. Moreover, the Fourth Amendment's prohibition against "unreasonable searches and seizures" requires that a search or seizure conducted by police in the absence of probable cause is unreasonable and, therefore, unlawful. In addition, the United States Supreme Court has interpreted the Fifth Amendment to require that a person may be charged with a crime in federal court only when probable cause exists to believe that the defendant is guilty. Courts in a majority of states observe a similar rule in reviewing prosecutors' decisions to bring formal charges against criminal defendants.

The Fourth Amendment to the U.S. Constitution states that a warrant authorizing either an arrest or a search of a person's property shall be issued only "upon probable cause. . . ." Thus, the Fourth Amendment reveals a general preference, though not a command, that arrests and searches occur only after law enforcement officials present to a judge or magistrate evidence sufficient to merit the issuance of a warrant. Prior to issuing an arrest warrant, a judge or magistrate must be satisfied that probable cause exists to believe that the suspect is guilty of the criminal activity alleged by law enforcement officers. Like arrest warrants, a judge or magistrate may issue a search warrant only when probable cause exists to believe that the places to be searched contain specific items regarded as contraband or evidence of a crime.

Often, delaying an arrest or search until a warrant can be secured severely burdens the processes of investigating crimes and apprehending suspects. Recognizing this, the Supreme Court has allowed that an arrest or search may be reasonable despite the absence of a warrant. As a result, many arrests and searches are conducted without warrants. Following a warrantless arrest of a suspect or warrantless search that uncovers evidence of a crime, law enforcement officers must present to a judge or magistrate evidence that probable cause existed prior to the arrest or search. This proceeding is often referred to as a first appearance. Thus, whether done before or after an arrest or search, courts evaluate police activities to determine if the intrusion resulting from a search or seizure is supported by an appropriate factual basis.

It is important that the Supreme Court has recognized a number of exceptions to the general rule that searches are allowed only upon a showing of probable cause. Among these exceptions are searches conducted immediately following a lawful arrest, instances when persons consent to a search of their clothing or property, and occasions when police officers perform a "frisk" or "pat-down" search of a suspect's outer clothing. Searches following an arrest may be conducted without probable cause—the presence of probable cause to justify the arrest is itself sufficient to merit a search of the suspect's body and clothing. Further, probable cause is not required when a suspect willingly and knowingly consents to a search of his or her person and belongings. "Frisks" are, by definition, not searches for evidence of a crime. Rather, a "frisk" is merely a search of a person's outer clothing, conducted for the purpose of determining whether the suspect possesses a weapon or other item that could be used to harm the officers. Performance of a "frisk" procedure does not require probable cause; police

may "frisk" a suspect upon a "mere suspicion" that the person is armed and dangerous.

Students of the law are often disappointed to learn that there exists no precise statement of the number or type of facts that constitute probable cause. The Supreme Court determined that probable cause exists when the "totality of the circumstances" lead a reasonable person to the conclusion that criminal activity is occurring, has occurred, or is about to occur. A "hunch" or mere suspicion that a criminal activity is afoot does not constitute probable cause.

It is important to note that although probable cause must exist in order for an arrest to be lawful, probable cause alone is not sufficient for an arrest to be considered reasonable. In addition to being supported by probable cause, lawful arrests are those during which suspects are not subject to unreasonable treatment by law enforcement. Moreover, the Supreme Court has interpreted the Fourth Amendment to mean that reasonable arrests include both probable cause and the use of acceptable police procedures.

For more information

Peltason, J. W. *Understanding the Constitution,* 14th ed. New York: Harcourt Brace College Publishers, 1997.

Samaha, Joel. *Criminal Procedure,* 4th ed. Belmont, Calif.: Wadsworth Publishing Co., 1999.

Bradley J. Best
Austin Peay State University

products liability is the area of tort law addressing the liability of manufacturers and sellers of products for injuries to consumers and others that result from the use of those products.

Entities that make or sell products may be liable to pay money damages to people injured by those products. Products liability is a species of tort liability. Until the 1950s, the standard of liability applicable to sellers of products resembled the standard that generally governed negligence lawsuits. In ordinarily negligence actions, such as those arising out of automobile accidents or failure to maintain real property in a safe condition, the plaintiff who brought the claim would have to prove that the person or entity that injured him had behaved unreasonably, that is, had not acted like a reasonable person would have under the circumstances.

As products liability law has developed from the 1950s until the present, liability is not based on the negligence of the manufacturer or seller of the product, but on the existence of a defect in the product. Thus, under strict products liability, product manufacturers or product sellers are liable for injuries caused by any product that was defective, even when they had acted reasonably in making and selling the product. The impetus for the development of strict products liability was the difficulty that plaintiffs faced in proving that the product manufacturers and sellers had acted negligently, even when the product they sold created unreasonable risks of physical injury to consumers and bystanders. This problem became even more serious as the system of distribution of products became increasingly more complex.

Justice Roger Traynor set forth the justification for creating strict products liability in his separate opinion in the case of *Escola v. Coca-Cola Bottling Co.,* decided by the California Supreme Court in 1944.

The courts have identified four types of product defects: manufacturing defects, design defects, warning defects, and warranty defects. A product has a manufacturing defect if it either does not perform as the manufacturer intends it to or if it fails to perform as identical products perform. Thus, if one in every million soft drink bottles explodes, the exploding soft drink bottle has a manufacturing defect—it does not perform as expected, nor does it perform like other soft drink bottles. A product has a design defect when its design is unreasonably dangerous. In such cases the product performs as expected and like other identical products, but the risks of injury from the product exceed the benefits that the product provides. A product has a warning defect if the product labeling either does not adequately advise the user of its danger or does not properly instruct the user of the product's safe use. A product has a warranty defect if it does not perform up to the standards set forth in the warranty provided with the product.

Every entity in a product's distribution chain, including manufacturers, wholesalers, retailers, and sometimes component parts manufacturers is subject to strict products liability, as are companies that rent products (such as cars). Providers of services (such as physicians), sellers of used products, and those who do not sell products as a business are generally not subject to products liability—they remain liable for negligence, however. Not only may purchasers of products bring products liability claims to obtain compensation for their injuries but others harmed by a product defect, such as pedestrians injured by defective automobiles, can bring strict products liability actions as well.

Strict products liability has proven controversial and has long provided a prime target for groups who pursue tort reform. Many states have enacted statutes modifying judicial doctrines regarding some aspects of products liability, but generally, such statutes have not significantly altered the broad outlines of liability described above.

For more information

Dobbs, Dan B. *The Law of Torts.* St. Paul, Minn.: West Group Publishing, 2000.

Phillips, Jerry J. *Products Liability in a Nutshell,* 5th ed. St. Paul, Minn.: West Group Publishing, 1998.

Shapo, Marshall S. *The Law of Products Liability.* 2nd ed. Salem, N.H.: Butterworth Legal Publishers, 1990.

Bernard W. Bell
Professor of Law
Rutgers Law School, Newark

prosecutor   typically refers to the legal counsel who represents the government in criminal proceedings. This type of prosecutor is also referred to as a public prosecutor. Public prosecutors can also be employed by the government in civil trials, although it is more rare. Alternatively, the term *prosecutor* can also refer to a private individual who initiates and participates in a legal action (referred to as a private prosecutor).

The first definition, however, is far more common. In this case, the prosecutor is the attorney employed by the government to act on behalf of the government in a criminal proceeding. Their job is to initiate and carry on legal proceedings against those accused of committing crimes. Prosecutors can work either for the state or federal government. Prosecutors in the federal courts are known as U.S. attorneys, while those employed by the state are known as district attorneys or state's attorneys. In essence, prosecutors, whether they are employed by the state or federal government, are supposed to serve the public by prosecuting those that have done something to injure the public.

Prosecutors are essential in criminal trials in the United States. The United States has an adversarial legal process which means that, at least in theory, the judge acts as a neutral decision maker between two opposing parties. It is up to the lawyers for either side to develop evidence and legal arguments. It is the prosecutor's job to present and argue the government's legal position and to prove the defendant guilty beyond a reasonable doubt.

Each federal judicial district in the United States has at least one U.S. attorney and at least one assistant U.S. attorney. The number of assistant U.S. attorney varies in each district according to the size of the population they serve. U.S. attorneys are appointed to office by the president and confirmed by the Senate. Their appointment lasts for a period of four years; however, reappointment is common. These positions are often seen as political rewards or stepping-stones into further political life.

In contrast, prosecutors at the state level, also called district attorneys, are mostly elected officials. District attorneys employ a number of assistant district attorneys to work on trials. Assistant district attorneys are mostly recent graduates from law school who use their positions to gain experience litigating. Many of these prosecutors will later move into private practice or on to criminal defense work. Some will move up to positions as judges or as U.S. attorneys.

Prosecutors, whether employed by the state or federal government, are not only lawyers for the government but they are also law enforcement officials. Many scholars have argued that the prosecutor is the most powerful official in the criminal courts. Prosecutors have influence at virtually every level of the criminal process. They help determine which defendants are prosecuted, which types of plea bargains are struck, which charges are filed, and the severity of the sentence imposed.

Prosecutors exercise wide discretion when making these choices, and their decisions can drastically affect those accused. For example, two of the most important decisions a prosecutor faces are whether or not to prosecute and what charges to file. Many factors may enter into the decision of whether or not to prosecute, including the sufficiency of the evidence, the importance of the case, and the availability of resources. If they do decide to prosecute, they must also then decide on which charges to file. Often, prosecutors will file as many charges as possible in order to have a strong ground on which to plea bargain. Which charges they file and whether or not they plea bargain can depend on several things, including the seriousness of the defense, the accused's past criminal record, and the strength of the prosecutor's case. Regardless, the prosecutor has and must use a large amount of discretion, which will impact those who stand accused.

For more information
Carp, Robert A., and Stidham, Ronald. *Judicial Process in America*. Washington D.C.: CQ Press, 1990.
Neubauer, David. *Judicial Process: Law Courts, and Politics in the United States*. New York: Harcourt Brace College Publishers, 1997.

Joy A. Willis
Graduate Researcher
Michigan State University

psychopath   is the term most often used to categorize what is more properly known in medical terminology as antisocial personality disorder. The word *psychopath* is often used interchangeably with the term *sociopath,* and in popular culture, it often is embodied by an individual who callously disregards social convention and morals, and pursues habitual criminal behavior.

However, the reality is that individuals with antisocial personality disorder are suffering from a mental illness. As defined by the American Psychiatric Association, individuals with antisocial personality disorder possess certain character traits, often initially exhibited at a young age, which help to diagnose the disorder in adulthood.

Those who suffer from the disorder will more likely be male than female and will exhibit strong signs of the disorder at the onset of adolescence, with a gradual decrease in symptoms as the individual gets older. Individuals who have the disorder may display the following traits: (1) failure to adhere to societal norms of acceptable behavior, which is often, but not always, manifested in criminal activity; (2) operating a high level of deceitfulness in interactions with others; (3) consistent irresponsibility in dealing with others and/or ventures such as school or career; (4) impulsive behavior with little thought or care for the consequences of such behavior; and (5) the inability to empathize with the feelings and emotions of others. The driving force behind an individual with the disorder is what will be of the most benefit to the individual. There is little concern, nor, more importantly, an understanding or comprehension, of the concepts that govern normal human social interaction with other individuals.

There is no concrete evidence that psychopaths as a whole display less than normal intelligence. In fact, a psychopath's level of intelligence may lead to his success in being able to manipulate individuals around him, as he is able to project a sincerity to victims that has no basis in real emotion. An individual with the disorder may be able to interact quite effectively on a superficial level with others; it is only upon closer examination of the individual's words and actions that contradictions may be spotted.

Those suffering from antisocial personality disorder often have difficulty forming any true intimate emotional relationships, whether it be with family or friends. Many also find themselves, as a result of their main disorder, suffering from added disorders, such as depression, anxiety, or paranoia. In addition, other behaviors, such as drug addiction, alcoholism, sexual promiscuity, or aggression and criminal behavior may be triggered in part by antisocial personality disorder.

While there is no known cure for the disorder, certain facets, or accompanying behaviors, such as anxiety, may be controlled by drug therapy.

For more information
American Psychiatric Association. *Diagnostic and Statistical Manual of Mental Disorders,* 4th ed. Washington, D.C.: American Psychiatric Association, 1994.

Raquel J. Gabriel
Associate Professor
Reference/Government Documents Librarian
City University of New York School of Law

public defender   is the individual paid by the state to represent indigent criminal defendants.

Public defenders represent individuals who cannot afford to pay for their own defense in criminal proceedings.

The United States relies on an adversarial form of justice. That is, the judge acts as a neutral party in a criminal case, while the prosecutor and defense attorney must argue evidence and the law before a jury. The state is always represented by a prosecutor who is paid by the state. Defendants pay defense attorneys to represent their interests and defend them against the charges of the state. Unfortunately, not all defendants can afford legal representation. Prior to 1963, some of these defendants faced trial without legal council.

In 1963 the United States Supreme Court held in *Gideon v. Wainwright,* 372 U.S. 335, that states are required to provide attorneys to indigent defendants in felony cases. In *Gideon* the Court recognized that the Sixth Amendment to the U.S. Constitution protects a defendant's right to counsel. The Court also recognized that court systems in the United States are so complex that justice may not be possible for defendants who do not have access to legal council. In 1972 the Court expanded its decision in *Argersinger v. Hamlin,* 407 U.S. 25, to cover misdemeanors for which incarceration is the sentence. States are currently therefore required to provide counsel to those defendants who cannot afford their own counsel in cases involving a sentence of jail time. Some states have gone even further, providing counsel to all indigents charged with a misdemeanor.

The Supreme Court, however, did not dictate how the states must set up their programs to provide lawyers for indigent defendants. As a consequence, there are three main ways of providing representation for indigent defendants: assigned counsel, the contract system, and the public defender (although some states use a combination of these three methods). The assigned counsel system is practiced most often in suburban areas (those areas with fewer criminal trials) and involves lawyers signing up with the state to do indigent defense work. The state then rotates these lawyers and pays them either on a case by case basis or on an hourly basis, although some attorneys do not request any fee and consider it a professional responsibility. The fairly new contract system provides indigent legal representation by having the state contract for a specific period of time with a law firm to provide legal services at a set price.

The most popular method for providing legal counsel to those who cannot afford it, however, is that of the public defender. A public defender's sole responsibility is to represent indigent defendants. These attorneys are appointed to their positions rather than elected and are state employees on a salary full-time. The public defender system is widely used in large cities and, although less so, in medium-sized cities.

There are benefits to this system. Public defenders, because they concentrate solely on criminal law, are able to keep up with new developments in the area that would most help their clients. In addition, the state has a population of lawyers theoretically available immediately when an indigent is charged. Finally, some proponents argue that lawyers paid full-time to represent indigents will pay more attention to them than court-appointed attorneys.

On the other hand, critics of the public defender system have argued that public defenders are too closely aligned with the state. Because they are continuously working with the same personnel (judges and prosecutors), there is more of an incentive for them to want to cooperate with those personnel. Unfortunately, this cooperation may not be in the interest of their client—the accused. Even more importantly, critics argue that public defenders are often underpaid and overworked. As a result, some argue that the attorneys attracted to public defender work, aside from a few dedicated people who are willing to work under poor conditions, are those attorneys who are not as competent. And those attorneys who are competent and committed may not have the experience or the time to devote to their clients.

For more information

Neubauer, David W. *Judicial Process: Law Courts, and Politics in the United States.* New York: Harcourt Brace College Publishers, 1997.

Tarr, G. Alan. *Judicial Process and Judicial Policymaking.* Boston: West/Wadsworth, 1999.

Joy A. Willis
Graduate Researcher
Michigan State University

punishment   is the suffering or legal price the state exacts for violating its laws.

Unlike civil suits that seek compensation, criminal law imposes hardship for wrongdoing. Punishment's unpleasant consequences are inflicted with condemnation by responsible agents upon an offender who is believed to have understood the nature of the offense and its moral character at the time of the misconduct.

The purpose of punishment is most commonly claimed to be reformation, deterrence, restraint, or retribution. Each has its defenders and detractors. Reformation as a form of punishment seeks to teach the individual not to engage in offensive behavior again. However, many believe that rehabilitation does not work.

Deterrence seeks to teach others not to do the penalized behavior. Heavy fines, imprisonment, and the death penalty are offered as object lessons to the general public often via the news media's reporting of criminal sanctions in order to deter others.

Restraint seeks to prevent an offender from having an opportunity to repeat his or her conduct. Long imprisonment, life without parole, and the death penalty all prevent for a duration, or permanently, repetition of the crime. Castration has also been occasionally practiced as a means to prevent repetition of sex offenses.

Retribution is simply vengeance. It may be cloaked in phrases such as "paying a debt to society." A large majority of American citizens believe that it is morally right to hate criminals, and as a consequence vengeance is also a strong feature in the criminal code of most U.S. law.

Punishment can take many forms. Misdemeanors can be punished with forfeiture, fines, restitution, jail time for less than a year and a day, and other forms. Felonies can be punished with forfeiture, heavy fines, imprisonment for more than a year in a penitentiary, and even with death.

Punishment that is disproportionate to the offense may be set aside. Some punishments outlawed by both the U.S. Constitution and the states are excessive fines, or cruel and unusual punishments. Punishments that are barbarous (branding), degrading (public stocks), or vicious (pressing) are usually considered as cruel and unusual.

Capital punishment has had a long history in American jurisprudence. Arguments that it is inherently cruel have not been widely accepted. However, the general trend is strongly toward lethal injection and away from hanging, electrocution, or the gas chamber. All the latter were adopted in earlier times as more humane forms of capital punishment.

Hidden sanctions often exist for the convicted after a prison sentence has been served. They may be required to register their presence, be denied the right to vote, drive a car, work for the government, serve in the military, or practice many licensed occupations, to name just a few such limitations.

Alternatives to punishment may include probation, parole, or community service.

For more information

Loewy, Arnold H. *Criminal Law in a Nutshell.* St. Paul, Minn.: West Group Publishing, 2000.

Gerber, Rudolph J., and Patrick D. McAnany. *Contemporary Punishment: Views, Explanations, and Justifications.* Notre Dame, Ind.: University of Notre Dame Press, 1972.

A.J.L. Waskey
Dalton State College

punitive damages is a sum of money awarded to a plaintiff in a civil lawsuit not to compensate for harm suffered but to punish the defendant's wrongful conduct and deter similar conduct in the future.

Punitive damages are only awarded in about 6 percent of civil cases in the United States, but they attract a great deal of public attention and have been the focus of much controversy in the final decades of the 20th century. Punitive damages are only allowed in civil cases, and they are not favored by the law. It is generally agreed that great caution should be used in awarding them and that they should only be granted if it will promote the public good. In some states, punitive damages are only available where expressly permitted by statute.

Although the rules governing punitive damages vary greatly from state to state and the entire issue is the subject of continuing debate, there is at least a majority of agreement on some basic principles. Punitive damages, also called exemplary damages, are not compensatory in nature and are not available as a matter of right. There is no independent cause of action for punitive damages, which may only be sought in cases where there is actual damage to the plaintiff. The purposes of punitive damages are punishment and deterrence, and in that sense they resemble a criminal fine more than civil compensation. The primary justification for punitive damages is public policy. According to the New York Court of Appeals, punitive damages "is a social exemplary 'remedy', not a private compensatory remedy" (*Garrity v. Lyle Stuart, Inc.,* 40 N.Y.2d 358 [1976]).

In cases involving punitive damages, the focus is on the character of the defendant's conduct rather than the nature and extent of the plaintiff's injury. Punitive damages may not be awarded where the defendant is guilty of only ordinary negligence, no matter how much harm the conduct caused. Instead, they are limited to cases in which the defendant acted with malice, gross negligence, or fraud and deceit. Thus, if 200 airline passengers were killed as a result of the ordinary negligence of an airline, punitive damages would not be available, whereas the conscious decision by the airline to deny a passenger a ticket for no good reason might justify the award of punitive damages.

Standards such as "malice" and "gross negligence" have been interpreted in many different ways. In general, conduct is considered to be malicious when a person's actions are willful, wanton, and deliberate, or show extreme recklessness or conscious disregard for the rights of others. In a case where the defendant acted with malice, any reasonable person would know that acting in that way would cause harm. Gross negligence is understood to be a conscious failure to use due care or conscious indifference to the rights or welfare of the victim. In both instances, the defendant's actions demonstrate the existence of a malign intent rather than a mere lapse of judgment.

Despite the fact that punitive damages awards are relatively rare, exceptional cases involving extremely large awards have been widely publicized and have contributed to demands for reform of the punitive damages remedy. Indeed, despite a 1996 ruling from the U.S. Supreme Court regarding excessive punitive damages awards, the total of the highest verdicts continues to rise. In *BMW of North America, Inc. v. Gore,* 517 U.S. 559, the Supreme Court overturned a $2 million punitive damages award in an Alabama case involving failure by the auto company to inform the buyer of a new car of minor repairs to the paint job. The Supreme Court called the award "grossly excessive" and held that it violated the constitutional guarantee of due process of law. In *BMW v. Gore* the Supreme Court stated that three factors must be considered in determining whether a punitive damages award is excessive: (1) the degree of reprehensibility of the defendant's conduct, (2) the ratio between the punitive damages awarded and the actual harm to the plaintiff, and (3) the existence of any state sanctions that could be imposed for comparable misconduct. Despite this decision, some recent punitive damages awards have risen into the billions of dollars. In 2000, a jury in a Florida class-action lawsuit against a tobacco company awarded $145 billion in punitive damages (*Engle v. R.J. Reynolds Tobacco Co.*, No. 94-8273, [Cir. Ct. Dade Co.]).

Such staggeringly large awards have fueled the movement to reform punitive damages, even though studies have found that large punitive damages awards are exceptional and that most are modest and bear a reasonable relationship to the compensatory damages awards. A major focus of protests has been large punitive damages awards in business contract cases involving fraud and deceit, many of which do not involve any physical harm to anyone. Critics also claim that punitive damages awards are too unpredictable, lack a reasonable relationship to the amount of actual damages awarded, provide an undeserved windfall to plaintiffs, and vary too much from case to case and jurisdiction to jurisdiction, making punitive damages awards a kind of lottery. Some states have enacted legislative caps on punitive damages awards and are considering establishing uniform guidelines to govern their application. Others have called for the U.S. Supreme Court to refine the punitive damages guidelines it set forth in *BMW v. Gore.*

For advocates of tort reform, punitive damages are held up as a prime example of how the U.S. civil justice system is "running wild," while defenders of the remedy argue that they are necessary to deter outrageous conduct that harms people and the environment. It seems highly probable that the rules governing punitive damages will undergo some serious reform in the future.

For more information

BMW of North America, Inc. v. Gore, 517 U.S. 559 (1996).

Peck, Robert S. "Punitive Damages 'Crisis' Is a Myth, Experts Say," *Trial* 32.12 (December 1996): 14.

Van Voris, Bob. "$145 to Send a Message," *National Law Journal* (July 31, 2000): A1.

Celia A. Sgroi
State University of New York, Oswego

R

racial profiling   is the stopping of individuals or suspected criminals based upon their race or skin color.

Racial profiling involves the claim that police are detaining individuals in traffic enforcement simply because of their race or skin color. Often times the pretext for the stopping is the claim that the individual fits some profile of a person wanted for a crime. Or individuals are stopped in their car on the basis that they have committed a minor traffic infraction. Evidence that racial profiling exists began to appear in the media in the middle to late 1990s when newspapers revealed that the New Jersey State Police were using racial profiles to stop and detain motorists. Since then, statistics gathered in other areas, such as New York City, Denver, Minneapolis and St. Paul, Minnesota, as well as other cities and states, demonstrate that people of color are disproportionally more likely to be stopped than are whites.

Those who point to profiling say that the issue raises important legal questions regarding racial discrimination. These issues may arise out of either the equal protection or due process clauses of the Fourteenth Amendment. In fact, racial profiling is sometimes referred to as "driving while black." The singling out of individuals solely based upon their race or skin color is unconstitutional. The statistics on who is stopped by the police is pointed to as evidence of either de jure or de facto discrimination.

Others deny that the statistics reveal discrimination. Instead, these stops are not motivated by race but are simply a sign of aggressive policing and efforts to apprehend criminals. Police are thus stopping individuals on the basis of reasonable suspicion that a crime has been committed, or that the person stopped is a criminal. In fact, in *Brown v. City of Oneonta,* 195 F.3d 111 (2nd Cir. 1999), a federal court ruled that in some cases race could be used as a reason to justify an investigatory stop.

While racial profiling has focused mostly on police stops, other statistics reveal that whites and people of color are treated very differently in the entire criminal justice system. This means that the initial stopping of people of color makes it more likely that they will face additional interaction with the criminal justice process. All of these instances could be considered examples of racial profiling.

For example, whites are more likely to be offered bail than people of color. Whites are much less likely to receive prison than people of color, and whites are much less likely to be prosecuted—and aggressively—for drug offenses than are people of color.

In the area of the death penalty, several studies have confirmed that whites are less likely to be placed on death row than people of color and that whites are much less likely to receive the prison sentence if they murder a person of color than if an African American murders a white person. For example, in 2000, 37 states, the military, and the U.S. government imposed the death penalty for a variety of crimes, with more than 40 percent of those on death row being African American. (African Americans are 12 percent of the population.)

From 1930 until 1993, 3,859 persons in the United States were executed. Of those, 2,066 were black. During this same time period, of 455 people executed for rape, 405 were black. From 1976 until 1993, 176 people in the United States have been executed. Of those, 40 percent were black. Even though whites and blacks are victims of homicide in about equal numbers, 80 percent of those sentenced to death and executed have been individuals who killed whites.

A 1990 Government Accounting Office (GAO) study entitled *Death Penalty Sentencing* concluded that "[t]hose who murdered whites were found to be more likely to be sentenced to death than those who murdered blacks." GAO and other studies by the American Bar Association, Congress, and the Death Penalty Information Center have found that those who murder whites are far more likely to be sentenced to death that those who murder blacks. Similarly, a 1994 House Judiciary Subcommittee on Civil and Constitutional Rights report indicated that prosecution of the 1988 federal Anti-Drug Abuse Act appears racially tainted. In general, of those prosecuted under the act, 75 percent have been white and 24 percent black. But in death penalty prosecutions, 78 percent have been black and 11 percent white.

Overall, racial profiling or racial disparities exist on several levels in the criminal justice system, raising questions regarding the explanation and possible remedy for this differing treatment.

For more information

"Civil Rights Commission Cites Improper Use of Racial Profiling by New York City Police," *Jet* 98 (July 3, 2000): 4.

Derbyshire, John. "In Defense of Racial Profiling: Where Is Our Common Sense?" *National Review* 53 (February 19, 2001).

Walker, Samuel, et al. *The Color of Justice: Race, Ethnicity, and Crime in America.* Belmont, Calif. Wadsworth, 2000.

David Schultz
Hamline University

R.A.V. v. City of St. Paul 505 U.S. 377 (1992) is a landmark United States Supreme Court First Amendment case that held unconstitutional a city ordinance prohibiting certain types of speech or expression based upon its content. The case began as a juvenile prosecution for violation of a bias-motivated crime ordinance of the city of Saint Paul, Minnesota.

In the early morning hours of June 21, 1990, R.A.V., a white juvenile, and several other white teenagers set fire to a large cross which they had made from chair legs and placed on the lawn of a black family that lived across the street from the house where R.A.V. was staying. The prosecutor had several laws from which to choose in prosecuting the juveniles. The prosecutor decided to proceed under a Saint Paul city ordinance that made it a crime to put on public or private property a symbol, an object, or graffiti, such as a burning cross or Nazi swastika, which one knew or should have known would cause in other persons anger, alarm, or resentment because of race, creed, color, religion, or gender. The specific crime was disorderly conduct.

In response to a rash of Nazi swastikas being painted on public and private property, the Saint Paul City Council in 1990 enacted the ordinance under which R.A.V. and the others were prosecuted. At that time the council expressed its outrage against the type of conduct described in the ordinance and stressed that it wanted to send a very strong message that conduct of this nature would not be tolerated. The solution was to make such conduct a criminal violation punishable by fine and/or imprisonment.

At the trial court R.A.V.'s attorney asked the court to dismiss the charge against R.A.V. because the conduct prohibited by the ordinance was protected by the right to freedom of expression guaranteed by the First Amendment to the United States Constitution. The trial court agreed and dismissed the charge. The prosecution appealed the case to the Minnesota Supreme Court, which reversed the trial court's dismissal and reinstated the charge. The rationale for the court's decision was that the ordinance prohibited expression not protected by the First Amendment and was written as narrowly as possible to promote the local government's interest in protecting persons from bias-motivated threats.

R.A.V.'s attorney appealed ultimately to the U. S. Supreme Court, which disagreed with Minnesota's and found that the ordinance violated the First Amendment. The Court found that the ordinance prohibited First Amendment protected expression and that the ordinance's content discrimination was not reasonably necessary to achieve governmental interest expressed by the City Council.

For more information

Cleary, Edward J. *Beyond the Burning Cross: The First Amendment and the Landmark R.A.V. Case.* New York: Random House, 1994.

R.A.V. v. City of Saint Paul, 505 U.S. 377 (1992).

Jane Calabria McPeak
Hamline University

reasonable doubt is a standard of proof required by criminal law.

In every criminal case, whether state or federal, the prosecution is required to prove that the accused is guilty of the crime with which he or she is charged *beyond a reasonable doubt.* This burden of proof is the most difficult standard of all, and the requirement to prove a criminal defendant's guilty beyond a reasonable doubt stems from the due process clauses of the U.S. Constitution's Fifth and Fourteenth Amendments. The burden in criminal cases is so high because an accused person stands to lose so much—liberty, civil rights, and, in those extreme cases, even life itself.

On the other hand, when a civil case goes to trial, most times the stakes are monetary. In civil cases, the plaintiff must prove his or her case by preponderance of the evidence, or by the greater weight of the evidence. When scales of justice tip in favor of the defendant, they are the prevailing party, and vice versa.

It takes a great deal more effort to meet the burden of proving a criminal case. If an accused is convicted without the prosecution having proven its case beyond a reasonable doubt, it is a violation of the defendant's due process rights. Although no precise definition of the standard "beyond a reasonable doubt" is constitutionally required, courts have strived to properly emphasize the gravity of the decision a jury must make in every criminal case, and to insure that trial proceedings do not trivialize the awesome duty to determine whether the defendant's guilt was proved beyond a reasonable doubt.

Even in a case where a jury holds an abiding belief that the accused is guilty, it does not necessarily require a guilty verdict, so long as some reasonable doubt still exists in the jury's mind. Reasonable doubt is, simply put, doubt that a reasonable man or woman might entertain. It has been defined by the U. S. Supreme Court as "an important life decision," and as the kind of doubt which people in the more serious and important affairs of their own lives might be willing to act upon (*Holland v. United States,* 348 US 121). Of course, the burden is not insurmountable, but a reasonable doubt is not fanciful or imagined doubt, and it is not doubt that one might conjure up to avoid performing an unpleasant task or duty as a juror. Any doubts must indeed be reasonable in light of the circumstances of the case, stemming from the jury's common sense arising out of some or all of the evidence presented or the lack or insufficiency of the evidence.

For more information

Robinson, Paul H. *Proving and Disproving Criminal Law Defenses—Burden of Persuasion.* Criminal Law Defenses (Treatise Main Volume), 1984.

Solan, Lawrence M. "Refocusing the Burden of Proof in Criminal Cases: Some Doubt about Reasonable Doubt," *Texas Law Review* 98 (November 1999): 105.

Kristin L. Stewart, J. D.
Craig Hemmers, Boise State University

Reconstruction is the historical period immediately following the Civil War, traditionally dated from 1865 to 1877 (although some scholars begin the period in 1863), during which the Union attempted to reconstruct the South, economically, structurally, and socially.

Reconstruction is divided into two major blocs: presidential reconstruction dating from 1863 to 1866, and congressional reconstruction 1867 to 1877. In 1873 and 1876 the Supreme Court also placed its marks upon the era.

Presidential Reconstruction began in 1863 when President Abraham Lincoln introduced the Ten Percent Plan. The Ten Percent Plan stated that when 10 percent of a Confederate state's prewar voters had taken an oath of loyalty to the U.S. Constitution, its citizens could elect a new state government and apply for readmission to the Union. It also called for state abolition of slavery through new state constitutions. In 1864 Congress passed the Wade-Davis Bill, in an attempt to expand Lincoln's Reconstruction Plan. The Wade-Davis Bill required that 50 percent, not 10 percent, of a state's voters declare loyalty to the Constitution before the state could create a new government, and also that these governments recognize the newly emancipated slaves as equal before the law: Lincoln indirectly vetoed the Wade-Davis Bill by leaving it unsigned until Congress adjourned in late March 1865.

The Thirteenth Amendment was approved by Congress in January 1865. The Thirteenth Amendment was to abolish slavery. In March 1865 Congress established the Bureau of Refugees Freedmen and Abandoned Lands, a relief agency for needy white and black refugees. In December 1865 the Thirteenth Amendment was ratified and slavery was constitutionally ended.

In April 1865 Vice President Andrew Johnson became the 17th president of the United States following Lincoln's assassination. Johnson began his term by pardoning all southern whites except for Confederate leaders and those whose wealth exceeded $20,000. Those in the latter category needed to apply directly to Johnson for a pardon. In order for states to be readmitted to the Union, Johnson required that the states need only to abolish slavery and repudiate both secession and the Confederate War debt. Under Johnson's reign Southern state governments issued Black Codes, laws that banned interracial marriages, and aimed to limit black mobility and with it economic options for the newly emancipated slaves.

In 1866 Congress sought the passage of the Freedmen's Bureau Act, extending the agency's life for another year, and the Civil Rights Act, which defined people born in the United States as national citizens, stating explicitly their rights regardless of race. President Johnson vetoed both bills, insisting that they violated states' rights. In another attempt to guarantee the civil rights of the newly freed slaves Congress introduced the Fourteenth Amendment, which was ratified in 1868. The Fourteenth Amendment defined U.S. citizenship in language similar to the vetoed Civil Rights Bill, while it also prohibited states from abridging the "privileges and immunities" of citizens without due process. The Fourteenth Amendment encouraged Southern states to allow black suffrage by reducing representation in states that disfranchised any male citizens.

Congressional Reconstruction began in March 1867 when Congress began passing the Reconstruction Acts, which divided the 10 unreconstructed states (the exception being Tennessee, which ratified the Fourteenth Amendment) into five military districts. Only after the states ratified the Fourteenth Amendment and new state constitutions provided for enfranchisement of all adult males would a state be considered reconstructed and readmitted to the Union. Congress at this time passed several laws to restrict President Johnson's power to undermine congressional policy. Johnson, responding, removed military officers who were enforcing the Reconstruction Act. Shortly thereafter, Congress began impeachment proceedings against Johnson, ultimately coming within one vote of conviction.

In 1869 Congress passed the Fifteenth Amendment protecting black voting rights, stating that no citizen could be denied the vote on the basis of race, color, or "previous condition of servitude." The Fifteenth Amendment was ratified in 1870. In 1875 Congress passed the Civil Rights Act of 1875, which barred discrimination by hotels, theaters, and railroads.

In 1873 the Supreme Court decided on two cases that interpreted the Fourteenth Amendment. In *Bradwell v. Illinois* (1873) the Court ruled against a female attorney who claimed that in prohibiting her from practicing law because of her gender, Illinois had violated the "privileges and immunities" clause of the Fourteenth Amendment. The more famous case decided in the shadow of Reconstruction was the *Slaughter-House Cases* (1873), the first major cases before the Supreme Court interpreting the Reconstruction Amendments. The cases dealt not with the

newly emancipated slaves but butchers and monopolies in New Orleans. The U.S. Supreme Court, with Justice Samuel F. Miller rendering the majority decision, decided against the slaughterhouse operators, holding that the Fourteenth Amendment had to be considered in light of the original purpose of its framers, i.e., guarantee the freedom of former black slaves. Although the amendment could not be construed to refer only to black slavery, its scope as originally planned did not include rights such as those in question.

In this case a distinction was drawn between United States citizenship and state citizenship. The holding declared that the amendment did not intend to deprive the state of legal jurisdiction over the civil rights of its citizens, stating, "The fourteenth amendment prohibits a State from depriving any person of life, liberty, or property, without due process of law; but this adds nothing to the rights of one citizen as against another. It simply furnishes an additional guaranty against any encroachment by the State upon the fundamental rights which belong to every citizen as a member of society." The *Slaughter-House Cases* set the tone for the Supreme Court in Reconstruction—state rights would predominate. Eventually, the Court decided *United States v. Cruikshank* (1876), in which the Court ruled the duty to protect citizens' rights rested with the individual states. The Court also mandated in *United States v. Reese* (1876) that the Fifteenth Amendment did not guarantee citizens the right to vote.

Reconstruction formally ended in 1877 with the inauguration of Rutherford B. Hayes as the 19th president of the United States. Hayes's nomination and presidency saw among other representations signaling the finality of Reconstruction, federal troops removed from the South, the prohibition of armed forces to monitor elections, and Hayes's assurance to southern Democrats his support for state rights, called "Home-Rule."

For more information

DuBois, W. E. B. *Black Reconstruction in America: 1860–1880*. New York.: Simon and Schuster, 1999.

Foner, Eric. *Reconstruction: America's Unfinished Revolution, 1863–1877*. New York: HarperCollins, 1989.

Franklin, John Hope. *Reconstruction after the Civil War*. Chicago: University of Chicago Press, 1995.

Higginbotham, Leon, Jr. *Shades of Freedom: Racial Politics and Presumptions of the American Legal Process*. New York: Oxford University Press, 1998.

Louise Adams Tyler
Unaffiliated Scholar

Regents of the University of California v. Bakke

438 U.S. 265 (1978), is the landmark United States Supreme Court decision that held that a university may use race as a factor in an affirmative action plan but cannot use race alone as the deciding factor in admission.

Mr. (now Dr.) Bakke, a white man, applied twice to the university's medical school, and twice was refused, although he had higher scores on the medical school's admissions point scale than many students who were admitted. This was the result of the medical school's "special admissions" plan under which 16 of 100 admissions were reserved for minorities. Bakke was therefore ineligible for any of those 16 places because of his race, despite his higher qualifications than some of the applicants who were admitted, and he argued that he was the victim of reverse discrimination. He showed that he would have been admitted but for the special admissions plan. The Court found that the plan discriminated on the basis of race and violated Title VI of the Civil Rights Act of 1964 and the Equal Protection Clause of the Fourteenth Amendment to the U.S. Constitution. The Court struck down the special admissions plan and ordered the medical school to admit Bakke (who successfully completed his training and practiced medicine for many years).

The *Bakke* decision has shaped many affirmative action programs. The Court ruled that while "racial and ethnic distinctions of any sort are inherently suspect" (and almost surely unconstitutional), a university could take race into account under appropriate circumstances. For example, a university could try to remedy past discrimination, even if it did not cause such discrimination; it need not be a "passive participant" in discrimination within the university community. However, the Court ruled out the use of quotas (for example, reserving 16 of 100 admissions for minorities) and the use of race as the sole determinant for admission.

After *Bakke*, many universities continued to use or institute affirmative action plans in order to achieve diverse student bodies and/or to remedy past discrimination, and by 1990 more than 11 percent of college students were African Americans, a figure that corresponds to their numbers in the general population. In the 1990s, however, further court decisions and many state laws tended to restrict affirmative action plans in both education and employment. In *Richmond v. Croson*, 488 US 469 (1989), the Supreme Court held that set-aside programs in city contracts are unconstitutional unless specific industry-wide discrimination can be proven. In *Adarand v. Pena*, 515 US 200 (1995), the Supreme Court adopted a strict scrutiny standard for proving race-based discrimination, a ruling that seriously undermined affirmative action.

In *Hopwood v. University of Texas Law School*, 78 F. 3d 932 (5th Cir. 1996), a federal appeals court overruled Bakke by ruling that race cannot be used as an admissions factor (the ruling is effective only within the 5th Circuit, Texas, Louisiana, and Mississippi; the Supreme Court has declined to hear an appeal of *Hopwood*). In 1997 California voters narrowly approved Proposition 209, an anti–affirmative action measure designed to end all such plans within the state. The result is that minority enrollments in universities have fallen. The Supreme Court is widely expected to revisit the question of university affirmative action plans within the next several years.

For more information

McDonald, Laughlin, and John A. Powell. *The Rights of Racial Minorities: The Basic ACLU Guide to Racial Minority Rights,* 2nd ed. Carbondale: Southern Illinois University Press, 1993.

ACLU Briefing Paper "Affirmative Action." American Civil Liberties Association, 125 Broad Street, 18th Floor, New York, NY 10004, 1999. On the web: http//www.alcu.org. E-mail: infoaclu.@aclu.org.

Elsa M. Shartsis, B.A., M.S., J.D.

regulatory crime is a crime committed against laws rather than persons or property. They may be federal, state, or local violations. Regulatory crimes have a number of features.

First, there are several synonyms, including "regulatory offenses," "regulatory transgressions," "regulatory violations," "statutory offenses," and "administrative crimes." Furthermore, regulatory crimes can be a type of "public welfare offense," "corporate crime," "environmental crime," or "white-collar crime." In these latter cases a regulatory crime violates the public's welfare, or harms the environment or some other area of life considered to be the concern of public affairs, and may be committed by a "white-collar" worker.

Second, the offender may be an individual or a legal entity. So a regulatory crime may be the result of an individual's act, or, it may be an offense committed by a corporation or by a public entity such as a government-owned utility or agency.

Third, regulatory crimes are supposed to be morally neutral. Traditionally crimes have been divided into acts which are inherently evil (*mala in se*), such as murder or robbery, and those that are wrong simply because they are prohibited by statute or administrative rule

(*mala quia prohibita*). Regulatory crimes are *mala prohibita* offenses. For instance, tearing the tag off of a mattress, fishing without a license, poaching, driving over the speed limit in a rural area, carrying a concealed weapon, or any number of acts are not inherently evil deeds involving moral turpitude. However, they are still treated as crimes by the law simply because the actions are prohibited.

A fourth feature is strict liability. This means that someone can be held guilty of violating a regulation even if they innocently performed some act, where there was no intuitively obvious moral clue that it was illegal, and even if it were an emergency act in extreme necessity to save life. The result is that regulatory crimes do not require criminal intent (mens rea), nor are circumstances a justification.

A fifth feature is that generally regulatory crimes that dispense with mens rea are minor infractions of statutes or rules such as traffic and parking regulations. They are usually not intentional crimes committed to harm someone or something. So the punishment for a violation may be minimal (*Morissette v. United States,* 342 U.S. 246 [1956]).

A sixth feature has developed in recent years. Critics argue that a new definition is forming. The new "regulatory state," using large bureaucracies to regulate financial markets, employment, utilities, broadcasting, product safety, workplace safety, the environment, transportation, taxation, and housing, has produced huge numbers of administrative rules backed by very serious civil and criminal sanctions. Critics charge that regulatory crimes are now harshly punitive for both innocent and minor infractions by either individuals or corporations.

For more information

Hill, Douglas J. *Federal Criminal Defendant's Handbook.* Berkeley, Calif.: Kensington Publishers, 1999.

Obermaier, Otto G., and Morvillo, Robert G., eds. *White Collar Crime: Business and Regulatory*

Offenses/With Update (Litigation Series). Denver, Colo.: Law Journal Seminars Press, 1990.

A. J. L. Waskey
Dalton State College

Rehnquist, William H. (1924–) was appointed chief justice of the United States Supreme Court in 1986 by President Ronald Reagan.

William Rehnquist was born in Shorewood, Wisconsin, in 1924, served in North Africa during World War II, studied at Kenyon College, Stanford University, and briefly at Harvard. On completing law school he worked as a clerk for Justice Robert H. Jackson. One of the most controversial acts of Rehnquist's career was his handing Jackson a memo while the Court was considering *Brown v. Board of Education,* arguing that *Plessy v. Ferguson* should be upheld. *Plessy* had held that the Constitution permitted "separate but equal" facilities. Controversy also continues to surround his opposition to passage of a public accommodations law in Arizona and his treatment of black voters at the polls.

Rehnquist served as counsel to President Nixon and participated in drawing plans for the roundup of some 12,000 demonstrators on May Day of 1971 in such a manner that no records existed of their behavior, resulting in release of all but 12 people, all of whom had been imprisoned but uncharged and unconvicted people.

Rehnquist was confirmed as an associate justice of the U.S. Supreme Court despite those controversies in 1971. He promptly attacked the Warren Court, claiming it had substituted its own principles for the Constitution and that he would interpret the Constitution without imposing his own principles. His protestations notwithstanding, he has been consistently conservative on the Court—a result one would not expect from the unbiased application of neutral principles.

Rehnquist has described his own approach to constitutional law in relativist, democratic, and positivist terms. But that self-description does not fit the pattern of his decisions.

Chief Justice Rehnquist has been a consistent opponent of the right to abortion, which the Court declared in *Roe v. Wade.* He has supported restrictions on homosexuality that have come to the Court. He has argued that the Constitution is not neutral toward religion and that government should favor religion over irreligion. And he has held that moral grounds alone, not the possibility of injury to non-consenting adults, are sufficient to justify otherwise protected activity like nude dancing.

Those cases would seem to establish Rehnquist's credentials as a moralist, rather than a relativist, on the Court. But he has also consistently taken the position that the government can execute men whom evidence shows are "probably innocent" so long as the proper legal formalities have been followed. It is difficult if not impossible to identify the moral criteria with which that conclusion fits.

Despite his claimed subservience to democratic norms, Rehnquist does not support claims of democratic rights. With the exception of one claim based on a statute drawn in the first decade of the 20th century, the only rights to participate in democratic governance that he has supported in his years on the Court have been in cases brought by white voters objecting to the drawing of district lines in such a way that black representation might approximate—but not exceed—its proportion in the population. Otherwise he has voted to support the exclusion of voters from special purpose districts, to support apportionment plans that included a 250 percent difference in district size, and against finding that the courts could consider the constitutionality of gerrymandering.

His protestations that he is a positivist, merely following the law as previously laid down, also do not ring true. On racial issues Rehnquist participated in greatly narrowing the meaning of discrimination until it became virtually impossible to prove in several areas. Where statutory amendments superceded those decisions he has participated in a narrowing of those statutes, overruling many prior decisions of the Court.

One of the major areas affected by Rehnquist's work has been federalism. Overruling more than half a century of precedent, he has led the Court to deny much of Congress's powers to regulate state activity, even in areas clearly delegated to Congress like patents and copyrights. He has led the Court in changing the power of Congress under the commerce clause from power to regulate activities that affect interstate commerce to power only over economic activity itself. And the Court under his leadership has cut back the powers of Congress to enforce the provisions of the Fourteenth Amendment.

At this writing, Rehnquist has served as a member of the Court for a relatively lengthy period. Largely as the result of his efforts, the Rehnquist Court will be remembered as one which made very significant changes in American law and did so in a consistently politically conservative direction.

For more information

Boles, Donald E. *Mr. Justice Rehnquist, Judicial Activist: The Early Years.* Ames: Iowa State University Press, 1987.

Davis, Sue. *Justice Rehnquist and the Constitution.* Princeton, N.J.: Princeton University Press, 1989.

Gottlieb, Stephen E. *Morality Imposed: The Rehnquist Court and Liberty in America.* New York: New York University Press, 2000.

Stephen E. Gottlieb
Albany Law School

religion   under U.S. law is protected in two ways. First, a majority of the people may not use government to force others to support religion; and second, the government may not prohibit a person from freely exercising religion.

Although some settlers came to America to escape religious persecution, a majority of the colonies and most of the original states used government to support religion. Now many state constitutions reiterate the language of the U.S. Constitution, which stipulates that (1) "no religious test shall ever be required as a qualification to any public office or public trust under the United States" (Article VI, clause 3); (2) "Congress shall make no law respecting an establishment of religion" (Amendment I); and (3) "Congress shall make no law . . . . prohibiting the free exercise [of religion]" (Amendment I). Further, the U.S. Supreme Court has incorporated the First Amendment's establishment and free exercise clauses into the due process clause of the Fourteenth Amendment, which provides that "no state shall . . . . deprive any person of . . . . liberty without due process of law" (Amendment XIV, section 1). Although most Americans uphold these ideals generally, many disagree about their specific application.

Does the establishment clause require a complete separation of church and state? Not exactly, says the Supreme Court, in a series of sometimes confusing cases. For example, a public school district may reimburse parents for the cost of their children riding buses to religious schools (*Everson v. Board of Education,* 330 U.S. 1, 1947). But public school personnel may not lead children in prayer or Bible-reading in class, while state legislators may hire chaplains to pray for them (*Engle v. Vitale,* 370 Y.S. 421, 1962; *School District of Abington Township v. Schempp,* 374 U.S. 203, 1963; *Marsh v. Chambers,* 463 U.S. 783, 1983). Further, a county may place a Christmas tree along with a menorah in front of a public building but may not display a crèche with a banner proclaiming "Gloria in Excelsis Deo" inside the courthouse (*Allegheny County v. ACLU,* 492 U.S. 573, 1989).

Since the Court refused to uphold a strict "wall of separation between church and State" advocated by Thomas Jefferson in 1802, it has searched for an alternate principle to support its establishment jurisprudence. The method it has used, perhaps more than any other to achieve some degree of consistency, is the so-called *Lemon* test. It provides that a government action will be upheld unless (1) it fails to have a secular purpose, (2) its primary effect either enhances or inhibits religion, or (3) it creates an excessive entanglement between government and religion (*Lemon v. Kurtzman,* 403 U.S. 602, 1971). Some justices today, however, reject *Lemon* in favor of some other guideline like a coercion test or an endorsement test.

The closest thing to an absolute right in the United States is the right to hold or not hold religious beliefs. But when beliefs lead to practice, government may use its power to prohibit those practices that disrupt social order, even when they are committed in the name of religion. For example, government may punish a person for practicing bigamy as a tenet of his religion (*Reynolds v. U.S.,* 98 U.S. 145, 1878), require persons to be vaccinated against their belief (*Jacobson v. Massachusetts,* 197 U.S. 11, 1905), forbid children from selling religious literature on the street (*Prince v. Massachusetts,* 321 U.S. 158, 1944), make an Air Force officer remove his yarmulke while on duty (*Goldman v. Weinberger,* 475 U.S. 503, 1986), deny public assistance to one who refuses to obtain a Social Security number for religious reasons (*Bowen v. Roy,* 476 U.S. 693, 1986), build a road on public land that interferes with Indian peoples practicing their religion (*Lyng v. Northwest Indian Cemetery Protective Assn.,* 485 U.S. 439, 1988).

On the other hand, states may not prevent parents from sending their children to religious schools (*Pierce v. Society of Sisters,* 268 U.S. 510, 1925), require a religious group to obtain a permit to proselytize door-to-door (*Cantwell v. Connecticut,* 310 U.S. 296, 1940), require a person to profess belief in order to become a notary public (*Torasco v. Watkins,* 367 U.S. 488, 1961), refuse to pay unemployment compensation to a person who cannot find a job because she will not work on the Sabbath (*Sherbert v. Verner,* 374 U.S. 398, 1963), compel Amish children to attend school after the eighth grade (*Wisconsin v. Yoder,* 406 U.S. 205, 1972), mask a prohibition against animal sacrifice under a health and anticruelty ordinance that is not generally applied (*Church of Lukumi Babalu Aye. Hialeah,* 508 U.S. 520, 1993). In addition, the Supreme Court has said that one may avoid military conscription if the individual conscientiously objects to war on the basis of a sincere belief equivalent to that of believing in God (*U.S. v. Seeger,* 380 U.S. 163, 1965).

The national government and the states may differ in the way in which they treat some religious practices. For example, Congress exempts "the use of peyote in the bona fide ceremonies of the Native American Church," while the Court has allowed Oregon to outlaw peyote (21 C.F.R. 1307.31 and *Peyote Way Church of God v. Thornburgh,* 922 F 2nd. 1210, Fifth Circuit, 1991; *Employment Div., Oregon Dept. of Human Resources v. Smith,* 494 U.S. 872, 1990).

In summary, U.S. law encounters religion in two ways. First, laws decide whether government will be secular, neutral toward religion, accommodate it, or promote it. Currently, most laws take a neutral or accommodating position. Second, laws determine whether general policies apply to all persons, or whether some may be granted exceptions from laws that conflict with their religious scruples. The Court often decides the latter upon the standard of strict scrutiny, whether a law has been narrowly tailored and is necessary to achieve a compelling state interest (*U.S. v. Carolene Products Co.,* 304 U.S. 144, 152–153, ftnt. 4, 1938).

For more information

Choper, Jesse H. *Securing Religious Liberty: Principles for Judicial Interpretation of the Religion Clauses.* Chicago: University of Chicago Press, 1994.

Eck, Diana L. *On Common Ground: World Religions in America.* New York: Columbia University Press, 1997.

Feldman, Stephen M. *Please Don't Wish Me a Merry Christmas: A Critical History of the Separation of*

Church and State. New York: New York University Press, 1997.

Kurland, Philip B., and Ralph Lerner, eds. *The Founders' Constitution: Amendment I (Religion).* Chicago: University of Chicago Press, 1987. http://press-pubs.uchicago.edu/founders/tocs/amendI_religion.html

Rosenblum, Nancy L. *Obligations of Citizenship and Demands of Faith: Religious Accommodation in Pluralist Democracies.* Princeton, N.J.: Princeton University Press, 2000.

Schotten, Peter, and Dennis Stevens. *Religion Politics and the Law: Commentaries and Controversies.* Belmont, Calif.: Wadsworth, 1996.

Schultz, David. "Church-State Relations and the First Amendment." In Schultz, ed. *Law and Politics: Unanswered Questions.* New York: Peter Lang, 1995, pp. 235–65.

Smith, Steven D. *Foreordained Failures: The Quest for a Constitutional Principle of Religious Freedom.* New York: Oxford University Press, 1995.

Thiemann, Ronald F. *Religion in Public Life: A Dilemma for Democracy.* Washington, D.C.: Georgetown University Press, 1996.

Witte, John, Jr. *Religion and the American Constitutional Experiment: Essential Rights and Liberties.* Boulder, Colo.: Westview, 2000.

JeDon Emenhiser
Humbolt State University

res judicata is a legal doctrine that prevents parties from re-litigating claims and issues that were the subject of prior cases.

There are two types of res judicata—claim preclusion and issue preclusion. Courts sometimes use the term *res judicata* when referring just to claim preclusion. Properly understood, however, res judicata encompasses both types of preclusion.

Claim preclusion, as its name suggests, precludes the re-litigation of claims. It is also known as "merger" and "bar." If a plaintiff wins a lawsuit, his or her claim is merged into the judgment, or final determination of the court. This means that the plaintiff may not file another case against the same defendant on the same claim seeking additional relief, such as more money. If the plaintiff loses the first lawsuit the claim is extinguished by the judgment, and he or she is barred from suing the defendant again on the claim.

A claim is often much broader than the specific points raised by a plaintiff in a lawsuit. It generally includes all legal rights that relate to the transaction at issue. Every part of a plaintiffs claim is merged into or barred by the judgment, including those aspects that were not argued by the plaintiff during the case. For example, if a company violates two employment discrimination statutes in firing an employee, and the employee brings a case under only one of the statutes, claim preclusion forbids him from filing another lawsuit under the other statute. The transaction in this example is the firing. All legal rights relating to that event constitute a single claim, and thus the terminated employee must assert them all in a single lawsuit.

Claim preclusion only applies if the first lawsuit is decided by a judgment on the merits. In the above example, if the employee's lawsuit ends with a determination of whether the company actually violated the employment discrimination laws or not, that would be a judgment on the merits. But if the employee's case is resolved on technical procedural grounds, such as a dismissal for a lack of jurisdiction or for improper venue, it is not on the merits and claim preclusion does not apply. (*See* Fed. R. Civ. Pro. 41(b).)

Issue preclusion, which is also called "collateral estoppel," bars the re-litigation of issues. To illustrate, suppose A and B get into a car accident. A sues B over the damage to A's car and the court finds that A wins because B was negligent. If B filed a second lawsuit against A for the damage to B's car, he would be precluded from re-litigating the issue of whether he was negligent or not because that issue was decided in the first case. In other words, since B was found to be negligent in the first case, the court would have to find that B was negligent in the second lawsuit.

For issue preclusion to apply, four elements must be satisfied. First, the issue in the two cases must be identical. In the example above, the question of whether B was negligent in causing the accident is the same in both cases. Second, the issue must have been actually litigated (i.e., contested) and decided in the first lawsuit. If A's lawsuit against B is dismissed because the court does not have personal jurisdiction over B, the issue of whether B was negligent was not litigated or decided and either party can raise the question again in a new case.

Third, the party against whom issue preclusion applies must have had a full and fair opportunity to contest the issue in the first proceeding. If the first lawsuit between A and B was in small claims court, where the rules and procedures are quite limited, the parties would generally be allowed to re-litigate B's negligence in a second case in a standard trial court where the rules and procedures are far more comprehensive. Fourth, the issue must be necessary to the judgment of the first lawsuit. Suppose the court in the first proceeding finds both that A is contributorily negligent and that B is negligent. Moreover, the rules of the state where the case was tried do not permit plaintiffs to recover where they are contributorily negligent. In this situation, the finding that B was negligent is not necessary to the judgment. A would have lost the case whether B was found to be negligent or not because the court ruled that A was contributorily negligent. However, the finding that A was contributorily negligent is necessary to the judgment. Accordingly, in a second lawsuit between A and B, the parties could re-litigate whether B was negligent but not whether A was negligent.

Both claim preclusion and issue preclusion apply to the parties in the first case and to those in privity with the parties. Persons are in privity if they have nearly identical legal interests. The clearest example is a successor in interest. Suppose that A lost to B in the first lawsuit concerning the car accident but then sold his car to P. As the new owner of the car, P is A's successor in interest and he could not re-litigate (1) any claims that A could have brought with respect to the damage to the car, or (2) any issues regarding the car that A in fact contested.

Unlike claim preclusion, issue preclusion can apply to persons who were neither parties to the first lawsuit nor in privity with a party. To illustrate, suppose that the car accident between A and B also involved a third car driven by C. A sued B and lost because the court found that A was contributorily negligent. If A then sued C, A would be issue precluded from re-litigating the issue of his negligence because that question was resolved in the first proceeding. This is called defensive issue preclusion because C is the defendant in the second case and is merely relying on issue preclusion to protect himself. But suppose instead that C sued A after the first lawsuit. In some instances, A would be issue precluded from re-litigating his negligence in this second context as well. This is called offensive issue preclusion, because C is the plaintiff and is using issue preclusion to obtain relief from A. Courts apply offensive issue preclusion less often than other types of preclusion because of concerns about fairness to parties like A.

Although issue preclusion is broader than claim preclusion, complete strangers to a lawsuit can never be issue precluded by the result because they did not have a full and fair opportunity to litigate the issue. Thus, while C can use issue preclusion against A or B, C could not be bound by the result of the first lawsuit between A and B unless he is actually in privity with either of them the way P was.

It is important to understand that claim and issue preclusion only apply to new lawsuits filed after a judgment is entered in a prior case. They do not restrict any of a party's rights in the original lawsuit, such as the rights to ask for a new trial or to appeal.

The rules constituting res judicata serve a critical purpose in our legal system. They guarantee that private disputes reach a final resolution. This saves scarce judicial resources and spares the parties from the prospect of endlessly litigating the same cases and issues over and over.

For more information

Corpus Juris Secundum, Vol. 50, *Judgement.* St. Paul Minn.: West Group Publishing, 1997, and Supp., 2000.

Wright and Miller, *Federal Practice and Procedure,* Vol. 18, sections 4301–4500, *Res Judicata.* St. Paul, Minn.: West Group Publishing, 1981, and Supp., 2000.

Joshua M. Silverstein
Freeborn and Peters, Chicago

restitution   sometimes called reparation, is a practice in which the offender compensates the victim for the damage or loss that the victim has suffered. Restitution originated in ancient times when the focus of punishment was on the injury to the victim. (For example, *see* the Code of Hammurabi, c. 1700 B.C.E.) More recently, punishment has focused on the harm the offender has caused to the political system or the state.

Modern restitution has proliferated since the 1970s. Compensation in the form of funds, services, or the replacement or repair of a damaged item may be the result of a private agreement between the parties, a plea bargain with the prosecutor's office, a supplement to a sentence for a criminal offense, an alternative to incarceration, or a condition of probation.

Restitution or reparation may also involve nations, institutions, or corporations who are compensating victims of war or persecution. In the early 2000s, negotiations were in progress to provide financial reparations for those who had lost bank accounts or property, were incarcerated, or were injured during the Holocaust.

According to advocates, restitution focuses the offender on the human consequences of his or her actions and promotes deterrence by holding the offender accountable for his or her behavior. Through restitution, the offender can "make peace" with the community, leading to connec-

tion (reintegration), rather than separation and ostracism (stigmatization).

Juvenile offenders are increasingly required to pay restitution by the courts, or informally by probation departments who are supervising offenders outside of the court system, most commonly for vandalism or burglary. When restitution is either agreed to or ordered for juvenile offenders, research suggests that recidivism (reoffending) is reduced.

Both youthful and adult offenders are often required to work in the public or private sectors to earn funds for restitution, especially those offenders who have no other resources with which to compensate victims. Such employment eliminates lack of work as an excuse for nonpayment of restitution and improves the rate and regularity of offender payment. Where restitution might be otherwise unavailable, some jurisdictions provide victim assistance funding for which victims may apply.

Victims are frequently left out of the criminal justice process after their victimization, leaving them feeling vulnerable and angry. Restitution is empowering because it gives the victim a role in the process and promotes feelings of fairness. Restitution may thus provide benefits for both the offender and the victim.

While the use of restitution is increasing, the lack of systematic planning, implementation, and evaluation continues to cause problems. The diversity of legislation and the broad discretion of courts and probation departments may also result in the exclusion of restitution programs. Further, the lack of importance with which some authorities view restitution may result in a reluctance to require restitution once it is ordered. As a consequence, the failure to pay restitution imposed as an alternative to incarceration may not have any repercussions.

For more information

Galaway, Burt, and Joe Hudson. *Criminal Justice, Restitution, and Reconciliation.* Monsey, N.Y.: Criminal Justice Press, 1990.

Tonry, Michael, and Hamilton, Kate. *Intermediate Sanctions in Over-Crowded Times*. Boston: Northeastern University Press, 1995.

Rosalie R. Young
Public Justice Department
State University of New York, Oswego

restraining order   is an order of a court in the form of an injunction that directs a party not to do a certain thing.

As with injunctions generally, a showing of irreparable injury and inadequate legal remedy is required. If issued on an emergency basis without notice or hearing, it is effective only until a full hearing can be held. Violation of a restraining order constitutes contempt of court and is punishable by a fine or imprisonment.

Restraining orders can be issued to protect individuals against violence, abuse, or harassment, often by restricting access or proximity to the protected party. For example, courts have issued orders restraining antiabortion protesters from intruding into "buffer zones" around entrances to abortion clinics. Former first lady Jacqueline Kennedy Onassis obtained a restraining order against a particularly intrusive photographer, prohibiting him from coming within 25 yards of her or 30 yards of her children.

Restraining orders also are issued in cases of domestic violence to protect a spouse from harm or a child from abuse. In divorce proceedings courts may issue restraining orders to enjoin, for example, removing children from the jurisdiction, damaging or disposing of family property, or molesting a spouse or child.

Some states have enacted statutes giving courts authority to issue a form of restraining order called a personal protection order, or PPO. Issued on the petition of a present or former spouse or domestic partner, PPOs restrain the other party from conduct that would interfere with personal liberty or cause an apprehension of violence. Under federal law, anyone named in a PPO is prohibited from possessing a firearm.

For more information
Dobbyn, John F. *Injunctions in a Nutshell*. St. Paul Minn.: West Publishing Co., 1974.

Norman Otto Stockmeyer, Jr.
Thomas M. Cooley Law School

Reynolds v. Sims   377 U.S. 533 (1964) was one of the cases decided by the U.S. Supreme Court in the "Reapportionment Revolution"—a series of cases in the 1960s in which the Court abandoned its hands-off approach to redistricting and reapportionment and required congressional, legislative, and local government districts to meet a "one person, one vote" standard.

In the first case, *Baker v. Carr*, 369 U.S. 186 (1962), the Court had decided that plaintiffs presented a justiciable claim when they sued under the equal protection clause of the Fourteenth Amendment to correct the malapportionment of their state legislative districts.

Alabama had last apportioned its legislative seats in its 1901 Constitution, despite a state constitutional requirement that the legislature reapportion itself every 10 years. Even as urban areas grew, political power remained concentrated in rural counties. By 1960 the largest state senate district had 42 times as many people as the smallest, and the ratio for the lower house was 16 to 1. A majority in either house could be elected by as few as one-quarter of the voters.

Charles Morgan, Jr., and George Peach Taylor, two Birmingham lawyers, filed suit on behalf of themselves and a dozen other members of the Young Men's Business Club of Birmingham in the summer of 1961, arguing that the failure to reapportion denied them the equal protection of the laws. Within five months after the *Baker v. Carr* decision, the federal district court hearing Morgan's suit adopted a new plan for Alabama's legislature. The district court's plan still left population disparities. While the ratio of the largest to smallest senate districts had been reduced to 4.7 to 1, it still only took

28 percent of the voters to elect a majority. The ratio of largest to smallest districts had actually increased in the house—to 20 to 1—but it would take 43 percent of the voters to elect a majority.

A group of county probate judges and two sets of intervening plaintiffs appealed the case to the Supreme Court. The probate judges called for the overturning of *Baker v. Carr*. The intervening plaintiffs, represented by David Vann (a former clerk to Justice Hugo Black and later mayor of Birmingham) and John W. McConnell, Jr., argued that the Supreme Court should grant more sweeping relief than the district court had. Vann argued for the Court to apply the basic districting principles of the Alabama Constitution, while McConnell argued for strict adherence to mathematical equality of districts. Morgan, too, argued for population as the only constitutional and practical basis for districting but was satisfied with the partial relief and asked that the case be returned to the district court to "finish the job."

The Supreme Court held 8–1 that population should be the basis for districting in both houses of the state legislature. It rejected the argument of the probate judges that the state senate could be apportioned on the basis of one senator per county under the so-called federal analogy. The decision of the Supreme Court said, "Legislators represent people, not trees or acres. Legislators are elected by voters, not farms or cities or economic interests." Still, the Court did not require strict mathematical equality of districts. It allowed states to vary from the equal-population principle based on a "rational state policy" such as constructing legislative districts along political subdivision lines.

The *Reynolds* ruling remains the bedrock of redistricting law to this day. The Supreme Court has toughened its stance toward equality of district sizes and has expanded the reach of the *Reynolds* ruling to more elected bodies, but it continues to follow the basic holding of the case.

For more information

Dixon, Robert G., Jr. *Democratic Representation: Reapportionment in Law and Politics*. New York: Oxford University Press, 1968.

Morgan, Charles, Jr. *One Man, One Voice*. New York: Holt, Rinehart and Winston, 1979.

The oral argument may be heard on the Northwestern University website: http://oyez.nwu.edu.

Edward Still
Lawyers' Committee for Civil Rights Under Law

right to counsel is granted by the U.S. Constitution's Sixth and Fourteenth Amendments and guarantees that, in every criminal case where a person could be incarcerated, an accused person is entitled to the assistance of a lawyer. If the accused cannot afford to hire a private attorney to represent him, one will be appointed by the court.

The Sixth Amendment states that in "all criminal prosecutions, the accused shall enjoy the right to . . . have the assistance of counsel for his defense." This right begins only after judicial proceedings have been initiated against the accused, whether by way of formal charge, preliminary hearing, indictment, or arraignment. Furthermore, the fact that police have focused upon a specific person in a criminal investigation does not trigger the Sixth Amendment right to counsel. Accordingly, the right to an attorney becomes applicable only when the character of the government's actions shifts from investigation to accusation.

The Fifth Amendment of the U.S. Constitution, and the United States Supreme Court's decision of *Miranda v. Arizona*, 384 U.S. 436 (1966), grants the right to those in custody of law enforcement and subject to interrogation to talk to an attorney, even if a judicial proceeding has not yet occurred. Commonly referred to as "Miranda rights," they include the right to remain silent, and the right to speak with an attorney before responding to any police questioning. Police may not ask any further questions of a person in custody who requests the assistance of an attorney unless and until an attorney is present with the accused during questioning or the accused reinitiates the questioning.

Likewise, once the Sixth Amendment right to counsel has attached after judicial proceedings are initiated, there may be no further interrogation by officials. A confession deliberately elicited by police after the right to counsel attaches is a violation of the accused's Sixth Amendment rights. The price of such a violation is severe—the court may simply refuse to allow use of the evidence of that confession at trial.

Of course, an accused may always waive her right to an attorney and confess to a crime voluntarily. Any damaging statement or confession obtained by police after a sufficient waiver will not result in a Sixth Amendment violation, and such statements may be admissible and used against the accused at trial. However, there are strict guidelines related to waivers of an accused's Sixth Amendment constitutional rights. Such a waiver must be knowing and voluntary and not the subject of police trickery or coercion.

The critical question when assessing whether a court should allow or exclude the defendant's confession at trial is whether such a confession was deliberately elicited by the police. Even after judicial proceedings have begun and the accused's Sixth Amendment rights have been triggered, whether or not there has been any waiver of rights, the court will not disallow a confession at trial unless the police have actually done something to violate the defendant's rights; for example, direct interrogation or questioning. If a law enforcement officer is a passive witness to a confession or other damaging statements made outside the presence of an accused's attorney, that evidence may be used against the accused at trial as there has been no violation of his or her right to counsel.

For more information

Distinguishing Fifth and Sixth Amendment Rights to Counsel during Police Questioning, 16 S. Ill. U. L. J. 101 (1991).

McNeil v. Wisconsin: The Supreme Court Has Another Bout with the Right to Counsel, 23 Pac. L. J. 1351 (1992).

Kristin L. Stewart, J.D.

right to die is a legal concept that has evolved from the right to refuse medical treatment. This, in turn, is derived from the concept of common-law battery, a basic principle that nobody should be allowed to engage in unwelcome touching or intrusive physical contact without a person's consent.

Consent as a central issue implicates the issue of lack of consent as well. However, in the right-to-die cases, this is usually asserted by a third party, such as parents, spouses, other family, or designated individuals assigned to protect the rights of the patient (who would be the first party).

In the line of seminal cases, including that of the New Jersey Supreme Court's ruling regarding Karen Ann Quinlan (who was in a persistent vegetative state after combining drugs and alcohol) and the United States Supreme Court decision regarding Nancy Cruzan (who was in a catastrophic car accident that left her in a persistent vegetative state), the ultimate question regarded what the patients would not have wanted, in terms of medical treatment. However, since these questions were raised by the parents of patients who were in a persistent vegetative state, the question of how to prove what the patients would have wanted was also an issue subject to litigation. In fact, many of the right-to-die cases emerge from situations where the patient has been in a persistent vegetative state for a minimum of six months, from which medical experts predict that the patient will never recover physical or mental competence, sensation, or capacity.

In essence, what is actually being sought is a judicial declaration (order) that has two central components. First, the patient is to have medical treatment, nutrition and hydration discontinued, so that the patient may die a "natural" death, without further intrusive medical intervention or interference. Second, the doctor, medical team, and medical facility are exempted from criminal prosecution and/or civil liability either for allowing the patient to die or for discontinuing life-sustaining treatment. This may also be further to a legal guardian's request for what amounts to lawful, nonvoluntary euthanasia, in which the act is performed without consent of the patient, because the patient is physically and mentally incapable of giving consent. An example of where this may happen is the case of Nancy Cruzan, where the patient was in a catastrophic car accident that resulted in brain death.

The issue of the right to die has largely arisen from advances in medical technology, which now provide for the indefinite continued maintenance of heart and lung function by machine, as well as artificial nutrition and hydration by tube. Before this, someone who met with a catastrophic accident, drug overdose, or coma would ultimately have degenerated and succumbed to their (natural) death within one to two weeks. Now that the medical profession has the ability to prolong the process of dying (as well as the capability to lengthen the time of living), we live in an age where a person who has no brain function can receive artificial nutrition and hydration and have biological functions be technologically induced, with the result that the person is "disenabled" from dying.

Right-to-die litigation and legislation by states such as that of "natural death acts" are targeted at preventing this result. It is important to realize, however, that state legislatures can determine, by creating legal tests or hurdles (which state courts can then interpret) under what circumstances people can refuse medical treatment, and the courts can decide whether the evidence presented by third parties is sufficient to meet the burden of proof in this regard.

Standards which have been applied by courts in determining whether a patient should be granted the right to die or to have treatment discontinued include substituting the judgment of a parent or legal guardian in place of the patient or holding a hearing where the court considers whether there is clear and convincing evidence to prove that the patient would not have wanted additional life-sustaining treatment under the current circumstances. Sometimes patients have previously drawn up living wills or advance directives, which are valuable documents for both treatment facilities and courts.

However, it should also be noted that where a physician, medical team, or treatment facility has a conscientious objection to discontinuing life-sustaining measures (one such example is for religious reasons), the legal remedy is to move the patient to another facility, rather than to force a physician or institution to engage in practices antithetical to their beliefs. In addition, many hospitals and treatment facilities have ethics committees, which consider the state of the law, the medical state of the art, and the physician and institutional perspectives in determining whether life-sustaining treatment should be discontinued, or whether a particular case is inappropriately being viewed as a right-to-die case.

For more information

Dworkin, Ronald. *Life's Dominion: An Argument about Abortion and Euthanasia.* London: HarperCollins, 1993.

Keown, John, ed. *Euthanasia Examined: Ethical, Clinical and Legal Perspectives.* Cambridge: Cambridge University Press, 1997 (first paperback edition, with revisions).

Demetra M. Pappas, J.D. M.Sc.
London School of Economics and Political Science

right to vote has been expanded and contracted over the history of this country by a variety of federal and state laws and constitutional provisions. An examination of the original U.S. Constitution and Bill of Rights reveals very little about who could vote. The Senate was to be chosen by the state legislatures, while the right to vote for members of the House of Representatives was linked to the individual state's decision about who could vote for the most numerous house in its own legislature.

On the eve of the American Revolution, most of the colonies used some variation of the British system of the day—suffrage based on wealth. Wealth was measured by ownership of a certain number of acres of land, the value of real or personal property, or the rental value of that property. Because of the different opportunities for accumulation of wealth in the mother country and the colonies, the right to suffrage extended to only about 15 percent of the English adult males but ranged from 50 percent to 97 percent of the free adult males in various colonies. Most colonies also limited the vote to Protestants.

During the Revolution and in the years to the end of the 18th century, most of the states changed to a requirement that a free adult male who paid a tax of a fixed amount (called a head or poll tax) could vote. This had the effect of simplifying the suffrage requirements while broadening them. Restrictions on voting by Catholics and free blacks were also relaxed in several states. Women (usually widows) who owned property worth 50 pounds were allowed to vote in New Jersey beginning in 1777.

During the first half of the 19th century, most states gradually moved toward universal white adult male suffrage while eliminating or restricting the right to vote of free blacks and women. For instance, North Carolina and Connecticut disfranchised free blacks entirely, while New York required that they own property worth $250. New Jersey simplified its suffrage requirements in 1807 by abolishing the property requirement and incidentally disfranchising women. Most of the new states admitted to the Union during this period had universal white adult male suffrage written into their constitutions.

The Civil War and Reconstruction changed the legal framework for suffrage. The Republican-controlled Congress in 1867 enfranchised blacks in the District of Columbia, federal territories, and each occupied southern state (while also disenfranchising former Confederate civil and military officials). After the election of 1868, when Democrats came close to defeating Republicans in many states in the North, the lame duck session of Congress in early 1869 (still controlled by the Radical Republicans elected in 1866) adopted the Fifteenth Amendment. It was ratified within 15 months. (Four southern states not yet readmitted had to ratify the amendment to secure their own readmission.) Its backers intended that this amendment would make permanent the enfranchisement of blacks in the South and require it in the North (where it was allowed in only a few states).

The women's suffrage movement tried to get Congress to adopt suffrage for women, as well as blacks, in the Fifteenth Amendment, but they were unsuccessful. The women's suffrage groups kept up the fight, both in Congress and the state legislatures. Wyoming adopted women's suffrage as part of its constitution upon being admitted in 1890. The number of states doing so increased gradually and sporadically until Congress adopted the Nineteenth Amendment in 1919. By August 1920 it was ratified, and women voted in the elections that fall.

In the meanwhile, the enfranchisement of blacks proved to be less permanent that the backers of the Fifteenth Amendment had hoped. With the end of Reconstruction, Democrats regained control in the South—often through violence, intimidation, and fraud. Beginning about 1880, southern legislatures adopted laws making it more difficult for blacks to vote. The new laws included registration laws (previously unknown in most places), secret ballots (combined with confusing ballot layouts and restrictions on who could assist the illiterate voter), literacy tests (with exclusions for those who owned a certain amount of property or who had served in the Confederate or U.S. Army), poll taxes (for which no effort was made at collection and which were due several months before candidates even qualified), and restrictions on voting by those convicted of certain crimes (usually chosen for their racial impact). From 1890 to 1910, most of the southern states held constitutional conventions to continue and institutionalize the disfranchisement.

The Democratic Party did its part by adopting primaries in place of conventions and restricting voting in those primaries to whites. During the 1930s and 1940s, the NAACP attacked the white primaries and succeeded in finally abolishing them in the 1944 Supreme Court case of *Smith v. Allwright,* 321 U.S. 649 (1944). Nevertheless, southern states still succeeded in keeping most blacks off the voter rolls through a variety of subterfuges and barriers.

As noted above, poll taxes were used in the early republic to expand the franchise and in the late 19th and early 20th centuries to restrict the franchise. Over the first two-thirds of the 20th century, the "poll tax" became synonymous with restriction of the franchise in southern states. Because many whites, as well as blacks, were poor and lived as sharecroppers with little or no cash money (for example, the fictional Mr. Cunningham in *To Kill a Mockingbird* who paid the lawyer Atticus Finch in produce rather than cash), the poll tax became an economic barrier and not a purely racial one. Southerners and northerners alike formed organizations to press for its repeal—either by the states or by federal legislation. The movement had a limited success when (from 1942 to 1956) Congress outlawed poll taxes as a condition for voting by members of the armed forces in time of war. After many unsuccessful attempts to pass other federal legislation (while the number of states actually using the poll tax dwindled), Congress adopted the Twenty-fourth Amendment in 1962. Within 17 months, it had been ratified. The amendment only forbade the imposition of a poll tax for federal elections but allowed states to collect it for registration for state and local elections.

About this same time, the movement to lower the voting age to 18 was reaching a point of fruition. Georgia had been the first to lower the voting age shortly after World War II, and only three states had followed suit over the next two decades: Kentucky, Alaska (at age 19), and Hawaii (at age 20). Congress amended the Voting Rights Act in 1970 to include an extension of the franchise to 18-year-olds in all elections. The Supreme Court quickly held that Congress had no authority to extend the franchise for state and local elections but could do so for federal elections (*Oregon v. Mitchell,* 400 U.S. 112 [1970].) On March 23, 1971, Congress proposed a constitutional amendment (the Twenty-sixth) to require all states to allow 18-year-olds to vote in state and federal elections. By July 5 of that year, enough states had ratified it and it became part of the constitution.

The passage of the Voting Rights Act of 1965 (*q.v.*) resulted in a large increase in the number of blacks registered to vote.

The most recent national advance in the right to vote has come through the National Voter Registration of 1993. The act requires states to make voter registration available through public benefits, motor vehicle, and driver licensing offices (thus its popular name of the "Motor Voter Act"). The act also requires states to accept a simple half-page application form published by the Federal Election Commission. While this act did not extend the franchise, as a practical matter it has made it easier for people to register to vote.

For more information
Kousser, J. Morgan. "Suffrage." In Greene, Jack P., ed. *Encyclopedia of American Political History.* New York: Charles Scribner's Sons, 1984.

Edward Still
Lawyers' Committee for Civil Rights Under Law

robbery is the forcible stealing or the use or threatened use of immediate physical force against another person during the commission of larceny.

A person is guilty of robbery when he employs force to prevent or overcome resistance during the act of taking property or uses or threatens the use of immediate force to coerce the owner of property to relinquish possession or control over the property.

Many states have passed criminal statutes that distinguish different categories of robbery. To be convicted of first degree robbery, a person must either (1) cause serious physical injury to persons who are not participants in the crime; (2) use or threaten to activate a dangerous instrument, or (3) be armed with a deadly weapon or (4) reveal possession of a loaded pistol, revolver, rifle, shotgun, machine gun, or other firearm.

Under federal law, if an individual is found guilty beyond a reasonable doubt of entering a bank or financial institution with the intent of committing a larceny and assaults any person or jeopardizes the life of any person by the use of a dangerous weapon, then he is subject to monetary fines and imprisonment of not more than 20 years. Most states have similar laws.

For more information

Brown, Stephen E., Finn-Aage Esbensen, and Gilbert Geis. *Criminology: Explaining Crime and Its Context*. Cincinnati, Ohio: Anderson Publishing, 1998.

J. David Golub
Touro College

Roe v. Wade   410 U.S. 113 (1973) recognized that even though states have some legitimate interests in regulating abortion procedures, a woman essentially has an unrestricted right to an abortion during the first trimester of her pregnancy.

Roe v. Wade gave the Supreme Court the opportunity to review a Texas abortion law, which made it a crime for women to obtain an abortion except in cases when it was necessary to save the life of the mother. Using the fictitious name "Jane Roe" in this suit, the plaintiff challenged the Texas criminal abortion statute for being unconstitutionally vague and for infringing on her right to privacy, which she argued was

protected by the First, Fourth, Fifth, Ninth, and Fourteenth Amendments of the U.S. Constitution. In a 7–2 opinion written by Justice Harry Blackmun, the majority of the Supreme Court ruled that the Texas statute was unconstitutional on the grounds that it violated a woman's right to privacy within the due process clause of the Fourteenth Amendment.

In defending this position, the Court pointed out that one of the arguments used to support most criminal abortion laws was that the procedure was hazardous to a woman's health. However, Justice Blackmun asserted that while it was true that the mortality rate of women obtaining abortions was high in the 19th and early 20th centuries, improvements in medical technology now made first-trimester abortions "relatively safe." In fact, Blackmun pointed out that medical data show that "until the end of the first trimester, mortality in abortion is less than mortality in normal childbirth." Consequently, the Court ruled that during the first trimester of pregnancy, states could not bar abortions. Rather, during this time period, abortion decisions were to be free from state interference and "left to the medical judgment of the pregnant women's attending physician."

Nevertheless, the Supreme Court noted that abortions performed in more advanced stages of pregnancy did in fact put a woman's health at an increased risk, and therefore states could regulate abortions after the first trimester. Justice Blackmun stated: "[T]he risk to the woman increases as her pregnancy continues. Thus the state retains a definite interest in protecting the woman's own health and safety when an abortion is proposed at a late stage of pregnancy." Hence, after the first trimester, states were permitted to regulate abortion procedures in ways that would reasonably protect the health of the mother.

Moreover, the issue was raised in this case as to whether or not states could bar abortions in an effort to protect the life of the fetus. Consequently, the Court was asked to consider whether a fetus was considered a "person" under the

Fourteenth Amendment. The Court concluded that historically the word *person* applied only postnatally, and thus, the unborn was not recognized under the law as a whole person. Despite this conclusion, the Court's majority still believed that states did have an important and legitimate interest in protecting human life. However, it was decided that the state's interest in protecting the unborn did not occur until the third trimester of pregnancy when the fetus had reached the point of viability. In other words, the states had a legitimate interest in protecting unborn life only when the fetus was capable of living outside the mother's womb. Thus, at the point of viability, states were permitted, if they desired, to ban abortions except when they were necessary "to preserve the life or health of the mother."

The *Roe v. Wade* decision made it clear that a woman's right to an abortion was not absolute and her right to the procedure depended on her stage of pregnancy. While a woman practically had an unrestricted right to choose abortion in consultation with her physician during the first trimester of pregnancy, after this time period the states could regulate abortion procedures to protect maternal health. Likewise, states could even prohibit abortions in the third trimester of pregnancy as long as the legislation permitted abortions in circumstances to save the mother's life.

The two dissenters in this 1973 case, Justices Rehnquist and White, were critical of the trimester framework established in the majority opinion. They argued that the framework was arbitrary, and they accused the Court's majority of exceeding its limited judicial power. More specifically, the dissenters asserted that the trimester framework was an act of judicial legislation and that creating legislation was the job of legislators and not unelected judges. Moreover, they contended that if the states did in fact have a legitimate interest in protecting the potential life of the fetus, then this interest should exist throughout the entire pregnancy and should not be limited to the third trimester of pregnancy.

Roe v. Wade did not put an end to the abortion debate in the U.S. political system. Legislation regulating abortion procedures has been passed on both the federal and state levels, which at times have been constitutionally challenged in the courts. Furthermore, the American people continue to be divided over the abortion issue. Strong pro-life and pro-choice movements exist in our political system, and these groups continue to work hard to acquire abortion policies that reflect their political interests. Thus, although *Roe v. Wade* traditionally is understood as the starting point for understanding the contemporary abortion debate, the Supreme Court decision did not put an end to the debate in our political practice.

For more information

Faux, Marian. *Roe v. Wade*. New York: Macmillan, 1988.

Tribe, Lawrence. *Abortion: The Clash of Absolutes*. New York: W. W. Norton, 1992.

Tushnet, Mark. *Abortion*. New York: Facts On File, 1996.

Francene M. Engel
University of Michigan

Romer v. Evans 517 U.S. 620 (1996), in which the U.S. Supreme Court struck down a Colorado constitutional provision exempting homosexuals from antidiscrimination laws and statutes, restricted the authority of states to limit the civil rights of targeted groups and marked a significant evolution in the Court's treatment of homosexuality and homosexuals as a distinct class under the Fourteenth Amendment.

In the 1970s and 1980s, a number of Colorado municipalities enacted ordinances prohibiting discrimination based on sexual orientation in housing, employment, education, public accommodations, health and welfare services, and other public and private activities. In 1992 Colorado voters adopted through a statewide referendum Amendment 2 to the Colorado State Constitution, repealing all existing homosexual rights laws and precluding all legislative, executive, or judicial action at the state or local level designed to protect the status of persons based on their "homosexual, lesbian, or bisexual orientation, conduct, practices or relationships."

Although its supporters maintained that the amendment was designed only to ensure that homosexuals not be accorded "special rights," a coalition of homosexuals, advocacy groups, and Colorado municipalities challenged Amendment 2 on the grounds that it violated the equal protection clause of the Fourteenth Amendment to the U.S. Constitution. Rejecting its supporters' argument that Amendment 2 was designed only to protect First Amendment rights to freedom of association, the Colorado State Supreme Court held that the U.S. Constitution protects the fundamental right to participate equally in the political process and that a state constitutional amendment infringing on such rights must be narrowly tailored and supported by a compelling state interest. Enforcement of the amendment was enjoined, and the case was appealed to the United States Supreme Court.

Oral arguments were heard on October 10, 1995, and on May 20, 1996, the Supreme Court in a 6–3 decision affirmed that the Colorado amendment was in fact violative of the equal protection clause of the Fourteenth Amendment. The Court held that prohibiting homosexuals from legal protections "inflicts on them immediate, continuing, and real injuries that outrun and belie any legitimate justifications that may be claimed for it." Writing for the majority, Justice Anthony Kennedy found that Amendment 2 bore no relationship to a legitimate government purpose and "withdraws from homosexuals, but no others, specific legal protections from the injuries caused by discrimination, and imposes a special disability on those persons alone."

The protections repealed by the initiative, Kennedy wrote, are "taken for granted by most people either because they already have them or do not need them; these are protections against exclusion from an almost limitless number of transactions and endeavors that constitute ordinary civic life in a free society." In rejecting the stated justifications for the amendment, including protecting the rights of landlords, Kennedy concluded that "Amendment 2 classifies homosexuals not to further a proper legislative end but to make them unequal to everyone else. . . . . A State cannot so deem a class of persons a stranger to its laws."

Kennedy was joined in the majority by Justices Stevens, O'Connor, Souter, Ginsburg, and Breyer. In dissent, Justice Antonin Scalia, joined by Justices Rehnquist and Thomas, maintained that Coloradans had the right to pass Amendment 2 in order to preserve traditional sexual mores.

For more information

Eskridge, William N. *Gaylaw: Challenging the Apartheid of the Closet.* Cambridge, Mass.: Harvard University Press, 1999.

Gerstmann, Even. *The Constitutional Underclass: Gays, Lesbians, and the Failure of Class-Based Equal Protection.* Chicago: University of Chicago Press, 1999.

Richards, David A. J. *Women, Gays and the Constitution: The Grounds for Feminism and Gay Rights in Culture and Law,* 1999.

William D. Baker
Arkansas School for Mathematics and Science

Roosevelt, Franklin Delano (1882–1945)
was president of the United States from 1933 to 1945.

Franklin Roosevelt was born on January 30, 1882, in Hyde Park, New York, into a family of wealth and privilege. Roosevelt attended Groton preparatory school, Harvard College, and Columbia Law School. He passed the bar, practiced law, and was elected to the New York state assembly. He served as assistant secretary of the navy under President Woodrow Wilson. He was the vice presidential nominee in 1920, but the Democratic ticket lost to Warren G. Harding. A year later he contracted polio and lost the use of his legs. Undeterred, FDR was elected to the governorship of New York in 1928. Following the stock market crash of 1929, the United States spiraled into depression. In 1932 he won his first of four presidential elections.

Roosevelt took immediate action to end the Depression, creating a new era in the relationship between the government and the economy. He proposed a "New Deal" for Americans and in the first 100 days of his administration he signed 15 major recovery and relief measures. The New Deal was a radical approach to the nation's economic woes. Millions of unemployed Americans were given work in new government projects, and federal money was pumped into public and private jobs through subsidies.

At first, the Court upheld some New Deal and state regulations such as in *Home Building & Loan Assoc. v. Blaisdell,* 290 U.S. 398 (1934), which allowed state laws providing relief for homeowners, and *Ashwander v. T.V.A.,* 297 U.S. 288 (1936), which upheld the power of Congress to construct dams for defense and to improve commerce. The Court, however, thwarted much of Roosevelt's early New Deal efforts. Four justices, Willis Van Devanter, James Clark McReynolds, George Sutherland, and Pierce Butler, sarcastically dubbed by reporters the Four Horsemen after the biblical reference, took a hard-line stance against the New Deal. The Four Horsemen could usually rely on Justice Owen Roberts and sometimes Chief Justice Charles Evans Hughes for the fifth and decisive vote they needed to invalidate New Deal legislation.

FDR saw one after another of his programs invalidated by the Court. For example, the National Industrial Recovery Administration, a cooperative effort by government, business, and labor, was struck down by the Court in *Schecter*

Franklin D. Roosevelt (NATIONAL ARCHIVES)

v. United States, 295 U.S. 495 (1935). The Agricultural Adjustment Act was invalidated in *United States v. Butler,* 297 U.S. 1 (1936). These and similar holdings, coupled with rulings striking down state regulations, convinced Roosevelt that the hostile Court needed to be radically altered.

In 1937 Roosevelt announced his plan to reorganize the federal court system, which ultimately became known as the court-packing plan. Roosevelt's idea was to add more federal judges and increase the number of Supreme Court Justices from nine to 15. The public reacted unfavorably to this plan and it was soon abandoned. Unbeknownst to Roosevelt, the plan was unnecessary. A significant switch occurred within the Court just prior to his announcement of the plan. No longer persuaded by the arguments of the Four Horsemen and aware of the changing economic landscape, Justice Roberts switched his position and began voting to uphold both New Deal and state regulation. When the 5–4 decision in *West Coast Hotel v. Parrish,* 300 U.S. 379 (1937) was announced, it was clear that Roberts, along with Chief Justice Hughes had had a change of heart. Later that year, in *National Labor Relations Board v. Jones & Laughlin Steel Corporation,* 301 U.S. 1 (1937), Roberts and Hughes confirmed their switch in upholding a major piece of New Deal legislation.

This switch signified a new era of liberal justices appointed by Roosevelt. By 1937 the Democrats controlled approximately 80 percent of the seats in both Houses, and Roosevelt was reelected with 97 percent of the electoral votes. In 1937 Roosevelt nominated Hugo Black, the first of his nine High Court appointments. These justices, combined with his appointments to the lower federal courts, solidified the triumph of the New Deal.

Roosevelt radically reorganized the American political landscape. He ushered in a new era in American politics that saw the emergence of such liberal notions as federal economic and social regulations; increased help for the underprivileged, such as poor, elderly, young, and handicapped; and civil rights. Roosevelt embodied the tension between personal liberty and the constructive power of democratic government. He assembled not simply a series of programs but a modern approach to government. Viewing the law as a tool, he used it to further develop the presidency and the United States. Not only did Roosevelt personally dominate American politics for a quarter of a century but the appointments he made to the Supreme Court and federal judiciary dominated the political landscape for decades beyond his death.

For more information

Leuchtenburg, William E. *The Supreme Court Reborn: The Constitutional Revolution in the Age of Roosevelt.* New York: Oxford University Press, 1995.

Ackerman, Bruce. *We The People II: Transformations.* Cambridge, Mass.: Harvard University Press, 2000.

James Wyer and Artemus Ward
California State University, Chico

S

San Antonio Independent School District v. Rodriguez

San Antonio Independent School District v. Rodriguez 411 U.S. 1 (1973) was an important Supreme Court case that helped to determine the scope of the Fourteenth Amendment by deciding whether a system of funding for public education through property taxes violated the equal protection clause by failing to distribute funds equally among school districts.

Because school funding is based primarily on property taxes, districts with more valuable property had a much larger base from which to fund their schools. Nowhere was this dilemma more pronounced than in the districts in this case. In San Antonio, Edgewood Elementary School, where Demetrio Rodriguez sent his children, was in a very poor area. While Edgewood's citizens taxed their houses at the state's highest rate, since their property value was so low, they raised only $26 per student when this challenge was first raised in 1970. Compared with the neighboring suburb of Alamo Heights, this seems even more extreme.

Despite having the state's lowest tax rate, citizens of Alamo Heights raised $333 per student. Even with the addition of state and federal funds to level some of this disparity, residents of Alamo Heights had nearly twice as much to spend per student on education. The impact of these numbers on the quality of education was just as dramatic. At the Alamo Heights schools, nearly half of the teachers had master's degrees. In Edgewood, half of the teachers had no certification at all. Where the school buildings in Edgewood were in disrepair, the Alamo Heights schools had tennis courts and swimming pools. Rodriguez claimed that the property tax system of public school finance violated the equal protection guarantee found in the Fourteenth Amendment by making educational expenditures, and thus educational quality, a function of money. The result of this system was to assure an inferior education to those who were poor. Since the state created the financing system, and this system created great inequality between schools, the state had denied the poor citizens of Edgewood equal protection of the law.

By a vote of 5–4, the Supreme Court rejected Rodriguez's argument holding that wealth is not a suspect classification. Justice Powell, writing for the majority, found that education is not a fundamental right since it is not guaranteed anywhere in the Constitution. Because it was not a fundamental right, the Court applied their lowest level of scrutiny, the rational basis test. Since the state did not deny a free public education to any citizen and there was some historical basis for the use of property taxes in this manner, the Court found no violation. While admitting that the system was not perfect, Powell argued that "the Equal Protection Clause does not require absolute equality or precisely equal advantages."

The dissenters, led by Thurgood Marshall, argued that there are many fundamental rights not specifically spelled out in the Constitution, such as the right to procreate or the right to appeal a criminal conviction. Still, the Court has recognized their importance to an evolving society. Rodriguez may have lost this battle; however, he ultimately won the war. The ruling forced him into state court to challenge this school funding system. Despite the decision of the United States Supreme Court, the Texas Supreme Court ruled in 1989 that while the U.S. Constitution may not have been violated by this funding plan, the Texas Constitution was. The court ordered the legislature to redesign their system so that every district would be relatively equal in per pupil revenues. Finally, in 1991, this order became a reality.

For more information

Hall, Kermit. *The Oxford Guide to United States Supreme Court Decisions.* New York: Oxford University Press, 1999.

Irons, Peter. *May It Please the Court.* New York: The New Press, 1993.

Paul Weizer
Fitchburg State College

Scalia, Antonin (1936–) was appointed by President Ronald Reagan in 1986 to be an associate justice of the United States Supreme Court.

Noted for his active questioning of lawyers during oral arguments and for his often pointed dissents, Justice Scalia is a reliable conservative voice on the Rehnquist Court, usually favoring the government over individual rights, state over federal power, property over civil rights, and using the intent of the framers as a way to interpret the Constitution.

Antonin Scalia was born in 1936 in New York City. He was the son of a professor of Romance languages at Brooklyn College. Growing up Roman Catholic, he was educated at Xavier High School, a Catholic military academy in Manhattan. After graduating first in his class at Georgetown University, Scalia attended Harvard Law School. He practiced law for eight years with a Cleveland firm before becoming a law professor at the University of Virginia. Scalia was an attorney in the Justice Department during President Richard Nixon's administration and an assistant attorney general in the Office of Legal Counsel during President Gerald Ford's administration.

From 1997 to 1981, Scalia taught law at the University of Chicago and was a commentator and editor of the American Enterprise Institute's journal, *Regulation.* President Reagan appointed Scalia to the U.S. Court of Appeals for the District of Columbia Circuit in 1982 and then elevated him to the United States Supreme Court in 1986 when William Rehnquist was picked to replace the retiring Warren Burger as chief justice. Both in 1982 and in 1986, he was easily and overwhelmingly confirmed by the Senate.

Antonin Scalia's background has been cited as being important to his legal thinking in several ways. His Catholicism is cited as important to his opposition to abortion and homosexual rights in such cases as *Planned Parenthood v. Casey,* 505 U.S. 833 (1992); *Webster v. Reproductive Health Services,* 492 U.S. 490 (1989); and *Romer v. Evans,* 517 U.S. 620 (1996). The influence of his father as a professor of Romance languages has been described as important to his use of specific techniques to interpret the law, and his own role as a law professor to his tendency to quiz lawyers and argue with his colleagues on the Court, on the bench, and through his opinions.

Justice Antonin Scalia (PHOTOGRAPH BY JOSEPH LAVEN-BURG, NATIONAL GEOGRAPHIC, COURTESY THE SUPREME COURT OF THE UNITED STATES)

Justice Scalia is considered part of a five-vote conservative majority on the Rehnquist Court that has often taken controversial positions. For example, he has joined the majority in placing limits on the application of federal commerce power and civil rights on states in cases such as *Seminole Tribe v. Florida,* 517 U.S. 44 (1996); *Kimel v. Florida Board of Regents,* 120 S.Ct. 631 (2000); *United States v. Morrison,* 120 S.Ct. 1740 (2000); and *Board of Trustees of the University of Alabama v. Garrett,* 531 U.S. 356 (2001). Yet Scalia has also earned a reputation as a supporter of free speech, with *R.A.V. v. St. Paul,* 505 U.S. 377 (1992) striking down an ordinance on hate speech on First Amendment grounds often cited as evidence. Yet opinions such as *Rust v. Sullivan,* 111 S.Ct. 1759 (1991); *Rankin v. McPherson,* 483 U.S. 378 (1987); and *Legal Services Corporation v.*

Velazquez, 121 S.Ct. 1224 (2001), limiting the speech rights of doctors, public employees, or lawyers contradict that claim.

Scalia's concurring opinion in the *Bush v. Gore* II, 531 U.S. 98 (2000) order halting the recounting of the 2000 presidential ballots in Florida was viewed by many as a very overt statement and indication of his willingness to bend the law to favor the election of George W. Bush. Despite being part of a voting bloc on the Court, Scalia, oftentimes with Justice Thomas, issued separate concurring opinions or stand-alone dissents.

For more information

Brisbin, Richard A., Jr. *Justice Antonin Scalia and the Conservative Revival.* Baltimore, Md.: The Johns Hopkins University Press, 1997.

Schultz, David A., and Christopher E. Smith, *The Jurisprudential Vision of Justice Antonin Scalia.* Lanham, Md.: Rowman and Littlefield, 1996.

David Schultz
Hamline University

Schenck v. U.S. 249 U.S. 47 (1919) was a major milestone in development of the U.S. Supreme Court's modern interpretation of the First Amendment's protection of free speech.

Decided in 1919, the *Schenck* decision was written by Justice Oliver Wendell Holmes and enshrined two important concepts in modern debate over the meaning of free speech—the "clear and present danger" test and the image of "falsely shouting fire in a theatre."

Although the "clear and present danger" test became part of the lore of First Amendment protection for radical, even revolutionary, speech, the test was not used that way when it was decided. Holmes used the test to curb free speech and to uphold the conviction of Schenck.

Schenck was an official of the Socialist Party. In 1917 with World War I well under way, Schenck was responsible for printing 15,000 leaflets and having them mailed to men who had just passed their draft board examinations. The leaflet on one side equated the draft with slavery and argued that it has been outlawed by the Thirteenth Amendment. On the other side, the leaflet urged men to assert their rights or be treated as little more than convicts. Schenck was convicted of violating the federal espionage law and was sentenced to six months in prison.

The Supreme Court unanimously upheld Schenck's conviction. Holmes conceded that in peacetime the leaflet might have been protected by the First Amendment, but he said free speech protection varied with the circumstances. "The most stringent protection of free speech would not protect a man in falsely shouting fire in a theatre and causing a panic," Holmes wrote. This image has come to symbolize the outer limit of free speech protection in the United States.

Holmes then announced the famous test that calls for a balancing of interests: "The question in every case is whether the words used are used in such circumstances and are of such a nature as to create a clear and present danger that they will bring about the substantive evils that Congress has a right to prevent." It did not seem to matter in the *Schenck* decision that the leaflets did not produce open resistance to the draft. It was enough, Holmes said, that the leaflets were intended to thwart the draft and that the words used might have a "tendency" to cause such resistance.

It did not take long for Holmes to decide that his test allowed too much restriction of free speech, and he began to dissent in other free speech cases. His dissents set the Supreme Court on a gradual path to a much more vigorous meaning for the "clear and present danger" standard that was far more protective of free speech. The journey took 50 years and culminated in 1969 with the decision in *Brandenburg v. Ohio*, sometimes called the modern restatement of the *Schenck* test. In *Brandenburg*, the Court said that speech advocating unlawful force or violence may still be protected by the First Amendment, unless it is both directed at inciting "imminent lawless action" and is "likely to incite" such action.

For more information

Kalven Harry, Jr., and Jamie Kalven, eds., *Worthy Tradition: Freedom of Speech in America.* New York: Harper and Row, 1987.

Smolla, Rodney A. *Smolla and Nimmer on Freedom of Speech.* St. Paul, Minn.: West Group Publishing, 1996.

Stephen Wermiel
American University Washington College of Law

Second Amendment See ARMS, RIGHT TO BEAR.

section 1983 actions are lawsuits under 42 U.S.C. section 1983, probably the most important federal civil rights statute.

Section 1983 provides, "Every person who, under color of any statute . . . of any State . . . subjects . . . any citizen of the United States . . . to the deprivation of any right . . . secured by the Constitution or laws, shall be liable to the party injured. . . ." In other words, a person who believes his federal civil rights have been violated may sue the violator under section 1983.

Congress enacted section 1983 as part of the 1871 Civil Rights Act to enforce the protections provided by the Fourteenth Amendment by protecting newly emancipated slaves from violence in the South, particularly as perpetrated by the Ku Klux Klan. Importantly, however, section 1983 was aimed not at the Klan but at state officials who were unwilling or unable to enforce the law in the face of Klan violence.

For much of its history, plaintiffs and courts largely ignored section 1983, based on the Supreme Court's narrow construction of the Fourteenth Amendment and its reluctance to apply the protections of the Bill of Rights to state governments. It was not until the Court's landmark decision in *Monroe v. Pape*, 365 U.S. 167

(1961), that section 1983 reclaimed its intended role as the primary means of enforcing federal civil rights. In *Monroe* the Court held that the plaintiffs had stated a valid cause of action under section 1983 by alleging that police illegally searched their home in violation of the Fourth Amendment. The Court expanded the reach of section 1983 and opened "deep pockets" to plaintiffs in *Monell v. Department of Social Services,* 436 U.S. 658 (1978), by holding that cities and local governments, as well as individuals, could be sued under section 1983. (States, however, cannot be sued under section 1983.) As a result of these and other cases, the number of section 1983 actions has increased dramatically.

To bring a section 1983 action, a plaintiff must allege that her federal civil rights were violated by someone acting "under color" of state law, such as a police officer, public school board official, or state social worker. (For defendants acting under color of federal law, a plaintiff may bring a similar claim, known as a *Bivens* action after the Court's decision in *Bivens v. Six Unknown Federal Narcotics Agents,* 403 U.S. 388 [1971].) A person acts under color of law when he acts according to some governmental authority, even when he abuses that authority. To sue a city or local government under section 1983, a plaintiff must allege that the city either authorized or condoned the civil rights violation through an official policy or custom.

A civil rights defendant may argue that he is immune from suit—that is, he cannot be sued by the plaintiff under section 1983. Prosecutors, judges, and legislators have absolute immunity from civil rights suits: They cannot be sued for carrying out their official functions. Other government actors, such as police officers and prison officials, have qualified immunity. They may be held liable only for conduct that violates a clearly established civil right, meaning that a reasonable official would have understood that his conduct violated that right under settled law.

Section 1983 plaintiffs may seek compensatory, punitive, or nominal damages, as well as injunctive relief—an order requiring a defendant to take certain action or forbidding him from taking certain action. Successful section 1983 plaintiffs also may be awarded their attorney fees under the 1976 Civil Rights Attorney's Fees Awards Act.

For more information

Nahmod, Sheldon H. *Civil Rights and Civil Liberties Litigation: The Law of Section 1983,* 4th ed. Colo. Colorado Springs, Colo.: Shepard's McGraw-Hill, 1999.

Prof. Kathryn R. L. Rand
University of North Dakota School of Law

Securities and Exchange Commission (SEC)

is the federal agency responsible for enforcement and administration of the federal securities laws.

The agency is composed of five commissioners and their staff, with its headquarters in Washington, D.C. There are also several regional and district offices located throughout the United States. Each commissioner is appointed by the president, with the advice and consent of the Senate. Commissioners serve five-year terms, but the terms are staggered so that only one position opens each year. Additionally, only three members of the same political party may serve on the commission at the same time, ensuring that the SEC remains nonpartisan. One commissioner is selected by the president to serve as chairman of the SEC. The commissioners meet regularly to resolve issues and make policy, and they have final authority on all decisions, but the bulk of the work is done by nearly 3,000 SEC staff members. In addition to clerical and administrative employees, the SEC staff includes lawyers, accountants, economists, examiners, paralegals, and other professionals. Most staff members work in the Washington headquarters, with the rest divided among the regional and district offices.

In response to the devastating stock market crash of 1929, Congress passed several major pieces of legislation designed to regulate and protect the capital markets and investors. The SEC was created by Congress through the Securities Exchange Act of 1934 to oversee and administer the newly created federal securities laws. These laws include the Securities Act of 1933, the Securities Exchange Act of 1934, the Public Utility Holding Company Act of 1935, the Trust Indenture Act of 1939, the Investment Advisers Act of 1940, and the Investment Company Act of 1940.

These acts were created and passed by Congress, and they remain the primary source of federal securities law, but one of the most important functions of the SEC is to promulgate new rules and regulations that interpret, clarify, and implement those broadly written acts. Because the SEC is an independent agency, it is able to respond to changing circumstances in the market and the industry much more quickly and effectively than Congress. Despite the age of the various securities laws, they remain dynamic and effective because of the SEC's ability to create new rules for changing situations. Many of the materials issued by the SEC have the force of law (especially the "rules"), and some have nearly the force of law, while certain publications contain only policies or interpretations of the SEC. Even the material that does not have the force of law is respected by the courts and the securities industry and plays an important role in federal securities regulation.

In addition to the SEC's rule-making capacity, the agency has two other important functions. It can act as a court and hold hearings and other proceedings when disputes arise under the various federal securities laws. The decisions of these courts act much like the decisions of any other court and can be appealed to the U.S. Court of Appeals. The SEC also has an important enforcement function. It has the power to investigate potential violations of the securities laws. This power includes statutory authority to subpoena witnesses and compel production of documents. The SEC is also authorized to take legal action and impose substantial civil penalties for violations of the securities laws, either through an internal administrative hearing or in federal district court. Although criminal penalties can result from securities fraud or other violations, the SEC does not prosecute these cases. Instead, the agency provides information and other assistance to the Justice Department.

For more information
The SEC's website at http://www.sec.gov.
Ratner, David L. *Securities Regulation in a Nutshell,* 6th ed. St. Paul, Minn.: West Group Publishing, 1998.

John H. Matheson
Melvin C. Steen and Corporate Donors
Professor of Law
University of Minnesota Law School

segregation   is the legal or actual separation of people based upon race, gender, or ethnicity. Oftentimes segregation occurs in housing, education, or other public or private accommodations or facilities.

Since the beginning of the American republic there have been varying attempts at segregation or the division of people based on inherent characteristics such as gender or ethnicity. The legal issue of segregation was a major issue before the Supreme Court during the 20th century. Most government efforts at segregation have occurred at the state and local level and were most pronounced after the period of Southern Reconstruction. Southern legislators passed what became known as Jim Crow laws, maintaining a division in government and community based on race. These laws were identified by the Court in *Plessy v. Ferguson* (1896). In *Plessy* the Court stated that segregation was not unconstitutional if conducted on the basis of

A drinking fountain on the county courthouse lawn, Halifax, North Carolina, 1938 (Library of Congress)

separate but equal public facilities. While *Plessy* dealt specifically with segregation in railroad cars, the decision was used to enforce segregation in education, public facilities, and accommodations.

Yet the Court did not use "separate but equal" to uphold all segregation laws. As some states broadened the segregation of the races, the Court looked closely at their impact. These laws included peonage, in which black defendants were forced to work on farms in order to pay off their fines. Other segregation laws restricted voting rights and included literacy tests, white primaries, and grandfather clauses. Each of these were challenged before the U.S. Supreme Court and struck down as a violation of the Fourteenth Amendment's equal protection clause.

But it was not until the *Brown v. Board of Education* decision in 1954 that the justices clearly defined the line between legally mandated segregation and societal segregation. The former, known as de jure segregation, is found in laws written by legislatures and in restricted use of public accommodations by blacks. De jure segregation was outlawed by the Supreme

Court and by congressional legislation. The Court struck down such things as restrictive covenants in *Sweatt v. Painter (1950)* and the white primary in *Smith v. Allwright* (1944). Congress acted later with the 1964 Civil Rights Act, prohibiting private discrimination that was enforced under the color of state law and local ordinance.

A counterpart to de jure segregation is de facto segregation, which refers to division of races based on residential patterns. De facto is not mandated by the state or required under law. Instead it is a voluntary form of segregation. De facto has been recognized by the Supreme Court, which ruled that because it was based on private action it did not allow for a judicial remedy. In the case of *Milliken v. Bradley* (1974), the Court ruled that de facto segregation in residential patterns could not be remedied by forced busing of students from suburban schools to urban schools.

For more information

Rasmussen, R. Kent. *Farewell to Jim Crow: The Rise and Fall of Segregation in America.* New York: Facts On File, 1994.

Warren, Robert Penn. *Segregation: The Inner Conflict in the South.* Athens: University of Georgia Press, 1990.

Douglas Clouatre
Kennesaw State University

self-defense   is a rule of criminal law that permits individuals to use force to protect themselves from others using unlawful physical force against them.

Self-defense does not apply if the person has used a proper amount of legally permitted force, e.g., in an arrest of a suspect or punishment of a child. Another rule, the defense of others, also allows people to use force to protect third parties in similar situations. These common-law rules are recognized by statutes and courts in virtually every state in the United States. If a person is found not guilty by reason of self-defense, his actions are considered legally justified. While self-defense can be raised in any case where the defendant claims he was protecting himself from another's unlawful physical contact, the most controversial self-defense cases have been in intentional homicides.

Most courts have developed a set of strict requirements a defendant must meet to justify the use of deadly force, force that will cause death or serious bodily injury. Usually, a defendant cannot be the aggressor in the conflict, the person who provokes the violence, although he may regain his right to self-defense by leaving the situation and communicating that he will not use force unless he is attacked. He must also show that he reasonably feared that he was in immediate or imminent danger of being killed or seriously injured, or in some states that he is about to be the victim of a serious crime such as robbery or kidnapping. Threats of even serious harm in the future, or threats of lesser physical harm, such as a broken nose, are not enough to justify using deadly force. The defendant must show that deadly force was necessary to repel the force against him. Therefore, if the defendant could have tripped the aggressor to stop him rather than killing him, he would not be acting in self-defense. Self-defense must also be proportional to the force offered by the aggressor: Shooting a person who is approaching with only his fists would not be self-defense unless it was reasonable to believe that the aggressor could and would kill with his bare hands. Finally, a minority of states require that defendants try to retreat, or leave the scene, if they can do so in complete safety, instead of standing their ground and fighting. However, most of these "retreat" states do not require people to retreat in their own homes, and some states do not require retreat in the defendant's workplace, although a few states do require retreat even in these settings if the aggressor also lives in the home or works in the same place.

People v. Goetz is a famous New York self-defense case involving a white subway rider who shot three unarmed black teenagers who asked him for money, claiming that he honestly feared that he was going to be robbed or maimed. Critics charged that Goetz's reaction was way out of proportion to his reasonable fears; or that if he was honestly afraid, his fear was based on the victims' race, not on any objective reasons. The New York Court of Appeals held that Goetz's belief must be more than honest, it must be reasonable, though the jury could consider his past mugging experience, his and his claimed attackers' physical strength and size, and other relevant circumstances in deciding if he was reasonable. This defense has also been controversial in battered women's cases in which a wife kills her abusive husband while he is asleep or not threatening her with death right at the time she kills. Many courts have held that the threat to these women is not imminent and deadly force is not necessary, since battered women can seek help from the police and social agencies. Women's advocates claim that in some longtime battering situations, wives can reasonably realize that their husbands' violence has escalated to the point of killing, and that government resources often turn their backs on the women. Others have argued that though a non-battered woman might realize that help is available so that killing is not necessary, many battered women come to believe that they are helpless to escape their abusers even with assistance from others and must kill in order to protect their lives. In these and other cases where the defendant cannot meet all of the requirements to be exonerated, some states will downgrade a murder to manslaughter and impose a lesser punishment.

For more information

Dressler, Joshua. *Understanding Criminal Law,* 2nd ed. New York: Matthew Bender, 1995.

Ewing, Charles Patrick. *Battered Women Who Kill: Psychological Self-Defense as Legal Justification.* Lexington, Mass.: Lexington Books, 1987.

Fletcher, George P. *A Crime of Self-Defense: Bernhard Goetz and the Law on Trial.* New York: The Free Press, 1988.

Marie Failinger
Hamline University Law School

self-incrimination   is the privileged protection (or right) found in the Fifth Amendment to the U.S. Constitution which provides that. "No person . . . shall be compelled in any criminal case to be a witness against himself." While the protection is also found in state constitutions, it is applicable to them through the due process clause of the Fourteenth Amendment.

The protection originated from English Puritan John Lilburne's refusal (1637) to testify against himself before the Star Chamber, which could (as could the ecclesiastical courts) use physical torture or compulsory oaths to gain evidence. The Fifth Amendment's clause expresses the founding fathers' view that such methods probably produce untrue confessions, because those tortured confess to escape pain or terror, rather than from a guilty conscience; furthermore, coercion insults basic human dignity.

The protection applies only in criminal matters that could result in prosecution. The U.S. accusatory system does not allow a person to be forced to give testimony or evidence that might result in criminal prosecution. The protection is a right to silence that applies to the investigation phase of a case, to grand jury proceedings, and during the conduct of a trial.

At various times numerous complaints have been made against Communists, mob leaders, and other unpopular persons "taking the Fifth," before televised congressional investigations, especially if involving national security. The impression gained among the general populace was that the Fifth shielded the guilty rather than sheltering the innocent.

Other complaints against the self-incrimination protection have arisen from those seeking to protect society from criminals. The *Miranda* case,

Miranda v. Arizona, 384 U.S., 436 (1966), applied the protection to the investigative stage of a case. Since then the claim has been frequently made that the Miranda rules hamper police work. Complaints that society's rights outweigh an individual's right to silence will usually look to be the stronger argument unless the telling history of the privilege is remembered.

The Fifth Amendment is not a protection against many evidentiary procedures such as fingerprinting, DNA testing, exhibiting one's body, voice exemplars, taking a sobriety test, or other such methods. Nor can it be invoked if the defendant is part of some regulatory system such as the regulation of the stock market or the supervision of a social service system (*Baltimore City Dep't of Social Services v. Bouknight*, 493 U.S. 549 [1990]). The protection cannot be claimed, and testimony or evidence withheld, if a grant of immunity from prosecution is issued. Nor does it apply to civil proceedings.

Difficult areas include the failure to immediately invoke the privilege, the limits of disclosure required, and when questions are incriminating and when they are not. There is still controversy between those who claim the protection is a right and those who see it as a privilege that government can suspend.

For more information

Berger, Mark. *Taking the Fifth: The Supreme Court and the Privilege against Self-Incrimination.* Lexington, Mass.: Lexington Books, 1980.

Levy, Leonard W. *Origins of the Fifth Amendment: The Right against Self-Incrimination.* New York: Oxford University Press, 1968.

A. J. L. Waskey
Dalton State College

sentencing of a criminal defendant occurs after a defendant has been found guilty of a criminal offense or offenses. This may happen as a result of guilty finding by a finder of fact, either a jury or a judge, or after a defendant has pleaded guilty.

The authority to sentence a defendant who has been convicted of a crime is granted by various legislative bodies to the courts. The range of sentences varies in degrees of severity, according to the seriousness of the offense of which the defendant was convicted. The range of available sentences include the following:

Death Penalty. "Capital punishment is authorized by statute in all but twelve states." Wayne R. LaFave, Jerold H. Israel, and Nancy J. King, *Criminal Procedure* vol. 5, sec. 26.1(b), 697 (2d ed., West Criminal Practice Series 1999). Capitol punishment is also authorized under federal law. The death penalty has long been a controversial subject in the United States.

Incarceration. Incarceration, or placing a convicted individual in jail, is a legislatively authorized form of punishment. "Legislation authorizing incarceration provides the range of allowable incarceration for each offense, specifies whether sentences will be indeterminate (parole eligible) or determinate (no parole available), and often prescribes alternative sentences or sentence enhancements for some offenses or offenders." Wayne R. LaFave, Jerold H. Israel, and Nancy J. King, *Criminal Procedure* vol. 5, sec. 26.1(c), 702 (2d ed., West Criminal Practice Series 1999). Offenders convicted of multiple offenses can be given terms of incarceration that run either concurrently or consecutively.

Community Release. Community release allows an offender to remain in the community after conviction. It involves the supervised release of offenders and can take various forms. Wayne R. LaFave, Jerold H. Israel, and Nancy J. King, *Criminal Procedure* vol. 5, sec. 26.1(d), 705 (2d ed., West Criminal Practice Series 1999). Community release can be as restrictive as home confinement. Under a sentence of home confinement, an offender's mobility is strictly curtailed, and he or she is only allowed to leave home for certain specified reasons.

Community release can also take the form of probation. The offender is released subject to the certain terms and conditions and required to be supervised by the court probation department. The level of supervision is tailored to the severity of the offense and the nature of the offender. When imposing a sentence of probation, the court can also impose a sentence of incarceration, which is suspended. The suspended sentence can then be imposed if the offender violates the terms and conditions of probation. Probationary terms for multiple offenses can be imposed either concurrently or consecutively.

Fines. "All jurisdictions provide for the use of fines in misdemeanor cases, and commonly allow the fine to be the only sanction for such offenses. Fines are also authorized for many felonies and are the primary sanction for corporate defendants. Despite its widespread use, the fine is not considered as serious a penalty as incarceration for individual offenders, and is usually imposed in addition to a term of incarceration." Wayne R. LaFave, Jerold H. Israel, and Nancy J. King, *Criminal Procedure* vol. 5, sec. 26.1(f), 715 (2d ed., West Criminal Practice Series 1999).

Legislatures often provide guidelines for use in the imposition of sentences to aid the sentencing authority in using its discretion in imposing sentences. However, some offenses carry mandatory sentences, and the sentencing authority is allowed no discretion in imposing sentences upon conviction of such offenses.

For more information

LaFave, Wayne R., Jerold H. Israel, and Nancy J. King, *Criminal Procedure,* 2nd ed. Vol 5, sect. 26. St. Paul, Minn.: West Criminal Practice Series, 1999.

Myra Orlen
Western New England College of Law

sentencing guidelines are recommended sentences or sentence ranges promulgated by the legislature, a sentencing commission, or the courts.

Some guidelines are purely advisory, while others are legally binding; however, even the latter permit "departures" based on exceptional circumstances. Guidelines are designed to make punishment decisions more uniform and avoid disparities in the treatment of similar cases. Some guidelines are also intended to serve other goals, including one or more of the following: encouraging implementation of particular sentencing policies for some or all offenders; promoting the development of more rational sentencing policy developed and monitored by an independent, expert agency (the sentencing commission) with some degree of insulation from short-term political and media pressures; and coordinating sentencing policy with available correctional resources (in particular, avoiding prison overcrowding).

Before there were sentencing guidelines, all U.S. states and the federal courts employed "indeterminate" sentencing systems. Under these systems, judges had almost complete discretion to impose any sentence up to the statutory maximum, and parole boards had broad discretion to decide how much of any prison sentence had to be served. These discretionary powers were based on the view that the most important goal of punishment was to rehabilitate offenders, and that this goal required sentences to be tailored to the particular treatment needs and risks posed by each offender. Judges would initially decide whether the offender was amenable to treatment in the community; if he was not, a substantial prison term would be imposed, and parole officials would then monitor the defendant's progress and determine when it was safe to release him.

In the 1970s indeterminate sentencing began to fall out of favor. Some critics argued that the broad discretion exercised by judges and parole boards permitted substantial disparities in the sentencing of offenders convicted of similar crimes, that case-specific assessments of offender amenability and dangerousness were unreliable, and that few treatment programs had been shown to be effective. Other critics felt that judges and parole boards used their discretion to impose unduly lenient sentences. A number of reforms, including sentencing guidelines, were proposed as a means of reducing disparities by reducing sentencing and parole discretion. In some courts, judges began experimenting with voluntary guidelines.

For example, guidelines for the crime of assault causing serious bodily injury might provide the following recommended prison sentences: for offenders with no prior convictions—80 to 90 months in prison (with the precise duration to be decided by the sentencing judge); for those with one prior felony conviction—90 to 100 months; with two prior felonies—100 to 110 months; and so on. For less serious assaults, the guidelines would recommend that offenders with no more than two prior convictions be placed on probation, perhaps combined with a short jail term, and with specified prison terms to be imposed on probation violators. Such judicial sentencing guidelines might be combined with abolition of parole release discretion; in that case, offenders would be required to serve their entire prison sentence, except for reductions for good behavior.

In 1980 the state of Minnesota became the first jurisdiction to adopt legally enforceable, statewide sentencing guidelines promulgated by a permanent sentencing commission. Since then, about 20 other states and the federal courts have adopted guidelines (although a few states subsequently repealed them). Most of the remaining states continue to use indeterminate sentencing but with some limitations on discretion; in almost all states (including those with sentencing guidelines), certain offenses or offenders (especially repeat offenders) are subject to mandatory sentencing laws, requiring the court to impose a prison term of at least a specified length (unlike sentencing guidelines, such mandatory-sentence laws do not permit "departures"). Many other states have limited or abolished parole release discretion, while retaining broad judicial sentencing discretion.

State and federal guidelines systems are very diverse (indeed, some state systems are not even called "guidelines"; instead, terms like "structured sentencing" are used). Over one-third of the state systems retain parole release discretion and only use guidelines to regulate judicial sentencing decisions. In more than half of the state systems, the recommended sentences are not legally binding (either because the guidelines are "voluntary," or because departures from the guidelines are not closely reviewed by appellate courts). Almost all systems are now using the greater predictability of guidelines sentences as a basis for estimating future prison populations, but systems use these estimates in different ways. Some use them both to adjust guidelines rules so as to reduce the need for additional prison capacity, and to determine how much to increase that capacity; in other systems, prison forecasts are primarily used to make prison-expansion decisions. Newer guidelines systems tend to be broader in scope. Whereas most of the early systems only regulated decisions about whether to impose a prison term and the duration of prison terms, some newer systems have also sought to regulate local jail sentences and/or to encourage increased use of "intermediate sanctions," such as intensive probation, home detention with electronic monitoring, fines, community service, and residential treatment. Most guidelines, new and old, are limited to the sentencing of felony crimes, but a few also cover some or all misdemeanors.

Although guidelines systems continue to expand both in number and in scope, they are not without critics. The federal guidelines have been particularly unpopular with judges, academics, and defense attorneys. Some of the judicial reaction may be due to the fact that federal judges are a powerful and prestigious group, unwilling to give up their traditional sentencing discretion. But most of the opposition is based on certain problematic features of the federal guidelines: They are much more complex than most state systems; they require judges to increase the sentence based on facts which were not part of any convicted offense; and they incorporate many severe mandatory minimum prison terms required by federal statutes, which only prosecutors have the power to avoid. As a result of the guidelines (in combination with changes in federal criminal statutes and law enforcement policies), the federal prison population more than doubled during the 1990s, increasing at a much more rapid rate than most state prison populations (although the latter were also increasing dramatically).

Unlike the federal guidelines, most state guidelines have been accepted by judges, attorneys, and academics. In part, this is due to the more modest nature of the state reforms—many are voluntary, and even the legally binding systems are quite flexible, leaving many areas unregulated. In particular, no state guidelines system places any major limits on sentence differentials related to plea bargaining, and most of these systems do not closely regulate conditions of probation.

Despite these limitations, many state guidelines systems have succeeded in bringing greater uniformity and rationality to sentencing policy and practice, while also using the greater uniformity of guidelines to predict and avoid prison overcrowding. And although all of the state systems remain committed to the goal of limiting sentencing discretion, many of these systems permit limited forms of indeterminate sentencing (e.g., allowing departures from recommended prison sentences, for offenders who appear particularly amenable to probation; giving particularly dangerous offenders longer prison terms and post-prison supervision). A number of the state systems have also found ways to incorporate newly emerging sentencing theories such as restorative justice.

In short, state guidelines provide a valuable structure and "starting point" for all sentences,

and an improved ability to manage correctional resources, while still leaving enough flexibility to take account of unusual offense facts, offender characteristics, and the needs of victims and the community. Since no other existing or proposed sentencing system accommodates all of these important goals and values, it is likely that more and more states will adopt sentencing guidelines designed to maintain a workable balance between the competing goals of uniformity and flexibility.

For more information

Frase, Richard S. "Sentencing Guidelines in Minnesota, Other States, and the Federal Courts: A Twenty-Year Retrospective," *Federal Sentencing Reporter* 12 (2000): 69–82.

Tonry, Michael. *Sentencing Matters.* New York: Oxford University Press, 1996.

Richard S. Frase
University of Minnesota Law School

separate but equal   was a legal doctrine used by the courts in the early 20th century to maintain state-enforced racial segregation.

The Supreme Court announced the "separate but equal" doctrine in *Plessy v. Ferguson,* 163 U.S. 537 (1896), establishing legally enforceable boundaries of interaction between races in the United States. The Court ruled that a law segregating whites and blacks using railroad transportation did not violate the equal protection clause of the Fourteenth Amendment. In the words of the Court, "laws permitting, and even requiring . . . separation in places where [whites and blacks] are liable to be brought into contact do not imply the inferiority of either race."

According to *Plessy,* states could pass segregation laws as long as these laws were reasonably related to public welfare, and the states provided separate and equal accommodations. Later, the Court defined equal as "substantially equal," not exactly equal, in quality or amount. In reality, this ambiguous definition compelled blacks and

NAACP youth and student members marching with signs protesting Texas segregation laws, Houston, Texas (Library of Congress)

other minorities to accept separate, but very often inferior, accommodations. In many cases, the Court determined that inferior facilities met the Fourteenth Amendment's requirement for equal treatment (*Cumming v. Richmond County Board of Education,* 175 U.S. 528 [1899]). However, in later cases the Court began to strike down segregation laws where states refused to provide facilities for blacks that actually were equal in quality (*McCabe v. Atchison,* 235 U.S. 151 [1914]).

Ultimately, the "separate but equal" doctrine became the basis for treatment of minorities under law in most matters of public accommodation, including transportation, hospitals, cemeteries, libraries, public restrooms, and especially in public schooling. Lawyers for blacks and other minorities, led primarily by the National

Association for the Advancement of Colored People (*see* NAACP), decided to attack "separate but equal" in court. They began by challenging laws requiring segregation in education.

First the NAACP brought cases attacking how the states treated college students. Three important cases highlight the NAACP's efforts. In *Missouri ex rel. Gaines v. Canada,* 305 U.S. 237 (1938), the Court found that states must provide equal opportunities for a law school education. In a later case, the Court found that states could not admit a black graduate student to the same school as white students and segregate him from those white students within the classroom and other facilities (*McLaurin v. Oklahoma State Regents for Higher Education,* 339 U.S. 637 [1950]). Finally, in *Sweatt v. Painter,* 340 U.S. 846 (1950), the Court effectively overturned "separate but equal" as applied to postgraduate college education. It ruled that blacks seeking graduate education could attend public universities where the state has no segregated institution of equal reputation.

After receiving these favorable rulings on college education, lawyers began to challenge the segregation of public school children. In the landmark case *Brown v. Board of Education I,* 347 U.S. 483 (1954), the Court rejected "separate but equal" as a doctrine justifying the segregation of public school children. The Court issued a unanimous opinion stating that separation of the races in public education was inherently unequal even where the state provided comparable facilities. According to the Court, segregation robbed minorities of opportunities and instilled a sense of inferiority. In a second case, *Brown v. Board II,* 349 U.S. 294 (1955), the Court considered how the integration of public schools should proceed. It declined to set a timetable but ordered that states proceed "with all deliberate speed" toward compliance with the original *Brown* ruling.

Although the task of ending segregation in other public accommodations fell to the U.S. Congress and president, the Court contributed significantly to the demise of legally enforced segregation under the "separate but equal" doctrine. The Supreme Court's rulings in *Brown I* and *Brown II* marked the end of court-mandated segregation. Clearly, the Supreme Court played a central role in creating the legal justification for widespread segregation, but it also played a crucial role in ending segregationist policies.

For more information

Haskins, James. *Separate but Not Equal.* New York: Scholastic, 1998.

Martin Waldo E. Jr. *Brown v. Board of Education: A Brief History with Documents.* New York: Bedford Press, 1998.

Hans J. Hacker
Adjunct Professor of Public Law
University of Maryland

Shapiro v. Thompson   394 U.S. 618 (1969) is a United States Supreme Court decision that declared unconstitutional policies in several states and the District of Columbia that imposed a one-year waiting period before welfare benefits would be paid to new residents.

In this case the Court combined several appeals from three-judge district court rulings challenging the residency requirements. In all of the cases (emanating from Connecticut, Pennsylvania, and the District of Columbia) the welfare applicants moved to the new state for reasons other than increased welfare benefits: Some moved to live with their parents, others to enter foster care, and still others to care for invalid grandparents. However, when they applied for Aid to Families with Dependent Children (AFDC) or other public assistance programs, they were denied for the sole reason that they had not resided in the state for at least one year prior to applying. They challenged these waiting periods as unconstitutional denials of equal protection and the Court agreed, holding that the one-year residency requirement "creates a classification which constitutes an invidious discrimination denying them equal protection of the laws."

Indeed, the Court found that there was no compelling governmental interest to justify such laws. The right of citizens to freely travel throughout the country is fundamental, according to the majority's opinion, and so is entitled to the strictest scrutiny whenever the government is accused of impinging on that right. The majority opinion goes on to examine each claimed governmental interest in the regulation only to determine that they are not compelling enough to allow for the substantial infringements on the constitutional rights of the applicants. Deterring indigent migration to higher paying states does not pass scrutiny; limiting assistance to those contributing to the community through taxation does not justify the classification; making the welfare budget more predictable is not sufficient reason; safeguarding against welfare fraud does not make the regulation necessary; encouraging employment is not a rational basis to impose a one-year waiting period restriction on new residents only; and finally, Congress did not, and constitutionally could not, approve the imposition of such a requirement in its legislation.

The Court quotes Justice Stewart's opinion in *United States v. Guest,* 383 U.S. 745: "The constitutional right to travel from one State to another . . . occupies a position fundamental to the concept of our Federal Union. It is a right that has been firmly established and repeatedly recognized . . . as a basic right under the Constitution."

While a portion of this decision was overruled in *Edelman v. Jordan,* 415 U.S. 651—that portion that tacitly approved, under the Eleventh Amendment, court-ordered retroactive payment of benefits—the substantive precedent stands today. However, with the elimination of AFDC and other welfare reforms, the relevance of this decision may be appreciably diminished.

For more information
Anderson, Linda, Paula Sundet, and Irma Harrington. *A Handbook of Social Welfare Policy & Programs.* New York: Prentice Hall, 1999.

Epstein, Lee, and Thomas G. Walker. *Constitutional Law for a Changing America: Rights, Liberties, and Justice,* 3rd ed. Washington, D.C.: CQ Press, 1998.

Noble, Charles. *Welfare as We Knew It: A Political History of the American Welfare State.* New York: Oxford University Press, 1997.

Shaw v. Reno   509 U.S. 630 (1963) held that voters had the right to challenge a congressional districting plan if they alleged that the plan "rationally cannot be understood as anything other than an effort to separate voters into different districts on the basis of race, and the separation lacks sufficient justification." This was the first of the "racial gerrymandering" cases.

The case was filed by several voters dissatisfied with the congressional districting plan adopted by the North Carolina legislature after the 1990 census showed that the state was entitled to 12 congressional districts (an increase from its prior 11). The legislature initially drew a plan with one majority-black district (the First) in the northeastern portion of the state. The state submitted the redistricting plan to the U.S. attorney general for preclearance under section 5 of the Voting Rights Act. That section requires certain states to submit any changes in their voting, registration, or districting laws to the attorney general for consideration of whether the plan will have a discriminatory effect on racial minorities or was passed with a discriminatory intent. (See VOTING RIGHTS ACT.) The attorney general objected to the act because the boundaries in the south-central and southeastern portions of the state split concentrations of African-American and Native American voting strength.

The legislature next adopted a plan with a second majority-black district (the 12th), not in the area noted by the attorney general but rather in the central area of the state running from Durham to Greensboro to Winston-Salem to Charlotte. The Supreme Court described the district this way: "It is approximately 160 miles long and, for much of its length, no wider than the I-85 corridor. It winds in snake-like fashion through tobacco country, financial centers, and manufacturing areas 'until it gobbles in enough enclaves of black neighborhoods.'" While the legislature did intentionally create a second majority-black district, the particular placement of this district was governed by a desire to maintain the districts of as many incumbent members of Congress as possible.

The *Shaw v. Reno* decision only decided that a federal court could hear a racial gerrymandering claim but did not establish the requirements of a successful claim. That was left to subsequent decisions, principally *Miller v. Johnson,* 515 U.S. 900 (1995) and *Bush v. Vera,* 517 U.S. 952 (1996). The litigation over the North Carolina districting plan has continued throughout the decade with subsequent decisions striking down the original 12th district and later plans with modifications of the 12th. In November 2000 the Court again heard an appeal concerning the revised 12th—*Hunt v. Cromartie,* No. 99–1864.

The *Shaw v. Reno* line of cases were widely seen as a reaction to efforts by courts, legislatures, and the U.S. Justice Department to increase the number of majority-black districts. Whether the reaction was proper or improper depended on one's view of the necessity and propriety of the districts that had been drawn by legislatures and courts. The number of districts with black and Hispanic majorities had increased markedly after the 1990 census. In 1992 an additional six Hispanic and 13 black members were elected to the U.S. House of Representatives—nearly all of these coming from majority-minority districts.

For more information

Peacock, Anthony A., ed. *Affirmative Action and Representation:* Shaw v. Reno *and the Future of Voting Rights.* Durham, N.C.: Carolina Academic Press, 1997. The oral argument may be heard on the Northwestern University web site, http://oyez.nwu.edu.

Edward Still
Lawyers' Committee for Civil Rights Under Law

Shelley v. Kraemer   334 U.S. 1 (1948) was a Supreme Court case that held that restrictive covenants barring home ownership to members of racial minority groups was an unconstitutional violation of the Fourteenth Amendment equal protection clause.

In 1945 J. D. and Ethel Shelley purchased a two-family house on Labadie Avenue in St. Louis. The Shelleys and their six children had moved from rural Mississippi prior to World War II. Both parents worked in industrial jobs during the war, saving their money to buy a house and move out of a crowded apartment in an all-black neighborhood. Their pastor, Robert Bishop, who sold real estate, helped them find the property and buy it for $5,700 from a white woman, Geraldine Fitzgerald. Two months after they moved, Ethel Shelley received notice that they were to be evicted, as their purchase had violated a neighborhood covenant, a 1911 agreement prohibiting persons of the "Negro or Mongolian race" from occupying the property. Louis and Fern Kraemer, white home owners who lived a few blocks away, had filed the suit on behalf of the Marcus Avenue Improvement Association.

The Circuit Court in St. Louis found that the restrictive agreement was invalid as it had never been signed by all the property owners in the district, and they held that it could not be effective without all signatures. The Missouri Supreme Court reversed, upholding the covenant and concluding that it did not violate any of the Shelleys' constitutional rights. Both the NAACP and the solicitor general of the United States, along with African-American attorney George Vaughn of St. Louis, argued the Shelleys' case before the Supreme Court. Six justices heard the arguments. The other three, Rutledge, Jackson, and Reed recused themselves, apparently because they owned property in restricted areas. Chief Justice Vinson delivered the opinion on May 3, 1948.

The constitutional question at issue in *Shelley v. Kraemer* was whether restrictive covenants, when enforced by state courts, violated the Fourteenth Amendment's equal protection clause. The Supreme Court found that they did. Those excluded from the property were defined by race or color alone, yet the framers of the Fourteenth Amendment had clearly intended to protect such civil rights of African Americans. The Civil Rights Act of 1866, contemporary with Congress's approval of the Fourteenth Amendment, had specifically mentioned the right to acquire, enjoy, own, and dispose of property. Kraemer's lawyers argued that restrictive covenants were strictly private contracts and therefore did not involve a state action to deprive a citizen of equal protection of the laws. The Court disagreed, holding that the covenants became state action when the state judicial systems enforced them. Chief Justice Vinson noted that the Fourteenth Amendment not only required procedural fairness from the states but also prohibited the state courts from enforcing rules that denied civil rights, even if the procedures were fair. The primary concern of the Fourteenth Amendment, the Court concluded, was to protect citizens from discrimination by the states, based on race or color.

As *Shelley v. Kraemer* prohibited the use of restrictive covenants based on race, such barriers to the ownership of property would no longer be legal. The case marked one of the significant victories in the NAACP's effort to dismantle the system of segregation and racial inequality.

For more information
Franklin, John Hope, and Genna Rae McNeil, eds. *African Americans and the Living Constitution.* Washington, D.C.: Smithsonian Institution Press, 1955.

Irons, Peter. *The Courage of Their Convictions: Sixteen Americans Who Fought Their Way to the Supreme Court.* New York: Penguin Books, 1990.

Mary Welek Atwell
Radford University

sheriff has ancient origins but is a vital and integral part of the criminal justice system today.

The office began with the development of local government in England and survived the centralization of power under the monarchy and parliamentary governments. Approximately 1,200 years ago, England was inhabited by small groups of Anglo-Saxons who lived in rural communities called "tuns" (later towns). Each group of 100 families, "hundreds," selected their chief or "grefa," which was later shortened to "reeve." Groups of hundreds were later formed into shires (the forerunner of modern counties) and elected a leader known as the "shire-reeve," eventually known as the sheriff.

The sheriff was one of the principal administrative officers of the shire, and his duties included collecting taxes and preserving the king's peace, although it was the duty of all citizens to assist the sheriff in keeping the peace. If a suspect or criminal was at large, the sheriff would raise the alarm, the "hue and cry," and everyone was then legally responsible for assisting in the capture of the wrongdoer. Following the Norman Conquest in 1066, William the Conqueror preserved the title and duties of sheriff although he replaced the incumbents with persons loyal to him. Great power often encourages abuses and misuse of that authority, and both monarchs and sheriffs were accused of such. The issue came to culmination in 1215 when King John was forced by his barons to sign the Magna Carta, a document that limited the absolute power of government as exemplified by the monarch and his minions. Sheriffs were repeatedly mentioned in provisions seeking to rectify or reform abuses of the office. The repute and authority of the sheriff continued to wax and wane over the next centuries.

The New World colonists established their governments by the pattern of governance in Great Britain, including the administrative position of sheriff. The first sheriff in the colonies, William Stone, was appointed as sheriff of Accomack County, Virginia, in 1634. The early sheriffs were the ranking police and financial officers in the counties. During the 18th and 19th centuries, state legislatures broadened and enlarged the sheriffs' traditional law enforcement and tax collection duties to include, among other things, supervision of jails and workhouses. By the 20th century, sheriffs were exercising independent political power, especially through the use of appointments, to enhance their own political stature and ascendancy.

Today more than 3,100 sheriffs' departments are operated by county or independent city governments in most, but not all, states. Sheriffs are considered state officials, although they are generally elected by county voters and have jurisdiction limited to their own counties. Their departments perform basic law enforcement activities such as patrol services, response to citizens' calls (including 911 calls), and enforcement of traffic laws. Nearly all sheriffs' departments have court-related functions such as serving notice of civil proceedings and providing court security. In addition, well over two-thirds of the departments operate and oversee jails.

The office of sheriff is the most ancient law enforcement office within the common-law system. Despite the variations in levels of power and prestige through the centuries, the office has survived as a viable, vibrant component of the legal system.

For more information

McMillan v. Monroe County, Alabama, 520 U.S. 781 (1997).

Reaves, Brian, and Pheny Z. Smith. *Sheriffs' Departments 1993.* Washington, D.C.: Department of Justice, Bureau of Justice Statistics, 1996.

Susan Coleman
West Texas A&M University

Sherman Act   refers to a group of federal laws that seeks to protect trade and commerce against improper restraints and monopolies. It is part of the cluster of laws referred to as "antitrust laws." This cluster also includes the Clayton Act and the Federal Trade Commission Act. The Sherman Act was enacted on July 2, 1890, and since has been amended only to update the penalties for proscribed behavior.

The Sherman Act prohibits any contract, agreement, or conspiracy in restraint of trade or commerce. The Sherman Act also prohibits monopolies and conspiracies to monopolize. By monopoly, the statute contemplates a consolidation of economic power that allows the suspect firm to set a price that is artificially high. In short, the legislative objective is to avoid an unfair domination of some sector of the economic market. The rationale behind the policy objective is that monopolies and cartels are economically inefficient. This inefficiency causes harm to consumers by creating higher prices and lessening competition.

The Sherman Act provides for criminal penalties for corporations of fines up to $1 million for each violation. Individuals may be fined up to $100,000 and sentenced to three years in prison for each offense. Each violation of the act is a felony.

The Clayton Act supplements the Sherman Act in part by providing a private cause of action for any person injured in violation of the proscribed behavior. That is, any person injured by an action that violates the constraints of the Sherman Act may bring a civil action against the company, individual, or group responsible for such action.

The remedies for private individuals who have been injured by violations of the Sherman Act include injunctive relief, compensatory relief for actual damages, and treble damages. Injunctive relief takes the form of a court order prohibiting continued violations of the act. Compensatory relief seeks to place the aggrieved party in the position they would have had if the violations had not occurred. Treble damages serves as a punishment for any violation of the act. The treble damages provision triples the award of actual damages.

The treble damages provision is the principle deterrent to and punishment of anticompetitive conduct. It also serves as an incentive for the private enforcement of the antitrust laws. Critics of the treble damages provision argue that the statute does not encourage those injured by anticompetitive behavior to mitigate, or lessen, their damages since it awards three times the actual damages suffered. Further, since the proscribed behavior is somewhat vague, the treble damages may create a disincentive for aggressive competition or encourage frivolous lawsuits.

For more information

Hovenkamp, H. *Federal Antitrust Policy, The Law of Competition and Its Practice,* 2nd ed. St. Paul, Minn.: West Publishing Co., 2000.

Ross, S. R. *Principles of Antitrust Law.* Westbury, N.Y.: The Foundation Press, 1993.

Sullivan, E. T., and J. L. Harrison. *Understanding Antitrust and Its Economic Implications,* 2nd ed. New York: Matthew Bender, 1994.

Charles Anthony Smith
University of California, San Diego

Slaughterhouse Cases   16 Wall. 36 (1873) were three companion cases decided by the United States Supreme Court in which it issued its first interpretation of the Fourteenth Amendment to the Constitution.

The cases, *The Butcher's Benevolent Association of New Orleans v. The Crescent City Live-Stock Landing-House Company, (et al.),* 83 U.S. (16 Wallace) 36 (1873), arose from a Louisiana law (1869) giving the Crescent City Live-Stock Landing and Slaughter-House Company a monopoly to own and operate livestock handling and slaughtering facilities in New Orleans. Butchers who were not members of the company could rent, at reasonable fees, space in the slaughtering facilities, quit the business, or face fines for defying the law. Extensive litigation sent the cases to the United States Supreme Court on appeal from the Louisiana Supreme Court.

At issue were the economic rights of the butchers versus the claims of the State of Louisiana to exercise its police power to regulate economic activity in order to protect the health, safety, and welfare of the people. John Archibald Campbell, a former United States Supreme Court Justice, who had resigned his seat in order to serve the Confederacy, represented the Butcher's Association. Campbell's brief argued for a broad interpretation of the Fourteenth Amendment, claiming that it gave to the federal government new powers to protect the individual rights of all citizens from state discrimination. Further, Louisiana's creation of a monopoly was not a legitimate exercise of its police power, because it violated the privileges and immunities, the due process clauses, and the equal protection clauses of the Fourteenth Amendment.

Justice Samuel F. Miller issued the majority opinion for a court divided 5–4 on the decision. He reasoned that the purposes of the Thirteenth and Fourteenth Amendments were to abolish slavery and to raise the former slaves to equal citizenship, while also protecting them from "black codes" and other acts of discrimination. Consequently, the Fourteenth Amendment, in the Court's view, was not intended to give the federal government extensive power to define and protect individual rights. Therefore, individual economic rights were subject to the power of the states.

In a dissenting opinion, Justice Stephen J. Field, recognizing the corruption in Louisiana's Reconstruction politics, saw the monopoly as economic privilege masquerading in the guise of police power. He opined that the Fourteenth Amendment had created a national citizenship, the rights of which the federal government could define and protect. In a separate dissent Justice Joseph P. Bradley reasoned that the due process clause was violated both procedurally and substantively.

Justice Miller's decision limited the effect of the Fourteenth Amendment for decades. Eventually the dissents of Field and others would be used to develop a doctrine of substantive due process with which the due process and equal protection clauses would be made applicable to the states. The privileges and immunities clause has remained of very limited scope since.

For more information

Nelson, W. F. *The Fourteenth Amendment: From Political Principle to Judicial Doctrine.* Cambridge, Mass.: Harvard University Press, 1988.

Saunders, Robert, Jr. *John Archibald Campbell: Southern Moderate, 1811–1889.* Tuscaloosa: University of Alabama Press, 1997.

A. J. L. Waskey
Dalton State College

small-claims court is a special court designed to handle civil actions for small sums of money.

Small-claims courts are streamlined courts of limited jurisdiction sometimes called conciliation courts. These courts may be city or state courts at the county level. They are usually a subdivision of a regular court, such as a magistrate court, municipal court, county court, justice of the peace court, or *pro se* (self-represented, without a lawyer) court.

The first small-claims court was opened in 1913 in Cleveland, Ohio. By the 1920s this form of court had spread to many states. By the late 20th century all the states, and Washington, D.C., had some form of small-claims court.

Small-claims courts are designed to handle cases promptly with efficient and inexpensive procedures. The cases are usually heard informally before a judge without a jury, although a few states (e.g., Texas) allow a case to be heard before a jury. The plaintiff who brings the suit and the defendant are often ordinary private citizens who will represent themselves without an attorney present. While some states allow attorneys to practice in small-claims court, many do not (e.g., California). In addition the small sums of money sought in small-claims courts usually do not warrant the legal expenses involved to use an attorney.

The monetary claims sought can be for only a few dollars. The upper limit has risen from $1,000 to as high as $25,000 in some states in recent years. Actions are usually for payment of a debt, recovery of damages, nonperformance of a contract, or recovery of something.

A small-claims action can be initiated when the plaintiff pays a small fee and files a complaint. The fees for filing and serving the complaint can be included in the judgment if the plaintiff wins. In some states mediation and arbitration are available to resolve disputes without resorting to the court.

In court each party will briefly argue their side of the case before the judge who will usually immediately issue a ruling. To promote access to the court for working people, court sessions may be held at night.

Some states allow appeals, but this is seldom done. In those states that allow appeals some require that the case begin *de novo* in a regular civil court. The appealed case will then be heard before a court of general jurisdiction.

Critics have charged that too often small-claims courts are simply collection agencies for businesses and utilities. To keep the small-claims court as an institution for consumers, some states bar corporations or utilities as plaintiffs. Others permit corporations and utilities to sue because they believe that it encourages the extension of credit by stores and others.

For more information

Brewer, William E. *Winning in Small Claims Court: A Step-by-Step Guide for Trying Your Own Small*

Claims Cases. Franklin Lakes, N.J.: Career Press, 1998.

Warner, Ralph. *Everybody's Guide to Small Claims Court,* 8th ed. Berkeley, Calif.: Nolo Press, 2000.

A. J. L. Waskey
Dalton State College

solicitor general is one of the least known and most important legal figures in the federal judicial system of the United States.

The only legal figure in America that is required by legislation to be "learned in the law," the solicitor general of the United States has been nicknamed "the tenth justice" because of the impact he has on the day-to-day work of the United States Supreme Court. Like cabinet officials and justices, the solicitor general is appointed by the president and confirmed by a vote of the Senate. Some of the most famous and skilled attorneys in America's history were solicitor generals, including William Howard Taft, Thurgood Marshall, Archibald Cox, Robert Bork, and Kenneth Starr. The solicitor general in 2001 was Seth P. Waxman.

The Office of the Solicitor General is housed within the U.S. Department of Justice and has the function of being the chief attorney for the United States of America. As such, the solicitor general typically has the function of representing the executive branch of government when it is a party to a Supreme Court case. As a result, the solicitor general has an additional office within the structure of the United States Supreme Court. Having offices in both buildings gives us a clue to the role and importance of the solicitor as a sort of diplomat between the attorney general and the Supreme Court.

In addition to trying cases in which the United States is a party to the suit, the solicitor general serves as a sort of "counselor" to the High Court when the office submits amicus curiae or "friend of the court" briefs. These briefs allow the solicitor general to provide additional legal arguments or opinions to the justices when the United States is interested in the outcome of a case but is not formally involved in the suit. These briefs have also been filed by the solicitor when the Supreme Court is deciding whether to take a case or not (by a vote of four out of nine members of the Court). In each case, the solicitor general provides information that the president's administration wants the Court to hear. Some have argued that this process is similar to lobbying the Court as interest groups can lobby the U.S. Congress.

A third role or power of the solicitor general is to judiciously screen the numerous cases and legal issues that executive agencies send through the office. Of the many legal problems that bureaucratic agencies face, the solicitor is there to decide which are the most important to the president and which are the most politically feasible to address as litigation. The power to funnel issues, then, is an enormous responsibility of the solicitor general.

In each of the roles of counselor and government attorney, the solicitor general has been viewed as one of the most powerful figures in the U.S. justice system. The power of the solicitor general as an insider to the legal process is found in evidence of political science studies. In general, the solicitor general wins more than 80 percent of the time when he argues a case before the Supreme Court. In addition, the solicitor general's amicus briefs are accepted by the Court almost 80 percent of the time. The solicitor general, then, truly has the "ear" of the Supreme Court on some of the most important legal issues that the president and his attorney general see fit to address. In recent years, the solicitor general has become one of the most important appointments of a president, and the office has been used by presidents to get case decisions that are similar to their ideas and values. For example, during the Reagan presidency, the solicitor general pushed an agenda that matched the Reagan policies on abortion, prayer in school, and affirmative action.

For more information

Caplan, Lincoln. *The Tenth Justice: The Solicitor General and the Rule of Law.* New York: Knopf, 1987.

Salokar, Rebecca Mae. *The Solicitor General: The Politics of Law.* Philadelphia: Temple University Press, 1992.

Roger Hartley
University of Arizona

special damages are a subdivision of compensatory damages, those damages that can be claimed by plaintiffs in civil lawsuits to repay them for harms resulting from legal injuries committed by defendants.

Some damages are considered so basic to certain types of injuries that they do not have to be listed and described specifically in the plaintiff's pleadings. These are known as general damages and are considered to be implied by law and not required to be specified in the plaintiff's complaint. However, there are many more items of damages that may be demanded in civil lawsuits. These are called special damages, which have been defined as "those damages, the amount and nature of which are peculiar to each individual plaintiff and might not be understood to be part of the damage claim without specific notice to the adversary" (Mintzer, et al. *Damages in Tort Actions* [1986]: 19). Special damages are the natural consequence of the defendant's wrongful act, but they do not necessarily occur in every case to every plaintiff. Thus, they are not foreseeable to the defendant and are not implied by law. Accordingly, they must be specified in the pleadings to give the defendant fair notice so that he or she can present an adequate defense.

To protect defendants against unfair surprise at trial, plaintiffs may not recover damages for special items that they have not specifically pleaded. Unfortunately, the definitions of general and special damages are sufficiently ambiguous that it is easy for plaintiffs to make errors about which items of damage are special and must be pleaded specifically. Plaintiffs' attorneys must research the law of their particular jurisdiction carefully to determine what items of damage are considered special damages, or else they must plead all items of damage specifically to avoid having items of damage excluded from consideration. What constitutes special damages varies from one jurisdiction to another, but the majority of courts agree that some harms arising in tort or contract actions must be regarded as special damages. These include past and future medical expenses, lost earnings, loss of earning capacity, future pain and suffering, physical impairment, damage to real or personal property, loss of goodwill, lost profits, and incidental damages and reliance damages in contract actions.

The constitutional principle of due process of law underlies the distinction between general damages and special damages. Requiring items of damage that are not immediately foreseeable to the defendant to be pleaded specially protects defendants from unfair surprise and gives them adequate notice of what claims they must defend against. However, some commentators question whether requiring special damages to be pleaded specially is necessary any longer. Today, civil lawsuits permit extensive pretrial discovery and other pretrial procedures that ensure that defendants know what is being alleged against them, so there is little likelihood that defendants will be unfairly surprised at trial. Given the ambiguity and resulting confusion surrounding the concept of special damages, plaintiffs may be placed at a disadvantage to redress an imbalance that no longer exists. In some jurisdictions, this problem is being considered as part of ongoing reforms of the civil justice system.

For more information

Cagle, Jeffrey R. "The Classification of General and Special Damages for Pleading Purposes in Texas," *Baylor Law Review* 51, no. 3 (summer 1999): 629–97.

Celia A. Sgroi
State University of New York, Oswego

speedy and public trial is guaranteed by the Sixth Amendment, and it is meant to protect criminal defendants from potential harm caused by pretrial delay.

Excessive or undue pretrial delay may prejudice a defendant because such delay increases the possibility that evidence may be lost or destroyed, witnesses may become unavailable (i.e., by moving or dying), or memories may fade. Deterioration of evidence with the passage of time may impair a defendant's ability to defend himself against the charges or to prove his innocence. Requiring the government to prosecute cases promptly also serves to avoid other potential injuries to criminal defendants awaiting trial, including (a) anxiety resulting from facing criminal charges, (b) discomfort due to unpleasant jail conditions, (c) restricted liberty, (d) lost employment and educational opportunities, and (e) impaired ability to maintain family relations. Finally, providing criminal defendants with speedy trials also serves to protect societal interests by ensuring that those who are eventually found guilty are tried and convicted before they can commit other crimes or flee the jurisdiction, and by ensuring that those who are eventually found innocent are not exposed to jail conditions and deprived of liberty for longer than necessary. There is no analogous right to a speedy trial in civil cases.

The right to a speedy trial is so important that it is guaranteed by both the Fifth Amendment's due process clause, which provides that "[n]o person shall be deprived of life, liberty, or property without due process of law," and the Sixth Amendment's specific promise that "[i]n all criminal prosecutions, the accused shall enjoy the right to a speedy and public trial." The right to a speedy trial is also protected in different ways by numerous state and federal statutes, such as the Federal Speedy Trial Act, 18 U.S.C. section 3164–3174 (specifying time limits between arrest, indictment, and trial, and permissible delays within each period), Rule 48(b) of the Federal Rules of Criminal Procedure (authorizing courts to dismiss indictments on the ground that the government caused unnecessary delay), the Interstate Agreement on Detainers Act, 18 U.S.C. App. section 2 (providing for expeditious disposition of charges against persons incarcerated in other jurisdictions), as well as by statutes of limitation.

Safeguarding a defendant's right against prejudicial pre-accusation delay (that is, delay between the date of the crime and the date on which the defendant is charged with the crime) is primarily the job of state and federal statutes of limitation. A statute of limitation requires that the government commence prosecution by bringing charges against a defendant within a specified amount of time after the commission of the crime. Where the statute of limitation does not provide relief, a defendant may resort to a Fifth Amendment due process claim. It is difficult, however, to establish a due process violation based upon pre-accusation delay. To do so, a defendant must demonstrate that the delay resulted in actual prejudice, and that the government's reasons for delay violate "fundamental conceptions of justice."

After a defendant has been arrested or formally charged with a crime, his or her speedy trial rights under the Sixth Amendment become operative. A court balances four factors in determining whether there has been a violation of the Sixth Amendment right to a speedy trial: (1) the length of the delay (generally, a delay of one year is sufficient to trigger further consideration); (2) the reason for the delay (purposeful delay by the government weighs in favor of finding a violation of the right to a speedy trial, but delay caused by the defendant will not); (3) the defendant's assertion of his or her rights (a defendant's failure to assert his speedy trial rights undercuts a Sixth Amendment claim by suggesting that the defendant did not want a speedy trial); and (4) the prejudice caused to the defendant (the most significant, of course, is prejudice impairing the defendant's ability to defend himself). (See *Barker v. Wingo*, 407 U.S. 514 [1972].) Once a speedy trial violation has been shown, the remedy is dismissal of the criminal charges. Dismissals due to speedy trial violations, however, are infrequent.

For more information

Misner, Robert L. *Speedy Trial: Federal and State Practice* Charlottesville, Va.: Lexis, 1983.

Shults, Kristen M. "Twenty-ninth Annual Review of Criminal Procedure, Speedy Trial," *Georgetown Law Journal* 88 (May 2000): 1208.

Jordonna Sabih
Law Clerk to the Honorable Andrew J. Wistrich
United States Magistrate Judge

stalking   is a distinctive behavioral pattern of repeated unwanted contact, which the stalker knows, or should know, is unwelcome by the victim or target.

Although stalking was not criminalized in the United States until the 1990s, that decade saw anti-stalking legislation sweep across the country, from California in 1991 to New York in 1999. This was done to make punishable acts previously viewed as the "crime before the crime," activity which was overwhelmingly gender-specific in nature (about 90 percent of stalkers are male, while approximately 90 percent of targeted victims are female).

Stalking behavior has been made famous by a relatively small number of cases in which famous people or celebrities have been stalked by starstruck obsessives. Similarly, there are a small group of "revenge stalkings," an example of which is a case where a man stalked individuals (including prosecutors and judges) involved in prosecuting him. However, the majority of stalking cases arise out of situations where the stalker was married, or romantically involved, or professionally involved as a colleague, or otherwise acquainted with the targeted victim, and the conduct has some similar dynamics to domestic violence. Because stalking is often a crime of stealth, it can be very difficult to trace the act to the stalker— one such example, which is quite frequent, is car

tampering. In addition, stalkers count on the targeted victim's perception of shame, so as to keep the targeted victim silent, or to force a negotiation or interaction (which police and prosecutors discourage, with the incantation of "never negotiate, period").

Moreover, because of their prior knowledge or studied learning, stalkers may know what activities will most unnerve a targeted victim. Some incidents, seemingly innocuous or unnoticed by others, can be especially distressing to a targeted victim. These can include staring incidents, "bumping into" someone at school, work, or the grocery store. One legislator who had personal experience in this regard recounted the story of going to the local market to buy a quart of milk and a pound of butter, only to find the man stalking her immediately behind her with a quart of milk and a pound of the same brand of butter— the most frightening aspect to her was that she never noticed him in the store prior to his appearance at the checkout.

Often conduct increases both in frequency and type, escalating in nature. Repeated hang up phone calls may turn to telephone death threats, which may turn to a car whose windshield wipers are stripped and discovered not to work on a dark and stormy night. "Presents" are also common (consider red roses that are followed by black roses), along with notes of either obsessive love or hate. While these are examples of stalking behavior, they are not exclusive. For example, in one case, a judge issued an order of protection listing 26 prohibited activities; shortly thereafter the protected ex-wife was awakened at 6 A.M. on Easter morning to hear her ex-husband hammering hinges on the kitchen door, allegedly to repair—when brought to court, the man protested that since this was not on the list, it was not a prohibited activity.

Targeted victims should keep logs of each event, save notes and gifts (however distasteful) to give or to show police and prosecutors (or to present in court when seeking a restraining order or prosecution), report each incident to the police and other authorities. One prosecutor intones at police and victim training sessions, "document, document, document." Targeted victims should try to get restraining orders or orders of protection against stalkers—even if the order is not granted, the record of the request serves as a predicate (or basis) for future prosecution. In cases where orders are granted, the protected party should keep copies at home, work, school, in briefcases and knapsacks, and immediately seek their enforcement (since violation of an order of protection is a strict liability crime, for which intent need not be proven).

Because the anti-stalking laws and legislation are so young, there is a dearth in the literature regarding the law in this growing area—a gap that will certainly change in the coming years. However, studies that discuss the anecdotal evidence and developing case law in articles and non-law books have been very similar in information and conclusions.

For more information

De Becker, Gavin. *The Gift of Fear: Survival Signals That Protect Us from Violence.* Boston: Little, Brown, 1997.

Mullen, Paul E., Michele Pathe, and Rosemary Purcell. *Stalkers and Their Victims.* Cambridge: Cambridge University Press, 2000.

Demetra M. Pappas
London School of Economics and Political Science

standing   is a jurisdictional issue that determines the ability of a court to hear a certain case.

Standing or "standing to sue" suggests that an individual or party has a sufficient stake in the outcome of a controversy to seek a resolution to that controversy in a court of law. As such, standing represents a threshold requirement for getting into court. The determination of standing can often be a complex matter that rests on the answer to several important questions. As Justice William O. Douglas put it, "generalizations about standing requirements are largely worth-

less as such." Despite that candid assessment, there are some more or less generalizable requirements in showing standing.

The most basic requirement to show standing is for the individual or party to demonstrate some injury. The injury that has been suffered must be of a real and personal nature, rather than simply hypothetical, abstract harm or even a general harm that is being committed against all. Traditionally courts have viewed the damage requirement as meaning "pocketbook" damages, i.e., monetary loss. That view of harm, as only monetary harm, has been relaxed in recent years, but it is still viewed as the most common type of harm sustained. Simply put, the individual or party must have a judicially protectable and tangible interest in the litigation that they are bringing to the court and must show a connection between that interest and the conduct complained of in the case.

A second requirement for standing requires that the individual or party show that all other remedies have been exhausted. This means that the possibility of the case being resolved in a lower court, or by an administrative tribunal or other competent venue, must have been explored fully. For practical purposes, this means, for instance, that the Supreme Court of the United States, as the court of last appeal in the federal judicial system, will not hear a case unless it has been heard first by a lower federal court or by a state court of last resort.

A third requirement for standing demands that the case being brought not be moot. This requirement ensures that controversy exists at all stages of the litigation procedure, not just at the time the action was filed with the court. If, during the course of the case the dispute is resolved so that the harm no longer exists, the case is deemed to be moot and therefore nonjusticiable.

The rules for standing are a combination of rules promulgated by the courts themselves and legislative enactments. Statutes conferring standing on individuals or groups usually contain broad language that leaves courts as the ultimate decision maker on standing issues. Furthermore, legislatures cannot force a court to hear a case that, in the opinion of the judges, lacks merit or is moot, simply by conferring standing on individuals.

The doctrines of standing, precisely because they lack clear definition, can be used by courts and judges to avoid hearing certain cases as well as being allowed to hear others. If a court wishes to avoid a particular case or even a broad area of law, it can do so by denying the parties' standing. In years past, courts have relaxed the standing requirements to allow individuals who could not show personal harm to act as surrogates for injured groups. This allowed an explosion of class action suits involving, for example, environmental damage. More recently, a conservative shift in the courts has led to a tightening of the rules surrounding standing. Generalizations are not terribly useful in the area of standing to sue precisely because the definitions are political as well as legal. It is clear that standing is a complex issue and that it can be used by courts for policy as well as legal purposes.

For more information

Grilliot, Harold, and Frank Schubert. *Introduction to Law and the Legal System.* Boston: Houghton Mifflin, 1992.

O'Brien, David M. *Constitutional Law and Politics: Struggles for Power and Governmental Responsibility.* New York: W. W. Norton, 1991.

David A. May
Eastern Washington University

stare decisis describes the legal principle that compels judges to adhere to the precedents of earlier cases as sources of law.

The term originates from the Latin phrase *"stare decisis et non quieta movere,"* which means "to stand by precedents and not to disturb settled points." Once a question has been settled by a judicial decision, stare decisis obliges lower courts within that jurisdiction to resolve similar disputes in the same manner.

This principle distinguishes common-law from civil-law legal systems. Stare decisis is the foundation of common-law systems, such as those found in the United States and England. Courts in civil-law systems, such as France, do not follow the principle. In these code-based systems, judges primarily apply the applicable code of laws and legal scholars' explanation of the codes.

Stare decisis requires lower courts to follow the supervisory court's applicable precedent. For example, a federal trial court must follow the case law of the federal court of appeals for the circuit in which it is located, and all federal courts must follow the case law of the U.S. Supreme Court. However, a federal trial court is not bound to apply the precedent established in a circuit in which it is not located. Even when a court is not obligated by stare decisis to follow precedent established in earlier cases, it may be persuaded by another court's legal reasoning. Thus a federal trial court may elect to follow another circuit court of appeal's decision.

Stare decisis is flexible when a court has previously established precedent. No federal or state court is absolutely constrained by its own decisions. It may overrule its previous decisions, except where overruling would cause the court's decision to conflict with precedent established by a higher court to which it is bound.

While stare decisis has been criticized because it can cause courts to apply antiquated precedent to current disputes, adherence to the principle serves three legal system objectives: fairness, certainty, and efficiency. Stare decisis encourages fairness because it ensures that "like cases will be treated alike." It prevents judicial arbitrariness by reducing a judge's ability to render decisions based on favoritism or bias. The principle also provides certainty to the legal system. Members of society can look to the past for guidance in what to expect from the courts in the future and can plan their actions accordingly.

Finally, stare decisis facilitates judicial efficiency. Applying the principle saves courts time and reduces costs for litigants by preventing courts from reexamining a legal question each time a dispute arises.

For more information

Bodenheimer, Edgar, John Oakley, and Jean Love, *An Introduction to the Anglo-American Legal System: Readings and Cases*, 2nd ed. St. Paul, Minn.: West Group Publishing, 1988.

Hanks, Eva, Michael Herz, and Steven Nemerson, *Elements of Law*. Cincinnati, Ohio: Anderson Publishing, 1994.

Robert W. Malmsheimer
SUNY College of Environmental Science and Forestry

state action   is restricted by the Constitution.

The Fourteenth Amendment to the Constitution declares, "No state . . . [may] deprive any person of life, liberty, or property, without due process of law; nor deny to any person within its jurisdiction the equal protection of the laws."

Because the Constitution applies only to state or governmental action, discrimination by a private entity does not constitute a constitutional violation. Nevertheless, both state and federal statutes provide for punishing a landlord who refuses to rent to minority tenants, a bank that denies credit to women, or an employer who fires an employee because of her religion.

State action comes in many guises—some obvious, some not. Courts try to determine who bears the greatest degree of responsibility—the state or a private actor—for the discrimination in question. If it is a state government or one of its subdivisions—such as a city, town, or county—there is state action. If it is not, there is none.

When state legislatures required African Americans and whites to attend separate schools, there was state action in violation of the equal protection clause of the Fourteenth Amendment (*Brown v. Board of Education* [1954]).

The Supreme Court has also found state action when officials administer a neutral law in a discriminatory fashion. In the latter part of the 19th century California officials granted laundry operating licenses to Caucasians but never to Chinese applicants, even though the application process was neutral on its face. In *Yick Wo v. Hopkins* (1886) the Court found that the practice of administrative discrimination violated the Constitution.

It can be difficult to determine whether there is state action when private parties bear partial responsibility for the violation of a person's rights. In one instance a neighbor asked a court to enforce a provision in a deed to a house. The deed stated that the property could be sold only to Caucasians. The Supreme Court declared that if the state court were to void the sale of the property to an African-American couple, there would be state action that violated the equal protection clause (*Shelley v. Kraemer* [1948]).

In another case a public parking authority in Delaware leased the bottom floor of its parking garage to a coffee shop that refused to serve African-American customers. In that case the coffee shop and the state were engaged in a joint venture, and responsibility for the discrimination could be laid at the feet of the state (*Burton v. Wilmington Parking Authority* [1961]).

By contrast the Court has found that neither partial government funding nor extensive government regulation, by themselves, necessarily turn private action into state action (*Moose Lodge #107 v. Irvis* [1972] and *Rendell-Baker v. Kohn* [1982]).

Some towns in the United States are "company towns." The company owns the homes, manages the parks, administers town elections, and employs a private police force. Since the private company exercises all the functions of a local government, its actions become state actions (*Marsh v. Alabama* [1946]).

For more information

Karst, Kenneth L. *Belonging to America: Equal Citizenship and the Constitution*. New Haven, Conn.: Yale University Press, 1989, pp. 58–61.

Tribe, Laurence H. *American Constitutional Law,* 2d. ed., chap. 18, "The Problem of State Action." Westbury, N.Y.: Foundation Press, 1989.

William H. Coogan
University of Southern Maine

state bills of rights   are found in all current state constitutions. They contain bills (or declarations) of rights, typically at the beginning of the document.

To some extent, state bills of rights resemble the Bill of Rights found in the U.S. Constitution. They protect many of the same fundamental rights—freedom of speech, religious liberty, rights of defendants, and the like—and some even employ the same language found in the federal guarantees. However, state bills of rights differ from their federal counterpart in important respects. Many state bills of rights contain provisions, typically originating in the 18th century, that do not resemble contemporary rights guarantees. These may include statements of political principle, structural provisions, and even recommendations. Thus, the Virginia Declaration of Rights (initially adopted in 1776) emphasizes that "no free government, or the blessings of liberty, can be preserved to any people but by a frequent recurrence to first principles"; mandates a separation of powers; and admonishes citizens to treat each other with "Christian forbearance, love, and charity."

State bills of rights also tend to include a wider array of rights than are found in the federal Bill of Rights. For example, 39 states guarantee access to a legal remedy to those who suffer injury, 11 expressly protect a right to privacy, and 17 ban gender discrimination. A state bill of rights may also address issues of particular concern to a state's residents. Thus, the New Jersey and New York bills of rights guarantee a right to collective bargaining, Wyoming's delineates water rights, and Mississippi's bans dueling. Even when state bills of rights safeguard rights analogous to those protected by the federal Bill of Rights, state guarantees may be more specific, more detailed, and more expansive than their federal counterparts. For example, 19 states not only forbid establishments of religion but also bar religious tests for witnesses and jurors, and 35 prohibit expenditures for "any sectarian purpose." Whereas all prohibit cruel and unusual punishments, some also prescribe that punishments be proportional to offenses or prohibit "unnecessary rigor" in punishments. Finally, states regularly amend their bills of rights, sometimes to expand rights protections and sometimes to narrow them. An example of the former is the adoption of victims' rights amendments in several states during the 1980s and 1990s, while an example of the latter is Colorado's amendment limiting gay rights, struck down by the U.S. Supreme Court in *Romer v. Evans* (1996).

Since the early 1970s, state bills of rights have become increasingly important in safeguarding rights. A few examples illustrate this "new judicial federalism." Many state supreme courts have recognized broader protections for the rights of suspects and defendants than are available under the federal Bill of Rights, and 15 have invalidated their states' systems of public-school financing. During the 1990s, the Vermont and Hawaii Supreme Courts struck down state statutes limiting marriage to heterosexual couples, although the Hawaii decision was subsequently overturned by constitutional amendment, and courts in three states struck down statutes limiting the damages that individuals could collect in personal-injury cases. There is good reason to believe that state bills of rights will continue to be important safeguards of liberty in the 21st century.

For more information

Tarr, G. Alan. *Understanding State Constitutions.* Princeton, N.J.: Princeton University Press, 1998.
Williams, Robert F. *State Constitutional Law,* 3rd ed. Charlottesville, Va.: Lexis Law Publishing, 1999.

G. Alan Tarr
Rutgers University, Camden, New Jersey

state constitutional law serves as the fundamental law of the states.

State constitutions establish state and local governments, limit the scope of state power beyond the few limits enshrined in the federal Constitution, allocate power among the branches of state government and between state and local governments, mandate certain state duties (e.g., education), and protect rights. Given the diverse responsibilities of state governments and the states' propensity to constitutionalize policy matters, state constitutions tend to be considerably longer and more detailed than their federal counterpart.

State supreme courts serve as the authoritative interpreters of state constitutions and hence as a prime source of state constitutional law. However, they share responsibility for the development of state constitutional law with other institutions. The states have regularly replaced their constitutions—only 19 retain their original constitutions—and current state constitutions have, on average, been amended more than 120 times. Thus, constitutional conventions and state legislatures (which propose amendments) have played a key role in the evolution of state constitutions. So too has the citizenry, which in 18 states can propose constitutional amendments by initiative, in 49 states ratifies proposed amendments (Delaware is the exception), and in all states votes on whether to call a constitutional convention and whether to ratify its proposals.

Historically, three issues have dominated state constitutional law. The first of these is the distribution of political power among groups and regions within each state. Conflict during the 19th century centered on the extension of the vote to propertyless males, African Americans, and women, and on the apportionment of state legislatures. Early in the century, the latter conflict pitted developed regions against frontier regions seeking representation commensurate with their burgeoning populations. Later, and well into the 20th century, it matched urban against rural areas. The extension of the franchise to all groups, plus U.S. Supreme Court rulings requiring apportionment based on "one person, one vote," have largely ended state constitutional disputes over the intrastate distribution of political power.

The second major issue in state constitutional law is the relation of the state to economic activity, including both the extent of direct support for enterprise and the appropriate balance between promotion and regulation of economic development. During the early 19th century, state governments encouraged development by rashly awarding subsidies to canal companies, railroads, and other corporations. But an economic collapse in 1837 forced several states to default on their debts and prompted constitutional changes designed to curtail state involvement with private corporations. During the late 19th and early 20th centuries, state constitution-makers introduced various provisions designed to curb the power of large corporations. By the late 20th century, many of these constitutional constraints had been removed, enabling states once again to take an active role in promoting economic development within their borders.

A final issue in state constitutional law involves the scope of state governmental power. Until the mid-19th century, state constitutions placed few restraints on state legislatures, relying on popular election to keep representatives in check. From mid-century onward, however, state constitution-makers imposed detailed restrictions on what state legislators could do and inserted policy prescriptions in the constitutions themselves in order to foreclose legislative action. For much of the 20th century, constitutional reformers campaigned against such restrictions and prescriptions, arguing that state legislatures needed flexibility in addressing the needs of a rapidly changing society. Although they achieved some successes, the "tax revolt" of the 1970s ushered in a new era of restrictions on state legislatures, extending from restrictions on taxing and spending to term limitations for legislators.

The primary judicial contribution to state constitutional law during recent decades has involved the reinvigoration of state bills of rights. State supreme courts are the authoritative interpreters of their states' constitutions, and thus under the doctrine of "adequate and independent state grounds," the U.S. Supreme Court generally cannot review state court decisions based on those constitutions. This insulation of state interpretations from federal review has allowed state judges to interpret their state guarantees to provide broader protections than are available under the federal Bill of Rights. Relying on state constitutions, state courts have played a major role in reforming the financing of public education. They have also announced pioneering decisions on issues as diverse as the rights of defendants, the right to die, the rights of same-sex couples, and religious liberty.

For more information

Tarr, G. Alan. *Understanding State Constitutions.* Princeton, N.J.: Princeton University Press, 1998.

Williams, Robert F. *State Constitutional Law,* 3d ed. Charlottesville, Va.: Lexis Law Publishing, 1999.

G. Alan Tarr
Rutgers University, Camden, New Jersey

states' rights   is the theory that states can declare acts of the federal government which they find to be unconstitutional null and void. Most often articulated by the southern states, states' rights rhetoric has been used to justify a variety of acts challenging federal authority, often in the area of racial relations. In some cases the Tenth Amendment or the concept of federalism has been invoked to justify states' rights.

States' rights arguments originated in the period just following the adoption of the Constitution and represent, in part, the arguments of the anti-Federalists who argued that the Constitution would seriously diminish the states'

powers. The first major statement of states' rights in the new republic came in the form of the Virginia and Kentucky Resolutions, authored by James Madison and Thomas Jefferson, in which those states disputed the constitutionality of the Alien and Sedition Acts of 1798 and signaled their refusal to enforce the law.

States' rights gave rise to two highly disputed constitutional doctrines, nullification and interposition. Nullification is the theory that states can declare federal laws invalid within their borders. In 1832 South Carolina declared federal laws raising tariffs on imports to be null and void after the southern states lost their battle against the higher duties, which were intended in benefit northern manufacturers. After several months of confrontation and negotiation, South Carolina backed down. Interposition is the idea that a state can use its sovereign powers to intervene in a dispute between federal officers and its institutions or residents. In another 1832 incident, the Georgia legislature declared that any attempt to enforce a U.S. Supreme Court decision which had overturned a Georgia law would be considered as "unconstitutional and arbitrary interference in the administration of [Georgia's] criminal laws."

The secession of the southern states during the Civil War was the ultimate extension of the theory of states' rights. Beginning with South Carolina, a hotbed of states' rights rhetoric, southern states justified secession by arguing that the Constitution had been a compact among the states, which had reserved the right to leave the Union if their rights were not respected. The Union victory in the Civil War seemingly settled the issue, but appeals to states' rights would reappear during the late 20th century. In 1948, in response to the more liberal racial policies of the Truman administration, Governor Strom Thurmond of South Carolina ran for president on the States Rights ("Dixiecrat") platform, winning in the states of Alabama, Mississippi, Louisiana, and South Carolina. Similar states' rights rhetoric justifying segregation was the central plank of the 1968 campaign for president by Alabama's governor, George Wallace.

The doctrines of nullification and interposition also reappeared in the context of race relations in the South during the late 20th century. After *Brown v. Board of Education* declared segregation to be unconstitutional in 1954, many southern states used the theory of nullification to declare the ruling to be unconstitutional or unenforceable. In 1957 Arkansas took the more dramatic step of exercising its self-asserted power of interposition, when its governor, Orval Faubus, deployed the Arkansas National Guard to prevent the desegregation of Little Rock's Central High School. After the local federal district court ordered the school reopened and desegregated, President Dwight D. Eisenhower sent U.S. Army paratroopers to implement the court's decision and open the schools.

For more information

Ellis, Richard E. *The Jeffersonian Crisis; Courts and Politics in the Young Republic.* New York: Oxford University Press, 1971.

———. *The Union at Risk: Jacksonian Democracy, States' Rights, and the Nullification Crisis.* New York: Oxford University Press, 1987.

Freehling, William W. *Prelude to Civil War: The Nullification Controversy in South Carolina, 1816–1836.* New York: Harper and Row, 1966.

Daniel Levin
University of Utah

status offense is any behavior that the state defines by statute as improper for juveniles to engage in by virtue of their immaturity.

The same behavior is lawful for someone who has attained the legal age of majority status. States differ in what they consider to be a status offense, but common examples include truancy, running away from home, curfew violations, drinking, smoking, gambling, driving, sexual activity, lewdness, immorality, and incorrigible behavior. The concept of a status offense recognizes that many adolescents yearn to have the privileges of adulthood but are too immature to handle the attendant responsibilities. While not as serious as criminal acts, repeated status offenses are considered by many authorities to be an early warning sign that, if left uncorrected, an incorrigible youth might graduate to more serious criminal behavior.

Status offenses are peculiar to the juvenile justice system, which was founded on the principle that children should not be treated the same as adults before the law; they should have a special status as children who are vulnerable to neglect and abuse and thus need the protection of the state. The juvenile justice system is guided by the principle of *parens patriae,* the legal doctrine that the state should become the surrogate father to the wayward child where parents were absent, neglectful, or abusive. In most cases, the primary goal is to provide treatment, rehabilitation, and education for status offenders. In isolation, many status offenses, such as smoking or drinking, are little more than the relatively harmless behavior of teenagers. Punishment is usually a secondary concern, but chronic status offenders may be institutionalized after an adjudicatory hearing— the juvenile equivalent of a trial—before a juvenile judge in juvenile court. While much attention is paid to violent crimes committed by juveniles, status offenses still make up approximately 40 percent of cases handled by the juvenile justice system.

Until the 1960s and 1970s, status offenders were routinely treated like juveniles who had committed more serious crimes. That is, there was a greater emphasis on punishment, and status offenders were incarcerated with more serious offenders and drug addicts, which oftentimes resulted in introducing the former to the more serious crimes of the latter. Today status offenders are variously called Children in Need of Supervision (CINS), Juveniles in Need of Supervision (JINS), Minors in Need of Supervision (MINS), Persons in Need of Supervision (PINS), and Youths in Need of Supervision (YINS). These terms reflect the effort of the movement during the 1960s and 1970s to reform the system by deinstitutionalizing the punishment of status offenders and emphasizing community-based treatments for wayward youths. The shortcomings of treating status offenders like more hardened juvenile criminals has persuaded many experts to recommend that status offenders be transferred to the jurisdiction of social care workers.

For more information

Handler, Joel F., and Julie Zatz, eds. *Neither Angels nor Thieves: Studies in the Deinstitutionalization of Status Offenders.* Washington, D.C.: National Academy Press, 1982.

Maxson, Cheryl L., and Malcolm W. Klein. *Responding to Troubled Youth.* New York: Oxford University Press, 1997.

Vernon Mogensen
Kingsborough Community College, CUNY

statute of frauds is the legal requirement that contracts of certain categories be in writing.

The purpose of the original statute, enacted in England in 1677, was declared in its title—"An Act for the Prevention of Frauds and Perjuries." The basic requirement to write those specified contracts was adopted by the United States and is written into the statutes of the various states.

Generally, the types of contracts that must be written are those for the conveyance of land, for the performance of an obligation of greater than one year, or for a sum of money greater than a statutorily established amount. The rule usually states that if the contract is one of those governed by the statute, the courts will not enforce it if it is not in writing. Oral agreements that do not fit within these categories are enforceable but are not usually a good idea. The common perception that contracts not in writing are unenforceable is false. Only those contracts that are required by statute to be written are unenforceable if not written.

What constitutes writing is given liberal interpretation. Notes on the back of an envelope, initialed by both parties, have been found to be sufficient. Handing over of a signed automobile title is often all that is necessary. An oral agreement to produce a writing is not sufficient to satisfy the statute and is therefore not enforceable if the written agreement is not subsequently produced. The courts will not supply terms not written into the contract unless the contract is fundamentally unfair without those terms.

However, given the age of the statute and its broad applicability, courts over almost three and a half centuries have stated a great number of exceptions to the requirement that contracts be written. In some ways the rule is more noted for its exceptions. A common expression of those exceptions is the idea of substantial performance. If the parties make an agreement, for example, such as Smith building a toolshed for a specific price on Brown's property, the courts will most likely find that there was a valid contract when Brown refuses to pay for the completed structure. A contract would be decreed if the shed was completed in a workmanlike manner and the price demanded was reasonable. To do otherwise would be unfair to Smith and would unjustly enrich Brown.

If the oral contract does not provide a stated time for performance of the agreement, and the contract could reasonably be performed within a year, then the law will not require a written agreement, provided the contract is not required to be written for some other reason. If the contract can only be partially performed within a year, it must be in writing. It is not clear that a written contract would be required if one side can perform within a year and the other side cannot. The solution to that situation would be most likely resolved by looking at whether the result is fair.

There are many other situations involving the requirement of a writing that can only be resolved by a much more complete exposition. The prudent rule is that if there is any doubt about whether a contract must be in writing it is best to take the time to write it down.

For more information

American Jurisprudence, 2nd. ed. Vol. 72, *Statute of Frauds.* St. Paul, Minn.: West Group Publishing. Consult the statutes in your state.

Stanley M. Morris
Attorney at Law
Cortez, Colorado

statute of limitations sets time limits for filing lawsuits.

Once the "limitations period" has ended, a party who was wronged may no longer sue, unless the party at fault waives his right to assert the statute as a defense.

Statutes of limitations are not legal technicalities designed to frustrate the rights of individuals. The purpose of these laws is to prevent the filing of stale claims. As time passes, evidence disappears, the memories of witnesses deteriorate, and witnesses often die or leave the jurisdiction. By setting a time limit for suing, statutes of limitations protect defendants from having to defend against claims where much of the evidence is no longer available.

Most states, as well as the federal government, have numerous statutes of limitations. Each statute governs a particular type of claim. For example, Illinois has a statute of limitations that governs cases involving written contracts (10-year limitations period), and one that governs personal injuries (two-year limitations period). States usually also have a "catchall" statute that sets the limitations period for any type of case not governed by the other, more specific laws.

The limitations period starts to run when the plaintiff's claim "accrues." Historically, accrual was the point in time at which a plaintiff could first file a lawsuit to prosecute his claim. This point in time varies depending on the type of claim. For example, the right to sue for breach of contract generally arises on the day the breach occurs even if the plaintiff has not been hurt yet. But in cases not involving contracts, a plaintiff generally may not sue until he has been harmed, even if the defendant breached a duty well before the date of injury. To illustrate, manufacturing a dangerous product may constitute a breach of duty, but until the plaintiff is hurt by the product, he may not sue the manufacturer for products liability.

The original accrual rule was often criticized for being unduly harsh. The limitations period could start and end before the plaintiff knew that he was injured and had a claim against the defendant. In addition, there were only a few exceptions. One worth noting was the doctrine of fraudulent concealment. Under this doctrine, if the defendant tried to cover up the grounds for the plaintiff's claim, the limitations period did not begin until the plaintiff became aware of those grounds.

Because of a concern that a strict application of the original accrual rule caused statutes of limitations to bar lawsuits where the plaintiff was blamelessly ignorant of his claims, state courts and legislatures began to adopt what is now known as the "discovery rule." Under this rule, a claim does not accrue, and the statute of limitations does not begin to run, until the plaintiff knows or should know that he has been wronged and has a right to sue. A person "should know" of his claim when he is presented with facts that would alert a reasonable person that he was wronged due to the fault of another.

To demonstrate how the discovery rule changed the law, suppose a neighbor broke into a house and stole a television while the owner was on a long vacation. Under the original accrual rule, the limitations period began to run the day the television was stolen because that was the day the owner first had a right to sue, and the limitations period could expire before the owner returned home. But under the discovery rule, the limitations period does not start to run until the day the owner gets back and discovers that his television is missing.

In addition to the discovery rule, statutes of limitations may be suspended, or "tolled," under certain circumstances in the interests of justice, particularly where the plaintiff is unable to assert his rights through no fault of his own. For example, most states toll the limitations period while a person is a minor, mentally incompetent, or in prison. A statute of limitations may also be suspended where (1) the defendant induces the plaintiff not to sue by offering to settle the claim, or (2) in certain extraordinary circumstances, such as when a war closes the courts. These last two cases constitute examples of "equitable tolling."

Filing a lawsuit within the limitations period obviously satisfies the requirements of the statute of limitations, but it does not necessarily mean that the lawsuit was filed in a timely manner. For example, the doctrine of laches provides that a court may dismiss a lawsuit if the plaintiff waited an unreasonable amount of time before suing, even if the plaintiff filed his case before the statute of limitations expired. Generally, a plaintiff acts unreasonably if he knows of his claim but waits to sue and during the delay important circumstances change. To illustrate, if a plaintiff knows that the defendant has started building a house on a piece of the plaintiff's land, but the plaintiff does not sue until the defendant has finished, the court may find that the plaintiff is barred by laches from claiming that the house and the land it is on are his even if the limitations period has not expired.

"Statutes of repose" are another type of legal time limit. These laws extinguish the right to commence a lawsuit after a period of time that is measured from the point a specific event occurs, regardless of whether the plaintiff's claim has accrued. The event that triggers the statute of repose is usually an act by the defendant, such as the manufacture or sale of a product or the performance of a service. To understand the differ-

ence between statutes of limitations and statutes of repose, consider the following example. A state might have a two-year statute of limitations for personal injuries and a 10-year statute of repose for product liability claims. Normally, if a plaintiff is hurt by a product, he may sue within two years of discovering his claim, as permitted by the statute of limitations. However, the statute of repose mandates that he file any lawsuit within 10 years of the day the product was sold. Therefore, if he discovers his claim 10 years and one day after the product was sold, the statute of repose bars him from suing.

The above example also illustrates the primary purpose of statutes of repose—they eliminate the possibility that the discovery rule will keep defendants under a permanent threat of being sued for something they did years before. Statutes of repose achieve this end by setting an absolute time limit after which a defendant cannot be sued even if the plaintiff is harmed or learns of his claim after the period of repose has ended.

Statutes of repose are not as common as statutes of limitation. They generally apply only to areas of the law where the discovery rule has proved to be especially troublesome, such as products liability, real estate development, and professional malpractice. However, because statutes of repose can bar a plaintiff's right before it has even accrued, some courts have ruled that statutes of repose are invalid on constitutional grounds.

For more information

American Jurisprudence, Vol. 51, Limitation of Actions (West 1970 and Supp. 2000).

Corpus Juris Secundum, Vol. 54, Limitations of Actions (West 1987 and Supp. 2000).

Joshua M. Silverstein
Freeborn and Peters, Chicago

statutory rape is sexual intercourse with an unmarried person who is under the "age of consent." Force is not required; the crime lies solely with the age of the victim. Today this age differs in each state. While most states set the age at 16, it ranges from 14 to 18 across the states. The main idea behind the laws is the presumption that young people are too immature to give valid consent to sexual intercourse.

Originally, the laws specifically named males as perpetrators and females as victims and set the age of consent at 10 or 12. Yet the prohibition on sexual activity extended only to people who were not married. The laws in some sense thus served to preserve female virginity, which was a valuable commodity, until marriage.

In the late 19th century, an alliance of organizations such as the Women's Christian Temperance Union, suffragists, and some conservative religious groups and workingmen's organizations lobbied to have the age raised to 16 or 18. This occurred most rapidly in the states in which women could vote. In response, male legislators made prosecutions more difficult. Some states required the female victim to be "of previous chaste character," i.e., a virgin, and be able to prove that fact. Others allowed perpetrators to claim that they had made a "mistake of age" and thought the female older than she was.

In the 1970s liberal feminists sought to do away with gendered inequities in a variety of laws, and statutory rape laws were amended in two ways. First, the laws were made "gender-neutral." While originally they prohibited only sexual intercourse by a male with an underage female, as amended the laws prohibited sexual intercourse by a person with an underage person. Second, "age-spans" required that the perpetrator be a certain number of years older than the victim. The spans vary across the 43 states that have adopted them, from two to six years, but are generally set at three or four years.

These changes did not go unnoticed or uncontested. The one Supreme Court case that focused on statutory rape, *Michael M. v. Superior Court of Sonoma County* (1981), intensified both the complexity and the controversy over the issue by upholding the conviction of a young male about the same age as the female victim. The majority opinion stated that statutory rape laws which punished only males were valid because they would serve as a deterrent to sexual activity equal to that faced by young females who were deterred by fear of pregnancy.

This kind of strained reasoning was exactly what radical feminists were concerned about. Unlike the liberal feminists, radical feminists felt that gender-neutral language and age spans would divert attention from the fact that males still held more power than females, including females their same age. Religious conservatives were also against both changes although for different reasons: In their view, the male was the dominant sexual partner and the parties' ages were less important than their marital status. Other feminists, often called sex radicals, as well as gay and lesbian groups, feared that gender-neutral laws might be used disproportionately against homosexual couples. They also felt that age spans did little to counter the laws' invasion of privacy of minors' sex lives.

Given the ideological crosscurrents surrounding this issue, it is no surprise that the laws contain contradictions. First, if the parties are married, the sexual activity is legal regardless of their ages. Second, underage females are legally able to consent to abortion but not to sexual activity. Third, the victim cannot stop a prosecution by claiming that he or she felt that the activity was consensual. Fourth, a number of young males in committed relationships with underage females have had to register as sex offenders under "Megan's Law" provisions and are thus barred from seeing their partners.

Despite these discontinuities, the laws remain in force. The question remains as to how one can increase protection against sexual abuse for children but at the same time allow consensual sexual activity among adolescents. Often, prosecutors use their own discretion as to whether or not to prosecute such cases.

For more information

Bienen, Leigh. "Rape III: National Developments in Rape Reform Legislation," *Women's Rights Law Reporter* 6, no. 3 (spring/summer 1980): 170–213.

Odem, Mary E. *Delinquent Daughters: Protecting and Policing Adolescent Female Sexuality in the United States, 1885–1920.* Chapel Hill: University of North Carolina Press, 1995.

Olsen, Frances. "Statutory Rape: A Feminist Critique of Rights Analysis," *Texas Law Review* 63 (1984): 387–432.

Carolyn E. Cocca
Assistant Professor of Politics
State University of New York
College at Old Westbury

Stevens, John Paul (1920–   ) was appointed to the Supreme Court by President Gerald Ford in 1975.

Stevens was born in 1920 in Chicago. He graduated Phi Beta Kappa from the University of Chicago in 1941, served as a naval officer during World War II, earning a Bronze Star, and studied law at Northwestern University, graduating first in his class in the space of two years instead of the usual three. He then worked as a clerk [or legal assistant] to Justice Wiley Rutledge on the U.S. Supreme Court.

Before joining the Court, Stevens also served as Republican counsel for the House Judiciary Subcommittee on the Study of Monopoly Power and later for the attorney general's antitrust study committee during the Eisenhower administration. He spent a number of years in private practice in Chicago, specializing in antitrust law, and taught that subject at both the University of Chicago and Northwestern University schools of law. He was appointed as a member of the U.S. Court of Appeals for the Seventh Circuit in 1970 where he acquired a reputation as a distin-guished judge who was admired for skill and intelligence.

Justice Stevens has sometimes been called a "maverick" because it proved difficult for many people to classify him. Sometimes he voted with the Court's conservatives like Rehnquist and at other times he voted with the Court's liberals like Brennan and Marshall. Stevens's approach to law focuses on the details. He combines a basic conservatism with an insistence on individual justice and procedural neutrality that often makes him appear to be the most liberal justice on the Rehnquist Court.

Adding to the complexity he brings to decisions, Stevens prefers to balance considerations in reaching decisions rather than to make categorical decisions that would control many future cases. He has supported a single balancing test rather than the division into the *rational basis test, intermediate scrutiny,* and *strict scrutiny,* which the Court uses to decide many First Amendment and equal protection cases. Stevens's attention to detail and his preference for balancing considerations comes from a pragmatic and utilitarian framework. For a utilitarian everything is contextual—it all depends on what works best.

As a result of his emphasis on context and social goals, Stevens is sometimes opposed to affirmative action but supports it when he believes it is relevant to institutional performance, like racial preferences in television ownership that might increase the diversity of televised programming, or where the system of preferences incorporated what Stevens thought were reasonable limits. But he excoriated his conservative colleagues for their inability to tell the difference between a "'No Trespassing' sign and a welcome mat."

Stevens joins in the fundamental shared conclusions of the more liberal bloc on the Rehnquist Court. He fights for accuracy in criminal judgments. Thus he was unwilling to send a convicted killer to his death when evidence found after trial suggests he was "probably innocent."

He fights for racial equality and has fought against districting systems that cancel out black votes. He has staked out a relatively liberal position with respect to freedom of speech, supporting rights to issue pamphlets anonymously, or to solicit contributions on sidewalks owned by the Postal Service. But here too he is sometimes found in opposition to speech rights, as in his famous vote to sustain convictions for burning the American flag as a symbol of protest.

Thus Stevens is a "maverick" because his philosophical approach to the work of the Court treats as factual questions issues that are ideological to many of his colleagues.

For more information

Gottlieb, Stephen E. *Morality Imposed: The Rehnquist Court and Liberty in America.* New York: New York University Press, 2000.

Popkin, William D. "A Common Law Lawyer on the Supreme Court: The Opinions of Justice Stevens," *Duke Law Journal* (1989): 1087.

Stephen E. Gottlieb
Albany Law School

Stone, Harlan Fiske (1872–1946) served as associate and chief justice of the U.S. Supreme Court from 1925 to 1946.

Stone received great acclaim as a justice for his protection of civil liberties and his legal craftsmanship. His tenure as chief justice, however, was marked by divisions within the Court and his inability to bring the justices together.

Harlan Fiske Stone was born in 1872 on a New Hampshire farm and was an Amherst College classmate of Calvin Coolidge. He became a professor of law at Columbia University in 1899 and remained there until 1923. Between 1910 and 1924 he served as dean of the Columbia University School of Law. Generally considered a conservative, he was selected by President Coolidge to become attorney general after the scandals of the Harding administration. He reorganized the department and later appointed J.

Edgar Hoover as director of the Federal Bureau of Investigation. He was nominated for the Supreme Court in 1925.

Considered a conservative at the beginning of his career, Stone quickly aligned himself with the more liberal wing of the Court. Always an advocate of judicial restraint, Stone rejected the idea of declaring economic legislation unconstitutional simply because he disagreed with it. He dissented from the Court's opinion in *United States v. Butler* (1936), which struck down the Agricultural Adjustment Act. Stone repeatedly dissented from decisions striking down state and federal economic legislation between 1925 and 1937.

In *United States v. Carolene Products Co.* (1938) Stone, in a famous footnote number 4, wrote, "There may be narrower scope for operation of the presumption of constitutionality when legislation appears on its face to be within a specific prohibition of the Constitution, such as those of the first ten amendments, which are deemed equally specific when held to be embraced within the Fourteenth." This has been hailed as an early expression of "preferred freedoms doctrine," which gave greater protection to civil liberties than to economic interest. Stone also had sensitivity to free speech concerns and civil liberties. In 1940 he was the lone dissenter from a Court majority upholding a requirement that students be forced to salute the American flag in *Minersville School District v. Gobitis.* His dissent in *Gobitis* was turned into a majority in 1943 when the Court reversed itself and adopted Stone's reasoning in *West Virginia State Board of Education v. Barnett.* Stone also advocated a belief that the First Amendment established "preferred freedoms" for American citizens.

After the retirement of Chief Justice Charles Evans Hughes in 1941, President Roosevelt ignored Stone's nominal Republicanism and elevated him to the position. Unfortunately his time as chief justice was not the most successful period of his career. Between 1941 and 1946 extreme differences of opinion and personality

Chief Justice Harlan Fiske Stone (HARRIS AND EWING, COLLECTION OF THE SUPREME COURT OF THE UNITED STATES)

clashes rocked the Court. Stone's approach to the judicial conference was one of unlimited debate and discussion and this style exacerbated the clash of egos and ideology.

During the war years the Supreme Court dealt with many issues dealing with the limit and scope of federal power. These cases revealed a split in the court between libertarians who wanted to protect individual liberties and those who stressed the need for government to have the power to deal with problems. This split would divide the court for a decade, and Stone's style of leadership tended to exacerbate differences rather than resolve them.

Stone died on April 22, 1946. His place in the history of the Supreme Court is secure as an expert judicial craftsman who stood on principle even in the face of intense opposition. His career as chief justice did not emphasize his strengths of intellectual integrity and commitment to open debate. Stone's legacy is one of intelligence and judicial vision rather than leadership.

For more information

Schwartz, Bernard. *A History of the Supreme Court.* New York: Oxford University Press, 1993.

Unofsky, Melvin I., and Herbert A. Johnson. *Division and Discord: The Supreme Court under Stone and Vision, 1941–1953.* Charleston: University of South Carolina Press, 1997.

Charlie Howard
Tarleton State University

strict liability   means that a person will have to pay—be liable—if he or she causes another person harm regardless of the care taken to avoid that harm.

The concept of strict liability is rooted in the beginnings of English common law when, for instance, a trespasser would have to pay for entering someone else's land even if the trespasser believed he was on his own land. As the industrial age began, strict liability would impose on the mining operation the cost of damages caused by using explosives on neighboring property or hold accountable the person who kept a dangerous animal that got loose and injured someone. Strict liability also extended to libel when a person falsely accused another and hurt the second person's reputation: If the statement was false, then the person making it would pay even if he had good reason to believe it was true. The rationale for this strict rule of liability in the law was that businesses or trespassers or defamers were best able to pay the costs of their transgressions. In the last 100 years in the United States, some of the harshness of strict liability under common law has been eased by statutes or by judicial decisions.

The law of negligence, by which fault can be assessed in accidents when the person causing the accident has done so because he failed to use reasonable care, was developed to ease the unyielding burden on the blameless. In modern society, the person who keeps a dangerous animal that gets loose may still be liable when it attacks and hurts someone else, regardless of how much care the owner took to keep the animal tied up. But the owner of a dog that gets out of its yard and bites someone may not be legally responsible if the dog had not shown vicious tendencies before. The U.S. Supreme Court, for the most part, has blunted on free speech grounds the strict liability imposed on the person who libels another when the libeler had a reasonable belief that what he wrote was true.

For more information
Vandall, Frank J. *Strict Liability: Legal and Economic Analysis.* New York: Quorum Books, 1989.

Wm. Osler McCarthy
Texas Supreme Court
University of Texas Department of Journalism

strict scrutiny   refers to the level of examination the courts give to legislation.

The concept originated in the arguments among the justices about judicial activism and judicial restraint. Justices Holmes, Brandeis, Cardozo, and Stone [later chief justice] argued that the Court had been second-guessing legislatures from the end of the 19th century into 1937 when they changed the terms of the debate. They argued that the Court should not find legislation in violation of any of several clauses of the Constitution if reasonable men might believe the legislation reasonable. This is the rational basis test.

In a seminal decision in 1938, Justice Stone wrote for the Court in a case concerning economic legislation, applying the rational basis test. But he added in one of the Court's most famous footnotes that it might be appropriate for the Court to review legislation more searchingly where it concerned either particularly clear provisions of the Constitution or the operation of democracy, so that those in power could not overrule the desires of the people to turn them out of office or otherwise countermand their decisions, and rights would be treated equally in religious, racial, and similar settings.

Eventually it became clear that where legislation threatens important rights, a critical review of legislation involves several components. The first component is that the values that the legislation is designed to pursue must be so important that they can be described as "compelling" or by similar adjectives. Constitutional rights should not be narrowed, limited, or curtailed for trivial reasons.

Second, the means chosen to implement the legislative objective must be necessary to accomplish those objectives. The third component is that there are no ways to reach the compellingly important legislative objectives without equivalent restriction of the constitutional right. This is known as the requirement of using the least restrictive means. The logic of the second and third components is that if the state could satisfy its important goals without infringing on liberty, then the goals that the state claims are so important are not what the state is actually accomplishing. Instead it may simply be taking the easy way, like banning demonstrations to keep the peace instead of policing them. In that case it is the cost of policing, not the value of public peace, that the state is really saving.

Thus it became the formula for strict scrutiny that the state's decision must be (a) *necessary* (b) to accomplish a compelling government interest and (c) there are *no less restrictive means*.

Strict scrutiny is a balancing test. Other balancing tests include rational basis, also known as the minimum scrutiny test, so-called ad hoc balancing, and intermediate scrutiny. In each form, the justices must weigh the importance of the government policy against the importance of the rights that are being restricted. Balancing tests, including strict scrutiny, are used in some fields of due process, equal protection, First Amendment, and other areas of constitutional analysis. Of all those tests, sometimes called "tiers of scrutiny," strict scrutiny is the most difficult to satisfy. It has been called "strict in theory, fatal in fact" although that is not always true.

For more information

Ely, John Hart. *Democracy and Distrust.* Cambridge, Mass.: Harvard University Press, 1980.

Gunther, Gerald. "Foreword: In Search of Evolving Doctrine on a Changing Court: A Model for a Newer Equal Protection," *Harvard Law Review* 1 (1972): 86.

Shelton v. Tucker, 364 U.S. 479 (1960).

United States v. Carolene Products Co., 304 U.S. 144 (1938).

Stephen E. Gottlieb
Albany Law School

student rights refer to the constitutional rights students have in public schools.

Student rights reached their peak in the U.S. Supreme Court in 1969, but they have been curtailed by the justices in subsequent decisions and are the subject of frequent controversy in high schools around the country. The term *student rights* applies to students at public schools and colleges and implicates the First, Fourth, and Fourteenth Amendments to the Constitution.

In 1969 the High Court decided the case of *Tinker v. Des Moines Independent Community School District.* A group of students in Des Moines, Iowa, wore black armbands to school to protest the Vietnam War. Their protest violated recently adopted school rules. The decision noted that the protest did not disrupt the school and said that the students were engaged in expressive conduct protected by the First Amendment. In an eloquent statement of rights, the Court said," It can hardly be argued that either students or teachers shed their constitutional rights to freedom of speech or expression at the schoolhouse gate." Not surprisingly, the

Supreme Court has also found First Amendment protection for a range of free speech at the college level.

In 1975 the Court ruled in *Goss v. Lopez* that students facing disciplinary suspension at public schools were entitled to due process under the Fourteenth Amendment and must be provided some form of notice and at least a brief hearing. Two years later, however, the justices declined to require any due process for students subjected to corporal punishment at school.

In the 1980s the Supreme Court took a narrower view of student rights and recognized more clearly the authority of schools to maintain order. In *New Jersey v. T.L.O.,* the Court ruled in 1985 that students may be subjected to searches in school with less justification than "probable cause," which the Fourth Amendment requires in other contexts. This has led, in turn, to courts upholding drug testing of students based on no individual suspicion and would likely be used to justify the use of metal detectors at school doors.

Deference to school officials has also extended to controlling the values taught. In *Bethel School District No. 403 v. Fraser* in 1986, the justices rejected free speech protection for a student who used sexual innuendoes in a speech nominating another student for school office. The Court said school officials could decide that the speech was vulgar and inappropriate for the age of the student audience. In *Hazelwood School District v. Kuhlmeier* in 1988, the Court upheld the principal's decision to bar two articles from the school newspaper. The Court said that the student newspaper was part of the school's activities and that the school could control the content.

Dress codes and other appearance regulations have also caused controversy. The Supreme Court has not resolved this aspect of student rights. Lower courts have found no constitutional right to a particular hair length and have upheld some dress codes or bans on clothes in known gang colors. Some courts have also found protected expression in T-shirts that bear messages.

For more information

Alexander, Kern, and M. David Alexander. *The Law of Schools, Students, and Teachers in a Nutshell.* St. Paul, Minn.: West Group Publishing, 1995.

Raskin, Jamin B. *We the Students: Supreme Court Cases for and about Students.* Washington, D.C.: Congressional Quarterly Books, 2000.

Stephen Wermiel
American University Washington College of Law

subpoena is a command, issued in the name of a court, ordering a person to testify or turn over evidence. If the recipient fails to comply with the subpoena without an excuse recognized by law, he or she may be held in contempt of court.

There are two types of subpoenas. A subpoena ad testificandum, often referred to simply as a "subpoena," compels the person designated to attend a hearing or a deposition for the purpose of testifying. A subpoena duces tecum orders the production of documents or other tangible things. Subpoenas are critical to the functioning of the judicial system. In civil matters, subpoenas are the primary means of obtaining testimony and tangible evidence from persons who are not parties to the case. They serve this function during both pretrial discovery and at trial. Unless a nonparty is served with a subpoena, he or she generally cannot (1) be compelled to testify at a deposition, a hearing, or a trial, or (2) be required to produce documents or things. In criminal cases, the government utilizes subpoenas to conduct investigations into illegal activity. Both defendants and the government must use subpoenas if a witness is unwilling to testify or produce documents and evidence.

The subpoena power is a broad one. A subpoena generally may seek any testimony or tangible evidence relevant to the case. This includes materials in the possession of a subpoena recipient that belong to someone else. Nevertheless, the subpoena power does have limits. Subpoenas may not direct that a person give testimony or produce tangible evidence that is irrelevant to the case or that is protected by a privilege, such as the attorney-client privilege or the Fifth Amendment privilege against self-incrimination. A subpoena duces tecum also may not order a person to produce tangible evidence if doing so would be unduly burdensome. While a court usually may enforce a subpoena served on any person in the same state, this authority does not extend beyond the boundaries of the state except in rare circumstances, such as federal criminal cases. To obtain testimony or documents from a person in another state, the subpoena must be issued by the court where the witness is located and enforced by that court.

When a party receiving a subpoena ad testificandum believes that the subpoena seeks testimony on irrelevant or privileged matters, he or she generally may not challenge the command to appear. Instead, the witness must wait and, during the examination, object to any questions that would require disclosing irrelevant or privileged information.

However, in the case of a subpoena duces tecum that requests privileged or irrelevant material, the recipient may ask the court to quash it. Where complying with a subpoena duces tecum would be unreasonable or burdensome, the court may either quash the subpoena or place conditions upon compliance, such as the payment of reasonable expenses incurred when producing the documents or things.

The subpoena form itself generally needs to list the name of the court from which it is issued, the title of the case, and the name of the court where the case is pending. It must also state whether the person designated is to appear and testify, produce tangible evidence, or both. A subpoena duces tecum has to specify the types of documents desired.

Subpoenas are issued in the court's name, but in most states and the federal system attorneys are permitted to fill out blank subpoena forms as needed and have them served. Subpoenas generally must be served by a person over the age of 18 who is a not a party to the lawsuit. See, for example, Fed. R. Civ. Pro. 45(b)(1).

Finally, a person receiving a subpoena must often be paid an appearance fee and travel costs at the time the subpoena is served. The precise amount is usually governed by statute. See, for example, 28 U.S.C. section 1821 (setting appearance fees and permitted travel costs in federal cases). Without these payments a subpoena is invalid and the recipient is not bound by it.

For more information

American Jurisprudence, 2nd ed. Vol. 81, *Witnesses* sections 7–33. St. Paul, Minn.: West Group Publishing, 1992, and Supp., 2000.

Wright, Charles, and Alan Miller. *Federal Practice and Procedure.* Vol. 2, sections 271–79, Rule 17. Subpoena. St. Paul Minn.: West Group Publishing, 2000.

———. *Federal Practice and Procedure.* Vol. 9A, sections 2451–56, Rule 45. Subpoena. St. Paul Minn.: West Group Publishing, 1995, and Supp., 2000.

Joshua M. Silverstein
Freeborn and Peters, Chicago

substantive due process   is a constitutional doctrine requiring fairness in the content of legislation.

As distinguished from the concept of procedural due process, which requires that government use reasonable methods in implementing and enforcing laws, the theory of substantive due process dictates that government may not regulate certain facets of private life. In this sense, the doctrine of substantive due process is an expression of American constitutionalism—the idea that the U.S. Constitution limits the range of government's authority to regulate the lives of citizens.

Both prior to and after the Civil War, the United States Supreme Court interpreted the Fifth Amendment's due process clause as prohibiting federal legislation that infringed on the property rights of citizens. Laws that constrained a person's use of his property, the justices reasoned, violated substantive due process rights protected by the Fifth Amendment. In the later decades of the 19th century, the Supreme Court interpreted the due process clauses of the Fifth and Fourteenth Amendments as circumscribing the power of government to regulate dealings between private businesses and workers. In short, conservative Supreme Court justices argued that the Fifth and Fourteenth Amendments guarantee to workers the right to engage in lawful employment activity free of government interference. Referred to as the "liberty of contract," this extension of the theory of substantive due process became in the late 1800s a principal component of the Court's Fourteenth Amendment jurisprudence.

During the early years of the 20th century, the Supreme Court handed down a series of decisions that elevated the theory of substantive due process, and the related right to "liberty of contract," to the status of a constitutional doctrine. Opinions written in *Lochner v. New York* (1905) and *Adkins v. Children's Hospital* (1923) reflected the Court's eagerness to use this reading of the Fourteenth Amendment to constrain the states in their attempts to regulate working conditions, create maximum hour regulations, and set minimum wage requirements. These subjects, the Court held, were outside the scope of government's lawful authority.

Although a majority of late 19th century and early 20th century justices embraced this application of substantive due process, the Court did not specify the extent to which the doctrine would be applied to government intervention in the economy. In *Munn v. Illinois* (1876) a majority of justices held that a state law was allowed under the principle of due process because the regulation was aimed at a business "affected with a public interest." The Court never settled on an exact definition of what constituted a business "affected with a public interest." Further, in *Muller v. Oregon* (1908) the justices revealed that other types of state regulation of economic activity would be allowed under the theory of substantive due process. *Muller* and subsequent decisions, however, shed no light on the standard the Court would use in discerning the types of business activities subject to government regulation. Arguably, the idea that the justices could delineate a universe of commercial activities legitimately within government's authority to regulate was little more than pretense.

Coupled with several personnel changes on the Court, the ambivalence concerning the reach of substantive due process facilitated the doctrinal shift that occurred in the mid-1930s. In deciding *West Coast Hotel v. Parrish* (1937), a majority of justices turned away from the substantive due process theory in cases involving government regulation of economic activity. Furthermore, the Court's decision in *United States v. Carolene Products Company* (1938) symbolized the new majority's position on government regulatory schemes: Regulation of commercial activity is presumed to be consistent with the Constitution and the government need only demonstrate that some rational basis exists for enacting such measures. The importance of this decision must not be missed: The *Carolene Products* ruling reflected the Court majority's view that economic regulations are presumed to be a legitimate exercise of government authority.

The diminution of the substantive due process theory coincided with a key shift in the Court's agenda. Since 1937 the Supreme Court has reviewed proportionally fewer business regulation cases, turning its attention toward civil liberties and civil rights issues. Moreover, the kind of rigorous judicial scrutiny once directed at instances of economic regulation is now employed in cases of other types. This heightened standard of review is now aimed at cases involving government limitations on political freedoms, cases implicating many of the Bill of Rights protections afforded to persons accused of crimes, and disputes involving some of the liberties encompassed by the equal protection clause of the Fourteenth Amendment.

For more information

Abraham, Henry J., and Perry, Barbara. *Freedom and the Court: Civil Rights and Liberties in the United States.* New York: Oxford University Press, 1998.

Ely, James W. *Property Rights in the Age of Enterprise.* New York: Garland Publishing, 1997.

Keynes, Edward. *Liberty, Property, and Privacy: Toward a Jurisprudence of Substantive Due Process.* University Park: Pennsylvania State University Press, 1996.

Bradley J. Best
Austin Peay State University

Swann v. Charlotte-Mecklenburg Board of Education

402 U.S. 1 (1971) upheld a far-reaching busing plan for school desegregation that was adopted by a U.S. District Court in North Carolina.

Charlotte-Mecklenburg School District covered not only the city itself but also all of surrounding Mecklenburg County. At the time of the Court's decree, the district still featured unconstitutional racial segregation produced by law. Of the 21,000 black schoolchildren in Charlotte, two-thirds attended schools that were at least 99 percent black.

One aspect of District Judge James McMillan's plan was that all elementary schools in the school district were to approximate an ideal figure of 71 percent white, 29 percent black, which was the ratio of whites to blacks in the district as a whole. Under his order, school attendance zones were redrafted and "black" schools in the inner city were grouped with "white" schools in Charlotte's outlying areas and its suburbs. Black students in grades 1–4 were bused to the white schools and white youngsters in grades 5–6 were bused to the black schools. The result was that all the elementary schools became genuinely integrated.

Chief Justice Warren Burger's unanimous opinion emphasized that race-conscious assignment of children to schools and busing might on occasion be needed if de jure segregation in a school district were to be uprooted. He pointed out that school busing was hardly an innovation in the United States, and that under the district court's plan the average trip was only about seven miles and did not take more than 35 minutes. He denied that Judge McMillan had imposed a racial quota on the elementary schools: The 71–29 percent figure was a target, not an "inflexible requirement" (402 U.S. at p. 25). He cautioned, moreover, that once a unitary school system was in place, the school board would not continually have to adjust school boundaries to take into account neighborhood racial changes.

On the same day, the Court invalidated a North Carolina law barring busing for purposes of racial integration (*North Carolina State Board of Education v. Swann*, 402 U.S. 43 [1971]). It also set aside a Mobile, Alabama, desegregation plan in which the eastern, heavily black neighborhood of the school district was treated as an isolated area and not enough consideration was given to busing from east to west and vice versa (*Davis v. Board of School Commissioners of Mobile County*, 402 U.S. 33 [1971]).

The *Swann* case was not popular. President Richard Nixon and members of Congress introduced bills to prevent the federal courts from ordering busing to promote racial integration, though no serious restraint on this power of the judiciary ever was enacted. The Supreme Court itself significantly weakened *Swann* in *Milliken v. Bradley*, 418 U.S. 717 (1974), where Burger's 5–4 opinion declared that a district court erred in ordering busing between heavily black Detroit and its predominantly white suburbs where the suburban school districts were separate from the city's and had not themselves been guilty of legally requiring segregation. Some feel that Burger joined the majority in *Swann* because he knew he did not have the votes for his antibusing views. He did say there that once legally required segregation was at an end, there would be no need for further intervention by the federal courts. Thus in September of 1999, a judge of the district court involved in *Swann* found that the Charlotte-Mecklenburg School District had eliminated all traces of intentional racial discrimination and so ordered it to stop its massive busing program.

For more information

Keynes, Edward, with Randall K. Miller. *The Court vs. Congress: Prayer, Busing and Abortion.* Durham, N.C.: Duke University Press, 1989.

Yellin, Amy, with David Firestone. "By Court Order, Busing Ends Where It Began," *New York Times,* September 11, 1999, p. A1.

Daniel C. Kramer
College of Staten Island, CUNY

T

Taft, William Howard (1857–1930) was the only president of the United States who also served as chief justice of the Supreme Court.

Born in Cincinnati, Ohio, Taft was raised in a family with a tradition of public service. Taft graduated from Yale University in 1878 and in 1880 was admitted to the bar. At the age of 30, he was appointed to the Ohio Superior Court, later winning reelection. This was one of the two times that Taft was elected to office, the other being the presidency. In 1890 President Benjamin Harrison named him U.S. solicitor general. Two years later Harrison tapped him for the newly established sixth circuit federal court of appeals. On the federal bench, Taft took a middle position in the area of organized labor law. While he supported worker's rights to unionize and strike if necessary, he opposed violence and was a staunch supporter of property rights.

Taft reluctantly left the bench eight years later to head a military commission on the Philippine Islands at the request of President William McKinley. He stayed on as civilian governor of the Philippines and was so absorbed by his responsibilities that he twice turned down nominations to the U.S. Supreme Court. In 1904 President Theodore Roosevelt named Taft to replace Elihu Root as secretary of war. Taft became one of Roosevelt's closest advisers.

As a cabinet member, Taft was responsible for the Panama Canal project and for investigating revolutionary activity in Cuba. Taft's influence on the Republican Party grew, and with President Roosevelt's backing, he won his party's nomination for president. On March 4, 1909, Taft was sworn in as the 27th president of the United States.

His single term in office saw the postal savings system and the Tariff Board institutionalized, the ratification of the Sixteenth Amendment to the Constitution, and continued breaking up of monopolies. Taft also appointed six justices to the Supreme Court, more than any single-term president in history. Though president, Taft longed to return to the judiciary, particularly as U.S. chief justice. His appointment of Justice Edward D. White to head the court was largely due to White being 12 years his senior. Taft hoped that he might succeed White as chief. In addition to White, Taft appointed associate justices Horace H. Lurton, Charles Evans Hughes, Willis Van Devanter, Joseph R. Lamar, and Mahlon Pitney.

Soon after Taft became president, he and former president Roosevelt began to have opposing views. The party split and in 1912 Theodore Roosevelt ran for president under his Progressive, or Bull Moose, Party. As Taft had expected, this new branch of the Republican Party split the Republican vote and Democrat Woodrow Wilson won the presidency.

Taft was relieved, and he could concentrate on fulfilling his real desire—to be nominated to the Supreme Court. After teaching law at Yale and making it clear to the next president, Warren G. Harding, that he would only accept nomination to the chief justiceship, he finally got his wish following White's death in 1921. On the Court, Taft contributed more to its efficiency than to constitutional law. For example, he lobbied for the Judiciary Act of 1925, which gave the justices nearly total discretion over which cases to hear.

On the Court, Taft couldn't keep the progressives or the conservatives happy. As president, Taft imposed more trust busting than his predecessor and on the Court he continued to break monopolies. For example, in *Stafford v. Wallace,* 258 U.S. 495 (1922) he applied the stream of commerce doctrine to uphold the Packers and Stockyard Act of 1921, which gave the federal government the authority to regulate the livestock industry. He also endorsed the Mann-Elkins Bill, which helped regulate the railroads more effectively. In *Bailey v. Drexel Furniture Co.,* 259 U.S. 20 (1922) he invalidated a federal law regulating child labor as outside the reach of Congress's taxation power. In *Adkins v. Children's Hospital,* 261 U.S. 525 (1923) Taft dissented from a Court majority invalidating a minimum wage law for women and children. He wrote, "The evils of the sweating system and of the long hours and low wages which are characteristic of it are well known. . . . . It is not the function of this court to hold congressional acts invalid simply because they are passed to carry out economic views which the court believes to be unwise or unsound."

Perhaps his most important contribution to constitutional law was his opinion in *Myers v. United States,* 272 U.S. 52 (1926) upholding the sole authority of the president to remove federal officials. "Each head of a department is and must be the President's alter ego in the matters of that department."

Taft's departure from the Court is among the handful that were clearly partisan. Though he became severely ill and was eligible for retirement, he chose to remain on the Court to counteract the liberal forces of Justices Holmes, Brandeis, and Stone. Furthermore, he viewed President Hoover as a dangerous progressive and did not want the president to name his successor. In 1929 he wrote, "I am older and slower and less acute and more confused. However, as long as things continue as they are, and I am able to answer in my place, I must stay on the court in order to prevent the Bolsheviki from getting control." His health deteriorating, Taft relented and retired on February 3, 1930, after nine years on the Court.

Taft's major contribution to U.S. law lies in his leadership in the area of court administration. He worked tirelessly, particularly in the first half of his tenure as chief, to modernize the Court.

For more information

Mason, Alpheus T. *William Howard Taft: Chief Justice.* New York: Simon and Schuster, 1965.

Pringle, Henry F. *The Life and Times of William Howard Taft,* 2 vols. New York: Farrar and Rhinehart, 1939.

Jeanine Neher and Artemus Ward
California State University, Chico

the takings clause   is the portion of the Fifth Amendment to the U.S. Constitution that declares "nor shall private property be taken for public use, without just compensation."

This provision of the Bill of Rights reflects the importance that Americans have traditionally placed on property rights. Although it authorizes the national government to take property through the power of eminent domain, it requires that owners be compensated for their loss. For example, if the government wants to build a road through your backyard, it can require you to vacate the land, but it must pay for the privilege. In *Armstrong v. United States* (1960), Justice Black summarized the purpose of the takings clause as assuring that no individual is forced to bear the cost of government projects "which in all fairness and justice, should be borne by the public as a whole." Since the whole community benefits from public projects such as the construction of roads, it is only fair that the whole community share in their cost.

Like the other provisions of the Bill of Rights, the takings clause originally applied only to the national government. The Supreme Court made this point clear in *Barron v. Baltimore* (1833). In this case, a wharf owner sued for compensation after city street improvements ruined his business. The Supreme Court declared that the takings clause was "intended solely as a limitation on the exercise of power by the government of the United States, and is not applicable to the legislation of the states." Many state constitutions had takings provisions of their own, but in the absence of state laws, there was no guarantee of compensation for government takings.

This situation changed in the 1890s, when the members of the Supreme Court were particularly concerned with protecting property rights. In 1897 the Court declared that the adoption of the Fourteenth Amendment (in 1868) had changed the law concerning takings. The justices considered compensation for property taken to be an essential part of "due process of law." They therefore applied the takings clause to the states. From then on, state governments were required to provide compensation when they took property. The takings clause thus became the first provision of the Bill of Rights "incorporated" against the states.

Courts use a number of legal standards in interpreting the takings clause. First, judges decide that a taking has occurred when an owner loses the ability to use or profit from the property. Second, property must be taken for a public purpose, which means that the government may take someone's property to benefit the community as a whole but not merely to benefit another private person or group. Third, the government must provide compensation equivalent to the property's "fair market value." Owners often complain that the amount offered is insufficient. Such complaints may be settled through negotiation or lawsuit. Fourth, government regulations that merely interfere with an owner's ability to use property usually do not constitute a taking that requires compensation. For example, the government may limit the amount of rent an apartment owner charges without having to pay compensation. Only when the government takes action which makes it nearly impossible for owners to derive an economic benefit from their property will the courts declare that there has been a "regulatory taking" that requires compensation. Fifth, the Supreme Court has recently ruled that the government must pay compensation when it requires owners to keep part of their land open to the public, since things such as bike paths and hiking trails constitute a "permanent physical occupation" of private property by the public.

For more information

Epstein, Lee, and Thomas Walker. *Constitutional Law for a Changing America,* 3rd ed. Washington D.C.: CQ Press, 1998, chap. 11.

Shannon Ishiyama Smithey
Department of Political Science
University of Pittsburgh

teen court programs are an alternative approach to juvenile justice, where first-time nonviolent offenders under age 18 are prosecuted, defended, and sentenced by other teenagers.

Teen courts are also called youth courts, student courts, or peer courts. Most of the cases involve status offenses, meaning those that are only illegal because of a person's age. Truancy is a status offense because adults do not have to attend school. Underage drinking is a status offense because adults over 21 are permitted to drink. Teen courts often also handle misdemeanors. Some handle destruction of property cases, but very few deal with violent offenses.

Teen courts are spreading rapidly around the country. They began at least 25 years ago, although no one is positive where or when the first teen court was started. There was a teen court in Grand Prairie, Texas, in 1976, and another was established the same year in Horseheads, New York. Both are still in existence. There is evidence that teen courts existed even before that time. Another program still operating is the Odessa Teen Court Program in Odessa, Texas. It began in 1983. It is a national model, so its purpose is probably the same as that of every teen court. The Odessa Teen Court Program was founded by Natalie Rothstein, in order to hold teens accountable for their own actions. The justice system often does not have the time or resources to handle juvenile cases, and juvenile court systems do not always hold teens responsible for their actions. Most receive only probation, even for violent crimes.

Teen court was created with the belief that if teens are held responsible for their actions, they will not develop a pattern of criminal behavior. The teenage years are very important since teens face a great deal of negative peer pressure. Teen courts provide positive peer pressure, sending the message that teens do not condone criminal behavior. They also provide meaningful learning opportunities for all of the participants.

Participation in teen court is voluntary, even for the defendant. The defendant may, with parental approval, choose to be sentenced in teen court rather than go through the regular court system. There are different advantages to each choice. In the regular court system, the defen-dant may have a real attorney. In teen court, the defendant's lawyer will probably be another teen. In the regular court system, the defendant may choose to plead not guilty and have a trial to decide guilt or innocence. Usually the defendant who chooses teen court must either plead guilty to the charges or plead no contest. A plea of no contest is not an actual admission of guilt but means that the defendant will not argue that he or she is innocent. All that remains for the jury to decide, then, is the sentence, or punishment. There are a few models of teen courts where the jury decides guilt or innocence, but these are not common.

There is still a trial, but it is held only to decide what sentence the defendant deserves. The prosecutor and defense attorney may call witnesses and submit evidence. The witnesses may testify about the teen's actions, or the effect those actions had on them. The prosecutor may also call a police officer or a school official who caught the defendant doing something illegal. The defense attorney may call witnesses to testify that the defendant has never been in trouble before, or that the defendant is sorry for what he or she did. The defendant may testify that he or she has already been punished enough. Each attorney has the opportunity to cross-examine the other witnesses. Just as in a regular trial, each lawyer is trying to get the jury to believe his or her side of the case. The difference in teen court is that the lawyers are usually not trying to prove guilt or innocence, but only trying to convince the jury to hand down a lighter or harsher sentence.

The sentences are another difference between teen court and the regular court system. Most teen court sentences include community service and restitution. Some require that the defendant apologize to the victim, write an essay, or attend special classes. Nearly all require the defendant to serve on the teen court jury a certain number of times. These sentences are meant to be punishment but also to be educational. All of the teens participating, even the defendant, learn about rules and laws, the consequences of breaking those rules and laws, and about our justice system itself. The teen volunteers all have adult volunteer mentors. The teen defense lawyer and prosecutor have lawyers as mentors. The court clerk and bailiff have adult mentors. In many cases, the judge is a practicing lawyer or retired judge, and the trial takes place in a real courtroom.

There are now teen courts of some sort in 46 states. Some are run by schools, some by nonprofit agencies, and some are run by the juvenile justice system. They all require a great deal of support from the community and many volunteers, both teens and adults. Although there has not been much research done on the effects of teen courts, early evidence shows that the defendants who participated in teen court are much less likely to end up back in court again.

For more information

Godwin, Tracy M. *Peer Justice and Youth Empowerment: An Implementation Guide for Teen Court Programs.* Lexington, Ky.: American Probation and Parole Association, 1996. Available free online only through the U.S. Department of Justice, Office of Juvenile Justice and Delinquency Prevention at: www.ncjrs.org/peerhome.htm.

Nessel, Paula A., program manager for School Programs of the American Bar Association Division for Public Education. *Teen Court: A National Movement.* Available online at www.abanet.org.

Mary F. Loss, Esq.
Bowles Rice McDavid Graff and Love PLLC
Fairmont, West Virginia

teenage curfew laws are rules adopted by many cities that make it illegal for individuals under a certain age to be out or on the street during the late night and early morning hours. Teen curfew laws are justified as a way to deter juveniles from committing crimes and also to protect them from being crime victims.

Generally teen curfew laws specify that it will be illegal for teens, generally those under the age of 18, to be out in public after a certain hour, such as 11:00 P.M. These laws also provide for exceptions to the curfew, permitting teens to be out if it is an emergency, if they are with their parents, running errands for their parents, are outside and in front of one's own home, or are coming from a legitimate school event. In addition, many of these curfew laws also permit teens to be out in public if they are exercising their First Amendment rights, such as freedom of speech, religion, or assembly.

Teen curfew laws raise two important questions. First, are the laws constitutional? Second, are these laws effective in cutting down juvenile crime and victimization?

Juvenile curfew laws raise important constitutional questions, including whether they violate the First Amendment right of teens to move about freely without being stopped and detained by the police. These laws also bring up Fourth Amendment questions about illegal search and seizure, as well as Fourteenth Amendment due process and equal protection arguments that police selectively enforce or detain certain youths based upon race, gender, or where they live, or that they interfere with the right of parents to raise their children. Courts around the country have taken a variety of approaches to these laws.

In *Qutb v. Strass,* 11 F.3d488 (5th Cir., 1993), a federal court upheld a Dallas curfew law, holding that it did not violate the First Amendment, but in *Nunez v. City f San Diego,* 114 F.3d 935 (9th Cir., 1997), a San Diego law was declared unconstitutional on the grounds that it impeded the right of parents to raise their children without government interference and that it also violated the equal protection clause.

In addition to constitutional claims, there is no clear evidence that juvenile curfew laws cut down on teen crime or victimization. For example, while these laws impose curfews during the late night and early morning hours, many if not most teen crimes and victimizations occurs in the late afternoon after school. Others claim that these laws will deter law-abiding teens from being out but do nothing to prevent those who wish to evade the law and commit other crimes from being out. Finally, some argue that these curfew laws turn otherwise law-abiding youths into criminals simply by virtue of being on the street or out in public.

For more information

Bey, Barbara, and Margot Smullyan-Capra. "Debate: Should Communities Set Teen Curfews?" *NEA Today* 13:5 (December 1994): 5.

Racine, Karl A. "Are Youth Curfew Laws Constitutional?" *CQ Researcher* 6:10 (March 15, 1996): 233.

David Schultz
Hamline University

temporary restraining order   or TRO is a type of injunction or court order and often the first step toward a preliminary or permanent injunction.

A TRO is an emergency order of brief duration that a judge may issue without giving the defendant notice or an opportunity for hearing. A judge may grant a TRO only in exceptional circumstances until hearing arguments or evidence and deciding if a preliminary or permanent injunction is appropriate. The TRO's purpose is to preserve the status quo until the hearing on the injunction. Typically, a TRO will last for 10 days if granted before notice to the defendant. The judge may not issue a TRO without requiring the applicant to give a bond or security to pay costs and damages the defendant may suffer if the court finds that it should not have granted the TRO. The United States and its officers do not have to put up security or bond.

There are numerous instances in which one may seek a TRO. One example would be when an employee has copied his employer's customer list, opened a similar business, and solicited the employer's customers. The employer may seek a TRO as the first stage in asking for a permanent injunction to prevent the employee from using or profiting from the customer list.

Labor law is probably the biggest area in which someone seeks a TRO. For instance, if a labor union has a "no strike" clause in its contract, and severe harm will result from an unofficial strike commonly known as a "wildcat strike," a judge may grant a TRO to keep the employees from striking and harming the business or industry. Another situation where a TRO is often used is in the case of an illegal strike, such as a teacher or police strike in a state that prohibits public employees from striking.

A party in the family law arena may seek a TRO. A parent may seek a TRO against another parent to prohibit moving a child from the state pending a determination of who will obtain custody of the child.

A TRO could be sought in the litigation arena to prevent destruction of evidence.

For more information

Black's Law Dictionary, 7th ed. St. Paul, Minn.: West Group Publishing, 1999.

Federal Rule of Civil Procedure, rule 65.

Paul D. Link
Daniel, Clampett, Powell and Cunningham
Springfield, Missouri

Terry v. Ohio   392 U.S. 1 (1968) is an important decision in which the U.S. Supreme Court created an exception to the Fourth Amendment requirement that searches and seizures be based on "probable cause." The Court has since expanded the exception to apply to a growing range of police practices.

The case was decided in 1968 at the end of the tenure of Chief Justice Earl Warren, who presided over a dramatic expansion of the rights of accused criminals. *Terry v. Ohio* bucked the trend and gave the police greater leeway to stop a person briefly for questioning and to pat down the individual for weapons without probable cause. The justices ruled that this "stop-and-frisk" practice commonly used by police could be based on a "reasonable suspicion," a lower threshold of justification than probable cause.

The case involved an incident in Cleveland in which a veteran police detective saw two men walk back and forth repeatedly in front of a convenience store, looking in the window and talking to each other and a third person. Believing that the men might be checking out the store to rob it and that they might have weapons, the detective approached them, asked their names, and then patted down their coats for weapons. When he felt a pistol in Terry's coat pocket, he removed it and also found a pistol in patting down a second man. He arrested them for carrying concealed weapons. The two men were convicted at trial.

In affirming their convictions, the Supreme Court said that the brief stop was a "seizure" under the Fourth Amendment and that the pat down of outer clothing for a weapon was a "search." However, the Court balanced these intrusions by police against the importance of the stop-and-frisk encounter to effective law enforcement. The justices said a police officer must be able to say what made the suspicion of an individual reasonable and that a simple hunch might not be enough. The Court stressed that its use of a reasonableness test was a narrow exception to the requirement for probable cause.

In subsequent decisions, the exception has been expanded in two important ways. First, the Court has allowed other types of searches based on reasonable suspicion because the justices found them to be a small intrusion like the stop-and-frisk procedure. For example, the Supreme Court has permitted searches of public high school students based on a reasonable suspicion that a law or school rule was being violated.

Second, the Court has used the same balancing test—the nature of the intrusion versus the needs of law enforcement—to permit a growing number of searches that are based on an even lower standard than reasonable suspicion. The most significant example is drug testing, which has been upheld in a number of cases based on no specific individual suspicion. The Court has upheld random drug testing based on no suspicion of specific individuals for Customs Service agents working on drug cases or carrying weapons, for railroad employees after train accidents or safety violations, and for high school student athletes.

For more information

Dressler, Joshua. *Understanding Criminal Law,* 2nd ed. Charlottesville, Va.: Lexis Law Publishers 1997.

Stephen Wermiel
American University
Washington College of Law

Texas v. Johnson   491 U.S. 397 (1989) holds that the First Amendment protects the burning of a U.S. flag as a means of symbolically expressing political opinions.

In order to signify his displeasure at the administration of Ronald Reagan, Johnson set fire to a flag and was prosecuted under a state law proscribing desecration of the flag. Fined and sentenced to prison, Johnson appealed his conviction, and the Texas Court of Criminal Appeals held that his actions were constitutionally protected. The U.S. Supreme Court, by a 5–4 margin, affirmed this judgment.

One of the last of the important First Amendment opinions written by Justice William Brennan during his lengthy career asserted that flag-burning amounted to "expressive conduct" that offered a political message. This case, then, dealt with a purer form of "expressive conduct" than had *United States* v. *O'Brien* (1968), a decision holding that the First Amendment did not protect draft-card burning because of the government's legitimate interest in conducting military conscription.

Moreover, Johnson's expression did not, on the basis of the trial record, constitute a "direct personal insult" to onlookers or an incitement to violence. In the absence of this kind of explosive context, Justice Brennan's opinion continued, "the First Amendment forbids" a state from limiting this kind of political commentary, even though a majority of its citizenry might find it "offensive or disagreeable." Here, the Brennan opinion relied on *Brandenburg v. Ohio* (1969) and distinguished or ignored other possible lines of precedent such as one going back to the "fighting words" doctrine of *Chaplinsky v. New Hampshire* (1942).

Although Justice Brennan claimed his opinion merely reiterated "bedrock" First Amendment principles, Justice William Rehnquist spoke for four dissenters in arguing that Texas was trying to protect the flag as a sacred symbol of national values and identity and that burning the flag was less a speech act than simply an "inarticulate grunt." Indeed, Justice Brennan's opinion sought to meet this claim by insisting that there was no conflict between the flag-burning desires of Johnson and the flag-protecting impulses of Texas officials. The First Amendment, in blocking Texas from proscribing flag burning, was actually helping, according to the Brennan opinion, to support the values that the flag itself symbolized. "The way to preserve the flag's special role" in American life, Justice Brennan concluded, "is not to punish those who feel differently. . . . It is to persuade them that they are wrong."

The decision in *Texas v. Johnson,* however, failed to persuade a majority of Congress who quickly enacted the Flag Protection Act of 1989. Once again, though, the Supreme Court, by the same 5–4 margin as in the *Johnson* case, ruled that the First Amendment did extend to flag burning and declared the congressional dissent unconstitutional in *United States v. Eichman* (1990).

Far from discouraged, opponents of *Texas v. Johnson* began to press state legislatures and Congress to support a "Flag Protection Amendment." By the opening of the 107th Congress in January 2000, the proposed amendment, which stated that "Congress shall have the power to prevent the physical desecration of the flag of the United States," had already passed the U.S. House of Representatives several times but floundered in the Senate. Meanwhile, proponents of the measure could point to the fact that 49 state legislatures had urged Congress to send them this amendment and that opinion polls suggested that nearly 80 percent of those surveyed supported the Flag Protection Amendment.

For more information
Goldstein, Robert Justin. *Flag-Burning and Free Speech: The Case of* Texas v. Johnson. Lawrence: University Press of Kansas, 2000.

Miller, J. Anthony. *Texas v. Johnson: The Flag-Burning Case.* Berkeley Heights, N.J.: Enslow Publishers, Inc. 1997.

Presser, Stephen B. "The Flag Protection Amendment and the Return to First Principles," at www.cfa-inc.org/edit19html.

Norman L. Rosenberg
Macalester College

Thomas, Clarence

Thomas, Clarence (1948–) is an associate justice of the United States Supreme Court who was appointed to the Court by President George Bush in 1991 when he was only 43 years old. Thomas is only the second African American to serve on the nation's highest court.

When Thomas was growing up in Georgia, African Americans suffered from widespread racial discrimination. Thomas came from a poor family and he had to work very hard to gain opportunities for success. After graduating from Yale Law School, he worked for the Missouri attorney general and a chemical company before moving to Washington. He was the chairman of the U.S. Equal Opportunity Commission during President Ronald Reagan's administration in the 1980s. President Bush appointed Thomas to serve on the U.S. Court of Appeals, but he served for just one year before Bush nominated him to fill a vacancy on the Supreme Court.

Thomas became the center of controversy during his confirmation hearings before the Senate Judiciary Committee because his former assistant, Anita Hill, accused him of harassing her when they worked at the Equal Employment Opportunity Commission. On national television, Thomas denied that he had ever harassed Hill. As people throughout the nation debated whether they believed Thomas or Hill, the U.S. Senate confirmed Thomas for a seat on the Supreme Court by a narrow 52–48 vote.

In his judicial opinions, Thomas advocates interpreting the U.S. Constitution according to the original intentions of the men who wrote the document in the 18th century. This controversial approach frequently leads to decisions that define constitutional rights very narrowly. Because of his decisions, Thomas earned a reputation as one of the Supreme Court's most conservative justices.

Thomas's views can differ from those of both his liberal and conservative colleagues. For example, Thomas is the only justice to argue that the Supreme Court should consider declaring that individual citizens have a constitutional right to own guns (*Printz v. United States,* 1997). Although Thomas became the Court's only African-American justice after 1991, he is the justice most critical of Supreme Court decisions regarded as advancing equality for racial minorities. In *Missouri v. Jenkins* (1995) Thomas became the first justice to criticize the reasoning of the Supreme Court's famous *Brown v. Board of Education* (1954) decision that outlawed racial segregation in public schools. Thomas also advocated reversing most of the Court's decisions supporting a broad interpretation of the Voting Rights Act, a law designed to prevent racial discrimination in voting and elections (*Holder v. Hall,* 1994).

Thomas established himself as a justice who seeks to advocate that the Court's decisions move in a more conservative direction. However, he is seldom assigned the task of writing decisions on behalf of the Supreme Court's majority in important cases, so he does not appear to be influential in shaping the Court's decisions.

For more information

Smith, Christopher E., and Joyce A. Baugh. *The Real Clarence Thomas: Confirmation Veracity Meets Performance Reality.* New York: Peter Lang Publishing, 2000.

Christopher E. Smith
Michigan State University

Tinker v. Des Moines Independent Community School District

393 U.S. 503 (1969) is a United States Supreme Court decision that held that students have first amendment rights just as adults do, even when they are at school, so long as their speech does not disrupt or impede the learning process.

Significant also is that the Court considers the wearing of a black armband in protest of the Vietnam War to be akin to pure speech. In other words, the Court says that wearing such an armband is just like talking about one's opposition to the war and so is similarly protected under the First Amendment to the Constitution.

In this case, a few families decided that they would make their opposition to the Vietnam War public and would wear black armbands on certain days and fast on certain others. Their children decided to take part in their protest as well and wore the armbands to school. Before the designated day, the administration of the school learned of their plan and enacted a regulation that anyone wearing black armbands to school would be expelled, not to return until the armbands were removed. The students and their fathers sought an injunction to prevent the expulsion and were denied by both the district court and the U.S. Courts of Appeals, and the Supreme Court decided to hear the case.

The Supreme Court's decision rested on two basic premises. First, the students' wearing of the armbands did not create any conflict nor was the policy forbidding them driven by such a

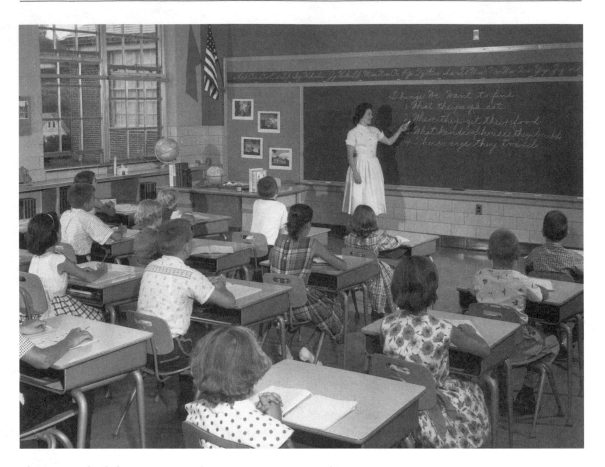

Elementary school classroom, 1940s (LAMBERT/HULTON ARCHIVE)

concern. The students were quiet and passive, and their wearing of the armbands did not impinge on any other students' rights. There was no speech here that intruded upon the school's education goals. The school authorities, in the Supreme Court's view, were merely trying to avoid the controversy inherent in the message. Avoidance of controversy is not a valid reason to deny First Amendment rights. In the words of Justice Fortas, the majority opinion author, ". . . [U]ndifferentiated fear or apprehension of disturbance is not enough to overcome the right to freedom of expression. . . . Any word spoken, in class, in the lunchroom, or on the campus, that deviates from the views of another person may start an argument or cause a disturbance. But our Constitution says we must take this risk . . . and our history says that it is this sort of hazardous freedom—this kind of openness—that is the basis of our national strength and of the independence and vigor of Americans who grow up and live in this relatively permissive, often disputatious, society" (at 508–509).

The second premise on which the Supreme Court's decision rested was that the school authorities did not regulate any other sort of symbolic speech—students were allowed to wear campaign buttons and other political paraphernalia (including the Iron Cross, traditionally a symbol of Nazism). Only the wearing of black armbands carried the penalty of expulsion. That this particular speech was singled out for prohibition was abhorrent to the Constitution. Fortas says, "Clearly, the prohibition of expression of one particular opinion, at least without evidence that it is necessary to avoid material and substantial interference with schoolwork or discipline, is not constitutionally permissible" (at 511).

While the Court made a large step both in freedom of speech and in the rights of students in this case, it did reserve the right to rule differently were the situation to be different. The majority opinion explicitly says that if there were a disruption in classwork or disorder in the school or invasion upon the rights of others, the school would be clearly within its right to prohibit the behavior. In this case, however, the students were peaceful and so the school trod on their constitutionally guaranteed rights when it prohibited the demonstration.

The Supreme Court distinguished several later cases from *Tinker,* however, in effect weakening the precedential value of this case. First, in *Bethel School District v. Fraser* (478 U.S. 675 [1986]), a majority allowed a student to be suspended for a speech given although it was questionable (at least to the dissenters) whether the speech disrupted education. The Court moved further from *Tinker* in *Hazelwood School District v. Kuhlmeier* (484 U.S. 260), where the Court allowed content regulation of a student-run newspaper to the dismay of Justice Brennan who, in dissent, said that the student expression at issue "neither disrupts classwork nor invades the rights of others" and so falls within protected speech outlined in *Tinker* (at 278). While *Tinker* continues to have precedential value, the Court seems to be continually more likely to allow for regulation of student speech to promote order in the nation's schools.

For more information

Epstein, Lee, and Thomas G. Walker. *Constitutional Law for a Changing America: Rights, Liberties, and Justice,* 3rd ed. Washington, D.C.: CQ Press, 1998.

Irons, Peter. *The Courage of Their Convictions: Sixteen Americans Who Fought Their Way to the Supreme Court.* New York: Penguin Books, 1990.

Irons, Peter, and Stephanie Guitton. *May It Please the Court: The Most Significant Oral Arguments Made Before the Supreme Court since 1955.* New York: The New Press, 1993.

Sara C. Benesh
University of Wisconsin, Milwaukee

torts are civil legal claims, initially created by judicial decisions, to redress violations of rights that do not involve agreements between citizens.

The field of torts encompasses an extremely wide variety of legal claims including negligence, medical malpractice, products liability, trespass and other forms of interference with property rights, defamation, invasion of privacy, assault, battery, false imprisonment, intentional infliction of emotional distress, and misrepresentation.

Torts differ from other types of legal claims in the following ways: Contract claims, unlike tort claims, involve assertions of rights under agreements made between parties. The law of property primarily defines individuals' rights to possess, use, and transfer real estate; tort law does so only indirectly (insofar as tort law provides for remedies for invasions of the rights defined by property law). Tort law can be distinguished from criminal law, though they address many of the same wrongs. Criminal law involves government punishment of individuals, often by incarceration or imposition of fines. Tort claims, however, are civil claims—they are claims by individuals to obtain money judgments or some other redress for themselves (rather than the public at large) and do not result in criminal sanctions. Torts can also be distinguished from many other civil claims for money damages or other redress by the differing origins of the claims. Tort actions were initially created by judicial decisions, frequently judicial decisions rendered by courts in Great Britain before the United States gained its independence. By contrast, Congress, by means of statutes, has in many fields initially defined legal rights and the legal claims available to vindicate those rights. Thus, for instance, claims for redress by people harmed by racial discrimination are not generally viewed as torts, even though they are legal claims for civil wrongs that do not involve agreements between citizens, because such legal claims have been created by statutes rather than by judicial decisions.

The subject of torts is generally broken into two categories: intentional torts and unintentional torts. Intentional torts involve intentional invasions of other's rights. For example, battery, which involves offensive or harmful physical touching, is an intentional tort because to show that a battery has occurred, the plaintiff must show that the defendant intended the harmful or offensive contact, or at the very least knew that such contact would result from his actions. Intentional torts include those designed to vindicate interests in: (1) bodily integrity, namely, assault, battery, false imprisonment, and false arrest; (2) emotional stability, namely, intentional infliction of emotional distress; (3) use and enjoyment of real property, namely, trespass and nuisance; (4) reputation, namely, defamation; and (5) privacy, namely, intrusion into seclusion and publication of private facts.

Most tort lawsuits, however, involve claims falling under the second category of torts—unintentional torts. Unintentional torts provide legal remedies even where the wrongdoer has not intentionally invaded the rights of another. For example, drivers who cause automobile accidents ordinarily do not intend to crash into other cars. Nevertheless, a driver can be found liable for money damages to compensate others who are injured if an accident resulted from his negligence. Ordinarily the standard of liability in unintentional tort cases is negligence; that is, defendants are liable when they fail to exercise the care a reasonable person would exercise under the circumstances. The negligence standard governs automobile accidents, medical malpractice, landowner liability for hazardous property conditions, and unintentional infliction of emotional distress. In order to prevail in a negligence action, the plaintiff must establish the existence of the following elements: (1) that the defendant had a duty to act in a manner that did not pose an undue risk of danger to the plaintiff, (2) that the defendant did not act as a reasonable person would have acted—in other words that the defendant acted negligently, (3) that the defendant's negligent acts caused the plaintiff's injuries, and (4) that the plaintiff suffered legally cognizable injuries.

Sometimes, however, actors may be held liable even when they have not been negligent. In such absolute or strict liability situations, an actor may be liable merely because his act caused harm, regardless of whether he acted prudently. Thus, in products liability, manufacturers are liable for injuries caused by defective products even if they were not negligent in making or selling those products. Similarly, actors who engage in abnormally dangerous activities, such as using explosives or holding wild animals in captivity, may be liable to those injured by the activity even if they were careful in conducting their abnormally dangerous activities.

In most tort actions, the plaintiff has the burden of proof—both the burden of producing evidence that is sufficient for a jury to decide that the defendant is liable and the burden of persuading the jury that his version of events is most likely correct. The burden of proof differs from that applicable in criminal trials. The torts plaintiff, unlike the government in a criminal trial, need not prove beyond a reasonable doubt that the defendant is liable.

For more information

Keeton, W. Page, Dan B. Dobbs, Robert E. Keeton, and David G. Owen. *Prosser and Keeton on Torts,* 5th ed., Westbury, N.Y.: Foundation Press, 1984.

Diamond, John, Lawrence C. Levine, and M. Stuart Madden. *Understanding Torts.* New York: Matthew Bender, 1996.

Bernard W. Bell
Professor of Law
Rutgers Law School, Newark

treason is a violation of the allegiance owed to one's sovereign or state.

In ancient England and even in some modern nations, speech or action offensive to the head of state may be treasonous and cause jailing, exile, or sometimes execution of the accused. Anything that seriously displeased the king might be described as "treasonous." Over centuries in Anglo-American courts this broad definition of treason has narrowed to the modern view that treason is limited to specific acts endangering national security.

This narrower view of treason is essential in democracies. Otherwise, those who criticize a president or prime minister might be committing treason! In fact, democratic theory requires that citizens have the opportunity to criticize their political leaders. The story of the shift in the Anglo-American legal tradition from the ancient broad definition of treason to the modern narrow definition is important for those favoring democratic procedures. The basic outline of that story follows.

In eighth-century Anglo-Saxon England, the "King's Peace" extended to certain occasions such as festival days and coronations. It also extended to certain places such as the king's castles and highways and to certain individuals: the king himself, his family, and others under royal protection. Serious harm on these occasions or at these places or directed toward these individuals might bring a charge of treason.

The Magna Carta, first agreed to in 1215 by King John I and later by his successors, states that when the king or his men have seized property illegally, a group of 25 barons and their aides may seize the king's "castles, lands and possessions . . . until amends have been made." Significantly, the king agreed not to charge these noblemen and aids with treason. The English Statute of Treasons (1352) for the first time distinguished "treason" from other serious crimes and specified what crimes were treasonous. This statute still provides the foundation for the English law of treason. Several of King John's successors sometimes ignored the noble intent of the Great Charter and the more specific Statute of Treasons.

Richard II (1397) vastly expanded the number of treasonous crimes in order to punish his enemies in Parliament. Henry VII, the first Tudor monarch, also expanded (1494) the list of treasonous crimes to make his hold on the English crown more secure. Henry VIII in 1534 had Parliament pass a law declaring that anyone challenging Henry's claim to the crown or his claim to be head of the English church would be judged high traitors and doomed to execution. Elizabeth I (1571) extended the laws of treason to both Roman Catholics and Protestants critical of the official position of the Church of England. This act later encouraged Pilgrim, Puritan, and English Catholic immigration to the American colonies. After Oliver Cromwell's victory, Charles I was accused of treason "against the people of England," convicted, and beheaded (1649). The enactment of the English Bill of Rights and the installation of William of Orange on a "forever Protestant" throne laid the groundwork for the Treasons Act of 1696, requiring anyone accused of treason to have legal counsel and providing that two lawful witnesses are needed for conviction.

In step with the English tradition, the U.S. Constitution carefully defines "treason" and requires two witnesses for conviction. Article III, section 3 of the U.S. Constitution states: "Treason against the United States shall consist only in levying war against them, or in adhering to their enemies, giving them aid and comfort. No person shall be convicted of treason unless on the testimony of two witnesses to the same overt act, or on confession in open court."

In the Civil War, Confederate soldiers and active sympathizers committed treason against the United States. Instead of enforcing treason statutes, President Lincoln had the military arrest some anti-Union civilian activists and suspended the habeas corpus rights of others. Confederate soldiers taken prisoner were treated as prisoners of war.

In the 20th century, the Supreme Court slightly expanded the definition of "treason" and American prosecutors continue to use other statutes to punish what some claim to be treasonous activities. In upholding the treason conviction of an American who worked for the Japanese during World War II, the Supreme Court asserted that an American could violate American treason statutes while abroad (*Kawakita v. United States,* 1952). Even with that clarification, treason statutes have been little used in the last half of the 20th century. The federal government used other statutes in seeking to punish American communists during the 1950s and, with greater success, used other statutes to punish American servicemen or civilians selling government secrets to other nations.

For more information

Kelley, Alfred H., et al. *The American Constitution; Its Origins and Development,* 7th ed. New York: W.W. Norton, 1991.

Smith, Goldwin. *A Constitutional and Legal History of England.* New York: Dorsett Press, 1990.

Gayle Avant
Baylor University

U

Uniform Commercial Code is the organization of the commercial law into a standard system so that there may be some certainty within the United States in matters between merchants and customers, banks and bank customers, and investors and entrepreneurs, as well as matters affecting credit accounts and documents of title.

The Uniform Commercial Code is commonly referred to as the UCC or "the Code." In all, 10 chapters cover the vast bulk of commercial law. Real estate transactions are not covered nor are any criminal laws. Since its introduction in 1952, all states except Louisiana have adopted the UCC. Louisiana bases its law on the Napoleonic Code and not on English common law. Various sections of the UCC have been modified somewhat by the state legislatures to fit local circumstances.

For example, a small garment supplier contracts with a multistate discount store, and the transaction depends on interstate credit arrangements. Because of the UCC, the garment supplier can be sure that the security interest he gives to the local bank for his supplies from another state meets nationwide standards. The banker can then rely on being able to market her credit accounts across state lines. An Internet stock transaction, a credit card used on vacation, or a car purchased in one state but registered in another are all affected by the UCC. This conformity to the same or similar standards nationwide eases the flow of commerce, thereby lowering the cost for the consumer.

The Code begins with an extensive list of general definitions used throughout the statutes. Terms specific to only one section are defined at the beginning of that section.

The Code provides that it is effective in a state at midnight on December 31 of the year it was accepted by that state so that a merchant or customer will need only to know the year the UCC became effective in a particular state to know most of the law of that state. In order to give certainty to the law applying to a commercial transaction, there is no provision for retroactivity in the UCC. All prior laws dealing with the subjects regulated by the UCC are repealed by the terms of the Code except those dealing with documents of title.

The UCC is meant to be read as one interrelated body of law, and reading of one section must take into account every other section where there may be an effect on any transaction under review. One feature of the UCC is to provide for a reservation of rights. A problem with the pre-code law is that if a dispute arose, the objecting party had to cease performance or risk waiving valuable rights by continuing to carry through with other provisions of the transaction. Under this modern statute, a party who performs after having made an explicit reservation of rights does not give up those rights. This innovation enables the party who objects to only parts of the other party's performance to resolve the dispute after all other parts are completed without the uncertainty of losing all rights.

The UCC does not, however, lock the parties into some rigid framework. While definitions and meanings must remain the same as prescribed by statute, the effects of the Code's provisions may be altered if specifically spelled out in the written instrument of the contract. The language of the statute directs courts to be liberal in construction so that the injured party may be put in as good a position as if the contract had been performed as intended.

The UCC was put forth as a method to facilitate commerce. A detailed study is needed to appreciate all of the innovations of the Code. Each section has appended to it a drafters' comment to aid in understanding each individual statute.

For more information

American Jurisprudence, 2nd ed. Vol 15A, *Uniform Commercial Code.* St. Paul, Minn.: West Group Publishing, 1988–.

Uniform Commercial Code, National Conference of Commissioners on Uniform State Laws.

Consult the statutes relating to commercial transactions in your state.

Stanley M. Morris
Attorney at Law
Cortez, Colorado

Uniform Crime Report   or UCR, consists of data sent to the FBI each month by 16,000 law enforcement agencies covering 95 percent of the American population. It has been our main source of information about crime in the United States since 1930.

The UCR focuses on eight "index crimes": homicide, forcible rape, robbery, aggravated assault, burglary, larceny (nonviolent theft except for stolen cars), motor vehicle theft, and arson (added in 1978). The FBI publishes tallies of the number of crimes reported to the police, the number cleared (generally by arrest), the percentage of increase or decrease for each crime, and the crime rate per 100,000 people. It also includes the number of law enforcement officers assaulted and killed. Not only do these statistics provide a useful view of the national crime picture, their longevity allows us to evaluate trends.

However, the UCR has come under criticism in recent years. Many crimes are not reported to the police. Different areas may define the same crime in different ways. For example, one jurisdiction may exclude attempted rapes from the total while another may not. Some critics claim police departments often manipulate the statistics for political purposes. Supporting their view was the withdrawal of Philadelphia from the UCR in 1996 and 1997 due to significant underreporting. Finally, important crimes such as federal and drug offenses are not included. The UCR concentrates on the more easily measured street crimes rather than white collar crime, which probably costs the public considerably more in monetary losses.

Changes have been made to meet these objections. Local police now include a brief description of each incident. Definitions of offenses have been tightened up. Crimes such as blackmail, embezzlement, and some drug offenses have been added, albeit not as index crimes. Although a 1990 federal law required the FBI to report hate crimes, it made compliance by local police departments voluntary, resulting in data that are of limited utility. For example, there was a decline of 300 incidents between 1997 and 1998, but this was probably because 500 fewer agencies reported. On the other hand, since 1992 the UCR has separated domestic violence from other assaults, resulting in more useful information.

Even more important was the development of the National Crime Victimization Survey (NCVS) in 1973. The NCVS polls 50,000 randomly selected households at six-month intervals, asking whether they have been crime victims. Thus, it includes crime that is not reported to the police but excludes homicide. The results suggest that only about 40 percent of violent and 30 percent of property crime is reported. However, the reliability of its data depends on the honesty and memory of its respondents.

While both the UCR and NCVS have their weaknesses, taken together the two have provided a good database for studying the incidence of crime in the United States. The consistency of results showing a decline in the crime rate in recent years gives us confidence in their accuracy.

For more information

Sherman, Lawrence, and Glick, Barry. "The Quality of Arrest Statistics," *Police Foundation Reports* 2 (1984): 1–8.

FBI web site: www.fbi.gov/homepage.htm

Bruce E. Altschuler
Professor and Chair, Department of Political Science
State University of New York, Oswego

United States Code   is a multivolume compilation of the text of statutes enacted by the Congress of the United States.

This set of statutes includes the complete and official code of the laws of the United States in 50 titles, which, in effect, represent the subject matter of the legislative work of the Congress.

The *United States Code* is published by the U.S. Government Printing Office. Prior to 1926, the statutory law of the United States had been published in the *Revised Statutes of 1875*. This

compilation of federal statutes was supplemented by the volumes of the *United States Statutes at Large,* which recorded the annual legislative output of the Congress. In 1926 Congress authorized the publication of the *United States Code* to include every statute still in effect in the years following the publication of the *Revised Statutes.* A new edition of the *United States Code* was published in 1934. Editions have been regularly published every six years since, with annual cumulative supplements enabling the edition to remain current and up-to-date. The editorial responsibilities for the *United States Code* have been given to the Office of Law Revision Counsel of the House of Representatives. The Committee on the Judiciary of the House of Representatives has overall supervision of the Congress's statutory codification work.

For more information

Jacobstein, J. Myron. *Fundamentals of Legal Research,* 7th ed. New York: Foundation Press, 1998.

Johnson, Charles W. *How Our Laws Are Made.* Washington, D.C.: U.S. Government Printing Office, 2000 (section XIX addresses the publication of United States laws).

Jerry E. Stephens
U.S. Court of Appeals (10th Circuit)
Oklahoma City, Oklahoma

United States Constitution   was drafted as the nation's charter in 1787. This document functions as the supreme law, which trumps any conflicting federal, state, or local laws.

Prior to the creation of the Constitution, the United States was ineffectively governed by the Articles of Confederation, which allowed states to remain sovereign governments and choose to work together only when it suited their needs. In contrast, the Constitution provides for a sovereign national government with subordinate yet somewhat independent state governments.

The Constitution consists of a preamble, seven articles, and 27 amendments. The preamble establishes that this document's purpose is to preserve the union by the rule of laws which emanate from the will of the people. The seven articles define the branches and powers of the federal government, specify that powers which are not assigned to the federal government are reserved for the states, and emphasize that no law may conflict with the federal Constitution. The first 10 amendments are known as the Bill of Rights because they focus on the rights of individuals, such as freedom of speech and the right to due process. Although specific individual rights are enumerated in the Bill of Rights, the Ninth Amendment explicitly guarantees that individuals retain other basic rights as well. Seventeen more amendments have been added since the creation of the Bill of Rights, dealing with issues ranging from the repeal of prohibition to voting.

Two methods for amending the Constitution are established in Article V. However, all of the amendments to date have resulted from the following method: two-thirds of both houses of Congress have voted to propose an amendment and then the amendment has been ratified by three-fourths of the states. The alternate method for amending the Constitution is that two-thirds of the states can request that Congress call a convention where amendments can be proposed. The ratification process for amendments proposed at a convention is the same as that for those proposed by Congress. That the Constitution has only been amended 27 times since it was written demonstrates the document's inherent adaptability to changing circumstances.

Because the Constitution is a concise document dealing with broad general issues, its meaning for current events must often be inferred from the text. The responsibility for this task lies with the Supreme Court, which first articulated and exercised this power in *Marbury v. Madison* (1803) by ruling that a law passed by Congress was invalid due to its inconsistency with the Court's interpretation of the Constitution. For example, one of the Court's most controversial

modern decisions, *Roe v. Wade* (1973), which established a woman's right to choose to have an abortion, stems from the Court's inference that privacy is one of the fundamental personal rights guaranteed by the Constitution.

For more information

U.S. founding documents at www.law.emory.edu/federal/
The U.S. Constitution Online at USConstitution.net

Martha M. Lafferty
Staff Attorney
Tennessee Fair Housing Council

United States v. Dennis   341 U.S. 494 (1951) was a landmark Supreme Court case on the issue of freedom of speech.

This 1951 ruling upheld the conviction of Eugene Dennis and 10 other high officials within the American Communist Party for "willfully and knowingly conspiring" to "advocate the overthrow and destruction of the Government of the United States by force and violence," a crime under the Smith Act of 1940. The petitioners argued that this law was a violation of the First Amendment because it punished ideas rather than action and because of its vagueness. Chief Justice Fred Vinson wrote the plurality decision, which was joined by Justices Stanley Reed, Harold Burton, and Sherman Minton and the separate concurring opinions of Justices Felix Frankfurter and Robert Jackson. Justices Hugo Black and William Douglas issued separate dissenting opinions. Justice Clark took no part in the case.

The chief justice wrote, "That it is within the power of the Congress to protect the Government of the United States from armed rebellion is a proposition which requires little discussion. . . . . We reject any principle of governmental helplessness in the face of preparation for revolution, which principle, carried to its logical conclusion, must lead to anarchy." He rejected the objection by petitioners that the Smith Act would punish even an academic discussion of the ideals of Marxism-Leninism, noting that the law was "directed at advocacy, not discussion." Because of this, Congress had a legitimate right to suppress a "clear and present danger," the doctrine announced in *Schenck v. United States* (1919), the first significant Supreme Court case on the scope of the free speech protection. Vinson went on to argue, "[I]f a society cannot protect its very structure from armed internal attack, it must follow that no subordinate value can be protected." In his concurring opinion, Justice Jackson wrote that the Communist Party was "realistically a state within a state, an authoritarian dictatorship within a republic" that was part of a vast international movement that had already taken control of a dozen governments around the world.

In separate dissenting opinions, Justices Black and Douglas attacked this rationale. Black noted that the petitioners were not charged with actually attempting to overthrow the government but merely to "talk and publish certain ideas at a later date." He believed that, "Such a doctrine waters down the First Amendment so that it amounts to little more than an admonition to Congress. The Amendment as so construed is not likely to protect any but those 'safe' or orthodox views which rarely needs its protection." Douglas agreed with Black's basic reasoning and went on to state that, since it would not be a crime to place books containing the objectionable ideas on a library shelf, "The crime then depends not on what is taught but on who the teacher is. That is to make freedom of speech turn not on what is said, but on the intent with which it is said." This last objection was noted by the chief justice in his opinion, when he noted that having a criminal state of mind (or mens rea) is quite often an element of a crime in the Anglo-American system.

Because there was no majority rationale in this case, it did not put an end to litigation on the scope of Congress's power to regulate speech it found dangerous. Several related cases would be decided over the next 18 years, most notably *Yates v. United States* (1957) and *Scales v. United States* (1961), until the current state of the law was reached in the landmark *Brandenburg v. Ohio* (1969) decision. During this period, the reliance on *Schenk's* clear and present danger doctrine fluctuated in response to the ideological shifts in the Court. *Brandenburg* enunciated a strong version of the doctrine, and a strict scrutiny standard has applied to all subsequent attempts to regulate dangerous speech.

For more information

Ducat, Craig R. *Constitutional Interpretation*. 7th ed. St. Paul, Minn.: West Publishing Co., 2000.

Tedford, Thomas L. *Freedom of Speech in the United States*, 3rd ed. State College, Pa.: Strata Publishing, 1997.

James H. Joyner, Jr., Ph.D.
Assistant Professor of Political Science
Troy State University

United States v. Nixon 418 U.S. 683 (1974) is an important Supreme Court case that required President Richard Nixon to comply with a judicial subpoena and turn over his personal papers.

The case arose out of the Watergate scandal of the early 1970s. Prior to the presidential election of 1972, a group led by Republican operatives broke into Democratic Party headquarters at the Watergate Hotel. After the break-in became public knowledge, President Nixon participated in a cover-up designed to conceal his administration's connection to it. Following a series of revelations by Nixon aides at congressional hearings, a special prosecutor subpoenaed tapes that the president had made in the oval office. The judge presiding over the trial of the men involved in the break-in ordered the president to release the tapes. The president refused, arguing that the Constitution protects "executive privilege," the power to keep sensitive information confidential. Thus, he argued, Congress and the courts lacked the power to require him to release the tapes.

The Supreme Court heard the case in July 1974. The justices focused on two main issues in their analysis of the case. First, the Court dealt with Nixon's argument that the courts should not decide the case because it was a political dispute rather than a disagreement about law. The justices rejected this claim. They agreed that courts are not qualified to make partisan judgments, but that courts are well qualified to interpret the laws using legal standards. Quoting *Marbury v. Madison* (1803) that it is "emphatically the province and duty of the judiciary to say what the law is," the Supreme Court held that it had the power, based on its role as interpreter of the Constitution, to hear and decide the case.

Next the Court turned to the president's claim of privilege. There is no mention of executive privilege in the text of the Constitution. However, the president argued that all governments require confidentiality to assure that government advisers will be candid, without fear of public exposure through devices like subpoenas. He also argued that the separation of powers in the Constitution protected him from having to follow this order from the judiciary.

The Court held that neither of these arguments was sufficient to support an absolute claim of executive privilege that would always trump a subpoena. While agreeing that "the President's need for complete candor and objectivity from advisers calls for great judicial deference from the courts," the justices were not willing to treat claims of executive privilege as automatic and absolute. The Court expressed concern that this claim of privilege was phrased generally, without demonstrating any particular need to keep the tapes secret. The Court argued that a claim of privilege based on the need to protect especially sensitive information, for example, information about the military, diplomacy, or national security, would have a greater chance of success.

This was the first time that the Supreme Court had recognized a constitutional claim of executive privilege. However, the justices ruled that the claim of privilege should be balanced against the legitimate needs of other government departments. In this case, the Court held that the judiciary's need for relevant evidence in criminal trials outweighed the president's general claim of privilege since the fairness of the judicial process depends heavily on a judge's ability to subpoena evidence. Since the judge would provide a confidential examination of the evidence, the loss of secrecy would be minimal.

The Court ruled 8–0 against the president, ordering him to turn over the tapes. The president complied with this order, though it meant the end of his presidency. He resigned on August 9, 1974, rather than face almost certain impeachment. The fact that Nixon complied, despite this high personal cost, is considered strong evidence that the Supreme Court enjoys a high degree of political legitimacy.

For more information
Kurland, Phillip. *Watergate and the Constitution.* Chicago: University of Chicago Press, 1978.

Shannon Ishiyama Smithey
Department of Political Science
University of Pittsburgh

United Steelworkers v. Weber   443 U.S. 193 (1979) was the Supreme Court's second major decision on affirmative action and the first to test voluntary affirmative action programs in private employment.

Justice William Brennan, writing for Justices Potter Stewart, Byron White, Harry Blackmun, and Thurgood Marshall, upheld a craft-training program created through a collective bargaining agreement between the Kaiser Aluminum and Chemical Corporation and the United Steelworkers Union. The program set aside half of the openings in the craft-training program for African Americans until the percentage of black craft workers approximated the percentage of blacks in the local labor force.

Brian Weber, an unskilled white production worker at Kaiser's aluminum plant in Gramercy,

Louisiana, applied to the craft-training program but lost to three black workers with less seniority. He sued, alleging that the craft-training program had violated his right to be treated without regard to race under Title VII of the 1964 Civil Rights Act. Both the federal district court and the Fifth Circuit Court of Appeals agreed.

Weber contended that the clear language of Title VII forbade even benign racial discrimination in employment training unless an authorized governmental body discovered a prior violation of the equal protection law. The pertinent section of Title VII reads: "It shall be an unlawful employment practice for any employer, labor organization, or joint management committee controlling apprenticeship or other training or retraining, including on-the-job training programs, to discriminate against any individual because of his race, . . . in admission to, or employment in, any program established to provide apprenticeship or other training" (section 703[d], 64 U.S.C. S2000e-2[d]).

Justice Brennan came to a different conclusion. Relying on the "language and legislative history" (200) of Title VII, Brennan found that it was not Congress's intent to restrict voluntary, private experiments to "abolish traditional patterns of racial segregation and hierarchy" (204) in private employment. Brennan pointed out that only two percent of the craft jobs at the plant were held by blacks while 40 percent of the local labor force was black (198–199). Given the lack of a congressional prohibition of such experiments and the absence of a Fourteenth Amendment equal protection issue, no statutory or constitutional restriction hindered Kaiser and the union's agreement.

Brennan made a special effort to acknowledge that "benign" programs could be abused, but he found sufficient safeguards in the challenged program. It did "not unnecessarily trammel the interests of white employees." No whites were fired to make places for blacks. Weber lost no preexisting entitlement or opportunity. Nor did the program impose "an absolute bar to the advancement" of whites; half of the trainees were white and Weber was still eligible for future openings in the training program. Finally, Brennan was reassured that the program was a "temporary measure," designed to end once the "manifest racial imbalance" in the labor pool was eliminated (208).

Justices Lewis Powell and John Paul Stevens abstained from the case. Powell was ill and unable to attend oral arguments. Stevens excused himself, reportedly because his former Chicago law firm worked for Kaiser. The dissenting justices, William Rehnquist and Warren Burger, found that the clear language, intent, and meaning of Title VII indicated that "*no* racial discrimination in employment is permissible" (emphasis in the original, 230).

Despite recent reverses for affirmative action programs by the Supreme Court (*Adarand Constructors, Inc. v. Pena*, 515 U.S. 200 [1995]) and lower courts (*Hopwood v. Texas*, 999 F. Supp. 872 [1998]), the Supreme Court has not rejected affirmative action programs in private employment.

For more information

Gertrude Ezorsky. *Racism & Justice: The Case for Affirmative Action*. Ithaca, N.Y.: Cornell University Press, 1991.

Timothy J. O'Neill
Southwestern University

V

vacate is a term whose legal meaning is to annul or void a court decision.

When a higher court vacates a lower court's judgment, it is setting the lower court judgment aside. When a higher court vacates the decision of a lower court, the higher court may simply set aside the judgment with no further action required on the part of the lower court. Alternatively, the higher court may order a lower court to void its own decision. For example, in the case of *Agostini v. Felton,* 521 U.S. 203 (1997), the United States Supreme Court ordered the federal district court to vacate an order the district court had issued on September 26, 1985, prohibiting the city of New York from using funds to provide secular services to students attending parochial schools. A higher court may also require the lower court to reconsider a decision by setting aside the lower court ruling and remanding the case back to that lower court. For example, in the case of *Miller v. California,* 413 U.S. 15 (1973), the California appellate court had summarily affirmed the trial court's conviction of Miller on obscenity charges. The United States Supreme Court vacated that summary affirmance and remanded the case back to the appellate court for further action in light of the obscenity standards articulated in the *Miller* decision.

For more information

Hazard, Geoffrey C., Jr., and Michele Taruffo, *American Civil Procedure: An Introduction.* New Haven, Conn.: Yale University Press, 1993.

Silberman Linda J., and Allan R. Stein. *Civil Procedure: Theory and Practice,* Gaithersburg, Md.: Aspen Publishers, 2001.

Wendy L. Martinek
State University of New York, Binghamton

vandalism is the willful damage or destruction of property for no apparent purpose.

The term derives from the Vandals, who were a tribe of Germanic people who invaded Western Europe in the 4th and 5th centuries. It was the Vandals who destroyed Rome in A.D. 455. In Latin, the word *vandal* came to mean anyone with an attitude of hostility or contempt for what is beautiful or venerated. Today the word is still used to express disapproval not only of someone's actions but also of an antisocial attitude.

English common law considered vandalism as "malicious mischief" and treated it as a form of tort. First considered only a trespass, claims for the destruction of personal property were limited to actions between two individuals and were not the subject of criminal prosecution. Today many states have laws imposing criminal penalties for the intentional destruction of property. Typically treated as misdemeanor offenses, conviction may result in a fine or less than one year in jail, depending on the severity of the offense and the extent of damage or loss. The court may also require that an offender pay restitution to the victim.

In some states, parents may be subject to a civil judgment if a child fails to pay restitution under an order by the juvenile court. However, juvenile court orders for restitution are often limited by statutory provisions that set specific dollar ceilings for children under a certain age, or by the requirement that the court impose no more in restitution than the child alone is financially able to pay. In some states, a parent may also be subject to a separate claim for damages caused by a child, if the child's actions can be characterized as willful, malicious, or wanton.

When is the willful destruction of personal property more than simply antisocial behavior? When does it become a form of social protest? In 1966 David Paul O'Brien stood on the steps of a Boston courthouse and burned his Selective Service registration certificate (his "draft card") in front of a large crowd. He was charged with violating federal laws that applied to any person who "knowingly destroys" these certificates. At his trial he argued that he had burned his card publicly in order to influence others to adopt his antiwar beliefs, and that his acts were therefore "symbolic speech" protected by the First Amendment to the Constitution of the United States. The Supreme Court affirmed O'Brien's conviction, holding that the "non-communicative impact" of his actions was the deliberate frustration of a justifiable government interest in the administration of its constitutional powers to raise armed forces. Since the incidental restriction on O'Brien's First Amendment right was no greater than was needed to further that government interest, the law prohibiting destruction of Selective Service certificates was constitutional.

For more information
Stromberg v. California, 283 U.S. 359 (1931).
United States v. O'Brien, 391 U.S. 367 (1968).

Ann C. Krummel, JD
Judicial Commissioner
Circuit Court for Columbia County, Wisconsin

venue   is the legal term denoting the geographical location (county, town, or other municipality) in which a case must be tried.

Venue and jurisdiction are related concepts, but whereas jurisdiction refers to the legal power of a court to hear a particular lawsuit, venue refers to the actual place where the trial must occur. The primary issue in determining venue is the convenience of the parties to the litigation. Today the venue of most actions, both civil and criminal, is established by statute. However, unlike jurisdiction, venue may be agreed upon by the parties or changed in the case of inconvenience or unfairness to one of the litigants. The major constitutional issues involved in venue are due process and equal protection of the laws. Accordingly, determinations of venue may not be arbitrary or discriminate unfairly against one of the litigants.

Although venue is a matter now left largely to the discretion of legislatures, some traditional concepts may still affect the choice of venue in certain actions. Traditionally, lawsuits involving matters related to a particular place, such as those involving title to real property, probate, or actions involving trustees and guardians, had to take place where the subject of the lawsuit was located. Most other lawsuits, including those involving contracts, personal injuries, and suits in equity, could be maintained wherever the defendant could be found and served with process. Today venue in most legal actions is regulated by statute. Sometimes venue is based on the residence or place of business of the parties, and other times on the place where the incident, transaction, or offense occurred. Ordinarily, the party initiating the lawsuit establishes the venue by starting the action in a particular place. Objections to venue may be made by the parties, and failure to object to an improper venue may constitute acceptance of the venue by waiver.

Venue may be changed by agreement of the parties or by an application to change the venue because of hardship, inconvenience, lack of connection to the forum *(forum non conveniens),* or prejudice against one of the parties. A major factor in determining whether to change the venue of an action is whether the ends of justice will be promoted by the proposed change. Some changes of venue may be granted as a matter of right, such as when a lawsuit was commenced in the wrong county or municipality, or by discretion when the applicant provides sufficient proof of hardship, inconvenience, or injustice. Sometimes applications for change of venue are objected to as "forum shopping," looking for the most favorable place to try a lawsuit, and some states, such as Pennsylvania, have restricted the ability to change venue on *forum non conveniens* grounds

Sometimes in criminal cases, but also in civil lawsuits, there may have been such widespread adverse publicity concerning the incident that is the subject of the lawsuit that venue may be contested on the basis of prejudice—that is, that the criminal defendant or civil litigant can no longer receive a fair trial in the place where the case is supposed to be tried. One prominent example would be the case involving the shooting by white police officers of the unarmed Amadou Diallo, a black man, in New York City, which was moved to Albany, New York, for trial. Other such factors might be conflict of interest or prejudice on the part of the prospective jurors or the judge who will try the case. The burden of proof in such instances is on the party applying for the

change in venue. Decisions involving change of venue may be appealed.

In most cases, however, the venue designated by the appropriate statute is, in fact, the one that best serves the interests of justice because the parties, witnesses, and evidence are located in that municipality and the trial can be held there in both an efficient and a fair manner.

For more information

Algero, Mary Garvey. "In Defense of Forum Shopping: A Realistic Look at Selecting a Venue," *Nebraska Law Review* 78 (1999): 79.

Celia A. Sgroi
State University of New York, Oswego

victimless crimes   are activities that supposedly involve willing participants and allegedly harm no one but the actors.

Examples of supposedly victimless crimes include drug use (including alcohol), a variety of sexual behavior (prostitution, homosexuality, adultery), and gambling. Some might also include fortune telling, loitering, polygamy, not wearing a seat belt or a motorcycle helmet, carrying a weapon, and abortion. In earlier eras the offenses included swearing, violating a curfew, dress unbecoming of godliness, holding dances or theatrical performances, and card playing.

Critics attack the imposing of one group's moral values on others in society. Defenders argue that criminalization performs an educational function for society, indicating behavior that is harmful. Lord Patrick Devlin, a British high court judge, thought it important to restrict practices that any "right-minded man" would find so offensive as to threaten the moral fabric of society. However, Professor H. L. A. Hart responded that mere offensiveness is not sufficient to justify criminal sanctions.

Proponents deny that the behavior affects only the participants. There is an erosion of social cohesiveness and a ruin of the lives of those who engage in it. The community is a victim.

Families suffer from neglect, impoverishment, etc. Sexually transmitted diseases like AIDS create a chain of victims. Those indulging in so-called victimless crimes may resort to other crimes to obtain money to support these activities. Law-abiding neighbors may have to flee (or be barricaded in) their neighborhoods to protect their families. They see the prostitute not as a freely acting entrepreneur but as someone kidnapped, drugged, and intimidated. They argue that there is a slippery slope from decriminalization: that gambling, marijuana use, prostitution, even the use of contraceptives, will lead to more hard-core criminal activities.

On the other hand, those urging decriminalization point to the demoralizing consequences of efforts to punish what the general public does not regard as offenses: police corruption, use of informers, blackmail, selective enforcement and hypocrisy (leading to erosion of respect for the law), opportunities for organized crime, invasion of privacy, or treating as criminal matters that could otherwise be treated as therapeutic.

For more information

Meier, Robert F., and Gilbert Geis. *Victimless Crime?: Prostitution, Drugs, Homosexuality, Abortion.* Los Angeles: Roxbury, 1997.

Gusfield, Joseph R. *Symbolic Crusade: State Politics and the American Temperance Movement,* 2nd ed. Urbana: University of Illinois Press, 1986.

Martin Gruberg
University of Wisconsin, Oshkosh

victims' rights   refer to the recognition and consideration of the physical, psychological, and financial impact of crime on victims and the basic right of victims to be treated with dignity and respect.

It is embodied in a movement that began in the 1970s, largely among feminists, with the opening of rape crisis centers. The mistreatment of rape victims led to a broader focus on how the criminal justice system treated all crime victims. This movement, then and now, is an attempt to ensure that crime victims are not victimized twice—once by the criminal offender and then by the criminal justice system itself. Victims' rights is an attempt to establish and protect "victim justice" or what is often referred to as "parallel justice."

In the past quarter century, the victims' rights movement has matured into a national and even international phenomenon. The National Organization for Victim Assistance (NOVA) was founded in 1975; in 1980 it proclaimed "National Victim Rights Week" and continues to sponsor an annual National Forum on Victims' Rights. NOVA also is a recognized nongovernmental organization of the United Nations. In 1982 President Ronald Reagan appointed a Task Force on Victims of Crime, which lobbied successfully for the passage of the 1984 Victims of Crime Act. In 1985 the United Nations adopted the Declaration on Basic Principles of Justice for Victims of Crime and Abuse of Power. In 1990 Congress passed the Child Victims' Bill of Rights and also the Victims' Rights and Restitution Act, which includes the right to be present at all public court proceedings, and in 1997, in the aftermath of the bombing of the Murrah building in Oklahoma City, Congress enacted the Victims' Rights Clarification Act. Within the Department of Justice in Washington, D.C., is the Office for Victims of Crime.

Much of this primarily legislative activity is aimed at mandating a greater role for victims and their families in the criminal justice system, including but not limited to testifying at the sentencing stage of a trial, attending the trial, being notified of the status of the case in the process, being notified of the terms of any plea bargain, being notified of any parole hearing or release date from incarceration or release from prison, and the right to restitution.

In recent years 29 states have enacted Victims' Rights Amendments to their state constitutions, and a federal constitutional amendment was introduced in Congress in 1999 but was withdrawn the following year. These amendments are attempts to solidify victims' rights by elevating them from statutory to constitutional foundations. The thesis advanced by victims' rights advocates is that these rights, no less than rights afforded criminal defendants, are most comprehensively protected by being enshrined in either state or national constitutions.

In 1981, in the case of *Payne v. Tennessee,* the United States Supreme Court provided additional momentum for the victims' rights movement by ruling 6–3 that a sentencing jury in a capital case may consider victim impact statements that address the impact of murder on the victim's family. The Court, through the opinion written by then Associate Justice William Rehnquist, decided that the Eighth Amendment did not prohibit a state from permitting the admission of such victim impact evidence during the sentencing phase of a capital trial. Since that time, such statements have become routine in the criminal justice system in such settings.

The movement for victims' rights began as a grass-roots movement initially on behalf of victims of rape, but it soon coalesced into a broader movement of rather unlikely allies: women's groups and more traditional "law and order" forces. The result has been a national and international movement of no small consequence.

Today victims rights are found in state statutes, many state constitutions, and there is once again pending legislation before Congress for a federal victims' rights constitutional amendment. Early victims' rights law encouraged justice systems to treat victims with dignity and respect and allow them access to information. It was suggestive language with no teeth. Today agencies are *required* to ask victims if they wish to be notified of and attend hearings, confer with prosecutors, demand restitution, provide victim impact statements, and become actively engaged in the legal process.

Many legislative acts have resulted in response to victims, such as "Megan's Law" and others addressing terrorism, stalking, child protection, sexual predation, etc. Victims and their advocates have continued to push forward and vow to continue to make the victims' voices even louder. Advancing concepts of coordinated community response teams, victim impact panels, restorative justice, and parallel justice are just a few of the recent attempts to keep the movement progressive. Great advances have been made and need to continue toward providing educational and training opportunities for service providers and others in the field who touch the lives of victims. Only if the legal system and service providers have knowledge and a real understanding of the immediate and long-term needs of victims can they respond appropriately to those needs.

For more information

Bedau, Hugo A., ed. *The Death Penalty in America: Current Controversies.* New York: Oxford University Press, 1997.

Office for Victims of Crime, U.S. Department of Justice, or the National Center for Victims of Crime, 2111 Wilson Blvd., Suite 300, Arlington, Va. 22201 or Internet at www.ncvc.org

Payne v. Tennessee, 501 U.S. 808 (1991).

Carol A. Day
Victim/Witness Services Coordinator
of the District Attorney's Office
Eau Claire County, Wisconsin

Stephen K. Shaw
Department of History and Political Science
Northwest Nazarene University
Nampa, Idaho

Vinson, Frederick Moore (1890–1953)

served as chief justice of the U.S. Supreme Court during one of its most contentious and controversial periods. He brought a wealth of political and administrative experience to the position as well as the full confidence of President Harry S

Truman. Unfortunately, Vinson's political skills failed to bring together a divided and decidedly unharmonious court.

Fred Vinson was born in Louisa, Kentucky, on January 22, 1890. He obtained a law degree in 1911 and practiced law in Kentucky until 1924. Vinson served in the U.S. House of Representatives from 1925 to 1938, the year he was appointed to the U.S. Court of Appeals. During World War II he served in a variety of administrative positions, including director of economic stabilization, federal loan administrator, and director of mobilization and reconversion. President Truman named Vinson secretary of the treasury in July 1945, and in June 1946 Truman elevated him to chief justice of the Supreme Court, after the death of Harlan Fiske Stone.

Chief Justice Fred Vinson (HARRIS AND EWING, COLLECTION OF THE SUPREME COURT OF THE UNITED STATES)

Truman had admiration for Vinson's common sense and quiet administrative ability, as well as his skill as a poker player. He apparently hoped that Vinson's personal skills would help unify an openly divided Court. The Supreme Court in 1946 contained such brilliant and opinioned men as Felix Frankfurter, Hugo Black, William O. Douglas, and Robert Jackson. The Court was sharply split along ideological and personality lines. From the beginning of his tenure Chief Justice Vinson seemed unable to deal with the intellectual cut and thrust of the Court as well as the intense personal antagonisms between some of the justices.

During his service on the Supreme Court, Vinson consistently took stands upholding the government's right to act and took a dim view of civil liberties. During the years 1945 to 1949, President Truman appointed three like-minded men (Justices Burton, Clark, and Minton) who strengthened the conservative pro-government wing of the Court.

One of the most important cases that arrived during Vinson's tenure was *United States v. Dennis* (1951). In his opinion for the majority upholding the convictions of several members of the American Communist Party Vinson argued that the clear and present danger test should be seen as, "whether the gravity of the 'evil,' discounted by its improbability, justifies such invasion of free speech as is necessary to avoid danger." The next year in the *Steel Seizure* case Vinson dissented when the majority ruled that the president did not have the inherent power to take over the nation's steel industry to prevent a strike during the Korean War.

The case that would come to be known as *Brown vs. Board of Education* would build on precedents established during early in Vinson's term. In the case of *Sweatt v. Painter* (1950) the Court had ruled that a state could not exclude Negroes from a law school unless equal facilities were available. The *Brown* case was originally argued on December 9, 1952. After months of deliberations the justices issued a call for a rehearing and added a series of questions it wished the lawyers to answer. A rehearing was scheduled for October 1953. In one of history's greatest ironies, Chief Justice Vinson suffered a heart attack and died in September 1953. This led to the appointment of California governor Earl Warren as chief justice.

History has not been kind to Fred Vinson as chief justice. He was praised for common sense, integrity, and administrative ability, but these qualities did not equip him to deal with the towering intellects and egos of the Supreme Court during this period of history.

For more information

McCullough, David. *Truman*. New York: Simon and Schuster, 1992.

Simon, James F. *The Antagonists*. New York: Touchstone, 1989.

Charlie Howard
Tarleton State University

Violence against Women Act

Violence against Women Act   or VAWA makes it a federal crime to cross state lines with the intent to injure a partner or spouse or to violate an order of protection.

The law also contains an anti-stalking provision, extends rape shield protection to victims of criminal acts, and requires states to honor orders of protection awarded in other states. In May 1995 a West Virginia man, who severely beat his wife and drove with her in the trunk of their car through West Virginia and Kentucky, was the first person convicted under the act. She suffered irreversible brain damage as a result of the attack.

The Violence against Women Act also contained a section, known as the "civil rights provision," that declared that "all persons within the United States shall have the right to be free from crimes of violence motivated by gender." Supplementing existing federal civil rights laws, this provision allowed victims of gender-motivated violence, such as sexual assault or domestic violence, to sue their attackers for damages in federal court.

VAWA was introduced by Senator Joseph Biden (Dem.-Del.) in 1990. After four years of hearings during which Congress heard testimony about the impact of violence on women's lives and the inadequate response by state law enforcement officials, Congress enacted VAWA as part of the Violent Crime Control and Law Enforcement Act of 1994. It was passed under Congress's authority to regulate interstate commerce as well as its Fourteenth Amendment power to guarantee equal protection of the law.

In an attempt to focus the efforts of state law enforcement agencies on gender-motivated violence, Congress also authorized $1.6 billion over six years to fund state programs to improve strategies among police, prosecutors, and prevention services to deal with crimes of sexual violence or domestic abuse. The law also established a Violence against Women Office in the Department of Justice and created a national 800 hotline number as well as a web site on the Internet.

The first case to test the constitutionality of the "civil rights provision" began in 1994 when a first-year student claimed she was sexually assaulted by two football players in her dormitory room at Virginia Polytechnic Institute and State University. She brought charges under the university's sexual assault policy; for a number of reasons, criminal charges could not be filed against the two men. Because she was dissatisfied with the disposition of the case, and fearing for her own safety, she left school and sued the university and her two attackers under the "civil rights provision" of VAWA. The defendants argued that this section of the law was unconstitutional because Congress exceeded its constitutional authority in enacting it and because laws punishing sexual assault were exclusively within the purview of state criminal justice systems.

The district court found the statute unconstitutional and dismissed the case; the appellate court affirmed the lower court. In its ruling, the appellate court relied on a 1995 case in which the U.S. Supreme Court struck a federal law that made it a crime to possess a gun within 1,000 feet of a school. The High Court said Congress had not sufficiently demonstrated the link between interstate commerce and gun possession near schools.

In May 2000, in *United States v. Morrison,* the Supreme Court affirmed the courts below, striking the "civil rights provision" of the act. The High Court ruled that despite congressional findings that gender-motivated violence has a serious impact on the economy, there is an insufficient link between interstate commerce and the criminal behavior to permit Congress to grant victims a federal right to sue the perpetrators of such violence. However, although *Morrison* struck VAWA's "civil rights provision," the Court left the remaining parts of the law intact.

For more information

United States v. Morrison, 120 S.Ct. 1740; 2000 U.S. LEXIS 3422; 146 L.Ed 2d 658.

The Department of Justice's Violence against Women web site is at http://www.ojp.usdoj.gov/vawo/welcome.html.

Susan Gluck Mezey
Department of Political Science
Loyola University, Chicago

voir dire   is a term American trial lawyers use in two ways. The first refers to the process, at the beginning of a trial, of selecting a jury. The second refers to the process, during a trial, in which the judge hears testimony from a witness, out of the hearing of the jury, in an effort to resolve a legal issue the judge must decide. Voir dire comes from the French, meaning, "to see to say" or "to speak the truth."

The court, at the beginning of a trial, calls numerous citizens for potential jury duty (the venire or panel). The judge, with the help of the attorneys, reduces the panel to the number the jurisdiction requires for the particular case. States may require six or 12 jurors for civil trials. Federal courts require only six. Both state and federal courts require 12 jurors to hear criminal cases. The judge may also select alternates.

The purpose of this type of voir dire, the jury selection process, is to select a legally qualified, unbiased, fair and open-minded jury capable of hearing the evidence and reaching a decision based on the evidence without considering outside influences. Each jurisdiction decides who may serve and what qualifications a potential juror must have. Many jurisdictions exclude lawyers, those who cannot understand English, and felons. Jurisdictions may excuse certain people, such as physicians, teachers, mothers with young children, and clergy, if the potential juror requests it. The judge may also excuse those for whom jury service would be a hardship.

This voir dire involves a series of questions the judge, attorneys, or both, ask the panel members about their backgrounds and qualifications. Each jurisdiction has its own jury selection procedure. The procedure may also vary from judge to judge. In many courts the judge asks general, preliminary questions to the panel as a whole, while the attorneys ask further, more detailed questions to the panel and individual panel members. In other courts, the judge asks questions the attorneys have suggested, in writing, beforehand. The attorneys may have only a limited opportunity to suggest further questions after the judge finishes.

The subjects of the questioning may include the potential jurors' family and work history, their experience with the law, attitudes toward people, and potential sources of bias. The attorneys will likely be interested in the potential jurors' previous jury service and experience with lawsuits, acquaintance with the parties, attorneys, and witnesses, their ages, and educational and economic levels. They will also be interested in the panel members' knowledge of the subject matter of the lawsuit, and whether they will be able to follow the instructions given by the judge. In some jurisdictions they may ask if any are officers, agents, employees, or shareholders of any insurance company involved in the litigation.

If the judge permits the attorneys to ask questions, they may seek to create rapport with the panel, inform the panel members of the nature of the case, and condition them to potential adverse evidence.

Based upon the answers to these questions, the attorneys may ask the judge to strike, or remove, a potential juror from hearing the case. Each party has an unlimited number of strikes for "cause," by which it asks the judge to remove a juror for a reason. The judge may or may not agree with a reason stated by the party's attorney. The judge has the discretion to remove the juror. Each party also has a limited number of "peremptory" challenges, by which it has a right to remove a potential juror for an unstated reason. The attorney is only limited by the case of *Batson v. Kentucky*, 476 U.S. 79 (1986), which holds that an attorney may not strike a potential juror solely on the basis of race and must have a nonracial reason for a peremptory challenge.

The second, and less frequent, use of "voir dire" describes the judge hearing the testimony of a witness away from the jury in order to determine a legal issue the judge must decide. Often this involves the admissibility of the witness's testimony. For instance one party may contest the relevance of a witness's testimony to the issues of the trial or whether a witness qualifies as an expert witness. The judge may hear what the witness has to say and then decide whether the jury should hear from the witness.

For more information

Black's Law Dictionary, 7th ed. St. Paul, Minn.: West Publishing Group 1999.
28 USC 1861–1878.

Warford B. Johnson III
Daniel, Clampett, Powell and Cunningham
Springfield, Missouri

Voting Rights Act of 1965 refers to the biggest statutory change in the relationship of the federal and state governments in the field of voting since the passage of the Reconstruction Acts, which enfranchised blacks in conquered southern states.

During the late 1950s and early 1960s, the U.S. Justice Department brought numerous cases across the South attacking restrictive registration practices under the Civil Rights Acts of 1957, 1960, and 1964, each of which contained some voting-related provisions. The department came to realize that these individual suits were largely ineffectual. First, after being enjoined to stop one restrictive practice, the sued jurisdiction usually resorted to another restriction. Second, the suits did not cause other jurisdictions to comply voluntarily with the federal law.

When the country's attention was centered on the African-American struggle for the right to register in Selma, Alabama, President Lyndon Johnson and the Justice Department took that opportunity to propose a radical departure from prior laws. They proposed that Congress outlaw certain restrictive registration practices, require certain states to obtain prior approval from the Justice Department or a federal court before adopting new election laws, authorize the appointment of federal voter registrars, and authorize the attorney general to attack the constitutionality of the poll tax in each state where it was still used. Congress approved the act and President Johnson signed it on August 6, 1965.

Several states quickly challenged the constitutionality of the act by bringing an original action in the U.S. Supreme Court. The Court upheld the constitutionality, stating:

Congress had found that case-by-case litigation was inadequate to combat wide-spread and persistent discrimination in voting, because of the inordinate amount of time and energy required to overcome the obstructionist tactics invariably encountered in these lawsuits. After enduring nearly a century of systematic resistance to the Fifteenth Amendment, Congress might well decide to shift the advantage of time and inertia from the perpetrators of the evil to its victims. *South Carolina v. Katzenbach,* 383 U.S. 301, 327–28 (1966).

Immediately after its passage, the Justice Department set about to enforce its provisions by appointing federal voter examiners who could register voters without using literacy tests or "voucher" requirements (having a registered voter vouch that the new applicant was a person of good character). The use of federal examiners secured an immediate increase in the number of blacks registered to vote in the southern states.

The poll tax had already been outlawed for federal elections by the ratification of the Twenty-fourth Amendment in early 1964. The Justice Department also brought suits against the use of the poll tax as a prerequisite to voting in state and local elections in Alabama, Mississippi, and Texas. A private suit was already pending in Virginia; the Justice Department filed an amicus ("friend of the court") brief in that case. These four were the only remaining states to impose a poll tax. The first of the cases to be decided by the U.S. Supreme Court was *Harper v. Virginia State Board of Elections,* 383 U.S. 663 (1966), in which the Court held that poll taxes violated the equal protection clause of the Fourteenth Amendment.

One of the most controversial provisions of the act is section 5, which requires some or all jurisdictions in 17 states to submit changes in their election laws or procedures to the Justice Department or the U.S. District Court for the District of Columbia before the state can enforce the new law. The states are not named in the act but are decided according to a formula: if the state or county used some discriminatory device (such as literacy test) in registration and less than 50 percent of its voting-age population voted in the 1964 presidential election, then it is covered by section 5. (In the 1970 and 1975 amendments, the formula was extended to other situations in the 1968 and 1972 presidential

elections.) Section 5 now covers the following states: Alabama, Alaska, Arizona, Georgia, Louisiana, Mississippi, South Carolina, Texas, and Virginia; and parts of the following: California, Florida, Michigan, New Hampshire, New York City, North Carolina, and South Dakota. The Justice Department receives between 14,000 and 24,000 election changes a year. On the other hand, fewer than a half-dozen judicial actions seeking preclearance of election changes are filed each year.

Section 2 of the act was initially based on the language of the Fifteenth Amendment. The Supreme Court held in *City of Mobile v. Bolden,* 446 U.S. 55 (1980), that plaintiffs had to prove the election system was adopted with the intent to discriminate against blacks. Congress amended section 2 in 1982 to remove the requirement of intent. The section now reads as follows:

(a) No voting qualification or prerequisite to voting or standard, practice, or procedure shall be imposed or applied by any State or political subdivision in a manner which results in a denial or abridgement of the right of any citizen of the United States to vote on account of race or color, or in contravention of the guarantees set forth in section 4(f)(2) [relating to bi-lingual ballots], as provided in subsection (b).

(b) A violation of subsection (a) is established if, based on the totality of circumstances, it is shown that the political processes leading to nomination or election in the State or political subdivision are not equally open to participation by members of a class of citizens protected by subsection (a) in that its members have less opportunity than other members of the electorate to participate in the political process and to elect representatives of their choice. The extent to which members of a protected class have been elected to office in the State or political subdivision is one circumstance which may be considered: Provided, That nothing in this section establishes a right to have members of a protected class elected in numbers equal to their proportion in the population.

This section is now used mainly to attack at-large elections and other election practices that have the effect of preventing blacks and other racial or ethnic minorities from electing their preferred candidates. Hundreds of jurisdictions have been sued and required to change from at-large elections to single-member districts so that minorities will have a fair chance of electing candidates.

The 1982 amendment also renewed the pre-clearance requirement of section 5. It is now scheduled to expire in 2007, although the more general requirement of section 2 is permanent.

The effect of the Voting Rights Act has been revolutionary. While in the early 1960s the registration rates of blacks lagged behind those of whites by 22 to 63 percentage points across the southern states, the registration rates for blacks and whites are nearly comparable now. Black elected officials were virtually unknown in the South before 1964. Now blacks hold at least one congressional seat in each of the old Confederate states and more than 15 percent of the legislative seats in those states. The Voting Rights Act lives up to the assessment of former attorney general Nicholas Katzenbach in 1975: "the most successful piece of civil rights legislation ever enacted."

For more information

Davidson, Chandler, and Bernard Grofman, eds., *The Quiet Revolution: The Impact of the Voting Rights Act in the South, 1965–1990*. Princeton, N.J.: Princeton University Press, 1994.

Garrow, David J. *Protest at Selma: Martin Luther King, Jr., and the Voting Rights Act of 1965*. New Haven, Conn.: Yale University Press, 1978.

Edward Still
Lawyers' Committee for Civil Rights under Law

W

Waite, Morrison Remick (1816–1888) was the seventh chief justice of the U.S. Supreme Court.

Waite was born in Lyme, Connecticut, on November 27, 1816. His father was a judge and farmer, eventually appointed chief justice of the Connecticut Supreme Court, who inspired him to enter the legal profession. Following his father's advice, Waite graduated from Yale College in 1837 and practiced law in Ohio, establishing a solid reputation representing railroad companies. Waite was active in Ohio politics, running for Congress, serving in the state assembly, and eventually turning down a seat on the state supreme court. He was appointed to a national tribunal, traveled to Geneva, and settled claims between the United States and Great Britain that had resulted from the Civil War. He returned with a $15 million victory, chaired Ohio's state constitutional convention in 1873, and was picked by President Ulysses Grant to fill the chief justice vacancy on the U.S. Supreme Court left by the death of Salmon P. Chase.

Waite took the bench in 1874 and, though confronted with contentious group of colleagues, became an able leader during his tenure. In general, Waite's constitutional philosophy favored the states, particularly in the key areas of regulation of business and civil liberties, and it marked the beginning of the retreat from Reconstruction-era ideals.

In civil rights cases, the Waite Court was unsympathetic to the claims of women and former slaves. In *Minor v. Happersett,* 88 U.S. 162 (1875), Waite held that because suffrage was not a right of citizenship, states could deny women the vote. In *United States v. Cruikshank,* 92 U.S. 542 (1876), he sided with the states in denying national protection for newly freed slaves. He again sided with the states in the area of voting rights for African Americans in *United States v. Reese,* 92 U.S. 214 (1876). Both *Minor* and *Cruikshank* paved the way for increased racial violence and Jim Crowism in the South.

In cases involving economic regulation, Waite was generally critical of national schemes and allowed states considerable leeway. In his most important opinion in this area, *Munn v. Illinois,* 94 U.S. 113 (1877), he upheld state power to regulate businesses. "Property does become clothed with a public interest when used in a manner to make it of public consequence, and

Chief Justice Morrison Remick Waite (LIBRARY OF CON-GRESS)

affect the community at large." He then argued for judicial restraint. "For protection against abuses by legislatures, the people must resort to the polls, not to the courts."

Waite was a notorious workaholic, laboring for long hours, weekends, and even taking his work on vacations. In March 1888 he became ill while working on the *Bell Telephone Cases,* 126 U.S. 1 (1888). Though in a fragile state, he endeavored to take his seat on the bench and deliver the opinion. He remarked that his absence from the bench would appear in the newspapers and his wife, then away on a trip to California, would needlessly worry. Once he reached the Court, however, he was unable to

draw enough strength to read the opinion. Attorney General Augustus H. Garland later recalled the scene, "It was evident to the observer that death had almost placed its hand upon him." Upon returning home, Waite was diagnosed with severe pneumonia. After 14 years on the Court, Chief Justice Waite died on March 23, 1888.

For more information

Magrath, C. Peter. *Morrison R. Waite: The Triumph of Character.* New York: Macmillan, 1963.

Trimble, Bruce R. *Chief Justice Waite: Defender of the Public Interest.* Princeton, N.J.: Princeton University Press, 1938.

Kimberly A. Williams and Artemus Ward
California State University, Chico

Wallace v. Jaffree   472 U.S. 38 (1985) was a Supreme Court decision that ruled that an Alabama statute authorizing public schoolteachers to hold a one-minute period of silence for "meditation or voluntary prayer" violated the establishment clause of the First Amendment.

Jaffree, a resident of Mobile County, Alabama, sent his three children to a Mobile public school. He complained of religious exercises that made his children uncomfortable. The Supreme Court priorly had held unconstitutional one of the Alabama statutes that required teachers to lead "willing students" in a state-written prayer. Another of Alabama's statutes, which allowed for a period of silence for meditation, was not challenged. Therefore, the only difference between the statute in question and a constitutional statute was the inclusion of the words *voluntary prayer* as a suitable activity in which students could engage during the moment of silence. Jaffree's brief was joined by the ACLU and the American Jewish Congress while the appellees were joined by several state attorneys general (including Joseph I. Lieberman, then attorney general for Connecticut) and the solicitor general of the United States.

Applying the *Lemon* test (developed in *Lemon v. Kurtzman*, 403 U.S. 602 [1971]), the Court decided that the statute had no secular purpose. Indeed, the senator who had sponsored the bill noted that it was an "effort to return voluntary prayer to our public schools" and that he had "no other purpose in mind" (at 43). The Court rejected the district court's opinion that a state had the right to establish a religion, calling it a "remarkable conclusion" (at 48) as states have no greater power to restrain individual freedoms than does the federal government. Even without establishing a religion a state may violate the establishment clause by endorsing religion over non-religion. Justice Stevens, speaking for the majority, said, "Just as the right to speak and the right to refrain from speaking are complementary components of a broader concept of individual freedom of mind, so also the individual's freedom to choose his own creed is the counterpart of his right to refrain from accepting the creed established by the majority . . . individual freedom of conscience protected by the First Amendment embraces the right to select any religious faith or none at all" (at 52–53). Though it remains acceptable to allow for a moment of silence and for a student to pray during that moment, this statute was seen as a "state endorsement and promotion of prayer" (at 58) and, therefore, deemed unacceptable.

In dissent, Justice Burger claimed that nullifying this statute "manifests not neutrality but hostility toward religion" (at 85). Rehnquist, also in dissent, claimed that the founders would never "require that the Government be absolutely neutral as between religion and irreligion" (at 99) but only that the state not establish a national religion to which all must adhere. Whether the dissenters or the majority were "correct" this precedent continues to be controlling.

For more information

Ally, Robert S. *Without a Prayer: Religious Expression in Public Schools*. Amherst, N.Y.: Prometheus Books, 1996.

Harrison, Maureen, and Gilbert, Steve. *Schoolhouse Decisions of the United States Supreme Court*. San Diego, Calif.: Excellent Books, 1997.

Ravitch, Frank S. *School Prayer and Discrimination: The Civil Rights of Religious Minorities and Dissenters*. Boston: Northeastern University Press, 1999.

Sano C. Benesh
University of Wisconsin, Milwaukee

war crimes   are actions performed by soldiers and others involved in military conflict that violate domestic law or international customs and conventions.

War crimes are generally enforced by the victors in tribunals held after the end of the conflict but may also be prosecuted by the home government of the person charged.

The idea that there should be rules limiting combatants, or justice in war (Latin *jus in bello*), dates at least from the writings of Thomas Aquinas (1225–74), but the application and enforcement of these rules continues to evolve. Initially, the principal concerns of the laws of war were to prevent "unnecessary suffering," that is, beyond that necessary to produce military advantage, and that the force should be "proportional" to the advantage gained. With the tremendous advances in military technology and increase in the number of people involved in conflict after the 19th century, attacks on population centers and infrastructure could produce enormous military advantage. The focus of international law shifted to protecting noncombatants, minimizing damage to private property, and even limiting the horrors of war for the soldiers themselves.

The 1856 Paris Declaration Respecting Maritime Law was the first large-scale effort to create written rules of warfare. Other notable agreements include the Hague Convention of 1907, the Pact of Paris of 1928, and the Geneva Conventions of 1929 and 1949. Collectively, these agreements extend common domestic law prohibitions against rape, slavery, plunder, and torture to wartime practice and attempt to limit the destruction of war to legitimate military targets. Among the actions prohibited by these conventions is torture and mistreatment of prisoners of war, intentional destruction of cultural objects, using the cover of surrender or a protected sanctuary to commit aggression, looting or otherwise maltreating corpses, wearing civilian clothing or enemy uniforms to conceal one's identity as a combatant, poisoning water supplies, killing or wounding surrendering or obviously incapacitated soldiers, and shooting at pilots who have ejected from their aircraft. While it is understood that civilians and nonmilitary targets might become casualties of war (so-called collateral damage), soldiers must take reasonable measures to prevent this from happening unnecessarily.

The concept of war crimes has long been rather controversial. Placing restraints on the conduct of soldiers can often expose them to increased risk, especially when engaged in guerrilla warfare and other operations against nontraditional forces. Michael Walzer, the preeminent just-war theorist of this generation, has drawn the following analogy: "Soldiers, it might be said, stand to civilians like the crew of a liner to its passengers. They must risk their own lives for the sake of others." Another significant argument against punishing soldiers who commit war crimes is that they often do so under the orders of superiors. This defense was traditionally thought to free subordinates from any responsibility. This argument was rejected by the Nuremberg and Tokyo Tribunals that investigated atrocities committed by the Axis powers during World War II but was considered a mitigating factor at the time of the sentencing of William Calley, the leader of the 1968 My Lai massacre in Vietnam.

In recent years, international law has begun to hold heads of state accountable for atrocities committed during wartime by their subordinates. Yugoslav president Slobodan Milosevic and several other political leaders have been charged with war crimes for their part in the ethnic cleansing and other illegalities committed in the Bosnia and Kosovo conflicts.

For more information

Glahn, Gerhard von. *Law Among Nations: An Introduction to Public International Law,* 7th ed. Boston, Mass.: Allyn and Bacon, 1996.

Malanczuk, Peter. *Akehurst's Modern Introduction to International Law,* 7th rev. ed. New York: Routledge, 1997.

Walzer, Michael. *Just and Unjust Wars: A Moral Argument with Historical Illustrations,* 3rd ed. New York: Basic Books, 2000.

James H. Joyner, Jr., Ph.D.
Assistant Professor of Political Science
Troy State University

War Powers Resolution is a law that was passed by Congress in 1973 in an attempt to limit the power of the president to commit U.S. troops without the consent or consultation of Congress.

Traditionally it was assumed in U.S. politics that presidents, as commanders in chief of the armed forces, are able to engage in defensive battles without the consent of Congress. During the years of the cold war, the exact nature of defensive wars as opposed to offensive wars began to be questioned. Presidents had begun using U.S. military power to protect the lives and property of U.S. citizens abroad as well as to pursue U.S. foreign policy interests even in the absence of a real, direct threat to the United States.

The extended exercise of military power by Presidents Johnson and Nixon in prosecuting the conflict in Vietnam and Cambodia was seen by the Congress as the last straw in this stretching of presidential power. In an effort to regain what they believed to be their rightful share of the war-making power, Congress passed the War Powers Resolution in 1973.

There are three main provisions to the War Powers Resolution. The first requires the president to consult with Congress "in every possible instance" before sending troops into hostilities. The second provision requires the president to report to Congress within 48 hours of introducing U.S. forces into hostilities. The third provision requires termination of military activity within 60 days unless Congress declares war, authorizes an additional 60 days, or is unable to meet because of an attack on the country. Even if Congress does not extend the time frame by an additional 60 days, the president may choose to extend the presence of U.S. troops by an additional 30 days if he determines that the forces are necessary to protect or remove U.S. troops. The intent of these provisions and the act itself was to "insure collective judgment" by both branches and to prevent the president from engaging in executive wars without congressional consent.

While perhaps laudable in intent, the War Powers Resolution has suffered from several significant flaws. Much of the language used in the resolution is vague and open to interpretation— interpretation that is ultimately left to the president. The requirement that the president consult with Congress in "every possible instance," for instance, leaves considerable discretion to the executive branch on both the timing and nature of the consultation. Similarly, the requirement that the president report to Congress within 48 hours of introducing forces into "hostilities" leaves the president free to define the meaning of *hostilities*.

The War Powers Resolution has also been questioned on constitutional grounds. Presidents have long argued that the power to commit troops to action is derived from the commander-in-chief power of Article II of the Constitution. If that is the case, then it does indeed seem odd that the Congress would be able to limit that constitutional authority through legislative enactment rather than by constitutional amendment. While the issue of constitutionality is quite serious, the Supreme Court to date has refused to address the question.

Military engagements such as Grenada in 1983 and Panama in 1989 have shown that the War Powers Resolution has not worked exactly as the Congress intended. As a result, members of Congress have sued in federal court to force compliance with the spirit, rather than just the letter, of the resolution. They have met with little success. Federal courts have generally declined to accept jurisdiction over these cases, arguing that questions such as when hostilities can be said to exist represent a factual dispute, an essentially political dispute between the other two branches of government that is not suitable for resolution in the courts.

If "collective judgment" is an essential component of good or democratic military policy, the War Powers Resolution has been only minimally successful. While presidents may feel compelled to seek congressional approval for longer term military engagements, they may feel no constraint at all when engaging in short-term activities.

For more information

Corwin, Edward S. *The President: Offices and Powers, 1787–1984.* New York: New York University Press, 1984.

Fisher, Louis. *Constitutional Conflicts between Congress and the President.* Lawrence: University Press of Kansas, 1991.

David A. May
Eastern Washington University

Warren Commission   refers to the informal name given to a presidential commission that investigated the assassination of President John Kennedy in 1963.

The name came from the chairman, U.S. Chief Justice Earl Warren, who was appointed by Kennedy's successor, President Lyndon B. Johnson, to lead the seven-member investigation commission to determine whether the accused assassin actually killed Kennedy and, if so, whether he acted alone. The commission's conclusion, delivered 10 months after Johnson appointed the body, was that Lee Harvey Oswald acted alone when he shot Kennedy in a motorcade through downtown Dallas. Oswald himself was killed two days after Kennedy by a Dallas nightclub owner with alleged ties to organized crime. Intended to dispel fears that Kennedy died as a result of a conspiracy, the Warren Commission's conclusion instead generated controversy that U.S. senator Richard Russell of Georgia, a commission member, said would endure for 100 years.

The conspiracy advocates saw three principal forces possibly behind the assassination: the Soviet Union, the leader of what was then the communist bloc allied against the United States and its role as democratic leader in the world; Cuban leader Fidel Castro, a communist, who could have acted alone or with Soviet help; or an organized crime syndicate in the United States, angry at Kennedy for his administration's prosecution of the Mafia schemes. (Kennedy's brother, Robert Kennedy, had been a tough congressional prosecutor of organized crime in the 1950s and was the president's attorney general.) The commission included Richard B. Russell, a staunch political foe of Warren's whom Johnson had to persuade to serve on the commission because Russell so despised Warren; three members of Congress, including Congressman Gerald Ford, himself destined to be U.S. president within a decade; Allen W. Dulles, former director of the U.S. Central Intelligence Agency, and John J. McCloy, former president of the World Bank. The Warren Commission investigated Oswald's background; Oswald's killer, Jack Ruby; and the possible conspiracies. It relied on tests from simulating the assassination to conclude that one person could have fired the three shots at Kennedy's limousine in rapid succession and that Oswald, an expert marksman who served with the U.S. Marines and who worked in the building from which the shots were fired, was the shooter.

For more information

Manchester, William. *The Death of a President.* New York: Harper and Row, 1967.

Wm. Osler McCarthy
Texas Supreme Court
University of Texas Department of Journalism

Warren, Earl (1891–1974) was chief justice of the United States from 1953 to 1969. He was appointed by President Eisenhower.

The son of a Norwegian immigrant railroad car inspector, Earl Warren received his undergraduate and law degrees from the University of California, Berkeley. After military service during World War I, he entered public service for what would be his lifetime. He became the district attorney (prosecutor) of Alameda County (Oakland, California) in 1925, and his vigorous prosecution of corrupt politicians and organized crime helped elevate him to the position of California's attorney general in 1938. In that role, he is best remembered for his strong advocacy of the relocation of Japanese Americans from their homes to prison-like camps for the duration of World War II. Although he never publicly acknowledged this as a civil rights error, he did so in posthumously published memoirs. In 1943 he became governor of California, and he ran for vice president of the United States in 1948 on the losing Republican ticket with Thomas Dewey of New York. Although he was a serious contender for the presidency in 1952, he threw his support to a pro-Eisenhower provision at the Republican nomination convention that assured Eisenhower's nomination. Warren was nominated by President Eisenhower as chief justice in September 1953, when Chief Justice Fred Vinson unexpectedly died of a heart attack.

Many have been puzzled by Chief Justice Warren's strong liberal record on the Supreme Court, given his background. A close inspection of his public career shows that as governor he had started out as an orthodox Republican, but he had soon shifted to moderate and progressive positions that by 1946 gained him both the Republican and the Democratic nomination to an unprecedented third term as California's governor. Also, although as a prosecutor he had been responsible for some actions that would have violated the rights of defendants that were established later by the Supreme Court, for the most part as county prosecutor and state attorney general he scrupulously upheld the rights of criminal defendants, especially disallowing electronic surveillance and the use of the "third degree" (beatings) to obtain confessions. Indeed, he refused to allow such techniques against a suspect in the murder of his own father, a crime that was never solved. Thus, his personal and political value systems had strong streaks of moralism and populism. He was also a superb administrator who knew how to motivate people and get things done. These tendencies came to the fore rapidly in his decade and a half as chief justice.

He is most remembered for his masterful ability to take a divided Court on the issue of school segregation and steer it toward a unanimous opinion in *Brown v. Board of Education* (1954). That case ruled that racially separate educational facilities were inherently unequal because segregation had a detrimental effect on African-American children. While the justices were morally opposed to racial segregation, several feared that the expected strident opposition from the Deep South would divide the nation and undermine the Court's credibility if it failed to enforce its ruling. Chief Justice Warren patiently led the justices to agree to produce a short, unanimous, and unequivocal decision that gave notice to segregationists that the Court was mustering the moral force of the nation behind its ruling, while giving segregated school systems a small amount of time to readjust. The decade of turmoil that followed the *Brown* case is an indication that the decision called on all of Earl Warren's talents as a judicial statesman.

The hallmarks of the Supreme Court under Justice Warren were activism, liberalism, and

Chief Justice Earl Warren (ABDON DAOUD ACKAD, COLLECTION OF THE SUPREME COURT OF THE UNITED STATES)

populism. During his tenure, the Court led the government in outlawing racial segregation; ended the ability of states to maintain misapportioned and unrepresentative voting districts; continued to extend First Amendment rights of free speech toward almost absolute limits; vigorously upheld antitrust laws; and revolutionized the rights of criminal defendants by making protections of the Bill of Rights applicable to suspects and defendants in state, as well as federal, courts. As a result of liberal ruling in these areas, local governments were required to desegregate public facilities such as swimming pools and buses. States were required to reapportion legislative districts so that a person's vote in one district would carry the same weight as a vote in another district. Local criminal justice practices were changed in major ways as *Mapp v. Ohio* (1961) disallowed the use of seized evidence illegally seized in violation of the Fourth Amendment; *Gideon v. Wainwright* (1963) mandated the appointment of lawyers for poor defendants under the Sixth Amendment; and *Miranda v. Arizona* (1966) required police officers to warn suspects of their Fifth Amendment right to remain silent prior to interrogation.

Earl Warren was not known as a great legal stylist or profound legal thinker, but his leadership abilities made him one of the most effective chief justices in the Supreme Court's history. In *Brown* and in all of his decisions, he displayed a result-orientation to judging based on common sense; an intuitive sense of justice, fairness, and equality; and a liberal theory of affirmative government. Thus, he departed from traditional modes of constitutional interpretation to ask what was the just outcome of a case, based on a theory of civics that held that the government existed for the benefit of its citizens. If so, federal and local governments had to bestow rights fairly and equally, even if the opposite result had been reached by the democratic process of legislation. The result, as one biographer explains, was a fusing of constitutional interpretation with a search for justice that harmonized the Constitution with current perceptions of what justice required.

For more information

Cray, Ed. *Chief Justice: A Biography of Earl Warren.* New York: Simon and Schuster, 1997.

Schwartz, Bernard. *Super Chief: Earl Warren and His Supreme Court—a Judicial Biography.* New York: New York University Press, 1983.

White, G. Edward. *Earl Warren: A Public Life.* New York: Oxford University Press, 1982.

Marvin Zalman
Wayne State University

Webster, Daniel (1782–1852) was a 19th-century senator and statesman from Massachusetts who argued several of the most important constitutional law cases in U.S. history before the United States Supreme Court.

Daniel Webster was born in 1782 in Salisbury, New Hampshire, in the hill country of the upper Merrimack River, to Ebenezer Webster and his second wife, Abigail Eastman. Daniel was the youngest son in a family of 10 children. While raised in a farming environment, the young Daniel preferred working in his father's tavern and conversing with the establishment's visitors. The integrity, devotion to political union, and political acumen of Ebenezer Webster would soon be evident in his son. As the boy became well known among the tavern patrons, he was given the nickname "Black Dan," owing to his dark hair and complexion.

Educated at local schools and through his voracious reading of great works, Webster attended Phillips Exeter Academy and Dartmouth College. At Dartmouth, Webster was an active student who was elected to Phi Beta Kappa. He proceeded to study law under Federalist teachers and to practice law in his native New Hampshire. After marrying Grace Fletcher in 1808, Webster became more interested in politics. After several unsuccessful campaigns, Webster was elected to the U.S. House of Representatives in 1812. Establishing himself as a critic of the Madison administration, he believed the country should practice self-restraint while maintaining national integrity. In approving the Hartford Convention's listing of complaints against the federal government, he did not endorse the secessionist elements within the gathering.

After moving to Boston and acquiring the reputation as an orator and defender of the nationalist tradition, Webster spent a great deal of time practicing law and presenting cases before the Supreme Court, including *McCulloch v. Maryland* and *Gibbons v. Ogden*. He was elected to the Senate in 1827. In 1828 he supported the prevailing tariff proposal, and this endorsement led to a famous debate with Senator Robert Y.

Hayne of South Carolina in 1830. In the course of the debate, Webster declared: "Liberty and Union, now and forever, one and inseparable!" These sentiments would embody his devotion to the importance of union for the remainder of his political career.

In 1836 and 1840 he would unsuccessfully attempt to obtain the Whig Party's presidential nomination; he would nevertheless serve as secretary of state under Presidents Harrison, Tyler, and Fillmore. He returned to the Senate from 1844 until 1850. He supported the Compromise of 1850, criticizing secessionists and abolitionists as not possessing enough devotion to the cause of union and as taking departures from the teachings of the fundamental law. He died in 1852.

For more information

Peterson, Merrill D. *The Great Triumvirate: Webster, Clay, and Calhoun*. New York: Oxford University Press, 1987.

Remini, Robert V. *Daniel Webster: The Man and His Time*. New York: W. W. Norton, 1997.

H. Lee Cheek, Jr.
Lee University

Weeks v. United States 232 U.S. 383 (1914) is the origin of the famous "exclusionary rule," the doctrine that evidence seized in violation of the Fourth Amendment's prohibition against unreasonable searches and seizures normally cannot be used as testimony in a criminal trial against the person whose privacy has wrongfully been infringed.

Defendant Fremont Weeks was convicted in the U.S. District Court for the Western District of Missouri of using the U.S. mails to send lottery tickets in violation of federal law. A U.S. marshal, in a warrantless search of Weeks's room, took from a desk drawer some letters that referred to the lottery and showed the latter's guilt. Before the trial the defendant asked that the government return these and other papers to him, which it refused to do. At the trial they were introduced into evidence over his objection. He was convicted and sent to jail. The trial judge admitted that the evidence had been illegally taken but permitted its use against Weeks since it was relevant to the charge against him.

The U.S. Supreme Court, in an opinion by Justice William R. Day, unanimously reversed Weeks's conviction. The Fourth Amendment, Day pointed out, was added to the Bill of Rights in reaction to searches during the colonial era under broadly worded warrants. The amendment enshrined in constitutional law the doctrine that every man's home is his castle. Applying these general principles to the case before him, Day said that if unreasonably seized letters could be used against a criminal suspect, the protection against unreasonable searches accorded by the Fourth Amendment would be valueless and might as well be stricken from the Constitution. Thus the letters should have been given back to the accused and not been used at the trial. (Since in 1914 the Fourth Amendment was not considered binding on the states, Day did not declare it improper for the trial court to have allowed into evidence lottery tickets wrongfully seized by local law enforcement officials.)

Despite its ringing libertarian tones, Day's opinion is thought by quite a few legal experts to be ambiguous on one crucial point: Is the doctrine that evidence illegally seized from a defendant cannot be used at her trial one required by the Fourth Amendment itself or is it simply a judicially created rule of evidence designed to safeguard the Fourth by discouraging the police from conducting fishing expeditions? If it is the latter, it can be discarded if it is shown to have no such deterrent effect. This alleged ambiguity was seized upon by Justice Felix Frankfurter in *Wolf v. Colorado*, 338 U.S. 25 (1949), declaring that though the Fourth was "incorporated," states did not have to adhere to the exclusionary rule. Nonetheless, Justice Tom Clark in *Mapp v. Ohio*, 367 U.S. 643 (1961), making the rule binding on the states as well as the federal government, asserted (p. 649) that "[T]he plain and unequivocal language of Weeks . . . [is] to the effect that the Weeks rule is of constitutional origin."

Later cases, e.g., *U.S. v. Calandra,* 414 U.S. 338 (1974), have readopted the position that the exclusionary principle is no more than a judicially formulated remedy. Actually, whatever the merits of the rule, Clark's interpretation of *Weeks* is the better one. Justice Day asserted outright that the refusal to give the letters back to Weeks at his request was "a denial of the constitutional rights of the accused . . ." (p. 398 of *Weeks*). He thus clearly implied that the closely related right to have them excluded at trial was a prerogative of equal stature.

For more information

MacDougall, Donald V. "The Exclusionary Rule and Its Alternatives: Remedies for Constitutional Violations in Canada and the United States," *Journal of Criminal Law and Criminology* 76 (1985): 608–65.

Daniel C. Kramer
College of Staten Island, CUNY

West Virginia State Board of Education v. Barnette

West Virginia State Board of Education v. Barnette 319 U.S. 624 (1943) is a United States Supreme Court decision that held that a school could not require members of the Jehovah's Witnesses religious group to salute the flag and recite the Pledge of Allegiance because it constitutionally violated their right to freedom of religion.

In *Minersville School District v. Gobitis,* 310 U.S. 586 (1940), the Supreme Court ruled that a state law making it compulsory for students to salute the flag and say the Pledge of Allegiance did not unconstitutionally interfere with their religious freedom even though the flag saluting was contrary to the teachings of their Jehovah's Witnesses faith. In that decision the Court stressed the importance of saluting the flag and reciting the Pledge of Allegiance as important to producing shared national values.

The ultimate foundation of a free society is the binding tie of cohesive sentiment. Such a sentiment is fostered by all those agencies of the mind and spirit which may serve to gather up the traditions of a people, transmit them from generation to generation, and thereby create that continuity of a treasured common life which constitutes a civilization. . . . The flag is the symbol of our national unity, transcending all internal differences, however large, within the framework of the Constitution. (310 U.S. 586, 596.)

Yet the *Gobitis* decision was controversial, with many individuals claiming that forcing them to say the Pledge of Allegiance violated their freedom of religion. In *West Virginia v. Barnette,* the Court agreed and reversed its decision in *Gobitis.*

While acknowledging that fostering national unity or shared values was important, the Court rejected the claim that it could force people to share or adopt values, stating that "National unity as an end which officials may foster by persuasion and example is not in question. The problem is whether under our Constitution compulsion as here employed is a permissible means for its achievement" (319 U.S. 624, 640).

The importance of the *Barnette* decision resides first in recognizing the right of freedom of religion of individuals, even in public schools. *Barnette* is even more significant in terms of its defense of freedom of conscience and the right of people to believe what they wish, without interference from the government, even if they represent or hold unpopular views. Justice Jackson spoke for the Court when he stated that "If there is any fixed star in our constitutional constellation, it is that no official, high or petty, can prescribe what shall be orthodox in politics, nationalism, religion, or other matters of opinion or force citizens to confess by word or act their faith therein" (319 U.S. 624, 642). Developing upon this theme, the Court stated that:

The very purpose of a Bill of Rights was to withdraw certain subjects from the vicissitudes of political controversy, to place them beyond the reach of majorities and officials and to establish them as legal principles to be applied by the courts. One's right to . . . freedom of worship . . . and other fundamental rights may not be submitted to vote; they depend on the outcome of no elections. (319 U.S. 624, 638)

Since the *Barnette* decision, the Court has used that opinion to justify freedom of conscience in numerous decisions, striking down laws that ban flag burning, forced teacher- or student-led prayer in public schools, and a host of other regulations.

For more information

Levy, Leonard W. *The Establishment Clause: Religion and the First Amendment.* New York: Macmillan, 1986.

Schultz, David. "Church-State Relations and the First Amendment." In Schultz, David, ed. *Law and Politics: Unanswered Questions.* New York: Peter Lang Publishing, 1994, pp. 235–56.

David Schultz
Hamline University

Wickard v. Filburn   317 U.S. 111 (1942) was a Supreme Court case upholding the power of Congress to regulate commerce. It is perhaps the best example of how totally the U.S. Supreme Court had changed from striking down to ultimately upholding President Franklin Roosevelt's New Deal policies.

By 1942 FDR had reshaped the Court by appointing eight justices who had been supporters of the New Deal. The dispute arose over the constitutionality of the Agricultural Adjustment Act of 1938 and its 1941 amendment. The purpose of the act was to control the price of wheat. By avoiding surpluses, the amount of wheat being exchanged in interstate commerce would bring stable prices. The secretary of agriculture determined the amount of wheat that farmers could grow. If a farmer's wheat production exceeded the limit set for him, he could either

dispose of the wheat by taking it to the secretary of agriculture or pay a fine of 15 cents per bushel. The 1941 amendment increased the penalty from 15 cents to 49 cents per bushel of excess wheat.

Roscoe Filburn owned a small farm in Ohio where he grew wheat and raised cattle and chickens from which he sold the milk, eggs, and poultry. While he sold some of his wheat, he retained most of it to feed his livestock, use in his home, and plant the next year's crop. Like other farmers, he had experienced a drastic drop in wheat prices due to the decline in wheat export from the previous 10 years. In 1941, in anticipation of another problem year for wheat sales, the secretary of agriculture set a quota for wheat production. Filburn was allotted 11.1 acres with an estimated yield of 20.1 bushels per acre, but he planted 11.9 excess acres of wheat. Under the 1941 amendment of the act Filburn was fined $117.11 for the excess he produced.

Filburn claimed that Congress had exceeded its power under the commerce clause in enacting the Agricultural Act. Filburn filed suit against the secretary of agriculture, Claude Wickard, claiming that regulation of the production of wheat for on-farm consumption was outside the authority of Congress since the activity is purely intrastate and only has an indirect effect on interstate commerce. In a unanimous opinion, the Court held that the term *market,* as defined in the act, included the disposal of wheat through sale, or "by feeding (in any form) to poultry or livestock which, or the products of which, are sold, bartered, or exchanged, or to be so disposed of." This meant that the quota given to Filburn included not only what he had intended to sell but what he would use on the farm. Writing for the Court, Justice Jackson explained that whether or not the activity was intrastate or interstate in character would no longer be a material factor in deciding commerce clause cases. He explained that although Filburn's activities were local, and would not traditionally be included in the idea of commerce, Congress had the authority to regulate them if they had a substantial economic effect on interstate commerce.

The Court further reasoned that the wheat Filburn produced might only have an insignificant effect on the demand for wheat when standing alone, but when combined with the effects of many other farmers, it would be far from trivial. The production of wheat for home consumption by farmers across the country has such a substantial effect on the market price of wheat that it is well within the authority of Congress to regulate such production and consumption.

Wickard was the first case in which the justices abandoned the balancing test between the direct and indirect effects on commerce and broadened the scope of congressional authority. Under this new framework, there was very little that could be construed as purely intrastate and therefore outside the scope of congressional regulation under the commerce clause.

For more information

Benson, Paul Revere. *The Supreme Court and the Commerce Clause, 1937–1970.* New York: Dunellen, 1970.

Frankfurter, Felix. *The Commerce Clause under Marshall, Taney and Waite.* Chicago: Quadrangle Books, 1964.

Susan F. Goodman and Artemus Ward
California State University, Chico

wills and trusts are methods of preserving property and transferring assets to others and are consequences of a system of individual ownership of property.

A will is the legal expression of a person's wishes regarding the disposition of his or her property upon the person's death. Preparing a will is a venerable custom, as wills were written by Egyptians as early as 2548 B.C.E. Testamentary distributions are referred to in the Book of Genesis, and both the Jewish and Islamic codes provided rules governing inheritances.

If someone dies without a will (intestate), the state will decide who is to receive the deceased person's property. This is done under a statutory scheme of fixed formulas that may not reflect the decedent's wishes. Preparing a will allows the author (the testator) to determine the recipients of his or her property.

Wills must be created with some degree of legal formality, but the level varies according to state law. Not all wills must be written or executed with great pomp to be valid. States that recognize nuncupative, or oral, wills often limit the amount or types of assets that can be transferred. Another form of wills, a holographic will or one that is wholly in the handwriting of the testator, is also accepted in most states. The legality of the will and its execution are determined by the laws of the state where the testator is domiciled.

All testators creating a will—of whatever kind—must have testamentary capacity. This is commonly known as being of "sound mind," that is, knowing the natural beneficiaries and extent of one's property and having the intent to designate the recipients of such. The act of creating the will must be voluntary and done without coercion, duress, or fraud. In most states, it is mandatory that the witnesses observe the will being signed by the testator and that they too sign the document. Most wills are also notarized.

Trusts are additional tools used to preserve and control the distribution of property. They may be created in a will—a testamentary trust—or during the lifetime of the trustor or person founding the trust—an inter vivos trust. A trust involves the transfer of property from the trustor to the trustee to manage the property for the benefit of the trustor or other beneficiaries. The most common reason for initiating a trust is to place the management of the assets in the hands of an impartial party as a form of protection for spouses, children, or grandchildren. The trust may be structured to meet the trustor's goals, but it cannot continue forever. It can last no more than 21 years past the lives of designated persons living when the trust is created.

The trustee has a legal duty to manage the trust, to maintain the corpus or body of the trust assets, and to comply with the terms of the trust instrument. Many trustees are corporate entities such as banks and other financial institutions because of their unlimited life spans, since a natural person might not survive as long as the trust. Trustees' actions are governed by the state's Trust Code, the trust instrument itself, and the common law. Trustees who fail in their fiduciary duties are subject to both civil and criminal penalties.

For more information

Atkinson, Thomas F. *Handbook of the Law of Wills,* 2nd ed. St. Paul, Minn.: West Publishing Co., 1953.

Calvi, James V. and Susan Coleman. *American Law and Legal Systems,* 4th ed. Upper Saddle River, N.J.: Prentice Hall, 2000.

Susan Coleman
West Texas A&M University

wiretapping is the traditional term for the interception of telegraph communications and telephone conversations.

The origins of wiretapping are found in eavesdropping and letter opening. With the advent of the electronic era in the late 19th and early 20th centuries, wiretapping, eavesdropping, and "bugging" all became intertwined in law and jurisprudence under the collective term *electronic surveillance.* Today neither government nor private citizens are allowed to wiretap at will. Made possible by scientific and technological inventions such as the telegraph and telephone, wiretapping and electronic surveillance began to emerge late in the 19th century and in the process produced one of the most important decisions in the history of the United States Supreme Court.

In 1928, in the case of *Olmstead v. United States,* the Supreme Court decided, by a margin of 5–4, that the Fourth Amendment's protection against "unreasonable searches and seizures" was not violated by law enforcement officials wiretapping the telephone conversations of a suspected bootlegger. Since there was no actual physical trespass nor seizure of anything tangible, the Court found no violation of the Fourth Amendment. In the words of Chief Justice William Howard Taft, "The language of the amendment cannot be extended and expanded to include telephone wires, reaching to the whole world from the defendant's house or office."

In response, and in one of his most famous dissents, Justice Louis D. Brandeis argued that, since the time of the adoption of the Fourth Amendment eavesdropping had evolved into "[s]ubtler and more far-reaching means of invading privacy[.]" Prophetically, he concluded, "The progress of science in furnishing the government with means of espionage is not likely to stop with wire tapping." Moreover, Brandeis contended, "The makers of our Constitution undertook to secure conditions favorable to the pursuit of happiness . . . . They conferred, as against the government, the right to be let alone—the most comprehensive of rights and the right most valued by civilized men."

The decision in *Olmstead,* however, was law for four decades, until the Court ruled in *Katz v. United States* in 1967 that evidence gathered from a warrantless electronic bug in a public phone booth was inadmissible in court. In the opinion of Justice Potter Stewart, in which the Court introduced and applied the notion of a "legitimate expectation of privacy," wherever one may be, "he is entitled to know that he will remain free from unreasonable searches and seizures." The Court overruled *Olmstead* in *Katz* by concluding that an unconstitutional search and seizure could occur without actual, physical trespass or seizure of real property.

Today the rule is that wiretapping is a form of search and seizure addressed by the Fourth Amendment, and that law enforcement officials may not use wiretaps without court authorization and only within the parameters of the Fourth Amendment. However, as technology in the digital age expands and evolves, so does the debate about the role of electronic surveillance in a constitutional democracy such as ours.

For more information

Amar, Akhil R. *The Constitution and Criminal Procedure: First Principles.* New Haven, Conn.: Yale University Press, 1997.

Olmstead v. United States, 277 U.S. 438 (1928).
Katz v. United States, 389 U.S. 347 (1967).
United States v. United States District Court for the Eastern District of Michigan, 407 U.S. 297 (1972).

Steven K. Shaw
Northwest Nazarene University
Nampa, Idaho

Z

Zenger, John Peter (1697–1746) was a New York newspaper publisher who was arrested and tried in 1735 for the crime of seditious libel. The Zenger case represents an important decision in the creation of what later would be the First Amendment right to free speech and the ability of the individual to criticize the government.

Seditious libel is the publishing of writings critical of a government that are designed to incite the overthrow of that government by force or other unlawful means. Zenger's case is historically significant for two reasons: First, it is a very early example of successful arguments in favor of the freedom of the press. Second, it is one of the earliest known examples of jury nullification. Jury nullification occurs when, despite clear evidence of guilt under a criminal statute, the jury refuses to convict the defendant, typically for political reasons or because the jury believes the law is unjust.

Zenger's newspaper, the *New York Weekly Journal,* was consistently critical of the oppressive policies of the English-appointed colonial governor William Cosby. After about a year of such publications, Cosby issued a proclamation condemning the newspaper and sought criminal indictments of persons responsible for the criticism. However, because the paper was popular with ordinary citizens, two grand juries refused to indict anyone affiliated with the paper, and so the Governor's Council ordered Zenger, as publisher, arrested and charged with seditious libel. Zenger's bail was set at an exceptionally high amount, which he was unable to post and so he was held in prison for months before his trial.

Zenger's trial was a high-profile event that attracted intense public interest and attention. Throughout, the trial judge, Chief Justice James Delancey (a royalist who was appointed by Governor Cosby), was antagonistic to Zenger's attorneys. After Delancey disbarred Zenger's first set of attorneys, he was represented by the well-known Philadelphia lawyer Andrew Hamilton. Keenly aware of Delancey's loyalty to the governor and hostility to Zenger, Hamilton (contrary to the legal procedure of the time) pleaded all aspects of the case directly to the jury. Despite the fact that Delancey directed the jury to return a verdict of guilty, it promptly returned a verdict of not guilty. It is vital to note that although under the law of the time Zenger was certainly guilty of seditious libel, the jury decided—despite the law—that because Zenger's writings were true he should go free. While Hamilton's use of jury nullification is celebrated in this case, in modern times it remains controversial. On the one hand, Hamilton's argument that jurors are the best representatives of the citizenry's sense of fairness, and are thus best situated to resolve mixed issues of fact and law, is powerful against patently unjust laws, such as were on the books in colonial America. On the other hand, the practice of jury nullification is rife with the potential for misuse and so juries today are sworn to uphold the law. Some argue that jury nullification is a "political right" of a jury to return a verdict of not guilty even in defiance of the judge's instructions and the law; others argue that jury nullification is inconsistent with a fair administration of the rule of law.

Under the colonial law of the time, it was no defense to a charge of libel that the statements were true. This was the law because colonial authorities believed that criticism of the government would undermine its stability. Ironically, truthful libel was considered an even greater crime because it constituted a greater threat to government stability since it was more likely to be believed. Appealing to the jury's sense of fairness and encouraging it to find Zenger not guilty, Hamilton established a precedent that a statement, even if harmful to someone's reputation, is not libelous if it is true. The right of the press to publish true statements without fear of prosecution is the core of the freedom of the press, which in turn is essential to a free society where citizens may criticize the government without fear of punishment. As such, the case of John Peter Zenger stands proudly in the American legal tradition as an early example of a jury of ordinary citizens affirming the right of a free press in the service of a free American society.

For more information

Putnam, William Lowell. *John Peter Zenger and the Fundamental Freedom.* Jefferson, N.C.: McFarland, 1997.

Alexander, James. *A Brief Narrative of the Case and Trial of John Peter Zenger, Printer of the New York Weekly Journal,* 2nd ed., edited by Stanley Nider Katz. Cambridge, Mass.: Belknap Press of Harvard University Press, 1972.

Marc D. Weiner
Rutgers University

zoning   is a type of land-use regulation whose objective is to keep development of land in a community under reasonable control for the benefit of the residents.

Zoning laws divide a community into districts and establish what uses of land are permitted in each district, e.g., residential, commercial, industrial, agricultural, or some combination of these. Zoning regulations generally determine what types of structures may be built in each district and may also prescribe the minimum lot size and how much of the lot must remain free of structures. The source of zoning power is the community's "police power," which enables the government to enact legislation to promote and protect the health, safety, morals, and general welfare of the community. Under the police power, zoning protects the health and welfare of the residents and promotes productive use of land for personal and business purposes. In the 20th century, zoning became an important tool of community planning. Most zoning regulation is carried out on the local level; however, the federal government's influence on zoning has increased in recent decades in the form of federal land-use regulation of the environment (such as laws affecting coastal zones, wetlands, and clean air and water).

Zoning places limits on the individual citizen's freedom to make use of his or her land and thus may affect the market value of that land. These factors have led to many legal challenges of zoning regulations. The validity of zoning requires that such regulations be a valid exercise of the police power, and zoning laws have been scrutinized under several important constitutional perspectives. Due process of law requires that zoning regulations may not be arbitrary, capricious, or unreasonable, and while reasonable zoning regulations are not considered to be a taking of land for governmental purposes without payment of just compensation, federal judicial decisions have held that zoning laws that deprive the landowner of the entire use value of his land and provide little benefit to the community are confiscatory. Many challenges to zoning have been made under the guarantee of equal protection of the laws. Zoning may not be discriminatory. It has to be fair and applied impartially in order to be legally valid. One type of zoning that has been consistently held invalid is so-called exclusionary zoning, which is zoning intended to exclude persons of a particular race or income level. Early in the 20th century, the United States Supreme Court invalidated racially motivated exclusionary zoning (*Buchanan v. Warley*, 245 U.S. 60 [1917]).

A major key to valid zoning is the creation of a comprehensive zoning plan that considers all the residents and potential land uses in a fair and reasonable manner. So-called spot zoning, zoning laws directed at particular persons or uses without being integrated into a comprehensive plan, are subject to invalidation as being outside the police power of the community. Zoning and other land-use regulations limit individual freedom in the interests of the community as a whole. As concerns about the quality of life in our communities grow, zoning regulations are likely to continue to be refined and expanded.

For more information

Bullard, Robert D. "Building Just, Safe, and Healthy Communities," *Tulane Environmental Law Journal* 12.2 (spring 1999): 373–404.

Celia A. Sgroi
State University of New York, Oswego

Zorach v. Clauson   343 U.S. 306 (1952) held that public school students could be released during school hours for religious instruction not held on school grounds.

A New York City program allowed students, at their parents' choice, to be excused from school to attend religious education held elsewhere during school hours; students who did not attend the classes remained in school. The Supreme Court considered whether this program violated the establishment clause of the First Amendment. Kenneth W. Greenawalt argued for Zorach that the program was impermissibly coercive and went too far toward establishing religion. Michael A. Costaldi and Charles H. Tuttle defended the program, arguing that it neither coerced individuals nor established religion. Numerous states filed their support for the New York City program. The case was argued on January 31 and February 1, 1952, and decided on April 28. In a 6–3 decision, Justice Douglas, speaking for the Court, ruled in favor of Clauson and upheld the New York City released-time program. Justices Black, Frankfurter, and Jackson dissented.

The *Zorach* decision was the Court's second released-time case. It came only a few years after the Court struck down a released-time program in *McCollum v. Board of Education*. In *McCollum*, the Court had held, with only one dissent, that a released-time program in which religious classes were held on school grounds violated the establishment clause. Justice Black wrote for the Court that such a program unconstitutionally promoted religion and had a coercive effect on students.

In his opinion for the Court in *Zorach*, Justice Douglas had to explain the Court's change of opinion—and his own—about released-time programs. Douglas argued that the cases differed crucially in that *McCollum* concerned the use of the school building for religious education and *Zorach* did not. Since the religious classes in *Zorach* were held elsewhere, the state was not unconstitutionally promoting religion. Furthermore, the socially coercive effects of having the religious classes held in the school were not present in the New York City program. Douglas also argued, contrary to his later writings, that religion was a part of American culture, and that religious education was in the public interest.

In his dissent, Justice Black opposed both Douglas's understanding of U.S. culture and his interpretation of *McCollum*. Black argues that a better understanding of the culture embraces the ideal of separation of church and state. He finds no significant difference between the programs in *Zorach* and *McCollum*. Black argues that the *McCollum* decision would have been no different had the classes been held outside the school, because the issue was the use of the administrative apparatus of the public school system to aid religious institutions. He argues that the public schools' released-time program helps religious institutions attract a body of young people who might not have attended such classes of their own volition.

In his dissent, Justice Frankfurter argues that simply letting school out early would be a constitutionally acceptable way of promoting religious education. Frankfurter sees *Zorach* as a Fourteenth Amendment equal protection issue. Religious and nonreligious students receive unequal treatment under the released-time program because formalized religious instruction is substituted for other school activity that students who do not join the release-time program are compelled to attend. Justice Jackson echoes many of Frankfurter's concerns, arguing that the state is attempting to accomplish indirectly what would be unconstitutional if done directly, and that the use of school district truant officers constitutes state support of religion. In later cases *Zorach* has been used to advocate permissible state accommodation to religion. However, in later religion cases Justice Douglas would reject his accommodationist argument in *Zorach* and advocate the strict separation of church and state.

For more information

Fraser, James W. *Between Church and State: Religion and Public Education in a Multicultural America.* New York: St. Martin's Press, 1999.

Hunt, Thomas C., and James C. Carper. *Religion and Schooling in Contemporary America: Confronting Our Cultural Pluralism.* New York: Garland Publishing, 1997.

Kahn, Ronald. *The Supreme Court and Constitutional Theory, 1953–1993.* Lawrence: University Press of Kansas, 1994.

Ronald Kahn
Oberlin College

APPENDICES

DECLARATION OF INDEPENDENCE

Action of Second Continental Congress, July 4, 1776.

The unanimous Declaration of the thirteen United States of America.

We hold these truths to be self-evident, that all men are created equal, that they are endowed by their Creator with certain unalienable Rights, that among these are Life, Liberty, and the pursuit of Happiness. That to secure these rights, Governments are instituted among Men, deriving their just powers from the consent of the governed. That whenever any Form of Government becomes destructive of these ends, it is the Right of the People to alter or to abolish it, and to institute new Government, laying its foundation on such principles and organizing its powers in such form, as to them shall seem most likely to effect their Safety and Happiness. Prudence, indeed, will dictate that Governments long established should not be changed for light and transient causes; and accordingly all experience hath shown, that mankind are more disposed to suffer, while evils are sufferable, than to right themselves by abolishing the forms to which they are accustomed. But when a long train of abuses and usurpations, pursuing invariably the same Object, evinces a design to reduce them under absolute Despotism, it is their right, it is their duty, to throw off such Government, and to provide new Guards for their future security. Such has been the patient sufferance of these Colonies; and such is now the necessity which constrains them to alter their former Systems of Government. The history of the present King of Great Britain is a history of repeated injuries and usurpations, all having in direct object the establishment of an absolute Tyranny over these States. To prove this, let Facts be submitted to a candid world.

HE has refused his Assent to Laws, the most wholesome and necessary for the public good.

HE has forbidden his Governors to pass Laws of immediate and pressing importance, unless suspended in their operation till his Assent should be obtained; and when so suspended, he has utterly neglected to attend to them.

HE has refused to pass other Laws for the accommodation of large districts of people, unless those people would relinquish the right of Representation in the Legislature, a right inestimable to them and formidable to tyrants only.

HE has called together legislative bodies at places unusual, uncomfortable, and distant from the depository of their public Records, for the sole purpose of fatiguing them into compliance with his measures.

HE has dissolved Representative Houses repeatedly, for opposing with manly firmness his invasions on the rights of the people.

HE has refused for a long time, after such dissolutions, to cause others to be elected; whereby the Legislative powers, incapable of Annihilation, have returned to the People at large for their exercise; the State remaining in the mean time exposed to all the dangers of invasion from without, and convulsion within.

HE has endeavoured to prevent the population of these States; for that purpose obstructing the Laws of Naturalization of Foreigners; refusing to pass others to encourage their migrations hither, and raising the conditions of new Appropriations of Lands.

HE has obstructed the Administration of Justice, by refusing his Assent to Laws for establishing Judiciary powers.

HE has made Judges dependent on his Will alone, for the tenure of their offices, and the amount and payment of their salaries.

HE has erected a multitude of New Offices, and sent hither swarms of Officers to harass our People, and eat out their substance.

HE has kept among us, in times of peace, Standing Armies without the Consent of our legislatures.

HE has affected to render the Military independent of and superior to the Civil power.

HE has combined with others to subject us to a jurisdiction foreign to our constitution, and unacknowledged by our laws; giving his Assent to their Acts of pretended Legislation:

FOR quartering large bodies of armed troops among us:

FOR protecting them, by a mock Trial, from Punishment for any Murders which they should commit on the Inhabitants of these States:

FOR cutting off our Trade with all parts of the world:

FOR imposing Taxes on us without our Consent:

FOR depriving us in many cases, of the benefits of Trial by Jury:

FOR transporting us beyond Seas to be tried for pretended offences:

FOR abolishing the free System of English Laws in a neighbouring Province, establishing therein an Arbitrary government, and enlarging its Boundaries so as to render it at once an example and fit instrument for introducing the same absolute rule into these Colonies:

FOR taking away our Charters, abolishing our most valuable Laws, and altering fundamentally the Forms of our Governments:

FOR suspending our own Legislatures, and declaring themselves invested with power to legislate for us in all cases whatsoever.

HE has abdicated Government here, by declaring us out of his Protection and waging War against us.

HE has plundered our seas, ravaged our Coasts, burnt our towns, and destroyed the Lives of our people.

HE is at this time transporting large armies of foreign mercenaries to compleat the works of death, desolation and tyranny, already begun with circumstances of Cruelty & perfidy scarcely paralleled in the most barbarous ages, and totally unworthy the Head of a civilized nation.

HE has constrained our fellow Citizens taken Captive on the high Seas to bear Arms against their Country, to become the executioners of their friends and Brethren, or to fall themselves by their Hands.

HE has excited domestic insurrections amongst us, and has endeavoured to bring on the inhabitants of our frontiers, the merciless Indian Savages, whose known rule of warfare, is an undistinguished destruction of all ages, sexes and conditions.

IN every stage of these Oppressions We have Petitioned for Redress in the most humble terms: Our repeated Petitions have been answered only by repeated injury. A Prince, whose character is thus marked by every act which may define a Tyrant, is unfit to be the ruler of a free people.

NOR have We been wanting in attention to our British brethren. We have warned them from time to time of attempts by their legislature to extend an unwarrantable jurisdiction over us. We have reminded them of the circumstances of our emigration and settlement here. We have appealed to their native justice and magnanimity, and we have conjured them by the ties of our common kindred to disavow these usurpations, which would inevitably interrupt our connections and correspondence. They too have been deaf to the voice of justice and of consanguinity. We must, therefore, acquiesce in the necessity, which denounces our Separation, and hold them, as we hold the rest of mankind, Enemies in War, in Peace Friends.

WE, therefore, the Representatives of the UNITED STATES OF AMERICA, in GENERAL CONGRESS, Assembled, appealing to the Supreme Judge of the world for the rectitude of our intentions, do, in the Name, and by Authority of the good People of these Colonies, solemnly publish and declare, That these United Colonies are, and of Right ought to be FREE AND INDEPENDENT STATES; that they are Absolved from all Allegiance to the British Crown, and that all political connection between them and the State of Great Britain, is and ought to be totally dissolved; and that as FREE AND INDEPENDENT STATES, they have full Power to levy War, conclude Peace, contract Alliances, establish Commerce, and to do all other Acts and Things which INDEPENDENT STATES may of right do. And for the support of this Declaration,

with a firm reliance on the Protection of Divine Providence, we mutually pledge to each other our Lives, our Fortunes and our sacred Honor.

JOHN HANCOCK.

Georgia
BUTTON GWINNETT
LYMAN HALL
GEO. WALTON
North Carolina
WILLIAM HOOPER
JOSEPH HEWES
JOHN PENN
South Carolina
EDWARD RUTLEDGE
THOMAS HEYWARD, JR.
THOMAS LYNCH, JR.
ARTHUR MIDDLETON
Maryland
SAMUEL CHASE
WILLIAM PACA
THOMAS STONE
CHARLES CARROLL
OF CARROLLTON
Virginia
GEORGE WYTHE
RICHARD HENRY LEE
THOMAS JEFFERSON
BENJAMIN HARRISON
THOMAS NELSON, JR.
FRANCIS LIGHTFOOT LEE
CARTER BRAXTON
Pennsylvania
ROBERT MORRIS
BENJAMIN RUSH
BENJAMIN FRANKLIN
JOHN MORTON
GEORGE CLYMER
JAMES SMITH
GEORGE TAYLOR
JAMES WILSON
GEORGE ROSS
Delaware
CAESAR RODNEY
GEORGE READ
THOMAS M'KEAN
New York
WILLIAM FLOYD

PHILIP LIVINGSTON
FRANCIS LEWIS
LEWIS MORRIS

New Jersey
RICHARD STOCKTON
JOHN WITHERSPOON
FRANCIS HOPKINS
JOHN HART
ABRAHAM CLARK

New Hampshire
JOSIAH BARTLETT
WILLIAM WHIPPLE
MATTHEW THORNTON

Massachusetts-Bay
SAMUEL ADAMS
JOHN ADAMS

ROBERT TREAT PAINE
ELBRIDGE GERRY

Rhode Island
STEPHEN HOPKINS
WILLIAM ELLERY

Connecticut
ROGER SHERMAN
SAMUEL HUNTINGTON
WILLIAM WILLIAMS
OLIVER WOLCOTT

IN CONGRESS, JANUARY 18, 1777.

ARTICLES OF CONFEDERATION

Agreed to by Congress November 15, 1777 then ratified and in force, March 1, 1781.

Preamble

To all to whom these Presents shall come, we the undersigned Delegates of the States affixed to our Names send greeting.

Articles of Confederation and perpetual Union between the states of New Hampshire, Massachusetts-bay Rhode Island and Providence Plantations, Connecticut, New York, New Jersey, Pennsylvania, Delaware, Maryland, Virginia, North Carolina, South Carolina and Georgia.

ARTICLE I

The Stile of this Confederacy shall be "The United States of America".

ARTICLE II

Each state retains its sovereignty, freedom, and independence, and every power, jurisdiction, and right, which is not by this Confederation expressly delegated to the United States, in Congress assembled.

ARTICLE III

The said States hereby severally enter into a firm league of friendship with each other, for their common defense, the security of their liberties, and their mutual and general welfare, binding themselves to assist each other, against all force offered to, or attacks made upon them, or any of them, on account of religion, sovereignty, trade, or any other pretense whatever.

ARTICLE IV

The better to secure and perpetuate mutual friendship and intercourse among the people of the different States in this Union, the free inhabitants of each of these States, paupers, vagabonds, and fugitives from justice excepted, shall be entitled to all privileges and immunities of free citizens in the several States; and the people of each State shall free ingress and regress to and from any other State, and shall enjoy therein all the privileges of trade and commerce, subject to the same duties, impositions, and restrictions as the inhabitants thereof respectively, provided that such restrictions shall not extend so far as to prevent the removal of property imported into any State, to any other State, of which the owner is an inhabitant; provided also that no imposition, duties or restriction shall be laid by any State, on the property of the United States, or either of them.

If any person guilty of, or charged with, treason, felony, or other high misdemeanor in any State, shall flee from justice, and be found in any of the United States, he shall, upon demand of the Governor or executive power of the State from which he fled, be delivered up and removed to the State having jurisdiction of his offense.

Full faith and credit shall be given in each of these States to the records, acts, and judicial proceedings of the courts and magistrates of every other State.

ARTICLE V

For the most convenient management of the general interests of the United States, delegates shall be annually appointed in such manner as the legislatures of each State shall direct, to meet in Congress on the first Monday in November, in every year, with a power reserved to each State to recall its delegates, or any of them, at any time within the year, and to send others in their stead for the remainder of the year.

No State shall be represented in Congress by less than two, nor more than seven members; and no person shall be capable of being a delegate for more than three years in any term of six years; nor shall any person, being a delegate, be capable of holding any office under the United States, for which he, or another for his benefit, receives any salary, fees or emolument of any kind.

Each State shall maintain its own delegates in a meeting of the States, and while they act as members of the committee of the States.

In determining questions in the United States in Congress assembled, each State shall have one vote.

Freedom of speech and debate in Congress shall not be impeached or questioned in any court or place out of Congress, and the members of Congress shall be protected in their persons from arrests or imprisonments, during the time of their going to and from, and attendence on Congress, except for treason, felony, or breach of the peace.

ARTICLE VI

No State, without the consent of the United States in Congress assembled, shall send any embassy to, or receive any embassy from, or enter into any conference, agreement, alliance or treaty with any King, Prince or State; nor shall any person holding any office of profit or trust under the United States, or any of them, accept any present, emolument, office or title of any kind whatever from any King, Prince or foreign State; nor shall the United States in Congress assembled, or any of them, grant any title of nobility.

No two or more States shall enter into any treaty, confederation or alliance whatever between them, without the consent of the United States in Congress assembled, specifying accurately the purposes for which the same is to be entered into, and how long it shall continue.

No State shall lay any imposts or duties, which may interfere with any stipulations in treaties, entered into by the United States in Congress assembled, with any King, Prince or State, in pursuance of any treaties already proposed by Congress, to the courts of France and Spain.

No vessel of war shall be kept up in time of peace by any State, except such number only, as shall be deemed necessary by the United States in Congress assembled, for the defense of such State, or its trade; nor shall any body of forces be kept up by any State in time of peace, except such number only, as in the judgement of the United States in Congress assembled, shall be deemed requisite to garrison the forts necessary for the defense of such State; but every State shall always keep up a well-regulated and disciplined militia, sufficiently armed and accoutered, and shall provide and constantly have ready for use, in public stores, a due number of filed pieces and tents, and a proper quantity of arms, ammunition and camp equipage.

No State shall engage in any war without the consent of the United States in Congress assembled, unless such State be actually invaded by enemies, or shall have received certain advice of a resolution being formed by some nation of Indians to invade such State, and the danger is so imminent as not to admit of a delay till the United States in Congress assembled can be consulted; nor shall any State grant commissions to any ships or vessels of war, nor letters of marque or reprisal, except it be after a declaration of war by the United States in Congress assembled, and then only against the Kingdom or State and the subjects thereof, against which war has been so declared, and under such regulations as shall be established by the United States in Congress assembled, unless such State be infested by pirates, in which case vessels of war may be fitted out for that occasion, and kept so long as the danger shall continue, or until the United States in Congress assembled shall determine otherwise.

ARTICLE VII

When land forces are raised by any State for the common defense, all officers of or under the rank of colonel, shall be appointed by the legislature of each State respectively, by whom such forces shall be raised, or in such manner as such State shall direct, and all vacancies shall be filled up by the State which first made the appointment.

ARTICLE VIII

All charges of war, and all other expenses that shall be incurred for the common defense or gen-

eral welfare, and allowed by the United States in Congress assembled, shall be defrayed out of a common treasury, which shall be supplied by the several States in proportion to the value of all land within each State, granted or surveyed for any person, as such land and the buildings and improvements thereon shall be estimated according to such mode as the United States in Congress assembled, shall from time to time direct and appoint.

The taxes for paying that proportion shall be laid and levied by the authority and direction of the legislatures of the several States within the time agreed upon by the United States in Congress assembled.

ARTICLE IX

The United States in Congress assembled, shall have the sole and exclusive right and power of determining on peace and war, except in the cases mentioned in the sixth article – of sending and receiving ambassadors – entering into treaties and alliances, provided that no treaty of commerce shall be made whereby the legislative power of the respective States shall be restrained from imposing such imposts and duties on foreigners, as their own people are subjected to, or from prohibiting the exportation or importation of any species of goods or commodities whatsoever – of establishing rules for deciding in all cases, what captures on land or water shall be legal, and in what manner prizes taken by land or naval forces in the service of the United States shall be divided or appropriated – of granting letters of marque and reprisal in times of peace – appointing courts for the trial of piracies and felonies commited on the high seas and establishing courts for receiving and determining finally appeals in all cases of captures, provided that no member of Congress shall be appointed a judge of any of the said courts.

The United States in Congress assembled shall also be the last resort on appeal in all disputes and differences now subsisting or that hereafter may arise between two or more States concerning boundary, jurisdiction or any other causes whatever; which authority shall always be exercised in the manner following.

Whenever the legislative or executive authority or lawful agent of any State in controversy with another shall present a petition to Congress stating the matter in question and praying for a hearing, notice thereof shall be given by order of Congress to the legislative or executive authority of the other State in controversy, and a day assigned for the appearance of the parties by their lawful agents, who shall then be directed to appoint by joint consent, commissioners or judges to constitute a court for hearing and determining the matter in question: but if they cannot agree, Congress shall name three persons out of each of the United States, and from the list of such persons each party shall alternately strike out one, the petitioners beginning, until the number shall be reduced to thirteen; and from that number not less than seven, nor more than nine names as Congress shall direct, shall in the presence of Congress be drawn out by lot, and the persons whose names shall be so drawn or any five of them, shall be commissioners or judges, to hear and finally determine the controversy, so always as a major part of the judges who shall hear the cause shall agree in the determination: and if either party shall neglect to attend at the day appointed, without showing reasons, which Congress shall judge sufficient, or being present shall refuse to strike, the Congress shall proceed to nominate three persons out of each State, and the secretary of Congress shall strike in behalf of such party absent or refusing; and the judgement and sentence of the court to be appointed, in the manner before prescribed, shall be final and conclusive; and if any of the parties shall refuse to submit to the authority of such court, or to appear or defend their claim or cause, the court shall nevertheless proceed to pronounce sentence, or judgement, which shall in like manner be final and decisive,

the judgement or sentence and other proceedings being in either case transmitted to Congress, and lodged among the acts of Congress for the security of the parties concerned: provided that every commissioner, before he sits in judgement, shall take an oath to be administered by one of the judges of the supreme or superior court of the State, where the cause shall be tried, 'well and truly to hear and determine the matter in question, according to the best of his judgement, without favor, affection or hope of reward': provided also, that no State shall be deprived of territory for the benefit of the United States.

All controversies concerning the private right of soil claimed under different grants of two or more States, whose jurisdictions as they may respect such lands, and the States which passed such grants are adjusted, the said grants or either of them being at the same time claimed to have originated antecedent to such settlement of jurisdiction, shall on the petition of either party to the Congress of the United States, be finally determined as near as may be in the same manner as is before prescribed for deciding disputes respecting territorial jurisdiction between different States.

The United States in Congress assembled shall also have the sole and exclusive right and power of regulating the alloy and value of coin struck by their own authority, or by that of the respective States – fixing the standards of weights and measures throughout the United States – regulating the trade and managing all affairs with the Indians, not members of any of the States, provided that the legislative right of any State within its own limits be not infringed or violated – establishing or regulating post offices from one State to another, throughout all the United States, and exacting such postage on the papers passing through the same as may be requisite to defray the expenses of the said office – appointing all officers of the land forces, in the service of the United States, excepting regimental officers – appointing all the officers of the naval forces, and commissioning all officers whatever in the service of the United States – making rules for the government and regulation of the said land and naval forces, and directing their operations.

The United States in Congress assembled shall have authority to appoint a committee, to sit in the recess of Congress, to be denominated 'A Committee of the States', and to consist of one delegate from each State; and to appoint such other committees and civil officers as may be necessary for managing the general affairs of the United States under their direction – to appoint one of their members to preside, provided that no person be allowed to serve in the office of president more than one year in any term of three years; to ascertain the necessary sums of money to be raised for the service of the United States, and to appropriate and apply the same for defraying the public expenses – to borrow money, or emit bills on the credit of the United States, transmitting every half-year to the respective States an account of the sums of money so borrowed or emitted – to build and equip a navy – to agree upon the number of land forces, and to make requisitions from each State for its quota, in proportion to the number of white inhabitants in such State; which requisition shall be binding, and thereupon the legislature of each State shall appoint the regimental officers, raise the men and cloath, arm and equip them in a solid-like manner, at the expense of the United States; and the officers and men so cloathed, armed and equipped shall march to the place appointed, and within the time agreed on by the United States in Congress assembled. But if the United States in Congress assembled shall, on consideration of circumstances judge proper that any State should not raise men, or should raise a smaller number of men than the quota thereof, such extra number shall be raised, officered, cloathed, armed and equipped in the same manner as the quota of each State, unless the legislature of such State shall judge that such extra number cannot be safely spread out in the same, in which case they shall raise, officer,

cloath, arm and equip as many of such extra number as they judge can be safely spared. And the officers and men so cloathed, armed, and equipped, shall march to the place appointed, and within the time agreed on by the United States in Congress assembled.

The United States in Congress assembled shall never engage in a war, nor grant letters of marque or reprisal in time of peace, nor enter into any treaties or alliances, nor coin money, nor regulate the value thereof, nor ascertain the sums and expenses necessary for the defense and welfare of the United States, or any of them, nor emit bills, nor borrow money on the credit of the United States, nor appropriate money, nor agree upon the number of vessels of war, to be built or purchased, or the number of land or sea forces to be raised, nor appoint a commander in chief of the army or navy, unless nine States assent to the same: nor shall a question on any other point, except for adjourning from day to day be determined, unless by the votes of the majority of the United States in Congress assembled.

The Congress of the United States shall have power to adjourn to any time within the year, and to any place within the United States, so that no period of adjournment be for a longer duration than the space of six months, and shall publish the journal of their proceedings monthly, except such parts thereof relating to treaties, alliances or military operations, as in their judgement require secrecy; and the yeas and nays of the delegates of each State on any question shall be entered on the Journal, when it is desired by any delegates of a State, or any of them, at his or their request shall be furnished with a transcript of the said journal, except such parts as are above excepted, to lay before the legislatures of the several States.

ARTICLE X

The Committee of the States, or any nine of them, shall be authorized to execute, in the recess of Congress, such of the powers of Congress as the United States in Congress assembled, by the consent of the nine States, shall from time to time think expedient to vest them with; provided that no power be delegated to the said Committee, for the exercise of which, by the Articles of Confederation, the voice of nine States in the Congress of the United States assembled be requisite.

ARTICLE XI

Canada acceding to this confederation, and adjoining in the measures of the United States, shall be admitted into, and entitled to all the advantages of this Union; but no other colony shall be admitted into the same, unless such admission be agreed to by nine States.

ARTICLE XII

All bills of credit emitted, monies borrowed, and debts contracted by, or under the authority of Congress, before the assembling of the United States, in pursuance of the present confederation, shall be deemed and considered as a charge against the United States, for payment and satisfaction whereof the said United States, and the public faith are hereby solemnly pleged.

ARTICLE XIII

Every State shall abide by the determination of the United States in Congress assembled, on all questions which by this confederation are submitted to them. And the Articles of this Confederation shall be inviolably observed by every State, and the Union shall be perpetual; nor shall any alteration at any time hereafter be made in any of them; unless such alteration be agreed to in a Congress of the United States, and be afterwards confirmed by the legislatures of every State.

CONCLUSION

And Whereas it hath pleased the Great Governor of the World to incline the hearts of the legislatures we respectively represent in Congress, to approve of, and to authorize us to ratify the said Articles of Confederation and perpetual Union. Know Ye that we the undersigned delegates, by virtue of the power and authority to us given for that purpose, do by these presents, in the name and in behalf of our respective constituents, fully and entirely ratify and confirm each and every of the said Articles of Confederation and perpetual Union, and all and singular the matters and things therein contained: And we do further solemnly plight and engage the faith of our respective constituents, that they shall abide by the determinations of the United States in Congress assembled, on all questions, which by the said Confederation are submitted to them. And that the Articles thereof shall be inviolably observed by the States we respectively represent, and that the Union shall be perpetual.

SIGNATORIES

In Witness whereof we have hereunto set our hands in Congress. Done at Philadelphia in the State of Pennsylvania the ninth day of July in the Year of our Lord One Thousand Seven Hundred and Seventy-Eight, and in the Third Year of the independence of America.

On the part and behalf of the State of New Hampshire:

Josiah Bartlett
John Wentworth Junior

On the part and behalf of the State of Massachusetts Bay:

John Hancock
Francis Dana
Samuel Adams
James Lovell

Elbridge Gerry
Samuel Holten

On the part and behalf of the State of Rhode Island and Providence Plantations:

William Ellery
John Collins
Henry Marchant

On the part and behalf of the State of Connecticut:

Roger Sherman
Titus Hosmer
Samuel Huntington
Andrew Adams
Oliver Wolcott

On the Part and Behalf of the State of New York:

James Duane
William Duer
Francis Lewis
Gouverneur Morris

On the Part and in Behalf of the State of New Jersey:

Jonathan Witherspoon
Nathaniel Scudder

On the part and behalf of the State of Pennsylvania:

Robert Morris
William Clingan
Daniel Roberdeau
Joseph Reed
John Bayard Smith

On the part and behalf of the State of Delaware:

Thomas Mckean
John Dickinson
Nicholas Van Dyke

On the part and behalf of the State of Maryland:

John Hanson
Daniel Carroll

On the Part and Behalf of the State of Virginia:

Richard Henry Lee
Jonathan Harvie
John Banister
Francis Lightfoot Lee
Thomas Adams

On the part and Behalf of the State of No Carolina:

John Penn
Corns Harnett
Jonathan Williams

On the part and behalf of the State of South Carolina:

Henry Laurens
Richard Hutson
William Henry Drayton
Thomas Heyward Junior
Jonathan Matthews

On the part and behalf of the State of Georgia:

Jonathan Walton
Edward Telfair
Edward Langworthy

THE CONSTITUTION OF THE UNITED STATES OF AMERICA

We the people of the United States, in order to form a more perfect union, establish justice, insure domestic tranquility, provide for the common defense, promote the general welfare, and secure the blessings of liberty to ourselves and our posterity, do ordain and establish this Constitution for the United States of America.

ARTICLE I

Section 1. All legislative powers herein granted shall be vested in a Congress of the United States, which shall consist of a Senate and House of Representatives.

Section 2. The House of Representatives shall be composed of members chosen every second year by the people of the several states, and the electors in each state shall have the qualifications requisite for electors of the most numerous branch of the state legislature.

No person shall be a Representative who shall not have attained to the age of twenty five years, and been seven years a citizen of the United States, and who shall not, when elected, be an inhabitant of that state in which he shall be chosen.

Representatives and direct taxes shall be apportioned among the several states which may be included within this union, according to their respective numbers, which shall be determined by adding to the whole number of free persons, including those bound to service for a term of years, and excluding Indians not taxed, three fifths of all other Persons. The actual Enumeration shall be made within three years after the first meeting of the Congress of the United States, and within every subsequent term of ten years, in such manner as they shall by law direct. The number of Representatives shall not exceed one for every thirty thousand, but each state shall have at least one Representative; and until such enumeration shall be made, the state of New Hampshire shall be entitled to choose three, Massachusetts eight, Rhode Island and Providence Plantations one, Connecticut five, New York six, New Jersey four, Pennsylvania eight, Delaware one, Maryland six, Virginia ten,

North Carolina five, South Carolina five, and Georgia three.

When vacancies happen in the Representation from any state, the executive authority thereof shall issue writs of election to fill such vacancies.

The House of Representatives shall choose their speaker and other officers; and shall have the sole power of impeachment.

Section 3. The Senate of the United States shall be composed of two Senators from each state, chosen by the legislature thereof, for six years; and each Senator shall have one vote. Immediately after they shall be assembled in consequence of the first election, they shall be divided as equally as may be into three classes. The seats of the Senators of the first class shall be vacated at the expiration of the second year, of the second class at the expiration of the fourth year, and the third class at the expiration of the sixth year, so that one third may be chosen every second year; and if vacancies happen by resignation, or otherwise, during the recess of the legislature of any state, the executive thereof may make temporary appointments until the next meeting of the legislature, which shall then fill such vacancies.

No person shall be a Senator who shall not have attained to the age of thirty years, and been nine years a citizen of the United States and who shall not, when elected, be an inhabitant of that state for which he shall be chosen.

The Vice President of the United States shall be President of the Senate, but shall have no vote, unless they be equally divided.

The Senate shall choose their other officers, and also a President pro tempore, in the absence of the Vice President, or when he shall exercise the office of President of the United States.

The Senate shall have the sole power to try all impeachments. When sitting for that purpose, they shall be on oath or affirmation. When the President of the United States is tried, the Chief Justice shall preside: And no person shall be convicted without the concurrence of two thirds of the members present.

Judgment in cases of impeachment shall not extend further than to removal from office, and disqualification to hold and enjoy any office of honor, trust or profit under the United States: but the party convicted shall nevertheless be liable and subject to indictment, trial, judgment and punishment, according to law.

Section 4. The times, places and manner of holding elections for Senators and Representatives, shall be prescribed in each state by the legislature thereof; but the Congress may at any time by law make or alter such regulations, except as to the places of choosing Senators.

The Congress shall assemble at least once in every year, and such meeting shall be on the first Monday in December, unless they shall by law appoint a different day.

Section 5. Each House shall be the judge of the elections, returns and qualifications of its own members, and a majority of each shall constitute a quorum to do business; but a smaller number may adjourn from day to day, and may be authorized to compel the attendance of absent members, in such manner, and under such penalties as each House may provide.

Each House may determine the rules of its proceedings, punish its members for disorderly behavior, and, with the concurrence of two thirds, expel a member.

Each House shall keep a journal of its proceedings, and from time to time publish the same, excepting such parts as may in their judgment require secrecy; and the yeas and nays of the members of either House on any question shall, at the desire of one fifth of those present, be entered on the journal.

Neither House, during the session of Congress, shall, without the consent of the other, adjourn for more than three days, nor to any other place than that in which the two Houses shall be sitting.

Section 6. The Senators and Representatives shall receive a compensation for their services, to be ascertained by law, and paid out of the treasury of the United States. They shall in all cases, except treason, felony and breach of the peace, be privileged from arrest during their attendance at the session of their respective Houses, and in going to and returning from the same; and for any speech or debate in either House, they shall not be questioned in any other place. No Senator or Representative shall, during the time for which he was elected, be appointed to any civil office under the authority of the United States, which shall have been created, or the emoluments whereof shall have been increased during such time: and no person holding any office under the United States, shall be a member of either House during his continuance in office.

Section 7. All bills for raising revenue shall originate in the House of Representatives; but the Senate may propose or concur with amendments as on other Bills.

Every bill which shall have passed the House of Representatives and the Senate, shall, before it become a law, be presented to the President of the United States; if he approve he shall sign it, but if not he shall return it, with his objections to that House in which it shall have originated, who shall enter the objections at large on their journal, and proceed to reconsider it. If after such reconsideration two thirds of that House shall agree to pass the bill, it shall be sent, together with the objections, to the other House, by which it shall likewise be reconsidered, and if approved by two thirds of that House, it shall become a law. But in all such cases the votes of both Houses shall be determined by yeas and nays, and the names of the persons voting for and against the bill shall be entered on the journal of each House respectively. If any bill shall not be returned by the President within ten days (Sundays excepted) after it shall have been presented to him, the same shall be a law, in like manner as if he had signed it, unless the Congress by their adjournment prevent its return, in which case it shall not be a law.

Every order, resolution, or vote to which the concurrence of the Senate and House of Representatives may be necessary (except on a question of adjournment) shall be presented to the President of the United States; and before the same shall take effect, shall be approved by him, or being disapproved by him, shall be repassed by two thirds of the Senate and House of Representatives, according to the rules and limitations prescribed in the case of a bill.

Section 8. The Congress shall have power to lay and collect taxes, duties, imposts and excises, to pay the debts and provide for the common defense and general welfare of the United States; but all duties, imposts and excises shall be uniform throughout the United States;

To borrow money on the credit of the United States;

To regulate commerce with foreign nations, and among the several states, and with the Indian tribes;

To establish a uniform rule of naturalization, and uniform laws on the subject of bankruptcies throughout the United States;

To coin money, regulate the value thereof, and of foreign coin, and fix the standard of weights and measures;

To provide for the punishment of counterfeiting the securities and current coin of the United States;

To establish post offices and post roads;

To promote the progress of science and useful arts, by securing for limited times to authors and inventors the exclusive right to their respective writings and discoveries;

To constitute tribunals inferior to the Supreme Court;

To define and punish piracies and felonies committed on the high seas, and offenses against the law of nations;

To declare war, grant letters of marque and reprisal, and make rules concerning captures on land and water;

To raise and support armies, but no appropriation of money to that use shall be for a longer term than two years;

To provide and maintain a navy;

To make rules for the government and regulation of the land and naval forces;

To provide for calling forth the militia to execute the laws of the union, suppress insurrections and repel invasions;

To provide for organizing, arming, and disciplining, the militia, and for governing such part of them as may be employed in the service of the United States, reserving to the states respectively, the appointment of the officers, and the authority of training the militia according to the discipline prescribed by Congress;

To exercise exclusive legislation in all cases whatsoever, over such District (not exceeding ten miles square) as may, by cession of particular states, and the acceptance of Congress, become the seat of the government of the United States, and to exercise like authority over all places purchased by the consent of the legislature of the state in which the same shall be, for the erection of forts, magazines, arsenals, dockyards, and other needful buildings;—And

To make all laws which shall be necessary and proper for carrying into execution the foregoing powers, and all other powers vested by this Constitution in the government of the United States, or in any department or officer thereof.

Section 9. The migration or importation of such persons as any of the states now existing shall think proper to admit, shall not be prohibited by the Congress prior to the year one thousand eight hundred and eight, but a tax or duty may be imposed on such importation, not exceeding ten dollars for each person.

The privilege of the writ of habeas corpus shall not be suspended, unless when in cases of rebellion or invasion the public safety may require it.

No bill of attainder or ex post facto Law shall be passed.

No capitation, or other direct, tax shall be laid, unless in proportion to the census or enumeration herein before directed to be taken.

No tax or duty shall be laid on articles exported from any state.

No preference shall be given by any regulation of commerce or revenue to the ports of one state over those of another: nor shall vessels bound to, or from, one state, be obliged to enter, clear or pay duties in another.

No money shall be drawn from the treasury, but in consequence of appropriations made by law; and a regular statement and account of receipts and expenditures of all public money shall be published from time to time.

No title of nobility shall be granted by the United States: and no person holding any office of profit or trust under them, shall, without the consent of the Congress, accept of any present, emolument, office, or title, of any kind whatever, from any king, prince, or foreign state.

Section 10. No state shall enter into any treaty, alliance, or confederation; grant letters of marque and reprisal; coin money; emit bills of credit; make anything but gold and silver coin a tender in payment of debts; pass any bill of attainder, ex post facto law, or law impairing the obligation of contracts, or grant any title of nobility.

No state shall, without the consent of the Congress, lay any imposts or duties on imports or exports, except what may be absolutely necessary for executing its inspection laws: and the net produce of all duties and imposts, laid by any state on imports or exports, shall be for the use of the treasury of the United States; and all such laws shall be subject to the revision and control of the Congress.

No state shall, without the consent of Congress, lay any duty of tonnage, keep troops, or ships of war in time of peace, enter into any agreement or compact with another state, or with a foreign power, or engage in war, unless actually invaded, or in such imminent danger as will not admit of delay.

ARTICLE II

Section 1. The executive power shall be vested in a President of the United States of America. He shall hold his office during the term of four years, and, together with the Vice President, chosen for the same term, be elected, as follows:

Each state shall appoint, in such manner as the Legislature thereof may direct, a number of electors, equal to the whole number of Senators and Representatives to which the State may be entitled in the Congress: but no Senator or Representative, or person holding an office of trust or profit under the United States, shall be appointed an elector.

The electors shall meet in their respective states, and vote by ballot for two persons, of whom one at least shall not be an inhabitant of the same state with themselves. And they shall make a list of all the persons voted for, and of the number of votes for each; which list they shall sign and certify, and transmit sealed to the seat of the government of the United States, directed to the President of the Senate. The President of the Senate shall, in the presence of the Senate and House of Representatives, open all the certificates, and the votes shall then be counted. The person having the greatest number of votes shall be the President, if such number be a majority of the whole number of electors appointed; and if there be more than one who have such majority, and have an equal number of votes, then the House of Representatives shall immediately choose by ballot one of them for President; and if no person have a majority, then from the five highest on the list the said House shall in like manner choose the President. But in choosing the President, the votes shall be taken by States, the representation from each state having one vote; A quorum for this purpose shall consist of a member or members from two thirds of the states, and a majority of all the states shall be necessary to a choice. In every case, after the choice of the President, the person having the greatest number of votes of the electors shall be the Vice President.

But if there should remain two or more who have equal votes, the Senate shall choose from them by ballot the Vice President.

The Congress may determine the time of choosing the electors, and the day on which they shall give their votes; which day shall be the same throughout the United States.

No person except a natural born citizen, or a citizen of the United States, at the time of the adoption of this Constitution, shall be eligible to the office of President; neither shall any person be eligible to that office who shall not have attained to the age of thirty five years, and been fourteen Years a resident within the United States.

In case of the removal of the President from office, or of his death, resignation, or inability to discharge the powers and duties of the said office, the same shall devolve on the Vice President, and the Congress may by law provide for the case of removal, death, resignation or inability, both of the President and Vice President, declaring what officer shall then act as President, and such officer shall act accordingly, until the disability be removed, or a President shall be elected.

The President shall, at stated times, receive for his services, a compensation, which shall neither be increased nor diminished during the period for which he shall have been elected, and he shall not receive within that period any other emolument from the United States, or any of them.

Before he enter on the execution of his office, he shall take the following oath or affirmation:—"I do solemnly swear (or affirm) that I will faithfully execute the office of President of the United States, and will to the best of my ability, preserve, protect and defend the Constitution of the United States."

Section 2. The President shall be commander in chief of the Army and Navy of the United States, and of the militia of the several states, when called into the actual service of the United States;

he may require the opinion, in writing, of the principal officer in each of the executive departments, on any subject relating to the duties of their respective offices, and he shall have power to grant reprieves and pardons for offenses against the United States, except in cases of impeachment.

He shall have power, by and with the advice and consent of the Senate, to make treaties, provided two thirds of the Senators present concur; and he shall nominate, and by and with the advice and consent of the Senate, shall appoint ambassadors, other public ministers and consuls, judges of the Supreme Court, and all other officers of the United States, whose appointments are not herein otherwise provided for, and which shall be established by law: but the Congress may by law vest the appointment of such inferior officers, as they think proper, in the President alone, in the courts of law, or in the heads of departments.

The President shall have power to fill up all vacancies that may happen during the recess of the Senate, by granting commissions which shall expire at the end of their next session.

Section 3. He shall from time to time give to the Congress information of the state of the union, and recommend to their consideration such measures as he shall judge necessary and expedient; he may, on extraordinary occasions, convene both Houses, or either of them, and in case of disagreement between them, with respect to the time of adjournment, he may adjourn them to such time as he shall think proper; he shall receive ambassadors and other public ministers; he shall take care that the laws be faithfully executed, and shall commission all the officers of the United States.

Section 4. The President, Vice President and all civil officers of the United States, shall be removed from office on impeachment for, and conviction of, treason, bribery, or other high crimes and misdemeanors.

ARTICLE III

Section 1. The judicial power of the United States, shall be vested in one Supreme Court, and in such inferior courts as the Congress may from time to time ordain and establish. The judges, both of the supreme and inferior courts, shall hold their offices during good behavior, and shall, at stated times, receive for their services, a compensation, which shall not be diminished during their continuance in office.

Section 2. The judicial power shall extend to all cases, in law and equity, arising under this Constitution, the laws of the United States, and treaties made, or which shall be made, under their authority;—to all cases affecting ambassadors, other public ministers and consuls;—to all cases of admiralty and maritime jurisdiction;—to controversies to which the United States shall be a party;—to controversies between two or more states;—between a state and citizens of another state;—between citizens of different states;—between citizens of the same state claiming lands under grants of different states, and between a state, or the citizens thereof, and foreign states, citizens or subjects.

In all cases affecting ambassadors, other public ministers and consuls, and those in which a state shall be party, the Supreme Court shall have original jurisdiction. In all the other cases before mentioned, the Supreme Court shall have appellate jurisdiction, both as to law and fact, with such exceptions, and under such regulations as the Congress shall make.

The trial of all crimes, except in cases of impeachment, shall be by jury; and such trial shall be held in the state where the said crimes shall have been committed; but when not committed within any state, the trial shall be at such place or places as the Congress may by law have directed.

Section 3. Treason against the United States, shall consist only in levying war against them, or in adhering to their enemies, giving them aid and comfort. No person shall be convicted of treason unless on the testimony of two witnesses to the same overt act, or on confession in open court.

The Congress shall have power to declare the punishment of treason, but no attainder of treason shall work corruption of blood, or forfeiture except during the life of the person attainted.

ARTICLE IV

Section 1. Full faith and credit shall be given in each state to the public acts, records, and judicial proceedings of every other state. And the Congress may by general laws prescribe the manner in which such acts, records, and proceedings shall be proved, and the effect thereof.

Section 2. The citizens of each state shall be entitled to all privileges and immunities of citizens in the several states.

A person charged in any state with treason, felony, or other crime, who shall flee from justice, and be found in another state, shall on demand of the executive authority of the state from which he fled, be delivered up, to be removed to the state having jurisdiction of the crime.

No person held to service or labor in one state, under the laws thereof, escaping into another, shall, in consequence of any law or regulation therein, be discharged from such service or labor, but shall be delivered up on claim of the party to whom such service or labor may be due.

Section 3. New states may be admitted by the Congress into this union; but no new states shall be formed or erected within the jurisdiction of any other state; nor any state be formed by the junction of two or more states, or parts of states, without the consent of the legislatures of the states concerned as well as of the Congress.

The Congress shall have power to dispose of and make all needful rules and regulations respecting the territory or other property belonging to the United States; and nothing in this Constitution shall be so construed as to prejudice any claims of the United States, or of any particular state.

Section 4. The United States shall guarantee to every state in this union a republican form of government, and shall protect each of them against invasion; and on application of the legislature, or of the executive (when the legislature cannot be convened) against domestic violence.

ARTICLE V

The Congress, whenever two thirds of both houses shall deem it necessary, shall propose amendments to this Constitution, or, on the application of the legislatures of two thirds of the several states, shall call a convention for proposing amendments, which, in either case, shall be valid to all intents and purposes, as part of this Constitution, when ratified by the legislatures of three fourths of the several states, or by conventions in three fourths thereof, as the one or the other mode of ratification may be proposed by the Congress; provided that no amendment which may be made prior to the year one thousand eight hundred and eight shall in any manner affect the first and fourth clauses in the ninth section of the first article; and that no state, without its consent, shall be deprived of its equal suffrage in the Senate.

ARTICLE VI

All debts contracted and engagements entered into, before the adoption of this Constitution, shall be as valid against the United States under this Constitution, as under the Confederation.

This Constitution, and the laws of the United States which shall be made in pursuance thereof; and all treaties made, or which shall be made, under the authority of the United States, shall be the supreme law of the land; and the judges in every state shall be bound thereby, anything in the Constitution or laws of any State to the contrary notwithstanding.

The Senators and Representatives before mentioned, and the members of the several state legislatures, and all executive and judicial officers, both of the United States and of the several states, shall be bound by oath or affirmation, to support this Constitution; but no religious test shall ever be required as a qualification to any office or public trust under the United States.

ARTICLE VII

The ratification of the conventions of nine states, shall be sufficient for the establishment of this Constitution between the states so ratifying the same.

Done in convention by the unanimous consent of the states present the seventeenth day of September in the year of our Lord one thousand seven hundred and eighty seven and of the independence of the United States of America the twelfth. In witness whereof We have hereunto subscribed our Names,

G. WASHINGTON: Presidt. and deputy from Virginia

New Hampshire: JOHN LANGDON, NICHOLAS GILMAN

Massachusetts: NATHANIEL GORHAM, RUFUS KING

Connecticut: Wm: SAML. JOHNSON, ROGER SHERMAN

New York: ALEXANDER HAMILTON

New Jersey: WIL LIVINGSTON, DAVID BREARLY, WM. PATERSON, JONA: DAYTON

Pennsylvania: B. FRANKLIN, THOMAS MIFFLIN, ROBT. MORRIS, GEO. CLYMER, THOS. FITZSIMONS, JARED INGERSOLL, JAMES WILSON, GOUV MORRIS

Delaware: GEO: READ, GUNNING BEDFORD JUN, JOHN DICKINSON, RICHARD BASSETT, JACO: BROOM

Maryland: JAMES MCHENRY, DAN OF ST THOS. JENIFER, DANL CARROLL

Virginia: JOHN BLAIR—, JAMES MADISON JR.

North Carolina: WM. BLOUNT, RICHD. DOBBS SPAIGHT, HU WILLIAMSON

South Carolina: J. RUTLEDGE, CHARLES COTESWORTH PINCKNEY, CHARLES PINCKNEY, PIERCE BUTLER

Georgia: WILLIAM FEW, ABR BALDWIN

BILL OF RIGHTS

The Conventions of a number of the States having, at the time of adopting the Constitution, expressed a desire, in order to prevent misconstruction or abuse of its powers, that further declaratory and restrictive clauses should be added, and as extending the ground of public confidence in the Government will best insure the beneficent ends of its institution;

Resolved, by the Senate and House of Representatives of the United States of America, in Congress assembled, two-thirds of both Houses concurring, that the following articles be proposed to the Legislatures of the several States, as amendments to the Constitution of the United States; all or any of which articles, when ratified by three-fourths of the said Legislatures, to be valid to all intents and purposes as part of the said Constitution, namely:

AMENDMENT I

Congress shall make no law respecting an establishment of religion, or prohibiting the free exercise thereof; or abridging the freedom of speech, or of the press; or the right of the people peaceably to assemble, and to petition the government for a redress of grievances.

AMENDMENT II

A well regulated militia, being necessary to the security of a free state, the right of the people to keep and bear arms, shall not be infringed.

AMENDMENT III

No soldier shall, in time of peace be quartered in any house, without the consent of the owner, nor in time of war, but in a manner to be prescribed by law.

AMENDMENT IV

The right of the people to be secure in their persons, houses, papers, and effects, against unreasonable searches and seizures, shall not be violated, and no warrants shall issue, but upon probable cause, supported by oath or affirmation, and particularly describing the place to be searched, and the persons or things to be seized.

AMENDMENT V

No person shall be held to answer for a capital, or otherwise infamous crime, unless on a presentment or indictment of a grand jury, except in cases arising in the land or naval forces, or in the militia, when in actual service in time of war or public danger; nor shall any person be subject for the same offense to be twice put in jeopardy of life or limb; nor shall be compelled in any criminal case to be a witness against himself, nor be deprived of life, liberty, or property, without due process of law; nor shall private property be taken for public use, without just compensation.

AMENDMENT VI

In all criminal prosecutions, the accused shall enjoy the right to a speedy and public trial, by an impartial jury of the state and district wherein the crime shall have been committed, which district shall have been previously ascertained by law, and to be informed of the nature and cause of the accusation; to be confronted with the witnesses against him; to have compulsory process for obtaining witnesses in his favor, and to have the assistance of counsel for his defense.

AMENDMENT VII

In suits at common law, where the value in controversy shall exceed twenty dollars, the right of trial by jury shall be preserved, and no fact tried by a jury, shall be otherwise reexamined in any court of the United States, than according to the rules of the common law.

AMENDMENT VIII

Excessive bail shall not be required, nor excessive fines imposed, nor cruel and unusual punishments inflicted.

AMENDMENT IX

The enumeration in the Constitution, of certain rights, shall not be construed to deny or disparage others retained by the people.

AMENDMENT X

The powers not delegated to the United States by the Constitution, nor prohibited by it to the states, are reserved to the states respectively, or to the people.

OTHER AMENDMENTS
TO THE CONSTITUTION

AMENDMENT **XI**

(1798)

The judicial power of the United States shall not be construed to extend to any suit in law or equity, commenced or prosecuted against one of the United States by citizens of another state, or by citizens or subjects of any foreign state.

AMENDMENT **XII**

(1804)

The electors shall meet in their respective states and vote by ballot for President and Vice-President, one of whom, at least, shall not be an inhabitant of the same state with themselves; they shall name in their ballots the person voted for as President, and in distinct ballots the person voted for as Vice-President, and they shall make distinct lists of all persons voted for as President, and of all persons voted for as Vice-President, and of the number of votes for each, which lists they shall sign and certify, and trans-mit sealed to the seat of the government of the United States, directed to the President of the Senate;—The President of the Senate shall, in the presence of the Senate and House of Representatives, open all the certificates and the votes shall then be counted;—the person having the greatest number of votes for President, shall be the President, if such number be a majority of the whole number of electors appointed; and if no person have such majority, then from the persons having the highest numbers not exceeding three on the list of those voted for as President, the House of Representatives shall choose immediately, by ballot, the President. But in choosing the President, the votes shall be taken by states, the representation from each state having one vote; a quorum for this purpose shall consist of a member or members from two-thirds of the states, and a majority of all the states shall be necessary to a choice. And if the House of Representatives shall not choose a President whenever the right of choice shall devolve upon them, before the fourth day of March next following, then the Vice-President shall act as President, as in the case of the death or other constitutional disability of the President. The person having the greatest number of votes as Vice-President, shall be the Vice-President, if such number be a majority of the whole number of electors appointed, and if no person have a majority, then from the two highest numbers on the list, the Senate shall choose the Vice-President; a quorum for the purpose shall consist of two-thirds of the whole number of Senators, and a majority of the whole number shall be necessary to a choice. But no person constitutionally ineligible to the office of President shall be eligible to that of Vice-President of the United States.

AMENDMENT XIII

(1865)

Section 1. Neither slavery nor involuntary servitude, except as a punishment for crime whereof the party shall have been duly convicted, shall exist within the United States, or any place subject to their jurisdiction.

Section 2. Congress shall have power to enforce this article by appropriate legislation.

AMENDMENT XIV

(1868)

Section 1. All persons born or naturalized in the United States, and subject to the jurisdiction thereof, are citizens of the United States and of the state wherein they reside. No state shall make or enforce any law which shall abridge the privileges or immunities of citizens of the United States; nor shall any state deprive any person of life, liberty, or property, without due process of law; nor deny to any person within its jurisdiction the equal protection of the laws.

Section 2. Representatives shall be apportioned among the several states according to their respective numbers, counting the whole number of persons in each state, excluding Indians not taxed. But when the right to vote at any election for the choice of electors for President and Vice President of the United States, Representatives in Congress, the executive and judicial officers of a state, or the members of the legislature thereof, is denied to any of the male inhabitants of such state, being twenty-one years of age, and citizens of the United States, or in any way abridged, except for participation in rebellion, or other crime, the basis of representation therein shall be reduced in the proportion which the number of such male citizens shall bear to the whole number of male citizens twenty-one years of age in such state.

Section 3. No person shall be a Senator or Representative in Congress, or elector of President and Vice President, or hold any office, civil or military, under the United States, or under any state, who, having previously taken an oath, as a member of Congress, or as an officer of the United States, or as a member of any state legislature, or as an executive or judicial officer of any state, to support the Constitution of the United States, shall have engaged in insurrection or rebellion against the same, or given aid or comfort to the enemies thereof. But Congress may by a vote of two-thirds of each House, remove such disability.

Section 4. The validity of the public debt of the United States, authorized by law, including debts incurred for payment of pensions and bounties for services in suppressing insurrection or rebellion, shall not be questioned. But neither the United States nor any state shall assume or pay any debt or obligation incurred in aid of insurrection or rebellion against the United States, or any claim for the loss or emancipation of any slave; but all such debts, obligations and claims shall be held illegal and void.

Section 5. The Congress shall have power to enforce, by appropriate legislation, the provisions of this article.

AMENDMENT XV

(1870)

Section 1. The right of citizens of the United States to vote shall not be denied or abridged by the United States or by any state on account of race, color, or previous condition of servitude.

Section 2. The Congress shall have power to enforce this article by appropriate legislation.

AMENDMENT XVI

(1913)

The Congress shall have power to lay and collect taxes on incomes, from whatever source derived, without apportionment among the several states, and without regard to any census of enumeration.

AMENDMENT XVII

(1913)

The Senate of the United States shall be composed of two Senators from each state, elected by the people thereof, for six years; and each Senator shall have one vote. The electors in each state shall have the qualifications requisite for electors of the most numerous branch of the state legislatures.

When vacancies happen in the representation of any state in the Senate, the executive authority of such state shall issue writs of election to fill such vacancies: Provided, that the legislature of any state may empower the executive thereof to make temporary appointments until the people fill the vacancies by election as the legislature may direct.

This amendment shall not be so construed as to affect the election or term of any Senator chosen before it becomes valid as part of the Constitution.

AMENDMENT XVIII

(1919)

Section 1. After one year from the ratification of this article the manufacture, sale, or transportation of intoxicating liquors within, the importation thereof into, or the exportation thereof from the United States and all territory subject to the jurisdiction thereof for beverage purposes is hereby prohibited.

Section 2. The Congress and the several states shall have concurrent power to enforce this article by appropriate legislation.

Section 3. This article shall be inoperative unless it shall have been ratified as an amendment to the Constitution by the legislatures of the several states, as provided in the Constitution, within seven years from the date of the submission hereof to the states by the Congress.

AMENDMENT XIX

(1920)

The right of citizens of the United States to vote shall not be denied or abridged by the United States or by any state on account of sex.

Congress shall have power to enforce this article by appropriate legislation.

AMENDMENT XX

(1933)

Section 1. The terms of the President and Vice President shall end at noon on the 20th day of

January, and the terms of Senators and Representatives at noon on the 3d day of January, of the years in which such terms would have ended if this article had not been ratified; and the terms of their successors shall then begin.

Section 2. The Congress shall assemble at least once in every year, and such meeting shall begin at noon on the 3d day of January, unless they shall by law appoint a different day.

Section 3. If, at the time fixed for the beginning of the term of the President, the President elect shall have died, the Vice President elect shall become President. If a President shall not have been chosen before the time fixed for the beginning of his term, or if the President elect shall have failed to qualify, then the Vice President elect shall act as President until a President shall have qualified; and the Congress may by law provide for the case wherein neither a President elect nor a Vice President elect shall have qualified, declaring who shall then act as President, or the manner in which one who is to act shall be selected, and such person shall act accordingly until a President or Vice President shall have qualified.

Section 4. The Congress may by law provide for the case of the death of any of the persons from whom the House of Representatives may choose a President whenever the right of choice shall have devolved upon them, and for the case of the death of any of the persons from whom the Senate may choose a Vice President whenever the right of choice shall have devolved upon them.

Section 5. Sections 1 and 2 shall take effect on the 15th day of October following the ratification of this article.

Section 6. This article shall be inoperative unless it shall have been ratified as an amendment to the Constitution by the legislatures of three-fourths of the several states within seven years from the date of its submission.

Amendment XXI

(1933)

Section 1. The eighteenth article of amendment to the Constitution of the United States is hereby repealed.

Section 2. The transportation or importation into any state, territory, or possession of the United States for delivery or use therein of intoxicating liquors, in violation of the laws thereof, is hereby prohibited.

Section 3. This article shall be inoperative unless it shall have been ratified as an amendment to the Constitution by conventions in the several states, as provided in the Constitution, within seven years from the date of the submission hereof to the states by the Congress.

Amendment XXII

(1951)

Section 1. No person shall be elected to the office of the President more than twice, and no person who has held the office of President, or acted as President, for more than two years of a term to which some other person was elected President shall be elected to the office of the President more than once. But this article shall not apply to any person holding the office of President when this article was proposed by the Congress, and shall not prevent any person who may be holding the office of President, or acting as President, during the term within which this article becomes operative from holding the office of President or acting as President during the remainder of such term.

Section 2. This article shall be inoperative unless it shall have been ratified as an amendment to the Constitution by the legislatures of three-fourths of the several states within seven years from the date of its submission to the states by the Congress.

AMENDMENT XXIII

(1961)

Section 1. The District constituting the seat of government of the United States shall appoint in such manner as the Congress may direct: A number of electors of President and Vice President equal to the whole number of Senators and Representatives in Congress to which the District would be entitled if it were a state, but in no event more than the least populous state; they shall be in addition to those appointed by the states, but they shall be considered, for the purposes of the election of President and Vice President, to be electors appointed by a state; and they shall meet in the District and perform such duties as provided by the twelfth article of amendment.

Section 2. The Congress shall have power to enforce this article by appropriate legislation.

AMENDMENT XXIV

(1964)

Section 1. The right of citizens of the United States to vote in any primary or other election for President or Vice President, for electors for President or Vice President, or for Senator or Representative in Congress, shall not be denied or abridged by the United States or any state by reason of failure to pay any poll tax or other tax.

Section 2. The Congress shall have power to enforce this article by appropriate legislation.

AMENDMENT XXV

(1967)

Section 1. In case of the removal of the President from office or of his death or resignation, the Vice President shall become President.

Section 2. Whenever there is a vacancy in the office of the Vice President, the President shall nominate a Vice President who shall take office upon confirmation by a majority vote of both Houses of Congress.

Section 3. Whenever the President transmits to the President pro tempore of the Senate and the Speaker of the House of Representatives his written declaration that he is unable to discharge the powers and duties of his office, and until he transmits to them a written declaration to the contrary, such powers and duties shall be discharged by the Vice President as Acting President.

Section 4. Whenever the Vice President and a majority of either the principal officers of the executive departments or of such other body as Congress may by law provide, transmit to the President pro tempore of the Senate and the Speaker of the House of Representatives their written declaration that the President is unable to discharge the powers and duties of his office, the Vice President shall immediately assume the powers and duties of the office as Acting President.

Thereafter, when the President transmits to the President pro tempore of the Senate and the Speaker of the House of Representatives his written declaration that no inability exists, he shall resume the powers and duties of his office unless the Vice President and a majority of either the principal officers of the executive department or of such other body as Congress may by law provide, transmit within four days to the President pro tempore of the Senate and the Speaker of the House of Representatives their written declaration that the President is unable to discharge the powers and duties of his office.

Thereupon Congress shall decide the issue, assembling within forty-eight hours for that purpose if not in session. If the Congress, within twenty-one days after receipt of the latter written declaration, or, if Congress is not in session, within twenty-one days after Congress is required to assemble, determines by two-thirds vote of both Houses that the President is unable to discharge the powers and duties of his office, the Vice President shall continue to discharge the same as Acting President; otherwise, the President shall resume the powers and duties of his office.

AMENDMENT XXVI

(1971)

Section 1. The right of citizens of the United States, who are 18 years of age or older, to vote, shall not be denied or abridged by the United States or any state on account of age.

Section 2. The Congress shall have the power to enforce this article by appropriate legislation.

AMENDMENT XXVII

(1992)

No law varying the compensation for the services of the Senators and Representatives shall take effect until an election of Representatives shall have intervened.

EMANCIPATION PROCLAMATION

First reading of the Emancipation Proclamation to the Senate.

WHEREAS, on the twenty-second day of September, in the year of our Lord one thousand eight hundred and sixty-two, a proclamation was issued by the President of the United States, containing, among other things, the following, to wit:

"That on the first day of January, in the year of our Lord one thousand eight hundred and sixty-three, all persons held as slaves within any State, or designated part of a State, the people whereof shall then be in rebellion against the United States, shall be then, thenceforward, and forever free; and the Executive Government of the United States, including the military and naval authority thereof, will recognize and maintain the freedom of such persons, and will do no act or acts to repress such persons, or any of them, in any efforts they may make for their actual freedom.

"That the Executive will, on the first day of January aforesaid, by proclamation, designate the States and parts of States, if any, in which the people thereof respectively, shall then be in rebel-lion against the United States; and the fact that any State, or the people thereof, shall on that day be in good faith represented in the Congress of the United States by members chosen thereto at elections wherein a majority of the qualified voters of such State shall have participated, shall in the absence of strong countervailing testimony, be deemed conclusive evidence that such State, and the people thereof, are not then in rebellion against the United States."

Now, therefore, I, Abraham Lincoln, President of the United States, by virtue of the power in me vested as commander-in-chief of the Army and Navy of the United States, in time of actual armed rebellion against authority and government of the United States, and as a fit and necessary war measure for suppressing said rebellion, do, on this first day of January, in the year of our Lord one thousand eight hundred and sixty-three, and in accordance with my purpose so to do, publicly proclaimed for the full period of one hundred days from the day first above mentioned, order and designate as the States and parts of States wherein the people thereof, respectively, are this day in rebellion against the United States, the following, to wit:

Arkansas, Texas, Louisiana (except the parishes of St. Bernard, Plaquemines, Jefferson, St. John, St. Charles, St. James, Ascension, Assumption, Terrebonne, Lafourche, St. Mary, St. Martin, and Orleans, including the city of New Orleans), Mississippi, Alabama, Florida, Georgia, South Carolina, North Carolina, and Virginia (except the forty-eight counties designated as West Virginia, and also the counties of Berkley, Accomac, Northampton, Elizabeth City, York, Princess Ann, and Norfolk, including the cities of Norfolk and Portsmouth), and which excepted parts are, for the present, left precisely as if this proclamation were not issued.

And by virtue of the power and for the purpose aforesaid, I do order and declare that all persons held as slaves within said designated States and parts of States are, and henceforward shall be, free; and that the Executive government of the United States, including the military and naval authorities thereof, will recognize and maintain the freedom of said persons.

And I hereby enjoin upon the people so declared to be free to abstain from all violence, unless in necessary self-defence; and I recommend to them that, in all cases when allowed, they labor faithfully for reasonable wages.

And I further declare and make known, that such persons of suitable condition, will be received into the armed service of the United States to garrison forts, positions, stations, and other places, and to man vessels of all sorts in said service.

And upon this act, sincerely believed to be an act of justice, warranted by the Constitution, upon military necessity, I invoke the considerate judgment of mankind and the gracious favor of Almighty God.

In witness whereof, I have hereunto set my hand, and caused the seal of the United States to be affixed.

Done at the city of Washington, this first day of January, in the year of our Lord one thousand eight hundred and sixty-three, and of the Independence of the United States of America the eighty-seventh.

ABRAHAM LINCOLN

L.S.
By the President:
WILLIAM H. SEWARD,
Secretary of State

LOCATING COURT CASES AND LAWS

Locating legal materials sometimes appears to be a very confusing task. However, for most court cases and laws, once one understands a few basic rules it is not too difficult to find them.

COURT CASES

All court cases cited are reported or published in a similar way. The general citation format is the name of the case printed in italics or underlined, followed by a comma, and then a citation to the volume number of the reporter it is in, the abbreviation of the name of the reporter the decision is in, the page number the decision starts on, and then the date of the decision in parentheses. The name of the case includes the two parties to the case.

For example, take a case such as *Baker v. Carr,* a famous case that deals with reapportionment. There are several ways that one can look up this case. Baker represented the plaintiff, the person appealing or bringing the case, and Carr was the defendant or respondent, the party against whom the court case was brought. The *v.* is an abbreviation for *versus.* "*Baker v. Carr*" is thus read as "Baker versus Carr."

Court decisions can be found in many public libraries. County courthouse, state law libraries, and college and law school libraries are other places where court opinions may be found.

The World Wide Web has many sites where court decisions can be found. The federal government, as well as many states and specific courts, also has a web site where many decisions are located.

UNITED STATES SUPREME COURT DECISIONS

United States Supreme Court cases are published in three different volumes. The official publication for the Court's opinions is in *United States Reports,* abbreviated as "U.S." The official citation to *Baker v. Carr* would thus be *Baker v. Carr,* 369 U.S. 186 (1962). What this citation means is that this decision can be found in volume number 369 of *United States Reports,* with the decision starting on page 186. The information in the parentheses, 1962, refers to the year the decision was issued.

The first 90 volumes of *United States Reports* also contain the name of the specific court reporter in the citation. While it is important to note that, for most people and lawyers, specific reference to that reporter is not needed.

United States Supreme Court Reports—abbreviated as "L.Ed" or "L.Ed.2d."—is a second place where Supreme Court decisions are reported. This is a private and unofficial reporter, but it is a very good and widely used source in which to cite and look up Court decisions. There is both a first and second edition of this volume, with the first edition cited as "L.Ed." and the second edition cited as "L.Ed.2d." *Baker v. Carr* is cited here as *Baker v. Carr,* 7 L.Ed.2d. 663 (1962).

Finally, the *Supreme Court Reporter,* abbreviated as S.Ct., is a third privately published source of Supreme Court opinions. *Baker v. Carr* is cited as *Baker v. Carr,* 82 S.Ct. 691 (1962).

Sometimes one might see a citation such as *Baker v. Carr,* 369 U.S. 186, 195 (1962), where a second number is cited after the beginning page number of the decision. That second page number refers to a specific page or reference in that decision; the "195" refers to some citation on page 195 of the *United States Reports'* decision in *Baker v. Carr.*

OTHER FEDERAL COURT DECISIONS

U.S. Federal Court of Appeals decisions are published in the *Federal Reporter,* abbreviated as "F.," "F.2d," or "F.3d."

U.S. District Court opinions are published in the *Federal Supplement,* abbreviated as "F.Supp."

Both federal court of appeals and district court decisions, as well as all other federal and states cases, are cited the same way as Supreme Court decisions, with the name of the case printed in italics or underlined, followed by a comma, and then a citation to the volume number of the reporter it is in, the abbreviation of the name of the reporter the decision is in, the page number the decision starts on, and then the date of the decision in parentheses.

There are many other federal court decisions for specialty courts such as bankruptcy, courts of claims, etc. Each of them have their own books or volumes where their decisions can be found.

STATE COURT DECISIONS

State court decisions can be located the same way as federal court opinions.

Most states have their own official reporters for their opinions. However, West Group, a private legal publisher, has created a series of nine different books where one can find state court opinions. New York court opinions are found in the *New York Supplement,* cited as "N.Y. Supp." or "N.Y.S. 2d.," and California decisions since 1960 are located in the *California Reporter,* cited as "Cal. Rptr." or "Cal. Rptr. 2d., "etc. The rest of the states are found in one of seven different volumes, grouped by geography, with each volume having is own abbreviation.

STATUTES AND LAWS

The *United States Code,* abbreviated as U.S.C., and the *United States Code Annotated* (U.S.C.A.) are the two main volumes where federal laws can be found. The *United States Code* is the official government of federal laws, while the *United States Code Annotated* is privately published and includes both federal law and references to major court decisions on each section of the law.

Federal law is organized under 50 separate titles covering subjects such as Congress, civil rights, and taxation. The basic citation system for the federal code is to first list the chapter number followed by the volume abbreviation U.S.C. or U.S.C.A., the specific section number of that chapter of the code, followed by the year, in parentheses, of the volume of the U.S.C. or U.S.C.A. one is using. Thus, 42 U.S.C. § 1983 (2000), indicates that one is looking up chapter 42 of the *United States Code,* section 1983, while 42 U.S.C.A. § 1983 (2000) indicates that one is looking up chapter 42 of the *United States Code Annotated.*

Most states have very similar systems for organizing their own laws.

Finally, in addition to federal and state laws, both also have rules and regulations that are created by administrative or regulatory agencies. The *Code of Federal Regulations,* abbreviated as "C.F.R.," is the place where federal regulations are published. There are 50 separate titles, and they are cited the same way as the *United States Code.* Thus, 16 C.F.R. § 25 is a reference to title 16, section 25 of the *Code of Federal Regulations.*

States have similar references to their own rules and regulations.

In addition to the above volumes in which to look up laws and rules, there are many other citation systems where one can look up a rule or law based upon its public law number or the popular name of the act or rule. Not all public libraries have these alternative reference materials, although law school and government libraries do. There are also many government and free commercial web sites that make it easy to find federal and state laws and rules.

LEGAL REFERENCE MATERIALS

There are many other legal reference materials that are helpful in looking up specific topics.

The *Index to Legal Periodicals* is the best book for yearly reference to legal articles of all types. The *Index* comes out monthly and it is organized by subject and author, by case, by statute, and by book review. Many public and school libraries have the *Index* in their reference collections.

The *Corpus Juris Secundum, American Jurisprudence,* and *American Law Reports* are three of the most comprehensive and detailed legal encyclopedias or reference books available on U.S. law. Each is composed of many volumes and is written primarily for lawyers and legal specialists. These books are generally found in law and law school libraries.

Black's Law Dictionary is the best one-volume dictionary of legal terms. It is written for lawyers and legal specialists, and copies of it are also found in most law and law school libraries.

Finally, every law school in the country publishes one or more law reviews. Law reviews are edited by law students, and these publications contain scholarly and students' articles on various aspects of law. They also may contain reviews of particular court cases, laws, and book reviews. Law reviews are generally found in law and law school libraries.

David Schultz
Hamline University

JUSTICES OF THE SUPREME COURT

Since 1789, 109 justices have served on the United States Supreme Court. The table provided here gives the names of these individuals, which president appointed them, and the years they served on the bench.

Justice	Appointing President	Years of Service
1. John Jay*	Washington	1789–1795
2. John Rutledge*	Washington	1789–1791
3. William Cushing	Washington	1789–1810
4. James Wilson	Washington	1789–1798
5. John Blair, Jr.	Washington	1789–1796
6. James Iredell	Washington	1790–1799
7. Thomas Johnson	Washington	1791–1793
8. William Paterson	Washington	1793–1806
9. Samuel Chase	Washington	1796–1811
10. Oliver Ellsworth*	Washington	1796–1800
11. Bushrod Washington	J. Adams	1798–1829
12. Alfred Moore	J. Adams	1799–1804
13. John Marshall*	J. Adams	1801–1835
14. William Johnson	Jefferson	1804–1834
15. Henry Brokholst Livingston	Jefferson	1806–1823
16. Thomas Todd	Jefferson	1807–1826
17. Gabriel Duvall	Madison	1811–1835

Justice	Appointing President	Years of Service
18. Joseph Story	Madison	1811–1845
19. Smith Thompson	Monroe	1823–1843
20. Robert Trimble	J. Q. Adams	1826–1828
21. John McLean	Jackson	1829–1861
22. Henry Baldwin	Jackson	1830–1844
23. James Moore Wayne	Jackson	1835–1867
24. Roger Brooke Taney*	Jackson	1836–1864
25. Philip Pendleton Barbour	Jackson	1836–1841
26. John Catron	Jackson	1837–1865
27. John McKinley	Van Buren	1837–1852
28. Peter Vivian Daniel	Van Buren	1841–1860
29. Samuel Nelson	Tyler	1845–1872
30. Levi Woodbury	Polk	1846–1851
31. Robert Cooper Grier	Polk	1846–1870
32. Benjamin Robbins Curtis	Fillmore	1851–1857
33. John Archibald Campbell	Pierce	1853–1861
34. Nathan Clifford	Buchanan	1858–1881
35. Noah Haynes Swayne	Lincoln	1862–1881
36. Samuel Freeman Miller	Lincoln	1862–1890
37. David Davis	Lincoln	1862–1877
38. Stephan Johnson Field	Lincoln	1863–1897
39. Salmon Portland Chase*	Lincoln	1864–1873
40. William Strong	Grant	1870–1880
41. Joseph P. Bradley	Grant	1870–1892
42. Ward Hunt	Grant	1872–1882
43. Morrison Remick Waite*	Grant	1874–1888
44. John Marshall Harlan	Hayes	1877–1911
45. William Burnham Woods	Hayes	1880–1887
46. Stanley Matthews	Garfield	1881–1889
47. Horace Gray	Arthur	1881–1902
48. Samuel Blatchford	Arthur	1882–1893
49. Lucius Quintus Cincinnatus Lamar	Cleveland	1888–1893
50. Melville Weston Fuller*	Cleveland	1888–1910
51. David Josiah Brewer	Harrison	1889–1910
52. Henry Billings Brown	Harrison	1890–1906
53. George Shiras, Jr.	Harrison	1892–1903
54. Howell Edmunds Jackson	Harrison	1893–1895
55. Edward Douglass White*	Cleveland	1910–1921
56. Rufus Wheeler Peckham	Cleveland	1895–1909
57. Joseph McKenna	McKinley	1898–1925
58. Oliver Wendell Holmes, Jr.	T. Roosevelt	1902–1932

Justice	Appointing President	Years of Service
59. William Rufus Day	T. Roosevelt	1903–1922
60. William Henry Moody	T. Roosevelt	1906–1910
61. Horace Harmon Lurton	Taft	1909–1914
62. Charles Evans Hughes*	Taft	1930–1941
63. Willis Van Devanter	Taft	1910–1937
64. Joseph Rucker Lamar	Taft	1910–1916
65. Mahlon Pitney	Taft	1912–1922
66. James Clark McReynolds	Wilson	1914–1941
67. Louis Dembitz Brandeis	Wilson	1916–1939
68. John Hessin Clarke	Wilson	1916–1922
69. William Howard Taft*	Harding	1921–1930
70. George Sutherland	Harding	1922–1938
71. Pierce Butler	Harding	1922–1939
72. Edward Terry Sanford	Harding	1923–1930
73. Harlan Fiske Stone	Coolidge	1925–1941
74. Owen Josephus Roberts	Hoover	1930–1945
75. Benjamin Nathan Cardozo	Hoover	1932–1938
76. Hugo Lafayette Black	F. Roosevelt	1937–1971
77. Stanley Forman Reed	F. Roosevelt	1938–1957
78. Felix Frankfurter	F. Roosevelt	1939–1962
79. William Orville Douglas	F. Roosevelt	1939–1975
80. William Francis (Frank) Murphy	F. Roosevelt	1940–1949
81. Harlan Fiske Stone*	F. Roosevelt	1941–1946
82. James Francis Byrnes	F. Roosevelt	1941–1942
83. Robert Houghwout Jackson	F. Roosevelt	1941–1954
84. Wiley Blount Rutledge	F. Roosevelt	1943–1949
85. Harold Hitz Burton	Truman	1945–1958
86. Frederick Moore Vinson*	Truman	1946–1953
87. Tom Campbell Clark	Truman	1949–1967
88. Sherman Minton	Truman	1949–1956
89. Earl Warren*	Eisenhower	1953–1969
90. John Marshall Harlan	Eisenhower	1955–1971
91. William Joseph Brennan, Jr.	Eisenhower	1956–1990
92. Charles Evans Whittaker	Eisenhower	1957–1962
93. Potter Stewart	Eisenhower	1958–1981
94. Byron Raymond White	Kennedy	1962–1993
95. Arthur Joseph Goldberg	Kennedy	1962–1965
96. Abe Fortas	Johnson	1965–1969
97. Thurgood Marshall	Johnson	1967–1991
98. Warren Earl Burger*	Nixon	1969–1986
99. Harry Andrew Blackmun	Nixon	1970–1994

Justice	Appointing President	Years of Service
100. Lewis Franklin Powell, Jr.	Nixon	1971–1987
101. William Hubbs Rehnquist*	Nixon	1971–
102. John Paul Stevens	Ford	1975–
103. Sandra Day O'Connor	Reagan	1981–
104. Antonin Scalia	Reagan	1986–
105. Anthony McLeod Kennedy	Reagan	1988–
106. David H. Souter	Bush	1990–
107. Clarence Thomas	Bush	1991–
108. Ruth Bader Ginsburg	Clinton	1993–
109. Stephen G. Breyer	Clinton	1994–

*SERVED AS CHIEF JUSTICE

Timothy R. Johnson
University of Minnesota

HOW CASES REACH THE UNITED STATES SUPREME COURT

How cases reach the U.S. Supreme Court depends upon a number of factors.

Since the national government has only those powers delegated to it by the people through the U.S. Constitution, its institutions, including the Supreme Court, may do only those things the Constitution prescribes specifically or implicitly. Article III of the Constitution limits the power of the Supreme Court to hear "cases and controversies," real disputes, regarding the interpretation of federal law (e.g., acts of Congress, treaties, presidential orders, agency rules, and the U.S. Constitution itself). Conflicts involving state laws are settled by state courts unless they somehow generate a federal question, at which time they may be reviewed by the Supreme Court.

Article III gives the Supreme Court authority to exercise its jurisdiction in two kinds of cases, those that come to it originally and those that come on appeal. Of the 7,000 or so cases that the Court reviews each year, no more than two or three, and often none, come under its original jurisdiction. These are cases that involve disputes between a state and another state.

Although the Constitution gives the Supreme Court original jurisdiction to hear cases affecting representatives of foreign nations and those between the national government and state governments, Congress has given lower courts concurrent jurisdiction in these latter cases. In other words, the Supreme Court's original jurisdiction is not considered exclusive. Congress may authorize lower courts to hear some of these cases. Thus, nearly all cases reach the Supreme Court under its appellate jurisdiction, which also, according to Article III, is subject to "such exceptions, and under such regulations as the Congress shall make."

Cases reach the Supreme Court under its appellate jurisdiction in three ways: a few by appeal and by certification, most by writ of certiorari. Congress all but repealed the *right* of appeal to the U.S. Supreme Court with PL 100-352 in 1988. A few cases still come on appeal directly from special U.S. District Courts, composed of three judges who issue or deny a writ of injunction. Rarely a case may reach the Court upon "certification," when a Court of Appeals

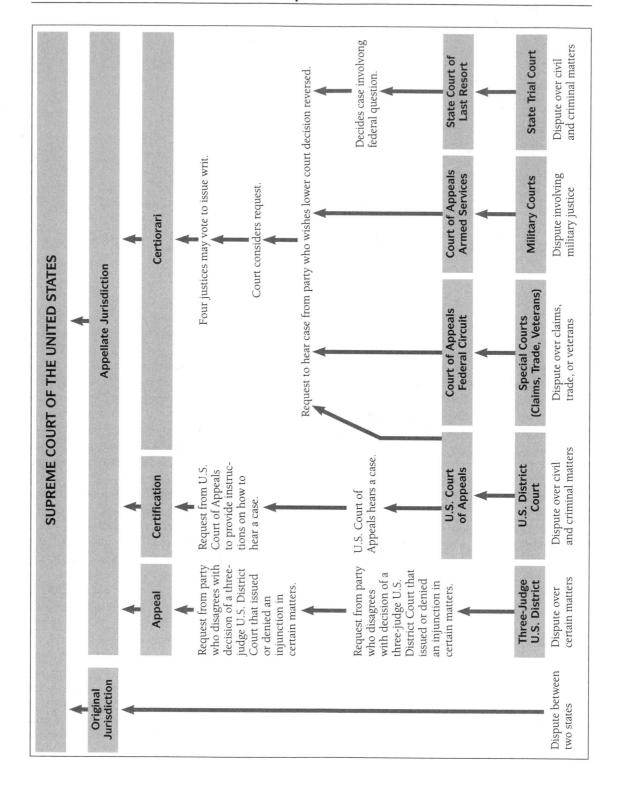

requests instructions on how to hear a case. Nearly all cases come to the Supreme Court when it issues a writ of certiorari to a lower court ordering the record of a case to be sent up for review. Those who disagree with a lower court's decision may petition the Supreme Court for review, but the chance of such a case being accepted is remote. According to the Court's own Rule 10: Review on a writ of certiorari is not a matter of right, but of judicial discretion. A petition for a writ of certiorari will be granted only for compelling reasons.

The Court's Rules say that it may review those cases in which lower courts have disagreed on the interpretation of a federal question or where there is "an important question of federal law that has not been, but should be, settled. . . ."

After considering briefs filed by parties to a case, the Court issues a writ of certiorari whenever four or more of its members deem it advisable to do so.

For more information

Article III, U.S. Constitution.

Eleventh Amendment, U.S. Constitution.

28 U.S.C. secs. 1251–1254, sec. 1257, sec. 1651(a), sec. 2241, and secs. 2254(a).

Rule 10, 11, 17, 18, 19, and 20, *Rules of the Supreme Court of the United States,* May 3, 1999, pp. 5–6 16–24.

(www.supremecourtus.gov/crtrules/rules.pdf).

JeDon Emenhiser
Humboldt State University

THE STAGES OF A CRIMINAL CASE

The various stages of a criminal case have specific rules that must be followed. These rules are part of an extensive framework of rules called criminal procedure.

While a person must be arrested before an actual criminal prosecution can take place, the government must follow certain laws during the investigation period. Criminal procedure laws protect people who are merely under investigation from unconstitutional actions.

The most important constitutional laws that arise during a criminal investigation are the Fourth and Fifth Amendments to the United States Constitution. The Fourth Amendment protects people from *unreasonable* searches and seizures by government officials (usually the police).

As a general rule, a search warrant is required before a police officer can search a person or that person's home. There are important exceptions to the search warrant requirement. Such exceptions include a search during a lawful arrest or a *stop and frisk* for weapons if the police officer has a reasonable suspicion that the suspect is armed. It is important to remember that the Fourth Amendment is a protection against *unreasonable*

searches and seizures; therefore, the police can conduct searches of people and property and seize property and evidence during these searches if it is a reasonable search. There is an important deterrent against the police engaging in unreasonable search and seizures. If it is determined that an unreasonable search and seizure occurred, evidence that was found can be excluded from trial.

The arrest of a person is the starting point for criminal prosecution. To arrest a suspect, the police must have an *arrest warrant* unless the police officer has probable cause to believe that a crime has been committed and there is not enough time to obtain a warrant. Also a warrant is not required if the crime is committed in the presence of the police.

The police are required to advise the arrested person of his or her Miranda rights during the arrest. Miranda rights consist of the right to remain silent and the right to have an attorney present during questioning. This fundamental right was reaffirmed in an important Supreme Court decision, *Dickerson v. United States,* in July 2000. In this case, the Supreme Court ruled that Miranda rights are constitutionally based and could not be overruled even by an act of Congress. It is important to point out that Miranda rights are only required during a *custodial interrogation*. A custodial interrogation occurs when the police question a detained person. If a suspect is not given the Miranda warning, a confession or other statements given to the police may be excluded from trial.

Arrested persons are searched to protect the safety of police personnel.

After being taken to the police station, the arrested person is *booked* and advised of the charges and held until being brought before a magistrate. Booking procedures include fingerprinting, photographing (commonly called a "mug shot"), and obtaining biographical information such as name and address. It is at this point that the arrested person is usually allowed to make a phone call.

After the arrest and booking, a police officer (or a prosecutor in some circumstances) prepares and files a *complaint*. A complaint is a written formal charge accusing a person of a crime and it sets forth the facts of the offense. However, a complaint is often written prior to arrest and is used to support a request for a warrant.

The suspect must be brought before a magistrate without *unnecessary delay,* and this is called the *first appearance* or the *initial appearance.* This first appearance usually must take place within 24 hours; however, if the arrest occurred on a Friday, the appearance may not occur until the following Monday. The magistrate will advise the accused of the charges that are set forth in the complaint as well as the accused's rights. If the accused is charged with a felony and cannot afford an attorney to represent him or her, the court will appoint an attorney, usually a public defender. If the arrest was made without an arrest warrant, the magistrate must determine whether probable cause exists to believe that the accused committed the crime. If there is a lack of probable cause, the accused must be set free. If probable cause exists, the magistrate may release the accused on bail unless it is determined that the

accused is a danger to the community or might flee. If it is determined that the accused is dangerous or might flee and not show up in court, then the accused will be held in *pretrial detention.* If the charge involves a misdemeanor, the initial appearance also constitutes an *arraignment*, where the defendant can plead guilty or not guilty to the charges.

In a felony case, the defendant is next brought before a judge for the *preliminary hearing.* The judge determines whether there is probable cause to believe that the defendant committed the crime. If the judge finds probable cause, the defendant is *bound over* for trial or grand jury review. If probable cause is not found, the case is dismissed; however, the prosecutor could refile charges later if for instance new evidence was found. In contrast to the initial appearance, the preliminary hearing is adversarial in nature. In an adversarial proceeding, both sides can present evidence including witnesses and both sides can question and cross-examine the other side's witnesses. While the initial appearance is a constitutionally required procedure, the preliminary hearing is not. However, the federal government and many states provide for preliminary hearings.

Prior to the preliminary hearing, the defense attorney and the prosecutor may engage in *plea bargaining,* a process in which the two sides bargain for concessions from each other. If they agree to a plea bargain, it usually involves the defendant agreeing to plead guilty to reduced charges or in exchange for some charges to be dropped or for a reduced sentence.

It is important to point out that a defendant that agrees to plead guilty in a plea bargain gives up his or her right to a trial. If a plea bargain is reached, it is presented for approval by the court at the preliminary hearing. The judge must determine whether the defendant's guilty plea was entered knowingly, voluntarily, and intelligently. A plea can also be reached anytime before or during a trial. Plea bargaining is a very important component of our criminal justice system, and it is has been estimated that 90 percent of all felony cases are disposed of by plea bargained guilty pleas.

After the preliminary hearing, if there is not a grand jury requirement, the prosecution will file an *information,* which is a formal criminal charge filed by the prosecutor when a grand jury is not involved. Most states utilize the filing of an information in misdemeanor prosecutions, and approximately half of the states use an information for felony prosecutions.

Some states require a review of the charges by a grand jury before a felony can be prosecuted. A grand jury is a body of private citizens (usually larger than a trial jury) who are convened to review the prosecution's evidence in closed meetings. If a majority of the grand jury decides that there is enough evidence to hold the suspect for trial it issues a *true bill* or *bill of indictment.* If a true bill is returned, the indictment is filed with the trial court by the prosecution.

Following the filing of an indictment or information, the defendant is *arraigned* before the trial court. During the arraignment, the defendant is informed of the charges and enters a plea of guilty or not guilty or *nolo contendere,* which means "I do not contest it." A nolo contendere or no contest plea is treated as a guilty plea. The reason a defendant would enter a no contest plea is that such a plea cannot be used against the defendant in a subsequent civil trial while a guilty plea could be used. If no plea is entered, the court will enter a not guilty plea for the defendant.

The next stage is called *discovery,* which is the process by which both the defense and prosecution reveal evidence to each other. The defendant has the right to obtain evidence that is needed to prepare the defense. In particular, the defendant will seek to obtain *exculpatory* evidence, which is evidence that is favorable to the defendant in terms of both guilt and punishment. The prosecution also has the right to obtain evidence, which could include the defendant's alibi, a witness list, and physical evidence such as blood samples.

Throughout the various stages of the process, the defense and prosecution may file motions that are requests to the court for favorable action.

In a felony case, the defendant has a Sixth Amendment right to a speedy trial by an impartial jury. Most misdemeanor defendants do not have the right to a jury trial. The first stage of a jury trial is when *jury selection* takes place and this is called *voir dire,* which means "to speak the truth." Although there are differences across jurisdictions, during jury selection each prospective juror is questioned in an attempt to determine whether he or she is qualified to be a juror in the case. If an attorney from either side decides that a juror cannot be fair or impartial then that juror can be *challenged for cause,* and if the judge agrees with the challenge that juror is released. There is no limit to the number of jurors that can be released for cause. Each side can also eliminate a specified number of jurors by using a *peremptory challenge.* A peremptory challenge can be used to eliminate jurors for any reason except race. In federal trial courts the defendant and the prosecution have 20 peremptory challenges in death penalty cases. In noncapital felony cases in federal trial courts, the defendant gets 10 such challenges and the prosecution gets six.

After a jury is selected and impaneled the trial is ready to begin. A trial begins with *opening statements* given by the prosecution and defense. During opening statements, both sides give the basic facts of the case but they do not make arguments. The prosecution goes first and puts on its *Case in Chief,* which is the state's main case against the defendant. The prosecution presents its evidence in the form of testimony by witnesses and other evidence that ties the defendant to the crime. The defendant does not have to present evidence because the defendant does not have to prove his innocence. However, the defense attorney may present evidence to dispute the prosecution's case. Both the prosecution and the defense can *cross-examine* witnesses.

The prosecution and the defense often argue about what evidence can be presented. There are rules of evidence that control what can be presented in court. After all the evidence is introduced, the prosecution and defense give their *closing statements*. During the closing statements, the attorneys can argue points of law but they cannot argue law that differs from the law that the judge will instruct the jury about.

The case goes to the jury after closing arguments. Proposed jury instructions are submitted by both the defense and prosecution and the judge decides which instructions to read to the jury before it begins deliberations. Jury instructions inform the jury of the law.

After the jury is given its instructions, it goes into deliberation. Jury deliberations are kept secret, and the jury is not supposed to have any contact with anyone outside the jury personnel during deliberations. Sometimes the jury is sequestered, especially in high-profile cases.

Most jurisdictions require a unanimous jury verdict. If the jury returns a guilty verdict, the defendant then faces the sentencing phase. If the jury cannot reach a unanimous verdict it is called a *hung jury*. In the event of a hung jury, the trial judge declares a mistrial and the prosecutor must decide whether to try the defendant again.

If the jury returns a guilty verdict in a felony case, there is a separate sentencing hearing. In death penalty cases the sentence is decided by the jury. In all other cases the trial judge decides the sentence.

After sentencing, the defendant has the right to appeal both the conviction and the sentence to the court of appeals for that jurisdiction. The appellate court will review the case for errors of law but it will not retry the case.

For more information

Cole, George F., and Christopher E. Smith. *Criminal Justice in America,* New York: Wadsworth, 2002.

INDEX

Boldface page numbers refer to main entries in the encyclopedia; *italic* page numbers indicate illustrations.